FIRSTHAND
AMERICA

WILEY-BLACKWELL

A John Wiley & Sons, Ltd., Publication

FIRSTHAND AMERICA

A History of the United States

EIGHTH EDITION ☆ VOLUME 1

DAVID BURNER

VIRGINIA BERNHARD

STANLEY I. KUTLER

Text copyright © 1980, 1985, 1991, 1992, 1994, 1996, 1998, 2000, 2002

Library of Congress Cataloguing in Publication Data

Main entry under title:

Firsthand America

Includes bibliographical references and index.
1. United States—History. I. Burner, David,
1937–   . II. Burner, David, 1937–   . American
people.
vol. 1, ISBN 1-978-1-9333-8502-0, 592 pp.
vol. 2, ISBN 1-978-1-9333-8503-7, 656 pp.
Combined edition, ISBN 1-978-1-8810-8973-5, 1136 pp.

Telephone Orders: 1-800-345-1776

Printed and bound in Malaysia by Vivar Printing Sdn Bhd

Second Printing 2011

About the Eighth Edition . . .

All comprehensive United States survey textbooks, including this one, give full coverage to standard political, economic, diplomatic, and legal events. But these elements of history are largely the story of elites. This textbook also provides social history captured in the recognizable lives of ordinary people. Presidents, congressmen, and corporate executives are quoted throughout the book. So are soldiers, slaves, indentured servants, cowboys, working girls and women, and civil rights activists. *Firsthand America*, using more than 2,000 quotations, therefore gives due place both to the traditional leaders and to the myriad Americans never named in formal histories.

In this eighth edition of *Firsthand America*, many of the firsthand quotations are placed in the margins in a contrasting color. This strategy is undertaken in cases where the materials might interrupt the main text narrative. The two-color format also improves the maps and graphs, and there are more of both. New dramatic incidents, including the Landscape of Confederate Defeat, the Harlem Renaissance, Disaster on the Plains, the Tet Offensive, and 9/11, improve the text along with innumerable smaller changes.

This eighth edition of *Firsthand America* contains a dialogue between two historians at the conclusion of each chapter. Contributors include Joyce Appleby, Bernard Bailyn, Michael Barnhart, Michael Les Benedict, Ira Berlin, Paul Boyer, Gene M. Brack, David Burner, Hosoya Chihiro, Catherine Clinton, Peter Collier, Paul Conkin, John S. D. Eisenhower, Peter G. Filene, David Hackett Fischer, Elizabeth Fox-Genovese, Paul Fussell, Eugene Genovese, Lawrence Goodwyn, Patricia Guerrin, Louis R. Harlan, Joan Hoff, David Horowitz, Carol P. Karlsen, Maury Klein, Thomas J. Knock, Alan M. Kraut, Walter LaFeber, Suzanne Lebsock, William Leuchtenburg, Manning Marable, Drew McCoy, Forrest McDonald, James M. McPherson, James Mooney, Gary B. Nash, Stephen Nissenbaum, Shari Osborn, Nell Irvin Painter, Edward Pessen, Thomas Reeves, Robert V. Remini, Martin Ridge, Daniel T. Rodgers, Michael Paul Rogin, Kirkpatrick Sale, Richard H. Sewell, Martin J. Sherwin, Kenneth M. Stampp, Richard B. Stott, Stephan Thernstrom, Hans L. Trefousse, Irwin Unger, Thomas R. West, Sean Wilentz, Gordon S. Wood, and Donald Worster.

American Letter for Gerald Murphy

It is a strange thing—to be an American
Neither an old house it is with the air
Tasting of hung herbs and the sun returning
Year after year to the same door and the churn
Making the same sound in the cool of the kitchen
Mother to son's wife, and the place to sit
Marked in the dusk by the worn stone at the wellhead—
That—nor the eyes like each other's eyes and the skull
Shaped to the same fault and the hands' sameness.
Neither a place it is nor a blood name.
America is West and the wind blowing.
America is a great word and the snow,
A way, a white bird, the rain falling,
A shining thing in the mind and the gulls' call.
America is neither a land nor a people,
A word's shape it is, a wind's sweep—
America is alone: many together,
Many of one mouth, of one breath,
Dressed as one—and none brothers among them:
Only the taught speech and the aped tongue.
America is alone and the gulls calling.

It is a strange thing to be an American.
It is strange to live on the high world in the stare
Of the naked sun and the stars as our bones live.
Men in the old lands housed by their rivers.
They built their towns in the vales in the earth's shelter.
We first inhabit the world. We dwell
On the half earth, on the open curve of a continent.
Sea is divided from sea by the day-fall. The dawn
Rides the low east with us many hours;
First are the capes, then are the shorelands, now
The blue Appalachians faint at the day rise;
The willows shudder with light on the long Ohio:
The lakes scatter the low sun: the prairies
Slide out of dark: in the eddy of clean air
The smoke goes up from the high plains of Wyoming:
The steep Sierras arise: the struck foam
Flames at the wind's heel on the far Pacific.
Already the noon leans to the eastern cliff:
The elms darken the door and the dust-heavy lilacs. . . .

This, this is our land, this is our people,
This that is neither a land nor a race. We must reap
The wind here in the grass for our soul's harvest:
Here we must eat our salt or our bones starve.
Here we must live or live only as shadows.
This is our race, we that have none, that have had
Neither the old walls nor the voices around us,
This is our land, this is our ancient ground—
The raw earth, the mixed bloods and the strangers,
The different eyes, the wind, and the heart's change,
These we will not leave though the old call us.
This is our country-earth, our blood, our kind.
Here we will live our years till the earth blind us—
                                        —ARCHIBALD MACLEISH

About the Points of View . . .

This country, as the poem by Archibald MacLeish reprinted opposite this page of your textbook has it, was born on a naked continent, and it has neither a single race nor a single family nor a single ancient tradition to make it a unity. The ancestors of some of us were here before Columbus, and their descendants have been driven from home after home by European immigrants or their offspring. Other Americans came in the wretched holds of slave ships. Countless others, from Europe, had a somewhat better and yet a miserable journey, packed in the poorer recesses of ships that also provided luxurious quarters for wealthy travelers. Asians among us have Chinese ancestors who worked on the railroads that bound the country in the nineteenth century, or Japanese who labored on California farms amidst vicious discrimination against them. More recently we have added to our numbers Southeast Asians, refugees from a war that we did not begin but enormously escalated, and along with them Koreans whose shops are becoming a visible feature of our cities. And we are also the migrants from south of our borders and from the Caribbean, children of various racial and national strains that have mixed over the centuries since Columbus. What we have to make us a nation besides the physical fact of dwelling here is an idea of what it means to be an American. And that in itself is a ceaseless question for debate.

This country was born of ideas, and innumerable Americans beginning with the Pilgrim and Puritan migrants to New England have thought that the very point of being here was to live one or another of them. A good way of summarizing them is to see in American history a continuing quarrel or partnership between the claims of individualism and the claims of community.

The American economy, for example, has championed the virtues of the self-contained individual: industry, foresight, ambition. It has at the same time been an immensely cooperative venture, stretching across the continent a tight web of roads, factories, electronic communication, and more recently computer networks. It is in contributing skills and effort to this web that personal industry and ambition have found much of their expression. Americans have craved private property. Yet twentieth-century American political conflicts have been over how to extend, limit, tax, or reconstruct institutions of private property for the general good. As popular phenomena, too, these polarities in American culture have varied in specific content. A labor organization is a community of sorts, but so is a lynch mob. A union-breaking financial buccaneer is an individualist of one kind; another sort is a southern small-town newspaper editor, denouncing the bigotry of his subscribers.

As opponents or as partners, individualism and community have in differing ways furnished much of our national political questioning. As an illustration of the breadth of the argument, this text provides a running debate among several dozen prominent American historians. The ability to read controversial argument and gain from the reading is at the heart of a college education. Hence the points of view in *Firsthand America*.

No number of interpretations, of course, could cover all the issues over which American historians have quarreled. This is particularly true today, as the tools of history become increasingly multilayered, while popular argument over the future of the nation grows both angrier and more confused than it has been for some time. It is the hope of the contributors to *Firsthand America* that readers will enjoy following the arguments of scholars as they struggle to give some clarifying order to the endlessly diverse and restless facts of history.

Dedication

For Thomas R. West

About the Authors . . .

DAVID BURNER has published several books on twentieth-century America including *Making Peace with the 60s* (1996), *John F. Kennedy and a New Generation* (1988), *Herbert Hoover: A Public Life* (1979), and *The Politics of Provincialism: The Democratic Party, 1918–1932* (1968). He is currently writing a history of West Point for Alfred A. Knopf, Inc.

VIRGINIA BERNHARD has published two historical novels, set in seventeenth-century Virginia and Bermuda, as well as a biography of a Texas governor's daughter. Her scholarly articles have appeared in *New England Quarterly, Virginia Magazine of History and Biography,* and *Journal of Southern History.* She has coedited the 1992 University of Missouri Press *Southern Women: Histories and Identities* and teaches at the University of St. Thomas in Houston. Professor Bernhard has served on the Advanced Placement test development committee for United States history.

STANLEY I. KUTLER is E. Gordon Fox professor of American Institutions at the University of Wisconsin and editor for more than twenty years of the influential *Reviews in American History.* Kutler brings to the book his familiarity with the most recent interpretations of American history from colonial times to the present. A constitutional historian, his published books include *Privilege and Creative Destruction: The Charles River Bridge Case, Judicial Power and Reconstruction Politics,* and *The Wars of Watergate.* Kutler's most recent book is *Abuse of Power: The New Nixon Tapes* (1997).

Acknowledgments

We are eager to receive comments on the seventh edition of this textbook from both teachers and students. We welcome corrections, suggestions, news of omissions, and general criticisms, which may be addressed to any of the authors. Or call the toll-free number of Brandywine Press at 1-800-345-1776.

For various kinds of help and encouragement thanks are gratefully extended to the following critics now teaching the United States history survey course: Francine Medeiros, Gus Seligmann, Jr., Thomas Schoonover, Lee Annis, Gary Bell, Ihor Bemko, Rick Donohoe, Gretchen Eick, Pat Gerster, Marilyn Halter, Barbara Posadas, John Belohlavek, Susan Hellert, Lottie Wilson, James E. Diestler, Raymond Hauser, Michael Mills, Chuck Wallenberg, James Mooney, Harlan Hoffman, Michael Krenn, Virginia Leonard, Elizabeth Kessel, Frank Alduino, Eric Jacobsen, Jane Johnson, Howard Jones, Cary Wintz, Lena Boyd-Brown, Louis Williams, Merline Pitre, Kathleen Munley, Patricia Mulligan, Mario Perez, Stan Phipps, Michael Kopanic, Robert Sayre, Constance Schulz, Marcia Synnott, Michael Strickland, James Willis, Kelly Woestman, Charles Zelden, Carl Meier, Anthony B. Miller, Ben Johnson, Raymond Wilson, Drew Holloway, Ron Hays, John H. Hutson, Stuart Knee, S. Carol Berg, Charles O'Brien, Douglas Firth Anderson, and Kathleen Byrne.

The Authors

Contents

1 Europe, Africa, and the Americas / 1

Preface: A New World, 1

The First North Americans, 4   The World Stage, 10   Africa, 15
Portugal's Crusade by Sea, 21   The Spanish Empire, 23   England:
The Sceptered Isle, 29   The Columbian Exchange, 32   Suggested
Readings, 33

Points of View: Christopher Columbus—The Conqueror of Paradise? 34

2 North America / 37

Preface: The Starving Time, 37

Early Southern Settlements, 38   Beginnings of New England, 40
New Colonies, 51   The Colonies and the Crown, 57   Indian Affairs, 60
The Dominion of New England, 63   Suggested Readings, 67

Points of View: Cultural Influences on the Early Colonies, 68

3   The Developing Colonies / 71

Preface: The Salem Witches, 71

New England Colonies, 74   Middle Colonies, 77   Southern Colonies, 83
Slavery, 86   The Great Awakening and the Enlightenment, 89   The
American Character, 95   English Colonies at Midcentury, 100
Suggested Readings, 105

Points of View: The Devil in the Shape of a Woman? 106

4   An Independent Spirit 1763–1776 / 109

Preface: The Plains of Abraham, 109

The French and Indian War, 111   Imperial Reform, 114   The Stamp Act
Crisis, 117   The British Blunder Again, 122   The Boston Massacre, 125
The *Gaspée* and the Boston Tea Party, 128   Resistance Turns to
Armed Conflict, 132   A Continental Army Takes Shape, 137
Common Sense and The Declaration of Independence, 140
Suggested Readings, 143

Points of View: Why Did the Americans Rebel? 144

5   Revolution and Independence 1776–1787 / 147

Preface: Liberty and Slavery, 147

The Armies, 149   The Fortunes of War, 152   Diplomacy and
Independence, 158   The War at Home, 159   How Revolutionary? 163
The Articles of Confederation and the Critical Period, 166   The Period of
the Confederation, 171   Daily Life, 174   Prelude to the Constitution,
177   Suggested Readings, 179

Points of View: How Radical Was the American Revolution? 180

6   We the People 1787–1800 / 183

Preface: The Bill of Rights, 183

Shays's Rebellion, 184   The Constitutional Convention, 185   Ratification, 189   The
Newly Formed Regime, 191   The Government Seeks a Foreign Policy, 199   The
Presidency of John Adams, 203   The Election of 1800, 209   Suggested
Readings, 211

Points of View: What Did Women Gain from the Revolution? 212

7   Independence Confirmed 1800–1816 / 215

Preface: Thomas Jefferson and Sally Hemings, 215

President Thomas Jefferson, 217   The Dawn of a Century, 226
France and England Once More, 229   James Madison Takes Over, 232
The War of 1812, 236   The Battle of New Orleans, 245   Suggested
Readings, 247

Points of View: How Republican Were the Jeffersonian Republicans? 248

8   Sinews of Nationhood / 251

Preface: The Erie Canal, 251

A New Society, 254   The Transportation Revolution, 254
Corporations, 258   Sources of Northern Labor, 259   Industrialism and
the Republic, 264   A Resurgent Nationalism, 265   Government and the
Economy, 267   The Panic of 1819 and the Bank, 270   Nationalism and
the Supreme Court, 273   Suggested Readings, 275

Points of View: American Living Standards in an Industrializing
Economy, 276

9   Sectionalism and Party 1816–1828 / 279

Preface: The Westward Movement, 279

A Resurgent Sectionalism, 281   John Quincy Adams and American
Continentalism, 287   The Monroe Doctrine, 290   The Election of 1824,
292   The Second President Adams, 294   Andrew Jackson and the
Election of 1828, 297   The Rise of the Common Man? 302   Parties and
the Republic, 303   Suggested Readings, 303

Points of View: North vs. South: A Clash of Cultures? 304

10   The Jacksonian Era 1828–1840 / 307

Preface: The Trail of Tears, 307

Removal of Indians, 309   Andrew Jackson's Inaugural, 311   Van Buren
vs. Calhoun, 312   Jackson and States' Rights, 314   A Conflict of
Interests, 315   The Second Bank of the United States, 319   The Bank
War, 320   Boom and Bust, 323   The Democrats vs. the Whigs, 325
The Election of 1840, 328   World Affairs in the Jacksonian Era, 331
Suggested Readings, 333

Points of View: Why Did Jackson Remove the Indians? 334

11   **An Age of Reform / 337**

Preface: The Women's Declaration of Sentiments, 1848, 337

Political and Economic Radicalism, 339   Religious Movements, 342
Secular Communitarianism, 347   Social Reform, 349   The Dark Side of
Reform, 359   The Arts, 361   The Antislavery Crusade, 364   Suggested
Readings, 367

Points of View: Women in the Antebellum South: Plantation vs.
City, 368

12   **Westward Expansion: The 1840s / 371**

Preface: The Battle of the Alamo, 371

The Nation in 1840, 374   Immigration, 374   The Land and the People:
The Northeast and Mid-Atlantic, 378   The Land and the People: The
West, 379   The Land and the People: The South, 382   The South Closes
Ranks, 388   Slavery in the Territories, 392   Whigs, Democrats, and
Westward Expansion, 395   The Mexican War, 399   Suggested Readings,
405

Points of View: What Caused the Mexican War? 406

13   **Impending Crisis: The 1850s / 409**

Preface: *Uncle Tom's Cabin* (1852), 409

The Compromise of 1850, 411   The Fugitive Slave Law, 415   Harriet
Tubman, 416   Manifest Destiny Revisited, 418   The Kansas-Nebraska
Act, 422   "Bleeding Kansas," 423   Political Cataclysm, 426   Sectionalism
Ascendant, 430   Abe Lincoln of Illinois, 434   The Election of 1860, 436
John Brown's Raid, 438   Suggested Readings, 439

Points of View: What Caused the Civil War? 440

14   **A Great Civil War 1861–1865 / 443**

Preface: Was the Civil War Necessary? 443

The South Secedes, 444   The Problem of the Forts, 448   War Strategies,
450   Stalemate: The Early Campaigns, 1861–1862, 453   War Fortunes
Turn, 1863–1864, 459   Life in the Confederacy, 469   Life in the
Union, 471   Army Life, 472   The End Stage, 1864–1865, 475
Suggested Readings, 477

Points of View: Who Freed the Slaves? 478

15   **"Been in the Storm So Long":**
Emancipation and Reconstruction / 481

Preface: The Klan's Lynching of Jim Williams, 481

The South after the Civil War, 482   Reconstruction, 484   Andrew
Johnson, 487   Early Reconstruction, 488   Radical Reconstruction, 490
Impeachment of Johnson, 493   Blacks and the Land, 494   The End of Racial
Progress and the Compromise of 1877, 502   Suggested Readings, 503

Points of View: Should Andrew Johnson Have Been Impeached? 504

Appendixes / I

The Declaration of Independence, III   The Constitution of the United
States, IV   Admission of States to the Union, XIV   Population of the
United States, 1790–2000, XV   The Vice Presidents and the Cabinet, XV
Presidential Elections, 1789–2000, XX

Glossary / XXV

Succeeding in History Courses / XXXIII

Index / XLIII

Cristoforo Colombo. Painter unknown. *(Courtesy, Uffizi Galleria, Firenze)*

Europe, Africa, and the Americas

A NEW WORLD

Christopher Columbus did not "discover" America. He was not even the first European to reach the New World. The Vikings, sailing in their small boats from Scandinavia around A.D. 1000, had reached Iceland and Greenland, but their brief presence there had no discernible effect on the rest of the world. The voyages of Columbus, on the other hand, set in motion an economic, cultural, intellectual, and political transformation that eventually revolutionized Europe, colonized the Americas, and ushered in the modern age.

Son of a Genoese weaver, Columbus was an extraordinary weaver of dreams. He envisioned himself sailing beyond the sunset, far beyond the horizons of his native Italy. Columbus was a fine mariner but an inaccurate geographer. Both qualities helped him to sell his dream to the monarchs of Spain. He badly underestimated the circumference of the globe, placing Asia about 2,400 miles from the Canary Islands of the eastern Atlantic: the actual distance is more than 10,000 miles, most of it vast oceans. Besieging King Ferdinand of Aragon and Queen Isabella of Castile, Columbus finally got his ships, his crews, and his quest for riches. On August 2, 1492, he sailed from Spain, setting his course west across the uncharted Atlantic Ocean, hoping to reach the fabled lands of the East Indies of Asia by sailing westward around the globe.

Instead, Columbus reached a "new world." It was not on any

HISTORICAL EVENTS

1100
Islamic forces conquer Morocco, western Algeria, Ghana, and parts of Spain and Portugal

Early 1200s
Mongols' Genghis Khan begins raids on China, Europe, and Islamic worlds

1260
Islamic forces stop Mongol invasion outside of Egypt

1348
Bubonic plague strikes Europe

1415
Prince Henry of Portugal begins explorations

1453
Constantinople falls to the Turks

1469
Queen Isabella and King Ferdinand marry, uniting Spain

1485
Henry VII becomes King of England

1487
Dias rounds the southern tip of Africa

continued

1

HISTORICAL EVENTS

1492
Columbus makes first voyage to
the New World • Moors and Jews
expelled from Spain

1494
Treaty of Tordesillas awards Brazil to
Portugal and rest of the New World
to Spain

1497
Cabot begins exploring the east
coast of North America

continued

map, and it was inhabited by millions of people whose languages and cultures were completely unknown to Europeans. Arriving on the island of San Salvador in the Caribbean on October 12, 1492, Columbus, believing that he had reached the East Indies, met some natives he called "Indians." He had no way of knowing that there was a vast mainland to the west. He would have been astonished to learn that there were approximately twelve to sixteen million native Americans living in what we now call Central and South America. Another five million or more inhabited North America.

Much to Columbus's disappointment, he could not find a sea route to the Far East from Europe. After further voyages in 1493, 1498, and 1502, he died in 1506 believing that he had failed in his

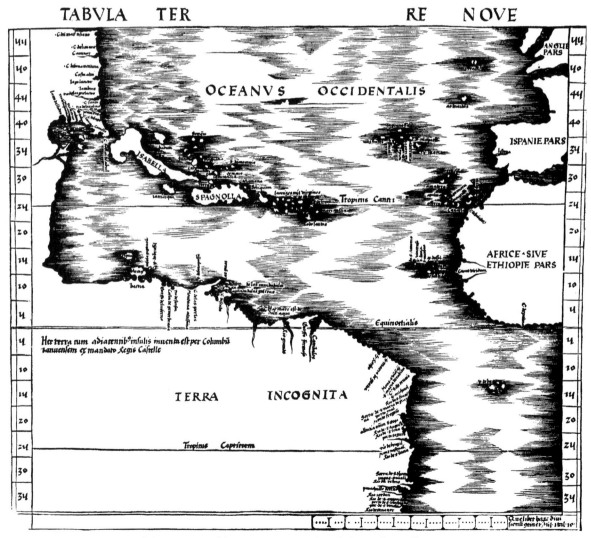

Tabula Terre Nove, **Map of the New World, ca. 1507–1513.** *(N. Phelps Stokes Collection. Prints Division. The New York Public Library, Astor, Lenox and Tilden Foundations)*

mission. He never knew that deep in the interior of the mainland beyond the Caribbean islands lay not the riches of China and Japan, but the fabulous treasures of the Aztec and the Inca empires. Their cities—the Aztecs' Tenochtitlán, where modern Mexico City now stands, and the Inca capital at Cuzco, high in the Andes Mountains of Peru—were flourishing centers of trade and culture at the time of Columbus's voyages. Before the Aztecs, the Mayan civilization, with sophisticated mathematics, astronomy, and architecture, had bloomed from about A.D. 300 to 900 in what is now Guatemala and the Yucatán peninsula. Royal palaces and ornate temples lavishly decorated with gold and silver, spacious public squares, gardens, terraces, paved roads, canals, and efficient systems of government existed in both Central and South America long before the first Europeans arrived in the Western Hemisphere. In North America, in the lands watered by the Rio Grande River, the Pueblo towns with their multilevel adobe structures, and in the valley of the Mississippi River, the huge earthen pyramids of the Mound Builders, abandoned before the coming of the Europeans, testified to the vitality of native cultures.

With the arrival of three small ships in 1492, the course of these native peoples' history, as well as that of Europe, would be forever changed. Christopher Columbus, whose given name means "Christ-bearer," saw himself as carrying Christianity to pagan peoples across the ocean. Christianity, in fact, would in its various institutions transform the Americas. In exchange, Europe was to be transformed by the Western Hemisphere. Much of the New World's first effect on the Old World was by way of its extraordinary wealth in resources. Gold and silver set in motion an economic revolution. Maize, or Indian corn, sometimes called the bread of the Americas, squash, beans, pumpkins, tomatoes, chili peppers, and chocolate enhanced European diets; and potatoes became a major sustenance to a growing European population. Tobacco altered Europe's social customs and helped colonial economies. Furs such as beaver pelts created fashions in dress. From the Old World to the New came hogs, horses, cattle, iron and steel weapons and tools, and wool for clothing and blankets, as well as beads, mirrors, alcohol, and other manufactured goods. But along with the knives, guns, axes, and copper kettles that changed the Stone Age societies of the Americas came another less welcome and accidental import: European diseases.

Smallpox, the scourge of Europe, was unknown in the Western Hemisphere until Europeans came. Native peoples had no immunity to this often fatal and always disfiguring disease. Indians were equally susceptible to plagues, measles, diphtheria, cholera, and typhus. They died by the millions. European bacteria and viruses reduced the native population of the Americas by as much

HISTORICAL EVENTS

1501
Vespucci explores east coast of South America

1513
De León explores Florida
• Balboa sights the Pacific

1517
Martin Luther posts his "Ninety-Five Theses," beginning Protestant Reformation

1519
Piñeda explores Texas Gulf Coast
• Cortés conquers Aztecs in Mexico

1522
Magellan's crew completes circumnavigation of globe begun in 1519

1524
Verrazano explores northeast coast of North America

1529–36
Henry VIII of England (1509–1547) uses Parliament to separate England from Rome

1532
Pizarro conquers Incas in Peru

1535
Cartier names the St. Lawrence River

Early 1540s
Coronado and de Soto search for gold in southern and western North America

1542
Cabrillo explores the North American west coast

1556
Philip II becomes King of Spain

1558
Elizabeth I becomes Queen of England

1565
St. Augustine founded by the Spanish

About 1570
Five Nations of Iroquois form confederation

1588
English defeat the Spanish Armada

as seventy-five to ninety percent. No wonder many early explorers described the new land as a "wilderness," and later historians would write of a "virgin land."

Europe's contacts with the lands across the sea initiated another kind of virus: the transatlantic slave trade. On his first voyage Columbus brought back seven Indians to display before his fascinated countrymen, "to learn our language and return . . . or to be kept as captives." A few years later a Spanish decree of 1503 allowed the enslavement of Indians in the Caribbean. In the 1520s Spaniards visiting the coast of what is now the Carolinas captured Indians there and sold them as slaves in Santo Domingo. By the1500s European traders who had "discovered" Africa a few years before Columbus's first voyage were bringing African captives to work as slaves on the New World's lands. That trade in Africans, much of it provided by African slave dealers, grew from hundreds, to thousands, to millions. Over the next 350 years an estimated ten to fifteen million African men, women, and children were transported to the Americas against their will. Another four to six million died on the way.

The First North Americans

For perhaps forty thousand years, people had been living in the world the Europeans called "new." Stone tools, spear points, and other artifacts unearthed at sites in modern-day Pennsylvania, Wisconsin, New Mex-

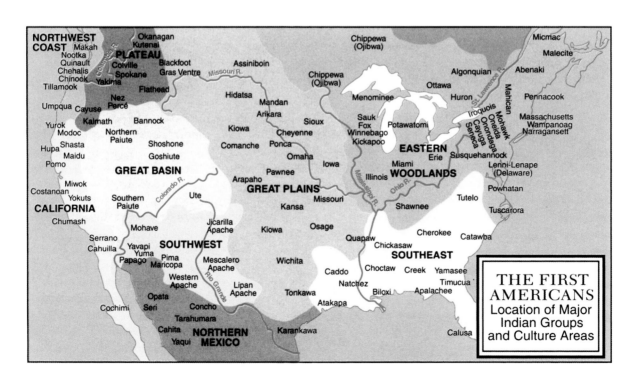

THE FIRST AMERICANS
Location of Major Indian Groups and Culture Areas

"They have likewise a notable way to catche fishe in their Rivers, for whear as they lack both yron, and steele, they faste unto their Reedes or longe Rodds, the hollowe tayle of a certain fishe like to a sea crabbe in steede of a poynte, wehr with by nighte or day they stricke fishes, and take them opp into their boates."—Thomas Hariot (1590). John White, *The Manner of Their Fishing*, drawing 1585. *(Courtesy, British Museum, London)*

ico, and Virginia show that human habitations were scattered across North America as early as ten or twenty thousand years ago. The first inhabitants had arrived from Asia thousands of years before that, gradually migrating into the interiors of North and South America.

The story of the millions of pre-Columbian Indians who inhabited the Americas is a puzzle for anthropologists, archaeologists, and historians. For the thousands of years before the Europeans arrived, there are no written records. The Mayans, whose culture flourished in Central America for six centuries prior to A.D. 900, made sophisticated mathematical calculations, accurate solar calendars, and pictorial representations, but they did not leave any written narratives. Neither did the Aztecs, who ruled Mexico from A.D. 1200 to 1500. The Incas governed an empire that extended from modern Ecuador to Chile by 1500 and built stone structures without mortar that survived earthquakes, but they had no alphabet. The history of these people, like that of the countless others who preceded them, is hidden in artifacts: carved images, strings of beads, pictographs. Painted pebbles dating from 6500 B.C. to A.D. 1400 have been found in the Pecos River valley in Texas, but the meaning of their linear designs remains a mystery.

In North America alone scholars have identified over 150 different language groups. These primitive North Americans were seed gatherers and game hunters. Some ten thousand years ago they learned to remove flakes from stone, making spears with what are called "Folsom points." Such weapons made them more efficient hunters. Yet they continued where possible to drive big game such as mammoths, bison, deer, and antelope off cliffs or into swamps preparatory for the kill. Gradually diets diversified to include raccoon, opossum, shellfish, and sea animals. As the Ice Age retreated about twelve thousand years ago and the continent dried, great forests grew in the north and east of North America; the bow and arrow aided in the kill of small, swift woodland animals. Hooks, nets, and weirs caught fish and snared ducks. Desert Indians relied increasingly on plants, ground seeds, berries, bulbs, and nuts. About seven thousand years ago North American natives, like peoples elsewhere around the world, developed agriculture. In comparison with modern technologies, basic agriculture seems simple. But in contrast with hunting and the gathering of wild plants, it is a major, sophisticated control of the environment. Efficiency in food growing increased populations and quickened village life. Plant domestication emerged first in the Mexican highlands, and then spread north and south. It probably reached the peoples north of Mexico about three thousand years ago.

Peoples of the Northwest In the coldest regions of North America dwelt the Inuits, or Eskimos. They were and are uncommon among human beings in their ability to accommodate themselves, by remarkable adaptations of clothing, housing, and

While Europeans were developing an interest in science and commerce, peoples half a world away were expressing cultures of their own. Mask. Nootka people. West Vancouver, Canada. *(Courtesy, The Menil Collection, Houston)*

A North Pacific Coast Indian village as depicted in a nineteenth-century painting by Arthur A. Jansson. Indians in this region probably never developed agriculture, relying instead on fishing and hunting for food. *(Courtesy, American Museum of Natural History)*

hunting, to regions of snow, ice, and long winters. Most quickly associated with Alaska, they spread across the extreme north of the continent and into Greenland. The Indians of the Far North, across Canada and Alaska, were few. Divided into two major language groups, Algonquian and Athabascan, they included such tribes as Algonquian, Beaver, Chippewa, Cree, Chowo, and Yellowknife by present designations. Since the growing season was short for agriculture, they gathered berries, plants, and nuts, and hunted caribou, moose, deer, elk, musk-ox, and buffalo. Nomadic Indians used portable tepees; others built sturdy log homes. The Far North Indians appear to have fought rarely.

A unique hunter-gatherer culture existed in the northwest corner of the present-day United States. The Northwest Coast Indians, their population stretching from northern California to southern Alaska, probably never developed agriculture. The Bella Coola, Chinook, Kwakiutl, Nootka, Quinault, and Tlingit Indians harvested the oceans and rivers, taking salmon, inland trout, shellfish, sea lions, sea otter, and whales. In the lush forests, they hunted bear, caribou, deer, elk, and moose. Unlike most Indians north of Mexico, these people were not egalitarian. A few families accumulated wealth in canoes, blankets, or hammered copper sheets. Lavishing wealth brought power over others, and these extraordinarily competitive Indians therefore held ceremonial feasts called "potlatches"; the hosts fed their guests and displayed, gave away, or even destroyed valued possessions. Like the hunter-gatherer Far North Indians, the Northwest Coast tribes had no pottery; they used wood for masks, grave markers, and utensils. The abundant redwoods, cedars, firs, and pines served as posts, beams, siding, and gables for their homes, and as raw material for the huge sixty-foot seagoing canoes that could carry up to sixty men. Religious dramas kept alive the myths surrounding the Northwest gods.

Indians of the West More technologically primitive tribes occupied the Great Basin of America—the region between the Rockies and the Sierra Nevada Mountains which comprises present-day Utah, Nevada, and southern and eastern Oregon. The climate was arid and the soil, without the use of complex irrigation systems, was unsuited for agriculture. Also, the desert did not support the big game populations to sustain a hunting economy. The people of the Great Basin—the Utes, Paiutes, Goshiutes, Modocs, Bannocks, and Shoshones—were foragers, living off the roots, insects, berries, rabbits, and small rodents they were able to collect or catch. They were nomadic, moving in small groups of twenty to thirty and sleeping under portable lean-tos. They lived a marginal economic existence in which starvation was always a threat.

A kaleidoscope of hundreds of small tribes lived along the California coast from what is today San Francisco south to San Diego. Although these Indians were neither hunters nor farmers, they enjoyed an adequate food supply. Most of them either foraged for clams and shellfish along the bays, inlets, and beaches of the Pacific Ocean or collected acorns from the oak tree forests. The weather was temperate and the food supply reliable for the California Indians. They lived in villages and handcrafted some of the finest basketry in the world.

The longhouse (bottom), made from bark stretched over a wood frame, was the standard home of the Iroquois. Most Algonquians of the eastern woodlands lived in wigwams (top), which were made by bending tree boughs and covering them with animal skin. Most Plains Indians lived in small, durable tepees (middle), usually made from buffalo hides.
(Courtesy, New York Public Library)

Columbus's voyages heralded an era of European expansionism that led to the development of new frontiers across the world. The first depiction of native Americans suggests Europe's fascination with the New World inhabitants. Note the elaborate ship, asserting the superiority of European culture. Unidentified artist. *Insula hyspana.* Woodcut, 1493. From *Carolus Verardus, In laudem serenissimi Ferdinandi* (Basel, 1494). *(Courtesy, Beinecke Rare Book and Manuscript Library, Yale University, New Haven, Connecticut)*

The land between the Mississippi River and the Rocky Mountains belonged to the Plains Indians. Until the mid-1500s the Plains Indians preferred a more settled agricultural life in villages near rivers. By the end of the sixteenth century the Plains Indians had domesticated the wild ponies, descendants of horses brought by the Spanish. They quickly became superb horsemen. As mounted warriors and hunters they would roam the plains for nearly three hundred years. When they stayed in their permanent villages, they built homes of log framing covered with brush and dirt. While traveling, they lived in portable tepees.

A combination of hunter-gatherer and settled agrarian culture occupied much of the Southwest. These Indians showed remarkable ability to adapt to the arid buttes, mesas, and steep canyons in the northern part of this area and the flatter desert country to the south. The Anasazi, whom the Navaho call "the Ancient Ones," and their general descendants, the Pueblos, Hopi, and Zuni, built cliff dwellings, some with as many as 800 units, centering around the point where Colorado, Utah, New Mexico, and Arizona meet. This more advanced agrarian culture developed specialization in work, yet sophistication did not lead to hierarchy: religious and military leaders worked much like anyone else. Pueblos were peaceable, preferring to pull up the ladders to their adobe homes when attacked. When an Anasazi killed someone, even in self-defense, elaborate purification preceded his reentry into the village. This peaceful, advanced culture faded, possibly because of a prolonged thirteenth-century drought and growing population pressures from the north.

Indians of the Midwest and the East   From about 400 B.C. to A.D. 1500, in the Mississippi and Ohio river valleys, in parts of what are now Wisconsin, Michigan, Missouri, Illinois, Indiana, Ohio, Louisiana, and on the Gulf Coast, a culture known as the Mound Builders flourished. It left behind hundreds of huge earthen mounds, some in the shapes of birds and snakes. Many were used as burial mounds. Ornaments and tools of bone, shell, and copper suggest that the Mound Builders traded with areas as far away as Mexico. From about A.D. 900 to 1500 the peoples along the Mississippi Valley built enormous flat-topped earthen pyramids, some containing exquisitely-made jewelry, pottery, and agricultural implements.

On the eve of European discovery several Indian cultures dominated the third of the continent bordering the Atlantic. The eastern Algonquians occupied the Atlantic Coast from Labrador to North Carolina. Deep in the interior, on the Western Great Lakes, a northern and western Algonquian culture shared many of the traits of its eastern relatives. The Iroquois peopled the area between the two Algonquian cultures, from the Great Lakes to the central Appalachians. They included the Hurons, located north of the lakes; the Five Nations (Cayuga, Onondaga, Oneida, Mohawk, and Seneca) of the Mohawk Valley; and a conglomerate of related tribes including the Cherokee, Tuscarora, Moneton, and Monacan in the central and southern Appalachian Mountains. The Muskogean culture occupied the lowlands of southeastern North America.

The Iroquois   The Five Nations Iroquois confederation, founded around 1570, numbered perhaps 10,000 people by the year 1600. Its purpose was to eliminate blood feuds and cope with conflicts with nearby Algonquians, which may have resulted from population growth generated by improved agriculture. According to Iroquois legend, the leader credited with solving these problems was a chief named Hiawatha. He apparently lost relatives around 1450 and, rather than taking blood revenge, recommended that a ritual bereavement replace the vendetta, that retaliations be forbidden, and that a council of forty-nine chiefs make decisions for all the villages. Thereafter villages of the Five Nations were bound together for internal peace and external defense. Communal sharing extended to land use, the hunt, and the home. Although plowed by a family, the land was not owned, and while one hunter might outdo another, the kill was distributed. Families might live together in one house, but no single family owned it.

Women dominated familial lineages and were influential in Iroquois politics, although the Senecas did not give women the right to vote or serve on tribal councils until the 1960s. The families included the oldest female and her daughters, immature male children, and sons-in-law. Married men joined the family of their wives. Women initiated divorce by throwing their husbands' belongings outside. In politics women influenced village decisions behind the scenes. The women farmed, controlling the villages while the men warred, fished, and hunted; women could sometimes veto military expeditions by refusing to supply footwear or food.

Although the Iroquois did compete among themselves in hunting, fishing, and fighting, child raising encouraged egalitarianism. Youngsters were rarely punished physically, and were expected to err as they imitated adults. This freedom continued as the children matured. Without specialized legal personnel, laws, or jails, acceptable behavior was maintained by the ostracism and consensus that are typical of many small agricultural communities.

Among themselves, then, the Iroquois were civilized people, in some ways more civilized than the Europeans. Yet they do not deserve to be romanticized as a lost, virtuous civilization destroyed by white invaders. Like Europeans and white Americans, they could be as ruthless toward people outside their polity and culture as they were civil to their own kind. Algonquians and others knew the Iroquois as cruel warriors.

Indians of the South and Southeast   South of the Iroquois, from Chesapeake Bay to the Gulf Coast were other tribes, some belonging to the Algonquian-speaking groups and the rest to the Muskogean language peoples in what is now the southeastern United States. The Susquehannocks, powerful in the Chesapeake Bay region, had links to the Iroquois, as did the Tuscaroras, who in 1720 became the sixth nation in the Iroquois confederation. Among the eastern Algonquians were the Delawares and the Powhatans, the latter being the Indians who met the English settlers at Jamestown in 1607. All of these tribes grew corn and vegetables, made pottery, hunted game with bows and arrows, fished, and lived in large communal houses made from reeds and saplings. The Muskogean groups to the south included the Cherokee, Caddo, Creek, Natchez, Chickasaw, Choctaw, and Seminole tribes. They, like the Algonquians, grew corn, dressed in deerskins, and were skilled at weaving and ceramics. Though these tribes had their own leaders, many with organized systems of tribute and considerable skills in making war, each tribe maintained a separate identity and had no interest in uniting with others.

The World Stage

At the time of Columbus's discovery of America, Europe was in a state of unending warfare. Europeans fought Europeans as well as Africans and Asians. Wars in defense of rival claims never ceased. Whatever unity held within European Christendom rested upon the hostility and contempt with which Europeans viewed all other racial, religious, and cultural groups. The contempt was unjustified. Europe, being one of the least unified, was also one of the most primitive and least potent of the world's major cultures. For some centuries its home territory had been shrinking.

In the twelfth century, the great civilizations had arrived at a temporary stalemate. Islam, the religion arising in Arabia early in the seventh century A.D., proclaimed Muhammad its prophet and the Koran (*qur'an,* or "book") its central religious text. Like Jews and Christians, Muslims believed in one God. They obeyed strict laws defining personal conduct and social justice, and yet were respectful of other religions, notably Judaism and Christianity, which they defined as true but incompletely understood faiths. Convinced that this world and this life are open to ordering by right reason and right conscience, Islam fostered philosophy, science, and such arts as did not violate the injunction against graven images. Islamic scholars in Spain, much of which had fallen under Muslim control, had a large part in providing the Christian West with philosophical texts of ancient Greece. For centuries Islam nurtured the most dynamic and aggressive culture on the planet. But after subduing the Iberian peninsula in Europe, all of North Africa, and southern Asia as far as northern India, Islam had temporarily spent its force. The Muslims retained a commanding superiority over the Europeans in science, technology, warfare, and general learning. It was the Muslims, in fact, who preserved the works of the ancient astronomer Ptolemy, whose estimates of the earth's size guided Columbus. In China, where printing, paper money, and gunpowder had already been invented, the Sung dynasty had presided over a culture differing from both the Islamic and the Christian world in the West but impressive on its own. Chinese philosophy flourished along with highly refined arts. But in the 1120s the Sungs lost half their territory through war and rebellion, and before the end of the twelfth century central Asia had spawned a new Mongol Empire that would rule for a hundred years.

The thirteenth century belonged to a fierce warrior army out of Asia. In the space of forty years, under the leadership of their ruler, Genghis Khan, the Mongols swept over two continents, totally subjugating China and pressing into both Europe and the Islamic world. In 1260 Islamic forces stopped them just short of Egypt. Thenceforth, the Mongols expanded no more; they held on for a century and then abruptly declined.

The European Economy   The Mongol occupation stimulated Europe's economy and in ways that would have vast consequences. When the Mongols seized land to the east, the wealthiest and most advanced centers in Europe were the great city-states of northern Italy. Venice and Genoa in particular had gained large profits by supplying and transporting the armies of the Crusades, a series of Christian wars against Islamic territory along the eastern Mediterranean and particularly in the ancient Holy Land. Venice and Genoa then established themselves as the principal trading centers for the importation of spices, silks, and other commodities from the Far East. During the Mongol years, the trade route for these many necessities and luxuries from the East had to shift southward, out of reach of the Mongol Empire, and a segment of that route went from the Byzantine Empire, the easternmost portion of the Christian world, by sea to Venice and Genoa. To exploit this trade, the Italians borrowed extensively from the technological and scientific storehouse of the Muslims. They learned to construct and use sails in a way that enabled vessels to sail toward the wind, and acquired a knowledge of mathematics, astronomy, and navigation that was far superior to any then current in Europe.

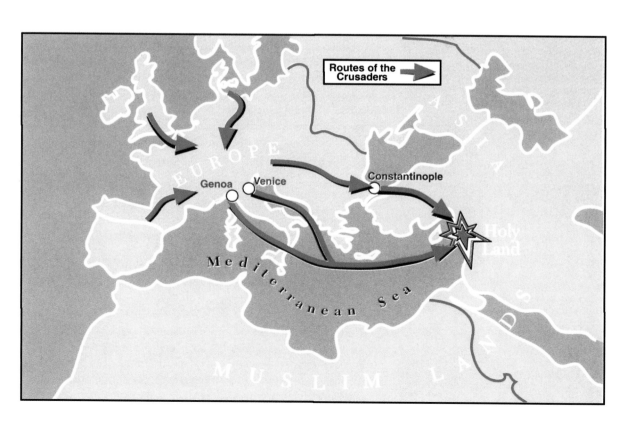

Late in the thirteenth century a Venetian, Marco Polo, spent nearly twenty years in the Far East, mostly in service at the court of Genghis Khan's grandson, the emperor Kublai Khan. Marco Polo's journal gave Europeans their first direct information about the geography and civilization of the Orient, quickened their curiosity, and introduced them to a host of Chinese technological and scientific advances, including gunpowder. Through such borrowings, and by their own ingenious improvements on them, the Italians started Europe along the way to the technological superiority that would, in time, make Europeans masters of the world.

The Ottoman Turks   But Europe's time of world power was yet to come. At the beginning of the fourteenth century, just as the menace of the Mongols was abating, the Muslims rose again, this time under the Ottoman Turks. Before this wave of Islamic zeal had spent itself, the Ottoman Empire would dominate a land mass extending ten thousand miles, from the Danube River to the Red Sea, and including North Africa, Egypt, Syria, Persia, and the Arab peninsula. Through their advanced seamanship, the Muslims dominated the entire Indian Ocean as well.

This expansion had drastic effects on economic conditions in Europe. Eastern commodities could no longer be carried overland to Constantinople, the city that today, as Istanbul in Turkey, is on both sides of the water between eastern Greece and Asia Minor. They now went by water to the Red Sea or the Persian Gulf, and thence overland, through a series of what were in effect toll stations, to Mediterranean ports in Africa and Asia Minor. The price of spices rose greatly, with severe consequences to Europe. Spices—cinnamon, cloves, pepper—were a necessity, not a luxury. Europe suffered from a chronic shortage of winter feed for cattle, and the spices were needed as preservatives for the huge amount of livestock slaughtered every autumn. The population of Europe, moreover, began to increase rapidly at this time, which meant that Oriental spices were becoming scarcer and dearer as the demand was becoming greater. By 1453, when Constantinople fell to the Turks, old trade patterns with the East had been thoroughly disrupted, and Europe's strength was at its lowest in centuries.

The European Social Setting   In the centuries preceding the entrance of the New World of America into the life of the Old, Europe was almost completely rural. Peasant life followed the seasons, along with recurrent celebrations determined by tradition and the Christian calendar. Society was strictly hierarchical, with rigid social classes and a Christian church equally structured from bishops down to clergy. Basic literacy was unavailable to the masses. Disease and other calamities threatened life at earlier ages than the more industrialized peoples of the world expect today. Craftsmen clustered in towns and sorted themselves into guilds—a carpenters' guild, a guild of goldsmiths, and so forth—that controlled standards for entrance and regulated quality and quantity of production.

Of misery, there was more than enough. Agricultural work wrestled from the earth often just enough food to fill stomachs, and sometimes less. Any shift in rain pattern or temperature could bring famine. The thinness of the margin that nature left for human survival got its most dramatic demonstration in the bubonic plague of 1348, which wiped out more than one-third of the people of Europe, townsfolk and villagers alike. This and reappearances of the disease kept the population down for more than a century—incidentally easing pressure on the land and thereby bettering the lives of the survivors. That it took such a disaster to improve the ratio of people to land indicates the delicacy of the balances of soil, effort, and biology amidst which Europeans eked out as many years of life as they could.

Yet there is another side to this grim European existence. Festivity and celebration informed the lives of Europeans. Both peasants and craftsmen worked by a less rigorous schedule than people of recent times. European immigrants to the United States in the late nineteenth century, inheritors of countless generations of labor on the land, would have difficulty adjusting to the clock-timed schedules of American factories. Training for work must have been difficult enough: peasants had to grasp the varied knowledge of planting, reaping, and the management of animals, and learning a craft meant being sent to live in the household of a craftsman. But the skills learned in either case were customary, handed down; they did not elicit the kind of formal literate and mathematical schooling that the work of present-day urban society requires.

| The Renaissance | Another way of life and thought was forming in the larger European towns, especially in Italy. Beginning in the fifteenth century, the phenomenon known as the Renaissance, the rebirth, radically altered the thinking of the classes having the luxury of literate and educated thought, and in time was to transform the existence of peasants and day laborers as well. |

The Renaissance — Another way of life and thought was forming in the larger European towns, especially in Italy. Beginning in the fifteenth century, the phenomenon known as the Renaissance, the rebirth, radically altered the thinking of the classes having the luxury of literate and educated thought, and in time was to transform the existence of peasants and day laborers as well.

For centuries Christians in western Europe had labored under the belief that humankind is miserably weak and sinful, subject to the overwhelming forces of temptation and physical nature. The Renaissance was a time in which a small portion of the European populace discovered, or rediscovered from the texts of the ancient Greeks, the powers of human creativity and the openness of nature to investigation and control. Yet the Renaissance itself was devoutly Christian, and harmonious with this Christianity that affirms the goodness of creation and the high place in it that is assigned to humanity.

The economic source of the Renaissance was the flourishing of Italian towns in the sea trade with Arabia, India, and the Far East. Their part in that commerce was to provide sea transport from the eastern Mediterranean, where goods arrived after overland travel. Perhaps the richness of the silks, the spices, and the other goods that passed through their hands on the way to the rest of Europe stimulated the imaginations of Venetian and Genoan merchants and townspeople. It must have revealed to them the splendid things of which nature and human skill are capable. Wealthy families paid painters and other artists for productions that today remain as tributes to the Renaissance.

In the midst of European peoples almost completely rural, Italian merchant cities offered the daily rush of activity, the interchange of

Printing and Exploration

The development of printing coincided with the age of discovery. Instead of shutting up explorers' accounts of their discoveries in dusty letter files, the fifteenth-century printing presses of Europe—Johannes Gutenberg's 1444 press in Mainz, Germany, was the first—broadcast them to the world. The technology of printing spread quickly through Europe, and eight million copies of books were printed by the end of the sixteenth century.

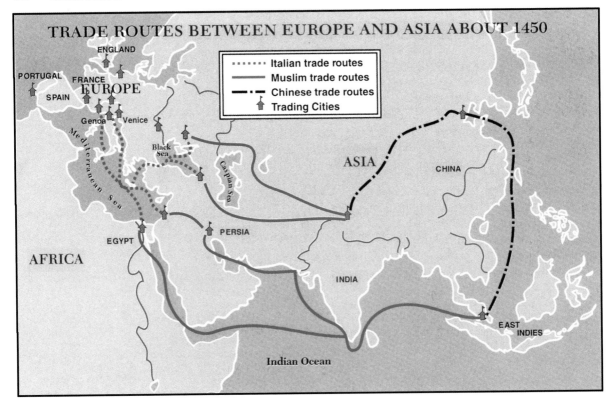

TRADE ROUTES BETWEEN EUROPE AND ASIA ABOUT 1450

········ Italian trade routes
———— Muslim trade routes
—·—·— Chinese trade routes
⚑ Trading Cities

**This salt dish made from gold is
attributed to Benvenuto Cellini.**
(Courtesy, Melville Library)

ideas, the vigor that make urban centers places of artistic and intellectual work. Towns too were centers of craftsmanship, from the simplest utilitarian kinds to the most refined metalworking. Renaissance artists belonged to this community of craftsmen, taking joy in the act of making, whether a great painting or the ornate salt dish that the sixteenth-century artist Benvenuto Cellini wrought of gold.

As thin as the line between craft and art was that between art and science. The Renaissance achievement of perspective in painting capturing the sense of depth on a two-dimensional canvas, was an aesthetic accomplishment. But it also reflected an essentially scientific curiosity about how the eye perceives space. The poet, painter, sculptor, and architect Michelangelo did not think it outside his province to examine the motion of horses, and so he did careful sketches of the leg positions of the animals as they ran.

**The
Reformation**   In the sixteenth century began a religious movement, the Reformation, that like the Renaissance changed European thought and behavior. In 1517 a German priest, Martin Luther, nailed to the door of the cathedral at Wittenberg—a common way of opening a debate—his Ninety-Five Theses, defining what he saw as abuses of the Catholic Church. In the years that followed, Luther developed a theology denying that the earthly Church and its sacraments are the means to salvation. That, Luther insisted, comes of God's freely given grace and the believer's

response in faith. The theologian John Calvin emphasized the individual's utter dependence on God's will. The Reformation captured much of northern Europe, setting Protestant countries against Catholic and generating conflicts within nations, including hostilities among the creeds and sects into which Protestantism itself splintered.

On the surface, the Reformation would seem opposite to the Renaissance in its definition of the human condition. The Renaissance celebrated the powers of intellect and talent; Protestantism brooded over the fallenness and helplessness of humanity. But the Reformation too increased productive activity. Protestant morality demanded work: not only strenuous but constant, methodical, carefully planned effort, a subjugation of the wayward impulses of the individual. The Renaissance awakened among artists and craftsmen an exuberant expression of human energies. Protestantism encouraged work for restraining and giving form to energies that might otherwise turn malicious. But together the two movements turned Christians to the world and the ways human skill and effort can master it. Without the scientific investigation and technological experimenting of the Renaissance and the Reformation, the European settlement of the Americas would have taken a far different course.

Africa

As Europe went through its long stretch of largely self-isolated history, much of the land known, even in the twentieth century, as the "Dark Continent" was growing wealthy, learned, and powerful. Yet Africa to Europeans was a land of "savages" that held riches, and the route to riches, that they coveted and as Christians felt entitled to.

Geography and Climate Man is believed to have originated from 4 to 1.5 million years ago in the high grasslands of eastern and central Africa. Gradually these early human beings spread out across Africa and to other continents.

The size of Africa is remarkable. It stretches 5,000 miles from its northernmost to its southernmost point and it is 4,600 miles at its greatest breadth. Several distinct geographical regions divide the continent. Starting with the northern coast, a narrow, fertile strip runs along the Mediterranean from the Atlantic to the Gulf of Tunis, east of present-day Algeria. A band of savanna or grassland runs beneath it and a bit farther east. Below this expands the Sahara, covering more than four million square miles, too dry to farm but larger than all of the United States by about 400,000 square miles. The central area beneath the Sahara, called the Sudan, is covered with grasslands down to the Equator, where they meet rain forests and mountains. The Kalahari Desert covers a large region near the southern tip. Grasslands, mountains, desert, and semi-desert complete the landscape in the southern region. The population of Africa in 1500 was approximately 78 million, nearly the same as that of Europe.

In many respects Africa is the most inhospitable of the populated continents. The ability of Africans to build complex cultures and survive

Figure of kneeling African woman with child. Western Sudan: Djenne culture. (*Courtesy, The Menil Collection, Houston*)

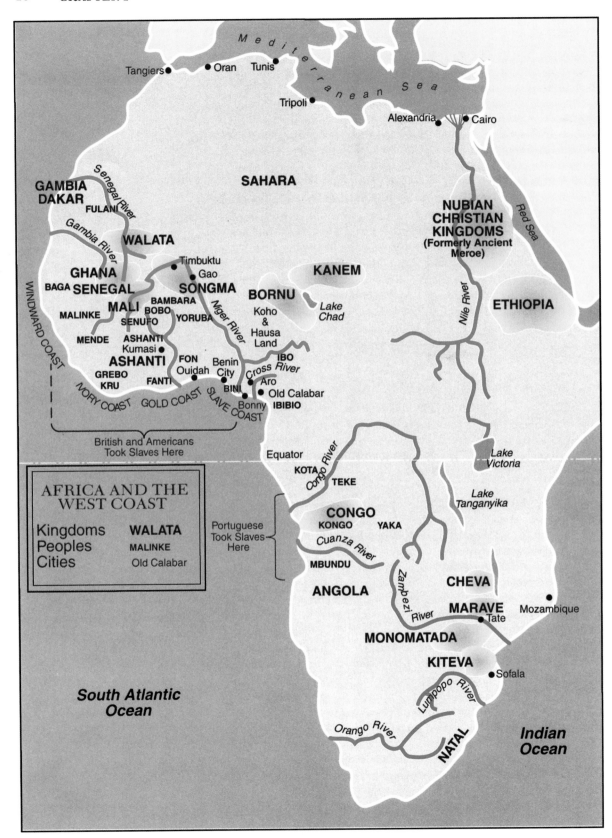

Mediterranean Sea

Tangiers • • Oran   Tunis •

Tripoli •

Alexandria •   • Cairo

SAHARA

GAMBIA
DAKAR
FULANI

Senegal River

Gambia River

WALATA

NUBIAN
CHRISTIAN
KINGDOMS
(Formerly Ancient
Meroe)

Red Sea

KANEM

GHANA
BAGA **SENEGAL**
MALINKE
MALI
MENDE
BAMBARA
BOBO
SENUFO
Timbuktu •
• Gao
SONGMA
YORUBA

BORNU
Koho
&
Hausa
Land

Lake
Chad

Nile River

ETHIOPIA

WINDWARD COAST

ASHANTI
Kumasi •

FON
Ouidah
Benin
City
BINI
Bonny
IBO
Cross River
Aro
Old Calabar
IBIBIO

Niger River

GREBO
KRU
FANTI

ASHANTI

IVORY COAST   GOLD COAST   SLAVE COAST

British and Americans
Took Slaves Here

Equator

KOTA
Congo River
TEKE

Lake
Victoria

Lake
Tanganyika

┌─────────────────────────────┐
│ AFRICA AND THE   │
│ WEST COAST   │
│   │
│ Kingdoms   **WALATA**   │
│ Peoples   **MALINKE**   │
│ Cities   Old Calabar   │
└─────────────────────────────┘

Portuguese
Took Slaves
Here

CONGO
KONGO   **YAKA**

Cuanza River

MBUNDU

ANGOLA

Zambezi River

CHEVA

MARAVE   • Mozambique
• Tate

MONOMATADA

KITEVA
• Sofala

South Atlantic
Ocean

Lumpopo River

Orango River

NATAL

Indian
Ocean

many hardships realizes the scope of human enterprise and purpose. The natural geography kept intruders away from its interior until the nineteenth century. Its deserts are hostile to habitation and travel. Throughout the whole of the continent, a plateau that rises swiftly from the coastline leaves few natural harbors. Even where entry is possible, the traveler is blocked by the desert, semi-desert, or nearly impenetrable forest that stands beyond the coast.

Africa has some of the world's longest and widest rivers, but the high elevation south of the equator makes river navigation difficult. Africans learned to adapt to a climate that ranged from the hot, dusty, dry summer weather and cold winter nights and bone-chilling winds of the desert to the hot and humid rain forest. In northern and southern Africa were areas with mild, rainy winters and warm summers, but diseases thrived for which the Europeans had no tolerance. The half-inch tsetse fly carried the deadly sleeping sickness that prevented animal transport as a means of travel south of the Sahara, and so interior travel was primarily on foot with porters. The interior was divided by the Great Rift Valley, a series of cliffs and troughs that separated the tribes on either side of it. The ability to eke a living out of this formidable landscape and not only to maneuver, but also to profit from its tangled interiors required skills that Africans developed over many thousands of years. It was a triumph of human ingenuity and persistence.

Empires Rise and Fall   Ancient Egypt is the African civilization most commonly known, but the continent nurtured numerous empires and states growing, shifting, and overlapping, then falling and rebuilding. What they held in common was an interest in trade among communities far and near, the development and refinement of artistic endeavors, and slavery.

The Nile Valley, whence sprang the civilization of ancient Egypt, had soil so fertile that it required but a minimum of labor to farm more productively than anywhere else in the continent or perhaps the world. The surrounding desert sands made ideal storage for cereal crops, in underground bins, and domesticated animals had ample riverside pastures to graze upon. These conditions created the opportunity for society to grow to a high population density. Records place some early dynasties as far back as 5000 B.C., and archaeologists have found hieroglyphics and skillfully wrought gold from that period.

The Egyptians learned to work copper as well as gold and created advanced tools, carefully constructed furniture, and the huge cross-cut saws that enabled them to cut large stones and to build the immense tombs, the pyramids, that housed their Pharaohs after death. For builders the Pharaohs used slaves. Typically these were war captives from neighboring populations, although from 3000 B.C. onward, slaves were also regularly bought and sold—as they were in many parts of the world.

Ancient Egypt was the largest and most advanced among the enduring civilizations in northern Africa. Others arose somewhat concurrently. Egyptian traders carried information and skills to Greece, Rome, Arabia, and India as well as to the regions west and south of them

Gou, god of war, a metal sculpture from the Fon culture in Dahomey. *(Courtesy, New York Public Library)*

in Africa. Meroë was the seat of a power, the kingdom of Kush, that rose to greatness. Iron making began in Kush, for the area, located south of the Nile Valley, was rich in iron ore. With iron weapons and iron tools, the kingdom became the richest and most influential in Africa during the first and second centuries A.D. Ancient Egypt had begun its decline long before that, finally falling in 332 B.C. to Alexander the Great. Later it became a province of the Roman Empire.

Generally, in Africa north of the equator, centralized states with hereditary rulers developed, while in regions isolated from exchange with other cultures, more egalitarian, decentralized communities came about essentially for ecological reasons. These were ruled, or rather regulated, by kinship groups such as clans and family lineages, and overall developed more slowly than the Sudan and northern Africa.

In those areas, civilization rolled forward swiftly. By the first century A.D., Greek merchants were trading with Axum, a rival of Meroë in the hills in the northern part of modern Libya. Art flourished throughout these rising civilizations. The rulers of Axum built stone obelisks as high as ninety feet, in addition to fine temples and palaces. In the fourth century A.D., the King of Axum imported iron weapons with which his armies were able to attack and destroy Meroë. Along the west coast, the kingdom of Ghana was formed about A.D. 200, reaching its height many centuries later. Since around the birth of Christ, both Jews and Christians settled along the coast of North Africa, and until early in the seventh century Christianity won some converts in North Africa and within Egypt and Meroë. The pattern of emerging rival states that traded, competed, and warred with one another was interrupted by the arrival of Arabs, aflame with the spirit of Islam and the will and means to conquer and convert.

Muslim Invaders   In A.D. 639, Muslim invaders swept through Egypt, easily subduing the country within two years. Thence they marched westward, were temporarily turned back by the Berbers, and eventually made their way into Berber territory and converted many. From there they conquered Spain and Portugal. In the eleventh century they seized all of North Africa and parts of both western and eastern coasts. It became the "Maghreb," or western part of the Arab world, and even the Berbers, who struggled to maintain their own language and racial identity, gave themselves over to the Arab religion, dress, speech, and customs. The vast Arab empire thus created had an enormous impact on Africa, bringing to it a unifying religion and many cultural elements critical to Africa's development up to the fifteenth century.

The conquest was followed by a period of political stability and economic growth. The Muslims brought learning to Africa at a time when much of Europe was illiterate and impoverished. Through them information about astronomy, advanced mathematics, medicine, clear and strict rules for governing and behaving, and a keenly managed and sophisticated system of trade passed to Africans. They also ran an active slave trade. Captives were sold throughout North Africa, into areas of Arabia, Spain, and Portugal, and to countries involved in the Arabs'

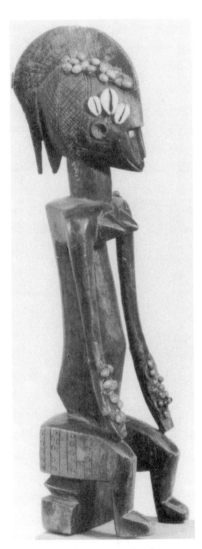

African Art (1200–1700). This figure is decorated with Indian Ocean cowrie shells, which were used as currency in many parts of Africa. (*National Museum of Denmark, Department of Ethnography*)

Indian Ocean trade route. Tens of thousands of slaves were dispersed this way.

The stability and trade engendered by the Muslim invasions and Islamic rule stimulated the rise of yet more African empires. The states that rose up during the period from about the eighth century to the fourteenth—the Hausa and Kanem-Baru, the Mali and Songhai, the Congo (also written *Kongo*) and Guinea—each had its goods to contribute to the trading system, each collected fees from those traveling through it, and each had fierce rivalries and frequent wars with the others. These states grew powerful and rich, their coffers built on international trade that went on, largely uninterrupted, until new waves of invasions began in the twelfth century.

The African   The decentralized regions of Africa, whose popula-
Slave Trade   tion met the harsh ecological challenge of their environments by engaging in subsistence agriculture,
were especially vulnerable to slave traders. These societies lacked central government structures and standing armies to protect themselves from the more powerful and predatory neighbors on their borders. As these neighbors took captives to sell as slaves, slavery became an essential part of African trade.

African slavery existed long before the Europeans initiated the transatlantic slave trade. From the seventh to the nineteenth century, more than a thousand years, Africans were bought and sold as slaves. In Islamic Africa as well as a few other areas, slaves of children could gradually free themselves, as could slave soldiers through the process of manumission preached in the Koran. In previous centuries many slaves had intermarried with their captors and so became integrated into a tribe. But this potential for liberation slowly changed. A general rule evolved that proclaimed that slaves born in captivity could not be sold, and this increased the need for slaves bought or stolen elsewhere. It also expanded the slave population to such an extent that, in some areas, slaves began to outnumber free people two or even three to one. Wars among the large states, or by large communities upon smaller ones (there were, according to one estimate, some one thousand smaller states), put more slaves into the rapidly expanding market, many of them needed as soldiers. The trade brought even more wealth to those states able to participate in it, and with that wealth came intensified rivalries and insatiable greed. The slave trade was profitable because of the trading networks and because slaves often cost little or nothing at the beginning of the market chain. The system could not work without African knowledge of the wild to traverse the unwelcoming land, African warriors to capture slaves, African merchants to facilitate the sales, and carefully managed agreements among populations and states.

Arab Africa controlled the spice trade and a large portion of the slave trade. Western and central Africans controlled the gold and the supply of slaves, as well as the flow of trade. So poised, Africa seemed to have everything that Europe wanted and needed, and it was available legitimately through trade, or illegitimately through plunder.

The diversity of the trade and the distance spanned to support that

One slave trader explained his operation:

"In the daytime we called at the villages we passed, and purchased our slaves fairly; but in the night we . . . broke into the villages and, rushing into the huts of the inhabitants, seized men, woman, and children promiscuously."

trade were stupendous given the time, difficulties, and dangers of travel. Yet European and African trade goods were distributed all over the northern half of the continent. While such trade had existed before the Arab invasions, Arab occupation and influence briskly increased commerce and made it more sophisticated. A merchant in the 1400s might start his trans-Saharan trek with beads and Egyptian cottons and exchange those at the first stop for camels. There he could pick up minerals, selling them for kolo nuts from the Yoruba kingdom on the southern edges of the savanna. Those he might sell to merchants in the centrally located Hausa states, picking up cotton and leather goods in that vicinity. Going eastwards again, he would perhaps exchange his merchandise for ostrich feathers and slaves, selling those in his home city, from which he might have been absent for as long as ten years.

Salt from the north and gold from the south were the most valuable commodities. Copper, cloth, beads, jewelry, horses, cattle, and dried fruit also came from the north, while commodities such as knives and swords, spices, and rugs came to East Africa and then west via the Arabian Indian Ocean trade, in exchange for gold, ivory, slaves, and skins. Through East Africa also came new foods from Indonesia, many of which—banana and coconut, for example—enabled the populations there to spread farther south and west. Iron, weaving, pottery, leather goods, slaves, grains, dried fish and mollusks, medicines, and baskets were but a few of the many goods that moved from south and west to north and east. Besides gold, cowrie shells from the Indian Ocean, iron bars, brass weights, and bolts of cotton cloth were used for currency, as was direct barter. An obligation to care for the elderly, widows, and orphans was pervasive throughout African society.

Olaudah Equiano. *(Courtesy, Collection of Hugh Cleland)*

OLAUDAH EQUIANO

Olaudah Equiano was kidnapped as a boy from what is now the Benin province of Nigeria. He was sold to British slavers in 1756, brought to Barbados, and then to Virginia. After service in the French and Indian War, he was able to buy his freedom and lived to publish his uniquely detailed memoirs in 1789. This part of his story, describing his capture in the 1700s, is a classic account of an experience shared by millions of Africans from the 1500s to the early 1800s.

[W]hen the grown people in the neighborhood [of Benin] were gone far in the fields to labor, the children assembled together in some of the neighboring premises to play; and commonly some of us used to get up a tree to look out for any assailant, or kidnapper, that might come upon us—for they sometimes took those opportunities of our parents' absence, to attack and carry off as many as they could seize. One day as I was watching at the top of a tree in our yard, I saw one of those people come into the yard of our next neighbor but one to

kidnap, there being many stout young people in it. Immediately on this I gave the alarm of the rogue, and he was surrounded by the stoutest of them, who entangled him with cords, so that he could not escape till some of the grown people came and secured him. But, alas! ere long it was my fate to be thus attacked, and to be carried off, when none of the grown people were nigh. . . .

The first object which saluted my eyes when I arrived on the coast, was the sea, and a slave ship, which was then riding at anchor, and waiting for its cargo. These filled me with astonishment, which was soon converted into terror, when I was carried on board. I was immediately handled, and tossed up to see if I were sound, by some of the crew; and I was now persuaded that I had gotten into a world of bad spirits, and that they were going to kill me. . . . When I looked round the ship too, and saw a large furnace of copper boiling, and a multitude of black people of every description chained together, every one of their countenances expressing dejection and sorrow, I no longer doubted of my fate; and, quite overpow-

Portugal's Crusade by Sea

Europe desperately needed a way of coping with the Muslims and trading with the East. Portugal found it. The people of that tiny kingdom, free for two centuries from Muslim domination but struggling for survival in a rocky and barren land, had turned to the sea, first as fishermen, then as traders. As seagoing traders whose home base was on the Atlantic, not the Mediterranean, they understandably thought of an indirect route to the spices that Europe needed. With Africa's gold and ivory Europe could buy spices. If Europeans could find a sea route around Africa to the East, they could bypass the Muslims who controlled North Africa's trade and establish trade directly with the black rulers of West Africa and the Sudan.

Geography was a reason Portugal and Spain were the leaders in the late fifteenth-century expansion of Europe. The Iberian peninsula, which Portugal and Spain occupied, jutted well out into the Atlantic and constituted the southwesternmost region of the continent of Europe. Seventy years before Columbus sailed, Portuguese and Spanish sailors had pushed far out into the Atlantic. The Canary Islands, which are located approximately seventy miles off the coast of West Africa, became Spanish territory in the 1420s. At the same time the Azores, a group of islands almost eight hundred miles out into the Atlantic, became Portuguese colonies. Portugal and Spain were both maritime powers long before the rest of Europe was even beginning to look westward beyond its shores.

It is also important that the two European powers were among the first to consolidate into nation-states. In the twelfth century, Portugal

ered with horror and anguish, I fell motionless on the deck and fainted. When I recovered a little, I found some black people about me, who I believed were some of those who had brought me on board, and had been receiving their pay; they talked to me in order to cheer me, but all in vain. I asked them if we were not to be eaten by those white men with horrible looks, red faces, and long hair. They told me I was not. . . .

I was soon put down under the decks, and there I received such a salutation in my nostrils as I had never experienced in my life: so that, with the loathsomeness of the stench, and crying together, I became so sick and low that I was not able to eat, nor had I the least desire to taste any thing. I now wished for the last friend, death, to relieve me; but soon, to my grief, two of the white men offered me eatables; and, on my refusing to eat, one of them held me fast by the hands, and laid me across, I think the windlass, and tied my feet, while the other flogged me severely. I had never experienced any thing of this kind before, and although not being used to the water, I naturally feared that element the first time I saw

it, yet, nevertheless, could I have got over the nettings, I would have jumped over the side, but I could not; and besides, the crew used to watch us very closely who were not chained down to the decks, lest we should leap into the water; and I have seen some of these poor African prisoners most severely cut, for attempting to do so, and hourly whipped for not eating. This indeed was often the case with myself. In a little time after, amongst the poor chained men, I found some of my own nation, which in a small degree gave ease to my mind. I inquired of these what was to be done with us? they gave me to understand, we were to be carried to these white people's country to work for them. I then was a little revived, and thought, if it were no worse than working, my situation was not so desperate; but still I feared I should be put to death, the white people looked and acted, as I thought, in so savage a manner; for I had never seen among any people such instances of brutal cruelty; and this not only shown towards us blacks, but also to some of the whites themselves.

had become an independent kingdom, and when Queen Isabella of Castile married King Ferdinand of Aragon in 1469, the two most powerful political entities in Spain came together. Both Spain and Portugal enjoyed the political unity and the economic resources necessary for exploration and colonization.

Both, moreover, were possessed of a crusading zeal unknown in the rest of Europe. In the eighth century, the Moors from North Africa had invaded Iberia, and they carried their Arabic, Muslim culture deep into Spain and Portugal. Over the next seven hundred years, Christian monarchs fought a bloody war to drive the Moors back into North Africa. In the process Spain acquired a religious identity bordering on fanaticism, imbued with a passion for expelling the infidels and upholding the Christian faith: a passion that after the Protestant Reformation would be committed to the defense of Roman Catholicism. Portugal expelled the last of the Moorish armies in 1245. Ferdinand and Isabella did not get rid of the Moors until 1492.

In the year Columbus headed for "the Indies," then, Spain and Portugal possessed the unity, maritime skills, and resources needed for exploration and empire.

Marine Monsters: from Olaus Magnus, Historia de Gentibus Septentrionalibus, 1555. (*Courtesy, New York Public Library*)

Prince Henry the Navigator   The man who directed Portugal's efforts to take advantage of the possibilities for pioneering by sea was Prince Henry the Navigator. Henry began his explorations in 1415. At the age of twenty-one this extraordinary young man retired from the court and from politics, became governor of the southernmost province of Portugal, and began building a strange settlement there, on Cape St. Vincent—"where endeth land and where beginneth sea." For the next forty years he gathered sailors, astronomers, mapmakers, instrument makers, and shipbuilders from all over Europe, and subsidized expeditions to explore the west coast of Africa, seeking to reach India by ocean. Overcoming the fears of superstitious sailors that ships would run into boiling hot waters at the equator, the grand and audacious Portuguese undertaking was only temporarily set back by Henry's death in 1460. In 1487 Bartholomeu Dias, his ship blown off course by a gale, rounded the southern tip of Africa. Then from 1497 to 1499, Vasco da Gama made his celebrated voyage around the Cape of Good Hope to India with a four-vessel fleet, returning two years later with a cargo of pepper and cinnamon. Within twenty more years Henry's dream was fulfilled, for Portugal had established a maritime empire that extended the full breadth of the Indian Ocean.

Other Europeans, inspired by the Portuguese, sought to share trade in the East. None reckoned that they could overtake Portugal in the race around Africa, but several thought they might find an alternate course. It was reasonably well known that the earth was round, and not knowing of the existence of America, they thought that a daring sailor might easily reach the Orient by sailing west from Europe. The most persistent of seamen who so reasoned was Christopher Columbus. His voyages profited from Prince Henry's development of a small sailing ship, the caravel. Its hull design and sail plan enabled the caravel to sail faster than earlier ships. Now mariners could go as far as they wished with assurance that they could return. And so Columbus made his spectacular voyages, thinking that he was finding the Orient but in fact opening a new continent to Europeans.

The Spanish Empire

The consequence of Columbus's voyages was a flurry of efforts by other Europeans to capitalize on his findings. The Portuguese did little, for they were convinced that Columbus had not reached Asia. Other European monarchs, including the Kings of England and France, backed voyages upon Columbus's mistaken belief that he had found the Indies, or a passage to them. Henry VII of England sponsored trips by the Italian John Cabot (Giovanni Caboto) in 1497 and 1498. Cabot explored the American coast from Labrador to Chesapeake Bay and discovered vast areas teeming with fish, but found neither spices nor a passage to India. Henry's England profited little from these and later explorations by John Cabot's son Sebastian. French and Venetian efforts were likewise unprofitable, and both states had pressing preoccupations, and so they, like England, soon abandoned the search for the Indies. Hence, for nearly a hundred years Spain had a virtual monopoly on exploration and discovery in the New World.

Explorers for Spain   The greatest of explorers sailing under the Spanish flag was, of course, Columbus himself. Columbus made four voyages in all: 1492–93, 1493–96, 1498–1500, and 1502–04. He visited most of the major islands of the Caribbean, the northern coast of South America, and the Central American mainland from Honduras to Panama, and planted colonies in several of these places. In Cuba one of Columbus's sailors reported "many people, with a firebrand in the hand, and herbs to drink the smoke thereof." By the 1600s tobacco smoking would become the rage all over Europe. In activities other than navigation, Columbus proved inept. He so neglected and mismanaged the colonies that he had to be removed as governor; and when he died in 1506 he was still convinced that what he had explored was part of Asia. Columbus's reports of the new land's abundance and its natives' childlike innocence planted in the European mind the image of an earthly paradise, a lost Eden inhabited by noble savages, that would shape ideas about the New World for centuries to come.

One of Columbus's contemporaries, an Italian navigator named Amerigo Vespucci, first convinced Europeans that Columbus had discovered a new continent. In 1507 a German cartographer, impressed by Vespucci's writings, named the new land "America" in his honor. Vespucci's detailed descriptions of terrain, plants, and people added greatly to European knowledge and understanding of the shape and size of the New World. Henceforth all Europe knew America for what it was, a new continent and a barrier between Europe and Asia.

Nothing of any recognized value had yet been found in America, and so the problem now was to find a strait through a land mass of unknown size. In 1513 a Spanish explorer, Juan Ponce de León, visited what is now the southeastern United States. He named the area Florida,

Sailing through the rich Grand Bank fisheries off Labrador, the explorer John Cabot wrote in his diary of "cod so thick they sometimes stayed my ship."

After sailing along the coast of what is now South America in 1501, Vespucci described the land and its people:

"The inhabitants of the New World do not have goods of their own, but all things are held in common. They live together without King, without government, and each is his own master. . . . If the terrestrial paradise be in any part of this earth, I esteem that it is not far distant from these parts."

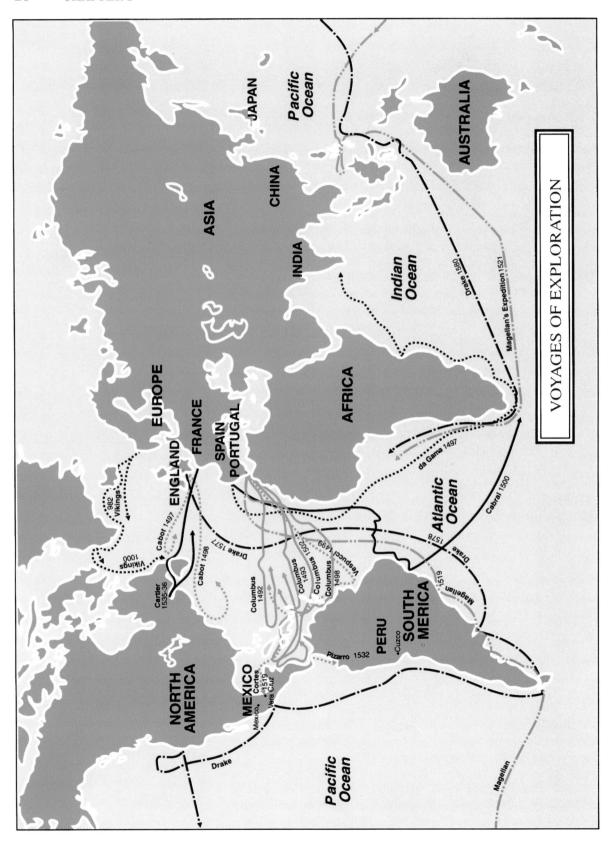

VOYAGES OF EXPLORATION

roughly translatable as "land of flowers." A chance discovery in 1513 stimulated the search for a passage to the Orient. Vasco Núñez de Balboa, a Spanish adventurer, led a band of followers in search of gold in Central America, crossed the Isthmus of Darien, and sighted the Pacific. Spain promptly planted a colony in the vicinity, and explorers, encouraged to learn that the two oceans were separated only by an extremely narrow strip of land, renewed their hopes. After the coast of Central America and Mexico had been fairly thoroughly cruised, it appeared that the most promise of finding a route lay to the south. And in 1519 Ferdinand Magellan, a Portuguese sailing under Spanish auspices, set out on a monumental voyage. On September 20 he embarked with five small ships and 275 men; three years later, on September 8, 1522, one worm-eaten ship and eighteen survivors sailed upriver into the harbor at Seville. Magellan had been killed by natives in the Philippines, but his place in history was assured. His expedition had discovered a passage to the Pacific lying between the southern tip of South America and the islands now named Tierra del Fuego: the narrow waterway has been named the Strait of Magellan. Thence the voyagers had sailed across the Pacific, through the Indian Ocean, around Africa, and back to Spain.

The first journey to circle the globe, it added enormously to Europe's knowledge of the world and demonstrated for all time that it was not feasible for Spain to try to compete with Portugal in the East by sailing west. The route was simply too difficult; and besides, by the time Magellan's vessels reached the Indian Ocean the Portuguese had already established the bases that made them dominant in the entire area. In 1519, while Magellan's ships were nearing Tierra del Fuego, another voyage of discovery brought the first Europeans to what is now the Texas Gulf Coast. Searching like Magellan for a route to the Orient, Alonso Alvarez de Piñeda and his 270 men visited the mouth of the Rio Grande River before returning to Spain.

Beginnings of World History   The exploratory voyages of the Spanish and Portuguese were seminal events in the history of the world. Until 1492 there was no "world," at least of a global stretch. Europeans, Asians, and Africans had only the vaguest notions of one another's existence, and the people of North America, South America, Australia, and the Pacific Islands were cut off almost completely. There were some tenuous commercial connections. European traders exchanged goods with West Africans. Arab businessmen in East Africa regularly crossed the Indian Ocean to trade with India. Italian merchants worked through traders in the Middle East to acquire Chinese products. And the Islamic religion by the fourteenth century was moving west into North Africa and east into Indonesia and the Philippines. What the Spanish and Portuguese voyages of exploration managed to do was bring together all of the previously separate regions of the world.

The process of creating a global community, of course, would take centuries to complete, but after 1500 no one part of the world was isolated from its distant neighbors. Religions, technologies, products, services, animals, plants, and people began spreading from one conti-

The Great Temple of Tenochtitlán reconstructed by Ignacio Marquina from descriptions by Spanish conquerors and existing Aztec monuments. *(Courtesy, American Museum of Natural History)*

Bartolomé de Las Casas (1474–1566) spent most of his long life attempting to protect native Americans against the massacres, tortures, slavery, tribute, and forced labor imposed on them by their Spanish conquerors. Modern scholars generally accept the accuracy of Las Casas's shocking portraits of devastation, some of which he personally witnessed. Today, however, many view these horrors not as the outcome of some peculiar Spanish cruelty but as characteristic of the "Columbian encounter" between Europeans and other cultures in the age of exploration and conquest.

"The natives are likewise the most delicate people, weak and of feeble constitution, and less than any other can they bear fatigue, and they very easily die of whatsoever infirmity; so much so, that not even the sons of our Princes and of nobles, brought up in royal and gentle life, are so delicate as they; although there are among them such as are of the peasant class. They are also a very poor people, who of worldly goods possess little, nor wish to possess: and they are therefore neither proud, nor ambitious, nor avaricious. . . .

Among these gentle sheep, gifted by their Maker with the above qualities, the Spaniards entered as soon as they knew them, like wolves, tigers, and lions which had been starving for many days, and since forty years they have done nothing else; nor do they otherwise at the present day, than outrage, slay, afflict, torment, and destroy them with strange and new, and divers kinds of cruelty, never before seen nor heard of, nor read of. . . . The reason why the Christians have killed and destroyed such infinite numbers of souls, is solely because they have made gold their ultimate aim."

nent to another, and so did disease, exploitation, and war. World history, in the sense of an interaction of all regions of the globe, had begun.

The Aztecs, Maya, and Incas

The early Spanish settlements in the West Indies proved reasonably prosperous, establishing some economies based on cattle raising with Spanish labor and others founded on sugar planting with Indian slave labor. But raising cattle and growing sugar were not the kinds of activities that quickened the imagination or filled the treasuries of the Spanish monarchs. Far more exciting were rumors of highly civilized kingdoms in the interiors of Mexico, Central America, and northwestern South America, and of their stores of gold and silver. An expedition set out in 1519 to find, conquer, plunder, and Christianize these kingdoms. In command was Hernán Cortés, a thirty-two-year-old soldier and adventurer.

The Aztec Indians had dominated the valley land of Mexico since the early 1300s. From their capital city of Tenochtitlán, now Mexico City, they sent out war parties to exact tribute from other tribes. In the capital the Aztecs had surgeons and hospitals as advanced as the best in Europe, but they also practiced human sacrifice. They worshiped many gods but particularly Quetzalcoatl, the feathered serpent, and the bloodthirsty Hummingbird. In the space of only four days the Aztecs once sacrificed from 20,000 to 60,000 human beings at the altar in Tenochtitlán. In 1519 as news of the Spanish encroachments reached them, the court astrologers forecast a war of the gods and the emperor Montezuma II stepped up the ritual killings. When the emperor finally realized that the Spanish were not gods, he fought ably and might have held them off. But during the siege of his city, smallpox imported from Europe decimated the Indian population. In a matter of months Cortés had penetrated the heart of the Aztec Empire, though it took two years to complete the systematic looting and destruction of Tenochtitlán and the total conquest of the Aztec people. The Aztecs, like the later Indian tribes Europeans encountered in America, had developed no immunity against the perennial European epidemics. Between 1500 and 1600 the native population of the New World declined, by various estimates, from as much as 70 to 90 percent.

After subduing the Aztecs, Cortés's men moved on to seize the Mayan lands of the southeastern Mexican peninsula of Yucatán and the present Central American republic of Guatemala. From about A.D. 300 to 900 the Maya had a culture advanced in architecture and representative arts and notable in astronomy: their calendar remains a marvel. Though the Maya, like the Aztecs, were warriors, the Aztecs had militarily overshadowed them. The relation between the empire-building Aztecs and the artistic Maya has been roughly compared to that between ancient Rome, skilled in organization and administration, and the culturally sophisticated Greek city-states. But the Maya had their own form of organization in the form of an aristocratic priesthood that lived off the labor of the populace. By the time of the Spanish conquest, Maya civilization had long since passed its greatness. Descendants of a people subjected to a priestly caste were now to be subject to adventurers and then to a Spanish colonial aristocracy. Even in the twentieth century, the Maya of Central America would live under regimes distinguished for the ruthlessness of their dominant classes and the military and police in the service of the wealthy.

South of the Maya and the Aztecs, the Incas ruled an area stretching from what is now modern-day Colombia through Peru to Chile, a distance equal to that from New York City to the Panama Canal. Inspired by rumors of Incan gold, in 1532 Francisco Pizarro, an illiterate adventurer in the service of the Spanish crown, entered Peru with a force of fewer than two hundred men. He seized and executed the Incan ruler, Atahualpa, placing himself at the head of an empire of six or eight million souls and fabulous riches of gold and silver. Pizarro was mur-

This description of a Peruvian garden, written by the illegitimate son of an Inca princess and a Spanish laborer, appeared in a work published in England in 1625:

"This Garden was in the Incas time a Garden of Silver and Gold, as they had in the Kings' houses, where they had many sorts of Hearbes, Flowers, Plants, Trees, Beasts great and small, wilde, tame: Snakes, Lizards, Snailes, Butterflies, small and great Birds, each set in their place. They had . . . Fruit-trees with the fruite on them all of Gold and Silver, resembling the naturall. They had also in the house heapes of wood, all counterfeit of Gold and Silver, as they had in the house royal: likewise they had great statues of men and women, and children . . . All the Vessel[s] . . . for the Temple's service, Pots, Pans, Tubs, Hogsheads, was of Gold and Silver, even to the Spades and Pickaxes for the Garden."

Machu Picchu, the fabled "Lost City of the Incas," clings to a ridge high in the Andes Mountains above the Urubamba Valley, eighty-five hundred feet above sea level. Built by the Incan ruler, Pachacuti, about 1450 and mysteriously abandoned around the time of the Spanish conquest, it was never found by the *conquistadores*. Once a vital part of the vast Inca Empire in the 1400s, Machu Picchu remained unknown to the outside world until a Yale history professor named Hiram Bingham discovered it in 1911. *(Braniff International)*

dered by one of his own men in 1541, but Peru, like most of South and Central America, would remain under Spanish rule for nearly three hundred years. Only Brazil, awarded to Portugal by the Treaty of Tordesillas in 1494, was outside Spain's vast New World domain.

In the years after Columbus, Spanish *conquistadores*, far outnumbered by the Aztecs, Incas, and other native peoples, subdued them with relative ease. Indian warriors on foot with weapons made of stone and bone were no match for Spaniards on horseback with steel swords and guns. With superior technology, and with bravado, cunning, and occasional treachery, the Spanish made themselves masters of all they invaded. They also deliberately destroyed most of the Indian cultures and imposed their own. Human sacrifice gave way to Holy Communion as intrepid friars and priests converted the natives to Christianity. Ornate Spanish buildings built by Indian laborers rose on the stone foundations of native structures. Roman Catholic churches, their altars carved by native artisans and encrusted with Indian gold and silver, replaced temples to the sun and moon. With remarkable efficiency and considerable cruelty, the Spanish established an empire that filled their coffers with gold and silver, while rumors of yet undiscovered New World treasures swept through Europe.

Coronado wrote to his monarch of the peoples in the kingdoms he visited:

"The people of the towns seem to me to be of ordinary size and intelligent, although I do not think that they have the judgment and intelligence which they ought to have to build their houses in the way in which they have, for most of them are entirely naked except the covering of their privy parts. . . ."

Exploration of the West   In the 1540s Hernando de Soto and Francisco Vásquez de Coronado separately explored parts of the present-day United States for gold. De Soto, after landing on the west coast of Florida, led his men into North Carolina, turning westward and ending somewhere at or just west of the Mississippi River, in what is now Tennessee, where he died in 1542. Ultimately, over three hundred of his followers made their way back to Mexico via the Mississippi River. Coronado moved northward out of Mexico and probably traveled as far as Kansas. When he returned he made clear that the fabled "seven Cities of Cíbola," cities said to be made of gold, did not exist and that there was little else in the area to attract settlement.

Spanish exploration of the California coast also occurred in the 1540s. In 1542 Juan Rodriguez Cabrillo, a Portuguese explorer in the employ of Spain, hoped to discover the Northwest Passage between the Pacific and the Atlantic. He first sailed into San Diego Bay and later went northward, perhaps as far as Oregon. Following Sir Francis Drake's claiming of California for the English, the Spaniards, fearing they might lose the region, sent Sebastián Vizcaíno in 1602 to report about California to the Spanish monarch. Vizcaíno recommended to the King that Spain establish colonies there, but further Spanish activity along the West Coast would await the passing of nearly a century.

Early French Explorations   In 1524 King Francis I of France sent an Italian navigator, Giovanni da Verrazano, to explore the coast of North America. Hoping to find a passage to the East Indies, Verrazano tried the Hudson River (where a bridge bears his name today), and other places from New York to Newfoundland, to no avail. But he did establish France's claim to the region, which he named "New France."

By 1535 a French explorer, Jacques Cartier, had discovered and named the St. Lawrence River. He also made friends with the Huron Indians there, who told him of a fabulously rich kingdom far upriver. Cartier then invited the King of the Hurons to return home with him and meet the King of France. After hearing the Indian King's story Francis I sent Cartier in 1541 with ten ships to explore the St. Lawrence. The expedition sailed as far as the site of present-day Montreal, but failed to find the storied kingdom. Far to the south, another group of Frenchmen in 1564 established a colony, Fort Caroline, near present-day Jacksonville, Florida. French Protestants, called Huguenots, remained in this colony until the Spanish massacred them. In 1565 the Spanish founded St. Augustine, the first permanent settlement in what would one day become part of the United States.

England: The Sceptered Isle

Henry VII   When Henry VII, the first King belonging to the House of Tudor, ascended the throne in 1485, the royal treasury had been depleted by a long civil war, the War of the Roses.

Henry might have been expected to secure his position in the traditional way, allying himself with groups of nobles. Instead, he built up the independent power of the Crown by taking a number of commoners into the government. As the principal instrument for his attack on the nobility he created the Court of the Star Chamber, through which people could be seized, tried without a jury, and punished by fines that amounted to confiscation of their property. In these early days the Star Chamber functioned and was looked upon as a protector of the common people against the tyranny of the nobles. By its means Henry weakened and divided the nobility. To replenish the royal treasury, Henry managed his fiscal affairs efficiently and frugally: for the 1497 voyage to America he paid John Cabot £10. He chose his wars carefully, acting only when he was likely not only to win, but also to reap profit from plunder. By the time he died in 1509 his dynasty was firmly secured, and the royal treasury was the richest in all Europe.

Henry VIII   Henry VII's son and successor, Henry VIII, began his reign by dissipating the royal treasury in little more than a decade. Then a number of circumstances induced Henry to a radical measure. Of the six children borne by Henry's wife Catherine of Aragon, only one daughter survived and Catherine was unable to have more. And so the Tudor dynasty was in danger of having no male successor to the throne. In addition, Henry fell passionately in love with Anne Boleyn, who was willing to marry the King but refused to become his mistress. Henry turned to the Pope with a request for an annulment of his marriage. That might have been granted except that the Pope was virtually a prisoner of Catherine of Aragon's nephew, who was both King Charles I of Spain and Emperor Charles V of the Germanic political entity known as the Holy Roman Empire. The King had his marriage to

English Exploration
The English clergyman Richard Hakluyt in 1584 presented her majesty, Elizabeth I, reasons for the state to take a hand in the western voyages:

"The soil yieldeth . . . all the several commodities of Europe, . . . that by trade of merchandise cometh into this realm.

The passage thither and home is neither too long nor too short, but easy and to be made twice in the year.

The passage . . . is safe passage, and not easy to be annoyed by prince or potentate whatsoever.

This enterprise may stay the Spanish King from flowing over all the face of America, if we seat and plant there in time. . . . How easy a matter may it be to this realm, swarming at this day with valiant youths, . . . to be lords of all those seas, . . . and consequently to abate the pride of Spain.

This voyage, albeit it may be accomplished by bark or smallest pinnace, . . . yet . . . the merchant will not for profit's sake use it but by ships of great burden; so as this realm shall have by that means ships of great strength for the defense of this realm. . . .

By making of ships and by preparing of things for the same, . . . by planting of vines and olive trees, and by making of wine and oil, by husbandry, and by thousands of things there to be done, infinite numbers of the English nation may be set on work, to the unburdening of the realm with many that now live chargeable to the state at home. . . .

We shall by planting there enlarge the glory of the gospel, and from England plant sincere religion, and provide a safe place to receive people from all parts of the world that are forced to flee for the truth of God's word. . . ."

Catherine dissolved and secretly married Anne Boleyn. In 1529 Henry called Parliament into a historic session that lasted seven years. Before it was discharged, the King had created the Church of England, or Anglican Church, and broke all ties with Rome and the Roman Catholic faith.

That opened the way for a solution to Henry's financial problems. He confiscated the property of the church monasteries, which brought him nearly a sixth of all the land in England. The releasing of land from the control of the Church, the consequent growth in the number of landholders, and the commercial activity that the sale of the lands awakened together energized the English economy.

The break gained for England the zealous enmity of its traditional ally, Spain. That enmity intensified with the accession of Philip II to the Spanish throne in 1556. Philip was fanatically dedicated to using all the wealth and power of the Spanish Empire to suppress Protestantism.

Elizabeth I   Queen Elizabeth, Henry VIII's daughter by Anne Boleyn, ascended the throne in 1558 after a turbulent and bloody eleven-year interval in which her half-brother Edward and her Roman Catholic half-sister Mary each occupied the throne for just over five years. By then England's internal order and external relations had been fundamentally rearranged.

Elizabeth faced spiraling prices and had no more monasteries to confiscate. One solution was for England to obtain a share of Spain's gold and silver through direct trade with Spanish colonies, and for Elizabeth to augment her treasury either by taxing or licensing this trade or by going into secret partnership with the English traders.

For a while such undertakings were entrusted to private enterprise. The first outsider to exploit this market was the Englishman John Hawkins. The two Old World commodities most in demand in Spanish America were cloth and slaves, the first a product of England and the other easily obtainable in Portuguese West Africa. In 1562 Hawkins acquired three hundred black slaves and sailed with them to the Caribbean, receiving payment in sugar and hides, which he sold profitably in Europe. On his second venture the Queen and several members of her Privy Council were Hawkins's secret partners, and he again made an enormous profit. Subsequent ventures were handicapped by a Spanish crackdown and by 1569 trade was thoroughly closed to outsiders. Within another four years, more or less open conflict between the Catholic and the Protestant countries had begun, the Dutch having allied themselves with England. For the next thirty years, British and Dutch ships engaged in smuggling to Spanish America and in systematic plunder of Spanish shipping.

The greatest of the English captains in these enterprises was Sir Francis Drake, kinsman of Hawkins. Drake conducted a brilliant and profitable privateering raid in 1573, viewed the Pacific Ocean from the Isthmus of Panama, and resolved "to sail an English ship in these seas." He launched his most spectacular venture five years later. With secret authorization and an investment from the Queen he crossed the Atlantic, passed through the Strait of Magellan, plundered Spanish shipping

Sir Walter Raleigh, encouraged by Queen Elizabeth to colonize North America, explored a new region which was named Virginia in honor of the monarch known to history as the Virgin Queen. *(Courtesy, New York Public Library, Picture Collection)*

off South America, captured a shipload of Peruvian silver, explored the Pacific coast of North America, crossed to the East Indies, concluded a treaty with a sultan who was at war with the Portuguese, bought several tons of cloves, and sailed home by the Portuguese route around Africa, returning with a magnificent treasure of £2,500,000. Meanwhile, Elizabeth encouraged Martin Frobisher and John Davis in their exploration of North America for a northwest water passage to Asia, and granted Humphrey Gilbert and his half-brother Walter Raleigh a charter to colonize "remote heathen and barbarous lands not actually possessed by any Christian prince or people," and providing for settlers to "enjoy all the privileges of free denizens and persons native of England." When Drake came home from his spectacular circumnavigation of the world in 1581, the Queen knighted him on the quarterdeck of his ship, the *Golden Hind,* and rejected all attempts by Spain to recover the stolen booty.

Open war with Spain soon followed. Spain under Philip II had had more than enough of Elizabethan sea dogs, and the somber Catholic zealot Philip was committed to rewinning Protestant England and Scotland for the Roman Catholic Church.

Naval warfare began in 1584. Elizabeth sent troops to Protestant Dutch states to aid in their struggle to retain independence from the Spanish crown. Drake set forth with more than twenty men-of-war to attack the Spanish position in America. In the ensuing year Drake wreaked considerable devastation in the West Indies and sacked Santo Domingo. In 1587 he conducted an audacious raid that sank much of the Spanish fleet in its home harbor at Cádiz.

Philip of Spain then ordered the construction of an "Invincible Armada" of 132 vessels carrying 3,165 cannon. The British hurriedly prepared for defense by constructing a fleet less heavily armed but more numerous and far better suited to fighting in rough seas. In a great naval battle in July 1588 the British outmaneuvered the Spanish in the English Channel and defeated the great Armada. Most of the Spanish vessels that escaped fled north hoping to return home by circling the British Isles, only to be destroyed by a storm off the Scottish Hebrides Islands.

At the time of Elizabeth's death in 1603, the English people, a scant three million but proud, aggressive, and prosperous, had gathered the energy that would propel them into virtual domination of the Western world.

While the Spanish were planting their colonies in the New World, Englishmen had given comparatively little attention to colonization. In the late sixteenth and the early seventeenth centuries, however, the idea of colonization found its promoters and publicists. The English after 1600 began crossing in large numbers to North America and the West Indies. In the first century of colonization, some 400,000 Britons embarked for the New World. Some searched for wealth, and some for a modest prosperity in the new lands. Many came for reasons connected with the religious controversies of the seventeenth century. Both the economic and the religious motives would leave their marks on American history, but first the English, like the Spanish, had to come to terms with the native Americans.

Population and Colonization

The emergence of England as a modern nation-state reflected more than changes in the role of the monarchy or the growth of a centralized bureaucracy. It also involved profound economic and social changes. In the first half of the sixteenth century British exports of woolen goods grew enormously. This new source of prosperity caused English landlords to shift from farming to sheepherding on a wide scale, a change that altered the society as well as the economy of the English countryside. Small farmers, most of them tenants, were driven from the land. These people wandered from place to place looking for work.

Colonies seemed the perfect solution to this and other new problems. Not only would they lead to increased trade, but they would also provide a place for the surplus population to go in the chartered trading colonies.

The Columbian Exchange

European exploration of the Americas brought about the worst demographic disaster in world history. Smallpox and other diseases for which the New World's natives had no immunity devastated regions from Canada to Chile, reducing Indian populations by as much as ninety percent by the eighteenth century. Within fifty years after Columbus, epidemics had killed off nearly all the native inhabitants of Santo Domingo, Haiti, and much of Mexico. After Francis Drake's ships visited the Caribbean and Florida in 1585, Indians in those regions died in great numbers, believing that "it was the Inglisshe God that made them die so fast." There were 150,000 Timucuan Indians in Florida when Europeans first came, but by the end of the seventeenth century their population had been reduced to around three thousand. In New Mexico the Pueblo Indians numbered around 130,000 in 1539 when Europeans first visited them; by 1706 there were 6,440 left.

As the years passed the native populations of the Americas were replaced by Europeans in three major patterns. In Central and South America the Spanish and Portuguese intermarried with highland Indians and lowland black slaves to form the mixed-race groups called mestizo, mulatto, and zambo. The English, French, and Dutch in the West Indies and the English on the southeast coast of the present-day United States, failing to enslave the Indians, established hierarchical societies based on the labor of blacks imported from Africa. And in the Northeast, English along with Dutch, German, French, and other European colonists and a few black slaves lived on farms or in villages separate from Indian communities.

Animal and food plant exchanges accompanied encounters between Indians and Europeans. Domesticated animals—pigs, goats, horses, cattle, and sheep—accompanied Europeans to America, along with wheat, rye, barley, oats, rice, melons, coffee, dandelions, sugar cane, and olives. Much of this was to the eventual benefit of the Indians. Another import was alcohol, bringing destructive consequences. The plants that American Indians made available to the rest of the world now constitute one-third of the world's food supply: Indian corn, beans, squash, pumpkins, tomatoes, peppers, and potatoes, the last an extraordinarily important food. The rich importation of American food was a factor in the growth and economic advance of the European population in modern times. Tobacco, drugs such as cocaine, novocaine, and quinine, and the strains of cotton in modern use also entered the world market from the Americas.

Some of the biological exchange also involved microscopic life in the form of diseases. Indians had developed no immunity to measles, chicken pox, smallpox, and whooping cough, from which they had been isolated by three thousand miles of ocean. These diseases devastated American Indians, killing far more than did conquest. And Europeans may have contracted syphilis from Americans or possibly Africans. The first recorded case appeared in Cádiz, Spain, soon after Columbus returned from America. In any event, as many as ten million Old World people died of syphilis within the next fifteen years.

Technical and Cultural Exchange

Central and South American gold and silver enriched European monarchies and stimulated trade and industry. European merchants prospered from the trade in American agricultural raw materials. America provided a storehouse of information in the natural sciences and contributed to the intensification of scientific inquiry. Europeans who prided themselves on such things as written languages, advanced weapons, and Christianity looked down on Indians. But others were captivated by the notion of the "noble savage" and took that mythic creation into political and moral philosophies that furthered modern concepts of liberty and democracy. The very idea of a new and open land enlarged the vision of human possibility.

In America, Europeans adopted Indian ways. Besides eating Indian foods, they wore moccasins, snowshoes, ponchos, and parkas, plied rivers and lakes with canoes, and rested in hammocks. They played lacrosse, built homes of adobe, and rode on dogsleds and toboggans. The early European settlers followed Indian trails, smoked native tobacco, and used native medicines. Indian names entered English usage. They would serve for about half of the eventual state names from Connecticut and Alabama to Iowa, Texas, and Wyoming and were used for many rivers and cities.

In addition to declining in numbers, the original Americans underwent enormous cultural changes. Indian lands shrank as the plow, lumbering, cattle, and sheep permanently transformed the eastern woodlands. Other changes in Indian life were largely a matter of choice. European knives and guns improved hunting. The horse gave the Plains Indians mobility to hunt buffalo and raid settlements. Iron pots replaced pottery and baskets. Sheep made possible the beautiful wool blankets of the Navahos. The iron hoe and plow increased agricultural productivity, and the metal fish hook enhanced catches. Many natives also responded to the lure of profit from the fur trade. European demand for pelts soon outstripped the animal population near the sea coast, and some tribes had to abandon older settlements in favor of new ones farther inland, eventually depleting animals there, too. In North America, Indians were not conquered and enslaved to the extent that occurred in Latin America, and so were able to maintain a largely separate racial and cultural existence. They interacted with the Europeans primarily in trade and war, with disastrous results for both sides.

Suggested Readings

The 500th anniversary of Columbus's 1492 voyage inspired a vigorous scholarly debate over the meanings of the initial encounters between Europeans and the indigenous peoples of the Americas. See William D. Phillips, Jr. and Carla Rahn Phillips, *The Worlds of Christopher Columbus* (1992), Donald T. Gerace, ed., *Columbus and His World* (1987), Paolo Emilio Taviani, *Christopher Columbus: The Grand Design* (1985), and Cecil Jane, ed., *The Four Voyages of Columbus* (1988). *The Columbian Exchange* (1972) by Alfred W. Crosby, Jr., shows how ways of life were altered in both hemispheres; see also Crosby's *Ecological Imperialism: The Biological Expansion of Europe, 900–1900* (1986). Kirkpatrick Sale gives the anti-Columbus view in *The Conquest of Paradise: Christopher Columbus and the Columbian Legacy* (1990). See also Tzvetan Todorov, *The Conquest of America: The Question of the Other* (1984).

Any study of the voyages of discovery can begin with Samuel Eliot Morison's works, *The European Discovery of America: The Northern Voyages*, A.D. 500–1600 (1971) and *The European Discovery of America: The Southern Voyages*, A.D. 1492–1616 (1974). A beautifully illustrated book on this period is Richard Humble, *The Explorers* (1979).

Colin G. Calloway's *New Worlds for All: Indians, Europeans, and the Remaking of Early America* (1997) explores the ways in which the cultures of indigenous peoples and immigrants affected each other. See also Karen O. Kupperman, *Settling with the Indians: The Making of English and Indian Cultures in America* (1980). Francis Jennings's *The Founders of America: How Indians Discovered the Land, Pioneered in It, and Created Great Classical Civilizations* (1993) is a provocative antidote to European-centered accounts. See also A. M. Joseph, Jr., ed., *America in 1492* (1992), David Carrasco, *Quetzalcoatl and the Irony of Empire* (1982), Brian M. Fagan, *The Great Journey: The People of Ancient America* (1987), and Robert Silverberg, *Mound Builders of Ancient America: The Archaeology of a Myth* (1968). Other recommended works are D. B. Quinn, *North America from Earliest Discovery to First Settlements* (1977), Samuel Eliot Morison's *Admiral of the Ocean Sea* (1942), a biography of Columbus, and James Axtell, *The European and the Indian* (1981) and *After Columbus* (1988).

On the Spanish in North America see David Weber, *The Spanish Frontier in North America* (1992), Joseph P. Sanchez, *Forging the Old Spanish Trail, 1678–1850* (1997), and Donald E. Chipman, *Spanish Texas, 1519–1821* (1992). See also John Miller Morris, *El Llano Estacado: Exploration and Imagination on the High Plains of Texas and New Mexico, 1536–1860* (1997).

John Thornton's *Africa and Africans in the Making of the Atlantic World, 1400–1680* (1992) is a pathbreaking study. See also Roland Oliver, *The African Experience* (1991), Phyllis Martin and Patrick O'Meare, eds., *Africa* (1986), and Anthony Sillery, *Africa: A Social Geography* (1972).

POINTS OF VIEW

Christopher Columbus—
The Conqueror of Paradise?

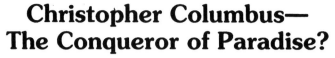

Kirkpatrick Sale

On his first voyage Columbus found himself in the middle of an old-growth tropical forest the likes of which he could not have imagined before, its trees reaching sixty or seventy feet into the sky, more varieties than he knew how to count much less name, exhibiting a lushness that stood in sharp contrast to the sparse and denuded lands he had known in the Mediterranean, hearing a melodious multiplicity of bird songs and parrot calls—why was it not an occasion of wonder, excitement, and the sheer joy at nature in its full, arrogant abundance? . . .

One measure that Colón [Columbus] could make, and did so frequently, was the utilitarian: if he was not up to describing natural beauty or distinguishing trees, he was a master at determining the potential use and value of all that he saw, even when (as so often) he was deluding himself. Nature for him was all one form of treasure or another, whether aloes, mastic, spices, cinnamon, nutmeg, dyes, or medicines, or gold and silver and pearls—it hardly mattered as long as it could be sold in Europe.

Colón was nothing more than "a businessman" describing resources for potential markets. Large European mammals were brought over on the Second Voyage. Nothing of the kind (nothing larger than a small dog) lived in the Caribbean, no competing species of any sort, so there were no established diseases to threaten them and, with the exception of sheep and goats, they bloomed spectacularly. Cattle reproduced so successfully on Española that, it was said, thirty or forty stray animals would multiply to three or four hundred in a couple of years. . . . Pigs were so numerous by 1500, just seven years after the first four pairs were introduced, that according to Las Casas they were called *infinitos*.

All these voracious animals naturally dominated and then destroyed native habitats, rapidly and thoroughly, with human help and without. The record is inadequate, since none among the colonists, even those who would take on the job of describing native species for audiences at home, ever noted the extensive alteration of the environment that was taking place literally beneath their feet. Las Casas, however, does mention that a certain grass common in Española at the turn of the century had vanished just forty years later, a victim of the hungry herds, and we may presume there were many similar floral die-outs. Crosby, without specifics, considers that the spread of these large species "doubtlessly had much to do with the extinction of certain plants, animals . . . and even the Indians themselves" who lost out "in the biological competition with the newly imported livestock." . . .

Many of those who know well the cultures that once existed in the New World have reason to be less than enthusiastic about celebrating the event that led to the destruction of much of that heritage and the greater part of the people who produced it; some have insisted on labeling the events of 1492 an "encounter" rather than a "discovery" and having it so billed for 1992; some others have chosen to make it an occasion to direct attention to native American arts and achievements, and others still are planning to protest the entire goings-on as a wrongful commemoration of an act steeped in bloodshed, slavery, and genocide.

And some of those who have sought to draw attention to the environmental destruction wrought in the aftermath of the Discovery, particularly members of various Green movements in the industrialized world, have decided to use the occasion to draw into question the nature of a civilization that could take the earth so close to ecocide.

Kirkpatrick Sale, *The Conquest of Paradise* (New York: Alfred A. Knopf, 1990). Reprinted by permission.

Stephan Thernstrom

A century ago, the United States celebrated the exploits of Columbus proudly. Some 24 million people—which amounted to about 40 percent of the U.S. population at the time—attended a great international exposition in Chicago marking the event. There, at a meeting of the American Historical Association, the young historian Frederick Jackson Turner delivered his famous paper on "The Significance of the Frontier in American History," sounding an appropriate theme for the commemoration of the explorer who opened up the most significant frontier in world history: the entire Western Hemisphere.

The 500th anniversary of 1492, by contrast, has touched off enormous controversy and endless political wrangling. The National Council of Churches has announced that 1992 should not be a time for celebration at all but rather for "repentance" for a great historical crime. Columbus, in the council's view, was a monster akin to Hitler, having been responsible for an "invasion and colonization with legalized occupation, genocide, economic exploitation, and a deep level of institutional racism and moral decadence."

The story of the European discovery, invasion, and conquest of the Western Hemisphere—a process that began with Columbus in 1492—certainly is not all sweetness and light. Crimes and follies are in the history of every people, including those who did not leave behind written records allowing historians to demonstrate their sins in detail. The Columbus story, like every other momentous historical event, calls not for easy moralizing and finger pointing but for an appreciation of a complex clash of cultures that was crucial to the emergence of the modern world we inhabit. . . .

Painful though it might be to accept, much of history is the story of what the strong have done to the weak—and of shifts in the bases of power that undermine the position of the once-strong and lead to their decline and fall. It would be nice if that were not so, but it has been so thus far in human history.

Contrary to romantics like Sale, who contrast the warlike Europeans of 1492 with the supposedly pacific natives, the history of the societies of the Western Hemisphere before Columbus fits this mold, too. Conquest and domination were not corruptions that Europeans introduced into a New World Eden. The great empires of the Aztecs in Mexico, the Incas in Peru, and those of the Mayas much earlier were not formed by a process of peaceful persuasion but by superior force. And their rule was as cruel and exploitative as anything Europeans were guilty of in the New World; in some ways more cruel. . . .

The newest addition to the indictment against Columbus is that he committed "ecocide." The native peoples of the Western Hemisphere, some current environmentalists claim, revered nature and lived in harmony with it. The European invaders instead raped and pillaged the land with reckless abandon.

Since environmentalists have been a healthy voice in contemporary public policy debates, it is regrettable to find some of them taking such a simplistic position on complex historical problems. It is generally true that the native peoples who lived at the most primitive technological level did less to alter the physical environment, for better or worse, than those who developed a more complex economy. But even small, semi-nomadic tribes practiced slash-and-burn agriculture, felling trees by stripping their bark along the base, letting them die and fall, and then setting them on fire. They violated the precept "Save the trees" and created some ugly scenes on the landscape, including forest fires burning out of control.

Reprinted with permission from the Spring 1992 issue of the *American Educator,* the quarterly journal of the American Federation of Teachers.

JAMESTOWN IN 1622
VIRGINIA

Jamestown, founded in 1607, fared better than the Roanoke settlement. Though ravaged by disease and Indian attacks, the settlement survived and Virginia became the preeminent southern colony. *(Courtesy, American Historical Society)*

John Smith, one of the original settlers of Jamestown, wrote a history of the colony. Smith's presidency of the local council was critical for the survival of the settlement. *(Scribner's Archives)*

A portrait of Pocahontas, painted in 1616, when she was 21. *(Courtesy, Smithsonian Institution)*

2
North America

THE STARVING TIME

In the fall of 1609 a group of English colonists huddled fearfully inside the log palisade of a small fort on the banks of a river. They had named this river the James, in honor of their King, James I. The local Indians called it the Powhatan, which was also the name of their ruler. The site of the fort was Jamestown, in the new colony of Virginia. It was the first permanent English settlement in the New World, a project undertaken by British businessmen who had formed the Virginia Company. A marshy, mosquito-infested place, it was nonetheless safe from Indian attacks, so the English thought, and it was close to a river that flowed to the ocean—the way back home.

Drought, disease, and death had plagued Jamestown from the beginning. Of the 104 men and boys carried by the ships *Susan Constant*, *Discovery*, and *Godspeed*, and left there in April 1607, only 38 were alive the following January. Governed by an un-wieldy and bickering council, they quarreled over their meager food supply, refused to work, grew sick from drinking the brackish water of the James, and antagonized the Indians. The next year, a brash twenty-seven-year-old named John Smith became president of the council and declared that "he that will not work shall not eat." Through his friendship with Pocahontas, the twelve-year-old daughter of Wahunsonacock, the ruler of the surround-ing tribes, Smith made a fragile peace with the Indians. Settlers exchanged glass beads with them for baskets of corn. The Virginia Company sent more colonists (including the first "Gentlewoman and woman servant" to arrive at Jamestown), but more died, and

HISTORICAL EVENTS

1587
Colony of Roanoke established; disappears by 1590

1603
James I becomes King of England

1606
Plymouth Company and London Company are formed

1607
Jamestown settled

1609
Spanish founded Santa Fe

1619
Virginia House of Burgesses established • First blacks arrive in English colonies

1620
Plymouth settled • Mayflower Compact

1622
Powhatan uprising in Virginia

1624
Virginia becomes a royal colony

1625
Charles I becomes King of England

continued

HISTORICAL EVENTS

1626
Dutch establish settlement called
New Amsterdam

1630
Members of the Massachusetts Bay
Company arrive in Massachusetts

1634
Maryland founded

1636
Roger Williams establishes
Providence (Rhode Island)

1637–38
Pequot War

1638
Anne Hutchinson banished from
Massachusetts

1642–47
Civil war in England (Puritans vs.
Royalists)

1649
Maryland passes Toleration Act
• Charles I executed

1651
First Navigation Act

1660
Charles II becomes King of England:
the Restoration • Navigation Act

1662
Half-Way Covenant enacted in
Massachusetts

1664
Charles II seizes New York from Dutch

1669
Locke and Ashley write "The
Fundamental Constitutions of
Carolina"

1675–76
King Philip's War

1676
Bacon's Rebellion

1680
Pueblo Revolt in New Mexico
• Virginia and Maryland export
seventeen million pounds of
tobacco

1682
Penn publishes *Frame of
Government*

continued

Smith himself was severely wounded by an exploding bag of gunpowder. In October 1609 he left for England, never to return.

Now, two years after the founding of the settlement, the colonists at Jamestown still had not managed to raise enough corn to see them through a winter, or to placate the Indians whose lands they occupied. John Smith was gone, and Pocahontas no longer came to visit the English. Now the inhabitants of the fort cowered inside, fearing the Indians outside its walls.

As cold weather approached, so did starvation. According to one of the colonists reporting on what has been remembered as the Starving Time, "Having fed upon horses and other beasts as long as they lasted we were glad to make shift with vermine, as dogs, cats, rats, and mice . . . boots, shoes, or any other leather . . . and those being spent and devoured, some were forced to search the woods and to feed upon serpents and snakes and to dig the earth for wild and unknown roots where many of our men were cut off and slain by savages. . . . And one of our colony murdered his wife, ripped the child out of her womb and threw it in the river and after chopped the mother in pieces and salted her for his foode. . . ." Once, when some of the men went in search of food, the Indians killed them and left them for the English to find: the mouths of the corpses had been stuffed with bread. Yet while the Jamestown colonists were shivering inside their log enclosure, thirty or forty of their countrymen, who had been sent to build a fort thirty miles downriver at Point Comfort, spent the winter in relative plenty. When spring came, there were "not past sixty men, women, and children" left in the fort at Jamestown.

In May 1610 two small ships arrived, carrying 150 more colonists, the survivors of a shipwreck in Bermuda. Among them was Virginia's new deputy governor, Sir Thomas Gates. Horrified at the condition of the people at Jamestown, Gates ordered the abandonment of the fort. But as his two ships made for the open sea, they were met by a longboat announcing the arrival of Lord De La Warr, the new governor, with more colonists—and enough food to feed the starving survivors. All returned, rejoicing, to the fort at Jamestown. England at last had a foothold on the coast of North America. But the English had made lasting enemies of the Indians.

Early Southern Settlements

The Roanoke Colony   Jamestown was not the first English effort to plant a colony in the New World. Late in the sixteenth century a group of adventurers, among them the courtier Sir Walter Raleigh, had developed plans for establishing settlements in the New World. Lusty and aggressive, the mercantile and maritime adventurers of the time were eager to exploit the American continent that Europeans only a few decades earlier had considered no more than an annoying obstacle on the route to the Orient.

In 1584 under Raleigh's sponsorship a voyage explored the coast of what is now North Carolina. One of the leaders of this expedition wanted to name the new land "Wingandacoa," a word he had heard the Indians use, but Raleigh chose "Virginia," in honor of Elizabeth, who was known as the Virgin Queen.

In 1585 Raleigh sent over a hundred men to establish a settlement at Roanoke, a small wooded island off the coast of present-day North Carolina. They quarreled with the Indians and returned home after a year. In 1587 Raleigh, still determined to set up a colony, sent 117 settlers, this time including seventeen women, under the leadership of John White, whose watercolors of the Indians and wildlife would furnish Europeans with some of their first views of the New World. At Roanoke, White's daughter Elenora, wife of Ananias Dare, gave birth to a girl, "the first Christian born in Virginia." The infant was named Virginia.

Sometime between 1587, when John White and the supply ships left Roanoke, and 1590, when he was finally able to return, Virginia Dare and all the rest of the colonists vanished. Research released in 1998 on the rings of centuries-old bald cypress trees suggest they—and a tribe of neighboring Indians—had the misfortune to be there during the worst three-year drought in some eight hundred years. Certainly this would have upset Raleigh's plans for a flourishing plantation agriculture. England's war with Spain and the battle of the Spanish Armada in 1588 had prevented a resupply mission to Roanoke until 1590. The letters CROATOAN the settlers left carved in a tree suggest some kind of involvement with an Indian tribe, perhaps a flight by stormy seas. Years later an English settler reported that coastal Indians told him that "several of their ancestors were white People."

Other reports from America nevertheless whetted English appetites for more colonizing ventures. One account described the shellfish as "exceeding good and very great," and characterized the Indians as "courteous" and "gentle of disposition." Another found the Atlantic coast's crabs "rather better in taste than ours, one able to suffice four men." In 1603 a sea captain exploring what would become New Hampshire reported seeing "goodly groves and woods and sundry beasts, but no people."

New Settlers   After the troubles of Jamestown's initial years, the Virginia Company and its investors were determined to see the colony prosper. Hardships and disease—salt poisoning from the saline James River, dysentery, typhoid—took a fearful toll. One colonist thought that "more doe die here of the disease of their mind, then of their body." In order to attract more investors and more settlers, the Company granted a "headright" of fifty acres of land per person to all individuals who came on their own or brought others to Virginia. With aggressive recruiting the Company poured some 3,500 newcomers into the colony between 1618 and 1621, more than twice the number who had emigrated since 1607.

At its own expense the Company undertook to send to Virginia a

John White's journal records his fruitless search for the lost settlers of Roanoke:

"We espied towards the north end of the island the light of a great fire through the woods, to which we presently rowed. When we came right over against it, we let fall our grapnel [anchor] near the shore, & sounded with a trumpet call, & afterwards many familiar English tunes of songs, and called to them friendly, but we had no answer. . . .

In all this way we saw on the sand the print of the savages' feet of 2 or 3 sorts trodden that night, and as we entered up the sandy bank upon a tree, in the very brow there were curiously carved these fair Roman letters, C R O: which letters presently we knew to signify the place, where I should find the planters seated, according to a secret token agreed upon between them & me. . . ."

Barbarism and cruelty occurred on both sides of the encounters between the English and the Indians in Virginia. George Percy recorded an incident of English treatment of a captured Indian queen and her children in 1610.

"And after we marched with the queen and her children to our boats again . . . my soldiers did begin to murmur because the queen and her children were spared. So upon the same a council being called it was agreed upon to put the children to death the which was effected by throwing them overboard and shooting out their brains in the water. Yet for all this cruelty the soldiers were not well pleased and I had much to do to save the queen's life for that time."

John Smith's General History of Virginia recorded the Indian uprising that took place in the spring of 1622.

"On the Friday morning that fatal day, being the two and twentieth of March . . . as at other times they came into our houses, with deer, turkeys, fish, fruits, and other provisions to sell us, yea in some places sat down at breakfast with our people, whom immediately with their own tools they slew most barbarously, not sparing either age or sex, man, woman or child, so sudden in their execution, that few or none discerned the weapon or blow that brought them to destruction . . . and by this means fell that fatal morning . . . three hundred forty seven men, women, and children, most by their own weapons, and not being content with their lives, they fell again upon the dead bodies, making as well as they could a fresh murder, defacing, dragging, and mangling their dead carcasses into many pieces, and carrying some parts away in derision, with base and brutish triumph."

variety of craftsmen and a number of female settlers, "young maids" who would make the colony's economy more self-sufficient and its life more tolerable. The Company relaxed its rules, provided that settlers continue to be governed by English law and have the rights of Englishmen, and gave settlers a voice in the management by allowing them to elect representatives to an assembly. The House of Burgesses, the first colonial legislature in North America, began meeting in 1619.

Also in that year, according to a letter written by colonist John Rolfe, a Dutch ship brought "20 and odd Negroes, which the governor and cape merchant bought . . . at the best and easiest rate they could." These were not the first blacks in Virginia; a census a few months earlier recorded 32 blacks—15 men and 17 women—before the arrival of the Dutch ship. The status of these people is not clear from the existing records, and it is possible that Virginia's blacks were treated much the same as the colony's white servants. The origins of slavery in North America are obscure, and the institution itself evolved slowly as the number of blacks in Virginia and other colonies grew in the seventeenth century.

Despite the determined efforts of the Virginia Company, the colony had not flourished. As the English tobacco fields spread, the Indians feared the loss of their lands, and in 1622 a surprise attack on English settlements killed 347 men, women, and children. A muster of English colonists in 1625 recorded a population of only about 1,210, including 23 blacks. The shocking mortality rate and the Virginia Company's virtually empty treasury led to a dissolution of the Company in 1624, and Virginia became a royal colony governed directly by the crown. Relations with the Indians worsened. One colonial official exulted that "now we have just cause to destroy them by all means possible." On one occasion, the colonists lured a band of peaceful Indians into drinking a toast with poisoned wine, killing "some two hundred." Indian-English relations were unstable for much of the seventeenth century.

Beginnings of New England

On the eve of European settlement, the Indian population of New England was possibly as large as 25,000, a density of about one person per four acres. The various tribes, none larger than 4,000 people, lived in relatively settled territories, moving between winter, summer, and autumn quarters to sustain their mixed farming and hunting economy and to escape into more sheltered valleys for the winters. During the winter of 1616–17 an epidemic of smallpox suddenly decimated many of the tribes, including the Massachusetts Indians, after whom the European colony would derive its name. No Indian would have connected this mysterious visitation with the occasional and usually friendly encounters with European fishermen drying their catches on the beaches in summer or trading a few items for furs and skins or food. But these were the source of the disease that wiped out as much as one-third of the area's population. Early settlers in New England found the land largely cleared of natives.

Religious persecution brought in 1620 the first permanent English colonists to present-day Massachusetts. By the 1630s thousands of religious dissenters known as Puritans were making their way across the Atlantic.

In England in the early 1600s the Separatists, so called for their desire to separate from the Church of England, incurred the wrath of King James I, who succeeded Elizabeth I in 1603. He declared that a Separatist was like "a rat to be trapped and tossed away." James was as good as his word. In Lincolnshire in 1607, the same year Jamestown, Virginia, was being settled, a Separatist leader named William Brewster and his young friend, seventeen-year-old William Bradford, were among those imprisoned for several months.

The Pilgrims and the Mayflower Compact   In 1611 Brewster, Bradford, and a small group of Separatists fled to the Netherlands, and in 1620 cemented an agreement with the London Company of Virginia to finance their emigration to America. In September 1620 the 180-ton *Mayflower* left Plymouth Sound with 102 men, women, and children. On November 9, they reached Cape Cod. The grateful Pilgrims celebrated their first Thanksgiving in October 1621. To secure their government in this unknown land, the leaders of these Separatists had drafted on shipboard an agreement that has come to be known as the Mayflower Compact. Every adult male who intended to be a part of the Separatist community signed it, and it has held a special place in the American imagination ever since as a model for the formation of government by free consent. And since contrary winds put the Pilgrims at Cape Cod, well outside the bounds of their London Company charter, that Company document could not serve as the basis of their government. The Pilgrims named their colony Plymouth, after the English seaport they had left behind. In 1691 Plymouth colony would become part of the larger Puritan colony of Massachusetts.

Despite the many obvious cultural differences and the language barrier between English settlers and Indians, the Pilgrims and after them the larger Puritan settlement in Massachusetts Bay received a generally friendly welcome. Puritans also made an effort to convert the Indians to Christianity. Trade, Indians perceived, made tribes rich and powerful and usually ended with their acquiring firearms. At first the needs of the two cultures seemed compatible. The English settlers carefully drew up land titles granting the Indians the right to continue to hunt or fish.

The Massachusetts Bay Colony   The Massachusetts Bay Company, organized in 1629 by a group of well-to-do English Puritans, received from the King a charter granting it land in present-day New England and elsewhere to the south. Hostile like his father to the Puritans, James's son and in 1625 his successor, Charles I, was doubtless happy to send some of them to the opposite shores of the Atlantic, also using them to populate and enrich parts of his American domain. Members of the Company signed a document, known as the Cambridge Agreement, to settle with their families in the

William Bradford, governor of Plymouth Colony, recorded in his journal the arrival in 1620 of the Pilgrims:

"Being thus arrived in a good harbor, and brought safe to land, they fell upon their knees and blessed the God of Heaven who had brought them over the vast and furious ocean, and delivered them from all the perils and miseries thereof, again to set their feet on the firm and stable earth, their proper element. . . . They now had no friends to welcome them nor inns to entertain or refresh their weatherbeaten bodies; no houses or much less town to repair to, to seek for succour. . . . And as for the season it was winter, and they that know the winters of that country know them to be sharp and violent, and subject to cruel and fierce storms, dangerous to travel to known places, much more to search an unknown coast. Besides, what could they see but a hideous and desolate wilderness, full of wild beasts and wild men—and what multitudes there might be of them they knew not."

Housing in Massachusetts Bay was primitive at first. Some colonists borrowed from the Indians and built wigwams. According to a settler's recollection:

"We built us our wigwam, or house, in one hour's space. It had no frame, but was without form or fashion, only a few poles set together, and covered with our boat's sails, which kept forth but a little wind, and less rain and snow."

Others dug cellars. The Puritan historian Edward Johnson wrote that they

"burrow themselves in the Earth for their first shelter under some Hillside, . . . make a smoaky fire against the Earth at the highest side, and thus . . . provide for themselves, their Wives, and little ones, keeping off the short showers from their Lodgings, but the long ones penetrate through to their great disturbance."

Some years later, Johnson described the finished houses, observing that

"the Lord hath been pleased to turn all the wigwams, huts, and hovels the English dwelt in at their first coming into orderly fair, and well-built houses, well furnished many of them, together with Orchards filled with goodly fruit trees, and gardens with variety of flowers."

new land, provided that they be allowed to take the charter and government of the Company with them. Nothing in the charter required the Company to maintain headquarters in England, and the transfer was arranged. This meant, in effect, that the structure of the Massachusetts Bay Company was to become the local government of the colony itself. The Company elected as its governor John Winthrop, a solid country squire. In 1630 Winthrop and ten other members of the Company had set sail for America with a fleet of eleven ships carrying 800 adults and children with them. They arrived in Massachusetts in July 1630. In the next decade, as persecutions of Puritans increased, more than 20,000 would come to New England. From the start, the immigration of families distinguished the settlement of New England. The presence of nearly as many women as men among the Puritans guaranteed that the settlement would grow in population. Women assured the accomplishment of basic domestic tasks necessary for survival. Perhaps because of that, these New England colonists, with the exception of those at Plymouth the first winter, did not suffer the dreadful mortality of Virginia's early years. By the end of 1630 the Puritans had established six towns in addition to Boston.

The Massachusetts Bay Company, like other English business corporations of the time, was governed by its voting members, or "freemen." At first the only members were the stockholders, but the government of the Company and therefore of the colony soon admitted as freemen all male members of Puritan congregations. Like the original government, this extended body was constituted on the assumption that men only were fitted for governance and would naturally speak for the women of their families. The charter provided that Company members gather as a General Court four times a year, and that between times management be in the hands of a governor, deputy governor, and council of eighteen "assistants," all elected annually by the freemen. As the colony expanded, legislation by the entire body of freemen became unwieldy, and after 1634 they annually elected representatives from each settlement. Government of the church was the domain of the male members of the church congregation; and the government of the town

Pilgrims Going to Church, a nineteenth-century painting by George Boughton. The original Massachusetts settlements were governed by and for the orthodox, but by the 1660s other settlers and congregations were laying the basis for religious pluralism. *(Courtesy, The New-York Historical Society. From the Robert L. Stuart Collection)*

was also their domain. Gaining admission to a congregation, however, was not automatic: the candidate had to give convincing indications of having experienced divine grace.

New England Democracy   It is easy, and in part correct, to trace American democracy to early New England institutions. But the Mayflower Compact, the government of Massachusetts Bay, and the church polity of the New England congregations did not spring from anything close to a conscious modern democratic theory. Each of the three came out of its own special circumstances and needs.

The *Mayflower* colonists were going to be far beyond the reach of established authority, and therefore the Pilgrim leaders feared that some of the settlers might "use their owne libertie, for none had the power to command them." A need for law and order, not a desire for democratic government, inspired the Mayflower Compact. To agree among themselves to have a government was a simple, necessary act. And the Compact did not project an independent government: it specifically declared allegiance to the King of England.

The suffrage in Massachusetts Bay represented the fusion of the organization of a business company with that of the New England Puritan congregations. That English joint-stock companies gave a vote to each shareholder for the conduct of business was a practical arrangement among people who had chosen to pool their resources for some enterprise. The purpose of such companies was not to establish a democracy, nor was democracy the purpose of the settlers who turned the shareholder voting system into a political system for the colony. Seventeenth-century Massachusetts Bay had few if any advocates of democracy. "If the people be governors," asked Puritan divine John Cotton, "who shall be governed?"

Within the Puritan and the Separatist congregations, members were spiritual equals, of a sort. While women could be full members of congregations, they could not be ministers or members of the governing body of the church, and they could not voice their opinions too loudly. The Puritan concept of equality derived from the doctrine, which no modern democrat would accept, that the members of the church congregations must be confined to the elect, selected for salvation from the beginning of time. Members were spiritual equals, but only because there can be no inequality among saints.

Yet even if the early institutions of New England did not derive from any philosophical notions of equality or democracy, they deserve a place in the history of American democracy. The manner of their formation represents the way in which many of the nation's political and social institutions came into being—neither by theory nor by ancient custom but by matter-of-fact response to conditions and needs.

Puritan Theology   Economic ambition had combined with religion in the founding of the New England colonies and many settlers had land or opportunity as their motive. The prevailing creed, however, was Puritan. This creed was heavily influenced by the French theologian John Calvin, best known for his belief in predestination: that those who were to be saved had been so chosen from the beginning of time. Calvin's premise might be taken to mean that there was no need to make any effort to be moral and good since salvation had already been granted. Not so: orthodox ministers in Massachusetts observed that religious conversion, an intense personal experience of salvation, would be attended by diligent pursuit of a "calling" or earthly occupation and a life of fervent prayer and good works. Industriousness, charity, and the other virtues were considered a consequence of salvation, a continuing act of gratitude, a joyful expression of the faith of the saved or, as Calvinists called them, the elect. The New England Puritans believed that God had made a covenant, or agreement, with the faithful to provide them with a clear and orderly redemption. Not only individuals but whole congregations and entire communities considered themselves as having entered into a convenant with God, promising to live together in love and harmony.

Not all Puritans reasoned the same way, and not all agreed even on the principle of cooperation among congregations. One who shared few of the values of the Pilgrims was Thomas Morton, an adventurer whose followers fraternized with the Indians and enjoyed drinking freely and dancing around a maypole at Mt. Wollaston, near Plymouth. The colonists disapproved of his conduct and shipped him back to England in 1628. Settlers who shared Puritan values but disputed specific points of the colony's religious practices were a good deal more troublesome.

New England Society   The Separatist Pilgrims at Plymouth and then the much larger body of Puritans around Massachusetts Bay continued to live as they had in England in tightly knit communities. The rural life of England had itself been close, peasants living in villages and working the surrounding fields under arrangements that made individual land tenancy subordinate to the will and need of the whole village. Those arrangements remained, reinforced by the Puritan determination to establish a model society on Christian principles, or, as John Winthrop called it, a "city upon a hill."

That model included enacting into Massachusetts law the injunctions against drunkenness (but not drinking in itself), adultery, murder, theft, and violations of the Sabbath. Neither these laws nor the powerful moral consensus of the community itself was sufficient to prevent New Englanders from committing the normal range of sins or worldly behavior; but they gave a certain righteous definition to the Puritan experiment.

Puritans would not have understood the modern tendency to distinguish between private and public morality. To be selfish toward your neighbor was a sin, exactly as was a private act of what Puritans considered sexual misconduct. Puritans were driven by a morality of work. But work, besides being a way of restraining otherwise rebellious impulses, was supposed to be for the common good. It was therefore not merely obedience to tradition that dictated the landed arrangements of Massachusetts Bay villages. Upon the signing of a contract, pledging the seriousness of their endeavor, a number of Puritans would receive from the Massachusetts General Court the authorization to form a town.

John Winthrop. *(Courtesy, New York Public Library)*

As early as 1630 John Winthrop was reminding the first Puritans of their mission:

"Wee must consider that wee shall be as a citty upon a Hille. The eyes of all people are uppon us. Soe that if wee shall deale falsely with our God in this worke wee have undertaken, and soe cause him to withdraw his present help from us, wee shall be made a story and a by-word through the world."

THE NEW ENGLAND
COLONIES

The responsible villagers would then apportion land to individuals on the basis of the size of the recipient's family and the usefulness of the land grant to the village as a whole. It was a remarkable fusion of private property and social obligation.

The word "Puritan" has come to be used, with some justification, to imply a rigid morality and a gloomy existence. But Puritans believed that conscience and effort could bring into good order both the individual self and the external world. Revering the Bible, which the printing press had made available to the masses, and other religious writings, they encouraged literacy, and communities supported common schools. Literacy brought not only Scripture reading but a degree of secular culture. The more educated Puritans read and wrote poetry. New Englanders developed a bright if decorous social life. They engaged in lively and profitable commerce—which in time, for better or for worse, broke up the original communal organization of the land. And it appears that, surely for the worse, they were early practitioners of the American habit of lawsuits.

Roger Williams and Rhode Island In 1631 Roger Williams, a clergyman of great personal charm, arrived in Massachusetts and became minister of the congregation at Salem. He began immediately to point out the numerous defects he saw in the Massachusetts scheme of things, declared the colony's charter invalid because it had not purchased the land from the Indians, and delivered such seditious doctrines as that no government should have authority over religious matters. When large numbers began to share those views the government found it necessary to banish him, lest the foundation for all authority in Massachusetts be undermined. In 1636 he went down the coast to Narragansett Bay, established a settlement he named Providence, which he said would be a "shelter for persons distressed of conscience," and for almost half a century presided as the spiritual head of what became the colony of Rhode Island and Providence Plantations—a haven for religious nonconformists. Roger Williams is sometimes mistaken for an early secular liberal. He was not. His opposition to government coercion of conscience was founded in a Separatist theology that had little specifically in common with the language of present-day defenders of civil liberties. But his sense of the integrity of private judgment does suggest something of later defenses of freedom of conscience.

Anne Hutchinson In 1638 the colony's authorities tried and banished another religious dissident. Anne Hutchinson, the daughter of a minister, wife of a prosperous cloth merchant, and mother of eleven children, had arrived with her family in 1634. She soon emerged as a charismatic amateur theologian. Holding informal meetings in her home to discuss the Sunday sermons, she argued that faith was more important than works in assuring salvation. She espoused a variety of what is commonly called Antinomianism, which by a rough translation means "against the law." It amounts to the belief that when love of Christ burns in the human spirit, the cold law of reason, custom, and government no longer prevails. Anne Hutchin-

---

A PURITAN MEDICAL REMEDY, 1656

"For all sorts of agues, I have of late tried the following magnetical experiment with infallible success. Pare the patient's nails when the fit is coming on; and put the parings in a litle bag of fine linen and tie that above a live eel's neck, in a tub of water. The eel will die and the patient will recover."

William Bradford, the Puritan historian, referred in his *History of Plimmouth Plantation* to Roger Williams as "a man godly and zealous, having many precious parts but very unsettled in judgment."

Roger Williams, banished from Salem for arguing that government has no authority over religious matters, founded Providence, Rhode Island. (*Courtesy, Ewing Galloway, New York*)

son's interpretation of Puritan theology challenged the very foundations of the community.

The words of this formidable and eloquent woman found a receptive audience. Even the most learned ministers had difficulty in countering the hair-splitting logic of her reasoning. As increasing numbers of Bostonians embraced Anne Hutchinson's doctrines, she became even more dangerous to the established authorities than Roger Williams had been. Moreover, in a society where women were supposed to be submissive and subservient to men, Anne Hutchinson spoke confidently. John Winthrop described her as "a woman of a haughty and free carriage, of a nimble wit and active spirit . . . more bold than a man." Spurred on by Winthrop, the authorities reacted sharply, accusing her and her followers of heresy. She was condemned by both civil and religious leaders and banished. She and her family, along with a number of loyal followers, moved to Rhode Island.

In the 1630s other Massachusetts colonists settled elsewhere, many simply out of an urge to have more room to move around in, physically and politically. In 1635 a group settled along the Connecticut River. The Reverend Thomas Hooker led his flock west also, to establish Hartford. In 1639 these new settlements, choosing to place themselves outside the jurisdiction of Massachusetts, drew up an agreement called the *Fundamental Orders of Connecticut*. Under this charter they established their own government, which differed from that in Massachusetts in a single important feature: suffrage was not confined to church members.

Puritans and Indians   In the early 1600s the Narragansett Indians of Connecticut and their neighbors were threatened by a powerful and warlike tribe from the upper Hudson River that had pushed its way into the Connecticut Valley. These people earned by their behavior the name Pequot: "destroyer" in the Algon-

***The Red Fox*, James Hope.**
(Courtesy, Museum of Fine Arts, Boston)

quian dialects of New England. By the 1630s they dominated the valley, terrorizing and exacting tribute from the neighboring tribes. But potential allies—white settlers equipped with modern firearms—were now arriving from Europe.

An eighteenth-century poet chronicler of the Pequot War made his sympathies clear:

First, helpless Stone! they bade thy
   bosom bleed,
A guiltless offering at th' infernal shrine.
Then, gallant Norton! the hard fate was
   thine,
By ruffians butcher'd, and denied a
   grave
Thee, generous Oldham! next the doom
   malign
Arrested; nor could all thy courage save
Forsaken, plunder'd, cleft, and burried
   in the wave.

The Pequot War

Misunderstandings nonetheless turned into resentments and finally conflict. Neither Puritan governors nor tribal sachems could control all that occurred in each trading venture or settlement. Massachusetts court records are full of attempts to punish and make restitution for the deception, sharp dealings, kidnappings, and little battles that marked many encounters between newcomers and natives. By the early 1630s the number of English colonists was far larger than that of any single Indian tribe; by mid-decade there were probably as many English as Indians in New England. And as the Massachusetts Bay colony grew in size, the disposition to impose order on Indians grew likewise. When settlement expanded into the Connecticut Valley, where the Pequots had already shredded the tissue of intertribal diplomacy, war broke out.

The war has been attributed to the killing of three Englishmen. That John Stone had already been banished from New England under penalty of death for larceny, adultery, and attempted murder of the governor of Plymouth lends some force to the Pequot claim that his killing was under dire provocation. Walter Norton was in cahoots with Stone; and John Oldham, apparently, met his fate at the hands of the Narragansetts—who remained allied to the colonists—rather than the Pequots. But the Puritans, goaded by their Indian allies, dispatched ninety men under John Endicott on a mission of destruction.

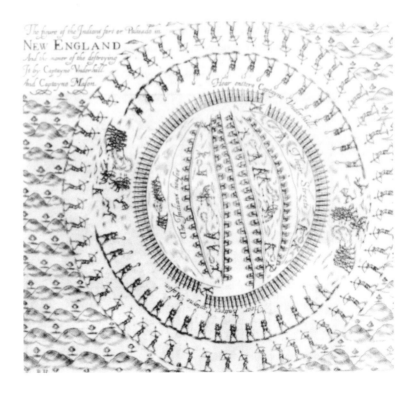

Diagram of the attack on the Pequot fort on Mystic River. Led by Captains John Mason and John Underhill the colonial forces set fire to the fort, burning alive all of the men, women, and children inside it. From an illustration, artist unknown, accompanying John Underhill's *Newes from America*, London, 1638. *(Courtesy, Rare Book Room, New York Public Library)*

Endicott's orders included putting to death all Indian men on Block Island. When the band of Englishmen with guns was frustrated by the Indians' retreat into swamps, they fired all their wigwams, destroyed all their possessions, then wantonly "destroyed some of their dogs." The Pequots replied in kind. Ambushing five men near Saybrook, they dispatched three immediately and roasted one alive; "the other came down drowned to us . . . with an arrow shot into his eye through his head." Similar fates befell about thirty white settlers in the next year before skirmishes and ambushes turned into a full-scale war of extermination, whose genocidal intent was expressed in the Reverend Thomas Hooker's admonition "not to do this work of the Lord's revenge slackly."

The Pequot War was not an early version of cowboys and Indians. There was not a white and an Indian side. The climactic battle pitted Mohegans, Narragansetts, and Englishmen against the Pequot fort on Mystic River within which somewhere between 400 and 700 men, women, and children perished by fire, musket ball, or arrow in less than an hour's time on May 26, 1637. God, so the Puritan commander reported, had "laughed his Enemies and the Enemies of his People to Scorn, making them as a fiery Oven. . . . Thus did the Lord judge among the Heathen, filling the Place with dead Bodies."

New England and the Chesapeake From the beginning the settlers in New England differed fundamentally from those in Virginia and in Maryland, the Chesapeake Bay colonies. The New Englanders lived in small, close-knit towns and villages with a common Puritan theology and devotional life. The Chesapeake colonists lived on small farms and plantations, located, as one of them put it, "scatteringly, as a choice veine of rich ground invited them, and the further from neighbours the better." They were united in little more than a devotion to tobacco as a money-making crop. Maryland, founded in 1634 as a haven for England's persecuted Roman Catholics, also attracted Protestants, but economics proved a better magnet than religion for drawing new colonists to the Chesapeake.

Maryland was the first proprietary colony, a colony founded not by a joint-stock company as were Virginia and Massachusetts Bay but by a close-knit group, a family, or an individual. Later the Carolinas, New York, New Jersey, Pennsylvania, and Georgia also would begin as proprietary colonies. In Maryland's case it was the family of George Calvert, Lord Baltimore. Calvert, a devout Roman Catholic, was also a good friend of King Charles I, who gave him a large grant of land in America. After his death in 1632, his son, Cecil, the second Lord Baltimore, carried out the plan for a colony in America. Lord Baltimore had the authority to set and collect rents, issue legal writs, appoint administrative officials, confirm laws, and supervise the defense of the colony. The only important limitation required the proprietor to make laws "with the advice, assent, and approbation of the freemen of the province," a provision that led Baltimore to establish an elective assembly similar to Virginia's House of Burgesses. The colony remained small. Founded with 2,000 colonists in 1634, it had fewer than 6,000 in 1660. Most heads of families were small planters, cultivating tobacco for export.

The Maryland Toleration Act of 1649, despite its advanced provisions, was nevertheless a document of the seventeenth century. It stated in part:

"Therefore . . . enacted that noe person or persons whatsoever within this Province, or the Islands, Ports, Harbors, Creeks, or havens thereunto belonging professing to believe in Jesus Christ, shall from henceforth bee any waies troubled, Molested or discountenanced for or in respect of his or her religion nor in the free exercise thereof within this Province or the Islands thereunto belonging nor any way compelled to the beleife or exercise of any other Religion against his or her consent, soe as they be not unfaithful to the Lord Proprietary, or molest or conspire against the civill Government established or to bee established in this Province under him or his heires. . . . [S]uch person or persons soe offending, shalbe compelled to pay trebble damages to the party soe wronged or molested, and for every such offence shall also forfeit 20ˢ sterling in money or the value thereof. . . , Or if the parties soe offending as aforesaid shall refuse or bee unable to recompense the party soe wronged, or to satisfy such ffyne or forfeiture, then such offender shalbe severely punished by publick whipping & imprisonment."

Roman Catholics never settled in Maryland in large numbers, and Protestants soon sought greater influence. During the 1640s England was in civil war. On the one side were the forces of Parliament, dominated by the Puritans and seeking to set up a republic and a state church purified of remnants of Catholic theology and practice. On the other was the army of King Charles I, defending the existence of monarchy along with the established church. That church was Protestant and technically considered Rome to be an enemy. But it was close enough to Catholicism in sacraments, liturgy, and hierarchy to have a degree of affinity with England's remaining Roman Catholics, at least so long as Puritans were a common foe. In 1649 the Maryland assembly adopted an act, framed by Lord Baltimore in response to pressures in England and America and in response to his own conscience, that guaranteed religious toleration to all Christians. Maryland, like the New England colonies and Virginia, felt the shock waves from civil war and revolution in England.

A Moment of American Independence: 1642–1660 In 1642 the Puritan Parliament in England began open warfare with the monarchy, holding it to be the defender of an unpurified church. Parliament triumphed in 1647, and in 1649 executed Charles I.

Then for eleven years a nation without a monarch was given over to experimentation in politics and in the shaping of a virtuous Protestant society. Parliament made the country into a Commonwealth that soon gave way to a Protectorate under Oliver Cromwell, who had been the essential leader of the Puritan forces. In 1660, not long after the death of Cromwell and the succession of his son to the Protectorate, Parliament invited a Stuart to resume the monarchy, and Charles II became King after years of exile in Europe.

From the Civil War until the restoration of the Stuarts, England was occupied with argument, war, and experiment, and the colonies were orphaned, virtually independent of the mother country. During these times they matured institutionally and socially.

The Chesapeake colonies of Virginia and Maryland, and the settlements in New England, evolved largely on their own, and then during the twenty years of the English Civil War the government largely ignored them. With little outside interference, the early British colonies developed a powerful sense of independence and self-sufficiency.

When the war broke out, the Puritan magistrates in New England formally dissolved their connections with the Crown. Various of the colonies, partly to establish more regular and consistent relations with the Indians in the wake of the Pequot War of 1637–38, formed the New England Confederation for mutual defense and general cooperation. Rhode Island was excluded, on the ground that it was a sinkhole of depravity and heresy. The sense of a common identity among the members of the Confederation hardened through their isolation from England. During the turmoil in England the New Englanders took to the sea, ventured into occasional trading activities with the West Indies, and therein laid the foundations for New England's robust maritime future.

During the 1650s both New England and the Chesapeake continued to grow. The outbreak of the Civil War had cut off the flow of

The Massachusetts General Court declared in 1650:

"Wee humbly conceive that the laws of England are bounded within the four seas, and doe not reach America. The subjects of his majesty here being not represented in Parliament, so we have not looked at ourselves to be impeded in our trade by them."

Puritans to New England, but by the time the war ended in 1647 the population of Massachusetts and the other New England colonies was increasing as fast as ever. In New England, where so many hundreds of Puritans had brought their families, that increase was largely due to a high birthrate. In Virginia and Maryland, women were scarcer, and family life took longer to develop. But a steady stream of immigrants swelled the population of the Chesapeake colonies. Some of the immigrants were fugitives from the Puritanical repression that was unfolding in England during the 1650s. Maryland's Toleration Act of 1649, guaranteeing freedom to all Christians, pulled immigrants of all denominations to Maryland.

The Half-Way Covenant   After about 1650, New England's economy began to boom. Industriousness, furthered perhaps by a Puritan commitment to the virtue of diligence, had brought material prosperity to John Winthrop's "citty upon a Hille." This quickening of economic activity turned heads away from the Puritan founders' original purpose and attracted profit seekers who remained outside the religious community. And by the 1650s Puritans uneasily noticed that many of their children were not undergoing the conversion experience required for church membership. If the trend continued, Puritans feared, a dangerously large portion of the population would soon be outside the church.

In 1662 a meeting of Puritan ministers arrived at a solution to the problem of declining church membership. The ministers agreed to admit the grown children of church members into partial fellowship even though they could not give evidence of grace. To preserve the church's purity, the ministers excluded these "halfway" members from participation in the sacrament of Holy Communion. This Half-Way Covenant did revive lagging church membership, but it also showed that the Puritans' early dreams were yielding to practicality. Churches must be kept filled, even though, as one Concord man complained, "in the extreme seasons of heat and cold we were ready to say of the Sabbath, 'Behold what a weariness.' " The colony of Massachusetts was no longer a community of saints.

Boston by the late 1660s was, in the observation of a merchant, a town

"furnished with many fair shops; their materials are brick, stone, lime, handsomely contrived, with three meeting houses or churches, and a town-house built upon pillars where the merchants may confer; in the chambers above they keep their monthly courts. Their streets are many and large, paved with pebble stone, and the south-side adorned with gardens and orchards. The town is very rich and populous, much frequented by strangers; here is the dwelling of their governor. On the northwest and northeast two constant fairs are kept for daily traffic [trade] thereunto. On the south there is a small but pleasant Common where the gallants a little before sunset walk with their *Marmalet*-madams . . . till the nine o'clock bell rings them home to their respective habitations, when presently the constables walk their rounds to see good orders kept, and to take up loose people."

New Colonies

While New England and the Chesapeake colonies were establishing settlements, other colonies were taking shape—some founded for religious reasons and some for a variety of other motives. Until the middle of the seventeenth century the division of British North America into colonies had been on a patchwork basis. In 1660, when a Parliament tired of the disruptiveness of the Puritan period brought back the Stuart monarchy, some settlements had no official sanction. The new King, Charles II, had to give these some legal status, and he also wished to reward his loyal supporters. His government and that of his successor James II also proceeded to provide for further colonization.

Earlier in the century lands lying within the present states of New Hampshire and Maine had gone to individual proprietors receiving

The Thirteen Original Colonies

Name	Founded by	Year	Made Royal	Status at Revolutionary War
1. Virginia	London Company	1607	1624	Royal
2. New Hampshire	John Mason and others	1623	1679	Royal
3. Massachusetts	Separatists and Puritans	1620–30	1691	Royal
4. Maryland	Lord Baltimore	1634	————	Proprietary (controlled by proprietor)
5. Connecticut	Emigrants from Massachusetts	1635	————	Charter
6. Rhode Island	Roger Williams	1636	————	Charter
7. North Carolina	Virginians	1653	1729	Royal (separated informally from S.C., 1691)
8. New York	Dutch	1613–24		
	Duke of York	1664	1685	Royal
9. New Jersey	Berkeley and Carteret	1664	1702	Royal
10. South Carolina	Eight nobles	1670	1719	Royal
11. Pennsylvania	William Penn	1681	————	Proprietary
12. Delaware	Swedes	1638	————	Proprietary
13. Georgia	James Oglethorpe	1733	1752	Royal

authority from the Crown, but that authority was shadowy and from time to time Massachusetts Bay had extended its government to settlers there. By 1679 New Hampshire became a royal colony, while Maine stayed with Massachusetts until 1820.

Connecticut and Rhode Island were quickly provided for. In 1662 the towns in the Connecticut Valley received a charter from Charles. The charter, to the displeasure of New Havenites, placed the strict Puritan town of New Haven within the same colony as the more liberal settlements of the Connecticut Valley. The Puritan government of England at Roger Williams's urging had given a patent to Rhode Island. In 1663 Charles granted a charter to that democratic collection of towns. The grant confirmed the policy of religious freedom that had made Rhode Island a haven for religious dissenters. Their charters gave to Connecticut and Rhode Island the privilege of governing themselves. Therein appeared a colonial form, the charter colony, taking its place alongside the proprietary colony such as Maryland, owned by a single individual or small group, and the colony owned by a joint-stock company, like Massachusetts. Before long the British American mainland would contain more royal colonies, with governors appointed by the Crown.

New York   Since the early 1600s the Dutch West India Company had owned New Netherland, the territory that is now the state of New York. A collection of Dutch, English, other Europeans, Africans, and Indians dwelt in the little village of New Amsterdam on the island of Manhattan, in a later century to become

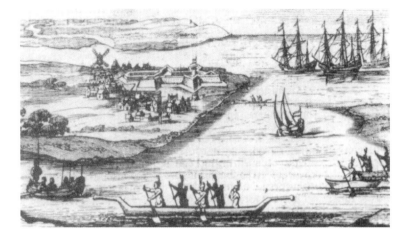

This 1651 engraving, the earliest known view of Manhattan Island, shows the fort of New Amsterdam in the 1620s. Indians are bringing beaver pelts in their canoes to sell to the Dutch.

one of the world's greatest cities: The future New York City lived off the fur and land trade and whatever other commerce the colony could offer. Farther up the Hudson River were the beginnings of a system that would leave its mark on New York society for two centuries and more, in which patroons—the word suggests the English "patron"—presided over huge farming estates and their workers. The Dutch West India Company had extended over New Netherland a loose control and provided local self-government and freedom of religion. The company was not able to turn a profit from the fees, taxes, and duties it imposed on the colony, and in 1654 it went bankrupt.

Charles II, continuing the commercial conflict with the Netherlands that the Puritan Commonwealth had entered, in 1664 seized New Netherland bloodlessly, the allegedly hot temper of its governor, Peter Stuyvesant, proving to have some mixture of prudence. (The Dutch would briefly retake the colony in the 1670s.) Charles II gave the province to his brother James, the Duke of York, and it became New York; the town of New Amsterdam also took that name. James's lieutenant in the colony proceeded to work out a set of laws. The scheme gave the freeholders—in essence, the landholders—of the colony the vote for town officials, but ensured that the Duke would hold ultimate power. There was to be freedom of religion, though each town was required to sustain a church. To two supporters, Lord Berkeley and Sir George Carteret, the Duke transferred the nearby conquered territory that received the name New Jersey. It was so named in honor of Carteret's earlier defense of the English Channel island of Jersey against the Puritans. Berkeley and Carteret then provided freedom of religion and granted to the freeholders the right to elect representatives who, along with a governor and council appointed by the proprietors, would legislate for the colony. The proprietors retained the authority to annul the laws.

Peter Stuyvesant. *(New-York Historical Society, New York City)*

The Carolinas   In 1663 a group that included Berkeley and Carteret became the proprietors of Carolina. In a charter of 1665, the King affirmed the right of the inhabitants to liberty of religion. The proprietors provided for a legislature elected by the freeholders, but retained the right to revoke laws. In 1669 Lord Ashley, one of the proprietors, and his secretary, the political philosopher John Locke, designed "The Fundamental Constitutions of Carolina," conceiving an elaborate and fanciful scheme for the colony, with a hereditary nobility and a feudal serfdom that were never realized. Toward the end of the century Carolina was centered in two unconnected locations: in the north, benefiting from migration from Virginia, a society of small farmers; and in the south, around the seaport of Charles Town (Charleston), a cluster of Virginians, migrants from the northern colonies, English immigrants, Scots, French Protestants called Huguenots, and planters from Bermuda and the British West Indies. The economy of the southern part of Carolina subsisted in part on the fur trade with the Indians, and the settlers around Charles Town were beginning to grow rice with slave labor. North and South Carolina both possessed self-government under ultimate proprietary control, but each would eventually become a royal colony with a Crown-appointed governor.

Pennsylvania   In 1681 an upper-class Quaker, William Penn, received from Charles II a proprietary grant to "Pennsylvania." Penn had already joined other Quakers in purchasing from Carteret the proprietary rights to part of New Jersey.

The Quakers, so called for the trembling religious fervor among their earlier members, believed that within each individual is a seed of truth and enlightenment. In pious living, contemplation, and a state of receptivity, a person can allow this seed to grow and spread its spiritual light. Quakers lived, then, in a condition of expectancy and inner questioning. Many Quakers were conspicuous for rejecting outward forms, customs, and social hierarchy. It was a common practice among Quakers, for example, to address even people of high social station with the familiar "thou" and "thee." They were persecuted in England and in Massachusetts Bay.

Penn's grant derived in part from the earlier friendship between Charles and Penn's father; Charles owed Penn for services rendered by

GABRIEL THOMAS'S ACCOUNT OF PENNSYLVANIA

Gabriel Thomas was a Quaker living in Pennsylvania during the late seventeenth century. Like many Quakers, he acted as a salesman for the new colony:

"The *Air* here is very delicate, pleasant, and wholesome; the *Heavens* serene, rarely overcast, bearing mighty resemblance to the better part of *France;* after Rain they have commonly a very clear Sky, the Climate is something Colder in the depth of Winter, and Hotter in the height of Summer; (the cause of which is its being a Main Land or Continent; the Days also are two Hours longer in the shortest Day of Winter, and shorter by two Hours in the longest Day of Summer) than here in *England,* which makes the Fruit so good, and the Earth so fertil.

The Corn-Harvest is ended before the middle of *July,* and most Years they have commonly between Twenty and Thirty Bushels of Wheat for every one they Sow. Their Ground is harrowed with Wooden Tyned Harrows, twice over in a place is sufficient; twice mending of their Plow-Irons in a Years time will serve. Their Horses commonly go with out being shod; two Men may clear between Twenty and Thirty Acres of Land in one Year, fit for the Plough, in which Oxen are chiefly us'd, though Horses are not wanting, and of them Good and well shap'd. A Cart or a Wain may go through the middle of the Woods, between Trees without getting any damage, and of such Land in a convenient place, the Purchase will cost between *Ten* and

Penn's Treaty with the Indians, **by Benjamin West. The Quaker William Penn's historic treaty with the Delaware Indians in 1682 created a peaceful settlement in Pennsylvania.** *(Courtesy, Pennsylvania Academy of Fine Arts)*

the father, an admiral, and the grant was made in payment of that debt. The charter to Pennsylvania required that William Penn enforce British trading acts, permit appeals from Pennsylvania courts to the King, submit all Pennsylvania laws to the King for approval, and upon request from twenty colonists, provide a minister of the established Church of England. The King reserved the power to impose taxes "by act of Parliament." In all other respects Penn was free to govern his colony as he pleased.

In an elaborate *Frame of Government* (1682), Penn provided that the governorship of the colony would go to the proprietor or his deputy, and that legislative power would be vested in a council and an assembly, both elected by the freeholders of the colony. He proposed to earn an income from his colony by collecting rents from the settlers, and to attract the settlers by advertising widely the good land, free government, and religious liberty available in the colony. The campaign was an immediate success. Quakers flocked to Pennsylvania from England, Holland, Germany, Wales, and Ireland. Many people of other beliefs

Fifteen Pounds for a Hundred Acres. Here is much Meadow Ground. Poor People both Men and Women, will get near three times more Wages for their Labour in this Country, than they can earn either in *England* or *Wales.* . . .

[There are also] Land Fowl, of most sorts, *viz. Swans, Ducks, Teal,* (which two are the most Graceful and most Delicious in the World) *Geese, Divers, Brands, Snipe, Curlew;* as also *Eagles, Turkies* (of Forty or Fifty Pound Weight) *Pheasants, Patridges, Pidgeons Heath-Birds, Black Birds;* and that Strange and Remarkable Fowl, call'd (in these Parts) the Mocking-Bird, that Imitates all sorts of Birds in their various Notes. And for Fish, there are prodigious quantities of most sorts, *viz. Shadds Cats Heads, Sheeps-Heads, Herrings, Smelts, Roach, Eels, Perch.* As also the large sort of Fish, as *Whales* (of which a great deal of Oyl is made) *Salmon, Trout, Sturgeon, Rock, Oysters,* (some six Inches long) *Crabs, Cockles,* (some as big as Stewing *Oysters* of which are made a Choice Soupe or Broth) *Canok* and *Mussels,* with many other sorts of Fish, which would be too tedious to insert.

There are several sorts of wild *Beasts* of great Profit, and good Food; *viz. Panthers, Woolves, Fither, Deer, Beaver, Otter, Hares, Musk-Rats, Minks, Wild Cats, Foxes, Rackoons, Rabits,* and that strange Creature, the *Possam,* she having a false Belly to swallow her Young ones, by which means she preserveth them from danger, when any thing comes to disturb them. There are also *Bears* some *Wolves,* are pretty well destroy'd by the *Indians,* for the sake of the Reward given them by the *Christians* for that Service."

went as well, and a group of German Mennonites, driven from their homes by the continental religious wars, also immigrated to Pennsylvania. The capital, Philadelphia, the City of Brotherly Love, had by 1720 a population of 10,000, and by the 1770s would be the largest city in North America.

Penn also possessed deeds to what is now Delaware, though the grounds of his legal claim to govern "the Territories," as the lower region was called for a while, were unclear. In the first decade of the eighteenth century, Delaware, settled in part by Swedes, in effect would separate from Pennsylvania, though both colonies continued to have the same governor. In 1776 Delaware was to become a separate state.

| **Spanish and French Settlements** | While England was colonizing much of the North Atlantic coast, other seventeenth-century European powers were settling portions of North America. |

Besides the Dutch in New Netherland (later New York) and the French in Canada, there were Spanish settlements in the Southwest. In 1598 Juan de Oñate had led a large expedition to the Rio Grande River into what is now New Mexico to claim that region for Spain. On August 20, 1598, Oñate and his entire company gathered with the priests to give thanks for their safe journey and successful settlement. Some say that this, and not the Pilgrims' more famous celebration in 1620, was the first Thanksgiving celebrated by Europeans in North America. The Spaniards also brought livestock with them: six hundred longhorn cattle and four hundred horses. Descendants of these longhorns were to become a legendary breed in Texas, and the descendants of the horses, the wild mustangs, would transform the Plains Indians into skilled horsemen and fearsome mounted warriors. Oñate's expedition led to the founding of Santa Fe, New Mexico, in 1609. Don Pedro de Peralta and a group of Franciscan missionaries established the settlement, but they were not the first to live there: the town was built on the site of an ancient Indian village.

Santa Fe was the northern outpost of Spain's vast empire. A branch of this main Spanish road led eastward across Texas to the French settlement on the Red River at Natchitoches, Louisiana, founded in 1713. Still another branch road went west to the Gila River and the Gulf of California. Along these roads, traders, Indians, and Spanish missionaries extended the influence of New Spain in North America.

By the early 1700s there was a scattering of small Spanish missions and presidios or forts in the river valleys of what are now the states of Texas, New Mexico, and Arizona. Jesuit and Franciscan priests worked at converting the Indians to Christianity, and Indians worked at growing beans and corn and meat cattle to supply the settlements' needs. Both enterprises had mixed results. In general, the Indians were not enthusiastic about leaving their native gods for a Christian deity, and the missions, far from the headquarters of New Spain in Mexico and even farther from the center of power in Spain, languished for want of converts and supplies.

In 1680 the Pueblo Indians of the upper Rio Grande valley staged a successful revolt against the Spanish settlers. Under the charismatic leader Popé, Indians killed priests, burned missions, and invaded the

Spanish explorations inspired by the French expedition to the Gulf Coast in the late seventeenth century gave the state of Texas its name. In 1686 Spaniards traveling in what is now east Texas met some hospitable Hasinai Indians, members of the Caddo nation. The Hasinai used a word for "friend" that sounded to Spanish ears like "tejas." The Spaniards, thinking themselves in the "great kingdom of the Tejas," called the entire region by that name.

Spanish capital at Santa Fe. Over four hundred Spanish colonists were killed, and the survivors fled. The refugees found safety at a place they called El Paso del Norte (the Northern Pass), now modern Juárez, Mexico, across the Rio Grande from the present city of El Paso, Texas.

Besides the Pueblo revolt, a French incursion into the Gulf of Mexico in 1685 potentially threatened New Spain. In 1682 a French explorer named Robert Cavelier, Sieur de La Salle, had traveled south from French outposts in Canada and claimed the Mississippi River Valley for France, calling the entire region Louisiana, after King Louis XIV. Two years later, supported by a grateful King Louis, La Salle sailed into the Gulf of Mexico, planning to establish a colony at the mouth of the Mississippi. Instead, his three ships missed their destination by about four hundred miles, arriving in early 1685 at Matagorda Bay near what is now the town of Port O'Connor in south Texas. The expedition's supply ship ran aground trying to enter the shallow bay, and another returned to France, leaving La Salle with 180 colonists and one small ship to search in vain for the Mississippi River. Their search ultimately proved unsuccessful, and disease and hostile Indians took their toll. In 1686 the French colonists' one remaining ship was wrecked in a storm. By 1687 only twenty settlers remained at Fort St. Louis as La Salle and seventeen others set off in search of help from a French outpost in Illinois. Discord as well as disease plagued these Frenchmen, and La Salle in 1687 was murdered by his disgruntled followers. In 1688 Indians attacked the few survivors at Fort St. Louis and destroyed the fort.

A year later the Spanish explorer Alonso de Leon, sent to search for Fort St. Louis, found the deserted site. All that remained were the main building, six huts of mud and buffalo hide, torn books, broken trunks, and parts of muskets. The Spaniards buried the remains of three dead bodies, two men and a woman. De Leon and his men also found eight cast-iron cannons, which they buried to keep them safe for future use.

Three major archaeological discoveries in the 1990s, three centuries after La Salle's ill-fated visit to Texas, verified the French presence on the Gulf Coast. In 1995 the wreckage of one of La Salle's ships, the sixty-five-ton *La Belle*, wrecked in 1686, was discovered in twelve feet of murky water in Matagorda Bay in south Texas. This shipwreck is one of the most significant ever found in North America. An eight-hundred-pound bronze cannon bearing the crest of King Louis XIV, and other recovered artifacts verified the ship's identity: *La Belle* had been a gift to La Salle from the French monarch. In 1996 a ranch hand with a metal detector unearthed three of the cannons that the Spanish had buried at Fort St. Louis in 1689. Archaeologists working in the same spot recovered all eight of the cannons, and the site of the long-lost French fort was conclusively identified. In 1998 the wreck of La Salle's supply ship *Aimable*, of three hundred tons, was discovered under water near the narrow channel of Cavallo Pass, the entrance to Matagorda Bay where the vessel had run aground in 1685.

The Colonies and the Crown

The Navigation Acts and Mercantilism   In 1651 the government of the Puritan Commonwealth passed a Navigation Act aimed at building up the shipping of England and the empire. The government was particularly interested in excluding from English and colonial ports the ships of the Netherlands, a fellow Protestant nation with which the Commonwealth was in close economic competition. The Act provided that no ships except those belonging to the people of England or her colonies could carry Asian, African, or American goods into England or the colonies.

After Charles II restored the English monarchy in 1660, his ministers and Parliament, building on principles established by the Navigation Act, enacted a broad program designed to stimulate England's economic growth and to transform into a world empire the scattered American settlements and East Indian trading posts. The primary aim of this mercantilist program was to make England and its overseas colonies a vast, closed trading area, as self-sufficient as possible, protected by an enlarged navy, and serviced by an expanded merchant fleet. Each part of the empire was supposed to specialize in supplying the products and services for which it was best suited, and thereby contribute to the well-being of all the other parts and to the strength of the whole. The colonies would provide the mother country with materials that England could not produce economically, such as lumber, naval stores, fish, tobacco, indigo, and West Indian sugar. The colonial products were supposed to be sent only to Britain, but would have a monopoly on the English market. Insofar as was feasible, the colonies were not to engage in manufacture. Instead they would buy their finished goods from England. All products would be subject to customs duties and be carried only in English or colonial ships.

Two major acts laid the legal foundations of the system: the Navigation Act of 1660 and the Staple Act of 1663. The Navigation Act restricted all colonial trade to vessels owned and manned primarily by Englishmen or British colonists, and required that certain named articles produced in the colonies—tobacco, sugar, indigo, and ginger—be shipped only to Britain or to another English colony. The Staple Act required that most goods imported into the colonies, whether they originated in Britain or in foreign parts, must be shipped from a British port. The Staple Act aimed to benefit the Crown by increasing the customs revenues on exports from England. It was supposed also to help English exporters by giving them a monopoly of the colonial market (even as the Navigation Act gave colonial producers a monopoly of the English market). And it was intended to protect the colonists by confining their trade to shipping lanes that could be patrolled and protected by the English navy.

A Trade Boom For all the laxity of its enforcement, the new commercial system was an immediate success. English commerce boomed and the merchant fleet became the largest and most profitable the nation had yet known. Besides the mainland colonies, England's island possessions prospered under this new system. These included Bermuda, founded in 1612, and the West Indies colonies of St. Christopher (1624), Barbados (1627), Nevis (1628), Montserrat and Antigua (1632), and Jamaica (1655). The West Indies, booming with the rapid expansion of slavery and sugar production, welcomed the naval protection afforded by the new system, for the Caribbean had been teeming with pirates. The Chesapeake colonies, Virginia and Maryland, paid perhaps a bit more for freight than they had before, and tobacco prices continued to decline until the 1690s. But the establishment of a great central marketing system in England facilitated an enormous increase in production that in the long run more than compensated. By 1680, for example, the Chesapeake colonies were exporting over seventeen million pounds of tobacco a year. The New England colonies, being free to elect their own governors, were also free to ignore the Acts of Trade when it was to their advantage. Thus they profited from trade with the enclosed imperial market as well as from the protection of the English navy, and otherwise did as they pleased. Consequently, the merchant fleet of New England, built by a burgeoning new local industry, grew even faster than that of Old England.

The Navigation Act of 1660 provided in part:

"That from and after the first day of *April,* 1661, no sugars, tobacco, cotton-wool, indicoes, ginger, fustick, or other dying wood, of the growth, production or manufacture of any *English* plantations in *America, Asia* or *Africa,* shall be shipped, carried, conveyed or transported from any of the said *English* plantations to any land . . . other than to such other *English* plantations as do belong to his Majesty. . . ."

By the 1620s Virginia was exporting in considerable quantity a valuable crop, tobacco, which appealed to Europeans. King James I published a pamphlet that denounced smoking as "a custom loathsome to the eye, hateful to the nose, harmful to the brain, dangerous to the lungs, and in the black stinking fumes thereof, the nearest resembling the horrible smoke of the pit that is bottomless." But the King's perception failed to dissuade seventeenth-century smokers, some of whom may have read a 1614 pamphlet by an Edinburgh physician. He claimed that tobacco would cure asthma, shortness of breath, coughs, ulcers, colic, "yea almost all diseases," and that smoking "prepareth the stomach for meat, it maketh a clear voice, it maketh a sweet breath, it cleareth the sight, it openeth the ears, it comforteth the nerves. . . ." Whatever the eventual impact on European lungs, tobacco ensured a long and prosperous history for the preeminent southern colony.

After what is known as the Restoration, the return of the Catholic Charles II to the British throne in 1660, the colonies cultivated the independence that they had already enjoyed when England, first under the Puritan Commonwealth and then under the Protectorate, left them for the most part alone. The Massachusetts Bay Puritan Colony led the way.

Charles II's resumption of discrimination against those who dissented from the Church of England also promoted New England's prosperity. A new wave of dissenters went to America in flight from this policy, and in the 1660s the population of New England increased from about 33,000 to some 52,000.

Resistance to the Crown   From the outset of the Restoration, Massachusetts was troublesome. It secretly harbored three of the men condemned to death for the execution of Charles I (though there was a £100 bounty on their heads and anyone caught assisting them would be executed). Massachusetts ignored the Navigation Acts; and it violated its charter by retaining on its statute books a number of laws, particularly those concerning religion, contrary to the laws of England. Very early, Charles II sent orders commanding Massachusetts to make its laws conform to those of England. The colony did temporarily stop persecuting the Quakers—it had executed three—and did modify its laws concerning suffrage, but neither action was taken in response to the King's orders, which the colonial assembly flatly ignored. And so, when the British mission to seize New Netherland from the Dutch was dispatched in 1664, Charles sent four commissioners along to investigate the New England governments.

The commissioners encountered no difficulty in Plymouth, Connecticut, or Rhode Island, but when they arrived in Boston they met a reception at once icy and bold. The magistrates referred the commissioners to the Massachusetts Bay Charter of 1629, refused to submit to investigation, and publicly forbade the citizens to offer any testimony. The commissioners returned to England, and three of them recommended to the King that the charter be revoked. The open defiance might have provoked not only a revocation of the charter but armed suppression of the colony as well. But the confrontation came just at the time England was suffering from the London plague, a great fire in that city, and military reverses abroad. For the next six years Massachusetts, together with the other colonies, was largely ignored, and could take advantage of the situation.

In 1667, when the price of tobacco fell to a low of less than half a penny a pound, New England's merchants began a practice they would continue off and on until the American Revolution. When it was to their advantage, they ignored the mother country's Acts of Trade. Tobacco by the late 1660s was a staple of the colonies' transatlantic trade, but its transport and sale were strictly regulated. Tobacco was subject to a customs duty of two pennies per pound, and could be shipped only to England, there to be taxed and put into English vessels bound for the European market. Under normal circumstances about half the tobacco shipped from the colonies to London was re-exported to the European continent through Holland. Though the English market had dwindled, European demand for tobacco continued. So the merchants of New

England, disregarding the Navigation Acts, loaded the Chesapeake's tobacco aboard their own vessels and sailed directly to Holland, where they and the colonial tobacco planters made handsome if illegal profits.

Virginia, of all the colonies most committed to the monarchy, and New England, the least, were equally dissatisfied with the government in London. By late in the seventeenth century, colonists in the two regions were to be in close to open rebellion against the English government. Both, too, had found something else to worry about: renewed hostilities with the Indians.

Indian Affairs

Indian Migration

The ultimate wellspring of the trouble was the ambition of France. Since the massacre of 1622 in Virginia and the Pequot War of 1637–38 in Massachusetts, the Indians had gradually and peacefully retreated to the interior rather than face the fire of English muskets. But in the late 1660s the French adopted a broad strategy of encircling the English colonies with settlements along the St. Lawrence, the Great Lakes, and the Mississippi, and forged alliances with the Indians between their own settlements and those of the English. The five Iroquois nations of New York had long been enemies of the French and their Indian allies. Hence the new French policy forced the Iroquois back. They, in turn, pushed back the Algonquian tribes of New England and the Susquehannocks of Pennsylvania, with the result that in the 1670s New England Indians clashed with the English to the east, and the Susquehannocks engaged in hostilities with the colonists to the south.

New England and King Philip's War

In New England the fighting was known as King Philip's War (1675–76). Metacom, whom the colonists called King Philip, a Wampanoag chieftain whose own people were already hemmed in between rival governments and land speculators in Rhode Island and Massachusetts, was pressed to the point of desperation by the Iroquois drive; and just at that time the Massachusetts government ordered the Indians to disarm. They responded in the only way they could, by attacking the English settlements.

The Indians did not fight according to the rules of formal territorial warfare, European-style: a contest in which the only combatants and subjects of attack were uniformed armies and both sides campaigned until one or the other surrendered. They crept up on unsuspecting villages, setting fire to houses and barns, driving away or killing livestock as well as unsuspecting colonists, and then retreating into the forests. Town after town was laid waste in the winter of 1675–76. The Indians fought only intermittently, and they regarded everyone, women and children included, as fair prey. There was considerable barbarism on both sides. But the colonists learned Indian ways of fighting, and they surprised the enemy in an attack deep within the swamps of Rhode Isand. Native Americans groups, meanwhile, suffered from disunity. Metacom met resistence from Indian competitors in the fur trade advancing against him from New York state, and some other tribes had

King Philip. *(Courtesy, Smithsonian Institution)*

allied with the colonists. His was the last Native American rebellion that seriously threatened New England settlers. By 1676 the Indians had been thoroughly defeated, though at great cost: King Philip's War destroyed over 20 towns and cost the English settlers a sixth of their adult males. During the entire campaign, the English government sent no help.

Instead of help, a special agent of Charles II, Edward Randolph, arrived in Boston to convey new royal instructions and to investigate the enforcement of the Navigation Acts. The obstinate Massachusetts General Court refused to recognize Randolph as customs officer, set up its own customs office, and imprisoned the deputies Randolph had appointed. When the colony did not satisfactorily reform its behavior, court proceedings began. In 1684 the Massachusetts Bay Company lost its charter and Massachusetts became a royal colony.

A map of Virginia in 1612, showing Powhatan. *(Courtesy, Smithsonian Institution)*

Virginia and the Powhatan Confederacy   After the bloody Powhatan uprising of 1622 in Virginia, throughout the 1620s and 1630s the Virginia militia methodically attacked native villages, destroying people, homes, and food supplies. Not until the mid-1630s did peace return. The aged Opechancanough, chief of the Powhatan Confederacy, then struck in 1644, his warriors killing more than 500 of Virginia's 8,000 settlers. With superior numbers and technology, the English quickly crushed the rebellion, capturing and killing Opechancanough and destroying the Powhatan Confederacy.

In a treaty that was to become typical of future such transactions between Indians and non-Indians in the United States, the English colonists and Virginia natives agreed in 1646 to end hostilities. For a variety of reasons, the colonists wanted to move the Indians to distant lands so that the two communities would be permanently separated. Some colonists supported such a plan because it would liberate native lands for development, while others saw it as a way to protect both Indians and Europeans from future violence. The treaty moved the tidewater tribes north of the York River and promised them permanent tenure on their new land. They were to be protected by Virginia courts and were expected to serve in the colonial militia. The reservation system in America had begun.

The reservation system would dominate for nearly three hundred years the relations between Indians and whites. The typical pattern was for white Americans to choose for an Indian tribal reservation land that they did not find desirable. Then over time new settlers, new technologies, or new discoveries of natural resources would make that piece of land suddenly valuable to whites. Violence or legal maneuvering would begin again as whites tried to settle on the reservations and Indians tried to prevent them. The Indians would then be moved to a new reservation farther west, until white land hunger brought still another cycle of invasion and removal.

Thomas Mathew of Virginia described the colonists' fears of Indians after a scare in 1675:

"In these frightfull times the most Exposed small families withdrew into our houses of better Numbers. . . . Neighbours in Bodies Joined their Labours from each plantation to others alternatively, taking their Arms into the Fields, and Setting sentinels; no Man Stirrd out of Door unarm'd."

Virginia and Bacon's Rebellion   In the summer of 1675, bands of Susquehannock Indians, fleeing the Iroquois, crossed the Potomac River into Virginia. Relations between the backcountry Indians and the Virginia planters deteriorated until a planter's herdsman was killed, several Indians (including five Susquehannock chiefs under a flag of truce) were killed in retaliation, and the whole Potomac frontier erupted in raids and counterraids.

As part of the restored royal authority, according to Governor William Berkeley of Virginia, Indians became subjects of the King, on an equal footing with the English colonists, and were therefore entitled to the protection of royal justice. No warfare upon the Indians was to be tolerated, despite the Indian attacks—which Berkeley regarded as minor frontier incidents and impediments to the lucrative fur trade. Berkeley met the crisis by raising funds to rebuild the frontier forts and to pay and equip a band of mounted rangers, and by prohibiting fur trade by any but a handful of traders whom he himself licensed. The new tax was ill calculated to please the frontiersmen, and the new trade regulations threatened the ambitions of a number of frontier fur traders, land seekers, and border barons.

The malcontents soon raised a leader who was willing to defy the governor: Nathaniel Bacon, recent settler in the interior of Virginia, artful demagogue, unscrupulous lawyer who had been trained at the Inns of Court in London. Bacon held that the Indians were not subjects of the Crown but were outside the law and could be attacked by any Englishman so disposed. In May 1676, without a commission from the governor, Bacon marched at the head of an expedition that descended upon the Roanoke River to destroy a Susquehannock village. He was promptly accused of treason, but the governor pardoned him when he acknowledged his offense.

"Bacon's Laws" Meanwhile Bacon, along with a goodly number of other radicals, was elected to the House of Burgesses. They proceeded to push through a series of enactments, collectively known as "Bacon's laws," which reversed most of Berkeley's policies by liberalizing voting, tax, and religious regulations. Bacon himself had little or nothing to do with all this. Instead, he took up his military career again. He raised an army of 500 men, marched on the colonial capital at Jamestown, forced Berkeley to commission him as a militia captain, and set about looking for more Indians to kill.

The planters professed no allegiance at all to Parliament, and their loyalty to the Crown had become only formal, devoid of any personal commitment. When Governor Berkeley again declared Bacon a rebel, many planters swore their allegiance to that frontiersman. In 1676, they held to their oath, enabling Bacon to drive Berkeley's forces out of Jamestown and burn the village to the ground. Loyalist forces threatened rebel families, and Bacon used loyalists' wives as hostages during his attack on Jamestown. The rebellion revealed class tensions as well as political differences. One female partisan of Berkeley wrote to a friend that the "differences within our selves [are] far greater [than with the Indians]."

Order was restored in the ensuing months, largely as a result of Bacon's death from the "bloody flux" (dysentery) in October. Berkeley regained control and proceeded to hang twenty-three of the rebels, causing Charles II to remark, "The old fool has hanged more men in that naked country than I have done for the murder of my father." The King sent a royal commission to Virginia to investigate the rebellion, and the seventy-year-old Berkeley was recalled to England, but he died before he could give his side of the story.

The Dominion of New England

With the death of Charles II in 1685, his brother James became King. James carried forward the project for the establishment of royal rule, and for bringing some coherence to the government of the colonies. He created the Dominion of New England. New Hampshire, Massachusetts, Plymouth (not yet absorbed into Massachusetts), Connecticut, Rhode Island, New York, and the Jerseys were all to be governed by one governor and his council, without the interference of representative assemblies. James appointed as governor of the Dominion Sir Edmund Andros, a former governor of New York and a staunch Church of England man, who arrived in Boston during 1686. "The fox," said the Puritan clergyman Cotton Mather, "has been made master of the hen house."

Sir Edmund Andros   The new system made a great deal of administrative sense. It had a defensive purpose as well. James II feared that the French in North America would threaten England's colonies, and wanted the Dominion of New England to unite those independent-minded colonists under one firm hand. For the first and only time in the history of the English empire in America, England had a colonial system that was, at least on paper, as efficient as those of France and Spain.

Andros's administration was in many respects both shrewd and enlightened. He left most of the existing laws in force. He respected the established churches and schools—though in his attempts to provide for the Church of England he antagonized Puritans. His observance of Christmas, which Puritanism rejected for savoring of ritual and Catholicism, drew the indignant notice of Samuel Sewall. A prominent and devout Puritan, Sewall made a dour comment in his diary on December 25, 1686 (a Sunday): "The Christmas keepers had a very pleasant day." For the most part Andros left the towns in control of their own local affairs: and the town and congregation constituted the primary unit of government in New England. Andros could also govern with a strong hand. He offered the merchants of his Dominion, for example, the protection of the Royal Navy if they cooperated with him. He also levied taxes without legislative approval, but they were no larger than they had been when duly elected representatives levied them. Andros further encroached upon the principle of local self-government by ordering that town meetings be held no more than once a year and that control of the militia be vested in the governor. But the towns customarily met officially only once a year anyway (they met once a week as church congregations, and that Andros did not change), and as it happened Andros never had occasion to call out the militia.

In short, Andros's innovations directly challenged the professed principles of the New Englanders, but altered little their daily lives. It is uncertain whether this experiment in enlightened despotism would have won over New Englanders inclined to hostility toward outside rule, and more especially rule by a communicant of the Church of England. The Dominion of New England was never put to the full test, for the Crown power that it needed for support collapsed.

Edmund Andros, governor of the Dominion of New England from 1686–1688, being taken prisoner in Boston. Though this was triggered by rumors of a popish plot, opposition to Andros stemmed from the colonists' belief that he was limiting local self-government. *(Courtesy, Scribner's Archives)*

James II's undoing came in 1688 after he alienated his strongest supporters by attempting to go too far too fast in his efforts to restore Roman Catholicism. Even the Tories, the party more sympathetic to the privileges of the Crown, were antagonists. Rich country gentry, who made up much of the strength of the Tories, were wedded to the Church of England. Some of them feared that full restoration of the Roman Church might include restoration of its lands, which happened now to belong to them. Even then, James might have prevailed but for a sudden change in the prospects for the royal succession.

The Glorious Revolution   James was in his fifties and his only children were two daughters, Mary and Anne, both by his first wife and both devoutly Protestant; his second wife, an Italian princess and a Catholic, had borne him no children. Most Englishmen, however much they despised the King, therefore thought it better to wait out the papist storm as they had the Puritan, on the theory that little permanent harm could be done before James died and the Crown passed to a Protestant. But in June 1688 the Queen had a son, and that opened the possibility of a permanent Catholic succession. English Protestantism seemed endangered: and so a group of prominent Englishmen conspired to invite William of Orange of Holland, husband of James's daughter Mary, to rescue England from Roman Catholicism. William accepted and on November 5 landed with a force of about 14,000. Great numbers of royal troops deserted, and much of the remainder of James's army refused to obey their Catholic commanders. James was left defenseless, and in December he fled to the continent. Eight weeks later William and Mary became joint sovereigns of England. The whole tame affair acquired a flamboyant title: the Glorious Revolution.

Governor Andros was in Maine when he got news of William's landing, and he returned to Boston to prevent an anti-royalist response. But he had neither army nor police, and rioting broke out in response not to James's removal but to rumors of a popish plot. Andros fled to the local fort, but before the end of the day he and the other royal officials surrendered and were jailed. A Puritan oligarchy governed the colony for two months, until a new General Court could be elected. In July Andros was ordered to return to England.

As soon as the news of Boston's uprising reached New York that colony too was swept with a great fear of a popish plot, and three of its counties, those populated mainly by Puritans, threw out the royal officials and elected their own. In New York, Jacob Leisler, a successful German trader, led a group that ousted Andros's deputy governor and established a provisional government. At first Leisler had little backing outside the city, but soon Indian raids in the upper part of the colony inspired by the French lent gruesome reinforcement to the rumors of a papist and Indian campaign to massacre Protestants. Leisler offered discipline, order, and military strength, and became in fact governor of the entire colony for two years, until a new royal governor arrived. Then Leisler and his son-in-law were hanged and drawn and quartered for treason.

The Jerseys and Pennsylvania adjusted to the new regime in England with little drama. In Maryland a group of colonists calling themselves the Protestant Association forced the resignation of the governor appointed by the Catholic Lord Baltimore, brought back the assembly, which had been dissolved, and petitioned the Crown to take over the colony. In Virginia the dominant planters announced their support of William and Mary and their confidence that James's governor would be removed, which soon happened. Settlers in northern Carolina turned on the proprietary governor, who fled to Charles Town and temporarily set up a government there. Soon afterward the proprietors suspended him.

The Ideology of Revolution The philosopher of the English revolution was John Locke. At the behest of various champions of the revolution, Locke published in 1689 and 1690 several essays, notably the *Second Treatise of Civil Government* and *An Essay Concerning Human Understanding*. Locke reasoned that man had once lived in a state of nature, in accordance with the laws of nature, which endow man with rights to life, personal freedom, and the property that he accumulates through honest labor. But in the natural state the strong prey upon the weak, and so men had formed societies and created governments. Governments exist by virtue of voluntary agreements, or contracts, between governed and governors, and their function is to protect the individual's natural rights to life, liberty, and property. The conclusion to which this argument points is that the government of James II broke the contract by depriving people of their natural rights, in effect declaring war upon his subjects. The people therefore had no recourse but to overthrow James's government and to establish a new contract with a new sovereign, William of Orange, who seemed more likely to abide by his agreements.

To make legitimate the Glorious Revolution, a Convention Parliament proclaimed early in 1689 a Declaration of Rights that a formal Parliament enacted, under the title of Bill of Rights; William and Mary approved it later the same year. The Bill of Rights established, for all time, limits upon the English monarchy and judiciary. The Crown could no longer make or suspend laws, levy taxes, or maintain standing armies without the consent of Parliament, which was guaranteed frequent meetings, free elections, and free debate. Some ecclesiastical courts were eliminated and others had their powers reduced, and in all courts every person was guaranteed trial by jury and protected from excessive bails and forfeiture of estates before conviction.

Equally important were measures to regularize, modernize, and render more flexible the system of public finance, which had previously occasioned such destructive conflict between the Crown and Parliament. Henceforth Parliament did not merely grant monies, but controlled their expenditure as well. To that end, it began to make specific appropriations for specific purposes, and to require estimates and accounts of expenditures.

Crown and Parliament, restructuring the government at home, attempted also to bring order to affairs in the colonies.

The Suffrage in the Colonies

While seventeenth-century European nations—with the partial exception of England—were becoming more autocratic, Americans were opening their political system to wide participation. That did not come of some radical democratic ideology. The colonies went on the fairly conservative conviction that participation in political decisions should be left to property owners. Since in the colonies ownership of property was widespread, so was the proportion of voters to the whole population. In the early settlement of Massachusetts Bay, the vote was vested in male members of Puritan congregations, and this too made for a fairly broad electorate. The eventual ideological commitment among Americans to popular rule resulted in good measure from their practical experience of it.

England Tries Again: The Navigation Act of 1696

In 1696 King William III of England commissioned the Board of Trade to supervise commerce, recommend appointments of colonial officials, and review colonial laws to see that none interfered with trade or conflicted with the laws of England. Since the 1660s the colonists had taken advantage of England's political preoccupations to profit from illegal trade. Enforcement of the earlier Navigation Acts had depended more upon private morality, supplemented by generous rewards to informers, than upon efficient administrative machinery. The new Navigation Act of 1696 sought to change that. Colonial governors were now held responsible, on penalty of forfeiture of office, for violations of the law. Regular customs officers were appointed for each colony, whereas previously there had been only a few officers who moved about from one colony to another. Trials for violations of the law were to be in admiralty courts, where proceedings were not encumbered by juries.

But the new system could not overcome the physical circumstances in English America, which were not conducive to efficient supervision of trade. Effective customs operations require concentration of shipping, and in much of America such concentration was not feasible. Tobacco, for example, by far the most valuable product of the mainland colonies, was normally loaded on ships directly at the plantations along the rivers of Virginia and Maryland and on Chesapeake Bay. Short of placing customs officers on every plantation or stationing armed ships at every river and inlet, it was virtually impossible to prevent masters of vessels from carrying tobacco anywhere they pleased.

For the enforcement of anything like the Navigation Acts England had as yet no tradition of civil service, royal or parliamentary, in the colonies or at home. Posts were filled through influence, bribery, or other corrupt means as quickly as through regard for honest and efficient administration. Colonial service attracted the least savory of a generally unsavory lot, not only because life in the colonies was far from desirable to most courtiers, but also because the rewards for legitimate service there were small. In all the mainland colonies except Virginia the governor was dependent upon the local assembly for his salary, and the customs officers were paid out of fees and fines, not the royal treasury. Accordingly, many of those who filled imperial positions were quite amenable to bribes, offered in exchange for looking the other way.

By and large, the imperial commercial system worked when it was to the mutual advantage of the colonies and the mother country to abide by it; which is to say, it worked for about three-quarters of the trade affected by the Navigation Acts. Otherwise it was generally ignored, except when the Royal Navy was not engaged in war and had nothing better to do than police the seas against pirates and smugglers.

In the years following the Glorious Revolution colonial governments underwent reorganization. Connecticut and Rhode Island retained their self-government, and the Penn family, after losing the original charter to Pennsylvania, regained the proprietorship of that colony. In 1691 the Crown took over Maryland, though the Calvert family retained property rights there. But then the Calverts converted from Roman Catholicism to the Church of England, and in 1715 they were given back proprietary rights to the government of Maryland. In the colony founded as a refuge for Roman Catholics, people of that faith lost the right to vote. Virginia, Massachusetts, and New Hampshire were now royal colonies. In 1702 New Jersey too became a Crown colony, and by 1729 North Carolina and South Carolina were separate Crown colonies.

Within a few years after the Glorious Revolution, then, British North America had the kind of government and the relationships to Great Britain that would determine its course until the American Revolution. In the eighteenth century governors and councils appointed by the monarch would often clash with elected assemblies that alone had the authority to tax the colonists, and therefore had the authority to withhold money from a governor in the pursuit of his policies. The Navigation Acts, with further legislation in the eighteenth century, would in time lead to major conflict with the government in Great Britain. The foundations had been laid for a grand but restless empire.

Suggested Readings

The study of the massive migration of Europeans to America must begin with Bernard Bailyn's *The Peopling of America: An Introduction* (1985). Patricia Seed's insightful *Ceremonies of Possession in Europe's Conquest of the New World, 1492–1640* (1995) explores the different ways in which the Spanish, English, Dutch, and French staked their cultural claims on the lands they colonized. See also David Hackett Fischer's provocative study, *Albion's Seed: Four British Folkways in America* (1989) and James Horn, *Adapting to a New World: English Society in the Seventeenth Century Chesapeake* (1994). Karen O. Kupperman's 1984 study, *Roanoke: The Abandoned Colony*, is a well-reasoned account of the lost settlers. Alden Vaughan, *American Genesis: Captain John Smith and the Founding of Virginia* (1975) and Edmund S. Morgan, *American Slavery, American Freedom: The Ordeal of Colonial Virginia* (1975), are classic works on early Virginia. Newer studies include Everett Emerson, *Captain John Smith* (1993) and A. J. Leo LeMay, *Did Pocahontas Save John Smith?* (1992).

On the founding of New England, Edmund Morgan's *The Puritan Dilemma: The Story of John Winthrop* (1958) has become a classic, as has John Demos, *A Little Commonwealth: Family Life in Plymouth Colony* (1970). Demos explores new territory in *The Unredeemed Captive: A Family Story from Early America* (1994). Useful town studies include Darrett Rutman, *Winthrop's Boston* (1965), Kenneth Lockridge, *A New England Town: The First Hundred Years* (1970), and Philip Greven, *Four Generations: Population, Land, and Family in Colonial Andover, Massachusetts* (1970).

Early New England's rich intellectual history may be sampled in Kenneth Silverman's *Cotton Mather: Puritan Priest* (1988), Sacvan Bercovitch, *The American Jeremiad* (1978), and the classic *Errand into the Wilderness* (1956) by Perry Miller. The standard study of the Anne Hutchinson controversy is still Emery Battis, *Saints and Sectaries: Anne Hutchinson and the Antinomian Controversy in the Massachusetts Bay Colony* (1962). See also Kenneth Lockridge, *Literacy in Colonial New England* (1974).

An important environmental study is William Cronon's *Changes in the Land: Indians, Colonists, and the Ecology of New England* (1984). Alden Vaughan's *New England Frontier: Puritans and Indians, 1620–1675* (1965) examines the confrontation of cultures, as does Gary B. Nash in *Red, White, and Black: The People of Early North America* (1992). Alfred A. Cave's *The Pequot War* (1996) is a recent account of that New England conflict.

On Virginia's Indians see Helen Rountree, *The Powhatan Indians of Virginia: Their Traditional Culture* (1989), and an important collection of essays edited by Peter Wood and others entitled *Powhatan's Mantle: Indians in the Colonial Southeast* (1989). See also Douglas Deal, *Race and Class in Colonial Virginia: Indians, Englishmen, and Africans on the Eastern Shore during the Seventeenth Century* (1993). Daniel Richter's *The Ordeal of the Longhouse: The Peoples of the Iroquois League in the Era of European Colonization* (1992) is a sympathetic study of northern tribes.

See the provocative new study by Jill Lepore, *King Philip's War* (1997). On Bacon's Rebellion see Stephen Webb's *The End of American Independence* (1983) and Wilcomb Washburn, *The Governor and the Rebel: A History of Bacon's Rebellion in Virginia* (1957).

Cultural Influences on the Early Colonies

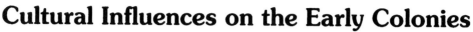

David Hackett Fischer

Our society is dynamic, changing profoundly in every period of American history; but it is also remarkably stable. The search for the origins of this system is the central problem in American history. . . .

The organizing question here is about what might be called the determinants of a voluntary society. The problem is to explain the origins and stability of a social system which for two centuries has remained stubbornly democratic in its politics, capitalist in its economy, libertarian in its laws, individualist in its society and pluralistic in its culture. . . .

During the very long period from 1629 to 1775, the present area of the United States was settled by at least four large waves of English-speaking immigrants. The first was an exodus of Puritans from the east of England to Massachusetts during a period of eleven years from 1629 to 1640. The second was the migration of a small Royalist elite and large numbers of indentured servants from the south of England to Virginia (ca. 1642–75). The third was a movement from the North Midlands of England and Wales to the Delaware Valley (ca. 1675–1725). The fourth was a flow of English-speaking people from the borders of North Britain and northern Ireland to the Appalachian backcountry mostly during the half-century from 1718 to 1775.

These four groups shared many qualities in common. All of them spoke the English language. Nearly all were British Protestants. Most lived under British laws and took pride in possessing British liberties. At the same time, they also differed from one another in many other ways: in their religious denominations, social ranks, historical generations, and also in the British regions from whence they came. They carried across the Atlantic four different sets of British folkways which became the basis of regional cultures in the New World.

By the year 1775 these four cultures were fully established in British America. They spoke distinctive dialects of English, built their houses in diverse ways, and had different methods of doing much of the ordinary business of life. Most important for the political history of the United States, they also had four different conceptions of order, power and freedom which became the cornerstones of a voluntary society in British America.

Today less than 20 percent of the American population have any British ancestors at all. But in a cultural sense most Americans are Albion's seed, no matter who their own forebears may have been. Strong echoes of . . . British folkways may still be heard in the major dialects of American speech, in the regional patterns of American life, in the complex dynamics of American politics, and in the continuing conflict between four different ideas of freedom in the United States. The interplay of four "freedom ways" has created an expansive pluralism which is more libertarian than any unitary culture alone could be. . . . The legacy of four British folkways in early America remains the most powerful determinant of a voluntary society in the United States today.

Reprinted from David Hackett Fischer, *Albion's Seed: Four British Folkways in America* (New York: Oxford University Press, 1989). Reprinted with permission.

"God is English." Thus John Aylmer, a pious English clergyman, exhorted his parishioners in 1558, attempting to fill them with piety and patriotism. That thought, though never stated so directly, has echoed ever since through our history books. As schoolchildren, as college students, and as presumably informed citizens, most of us have been brought up on what has passed for the greatest success story of human history, the epic tale of how a proud, brave offshoot of the English-speaking people tried to reverse the laws of history by demonstrating what the human spirit, liberated from the shackles of tradition, myth, and oppressive authority, could do in a newly discovered corner of the earth. . . .

This is ethnocentric history, as has been charged frequently and vociferously in the last few decades, both by revisionist white historians and by those whose citizenship is American but whose ancestral roots are in Africa, Asia, Mexico, or the native cultures of North America. Just as Eurocentrism made it difficult for the early colonizers and explorers to believe that a continental land mass as large as North America could exist in the oceans between Europe and Asia, historians in this country have found it difficult to understand that the colonial period of our history is the story of a minority of English colonizers interacting with a majority of Iroquois, Delawares, Narragansetts, Pequots, Mahicans, Catawbas, Tuscaroras, Creeks, Cherokees, Choctaws, Ibos, Mandigos, Fulas, Yorubas, Ashantis, Germans, French, Spaniards, Swedes, Welsh, and Scots-Irish, to mention only some of the cultural strains present on the continent. . . .

[A] fuller and deeper understanding of the colonial underpinnings of American history must examine the interaction of many peoples, at all levels of society, from a wide range of cultural backgrounds over a period of several centuries. For the "colonial period" this means exploring not only how the English and other Europeans "discovered" North America and transplanted their cultures there, but also how societies that had been in North America and Africa for thousands of years were actively and intimately involved in the process of forging a new, multistranded culture in what would become the United States. Africans were not merely enslaved. Native Americans were not merely driven from the land. As Ralph Ellison, the African American writer, has reasoned: "Can a people . . . live and develop for over three hundred years by simply *reacting*? Are American Negroes simply the creation of white men, or have they at least helped to create themselves out of what they found around them?" To include Africans and Indians in our history in this way, simply as victims of the more powerful Europeans, is hardly better than excluding them altogether. It is to render voiceless, nameless, and faceless people who powerfully affected the course of our historical development as a society and as a nation.

To break through the notion of Indians and Africans being kneaded like dough according to the whims of the invading European societies, we must abandon the notion of "primitive" and "civilized" people. There is still some utility in pointing out differences in technological achievement—the Europeans' ability to navigate across the Atlantic and their ability to process iron and thereby to manufacture guns, for example. But if we take these achievements as constituting the marks of a "superior" culture coming into contact with an "inferior" one, we unconsciously step in a mental trap in which Europeans are the active agents of history and the African and Indian people are the passive victims.

. . . "Savages we call them," wrote Benjamin Franklin more than two centuries ago, "because their Manners differ from ours, which we think the Perfection of Civility; they think the same of theirs." To think of Indians simply as victims of European aggression is to bury from sight the rich and instructive story of how Narragansetts, Iroquois, Delawares, Pamunkeys, Cherokees, Creeks, and many other nations, which had been changing for centuries before Europeans touched foot on the continent, responded creatively and powerfully to the newcomers from across the ocean and in this way reshaped themselves while reshaping the course of European settlement.

Gary B. Nash, *Red, White, and Black: The People of Early North America,* 3rd ed. (Englewood Cliffs, N.J.: Prentice Hall, 1992). Reprinted with permission.

Gallows Hill, Salem, Massachusetts, where the "witches" were hanged.

The Developing Colonies

THE SALEM WITCHES

In 1692 the Devil assaulted the seaport town of Salem, Massachusetts, north of Boston. This village of a few hundred people was invaded by scores of warlocks and witches, men and women who had covenanted with the Devil to make mischief, to drive little children mad, to sicken and kill livestock and people. One witch, it seemed, had caused the deaths of fourteen members of a single family. The jails bulged with over a hundred prisoners awaiting trial, including a four-year-old child bound for nine months in heavy iron chains. Twenty-seven people eventually came to trial; the court hanged nineteen—fourteen women and five men—as witches. One man refused to enter a plea, and suffered *peine forte et dure:* heavy weights were laid on Giles Cory's body until, still refusing the plea, he was pressed to death.

The trouble had begun innocently enough: "Conjuration with sieves and keys, and peas, and nails, and horseshoes" at first seemed harmless activities with which to pass the New England winter. But these games turned serious when grim-visaged parents tried to discover what was causing their children's "fits" and "distempers."

Everyone knew about witchcraft. Witches and their male counterparts the warlocks had made a pact with the Devil. They "wrote in his book," joining his legions for the thrill of conjurations, midnight frolics, obscure or perhaps obscene rituals, and the power to harm their neighbors. Do not "suffer a witch to live," the Bible commanded, and in Europe, tens of thousands, most of them women but many men as well, had been executed as the Evil One's followers.

HISTORICAL EVENTS

1636
America's first college founded (Harvard)

1692
Salem witch hunts

1699
Wool Act

1704
America's first newspaper published (*Boston News-Letter*)

1712
Slave uprising in New York City

1715
Yamasees of South Carolina rebel

1718
Spanish founded San Antonio • French founded New Orleans

1732
Hat Act

1733
Sugar Act • last British colony in America founded (Georgia)

1734
The Great Awakening begins in Massachusetts

1735
The Zenger Case

continued

HISTORICAL EVENTS

1737
The Reverend Jonathan Edwards publishes *A Faithful Narrative of the Surprising Work of God*

1739
Stono Rebellion in South Carolina • George Whitefield makes evangelical tour of English colonies

1743
American Philosophical Society established

1750
Iron Act

1752
Benjamin Franklin's kite experiment

Before 1692, the Devil had paid small attention to New England. Forty-four cases, three hangings—such was the entire history of New England witchcraft before the malady spread to nine adolescent girls in Salem. Under intense questioning, and responding to this attention with yet further manifestations of demoniac possession, the girls named three women as the source of their sufferings. These were likely candidates.

Sarah Good, daughter of a well-to-do innkeeper, had steadily tumbled down the social ladder; she was in 1692 a surly, pipe-smoking beggar whose "muttering and scolding" seemed to cause cows to die. Sarah Osborne's name swirled in contention and scandal: her battle with her own sons for control of her first husband's estate, her liaison with the Irish indentured servant who became her second husband.

And there was Tituba, the Indian slave woman, who represented a culture both fascinating and frightening to the Puritans. She had been brought to Massachusetts from Barbados in 1680 by the Reverend Samuel Parris, and when the girls accused her of witchcraft, her testimony sent waves of fear throughout Salem. For five days, she regaled her questioners with stories of comportings with the Devil, with witches Sarah Good, Sarah Osborne, and with two Boston women she did not name. Tituba told of nightly spectral meetings and rides through the air. In vivid, fearsome detail, Tituba described one of Satan's minions as "a thing all over hairy, all the face hairy and a long nose," a creature "about two or three foot high." She had seen the Devil's "book," she said, and although she could not read, she had counted nine names in it. Drawing on the Indian and African lore she had learned in the West Indies, Tituba told her fearful, fascinated audiences what she thought they wanted to hear.

Tituba's dark complexion and dark hair reminded her Puritan hearers that she was an Indian—one of a people they associated with Satanic practices. They were more than willing to accept her imaginative fantasies as truth. As Tituba tried to protect herself, she unfolded a tale of Satanic conspiracy that confirmed the deepest suspicions of the anxious Puritan community. A recent biography of Tituba points out that it was this Indian slave woman's confession, not her alleged teaching of witchcraft practices to the young girls, that so inflamed the Puritan community.

Soon the girls, shrieking, contorting, sobbing hysterically, dredged up still more names. Not all were outcasts like Sarah Good, Sarah Osborne, and Tituba; not all were from Salem. The jails groaned; the gallows rope snapped. The madness, for the better part of a year, infected a whole society. When the accusers began to name prominent citizens—some Boston clergymen, for instance, and the governor's wife—the Reverend Cotton Mather, his father, the Reverend Increase Mather, and some other ministers recommended the cessation of the trials. (Cotton Mather, as was common in the seventeenth century, believed in witches, but he also believed in science. He would have his day in 1721, when to combat popular fears of the new medical practice of inoculation for smallpox, he allowed his son to be inoculated.) Reason returned to Salem; probing questions were asked; the jailed were sent home and pardoned.

The girls' part in it is easiest to explain. The life of young girls in Massachusetts Bay was dull in the best of times. "I am not fond," wrote Cotton Mather, "of proposing *Play* to children, as a Reward of any diligent Application to learn what is good; lest they should think *Diversion* to be a better and nobler Thing than *Diligence*." While young men, sent to school and taught to pray and work, could at least look forward to the adventure of choosing careers, girls could do little more than wonder "what trade their sweethearts should be of." It is understandable that when the little girls dabbled in magic with Tituba, their slightly older friends and relatives joined the only excitement midwinter had to offer. (Many teen-aged girls—including most of the "afflicted" ones—did not live at home where parents might spoil them, but were sent to relatives' or neighbors' houses to learn their adult roles and to be evenly disciplined.) Once the adults began to fuss over their fits, how could the young resist pursuing their adventure and showing their power over the adult community, particularly over the married women who laid on endless chores and discipline? Even these antics would have been relatively harmless had not the adults panicked.

One explanation that has been offered of the witchcraft turmoil in Salem is that it fed upon local conflicts. People from differing political and clerical factions hurled accusations back and forth. For Salem was an angry place. Town and countryside were sharply diverging. Conservative backcountry farmers smarted under the growth of commercial capitalism and its accompanying secular style. Sons coming of age found difficulty establishing themselves as land became increasingly scarce. The values of Puritanism itself seemed more and more in question as ministers bemoaned the "declension" from the piety of the colony's founders three generations before. And from 1684 to 1691 the colony of Massachusetts had been without a charter. Would the old land claims be valid under a new one? Would voting still be restricted to church members? Nearly every adult must have been startled at a changing world crowding in on what had been for two generations a largely fixed culture. Men and women who were supposed to practice Christian unity engaged year after year in lawsuits over boundaries and legacies. Like the witches, they were at war with their neighbors, disrupting the church and government, bursting the old molds. Were they too possessed? How much easier it must have been to blame everything on the literal bewitchment of enemies rather than on their own bewitchment with the new and perhaps dubious values and goals that were transforming John Winthrop's "citty upon a Hille" into a secular society.

One recent writer correlates the witchcraft scare with an Indian war that began in 1689. Here was a main cause of dislocation. People who survived the frontier massacres abandoned their exposed positions and retreated to older settlements. Fear of Indian attack spurred by French Catholics to the north was quite thoroughly mixed up with fear of the Devil in the minds of seventeenth-century Protestants.

Massachusetts a few years after the Salem trials passed an act reversing the convictions of those executed. Though this did not help the victims, it lifted a stigma from the townspeople. No community before had ever issued a repentance for destroying witches.

New England Colonies

Everyday Life   The early New England settlers gathered into communities that duplicated something of the physical arrangement of the English villages they had known. An English family did not live in isolation on the land it worked. Homes were close together in the village, and each family worked plots of the surrounding lands. The system was well suited to the needs of the first generation in New England. On a stubborn soil in a harsh winter climate and under threat of Indian attack, that generation sought to establish a stable and comfortable life. For several decades in Massachusetts, attendance at church was required of everyone, including nonmembers; and the centrality of the churches in the life of the colony was further reason for the colonists to cluster into villages. By the eighteenth century, however, young men seeking farm land had to go farther afield, or be content with smaller plots as fathers parceled out family holdings to sons. Neighbors sometimes coveted one another's land, and social tensions rose. But the village pattern that had developed in the early years left its permanent stamp on New England. The system of town meetings, in which local citizens directly make decisions that elsewhere in the country are left to elected or appointed officials, persists to this day.

Even in the seventeenth century New England, at least in its most settled portions, contained one of the most remarkably well-educated populaces in the English world. Harvard College, America's first institution of higher learning, was founded in 1636, primarily to educate young men for the clergy. The government of Massachusetts Bay had the towns provide free elementary schools—although girls were not expected to benefit from them and women's literacy lagged far behind that of men. Sermons could employ an imagery beautiful in its home-

Boys and girls alike read the New England Primer, published in 1691:

In *Adam's* fall
We sinned all.

Thy life to mend
This *Book* attend.

The *Cat* doth play
And after slay.

A *Dog* will bite
The thief at night.

An *Eagle's* flight
Is out of sight.

The idle *Fool*
Is whipped at school.

As runs the *Glass*,
Man's life doth pass.

spun plain style, and educated New Englanders read not only religious but secular literature written in the language of everyday life. Sermons and history dominated colonial reading, but there was also an audience for poetry that ran from the religious doggerel of Reverend Michael Wigglesworth's "Day of Doom" to the delicate lyrics of Anne Bradstreet's "To My Dear and Loving Husband." Colonists also read newspapers, beginning in 1704 with the *Boston News-Letter* and the *New England Courant* (run by Benjamin Franklin's brother) in 1721.

Scholars have rejected the notion that New Englanders were black-clad haters of life, the world, and pleasure. The diarist Samuel Sewall might grumble at Edmund Andros for celebrating Christmas, but Sewall and other Puritans enjoyed good food and drink. In 1725 the *Boston News-Letter* complained that people "could hardly hear the minister's first prayer for the rustling of silk gowns and petticoats." That same year a horse race on Boston Common offered a prize of "a velvet Saddle with Silver Lace." Most New Englanders did not even wear black, although they would have been happy to do it. Black was the color not of grimness but of wealth and prominence. As New England's economy matured, colonial merchants found it necessary to buy large quantities of manufactured goods from England. The region was almost entirely dependent upon the mother country for clothing, for almost all tools beyond the most primitive, for muskets and other firearms, and for clocks, compasses, and a host of other instruments. The New Englanders drank oceans of tea and used considerable quantities of spices, which could be legally obtained only through the East India Company in London; and despite recurring waves of puritanical hostility toward the consumption of luxuries, they sought and bought the finer things of life when they were able.

New England settlers imported English class distinctions, yet here as in other matters the land and conditions of the New World modified the institutions of the old. Class distinction in New England meant not the presence of a powerful aristocracy but a somewhat milder component of the English system of class, a deference on the part of the majority toward people of greater wealth, schooling, and political position. But class distinctions were difficult to maintain. As one New England minister observed, "The Misery and Iniquity of it is, the inferior sort of People will be clad in as Costly Attire as the Rich and Honourable."

Prosperity   The years from about 1715 to 1755 were a time of great prosperity. New England's commercial success was not based upon hauling freight or directly upon the slave trade. The colonial merchants were never more than marginally engaged in either of these maritime activities. The key to the New Englanders' system was the great sugar plantations of the West Indies. These were not self-sufficient, for it was uneconomical to waste the labor of slaves on growing staple food when it could be bought so cheaply and land was so valuable. The sugar islands were also deficient in timber suitable for providing the bare necessity of wood products, even including staves for making containers in which to ship their sugar. By supplying the West

If ever two were one, then surely we,
If ever man were lov'd by wife, then thee;
If ever wife was happy in a man,
Compare with me ye women if you can.

—Anne Bradstreet
d. 1672

Felling axe, New England, ca. 1725. With tools like this colonists cleared their land of trees and hewed their wood into shape for use in domestic construction. *(Curtesy, Essex Institute, Salem, Massachusetts)*

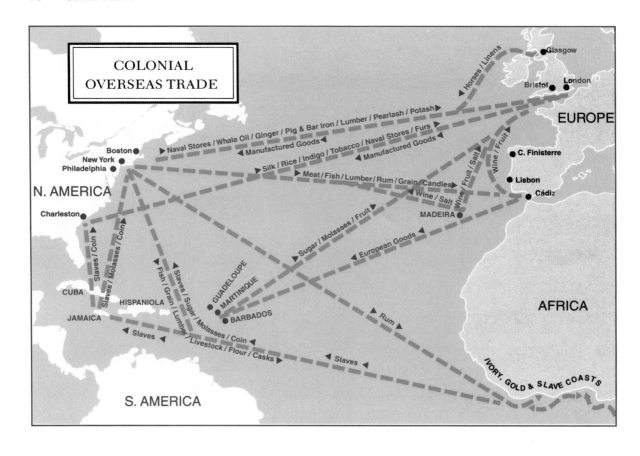

Indies, New England's entrepreneurs made enough profit not only to pay what they owed for imports, but to provide employment for their whole population.

New England farmers produced fruit, beef, pork, butter, and cheese for the West Indian market, and many also raised cattle, horses, and chickens for live export. Fishing expanded enormously and became highly commercialized after 1715. By the 1730s as many as 150 new fishing vessels were being built annually, and the number of people employed in the fisheries was more than 5,000. Whaling developed as an additional specialty in some places, notably Nantucket, where it was even more valuable than fishing.

In the early days, when settlements were concentrated along the seacoast and immediately to the interior from Boston and the other ports, farmers produced marketable timber from the trees they felled to clear their lands for the plow. But timber is a bulky commodity and the only practical way to transport it is by river; and south of Salem the Massachusetts coast was almost entirely devoid of streams that extended as much as five miles into the interior. New settlers in towns beyond that distance developed the practice of burning the trees they felled and making the ashes into potash; this could easily be carried to port towns for merchants who found a ready market for it in England. But the change also meant that the supply of lumber from Massachusetts and Connecticut dwindled just at the time the demand for lumber products in the West Indies was expanding rapidly. For this growing market, a commercial lumber industry was developed after about 1720 in New Hampshire and the province of Maine, where there were magnificent stands of white pine and the river systems afforded convenient transportation.

The merchants of New England secured their provisions for the West Indies from the local farmers by selling them goods imported from England, but the owners of fishing fleets and lumber camps and their employees consumed little of such commodities. The fishermen and lumber workers did, however, consume one thing abundantly, and that was rum. Accordingly, New England merchants made a practice of importing West Indian molasses for part of the goods they sold in the islands; the molasses was then manufactured into rum to trade for more lumber or fish.

Payment of the duty on molasses that the British government imposed under the Sugar Act of 1733 would have been detrimental to New York and Pennsylvania and ruinous to New England. So merchants did what American businessmen would do ever after when British law ran counter to their interests: they simply ignored the law. It was easy enough to do, for Britain's machinery for collecting customs and preventing smuggling in America was as yet primitive, and many customs officials were amenable to bribery. The passage of the Sugar Act of 1733, therefore, in no way altered the course of New England's economic growth, except to place the entire economy upon illegal foundations.

Middle Colonies

New York, Pennsylvania, New Jersey, and Delaware contained by the mid-eighteenth century a varying mix of population. People of Dutch ancestry in New York were retaining their ethnic identity, Scotch-Irish and Germans had settled in Pennsylvania west of the Quakers, and there were Swedes to their south. Philadelphia was a principal landing place for immigrants who in the eighteenth century moved to British America by the hundreds of thousands. Each successive wave of immigrants sought land for settlement in the immediate vicinity, until all the cheaply available land in the middle colonies was taken up and it became necessary to push toward the interior and toward the backcountry of the South.

German Immigrants Many if not most German immigrants came as indentured servants—also called redemptioners— paying for their passage by binding themselves to serve as laborers for a number of years before becoming freemen and ordinary settlers. Then, migrating to the backcountry, former German redemptioners settled in a broad area extending twenty to a hundred miles west of the Delaware River. They picked the choicest lands, especially those in the limestone valleys, cleared their farms slowly but thoroughly, and built solid buildings upon them. Because of the care with which they proceeded, by the time they were able to produce for market they could bring in regular and bountiful harvests. Their princi-

Gottlieb Mittelberger, a German immigrant, described the arrival of indentured servants in Philadelphia around 1750:

"When the ships finally arrive in Philadelphia after the long voyage only those are let off who can pay their sea freight or can give good security. The others, who lack the money to pay, have to remain on board until they are purchased and until their purchasers can thus pry them loose from the ship. In this whole process the sick are the worst off, for the healthy are preferred and are more readily paid for. The miserable people who are ill must often still remain at sea and in sight of the city for another two or three weeks."

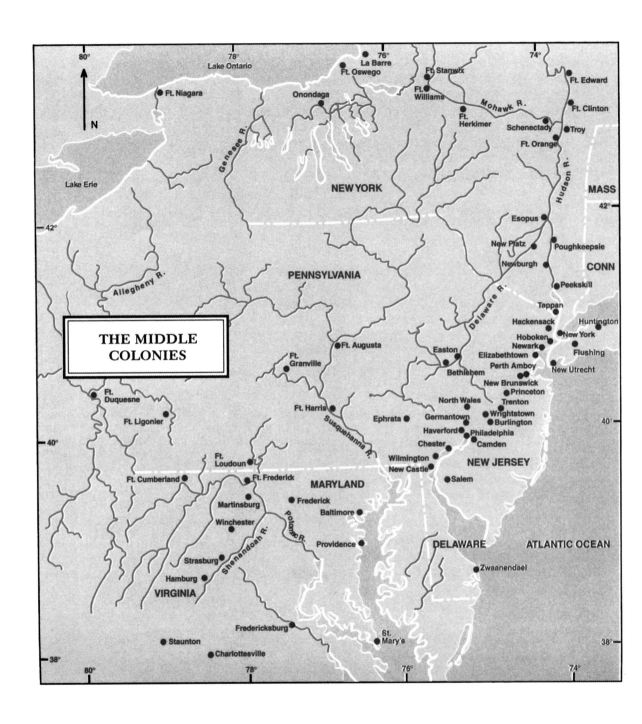

pal crop was wheat, which became the second great staple (or third, if New England fish is counted) to be produced in British North America. Virginia tobacco of course was the first.

The Germans continued to arrive at a steady rate, around 2,000 a year, from 1717 until about 1750. By the 1730s they were beginning to overflow the middle colonies. Thenceforth, they proceeded to the Pennsylvania backcountry and headed south, settling the Cumberland Valley in Pennsylvania and Maryland and much of the Shenandoah Valley of Virginia.

By and large, wherever they went the Germans kept to themselves, retaining their own ways and making no effort to become involved in the political or social life of the colonies they inhabited. They tended to cluster in groups that had little to do even with one another. They represented a wide variety of religious sects, Reformed, Mennonite, Dunker, Moravian Brethren, and even Roman Catholic.

The Scotch-Irish Considerably more numerous and far more disruptive were the descendants of the Scottish Protestants from Ulster in the North of Ireland. The total number of Scotch-Irish immigrants was around 250,000.

The first wave headed for New England. The Ulstermen, like the Puritans, were Calvinist, though the congregation-based church polity of New England was incompatible with the Scotch-Irish polity, with its more centralized Presbyterian church structure. Boston and its vicinity, at any rate, had no excess land and no shortage of labor; the inhabitants feared that immigrants would become just so many paupers to feed from the resources of their meager land; and New Englanders generally regarded the Ulstermen as less civilized. A few thousand immigrants of the first wave landed in Boston and, with difficulty, founded settlements around Worcester and along the Merrimac Valley of New Hampshire, but irate mobs greeted at the docks subsequent Scotch-Irish intended settlers and refused to let them land. Here was an early instance of a phenomenon that continues to this day: hostility on the part of an established American ethnic group to the immigration of another.

The remainder of the first wave of Ulstermen and the overwhelming majority of future shiploads headed for Philadelphia, along with the Germans. The Scotch-Irish also followed the same routes to the interior, but there the resemblance between them and the Germans ends. For reasons of preference as well as circumstance, the two groups of immigrants did not mix. The pattern of settlement, all the way down through the Virginia valley, was that the German firstcomers farmed staples on the rich bottom lands and the Ulstermen who came later raised cattle and corn on the hillsides and poorer lands.

By the late 1730s Ulstermen were filling the Shenandoah Valley of Virginia. Late in the next decade they were spilling out over the Piedmont Plateau of southern Virginia and central North Carolina. A decade later they were invading the uplands of South Carolina.

In constant friction with the Indians, Scotch-Irish often did not hesitate to slaughter them or involve colonial authorities in wars with them. They became avid politicians, skillful and disputatious, and regu-

As late as the mid-eighteenth century the practice of indentured servitude was still common as this newspaper account indicates:

Philadelphia, April 14, 1748.

Run away from Samuel Lippincott of Northampton in the county of Burlington, an Irish servant Maid, named Mary Muckleroy, of a middle Stature: Had on when she went away, a blue and white striped gown, of large and small stripes, cuffed with blue, a white muslin handkerchief, an old blue quilt, a new Persian black bonnet, a new pair of calf-skin shoes, a fine Holland cap, with a cambrick border, an old black short cloak lined with Bengal, blue worsted stockings, with white clocks, a very good fine shirt, and a very good white apron. She took with her a sorrel horse, about 14 hands high, shod before, and paces very well. It is supposed there is an Irishman gone with her. Whoever takes up and secures the said woman and horse, so that they may be had again, shall have Three Pounds reward, and reasonable charges paid by

Samuel Lippincott
—The Pennsylvania Gazette

larly demanded a voice in the lawmaking process when the law affected their way of life, but they disregarded the law when it did not suit them. While many Scotch-Irish showed what frontiersmen could be at their worst, others had a zeal for education deriving from their Presbyterianism, and founded schools and colleges on a scale that no other group of Americans ever approached.

Economic Life in the Middle Colonies   Amidst enormous growth in population—from more than 75,000 in 1715 to 400,000 by the 1750s—the economic and political life of the middle colonies developed rapidly. The economy grew even faster than the population and, as had been the way in New England and the tobacco colonies, proceeded along two lines: development of small-scale production of tools and other equipment for the expanding population, and development of production for trade in international markets.

In the colonies to the north and the south, by far the biggest portion of the business was selling land, but in the middle colonies the population at large could not participate in this lucrative enterprise. In New York the governors and assemblies continued the policy, originated by the Dutch, of granting land only in huge tracts—and only to themselves and their friends and relations. The great patroons, as the Dutch called them, who received the grants were interested more often in leasing the lands than in selling them. In Pennsylvania and Delaware the land belonged originally to the Penn family as proprietors, and all proceeds from sales and rentals went to them. In New Jersey, too, the land belonged to small groups of proprietors, and though the system of land disposition was always complex the profits from land sales went to these small groups.

Indians in the Middle Colonies   King Philip's War in 1675–76 had all but destroyed the Indian communities in New England, but in the middle colonies relations between Indians and whites evolved differently, for a while at least. By the time the English took over in 1664, the Dutch in southern New York and the Swedes in New Jersey had nearly eliminated the Indians as a force. In Pennsylvania the situation was different. A persecuted people dedicated to nonviolence and the belief that all men and women were children of God, the Quakers along with their leader William Penn wanted a colony in which everyone could live in harmony. They respected the right of the Delaware Indians to the land and purchased it from them only after careful negotiations. Word spread, and in the 1690s and early 1700s the Tuscaroras, Shawnees, and Miamis all migrated to Pennsylvania. Eventually, as Scotch-Irish Presbyterians, German Lutherans, and more English Protestants pushed west in Pennsylvania and squatted on tribal land, tensions increased. And when the colonial rivalry for control of the Ohio Valley erupted during the 1750s between the English and the French, open warfare commenced between the Indians and the European settlers, who were far distant in space and mind from the Quaker establishment of eastern Pennsylvania. Eventually, the Indians of Pennsylvania, like those of New England, New York, and New

ESTIMATED POPULATION OF AMERICAN COLONIES:
1630 TO 1750

	1630	1650	1670	1690	1730	1750
White						
New England	1,796	22,452	51,521	86,011	211,233	349,029
Middle Colonies	340	3,786	6,664	32,369	135,298	275,723
Southern Colonies	2,450	22,530	49,215	75,263	191,893	309,588
Black						
New England	0	380	375	950	6,118	10,982
Middle Colonies	10	515	790	2,472	11,683	20,736
Southern Colonies	50	705	3,370	13,307	73,220	204,702
Total White	4,586	48,768	107,400	193,643	538,424	934,340
Total Black	60	1,600	4,535	16,729	91,021	236,420

Jersey, were either killed or driven to points west, where their children awaited the arrival of the next generation of white settlers.

Philadelphia   The supply of craftsmen, the abundance of raw materials, and the insatiable market combined in the middle colonies to breed a thriving industry in farm implements, locks, guns, nails, and other hardware, as well as clocks, flints, glass, stoneware, paper, and woodwork. The port of Philadelphia burgeoned: by the mid-1730s several hundred vessels were entering and clearing the port every year. At first most of these vessels belonged to others, but then Philadelphians began to acquire their own ships. With this development came another, the establishment of a shipbuilding industry and such linked activities as importing and processing naval stores and manufacturing ropes, anchors, and sails.

By the 1730s, Philadelphia, like New York City to a lesser extent, had begun to emerge as a major export and import center. Among the exports were beef and pork, which, along with the livestock, were produced mainly by the Scotch-Irish. These products found ready markets on the sugar plantations of the West Indies. More important were wheat and flour, produced by the industrious Germans and the scores of mills that sprang up along the Delaware and Schuylkill rivers. The Navigation Acts did not confine colonial wheat and flour to the English market. Some went to the West Indies and much to the European continent, where Philadelphia merchants could acquire bills of exchange and goods for trade in England. This made Philadelphia a principal importing center for English manufactures in North America.

Quaker   William Penn's plans late in the seventeenth century
Influences   for Pennsylvania had been ambitious. The colony would be a place of love and harmony. Penn had established friendly relations with the Indians. The very act of establishing a government that could back up its laws with force meant, of

course, that whether or not Penn, like other Quakers, would oppose all wars among nations, he was not prepared to practice a Quakerism of total nonresistance at home. Yet one of his schemes provided that imprisonment would be humane and seek the reformation of criminals. For a short period Pennsylvania actually attempted a system of imprisonment for reform of criminals—an experiment that prefigured the modern penitentiary. The earliest Quakers had been given to fits of emotionalism accompanied by disruptive behavior, but Penn prized more sober virtues and conduct. An account that he wrote of Pennsylvania, translated into German, Dutch, and French and published on the European continent as well as in Britain, invited solid, industrious farmers and craftsmen to settle in the colony. His Quakerism, then, cherished the compound of spirituality and virtuous worldliness that has been characteristic of the Society of Friends ever since.

After Penn's death the colony became quite different from the harmonious commonwealth he had envisioned. The presence of the Scotch-Irish on the frontier guaranteed that the Indians would receive something other than the treatment Penn would have wanted for them. The tide of immigration made the Quakers a minority in the colony, though a wealthy and powerful one, and Quakers lost favor with the proprietors when the sons of William Penn left the Society of Friends for the Church of England. To promote and protect their interests in the face of these reversals, the Quakers gathered allies and formed a political faction called variously the Quaker party and the Anti-Proprietary party. Their wealth and influence normally gave them control of the legislature. Arrayed against them in the Proprietary party were the Scotch-Irish, many frontiersmen, and a considerable number of non-pacifist Germans.

New York   By the late eighteenth century Philadelphia would be the second largest city and second busiest port in the entire English-speaking world. New York's port also thrived, though it developed much more slowly. The colony's restrictive immigration and land policies kept New York City from developing anything like Philadelphia's business of transporting and supplying newcomers, and it also had a smaller productive base for its international trade. But the Iroquois Indians in New York's interior did trap some furs themselves and also served as middlemen between the Albany traders and many of the western Indians, who trapped in enormous quantities and were eager to sell.

In contrast to the popularly based politics of Pennsylvania, politics in New York was aristocratic. The colony did have numerous and vociferous lower elements, fighting one another as well as the upper classes and clamoring for a voice in government. But the lower classes largely canceled one another out in antipathies among Scotch-Irish and New Englanders and New Yorkers, among Presbyterians and Congregationalists and Dutch Calvinists, among tenant farmers and squatters and the plain folk of the city. Such of these inhabitants as could vote were normally easy for the landed aristocrats to manage, for they voted orally, in public, and were therefore amenable to bribery and pressure when mere deference failed to secure their vote.

Southern Colonies

The upper South, unlike New England, had land suitable for the growth of a great commercial staple crop. And since Virginia planters had never been interested in setting up villages with churches as the focus of their life, society in Virginia spread out into tobacco plantations of various sizes—the average was about 200 acres. The majority of Virginia's colonists were small farmers, the independent yeomen whom Thomas Jefferson, years later, would call "the chosen people of God."

Economic Boom in Virginia
In the early 1730s there began a remarkable economic boom in Virginia. Before it had ended the entire area from Pennsylvania to Georgia had been transformed.

Part of the boom was in tobacco prices. The plantation system spread rapidly, and slavery spread with it. An enormous volume of importations as well as natural increase doubled the number of slaves in Virginia to 60,000 in 1740, pushed it substantially past 100,000 in 1750, and took it to 140,000 in 1760.

Meanwhile, land sales surged in Virginia. When the Penn family in the 1730s raised the prices and rents on Pennsylvania lands, Scotch-Irish and German immigrants flooded to the west and south. As they poured southward down the great valley of Virginia, North Carolina and Virginia both promised freedom of worship for Presbyterians, and Virginia and Maryland liberalized their land policies. These measures stimulated a thriving sale of land, and Virginia in particular moved to capitalize on it. Planters and other influential inhabitants of the old tidewater settlements began to realize that there was as much money to be made from selling land as from selling tobacco, and perhaps a great deal more. The members of the House of Burgesses, in collaboration with the governor and his council, began to grant large blocks of interior lands to themselves: sometimes for nominal sums, sometimes for nothing, sometimes in exchange for their services in attracting new settlers to the colony.

The social system that evolved in Virginia was designed to ensure the primacy of a class that can best be termed gentry. The gentry were not of the same class as the royal officials, and did not possess the wealth of the largest planters and land speculators. But by education and the size of their lands they stood apart from their neighbors and from the Scotch-Irish and Germans of the backwoods. Their position of leadership came in large part from the willingness of their humbler neighbors to grant it to them, a habit of deference on the part of the lowly toward people of education and political training. That deference was easily given, for the gentry were generous to those below them. A Fairfax County candidate for the House of Burgesses named George Washington once provided 160 gallons of liquor for the county's 400 voters and, after an election, invited his supporters to a victory ball and supper.

The Carolinas and Georgia
Early in the eighteenth century the institution of slavery was rapidly spreading in another quarter, on the rice plantations of South Carolina (and, a little later, of Georgia). Slavery was a part of life in South Carolina almost as

In 1716 Virginia's Governor Spotswood and a party of Virginians explored the Blue Ridge Mountains. One of them, John Fontaine, noted in his journal:

"We had a good dinner, and after it we got the men together, and loaded all their arms, and we drank the King's health in champagne, and fired a volley; the Princess's health in burgundy, and fired a volley; and all the rest of the Royal Family in claret, and a volley. We had several sorts of liquors, viz., Virginia red wine and white wine, Irish whiskey, brandy, shrub, two sorts of rum, champagne, canary, cherry, punch, water, cider, etc. I sent two of the rangers to look for my gun, which I dropped in the mountains. . . ."

A visitor to Virginia in the 1680s described life there:

"They usually plant tobacco, Indian corn, wheat, peas or beans, barley, sweet potatoes, turnips, which grow to a monstrous size and are very good to eat. They make gardens as we do in Europe. . . . So much timber have they that they build fences all around the land they cultivate. A man with fifty acres of ground, and others in proportion, will leave at least twenty-five wooded, and of the remaining twenty-five will cultivate half and keep the other as a pasture and paddock for his cattle. . . . Some people in this country are comfortably housed; the farmers' houses are built entirely of wood."

Of the houses of the wealthier planters, this observer commented:

"Those who have some means, cover them inside with a coating of mortar in which they use oyster shells for lime; it is as white as snow, so that although they look ugly from the outside, where only the wood can be seen, they are very pleasant inside, with convenient windows and openings. They have started making bricks in quantities, and I have seen several houses where the walls were entirely made of them. . . . They build also a separate kitchen, a separate house for the Christian slaves, one for the Negro slaves, and several to dry the tobacco. . . ."

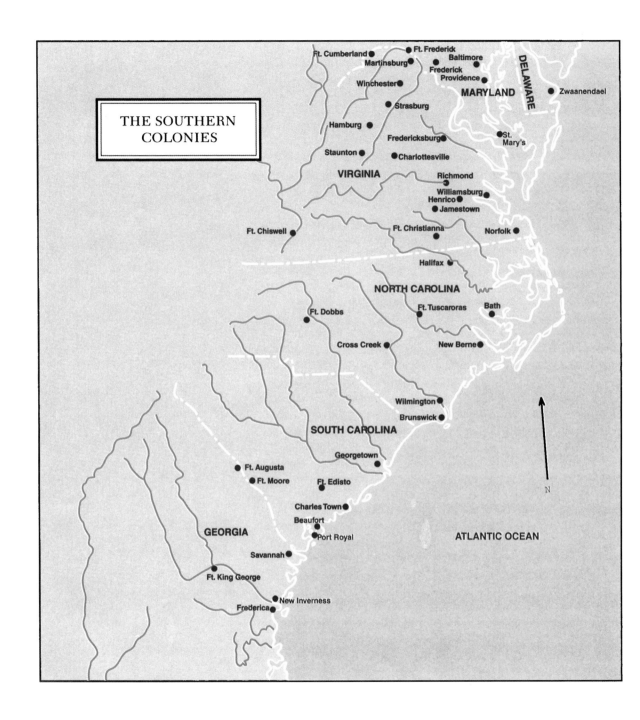

THE SOUTHERN
COLONIES

Ft. Cumberland
Ft. Frederick
Martinsburg
Baltimore
Frederick
Providence
Winchester
MARYLAND
DELAWARE
Zwaanendael
Strasburg
Hamburg
Fredericksburg
St. Mary's
Staunton
Charlottesville
VIRGINIA
Richmond
Williamsburg
Henrico
Jamestown
Ft. Chiswell
Ft. Christianna
Norfolk
Halifax
NORTH CAROLINA
Ft. Dobbs
Ft. Tuscaroras
Bath
Cross Creek
New Berne
Wilmington
Brunswick
SOUTH CAROLINA
Georgetown
Ft. Augusta
Ft. Moore
Ft. Edisto
Charles Town
Beaufort
GEORGIA
Port Royal
ATLANTIC OCEAN
Savannah
Ft. King George
New Inverness
Frederica

N

soon as the colony passed beyond its primitive frontier stage. Many of the early settlers were immigrants from Barbados, where slavery had long been firmly established, and they brought their slaves with them. Of the roughly 3,900 inhabitants of the colony in 1690, about 1,500 were slaves. Then, in the early decades of the eighteenth century the South Carolinians began large-scale rice cultivation in the coastal swamps, and with a phenomenal increase in rice production, slavery increased apace. South Carolina exported 394,000 pounds of rice in 1700 and 43,000,000 in 1740; in the same years the number of slaves in the colony increased from 2,400 to 30,000. From 1720 until the Civil War, slaves outnumbered whites about two to one in South Carolina.

Rice was grown in the coastal swamps, where the climate was hot and humid and malaria and other diseases were common. The work was possible only for strong young adult males, and even many of these died from overwork and disease. For the few slaves, most of them women and children, who lived in or near the master's house and worked as menial servants, life was tolerable, but for the field hands it was monstrous. Despite a law permitting any white to shoot on sight a slave who left his plantation without a written pass from his owner, many a Carolina slave escaped from his master and found refuge among the Creek and Seminole Indians to the south. There were isolated uprisings, and in 1739 slaves on several plantations rose in a rebellion that was not put down until twenty-one whites and forty-four blacks had been killed and scores more of both races had been wounded. Thirty more slaves were killed in the Stono Rebellion that same year.

In the early 1700s North Carolina rapidly became even more separate socially and economically from its sister colony. Plantation slavery was slow to take root, for the colony was covered with thick pine forests, was too dry to permit rice cultivation, and lacked the access to the sea that was then necessary to the growth of tobacco plantations. Until well into the eighteenth century North Carolina's principal products were the naval stores that could be extracted from the pines: tar, pitch, rosin, turpentine, and masts and spars. After 1705, the British government subsidized the production of all these commodities.

Georgia, founded in 1733, the last British colony to be established in America, developed slowly until the 1760s. In 1732 James Oglethorpe, a Tory member of Parliament, had received a charter to plant the colony. He conceived of it as a refuge for paupers and debtors, and as a laboratory for experiments in social and religious reform. But for the first twenty years of its existence the colony served mainly as a buffer between South Carolina and the hostile Indians to the immediate south along with the Spanish colony in Florida. Thereafter, Georgia began to develop on a more permanent basis, largely through the establishment of slavery and a rice plantation system much like that of South Carolina.

Indians in the Southern Colonies   In the southern colonies occurred tribal resentment at the proliferation of English settlements similar to the fury of the New England Indians. Bacon's Rebellion in Virginia in 1676 aimed at nothing less than the destruction or expulsion of the Virginia tribes. Although Governor

William Byrd. (*Courtesy, Library of Congress*)

The Virginia planter William Byrd looked down upon the backcountry denizens of North Carolina and Virginia, condemning them for their idleness:

"Indian corn is of so great increase, that a little pains will subsist a very large family with bread, and then they may have meat without any pains at all, by the help of the low grounds and the great variety of mast that grows upon the high-land. The men for their parts, just like the Indians, impose all the work upon the poor women. They make their wives rise out of their beds early in the morning, at the same time that they lie and snore, till the sun has run one third of his course, and dispersed all the unwholesome damps. Then, after stretching and yawning for half an hour, they light their pipes, and, under the protection of a cloud of smoke, venture out into the open air; though if it happens to be ever so little cold, they quickly return shivering into the chimney corner. When the weather is mild, they stand leaning with both their arms upon the cornfield fence, and gravely consider whether they had best go and take a small heat at the hoe: but generally find reasons to put it off till another time."

William Berkeley eventually crushed this rebellion, the assault on the Indians continued in the 1670s and 1680s. By 1690, only 1,000 of an original 30,000 Indians were still in Virginia. The others either were dead or had moved, voluntarily and involuntarily, into the western forests.

There were no powerful Indian confederacies in Maryland, and the tribes living along the southern seaboard had been defeated and driven away in the seventeenth century. But it was not that easy in the Carolinas. In 1711 the Tuscaroras in North Carolina finally rebelled after years of exploitation at the hands of fraudulent traders and slave-raiding parties, as well as the inexorable expansion of English settlement. After two years of hard fighting, a colonial militia finally crushed Tuscarora resistance, killing hundreds of Indians and enslaving hundreds more. The survivors moved north and eventually settled in Pennsylvania or joined the tribes of the Iroquois Confederacy in New York.

The Yamasee of South Carolina rebelled in 1715. Once friendly allies with the English, the Yamasee were outraged when English traders cheated them and seized and sexually exploited their wives and daughters, while English settlers presumptuously took control of tribal land. In their uprising, the Yamasee gained the support of several other tribes, including the Creeks and Catawbas, and inflicted heavy casualties on the colonists, at one point threatening the very future of South Carolina. With the assistance of the Cherokees, the colonial militia finally ended the rebellion by a nearly genocidal assault on the Yamasee. Relations with the Creeks later improved after the founding of Georgia in 1733. The relationship of James Oglethorpe, the proprietor, with a mixed-blood woman named Mary, a close relative of a Creek chief, helped alleviate tensions between the Creeks and the English.

An Indian is taken into slavery by South Carolinians in the late seventeenth century. *(Courtesy, The Illustrated London News)*

Slavery

Through most of the seventeenth century slavery was not of major importance on the American mainland. There was a perpetual shortage of labor in most of the colonies, but as long as the farm unit remained small and was worked by the owner alongside his family and such indentured servants as he could afford, servants who spoke English were preferred to others. At first even large planters shunned slaves as expensive and subject to a high mortality in a new land.

For a time, then, the black population in the English colonies grew only slowly. The first blacks in the English colonies had arrived in Virginia in the early 1600s. But in that colony at midcentury, out of a population of 15,000 there were only about 300 blacks in Virginia and not all of these were slaves. In Virginia's early years some of them lived as free men and women, and some acquired land of their own. As late as 1671 there were still no more than 2,000 in Virginia within a population of 40,000 and fewer than 7,000 slaves in all the mainland colonies combined.

But then in the 1680s and the following decades a series of developments combined to establish slavery firmly, though still on a modest scale, in the tobacco-growing colonies of Virginia and Maryland, and at the same time to establish a prosperous gentry as the governing class. A change in the laws of both colonies finally made it legal and even easy to buy land in large tracts. Despite rapid increase in production, tobacco prices remained fairly high from 1684 to 1703. In these circumstances small farm units began to give way to sizable plantations, where workers could be employed efficiently in gangs. At just this time, the Royal Africa Company and other groups of English merchants were beginning to dominate the African slave trade and were looking for markets. Competition among slave traders of several nations, moreover, temporarily reduced the profits of supplying blacks for West Indian sugar plantations, so the English were willing to sell slaves in Virginia and Maryland at bargain prices. After moving up and down the coast of West Africa acquiring slaves, the English slave ships turned west and headed for America. The trip across the Atlantic was the dreaded "Middle Passage." Hundreds of slaves were crowded into the dark, damp holds of a slave ship for months at a time, with subsistence diets, little or no exercise, and no sanitary facilities. The mortality rate from flu, dysentery, pleurisy, pneumonia, and smallpox was devastating. Thousands of Africans died from what the shipowners called "fixed melancholy," a severe mental depression. As many as ten to fifteen million slaves were transported from Africa to all the colonies in the Western Hemisphere between 1600 and 1800, and another four to six million died on the way. The vast majority of the survivors ended up working the sugar plantations of Brazil, Cuba, Hispaniola, and Puerto Rico, but during the colonial period approximately 400,000 came to British North America.

The Character of Colonial Slavery

In the beginnings of colonial settlement, Africans and whites had needed to work closely together to survive. West Africa, the homeland of most of the slaves, was a settled area in which agriculture, mining, and handicrafts were well established, and slaves from there adapted reasonably well to work on American farms and plantations. Since West Africa resembled the South in climate and flora, Africans made conspicuous contributions to the economy. They helped introduce rice cultivation to South Carolina, and Guinea corn was mixed with native Indian varieties. Experienced in animal husbandry, Africans were put in charge of the livestock. The use of gourds for drinking, grass and reeds for baskets and mats, and palmetto leaves for fans, brooms, and chairs all came from Africa. Familiar with swamps and marshes, Africans dominated fishing and passed on to Europeans their knowledge

Percentage of African Americans in the Total Population of the British Colonies, 1660–1780					
Year	New England	Middle Colonies	Upper South	Lower South	West Indies
1660	1.7	11.5	3.6	2.6	42.0
1700	1.8	6.8	13.1	17.6	77.7
1740	2.9	7.5	28.3	46.5	88.0
1780	2.0	5.9	38.6	41.2	91.1

LIST OF THE SLAVES who died on board the ship *St. John* from 30th June to 29th October in the year 1659.

1659		Men	Women	Children
June	30	3	2	
July	1	2	1	
	3		1	
	5		2	1
	6		1	
	7	1		
	8	2	1	
	9	2		
	10		2	
	12		1	
	13	2		1
	14	1		
	16	3	2	
	17	2		
	18	3	1	
	19	1	3	
	20	1		
	21	1	1	
	23		2	
	24	1	1	
	25	2	1	
	26	1		
	28	3		
	29		2	
Aug.	2	2		
	3	1		
	6	1		
	8	2		1
	9		1	
	11		1	
	16	1 man leaped overboard		
	18	1		
	20		1	
	22		1	
	23		1	
	24	1		
	29	1		
	31	1	1	
Sept.	3		1	
	6	2		
	7	1		
	8	1	1	
	13	1	1	
	14	2	2	1
	16	1		
	19	1		
	23		2	
	24	1	3	
	26		1	
Oct.	1	2		
	3	1	1	
	4		1	
	10	1	2	
	12	1		
	13		1	
	19		1	
	23	1		
	29	1		
		59	47	4

As this eighteenth-century advertisement suggests, tobacco-smoking was popular in Europe. Tobacco profits, based on the labor of slaves, were popular in Virginia.

Among slaves, resistance mixed with acquiescence. An English visitor in 1746 observed that

"a new Negro, if he must be broke, either from obstinacy, or, which I am more apt to suppose, from greatness of soul, will require more hard discipline than a young spaniel. You would really be surprised at their perseverance; let an hundred men show him how to hoe, or drive a wheelbarrow; he'll still take the one by the bottom, and the other by the wheel, and they often die before they can be conquered."

of temporarily poisoning rivers and streams with quicklime to catch fish. Europeans feared alligators, but Africans knew that, like the crocodiles back home, they could be used to protect livestock. Africans also introduced to the colonies the use of certain herbs and natural medicines, dominated the fur trade as Indians disappeared, and served in the colonial militias well into the 1700s.

Slavery acquired in time a sharper legal definition. A Virginia law of 1662 declaring that "all children born in this country shall be held bond or free only according to the condition of the mother" ensured that children of slave women would be slaves as well. Other legislation restricted slaves from "walking abroad on nights meeting together" without their master's permission. By the early eighteenth century slavery was fully defined as a legal institution in the colonies. Virginia and Maryland were importing thousands of African slaves and laying the foundation for the plantation system of southern agriculture. In 1710 there were well over 30,000 slaves in Maryland and Virginia in a total population of about 120,000. By 1740 the numbers had grown to 84,000 blacks in a population of 296,000. New England, by contrast, had only 8,500 blacks in a population of nearly 290,000. Slavery spread throughout the colonies, but never in the concentration it achieved in the plantation economies of the South.

On a tobacco plantation the atmosphere was generally healthy and the labor to be done, though fussy and tedious, was not backbreaking. It became possible and profitable for a plantation owner to encourage both breeding and some semblance of family life among his slaves. Around the 1720s the slave population in the Chesapeake colonies began to reproduce itself, kinship networks formed, and a slave community developed. Slaves on small plantations might visit friends or relatives on larger ones; husbands and wives (slave marriages were not recognized by law) if owned by different masters might spend Sundays together.

Opinions of Slavery   The English who settled in North America did not go there with the intention of enslaving other human beings for life. After all, chattel slavery did not exist in England. But in English America by the end of the seventeenth century it was a well established institution. From Puritan clergymen in New England to rice planters in Georgia, slave holders could be found in every colony. New Englanders, who did not need a large labor force, nonetheless held slaves and perceived slavery as one of the conditions appropriate to the human race. South of New England, farmers and planters who desperately needed labor turned to slavery when supplies of white servants dwindled.

Few colonists protested the use of slaves. Quakers in Pennsylvania denounced slavery, but many Quakers themselves acquired slaves. A Puritan pamphlet attacking slavery, Samuel Sewall's *The Selling of Joseph*, was published in Boston in 1701, but the Reverend Cotton Mather informed a group of Boston slaves that slavery was "what God will have to be the thing appointed for you."

In the Northeast, where by the middle of the eighteenth century a small but substantial portion of the populations of Boston, Philadelphia, New York City, and Newport, Rhode Island were slaves, most worked as craftsmen, laborers, or personal servants rather than as field workers. In New York City in 1712 a slave uprising involving two dozen blacks resulted in the deaths of nine whites. Punishment was swift and cruel: thirteen slaves were hanged, one left to die in chains, three burned at the stake, one burned over a slow fire for ten hours, and one broken on the wheel.

In the colonies as a whole, white indentured servants could look forward to freedom and perhaps to entry into the propertied classes. A large part of the population could vote or otherwise engage in local government. And yet, while so much of British civilization was becoming freer in North America, the new land had begun to cultivate the institution of slavery, unknown in Britain for centuries. Freedom and slavery were growing up together.

John Woolman, a prominent Quaker, wrote in his diary:

"A neighbor received a bad bruise in his body and sent for me to bleed him, which having done, he desired me to write his will. Amongst other things he told me to which of his children he gave his young Negro. I considered the pain and distress he was in, and knew not how it would end, so I wrote his will, save only that part concerning his slave and carrying it to his bedside read it to him. I then told him in a friendly way that I could not write any instrument by which my fellow creatures were made slaves without bringing trouble on my own mind. I let him know that I charged nothing for what I had done, and desired to be excused from doing the other part in the way he proposed. We then had a serious conference on the subject; at length, he agreeing to set her free, I finished his will."

The Great Awakening and the Enlightenment

In the 1730s, a new enthusiasm for religion and moral reform appeared almost simultaneously in continental Europe, Great Britain, and the colonies. The message was essentially the same, whatever its form: that the way to salvation lay not in faithful performance of sacraments and rituals as the Catholics and Anglicans had always maintained, or a life of good works, but simply in opening the heart to God through prayer. A simple and total act of faith in God's goodness and mercy would bring to the faithful an unspeakably profound experience of personal conversion and salvation. And while good works were not the means to

The Rev. Jonathan Edwards awakened many congregants to their plight in sermons such as "Sinners in the Hands of an Angry God" *(Courtesy, Library of Congress)*

The eloquent British revivalist preacher George Whitefield fueled the Great Awakening on his evangelical tours. *(Courtesy, National Portrait Gallery)*

redemption, they would follow, issuing from the cleansed and grateful heart of the convert. As John Winthrop and those who banished Anne Hutchinson had argued in the 1630s, any such doctrine is potentially dangerous to an established social order, for it implicitly vests in individuals the capacity to judge the moral rectitude of their own behavior.

In the colonies the Great Awakening had its beginnings in 1734, when the Reverend Jonathan Edwards, pastor of the church in the small frontier town of Northampton, Massachusetts, a community of about 200 families, noted a "religious concern on people's minds." As the winter of 1734 progressed, Edwards noticed that "There was scarcely a single person in the town, either old or young, that was left unconcerned about the great things of the eternal world. Those that were wont to be the vainest, and loosest, and those that had been most disposed to think and speak slightly of vital and experimental religion, were now generally subject to great awakenings." Edward's account of the Northampton revival, *A Faithful Narrative of the Surprising Work of God,* published in 1737, may have prepared the way for the preaching of George Whitefield, the eloquent young English clergyman who arrived in America in 1739.

George Whitefield

Various French, German, and Dutch ministers were associated with revivalism, and John and Charles Wesley were the most important figures involved in England. The most influential of all in British America was George Whitefield.

After receiving some training at Oxford, Whitefield had persuaded his bishop of the Church of England to ordain him before he was of the customary age. In his maiden sermon, this restless, charismatic preacher raved and exhorted, sang and shouted, wept and thundered. Whitefield made his first evangelical tour to America in 1739 at age twenty-five, preaching under the open air and converting hundreds in Georgia. He returned two years later to conduct a great revival in New England. The New England and mid-Atlantic tour was the greatest triumph of Whitefield's career, though he made several successful trips to America during the next thirty years. In 1740 the populace was ready for him, if only out of restlessness, boredom, or economic troubles.

Enthusiastic Religion

The impact of the Great Awakening was not quite what the ministry that welcomed Whitefield had expected. The number of active participants in church affairs doubled, trebled, and quadrupled, and for the first time in years religion attracted the enthusiasm of the young. But much of New England became divided into fiercely hostile camps of "Old Lights," or defenders of the existing order, and "New Lights," who embraced the new piety.

The Great Awakening had its philosophical connections with more sober forms of Protestantism that had preceded it. Puritans, like other Protestants, had taken the conversion experience very seriously. Even after the Half-Way Covenant of 1662, which accepted as restricted church members the unconverted children of full members, a conversion experience was a requirement for full admission. But the Puritan congregations had not demanded the violent outpourings of emotion that revivalism usually identifies with religious experience. The New Lights sought to convert through their sermons, thereby taking what had been an intensely private experience and making it public. People cried out—presumably under the conviction of sin. They wept, they groaned, they fell to their knees. Some lost consciousness. And, most critically, the excitement was contagious. Whole gatherings experienced the drama of conversion together. The Great Awakening was the earliest instance of a recurrent phenomenon in American Protestantism. Like the Great Awakening, moreover, American religion since has emphasized the experiential component of religion. In breaking open churches that had been stable and undivided, the Awakening is suggestive of the tendency within Protestantism to multiply churches and sects. And the Awakening introduced America to a movement that John and Charles Wesley were spreading within the Church of England: a faith that stressed both religious feeling and a consequent morality of self-discipline and hard work. Soon, adherents to that form of piety left the Anglican church and formed their own, the Methodist. In the nineteenth century the Methodist and Baptist churches, well adapted in structure, practice, and belief to spread to the frontier and the backcountry, would become two of the largest denominations both in cities and in the countryside. Throughout Great Britain and the United States, Methodism had a powerful influence on popular morality, spreading habits of sobriety, thrift, and diligence, turning its members to acts of social reformation. Numbers of Methodists in the northern states, for example, were active in the antislavery movement, and later generations worked for prohibition of alcohol. In Britain, Methodists had an important part in the labor movement.

The Enlightenment   The energies of revivalism were directed against reason, or at least the cool, detached reason that opposed bursts of emotion. But there began in Europe around the middle of the eighteenth century a movement, called the Enlightenment, that celebrated reason and viewed the times as an age of social and scientific rationality. The Enlightenment soon reached American shores.

It began to glimmer there in the glass jars of Benjamin Franklin's electrical experiments in Philadelphia. In 1749 Franklin was "chagrined a little that we have hitherto been able to discover nothing in the way of use to mankind," but by 1752, with his now-famous kite experiment, he had proved that lightning and electricity were one and the same. His practical invention of the lightning rod soon followed. On one occasion he nearly electrocuted himself attempting to roast a turkey. By the late 1750s Franklin had acquired an international reputation for his contributions to science.

In its European form the Enlightenment practiced an abstract kind of thinking known as deductive logic, a reasoning that begins with general principles and then applies these to particular cases or details. Philosophers of the Enlightenment, for example, abstractly defined large, general "laws of nature," which could be laws governing the material world or natural laws fixed in human beings. Having deter-

In Philadelphia Whitefield managed to affect even that lover of reason, Benjamin Franklin, who recorded in his Autobiography:

"I happened . . . to attend one of his sermons, in the course of which I perceived he intended to finish with a collection, and I silently resolved he should get nothing from me. I had in my pocket a handful of copper money, three or four silver dollars, and five pistoles in gold. As he proceeded I began to soften, and concluded to give the coppers. Another stroke of his oratory made me ashamed of that, and determined me to give the silver; and he finished so admirably, that I empty'd my pocket wholly into the collector's dish, gold and all."

George Whitefield and John Wesley promised salvation to those who opened their hearts to God through prayer. To them was offered eternal life in the New Jerusalem depicted in this drawing; to others the door to Hell stood open. *(Courtesy, Scribner's Archives)*

GEORGE WHITEFIELD'S PREACHING

Nathan Cole, a farmer and carpenter of Connecticut, sought out the evangelist George Whitefield.

"There came a messenger and said Mr. Whitfield preached at Hartford and Weathersfield yesterday and is to preach at Middeltown this morning at 10 o clock. I was in my field at work [and] I dropt my tool that I had in my hand and run home and run thru my house and bade my wife get ready quick to goo and hear Mr. Whitfield preach at Middeltown. And [I] run to my pasture for my hors with all my might, fearing I should be too late to hear him. I brought my hors home and soon mounted and took my wife up and went forward as fast as I thought my hors could bear, and when my hors began to be out of breath I would get down and put my wife on the Saddel, and bid her ride as fast as she could, and not Stop or Slak for except I bade her. And so I would run until I was almost out of breth, and then mount my hors again, and so I did severel times to favour my hors. . . .

When we came within about half a mile of the road that comes down from Hartford, Weathersfield and Stepney to Middeltown, on high land, I saw before me a Cloud or fog, rising—I first thought—off from the great river. But as I came nearer the road I heard a noise, something like a low rumbling thunder, and I presently found it was the rumbling of horses feet coming down the road and this Cloud was a Cloud of dust made by the running of horses feet. It arose some rods into the air over the tops of the hills and trees. And when I came

mined the laws of nature that applied to human beings, Enlightenment thinkers considered what particular kind of government would best serve or express these laws. The European Enlightenment would make for great advances in science. Its political thought, much of which presumed that the laws of nature make all human beings equal in rights, contributed to the modern political revolutions seeking freedom and legal equality.

Empiricism   Numbers of American writers were much under the influence of the political as well as the scientific Enlightenment in Europe, talked of the general "laws of nature," and argued in the language of the Enlightenment for liberty and equality. But some historians have identified a difference in emphasis between the European Enlightenment and its American counterpart. Americans tended more than European philosophers of the time to follow not deductive reasoning but a kind of thought that is now called empiricism, a reasoning that begins with the observation of particular details rather than with speculation about general principles. American thinkers confined much of their work to looking at plants and animals, to experimenting with gadgets, and to solving practical problems of government.

Empiricism produced early and important scientific studies in America. In 1715 eleven-year-old Jonathan Edwards studied a spider's habits and recorded his observations in an essay, "Of Insects." But he forsook science for theology. Late in the seventeenth and early in the eighteenth century the New Englanders Thomas Brattle and Thomas Robie made a number of astronomical observations that proved useful to Newton and other Europeans, and the Royal Society in London published papers by John Banister, Cotton Mather, and Paul Dudley on American flora and fauna. Eliza Lucas Pinckney's observations pioneered the cultivation of indigo, which became widespread as a cash crop. Mathematical observations of note came from John Winthrop IV, Ezra Stiles, and David Rittenhouse. Possibly as important as these scientific within about twenty rods of the road, I could see men and horses Slipping along in the Cloud like shadows. And when I came nearer it was like a stedy streem of horses and their riders, scarcely a horse more than his length behind another, all of a lather and fome with swet, ther breth rooling out of their noistrels. . . . Every hors semed to go with all his might to carry his rider to hear the news from heaven for the saving of their Souls. It made me trembel to see the Sight.

We went down in the Streeme. I herd no man speak a word all the way, three mile, but evry one presing forward in great haste. And when we gat down to the old meating house, thare was a great multitude. It was said to be 3 or 4000 of people assembled together.

We gat off from our horses and shook off the dust, and the ministers was then coming to the meating house. I turned and looked toward the great river and saw the fery boats running swift forward and backward, bringing over loads of people. The ores rowed nimble and quick. Everything—men, horses and boats—all seamed to be struglin for life. The land and the banks over the river looked black with people and horses all along the 12 miles. I see no man at work in his field, but all seamed to be gone.

When I see Mr. Whitfield come upon the Scaffold, he looked almost angellical—a young, slim, slender youth before some thousands of people, and with a bold, undaunted countenance. And my hearing how God was with him everywhere as he came along, it solomnized my mind, and put me in a trembling fear before he began to preach, for he looked as if he was Cloathed with authority from the great God."

discoveries were the media through which scientific knowledge was introduced and spread.

Higher Education   The most advanced were the colleges, along with philosophical and scientific societies, notably the American Philosophical Society, established in Philadelphia in 1743. Most colleges started during the colonial period were founded by religious groups. Harvard (1636) and Yale (1701) were what is now termed Congregationalist, the word that has come to designate New England churches of Puritan ancestry that placed church government in the hands of the congregation. William and Mary (1691) and King's College (1754, later renamed Columbia) were founded by Anglicans. Rhode Island College (1764, later Brown) was Baptist, Queen's College (1766, later Rutgers) was Dutch Reformed, and the College of New Jersey (1746, later Princeton) was Presbyterian. The only nonsectarian college founded in the colonial period was Franklin's Academy, established in 1754, which became the University of Pennsylvania in

Captains from Surinam, by John Greenwood. (*Courtesy, Art Museum of St. Louis*)

AN EARLY HARVARD RIOT

College students have long complained about the quality of food in university dining rooms. If this very first American instance in 1639 of an incipient food riot is typical, they have good reason for their complaint. Mistress Eaton, the cook and author of this letter, was wife of Harvard's first headmaster, Nathaniel Eaton. Both lost their jobs when students protested the severe discipline that Mr. Eaton dispensed and the atrocious food that his wife served.

"For their breakfast, that it was not so well ordered, the flour not so fine as it might, nor so well boiled or stirred, at all times that it was so, it was my sin of neglect, and want of that care that ought to have been in one that the Lord had intrusted with such a work. Concerning their beef, that was allowed them, as they affirm, which, I confess, had been my duty to have seen they had it, and continued to have had it, because it was my husband's command; but truly I must confess, to my shame. I cannot remember that ever they had it, nor that ever it was taken from them. And that they had not so good or so much provision in my husband's absence as presence, I conceive it was because he would call sometimes for butter or cheese, when I conceived there was no need of it; yet, forasmuch as the scholars did otherways apprehend, I desire to see the evil that was in the carriage of that as well as in the other, and to take shame to myself for it. And that they sent down for more, when they had not enough, and the maid should answer, if they had not, they should not, I must confess, that I have denied them cheese, when they sent for it, and it have been in the house; for which I shall humbly beg pardon of them, and own the shame, and confess my sin. And for such provoking words, which my servants have given, I cannot own them, but am sorry any such should be given in my house. And for bad fish, that they had it brought to table,

---

1791. Dartmouth became a college in 1769 after having been established much earlier as an Indian missionary school. King's College and Franklin's Academy introduced practical courses in agriculture, navigation, and astronomy.

Higher education was available to a much wider spectrum of classes in the colonies than in England, though the prestigious institutions of higher learning were reserved for males. During the eighteenth century, a few private academies for women were founded, but systematic attempts to provide even for the education of upper-class girls would not emerge until after the Revolution. The colonies did produce some well-educated and even learned women, but it was typical among them to have benefited from private instruction from tutors who had been hired for their brothers or cousins. Female literacy lagged far behind the rate among men.

The Press and the Zenger Case On the popular level, scientific and other information was spread mainly through newspapers. Laws in Massachusetts and Connecticut required every town to provide a school at which children could learn reading and writing. Elementary schools, established most zealously by Congregationalists and Presbyterians, gave America a much higher literacy rate than Europe possessed: ninety percent or more could sign their names in New England, fifty to sixty percent in Virginia.

In 1725 the British mainland colonies had only five newspapers. Then along with the rapid expansion of commerce and land settlement came a proliferation of papers: by 1765 there were twenty-five. Four-page weeklies were filled with advertisements, notices of arrivals and departures of ships, and reprints of news that had appeared months earlier in European journals. But as time went by the colonial news-

I am sorry there was that cause of offence given them. I acknowledge my sin in it. And for their mackerel, brought to them with their guts in them, and goat's dung in their hasty pudding, it's utterly unknown to me; but I am much ashamed it should be in the family, and not prevented by myself or servants, and I humbly acknowledge my negligence in it. And that they made their beds at any time, were my straits never so great, I am sorry they were ever put to it. For the Moor his lying in Sam. Hough's sheet and pillowbier, it hath a truth in it: he did so one time, and it gave Sam. Hough just cause of offence; and that it was not prevented by my care and watchfulness, I desire [to] take the shame and sorrow for it. And that they eat the Moor's crusts, and the swine and they had share and share alike, and the Moor to have beer, and they denied it, and if they had not enough, for my maid to answer, they should not, I am an utter stranger to these things, and know not the least footsteps for them so to charge me; and if my servants were guilty of such miscarriages, had the boarders complained of it unto myself, I should have thought it my sin, if I had not sharply reproved my servants, and endeavored reform. And for bread made of heated, sour meal, although I know of but once that if was so, since I kept house, yet John Wilson affirms it was twice: and I am truly sorry, that any of it was spent amongst them. For beer and bread, that it was denied them by me betwixt meals, truly I do not remember, that ever I did deny it unto them; John Wilson will affirm, that, generally, the bread and beer was free for the boarders to go unto. And that money was demanded of them for washing the linen, it's true it was propounded to them, but never imposed upon them. And for their pudding being given the last day of the week without butter or suet, and that I said, it was miln of Manchester in Old England, it's true that I did say so, and am sorry, they had any cause of offence given them by having it so. And for their wanting beer, betwixt brewings, a week or half a week together, I am sorry that it was so at any time, and should tremble to have it so, were it in my hands to do again."

papers printed more and more articles, written by their readers, in which the nature of man, society, and government was endlessly explored. So it was largely through the newspapers that Americans formed their opinions of themselves and their world. Following the English lead, the colonies also began to produce a few journals such as the *Lady's Magazine* and the *Gentleman's and Lady's Town and Country Magazine* that catered to the female members of polite society.

Colonial America provided an important incident in the development of freedom of the press. In 1735 John Peter Zenger faced a charge of libel for publishing in his newspaper an attack by the former chief justice of New York on actions of the governor of the colony. The counsel for Zenger argued that since the statements printed in the paper were true they were not libelous. The jury agreed, and returned a verdict of not guilty. The effect of the verdict was to establish the principle that only false statements are libelous, and thereby to free newspapers to widen the range of their commentary and criticism.

The lawyer Andrew Hamilton argued the case for John Peter Zenger:

"Power may justly be compared to a great river which, while kept within its due bounds is both beautiful and useful; but when it overflows its banks, it is then too impetuous to be stemmed, it bears down all before it and brings destruction and desolation wherever it comes. If this then is the nature of power, let us at least do our duty, and like wise men use our utmost care to support liberty. . . . The question before the court and you gentlemen of the jury is . . . the cause of liberty . . . by . . . writing Truth."

The American Character

An English visitor in Connecticut in 1750 remarked of Americans that "their government, religion, and manners all tend to support an equality. Whoever brings in your victuals sits down and chats with you." Europeans were inclined to view Americans as bumpkins lacking the social graces. The commercial and urban sectors and the more well-to-do planters were in fact quite sophisticated in their awareness of events on both sides of the Atlantic. They had to be. Their prosperity depended on knowledge of European markets; their political well-being on the doings of factions within the British Parliament. And having a higher literacy rate than perhaps any nation of Europe, Americans read newspapers and exchanged letters avidly.

British America was diverse not only in ethnic and religious background but in regions and societies changing over time, from the plantations of the Virginia tidewater section a century and a half old to the newly-plowed red fields of Georgia, from the urban bustle of Boston and Philadelphia to the remote villages and farms on the frontier. Multiple forms of social stratification existed. Each community—the town in New England, the manor in New York, the county or parish elsewhere—had its own hierarchy, which sometimes did and sometimes did not correspond to the gradations of power and status in the colony as a whole.

POST SCRIPT
1771-99

June 30, 1771: . . . went this afternoon into the Bath, I found the shock much greater than I expected. . . .

July 1, 1799: . . . Nancy came here this evening, she and self went into the Shower bath. I bore it better than I expected, not having been wett all over at once, for 28 years past.

A Woman's Place

According to the Puritan leader John Winthrop, a woman's husband "is her lord, and she is subjected to him, yet in a way of liberty, not of bondage: and a true wife accounts her subjection her honor and freedom." A Puritan clergyman likened the family to "a little commonwealth" with the father as its undisputed head. Women when they married normally lost whatever property rights they might have had. As the eighteenth-century British jurist William Blackstone put it: "Husband and wife are one and that one is the husband." Husbands were expected to govern their wives with gentleness and love whenever possible, but an unruly wife required stronger measures.

The laws of Massachusetts differed from those of England in restricting the husband's right to correction. Wife-beating with a stick that was larger than one inch in diameter was prohibited. But even the gentler laws of the new world did not interfere with "corrections" or "chastisements" administered with switches of the proper size. And the Puritan emphasis on the responsibility of the individual to God did not encourage women's equality in religious institutions. Puritan fathers were especially fond of St. Paul's dictum: "Women, keep silent in the churches." By the end of the seventeenth century, women usually outnumbered men in church congregations, and in the nineteenth century the predominance of women in church attendance would be noticeable in many congregations, but it did not open to women the role of minister or church leader. And women were almost entirely excluded from all forms of politics.

The inferiority of women to men, like women's necessary subordination to men, was the dominant view of gender relations and one of

Puritan women in their Sunday best. Some wore masks to protect themselves from wind and sun.
(Courtesy, Scribner's Archives)

the most widely shared assumptions throughout the colonies. It has nonetheless been argued that women enjoyed a better position in the New World than women in the old, then or earlier. This view rests in part on the assumption that since women remained in short supply throughout the seventeenth century they were especially valued. But there is little evidence to suggest that simply because the authorities tried very hard to encourage women to go to the colonies the reigning idea of women's nature and worth actually changed very much. The incentives offered to women had to do more with improving their social and economic position among other women than with improving the status of women relative to men.

The distinction between male and female remained a fundamental determinant of an individual's social opportunities, but in any given instance wealth, inherited social status, and family membership could outweigh gender. Women of high social stature were desirable as wives for ambitious men seeking to ally themselves to influential families. Family connections could also permit women, either married or single, to take significant political roles in exceptional circumstances. Most women, however, spent their lives firmly under the governance of their fathers, husbands, and male kin to whom they were considered constitutionally and intellectually inferior.

Indentured Servants and Slave Women

Female indentured servants were doubly subordinate. Indentured women were seldom allowed to marry, and in some places the "secret marriage of servants" was forbidden by law. Masters reserved the right to lengthen the period of service if the woman became pregnant. The possibility of marrying better than they might have married in England was the major attraction for single female immigrants. But delaying marriage for the normal minimum of the seven years of indenture often meant that the female servant might marry only after several of her childbearing years had passed and after brutal work in a harsh climate had perhaps undermined her health.

The hardships that weighed on female indentured servants weighed even more heavily on slave women who lacked the minimal rights and promise of eventual freedom that masters accorded to indentured servants. Initially, slave women were as scarce relative to slave men as indentured females were to indentured men. African societies placed a high value on women, or at least on their productive and reproductive abilities, and so African slave-traders often withheld women from the slave trade. Many women who were transported to the New World had been separated from their families. In the early years of slavery in the colonies, the ratio of men to women was too high for the newly enslaved population to reproduce itself. Only in the eighteenth century did a considerable community of slaves begin to take shape in the Chesapeake colonies and South Carolina. By then, some slave women were forming stable unions with slave men and bearing their children. But the legality of slave marriages was never recognized in law. And slave women, even more than indentured women, lacked any resources to oppose sexual exploitation by the master or other white males. Most slave colonies forbade interracial sex, but enough black women bore mulatto chil-

A Virginia colonist advised single women to

"sojourn in a house of good honest repute, for by their good carriage, they may advance themselves in marriage . . . loose persons seldome live long unmarried, if free, yet they match with as desolate as themselves, and never live handsomly or are ever respected."

In 1756 a young serving-girl in Maryland wrote to her father that she was "toiling almost day and night," had "scarce any thing but Indian corn and salt to eat," and had "no shoes nor stockings to wear . . . what rest we can get is to rap ourselves up in a blanket and ly upon the ground."

A poem speaks in the voice of an indentured servant who, after recalling her happier days in England, laments her condition in the New World:

In weeding Corn or feeding Swine,
I spend my melancholy Time,
Kidnap'd and Fool'd, I thither fled,
And to my cost already find,
Worse Plagues than those I left behind.

Jersey Nanny, **by John Greenwood.** *(Courtesy, Museum of Fine Arts, Boston)*

dren—either because they had been raped, or because they had established a relationship with a man who was not black—to make the status of mulatto children a pressing legal question. In most Latin American slaveholding countries many masters acknowledged their mulatto offspring and freed them, so a distinct class of free mulattoes emerged. In English America, such acknowledgments and manumissions were less common: there were many mulatto slaves, and free mulattoes simply joined the class of free blacks.

Women's Legal Rights   The law severely circumscribed the status of most women whether their status be slave, indentured, or free. Only adult single or widowed free women could act in their own name or hold or dispose of property for themselves. These legal barriers to all forms of female independence derived primarily from the English common law, which assigned all minor children to the authority of their fathers and viewed all married women as "femmes coverts"—or, literally, covered women. New World practice apparently modified the severity of this legal doctrine; some widows who remarried signed contracts with their husbands-to-be prior to marriage and thus preserved control of their own property. In Braintree, Massachusetts, John French upon his marriage to Eleanor Veazie in 1683 had to agree "not to meddle with or take into his hand any part of her estate wherein she is invested by her former husband. . . ." Women were also known to act in a legal capacity on their own or their family's behalf. Wills reveal that at least some women did bequeath property to heirs of their own choosing. Law in some colonies such as Massachusetts and Connecticut also permitted women somewhat easier access to divorce than they had in England, and the records reveal that at least some women took advantage of the opportunity. But formal divorce was never common; some colonies prohibited it absolutely except by act of the legislature.

In a predominantly rural society, most women had few opportunities to live comfortably on their own. Men had difficulty managing an agricultural household without a woman; women alone faced even greater obstacles. But by the eighteenth century, some single and widowed women were running small businesses, managing shops, or otherwise supporting themselves and perhaps their children. And whatever the limitations imposed by the law, in practice married free women probably enjoyed considerable feelings of importance to the survival of their households. Their work was as essential to the survival and solvency of those households as was that of their men. White women who survived their childbearing years had on the average about eight children. Some bore more, and many lost one or more in childbirth or infancy. In addition to this vital contribution, most women shouldered a significant portion of the labor necessary to the household. They were responsible for cooking, for the making of many household necessities such as candles and soap, for washing, for sewing, and frequently for making clothes. This labor could include heavy tasks, among them carrying the water for cooking and washing from stream or well to the house. Women also usually assumed responsibility for certain kinds of agricultural labor, such as milking cows, tending gardens, and keeping chickens. When circumstances required, especially at harvest time, they worked in the fields beside men.

The woman of the day who enjoyed the greatest freedom did not work alongside her husband, but could enjoy the more leisured life of the colonial aristocracy. She might acquire something of the more serious education provided for her brothers. By the eighteenth century, she was likely to have silver instead of pewter, an ample supply of linen for beds and tables, silks and laces to wear, looking glasses, cupboards and chests from Europe, books, periodicals, and more. But the comfort of her life depended upon the labor of other women—slaves or servants—who performed the tasks from which wealth had liberated her.

The Young   In a land where labor was scarce, offspring also contributed to the livelihood of the family. Colonial Americans had little if any concept of a time of suspension between childhood and maturity that today goes by the name of adolescence. But if family responsibilities came early, the opportunities of a new land also frequently pulled the young away from home.

Every colony had laws demanding obedience from young offspring; the potential punishment for disobedience in Massachusetts and Connecticut was nothing less than death. In New Haven in 1656, for example, the law stated that "If any child or children above sixteen year[s] old, and of competent understanding, shall curse, or smite, his, her, or their natural father or mother, each such child shall be put to death. . . ." "Stubborn rebellious" sons sixteen or older who refused to obey the "voice and chastisement" of their parents were also subject to the death penalty. Existing records do not reveal that any court ever resorted to such extreme punishment. In fact, by allowing such cases to be tried, these laws guarded against parental abuse at the same time that they sought to curb recalcitrant youth. Colonial law reflected the belief that the community, acting through the courts, had an interest in maintaining order within individual families.

New England also assumed the burden of providing formal education. A Massachusetts statute of 1641 anticipated the nineteenth-century community provision of schooling for all members of society. And as society became more secular, so did education; the inculcation of civic virtue and good citizenship took priority over religious instruction.

Yet most young people learned pedagogical and vocational skills within their families. If a son did not want to learn his father's trade, he might be apprenticed into another family for study under the direction of the master. Whatever young colonials failed to absorb from elders they had to learn on their own. Colonial newspapers and almanacs, such as Ben Franklin's *Poor Richard's Almanac*, served as early home study guides.

Courtship   Though marriages were often arranged by parents or at least had to have parental approval, courtship had its prescribed rituals. The custom of "bundling," a betrothed couple's spending the night in bed together—but fully clothed—was much practiced, especially during the cold New England winters. Particularly in the cities, courting customs changed rapidly, disturbing the older

Alice Mason, **1670. Massachusetts. Artist unknown. Puritans focused on the moral development of their children.** (*National Park Service, Adams National Historic Site, Quincy, Massachusetts*)

Courtship and marriage across racial boundaries were discouraged, and in some colonies illegal. A 1691 Virginia law aimed to prevent

"that abominable mixture and spurious issue which hereafter may increase in this dominion, as well by negroes, mulattoes, and Indians intermarrying with English, or other white women, as by their unlawful accompanying with one another. . . ."

Such couples were to be "banished and removed from their dominion forever."

Compare the lyricism of the English "Greensleeves" ("Alas, my love / You do me wrong / To cast me off / Discourteously. . . .") with the blunter expression of "Springfield Mountain," the first popular folk song known to be native to the colonies in both words and music:

On Springfield Mountain there did
    dwell
A lovelie youth I knowed him well. . . .
He had scarce mowed half round the
    field
When a poison serpent bit at his
    heel. . . .
They took him home to Mollie dear,
Which made him feel so verie queer. . . .
She also had a rotten tooth
And so the poison killed them both.

generation, shocking rural visitors, and even surprising foreign observers. A young man described a party he went to in Quaker Philadelphia: "Seven sleighs with two ladies and two men in each, preceded by fiddlers on horseback" rode to a public house where "we danced, sung, and romped and ate and drank, and kicked away care from morning till night, and finished our frolic in two or three sideboxes at the play." A British traveler in Virginia in 1755 reported that "dancing is the chief diversion here," and another was shocked at the widespread dancing of "jigs." Claiming that the dance was borrowed from the slaves, the proper Englishman found it "without method or regularity: a gentleman and lady stand up, and dance about the room, one of them retiring, the other pursuing, then perhaps meeting, in an irregular fantastical manner." Serenading under the window of a favored lady also came into vogue during the late colonial period. Sometimes the gentlemen first lubricated their throats at a local tavern, yet women reportedly considered the midnight visitation, however predictably inharmonious, a high compliment.

Like folk songs everywhere, those of colonial America revolved around courtship, unrequited love affairs, or doomed lovers. Many American ballads came from Britain. "Greensleeves" was one of the most popular and graceful tunes, and it provided the melody for about eighty different sets of lyrics.

English Colonies at Midcentury

Indians, Africans, and Europeans

The wars of the 1600s and early 1700s had either killed or driven most of the Indians out of the thirteen colonies and into the western frontier. There were still large groups: Cherokee, Creeks, Choctaws, and Chickasaws on the North Carolina and Georgia frontiers, and surviving members of the Iroquois Confederacy in upstate New York and western Pennsylvania. But the rest of the Indians were gone. They were living near the foothills of the Appalachian Mountains or had already crossed the mountains.

In 1750 blacks, both slave and free, made up a fifth of the population of Britain's mainland colonies. In the southern colonies, however, the population consisted of just under two blacks for every five whites. In the northern colonies in 1750, less than one person in twenty was black. Of the entire black population in all of the colonies, only one in twenty was free.

By 1750 America had become an ethnic kaleidoscope of competing racial, religious, and linguistic groups. Although representatives of most groups were scattered throughout the colonies, there were visible ethnic concentrations in particular regions.

English settlers lived everywhere, but they were especially dense along the Atlantic seaboard of all thirteen colonies and throughout New England. Although they shared a heritage of language and national origins, the English settlers were deeply divided along religious lines. Most of the English residents of New England were Congregationalists—of Puritan descent—but in the middle colonies dwelt sizable numbers of Anglicans and Quakers. Anglicans dominated the English settlements of the South, although Maryland still had a contingent of Roman Catholics.

The Scotch-Irish were Presbyterians. Their greatest numbers were in the western reaches of the colonies, from Pennsylvania south to Georgia. Although they spoke English, the Scotch-Irish did not have much else in common with their neighbors on the eastern seaboard. Political life in the colonies with large Scotch-Irish populations was characterized by extreme factional struggles between the English settlers on the East Coast and the Scotch-Irish settlers on the western frontier.

The German settlers in colonial America were largely confined to Pennsylvania and Maryland, where they prized the rich limestone soil. Most Germans were Lutheran or "Dutch" Reformed, but significant numbers of Quakers, Moravians, and other groups stressing personal, inward devotion lived among them. The Germans retained their language and separate identity throughout the colonial period: among some of their descendants in Pennsylvania, a form of the German language survives today. By 1750 approximately 200,000 people of German descent lived in America. The Germans of south central Pennsylvania became known as "Pennsylvania Dutch," "Dutch" referring, as with the Dutch Reformed Church, not to natives of the Netherlands but to the *Deutsch*, as Germans speak of themselves in their own language.

The Dutch of the Netherlands were still located in the New York colony, where their ancestors had settled back in the 1620s or later. Approximately 60,000 people of Dutch descent resided in New York City and on farms bordering the Hudson River between New York City and Albany. Several thousand other Dutch lived on the west side of the Hudson River in New Jersey. Most were Dutch Reformed in religion and earned reputations for hard work, prosperity, and clannishness.

The Colonies and the Empire   By the middle of the eighteenth century the thirteen contiguous British colonies clustered on the North American mainland contained well over a million inhabitants. The Board of Trade, a fifteen-member agency of the Crown, exercised general supervisory power over the entire overseas empire. It selected most royal officials for the colonies and reviewed all legislation passed by the colonial assemblies. Of about 8,500 colonial laws passed in the entire period prior to 1776, all were at least nominally reviewed and 469 were rejected. The Board had established vice-admiralty courts in five mainland colonies, with jurisdiction over the acts of Parliament and the various orders concerning trade, other maritime activity, and the conservation of timber for the Royal Navy. For a time appeals from these courts went to the High Court of Admiralty in London. After 1748, the Admiralty court shared jurisdiction with the Board of Trade. Appeals from colonial courts on all other matters went to the King's Privy Council. All told, something like 1,500 court decisions were appealed prior to 1776. This jerry-built structure, cumbersome enough in theory, was doubly so in practice, for officials were generally slipshod, inefficient, and negligent in executing their duties. That left the royal governors as the principal instruments of the royal will in the colonies, but since the governors normally received their salaries from the local legislatures they were prone to identify themselves less with the Crown than with the richer and more powerful colonials.

The Imperial System and Mercantilism   The system of imperial regulation that the colonies followed or evaded as expediency demanded was not merely an effort to build up the prosperity of the mother country at the expense of the colonies. It aimed at protecting the empire as a whole and encouraging each part to do what it could do best.

The Navigation Acts gave a monopoly of the carrying trade within the empire to ships of England and the colonies, with crews made up mostly of colonists or Englishmen. The acts not only protected the American carrying trade but stimulated the shipbuilding industry in British America. Another measure of the imperial system gave the tobacco colonies a monopoly for their product. The Wool Act of 1699, the Hat Act of 1732, and the Iron Act of 1750 did shield producers in the home country against potential competition from American makers of these goods. But at the moment there was not enough colonial production of wool, hats, or iron to make them competitive with British products. The Molasses Act injured the colonial manufacture of rum, or would have done so if colonists had obeyed it, but its object was to protect other colonists, those of the British West Indies, against foreign competition.

The imperial system, then, was designed to nourish the whole empire and each of its parts. But to colonists aware that the imperial system was the work of a government in which they had no direct voice, every item of the system that seemed to clash with their interests could turn them suspicious of the motives of the mother country. In the meantime, Britain and the colonies alike profited from a vast, enclosed common market.

The informal adhesives of the empire were somewhat stronger than the formal. The colonies and the mother country had common enemies, France and Spain, and that alone was enough to cement the empire. Beyond such tangible considerations were common language, customs, constitutional and legal institutions, and above all pride in a heritage of freedom, of sharing the celebrated "rights of Englishmen."

Political Theory   All British subjects, whether they resided in England or the colonies, shared a pride in the British constitution. This unwritten foundation of Britain's political system was an aggregation of custom, law, and precedent developed over centuries. By the 1700s it had achieved a fine balance among the classic forms of government: monarchy, rule by the one; aristocracy, rule by the few; and democracy, rule by the many. Englishmen believed that each needed to be checked by the other two, or it would degenerate into an evil: monarchy would fall into tyranny, aristocracy into selfish domination by the wealthy and powerful, democracy into mob rule. The British government, according to this concept, contained an element of each of the three forms. The Crown represented rule by the one; the House of Lords represented the titled aristocracy, the privileged few; the House of Commons represented the democracy. In the British system, the theory went, each of the three was properly restrained by the other two.

Theory was one thing, practice another. The House of Commons did represent, directly or indirectly, a considerable range of British public opinion. But it was not democratic. For the most part only the propertied classes, and not all individuals within these, had the privilege of voting for members of the Commons. And the Commons did not balance neatly against the Lords. Interests represented in the House of Commons could be as hostile to one another as to the aristocracy. The monarchy in the later years of the century did wield much power, but it was no longer able to rule by sheer sovereign will and command. Its strength now lay in its ability to influence Parliament through the appointments and other royal favors at its disposal.

Much of what remained of the presence of the Crown in British political thought was a fiction that theorists thought it convenient to abide by. It was believed that for every country, there must be a sovereignty, a single individual source of all legal authority. The British throne, so tradition claimed, constituted this sovereignty within the empire. Whatever legitimate power the Lords, the Commons, or the courts possessed was by grant of authority from the monarch. Those who held to this idea were perfectly aware that in fact Parliament could pretty much do as it pleased, constrained only by the monarch's power to make appointments and to influence parliamentary votes. But champions of the King believed that the idea of a monarchy from which all legitimate authority flows made for loyalty, unity, and obedience to law.

Eighteenth-century observers perceived the politics of their time as a corruption of a system that had once been pure. Beginning in the 1720s, when party politics was developing in the mother country, political essays attacking the King's ministers and claiming evil designs against English liberties were common in London periodicals. Literate and concerned colonists read these, too, and kept a watchful eye on ministerial policies. By the 1760s it would take little to convince Americans that they, too, were endangered by a vast, evil conspiracy of corrupt officials to take away the sacred rights of Englishmen everywhere. The belief that an ideal government should combine three elements—monarchy, aristocracy, and democracy—and that the British system had once possessed the right combination persisted into the early days of the independent United States. It would be a model for the Constitution, the President providing government by the one, the Senate—for which the Constitution did not require popular elections—embodying rule by the few, and the House of Representatives supplying rule by the many.

By 1750 the governments of the royal colonies—all the colonies except Rhode Island and Connecticut—also appeared to reflect the structure of the British government. The governor, appointed by the Crown, had the authority to veto legislation passed by the colonial assembly and to call or dissolve the assembly. The governors' powers in the colonies were not identical to those of the monarch in Britain, but the governors, like the Crown, could be described as providing government by the one. While some governors were upper-class Americans, the Crown commonly appointed someone from Britain. A council, drawn for the most part from among the wealthier or more distinguished colonists and in most royal colonies appointed by the governor, could amend or reject measures passed by the other branch of the colonial legislature, called in most colonies the assembly, and served as the highest court in the colony. The assembly provided government by the many. Throughout British America between fifty and seventy-five percent of adult white males possessed enough property to vote for members of that branch of government.

How Much Democracy? Why were the colonies so much more nearly democratic politically than Great Britain? No passionate commitment to the idea of universal equality had moved proprietors, companies, and colonial leaders to provide for broad distribution of the right to vote, or led Kings and the rest of the British government to accept the arrangement. Voting in much of England was restricted to people owning at least a "forty-shilling freehold" (land that produced a yearly income of forty shillings). But land was scarce in England, and comparatively few people could vote. In America land was abundant, and a modest property requirement comparable to that in England was easily met. Thus the franchise in the colonies was wider by accident, not by design. Not only was voting more widespread in America, but the number of voters was constantly growing as new immigrants became settlers, as new communities formed and elected their own representatives to colonial legislatures. And so much of colonial British America enjoyed a democracy that had little ideology to it, representing instead something of British tradition and much of the reality of colonial life.

Still, the colonies were not democratic by modern standards. People voted, but governors not chosen by the people could veto legislation. Wealthy elites ruled, but ordinary folk were untroubled by that rule, since, being democratic by circumstance rather than by ideology, they had no philosophical reason to be troubled; they were prepared to offer to people of wealth and standing a certain deference.

By no means all white American males could vote. There were laborers and seamen with almost no property, and paupers with none. Women were similarly disfranchised, but there is no record of their having protested their condition. Since in principle married women could own no property without very special legal arrangements, and since officially no women performed military service, they could not claim the two main justifications for a vote. Colonists of both genders widely shared the assumption that public affairs were the business of men. And finally, throughout British America the institution of slavery mocked whatever democracy white Americans practiced.

And so democracy in British America was incomplete and, in considerable part, unintentional.

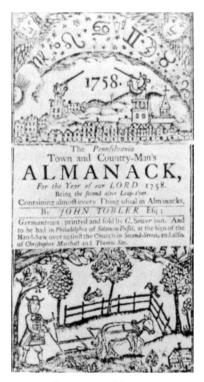

Literate farmers and businessmen craved practical information and made almanacs best-sellers. Nathaniel Low wrote in 1786: "No book we read (except the Bible) is so much valued, and so serviceable to the community. Almanacs serve as clocks and watches for nine-tenths of mankind." *(Courtesy, New York Public Library)*

Suggested Readings

On the development of New England and the Chesapeake colonies, see Michael Zuckerman, *Peaceable Kingdoms: New England Towns in the Eighteenth Century* (1970) and Allan Kulikoff, *Tobacco and Slaves: The Development of Southern Culture in the Chesapeake, 1680–1800* (1986). See also Lois Green Carr, Philip D. Morgan, and Jean B. Russo, *Colonial Chesapeake Society* (1989), Francis Bremer, *The Puritan Experiment* (1976), Stephen Foster, *Their Solitary Way: The Puritan Social Ethic in the First Century of Settlement in New England* (1971), Charles Hambrick-Stowe, *The Practice of Piety: Puritan Devotional Literature in Seventeenth-Century New England* (1982).

As for witchcraft, Bernard Rosenthal's *Salem Story: Reading the Witch Trials of 1692* (1993), sees adolescents and elders collaborating in a scheme of lies and fraud. Paul Boyer and Stephen Nissenbaum find the cause in social and economic tensions in *Salem Possessed: The Social Origins of Witchcraft* (1974), while Carol Karlsen offers a feminist view in *The Devil in the Shape of a Woman: Witchcraft in Colonial New England* (1987). Elaine Breslaw offers a fresh perspective in *Tituba, Reluctant Witch of Salem: Devilish Indians and Puritan Fantasies* (1996). See also John Demos, *Entertaining Satan* (1983).

On slavery see Hugh Thomas, *The Slave Trade* (1997). Standard works on the origins of slavery in the colonies are David Brion Davis, *The Problem of Slavery in Western Culture* (1966) and Winthrop Jordan, *White Over Black: American Attitudes towards the Negro, 1550–1815* (1968). A good overview is Betty Wood, *The Origins of American Slavery: Freedom and Bondage in the English Colonies* (1997). See also Peter Kolchin, *American Slavery 1619–1877* (1993).

Gender roles are the focus of Mary Beth Norton's *Founding Mothers and Fathers: Gendered Power and the Formation of American Society* (1996). Kathleen Brown examines gender issues in the South in *Good Wives, Nasty Wenches, and Anxious Patriarchs: Gender, Race, and Power in Colonial Virginia* (1996). This work should be set beside Julia Cherry Spruill's earlier pathbreaking *Women's Life and Work in the Southern Colonies* (1938). A rich collection of articles set in the southern colonies is Catherine Clinton's and Michelle Gillespie's *The Devil's Lane: Sex and Race in the Early South* (1997). On the northern colonies see Laurel Thatcher Ulrich, *Good Wives: Image and Reality in the Lives of Women in Northern New England, 1650–1750* (1982) and Lyle Koehler, *A Search for Power: "The Weaker Sex" in Seventeeth Century New England* (1980).

On the colonial economy, see Michael Kammen, *Empire and Interest: The American Colonies and the Politics of Mercantilism* (1970), Richard R. Johnson *Adjustment to Empire* (1981), and John J. McCusker and Russel R. Menard, *The Economy of British America 1607–1789* (1985).

The Devil in the Shape of a Woman?

Paul Boyer and Stephen Nissenbaum

More than a hundred years ago, Charles W. Upham, a public figure in Salem whose lifelong avocation was the study of the witch trials, published a map which located with some precision the home of nearly every Salem Village resident at the beginning of 1692. Using Upham's careful map as basis, it is possible to pinpoint the place of residence of every Villager who testified for or against any of the accused witches and also of those accused who themselves lived within the Village bounds. A pattern emerges from this exercise. . . .

There were fourteen accused witches who lived within the bounds of Salem Village. Twelve of these fourteen lived in the eastern section of the Village. There were thirty-two adult Villagers who testified against these accused witches. Only two of these lived in that eastern section. The other thirty lived on the western side. In other words, the alleged witches and those who accused them resided on opposite sides of the Village. . . .

What are we to make of this pattern? To begin an answer, we must take a close look at Salem Village before its moment of notoriety. . . . [T]he town of Salem, Massachusetts, began as a commercial venture. From the first its gaze was directed outward toward Europe, the West Indies, and the sea. . . . With the tide of Puritan immigrants to Massachusetts after 1630, Salem prospered, soon outgrowing the narrow neck of land that was its original site. Responding to these pressures the Town selectmen began to make grants of land several miles in the interior. . . . This was the beginning of what in time would be called Salem Village [as opposed to the more mercantile Salem Town].

At least some of these farmers . . . soon began to chafe beneath the power which Salem Town held over them. . . . Salem Village's uncertain status seems, too, to have contributed to a strikingly high level of internal bickering and disarray. . . . Given the ineffectiveness of the Village's institutional structures, private grievances and disputes escalated with a rapidity which must have startled even those embroiled in them. . . .

The witchcraft episode did not generate the divisions within the Village, nor did it shift them in any fundamental way, but it laid bare the intensity with which they were experienced and heightened the vindictiveness with which they were expressed. . . .

[Afterwards] a genuine effort was made by a chastened community to give voice to all factions in the search [for a replacement for Samuel Parris, a controversial minister]. . . . The long cycle of acrimony was at last winding down. . . . The nineteen bodies that swung on Witches' Hill in the summer of 1692 were part of the price Salem Village paid. . . .

By the end of the seventeenth century the sense that there was a dangerous conflict between private will and public good had become seriously eroded in many quarters by two generations of population growth, geographic dispersal, and economic opportunity. . . . New England towns of the 1700s conceded that they were made up of a diverse mixture of imperfect and self-seeking human beings, and they largely abandoned the effort to be anything more.

Paul Boyer and Stephen Nissenbaum, *Salem Possessed: The Social Origins of Witchcraft* (Cambridge, MA: Harvard University Press, 1974), pp. 35, 36, 37, 39, 44, 45, 69, 75, 105.

The single most salient characteristic of witches was their sex. At least 344 persons were accused of witchcraft in New England between 1620 and 1725. Of the 342 who can be identified by sex, 267 (78 percent) were female. Roughly half of the seventy-five males accused (thirty-six), as the historian John Demos has pointed out, were "suspect by association": they were the husbands, sons, other kin, or public supporters of female witches. . . .

During severe outbreaks, the reaction of the authorities to witchcraft accusations presents a more complicated, if finally consistent, picture. Though proportionately more men found themselves under suspicion during outbreaks than at other times, officials seem to have been even more reluctant than usual to give credence to these suspicions. While they decided to try fifty-eight of the 156 women accused (37 percent), they indicted only eight of the forty-nine men (16 percent). . . .

Statistics can establish the extent to which New Englanders considered witchcraft the special province of women, but they cannot convey the vindictiveness that characterized the treatment of female suspects. This sexual double standard is perhaps most vividly seen in the different punishments meted out to confessed witches outside of the Salem outbreak.

Deeming voluntary confession one of the best "proofes sufficient for Conviccon," ministers and magistrates put considerable pressure on women to admit they had covenanted with the Devil. No comparable coercion was used with men.

Men who confessed to witchcraft outside of the Salem outbreak were punished, to be sure—but whereas most confessing women were taken at their word and executed, confessing men were almost all rebuked as liars. . . .

Some women who questioned the authority of their husbands were also considered witches. Colonial culture strongly discouraged the use of witchcraft accusations as a way of severing marital bonds. Nevertheless, a wife's insubordination to her husband is implicit in many of the sins that New Englanders saw as witchcraft, from adultery to the murder of one's own spouse and children to the pursuit of independent economic activities.

Witchcraft in colonial New England meant more than women's refusal to subordinate themselves to men with institutional authority over them: it suggested their refusal to subordinate themselves to all persons whom God had placed above them in the social hierarchy. In some cases, women came under suspicion for acting as if they were above other women whom society had defined as their betters. Most often, though, suspicion originated in women's interactions with men, whom society implicitly held to be superior to all women. While Puritans surely would have denied the principle that *all* women were subject to *all* men, the record shows the lack of deference for male neighbors to be a common thread running through the many sins of witches. It was not just pride that most fundamentally distinguished witches from other people; it was female pride in particular. . . .

By treating female [religious] dissent as evidence of witchcraft as well as heresy, the authorities may have effectively silenced Puritan women's opposition. Indeed, by 1660 the debate over women's participation in the church had all but ended—and women had lost many of the gains of the early years. After 1660 Puritan ministers increasingly found reasons to celebrate rather than vilify their most active female congregants, but women's religious activity had taken on a decidedly submissive character. Women continued to join the church in proportionately larger numbers than men for the rest of the century, but if the ministers can be believed, female congregants now listened more than they spoke.

Carol P. Karlsen, *The Devil in the Shape of a Women: Witchcraft in Colonial New England* (New York: W. W. Norton & Company, 1987). Reprinted with permission.

The Death of Wolfe, by Benjamin West. Though General James Wolfe was killed in action at Quebec, the British victory there marked a turning point in the French and Indian War. *(Courtesy, National Gallery of Canada)*

An Independent Spirit
1763–1776

continued

THE PLAINS OF ABRAHAM

At 2:00 a.m. on September 13, 1759, Major General James Wolfe ordered two lanterns raised to the maintop shrouds of his British flagship, the *Sutherland,* anchored on the St. Lawrence River. It was the signal to attack the French fortress of Quebec. The city lay on the heights 175 feet above the dark river. Its high rock cliff made it the most formidable natural fortress in North America.

The attack had been long delayed. Wolfe and his army of redcoats, Scottish highlanders, and American rangers had arrived before the French stronghold the previous June, fighting a score of skirmishes with the French-Canadian militia, their Indian allies, and the crack French regulars of the Guyenne, Royal Roussillon, Bearn, La Reine, and La Sarre regiments. By now the brief Canadian summer was nearly spent, and the bitter northern winter would soon descend. The British naval commander, faced with the prospect of being trapped by ice, was threatening to sail home with his fleet.

Wolfe and his men were quite confident. They were fewer than the French, but what they lacked in numbers they made up in morale and experience. Also, they had been laying siege to the city for weeks. Yet in the boat taking him to the French side Wolfe himself, as though with some premonition of what was about to happen to him, recited Gray's "Elegy in a Country Churchyard." It contained the line "The paths of glory lead but to the grave."

As the small boats carrying the British troops edged along the

1689–97
War of the League of Augsburg

1702–13
War of the Spanish Succession
(Queen Anne's War)

1740–48
War of the Austrian Succession
(King George's War)

1756
French and Indian War begins

1760
Montreal surrenders to Britain

1763
France and Britain sign the Treaty of Paris • American settlers begin moving west of the Appalachians • Chief Pontiac attacks British at Detroit • Proclamation of 1763

1764
Revenue Act • Currency Act • Sugar Act

1765
Quartering Act • Stamp Act • Stamp Act Congress

continued

HISTORICAL EVENTS

1766
Stamp Act repealed
• Declaratory Act

1767
Townshend Duties

1768
John Dickinson's "Letters of
a Pennsylvania Farmer
to the Inhabitants of the British
Colonies" • Britain sends
troops to Boston

1770
Boston Massacre
• Samuel Adams proposes
Committees of Correspondence

1772
Burning of the *Gaspée*

1773
Tea Act of 1773 • Boston Tea Party

1774
Coercive or Intolerable Acts
• Quebec Act • First Continental
Congress

1775
Battle of Lexington and
Concord • Second Continental
Congress • Fort Ticonderoga
captured from British • Washington
appointed commander of the
Continental army • Battle of
"Bunker Hill" • Continental Congress
adopts Olive Branch Petition and
"Declaration of the Causes and
Necessities of Taking Up Arms"
• Montgomery captures Montreal

1776
Common Sense • Declaration of
Independence

darkened north bank of the St. Lawrence, a French sentry shouted: "what regiment?" "The Queen's," responded a highland officer in fluent French. The boats were allowed to pass. Soon after, they touched the bank close to where Wolfe some days before had spied a zigzag path up the steep cliff that separated the river from the plain stretching before Quebec city. Twenty-four volunteers leaped out and, grabbing trees and bushes, pulled themselves up the plateau. Hundreds more followed.

The invaders spied a small French encampment. They immediately attacked, captured two of the French soldiers, and put the rest to flight. Hearing the triumphant shouts of his men above, Wolfe and his remaining force disembarked and scaled the cliff by way of the path to join the advance party. As morning broke with clouds and threatening rain, 4,000 British troops drew themselves up in battle order on the Plains of Abraham a mile west of Quebec, the center of French power in America, where General Louis Montcalm commanded 14,000 troops.

In the walled city itself, news of Wolfe's surprise move provoked great alarm. For many weeks the *Quebeçois* had endured bombardment from the British fleet and army. Much of the city was in ruins, and it was packed with refugees from the countryside who jammed into every remaining dwelling and spilled over into the town's hospitals, convents, and public buildings. As news spread of the British success in scaling the heights, the French and Canadians poured out of the town to assemble on the plain outside the walls. Montcalm asked the city commander to send him big guns from the palace battery, but was given only three on the plea that the rest were needed to defend the town itself. Montcalm might have waited for more troops, but the local commander held back. As his men formed ranks, Montcalm rode back and forth along his lines brandishing his sword and urging his troops to show their mettle for France and for the King.

At 10:00 a.m. the French, with the white-clad regulars in the center and the Canadians at either end, started forward against the double-ranked British, firing and shouting. The redcoats and highlanders advanced a few yards and then stopped. When the two lines were within forty paces the British commander ordered his men to fire. Two precise volleys rang out like single shots, and then a ragged clatter as the men reloaded and fired at will. When the smoke lifted, it was clear that the battle was over. As far as the eye could see, the field was strewn with French dead and wounded, 1,400 in all. The French troops still on their feet had stopped short and were milling around in a confused mob. The British officers now gave the order to charge. The cheering redcoats ran forward with their bayonets poised. The highlanders dashed ahead yelling in Gaelic and brandishing their broadswords. Leading one force was Wolfe himself. At that moment of

French troops being reviewed in Quebec, an almost impregnable fortress commanded by Louis Joseph Montcalm. *(Courtesy, William H. Coverdale Collection, and the Canada Steamship Lines Limited, Montreal, Canada)*

triumph the British general was struck in the chest by a French bullet and taken to the rear. A few minutes later he died.

By now the French were fleeing pell-mell to the safety of Quebec's walls. Borne along with the human tide was Montcalm, still mounted. Close to the walls a British shot hit him in the thigh and passed along it to lodge in his stomach. The French commander was escorted through the city gate by three soldiers and brought to the military surgeon. But nothing could be done, and he died the next day. Montcalm's successor surrendered the city. The great war between France and Britain went on officially for three and a half more years before the negotiators at Paris signed a peace treaty in 1763. In reality, it had ended on the cloudy battlefield at Quebec, where both brave commanders surrendered their lives.

News of Wolfe's victory deeply affected the North American public. The young hero had given his life to save Protestant America from Catholic France and his sacrifice took on epic proportions.

The French and Indian War

A World War for Empire   Though they had claimed and occupied much of North America for more than a hundred years, the French had by no means settled it. In the mid-eighteenth century there were only about 55,000 French settlers in North America, the overwhelming majority in the far northeast and along the St. Lawrence River and the remainder distributed in widely scattered trading posts on the Great Lakes and the Ohio and Mississippi rivers. Quebec and Montreal were the only towns of consequence on

As time went on it became apparent that the Iroquois tribes were more friendly to the French settlers of North America than they were to the English. In the eighteenth century Governor James DeLancey of New York stood before Iroquois chieftains and read a proclamation pledging to "brighten the Chain of Friendship . . . Inviolate and Free from Rust." As each part of the speech was translated, the Indians were presented with a decorative belt, to which they gave a ceremonial "*yo-heigh-eigh*" in unison. Normally the tribes voice their agreements individually, *yo-heigh-eighs* coming one after another. By mixing them together, noted a member of the audience the Iroquois delegates "had a mind to disguise that all the nations did not give their hearty assent to the Covenant."

J. Hector St. John de Crèvecouer, a Frenchman who came to the colonies in 1759 and lived there until 1780, wrote Letters from an American Farmer. *Here he describes society in British North America.*

"Here are no aristocratical families, no courts, no kings, no bishops, no ecclesiastical dominion, no invisible power giving to a few a very visible one; no great manufacturers employing thousands, no great refinements of luxury. The rich and the poor are not so far removed from each other as they are in Europe. Some few towns excepted, we are all tillers of the earth, from Nova Scotia to West Florida. We are a people of cultivators, scattered over an immense territory, communicating with each other by means of good roads and navigable rivers, united by the silken bands of mild government, all respecting the laws, without dreading their power, because they are equitable. . . ."

the St. Lawrence, and New Orleans the only important town on the Mississippi. The vast area of New France, comprising most of present-day Canada, the Ohio Valley, the Mississippi, and lands to its west, constituted nonetheless a serious threat to the English colonies. France established a brisk fur trade with Algonquian-speaking Indian tribes and supplied guns to their Indian allies. As French traders moved along the St. Lawrence and into the Great Lakes region, they established Indian alliances that would later aid them in fighting the English.

Since the last years of the seventeenth century Britain and France had been rivals in Europe and wherever their empires clashed. The War of the League of Augsburg, waged from 1689 to 1697, had led to French and Indian raids on New England's frontier and attacks by New Englanders on the French in Canada. The British colonists called this conflict King William's War. The War of the Spanish Succession, from 1702 to 1713, again produced its small counterpart in America, Queen Anne's War. So far the colonial fighting had consisted of border raids between British and French colonists, sometimes employing their Indian allies. The American phase of the War of the Austrian Succession, which took place from 1740 to 1748, was called King George's War. New England troops won an important victory in the capture of Louisburg, which guarded the entrance to the St. Lawrence River. Colonists were disappointed when Britain returned Louisburg in the Treaty of Aix-la-Chapelle. Territory the British retained, now called Nova Scotia, the French had named l'Acadie. Many of the French colonists, the Acadians, remained hostile to British rule, and in 1749 the conquerors undertook a deportation of Acadians. Between six and seven thousand left, some to France, others later to return to Nova Scotia, still others going to Louisiana, where to this day their descendants are known as Cajuns, a variant of "Acadians." Then in 1756 Britain and France began their seven-year world war for empire. The fighting in North America became known as the French and Indian War.

Skirmishes in the Ohio Valley

A new governor of Virginia, Robert Dinwiddie, had instructions to promote the concerns of Britain in the Ohio Valley, but to do so without antagonizing the French. Accordingly he dispatched a seven-man mission, which included a twenty-one-year-old surveyor named George Washington, to urge the French to respect British rights in the area. The mission was politely received and, with equal politeness, informed that the construction of Fort Duquesne would begin in the spring. The place where the fort was to be located, the site of present-day Pittsburgh, was in territory then claimed by Virginia. Upon being told of the French intention, Governor Dinwiddie rushed a workforce to the area with instructions to build a British fort on the spot. To protect the workers young Washington followed with troops a little later, quite unaware that the French had expelled the workforce almost immediately upon its arrival. In May 1754 Washington was encamped on the Monongahela River when he learned of the existence of a small French contingent a few miles ahead. He ordered a night march and attacked the French, capturing twenty-one and killing ten. Then he pushed on until he learned that the French were about to attack him in force. He retreated and hastily threw up a stockade, imaginatively called Fort Necessity. In June his troops of 150 grew by 200 more men, and on July 3 he was attacked by 500 French and 400 Indians. After a nine-day siege Washington surrendered. The future commander of the American forces had gotten his first taste of battle. "I heard the bullets whistle," Washington wrote to his half-brother, and there was "something charming in the sound."

Albany Plan of Union   Even before Washington's abortive expedition, the Board of Trade had ordered a conference of colonial officials, and even as Washington was blundering in the wilderness a colonial congress was in session in Albany, New York. Schemes for uniting the colonies were afloat at the congress. The Pennsylvania delegation, led by Benjamin Franklin, proposed what is known as the Albany Plan of Union. The plan called for a president-general for the British colonies, to be chosen and supported by the Crown, and a grand council, representing the several colonies in proportion to their contributions to the colonial treasury. This agency was to have general legislative and taxing powers for defense costs and improving Indian relations. The delegates approved the plan with modifications, but the colonies rejected it. The first effort to establish an American union was stillborn. The colonial legislatures had been jealous above all of sharing their power to tax. That jealousy would later involve them in a revolution against Great Britain.

General Braddock's Defeat   As hostilities continued on the frontier it remained obvious that some sort of plan would have to be devised for coping with the French in America. Official British policy was to engage in what, at a later day, would be called limited warfare. Two British regiments at half strength, the rest to be made up of colonial militiamen, would march up from Virginia to attack Fort Duquesne. Another similar force, to be gathered in New England and New York, would seize Fort Niagara. General Edward Braddock, sixty years old with forty-five years' military experience, was put in charge of the campaign.

Braddock arrived in Virginia early in 1755, then delegated responsibility for raising troops for the multiple attack, and chose Washington as one of his aides-de-camp. In June he started over the mountains with a force of over 1,400 men and 150 wagons, cutting a road through the wilderness as he went. In an open space near Fort Duquesne on July 9 French and Indian forces fighting from behind cover surprised Braddock's troops. Some Virginia troops abandoned the close-ranked, conventional eighteenth-century military formation and tried to fight in the frontier manner, which meant using cover. Some of the British regulars attempted the same thing, but Braddock and his officers ordered them back into line, where they were slashed by enemy fire until they broke. Many ran, as George Washington said, "as sheep pursued by dogs." By the next evening Braddock's forces had been destroyed; Braddock himself was killed. Of 1,459 men, 977 were dead or wounded. In the

Virtual Representation

In the eighteenth century the popularly elected lower houses of the legislatures in the royal colonies protested against whatever they found to be heavy-handed in imperial policy or in the conduct of governors. In time the lower houses came to argue that since colonists were entitled to "the rights of Englishmen," they were entitled to representation in any body that governed them. The full implication of this argument, which it took a generation or more to realize, was that, since colonists were not properly represented in Parliament, only the lower colonial houses could legitimately pass laws for British America.

Some British defenders argued that the colonists were already "virtually" represented in Parliament and needed no other voice in the imperial government. A member of Parliament, so the concept of virtual representation argued, spoke not only for his own constituency but for other constituencies with similar interests. This reasoning would hold that a member of Parliament from a seaport town in England also represented Bostonians or New Yorkers. It made a certain sense to the English because the franchise in Britain was severely limited. But on the other side of the Atlantic, virtual representation made no sense.

North, the planned expedition on Fort Niagara, directed by the new Governor William Shirley of Massachusetts, got as far as Oswego, half the distance, before being defeated.

Attack on Canada

By the middle of 1756 the French had taken the offensive, and throughout 1757 French forces won victory after victory. Then a new expedition, commanded by General John Forbes, took the remains of Fort Duquesne, which the French, deserted by their Indian allies, had blown up before retreating. Forbes immediately began to reconstruct the fort, rechristened Fort Pitt after the great British statesman. In 1759 an expedition of 3,500 Americans, 2,500 British regulars, and 1,000 Indians under Sir William Johnson seized Fort Niagara, cutting off Montreal and Quebec from the Great Lakes region. A force commanded by Sir Jeffrey Amherst was directed to clear the French posts on Lake Champlain and lay siege to Quebec from the southwest. General James Wolfe was ordered to move with a combined army and naval force up the St. Lawrence and attack Quebec from the other side. Amherst's expedition took both Ticonderoga and Crown Point, but was so slow in the doing that it was forced to stop on Lake Champlain for the winter of 1759–60. That left Wolfe to attack Quebec alone. Montcalm remained inside the fortress, confident that high cliffs would prevent any attack on Quebec from the southwest by way of the Plains of Abraham. The ensuing battle and English victory were a momentous occasion for the future of North America.

Armies had to drag their artillery with them, sometimes through deep snow. (*Courtesy, Scribner's Archives*)

Imperial Reform

The Treaty of Paris (1763)

The French and Indian War was an invigorating experience for Americans. They had fought well in a score of battles from Canada to the Caribbean. After 1763 they would exhibit a new confidence and pride in what they, mere provincials before, could accomplish. For a century New France and then Louisiana, representing absolutism and clericalism, had hung like a sword over Anglo-America, forcing the colonists to acknowledge dependence on the British army and navy. The Treaty of Paris in 1763 changed all this. To Great Britain, which had already won Canada by the surrender of Montreal in 1760, France now relinquished all claims to America east of the Mississippi. Spain, an ally of France, turned over Florida to the British. In compensation for Spanish losses, the French gave Spain New Orleans and all their possessions west of the Mississippi. Now that the most dangerous foreign power had been removed, the colonists were free to reassess their relationship with the mother country.

The British were aware of the possibility of change in the colonial temperament. During the negotiations at Paris the Duke of Bedford spoke for returning Canada to France to prevent Americans from growing too mighty and asserting their independence. Bedford's views were overruled, but in later years there were those who believed that the conquest of New France had been a mistake.

During the fierce debate between the colonies and Britain that preceded independence, the loyalist governor of Massachusetts, Thomas Hutchinson, noted:

"Before the peace of 1763 I thought nothing so much to be desired as the cession of Canada. I am now convinced that if it had remained to the French none of the spirit of opposition to the Mother Country would have yet appeared and I think the effects of it worse than all we had to fear from the French or Indians."

Renewed Conflict with Indians

During the war American settlers and Indian traders had moved into the trans-Appalachian region in the wake of British victories over the French. The new-comers often plied the Indians with rum and then "bought" their lands for a few cheap goods and rifles and powder. Once the Americans poured across the mountains in force after 1763, the Indian frontier exploded. One of the Indian leaders was the Delaware Prophet, a visionary and seer who assured his followers that if they rejected the European's ways, they would regain their former strength and former lands. The other, the Ottawa chief Pontiac, led his warriors in May 1763 against the British fort at Detroit and came close to taking it. Pontiac's attack commenced a massive Indian uprising all along the northern frontier; by June only three major British military posts remained.

The British quickly struck back. Two columns went to the relief of the surviving posts. One, led by Colonel Henry Bouquet, forced Pontiac to accept a truce. Soon after, Pontiac's chief allies made peace with the English, and before long Pontiac himself came to terms with the British and Americans. On the Pennsylvania frontier in 1764 a band known as the Paxton Boys attacked some peaceful Indians and then marched on Philadelphia, "uttering hideous cries in imitation of the war whoop" and bent on killing the Indian refugees who had fled to the capital for protection. Benjamin Franklin persuaded them not to invade the city.

The End of Salutary Neglect

The French forced the British government to focus attention on American affairs as never before, and the experience was an eye-opener. As British officials saw it, the Americans had behaved badly. Their illegal trade with the enemy had profited them and made the war more costly in men and money. British officials argued that the easy and benign policy of governing the colonies by "salutary neglect," a policy of leaving the colonies alone, would have to be replaced by a tighter, more rational, and financially sounder system. Spokesmen for the Americans pointed out that heavy local taxation for the repayment of the colonial war debt already burdened British America. Colonists were also prepared to argue that the Navigation Acts pulled wealth from the colonies into Britain.

The chief advocate of the British position was George Grenville, Chancellor of the Exchequer and King George III's chief minister following the retirement of William Pitt, the great wartime leader. Grenville was a man of limited vision who treated the empire as if it were a business concern. As a contemporary noted, Grenville judged "a national saving of two inches of candle . . . a greater triumph than all Pitt's victories." He soon initiated measures to reduce British expenses and to generate income for the mother country.

Grenville first took aim at policy toward the West and the Indians. To generate orderly settlement and in an attempt to prevent further Indian wars caused by land-hungry settlers, the Proclamation of 1763 set the limit of colonial settlement at the crest of the Appalachians. All colonists west of that line must "forthwith . . . remove themselves." British military authorities would now be in charge of all Indian territory

King George III, at age thirty-three.
(Courtesy, Library of Congress)

west of the mountains; all traders in Indian territory would have to be licensed, and they could trade only at designated points under British military supervision. The Proclamation was soon followed by a flurry of measures designed to raise revenue in America whenever the colonists might refuse to provide for their own defense.

The intention of the Sugar Act of 1764, a revision of the Molasses Act of 1733, was to increase the scanty receipts of the British customs service in America. The law added a dozen items to the list of enumerated American exports that must go first to Britain to be taxed before they could be sent elsewhere. The law also established a new set of taxes for goods imported into the colonies and set up new admiralty courts with power to enforce their collection with the aid of general search warrants, called "writs of assistance." The most important change affected the trade between the mainland colonies and the West Indies. Molasses was the chief raw material in the making of rum, a major New England industry. For many years American merchants had relied on the French and Dutch Caribbean islands for this product, which was cheaper there than in the British Caribbean islands. By smuggling, the colonists had evaded the high tax Britain had imposed on foreign-produced molasses. Because the duty of sixpence a gallon had been

British Legislation Affecting the Colonies, 1764–74			
Legislation	*Date*	*Provisions*	*Colonial Reaction*
Sugar Act	April 5, 1764	Revised duties on sugar, coffee, tea, wine, other imports; expanded jurisdiction of vice-admiralty courts	Several colonial assemblies protest taxation for revenue
Stamp Act	March 22, 1765; repealed March 18, 1766	Printed documents issued only on stamped paper purchased from appointed distributors	Riots in some cities; collectors forced to resign; Stamp Act Congress (October 1765)
Quartering Act	May 1765	Colonists must supply British troops with housing, candles, firewood, and so on	Protest in assemblies; New York Assembly punished for failure to comply
Declaratory Act	March 18, 1766	Parliament declares its authority "in all cases whatsoever"	Ignored
Townshend Revenue Acts	June 26, 29, July 2, 1767; all repealed—except duty on tea, March 1770	New duties on glass, lead, paper, paints, tea; customs collections tightened	Nonimportation of British goods
Tea Act	May 10, 1773	Parliament gives East India Company the sole right to sell tea directly to Americans (some duties on tea reduced)	Tea destroyed in Boston (December 16, 1773)
Coercive Acts (Intolerable Acts)	March–June 1774	Closes port of Boston; restricts town meetings; troops quartered in Boston	Boycott of British goods; First Continental Congress convenes (September 1774)

uncollectable, the British now cut the duty in half—but determined to collect the money.

A second measure of 1764, the Currency Act, struck at the practice of issuing legal tender, or paper money. The colonials believed paper to be an indispensable medium of exchange in a chronically coin-poor community. British merchants had long complained, however, that the paper issued under the colonial legal-tender laws was a cheap and flimsy currency. Its use by Americans, especially southern planters, in payment of their debts to British creditors amounted to a scaling down of the debt. The right to issue legal tender had already been forbidden the New England colonies. Now, the prohibition would extend to the middle and southern colonies as well.

The Proclamation of 1763 threatened the ambitions of land speculators, Indian traders, and would-be settlers in the West alike. For the moment, Americans interested in western development simply ignored British policy and went ahead with their own plans. As George Washington wrote a fellow land speculator: "any person who . . . neglects the present opportunity of hunting out good Lands and in some measure marking and distinguishing them for his own . . . will never regain it." Reaction to the Revenue and Currency Acts was more vigorous. A Boston town meeting listened to James Otis's impassioned attack on writs of assistance and condemned the Revenue Act as taxation without representation. A group of Boston merchants, joined by the city's artisans, resolved to boycott several items imported from Britain. By the end of 1764 a limited boycott of British goods had spread to several other colonies.

The New York Gazette *reported that in New Haven, as a patriotic act,*

"the young Gentlemen of Yale have unanimously agreed not to make use of any foreign spiritous liquors. . . . This will not only greatly diminish the Expences of Education, but prove, as may be presumed, very favourable to the Health and Improvement of the Students."

The Stamp Act Crisis

Trouble awaited the Grenville program. But few people could have anticipated the full extent of American hostility to British policy. Then came the Stamp Act—the first attempt to impose an internal tax on American colonists, a tax on their activities within their own localities. Previous taxes had been external; they had applied to American commerce with the outside world.

Grenville must have realized the danger in the new policy, for when he asked for a tax that would apply directly to transactions in America rather than to overseas trade, he promised to consider other means of raising revenue in the colonies if Americans objected. But he gave the colonial legislatures little time to respond. When their London agents, including Benjamin Franklin, the agent for Pennsylvania, tried to induce Grenville to withdraw the stamp tax proposal, he refused.

In February 1765 the fatal measure came before a poorly attended session of the House of Commons. The debate, though brief, was significant as an expression of the differing views of the colonies that were then current among Englishmen.

Speaking for Grenville, Charles Townshend gave voice to a widespread condescension toward Americans that would poison relations between the two peoples. Townshend called Americans "children

Demonstrations erupted
throughout the colonies in
response to "taxation without
representation." In New England,
suspected supporters of the hated
Stamp Act were hanged in effigy.
(Courtesy, Scribner's Archives)

(Courtesy, Scribner's Archives)

planted by our care." They had been "nourished up" by British "indulgence" and protected by British arms. Would "they grudge to contribute their mite" to relieve the British people from "the heavy burdens" they suffered?

Townshend's remarks offended Colonel Isaac Barré, an officer who had fought under Wolfe and unlike other upper-class Englishmen argued for relaxing the bonds of empire. Townshend was seriously mistaken, Barré declared. The Americans had been planted not by British care, but rather by British oppression, which had driven refugees to the New World. Nor were they nurtured by British indulgence. Rather they "grew by your . . . neglect of 'em." These "sons of liberty," Barré said, had suffered under greedy British officials for many years. Nor had they been protected by British arms; they had nobly fought for themselves.

Americans would cheer Barré's words, and rebel organizations would soon adopt "Sons of Liberty" as their name. But Parliament was unmoved. On March 22, 1765, it passed the Stamp Act, taxing newspapers, almanacs, pamphlets, legal documents, insurance policies, dice, playing cards, and other items. These taxes would be paid in the form of a stamp, purchasable from officials to be chosen from among Americans residing in the colonies, and placed on the specified documents. England had a similar tax, and Grenville expected the law to raise £60,000 of the £300,000 needed to maintain the British military establishment in North America. Tax evaders could be tried in vice-admiralty courts, which had no juries.

News of the Stamp Act's passage reached America in mid-April. Although the act would not take effect until November 1, consternation was immediate.

In the Virginia House of Burgesses at Williamsburg the young lawyer Patrick Henry denounced the measure in a speech that has become famous. "Caesar had his Brutus; Charles the First his Cromwell; and George the Third—[here tradition has it that the House Speaker interrupted with a shout of "Treason!" whereupon Henry continued] may profit by their example. If this be treason, let us make the most of it." Although some doubt exists that the eloquent and ringing version well known to generations of American schoolchildren represents Henry's actual words, he apparently came close to suggesting rebellion. After this speech the delegates at Williamsburg adopted a set of resolutions proclaiming that the House of Burgesses possessed the "only and sole power to lay taxes . . . upon the inhabitants of this colony," and that Virginians were "not bound to yield obedience to any law" that Parliament might pass to tax them. Various of these Virginia Resolves appeared in colonial newspapers, serving as "an alarum bell to the disaffected." Soon almost all the other colonies had adopted similar resolutions. In June 1765, when the Massachusetts General Court proposed that representatives of all the colonies meet in New York in October to consider joint action against the detested measure, nine of the colonies quickly and enthusiastically accepted the invitation.

Long before the Stamp Act Congress assembled, Americans resorted to more than words to express their indignation.

Sons of Liberty   In August 1765 Boston's Sons of Liberty hanged in effigy the man who was to be the new tax commissioner, Andrew Oliver. Oliver was a brother-in-law of Lieutenant Governor Thomas Hutchinson, who was also chief justice of the Superior Court of Massachusetts. Later the mob tore down a house that Oliver had allegedly built to serve as his tax office. The crowd next marched on his home and broke all the windows. The following day Oliver resigned his tax commission. The Boston Sons of Liberty next attacked the house of William Story, deputy register of the admiralty court, smashed down the doors, and burned Story's public and private papers. Another contingent sacked the home of the comptroller of customs, carried away his records, and pillaged his wine cellar. On August 26 the mob targeted Hutchinson's three-story brick mansion. The swarm battered down the walls, burned the furniture, destroyed the library, tore windows and doors from their frames, drank all the liquor, and even cut down the trees in the Hutchinson yard. Individuals also stole £900 in cash and walked off with the family silver. Hutchinson, who escaped through his back garden, had actually opposed both the Revenue Act and the Stamp Act.

At the State House the morning after, a disheveled Thomas Hutchinson took his place in court without his chief justice's robes. It was the second time a member of the family had faced the wrath of Boston. Thomas Hutchinson was the great-great-grandson of Anne Hutchinson. She had stood up to the governmental and ministerial establishment of the colony. With an equally stubborn courage that he would display in the aftermath of the Boston Massacre of 1770, he was prepared to stand up to the mindless fury of the mob.

The violence appalled even some opponents of British policy. The Boston town meeting condemned the rioting, and the authorities issued a warrant for the arrest of Ebenezer McIntosh, the leader of the Sons of Liberty, but the damages were never repaid.

In Newport, Rhode Island, a crowd burned and sacked the homes of "Tories" (so called after the more conservative of Britain's political parties), who defended British authority. In Newport as in Boston, the mobs forced the Stamp Act collector to resign. In Connecticut, citizens conducted a mock trial of stamp distributors. New York Sons of Liberty vented their fury on the house of the British military commander who had sworn to "cram the Stamp Act down the people's throats." In Charleston, capital of South Carolina, a mob attacked the house of the prominent merchant Henry Laurens, suspected of being the future stamp distributor. Only Laurens's bold denials kept the crowd from doing harm to him and his property.

So it went from colony to colony. Everywhere Tories were intimidated, and collectors forced to surrender their commissions. When the stamps finally arrived, there was no one to sell them or to see that they were affixed to the designated documents.

Crowds like those that roamed the streets during the Stamp Act crisis would appear in later confrontations between colonists and the British government. They were, in fact, a feature of eighteenth-century politics. Across the Atlantic, the London mob was a menacing presence to the government. And before the end of the eighteenth century, the Paris mobs of the French Revolution would enter history.

The Stamp Act Congress   In the early fall of October 1765, twenty-seven delegates from nine colonies—all but New Hampshire, North Carolina, Virginia, and Georgia—convened in New York to consider united action against the detested law. This Stamp Act Congress was relatively conservative, but its Declaration of Rights and Grievances effectively summed up most of the colonists' complaints. Taxation, the Declaration asserted, could be imposed only by the people's consent, "given personally, or by their representatives." Trial by jury, ignored by the new admiralty courts, was an inherent right of Englishmen. The Stamp Act as well as the other recent measures restricting American commerce, the Congress declared, must be repealed.

Far more effective than the words of the Stamp Act Congress were the actions of businessmen in the major American port cities. Two hundred New York merchants agreed not to take new orders for British goods so long as the Stamp Act remained. They were joined by the traders of Philadelphia, Boston, Salem, and other ports. Meanwhile, November 1, the date when the Act was supposed to take effect, rolled around. For a while business was disrupted, since very little could be done legally without the stamps. Slowly it resumed without them. The law was dead.

The British government could not ignore the American response to the Stamp Act. Some Englishmen were outraged at American defiance. Dr. Samuel Johnson, the critic and lexicographer, called the opponents of the Act "incendiaries" and "fractious demagogues." But others, particularly merchants who found their American business dwindling, sympathized with the Americans and bombarded Parliament with petitions for repeal of the measure. In Manchester, Leeds, Nottingham,

THE STAMP ACT CRISIS

The Stamp Act crisis was in several senses the "prologue to the Revolution." What made it particularly so was that, as in later conflicts, the disgruntled colonists along with their opponents were stating the clash as a matter of absolute principle. It was a foretaste of the peculiarly intellectual flavor that characterized the American Revolution.

The colonists objected not simply to the particular exercise of power (which, however ill-advised, was anything but tyrannical), but to what it boded for the future. Americans of the revolutionary generation had a positive genius for searching out the farthermost implications of every British action. Hence they devoted their most vigorous condemnations not to the Stamp Act but to the principles it embodied. The British were equally sensitive to questions of principle. For them, too, the Stamp Act quickly ceased to be a mere means of raising revenue

and became instead a test of parliamentary authority. Each party, believing that the other was aiming at the total overthrow of legitimate law and justice, assumed that it had to defend itself by the assertion of its absolute and inviolate rights.

Both sets of suspicions were initially mistaken. Parliament did not wish to enslave America. It wished merely to oblige the colonists to pay a larger share of the expenses of running the empire. The colonists did not wish to be independent. They wished simply not to be taxed internally without their consent. But the intense suspiciousness on both sides meant that their expectations, however wrong initially, quickly became self-fulfilling prophecies. Colonial intransigence provoked ever sterner measures from Parliament. The colonists in reaction advanced ever greater claims to home rule, culminating in the Declaration of Independence.

and other English industrial towns, thousands of workingmen lost their jobs as the workshops and mills dependent on the American market slowed and then stopped.

The man who now had to face the uproar was the Marquis of Rockingham, who had succeeded Grenville as prime minister in July 1765. Rockingham's group drew its support largely from the merchants and manufacturers and was particularly sensitive to their plight. Leading the battle for repeal in Parliament was William Pitt, the great wartime prime minister. Pitt eloquently defended the colonists' rights. "The Americans," he declared, "are the sons, not the bastards of England." The Stamp Act must "be REPEALED ABSOLUTELY, TOTALLY, IMMEDIATELY...." In March 1766 Parliament complied. But at the same time it passed the so-called Declaratory Act, asserting its power to make laws binding the American colonies "in all cases whatsoever."

Amid general rejoicing at the end of the detested stamp tax, few Americans took note of the Declaratory Act. Merchants immediately abandoned their nonimportation agreements and placed large orders with British suppliers. New York City voted to erect statues to Pitt and George III. Other towns and villages put up monuments to Pitt, the "Great Commoner." The ordinary people rang church bells, put lighted candles in their windows, and fired off guns. The Boston Sons of Liberty built on Boston Common "a magnificent pyramid, illuminated with 280 Lamps." Crowning the pile was a box of fireworks that went off at dusk to splendid effect.

A popular song was written for the celebration in Boston of the repeal of the Stamp Act:

In spite of each parasite, each cringing slave,
Each cautious dastard, each oppressive knave,
Each gibing ass, that reptile of an hour,
The supercilious pimp of abject slaves in power,
We are met to celebrate in festive mirth,
The day that gave our freedom second birth,
That tells us, British Grenville never more
Shall dare usurp unjust, illegal power,
Or threaten America's free sons with chains,
While the least spark of ancient fire remains.

Whig Political Philosophy   By the 1760s many Americans were adhering to the Whig political theories popular among so many British citizens. Whig philosophy proceeded on the assumption that all human beings are vulnerable by nature to the seductions of money and power. Governments are necessary evils, needed for guaranteeing order and protecting basic liberties. But governments are tainted by the same human evils that make governments necessary. Government was synonymous with political and economic power. Individuals who hold public office, unless they are rigidly limited by constitutional restrictions, are virtually certain to abuse their power eventually. They will use the power of government to promote their own personal interests or to hurt their political opponents. Every institution and tradition that limits the arbitrary power of government deserves therefore the most careful preservation.

Naturally suspicious of politicians, Americans were always worried about government's using its authority in abusive and unconstitutional ways. Their own British heritage had given them strong beliefs in representative government, jury trials, and freedom from unreasonable searches and seizures. Both the Sugar Act of 1764 and the Stamp Act of 1765 had, in the opinion of many Americans, compromised those liberties. They were ready to resist any future violations.

Even angry colonists, then, still saw themselves as part of the empire, subjects of the King, sharing in the rights that belonged to the British nation and history. But recent events had made them touchy; they were developing a habit of asking large questions about the legitimacy of the actions of the British government. And in the Stamp Act

A teapot celebrating Parliament's repeal of the Stamp Act in March 1766. *(Courtesy, Essex Institute, Salem, Massachusetts)*

Congress they had gained experience in confronting Great Britain not as Virginians or people of Massachusetts but as united colonists, as Americans.

The British Blunder Again

The Quartering Act Crisis In 1765 General Thomas Gage, the commander of all British forces in North America, asked Parliament to pass an act that would reduce the financial burdens associated with the defense of the colonies. In March Parliament passed the Quartering Act. It required colonial officials, for a two-year period, to provide barracks and supplies for the British troops. While the Stamp Act was lighting a political firestorm in the colonies, the new law was further stoking the flames.

The French and Indian War, by eliminating France as a North American power, appeared substantially to reduce the need for the permanent stationing of British troops in the thirteen colonies. The Indians had been driven far away into the western lands. Most British troops, however, were still billeted in or near the major American population centers. Were the troops really there to protect the colonies or to control them?

In December 1765 General Gage asked the New York legislature to obey the Quartering Act and provide the funds necessary to support his troops. The legislators refused, arguing that because so many British troops, as well as Gage's headquarters, were located in New York, the financial burden fell too heavily on them. Tensions mounted throughout 1766, aggravated when Parliament passed a second Quartering Act providing for the billeting of soldiers in inns, alehouses, and vacant buildings. Brief skirmishes occurred between New York citizens and British soldiers in August 1766, and in December the legislature refused to appropriate any money for the troops. In retaliation, Parliament suspended the New York assembly, an act many New Yorkers considered a violation of their constitutional rights. The controversy did not subside until October 1, 1767, when the New York assembly finally appropriated £3,000 for the support of Gage's troops.

Townshend Duties Many British leaders still wanted colonials to pay a larger share of their administrative and military costs. In early 1767, Charles Townshend, Chancellor of the Exchequer, unveiled his program. The colonies had successfully resisted the Stamp Act, which had taxed their internal business without their consent. But the colonials themselves had not yet challenged Parliament's right to tax their external commerce, which could be perceived as coming within Parliament's authority to regulate the affairs of the empire as a whole. It might therefore still impose an import tax. Capitalizing on the distinction between "internal" and "external" taxation, Townshend proposed taxing a wide range of colonial imports including glass, paper, lead, and tea. These duties, he argued, would raise badly needed funds and also teach the disruptive colonials that Parliament had the authority to tax them. He further proposed creation

Grant Wood, *Daughters of Revolution.* **In this twentieth-century painting, the artist captured a later proud group of upper-class women who could trace their ancestry to the American Revolution.** *(Courtesy, The Edwin and Virginia Irwin Memorial)*

of a new American customs service as well as a crackdown on New York's continually defiant assembly. After Parliament enacted all these potentially explosive measures, the ministry indicated its determination to enforce the trade laws. In the fall of 1767 when the Acts went into effect, Parliament appointed several unpopular officials to the new customs board and established the body's headquarters in Boston, the center of opposition to stricter commercial regulation.

In some areas, enforcement of commercial regulations broke down almost completely. A Boston ship's captain, Daniel Malcolm, drew a pistol on two revenue agents searching for illegal wine in his basement. Returning with the sheriff and a search warrant, the agents discovered the captain's house surrounded by a crowd of his friends, and the harried sheriff avoided a direct confrontation only by stalling for time until the search warrant expired. After the officials departed, Captain Malcolm treated his protectors to buckets of smuggled wine. Such cases were not infrequent.

Investigating previous cases of enforcement, Townshend's customs board discovered only six seizures and one smuggling conviction in all of New England during two and one half years. Mobs had rescued three of the seized ships, and colonial juries acquitted two other defendants. Initially the new customs officials fared little better, enforcing restrictions only enough to enrage colonial merchants. The same Captain Malcolm brought an entire load of illegal wine into Boston on small boats during the night and then boldly sailed his empty ship into port the next day. The vessel's water line revealed his subterfuge, but enraged customs officers could find no Bostonian who would testify against him. In June 1768 a British customs official was locked in the cabin of John Hancock's sloop *Liberty* while the crew unloaded untaxed madeira wine. When customs officials tried to seize the vessel, citizens forced them to flee to the British garrison at Castle William, where they appealed for British troops to help keep order.

Another Boycott   Conditioned by the Stamp Act, Americans were sensitive about any further extension of British power, and an outcry greeted the Townshend Duties. That the duties did not constitute an internal tax failed to impress the colonists. This time, though, leading merchants and lawyers kept

In Virginia "An Address to the Ladies"
asked them to forswear imported finery:

And as one all agree that you'll not mar-
    ried be
To such as will wear London factory,
But at first sight refuse, tell them such
    you do choose
As encourage our own manufactory.
No more ribands wear, nor in rich dress
    appear,
Love your country much better than
    fine things,
Begin without passion, 'twill soon be the
    fashion
To grace your smooth locks with a twine
    string.

dissent under control. In each colony, the Sons of Liberty and the merchants adopted strict nonimportation agreements. In Massachusetts early in 1768 the popular Samuel Adams drew up a "circular letter" laying out British misdeeds and suggesting united colonial actions. The Massachusetts General Court approved it, and so did several other colonial assemblies. Governor Francis Bernard of Massachusetts did not approve, and dissolved the General Court. In South Carolina, the legislature resolved that until the colonies were restored to their former freedom by repeal of the Townshend Duties the people of the colony would refuse to import any of the manufactures of Great Britain. South Carolinians would practice the "utmost economy in our persons, houses, and furniture, particularly that we will give no mourning, or gloves, or scarves at funerals."

The Townshend Duties and the nonimportation movement encouraged a great deal of pamphleteering advocating a new imperial relationship with more freedom for the colonists—or, rather, with the liberties of Englishmen that they claimed already to possess. The most effective and eloquent of these arguments was John Dickinson's "Letters of a Pennsylvania Farmer to the Inhabitants of the British Colonies" (1768). Posing as a simple Pennsylvania yeoman, Dickinson cautioned against violence and expressed an affection for "mother Britain" that foreshadowed his later refusal to sign the Declaration of Independence. But on the question of British taxation he was adamant. And Dickinson meant all taxation, taxes on imports as well as on internal business.

Lord North   In the summer of 1768 Governor Bernard called on British authorities for troops to restore order in unruly Boston and prevent a repetition of the *Liberty* incident. In September the new British prime minister, Lord Frederick North, ordered two regiments of redcoats from Ireland to the rebellious Massachusetts capital despite threats of armed resistance by the Sons of Liberty.

North and his colleagues were having second thoughts about the Townshend Duties. Widely evaded, the taxes brought in virtually no revenue. Particularly galling was the smuggling of untaxed Dutch tea into the colonies. And nonimportation agreements had reduced annual exports to America. The British government was in a quandary: repealing the duties would end nonimportation, but it would also be the second time the British government had backed down.

In the end, the North ministry yielded to American pressure, but in a grudging and halfhearted way that only highlighted British weakness without calling forth American gratitude. In 1770 Parliament allowed the Quartering Act to expire and rescinded the taxes on glass, paper, and painters' colors; it also reduced the tea tax from twelve to three pence a pound, but did not repeal it.

This partial repeal ended the boycott. It did little to end resentment of Britain. As one American merchant remarked about the repeal: "Doing things by Halves of all others [is] the worst Method." Many fundamental disagreements with Britain persisted. The whole question of the constitutional relationship between mother country and colonies was still unsettled. What body, colonists asked, was the ultimate source of authority in America, the colonial legislatures or Parliament? By now some colonials were advocating an American relationship with Great Britain resembling that of the later British dominions within the British Commonwealth. The King of England would also be King of the colonies, but each American colony would be autonomous in all its domestic affairs. Few, if any, thought of complete independence. Americans remained proud of their British heritage and of the rights of "free-born Britons." Even the most ardent champions of colonial freedoms still insisted that they merely wished to preserve these rights from the arrogant usurpers who had gathered around the King.

The Boston Massacre

Quartering British Troops   In the months following repeal of the Townshend Duties, resentment toward Britain remained particularly strong in Boston. Aside from the long-standing grievances the Boston townspeople shared with other communities, there was the question of the recently arrived troops. If Massachusetts was not at war, what justified the sending of nearly 2,000 soldiers to Boston Common?

" 'The Bloody Massacre perpetrated in King Street, Boston on March 5th, 1770, by a party of the 29th Reg [iment].' Engrav'd, Printed and Sold by Paul Revere, Boston." (*Courtesy, Museum of Fine Arts, Boston*)

THE BOSTON MASSACRE

John Tudor, a Boston merchant, described the "Massacre" in his diary:

"On Monday Evening the 5th current, a few Minutes after 9 O'Clock a most horrid murder was committed in King Street before the Customhouse Door by 8 or 9 Soldiers under the Command of Capt Thos Preston drawn of from the Main Guard on the South side of the Townhouse.

This unhappy affair began by Some Boys & young fellows throwing Snow Balls at the sentry placed at the Customhouse Door. On which 8 or 9 Soldiers Came to his assistance. Soon after a Number of people colected, when the Capt commanded the Soldiers to fire, which

they did and 3 Men were Kil'd on the Spot & several Mortaly Wounded, one of which died next morning. The Capt soon drew off his Soldiers up to the Main Guard, or the Consequencis mite have been terable, for on the Guns fiering the people were alarm^d & set the Bells a Ringing as if for Fire, which drew Multitudes to the place of action. Leu^t Governor Hutchinson, who was commander in Chefe, was sent for & Came to the Council Chamber, w[h]ere som of the Magistrates attended. The Governor desired the Multitude about 10 O'Clock to sepperat & go home peaceable & he would do all in his power that Justice shold be done &c. The 29 Rigiment being then under Arms on the south side of the Townhouse, but the people insisted that the Soldiers should be ordered to their Barracks 1st

Before the British regiments arrived in the fall of 1768, the Boston town meeting urged the people of the city to arm themselves and demanded that Governor Bernard call a meeting of the General Court, which he had dissolved in June. When he refused, spokesmen for Massachusetts called an assembly of the colony's towns as a substitute for the General Court. This "convention" helped to acquaint the citizens of smaller communities with the view of the radical leaders of the capital, and it demonstrated that John Hancock (Harvard '54), Boston's richest merchant, John Adams (Harvard '55) the prominent lawyer, his cousin Samuel Adams (Harvard '40), the failed brewery owner who found his true calling in political activism, and the rest spoke for a large number of the colony's people, not just for the merchants and artisans of the metropolis.

The day the convention adjourned, the British troops dispatched by North arrived in Boston harbor, protected by guns of British men-of-war. While the city's dubious citizens looked on, the soldiers debarked at the Long Wharf and marched up King Street to the music of drums and fifes. It was a moving sight, even for the most dedicated radicals. The men's red tunics, criss-crossed by white straps, and their black three-cornered hats were far more colorful than modern uniforms. Towering over the regular troops were the grenadiers, chosen for their height, a feature emphasized by their tall, mitre-shaped bearskin caps. The grenadier officers wore crimson sashes and carried swords at their sides.

Boston's pleasure at the bright display soon faded, however, and the troops found it no pleasure to be quartered among a hostile populace. While their officers had no difficulty finding good lodgings with wealthy Tories, the city council refused to assign barracks for the troops, and soldiers had to be scattered around the town at whatever empty buildings, generally workshops and warehouses, the British could rent. In a town of about 17,000 the redcoats were conspicuous.

before they would sepperat, Which being don the people sepperated about 1 O'Clock.—Capt Preston was taken up by a warrent given to the high Sherif by Justice Dania & Tudor and came under Examination about 2 O'clock & we sent him to Goal [jail] soon after 3, having Evidence sufficient, to committ him, on his ordering the soldiers to fire: So aboute 4 O'clock the Town became quiet. The next forenoon the 8 Soldiers that fired on the inhabitants was allso sent to Goal. Tuesday A.M. the inhabitants mett at Faneuil Hall & after some pertinant speches, chose a Committee of 15 Gentlem^n to waite on the Leu^t Governor in Council to request the immediate removeal of the Troops. . . .

(Thursday) Agreeable to a general request of the Inhabitants, were follow'd to the Grave (for they were all Buried in one) in succession the 4 Bodies of Mess^s Saml Gray Saml Maverick James Caldwell & Crispus Attucks, the unhappy Victims who fell in the Bloody Massacre. On this sorrowfull Occasion most of the shops & stores in Town were shut, all the Bells were order'd to toll a solom peal in Boston, Charleston, Cambridge & Roxbery. The several Hearses forming a junction in King Street, the Theatre of that inhuman Tradgedy, proceeded from thence thro' the main street, lengthened by an immence Concourse of people, So numerous as to be obliged to follow in Ranks of 4 & 6 abreast and brought up by a long Train of Carriages. The sorrow Visible in the Countenances, together with the peculiar solemnity, Surpass description, it was suppos'd that the Spectators & those that follow'd the corps amounted to 15,000, som supposed 20,000. Note Capt Preston was tried for his Life on the affare of the above Octob^r 24 1770. The Trial lasted 5 Days, but the Jury brought him in not Guilty."

Lobsterbacks   Before long, the bored troops turned for solace to Boston's cheap rum and loose women. To get money for their dissipations, many engaged in petty theft. Inevitably they got into fights, especially with sailors in the local taverns. When winter came many soldiers deserted. The citizens of the Massachusetts countryside had little love for the "lobsterbacks," as they termed the British troops with their long red coats. But they also refused to help the military authorities return deserters to duty. The colonists saw the redcoats as an army of occupation and both sides often traded insults.

On Friday, March 2, 1770, a civilian ropemaker, William Green, asked a soldier passing by, Patrick Walker of the Twenty-ninth Regiment, whether he wanted work. Such part-time jobs were permitted to off-duty soldiers, and Walker said yes. Green responded: "Then go clean my shithouse." Walker retorted in kind and left, threatening to come back with some friends. Soon afterward he appeared with forty of his mates, led by a tall, black regimental drummer. The soldiers, armed with clubs, sailed into Green and his friends, who defended themselves with sticks. When other civilians joined in, the soldiers retreated.

All that weekend rumors circulated that the soldiers intended revenge. And so they did. On the night of Monday the 5th, bands of soldiers and of citizens roved the icy streets of Boston looking for trouble. It came at Private White's sentry post adjacent to the Custom House, when a wigmaker's apprentice baited White until the sentry hit him with the butt of his gun. When the apprentice fled, a British sergeant pursued him, brandishing his musket.

News of the fight spread quickly, and a half-dozen young men descended on the sentry post screaming "Lousy rascal! Lobster son of a bitch!" Soon the swelling crowd pelted White with snowballs and jagged chunks of ice, crying "Kill him, kill him, knock him down." Finally Captain Thomas Preston, officer of the day, decided he must save White even at the risk of a serious confrontation. With six grenadiers he marched on the beleaguered sentry post and surrounded White. But

Phillis Wheatley, a seventeen-year-old slave girl who had published her first poem in Boston at age thirteen, wrote of the Boston Massacre, "AMERICANS were burden'd sore / When streets were crimson'd with their guiltless gore!"

Phillis Wheatley the poet.
(Courtesy, Library of Congress)

with angry civilians pressing on him from every direction, Preston now found that he could not return to the safety of the barracks. He tried to persuade the crowd to disperse; its response was to dare the soldiers to shoot. At this point someone struck one of the redcoats with a club, knocking him off his feet. The soldier fired, and then another. A third pulled the trigger of his musket and hit Crispus Attucks, a black man, in the chest. By the time the shooting stopped, three Bostonians lay dead and two others were mortally wounded.

The whole city might have erupted in a bloody rebellion, but Lieutenant Governor Hutchinson intervened, and by promising a quick investigation and punishment of the guilty parties prevented a blow-up. Preston and his men were arrested and confined to jail pending trial. The silversmith Paul Revere quickly made an engraving of the "Bloody Massacre." The trial itself was conducted with propriety and fairness. Captain Preston hired as counsel two prominent Boston patriots, John Adams and Josiah Quincy, who took the case out of a combined concern for the colony's and their own good names. Bostonians wished to avoid any suspicion that the Massachusetts courts would not give the accused a fair trial. Adams demolished the charge that Preston had given the order to fire. He and Quincy appealed for fairness. "The eyes of all are upon you," Quincy told the jurors. The two defense lawyers called witnesses who demonstrated that the soldiers had been taunted and abused beyond bearing. Some soldiers were convicted of manslaughter but punishments were light. Massachusetts justice had been vindicated.

The trial eased angers in Boston and the colonies as a whole. It was followed by a period of relative calm in relations between Britain and the colonies. During these months the nonimportation agreements totally collapsed, despite the attempts of more radical colonials to continue them until tea too was exempted from duty. At Samuel Adams's suggestion the Boston town meeting organized a "committee of correspondence" to keep other towns informed of what the British were up to. "Let every town assemble" said Adams. "Let associations and combinations be everywhere set up, to consult and recover our just rights."

The *Gaspée* and the Boston Tea Party

The Burning of the *Gaspée* Then in June 1772 came the *Gaspée* affair. Rhode Island, one of the two colonies whose charter did not require a governor appointed by the Crown (Connecticut was the other), had long been notorious for ignoring imperial trade laws. For years, Rhode Island's many coves and inlets had sheltered smugglers who defied the customs authorities with impunity. To stop the traffic, the British authorities finally dispatched the ship *Gaspée* to Narragansett Bay. Tricky tides ran the ship onto a sandbar near Providence. That night a band of Rhode Island Sons of Liberty boarded the stranded *Gaspée,* overwhelmed its captain and crew, and burned the vessel to the waterline.

The British were outraged. Civilians had attacked one of the King's naval vessels in performance of its lawful duties. British authorities immediately appointed a commission of inquiry, with power to send suspects to England for trial. Despite a £500 reward, the commission—stymied by the refusal of witnesses to testify against the suspects, many of them substantial citizens of the colony—adjourned without fulfilling its mission.

The *Gaspée* affair had important consequences. British officials concluded that colonists would stop at nothing, and resolved to take a harder line. Colonials themselves were angered by the authorities' intention to drag men off to England to stand trial for crimes committed in America. It violated one of the elementary "rights of Englishmen," and they determined to prevent it from taking place. British officialdom announced, moreover, that the salaries of both the governor and the judges of Massachusetts were now to be paid by the Crown, which would free them from dependence upon the good will of the colonists.

The East India Company   Another brief period of calm followed the *Gaspée* affair. Then came swift events that ripped apart the old empire. The shock came from an unexpected source.

In 1773 the East India Company was on the verge of financial collapse. Since the seventeenth century the company had traded in India as its private corporate enterprise. Many company officials had become rich through bribery and special privileges, but the company itself had suffered. One of its few remaining assets, seventeen million pounds of tea held in its London warehouses, remained unsold because of the American boycott, and also because heavy taxes made it too expensive in Britain itself. Why not, Lord North asked, drastically reduce the import tax on tea? With only three pence per pound to be paid on arrival in America, the tea would become so cheap that it would undersell smuggled Dutch tea. The tea would sell widely, its profit saving the East India Company from ruin and its tax bringing the government at last some much-needed revenue from the troublesome mainland colonies. This plan received legislative form in the Tea Act of 1773.

What North did not foresee was that Americans were opposed on principle to paying any tax, however cheap, to which they had not consented. To make matters worse, he consigned the East India Company tea exclusively to colonial merchants who favored British policies and obeyed the trade laws.

News of the new British affront enraged the radicals. In New York City, most of the merchants resolved that the tea would not be sold. Philadelphians adopted resolutions declaring that since "the duty imposed by Parliament upon tea landed in America is a tax on the Americans, or levying contributions on them without their consent, it is the duty of every American to oppose this attempt." Along the Delaware River, a "Committee of Tarring and Feathering" threatened captains of vessels carrying tea that their cargo would bring them "into hot water." In Charleston, patriot pressure also frightened off tea importers. As usual, Boston responded more violently than any other town.

Governor Hutchinson warned the British authorities soon after the Tea Act passed that "at and near Boston the people seem regardless of all consequences. To enforce the Act appears beyond all comparison more difficult than I ever before imagined." If Hutchinson had allowed

Women were essential in the pre-Revolutionary War protest against Great Britain. One composed:

"A Lady's Adieu to Her Tea-Table."

FAREWELL the Tea-board with your gaudy attire.
Ye cups and ye saucers that I did admire;
To my cream pot and tongs I now bid adieu;
That pleasure's all fled that I once found in you.
Farewell pretty chest that so lately did shine.
With hyson and congo and best double fine;
Many a sweet moment by you I have sat.
Hearing girls and old maids to tattle and chat;
And the spruce coxcomb laugh at nothing at all,
Only some silly work that might happen to fall.
No more shall my teapot so generous be
In filling the cups with this pernicious tea,
For I'll fill it with water and drink out the same.
Before I'd lose LIBERTY that dearest name.
Because I am taught (and believe it is fact)
That our ruin is aimed at in the late act,
Of imposing a duty on all foreign Teas.
Which detestable stuff we can quit when we please.
LIBERTY'S The Goddess that I do adore,
And I'll maintain her until my last hour,
Before she shall part I will die in the cause,
For I'll never be govern'd by tyranny's laws.

this perception to guide him, disaster might have been avoided. But though he was American born, as governor of a British colony he felt bound to enforce the law, and when three cargo ships carrying tea arrived in Boston harbor he determined that they must unload.

The Tea Party   On the evening of December 16, 1773, a gathering of perhaps 8,000 men, much of the town's contingent of able-bodied males, assembled at Old South Church. They were there to hold a town meeting, to ask that the hated tea not be landed. Their request was not granted, and at the end of the meeting Sam Adams rose from his seat and said "This meeting can do nothing to save the country." As if by prearranged signal, as soon as the meeting adjourned, a band of men disguised as Mohawk Indians rushed down Milk Street to Griffin's Wharf. Three companies of these instant Indians rowed out to the anchored tea ships, boarded them, split open the tea chests, and dumped their massive contents into the waters of the harbor. Their mission accomplished, the men quickly and quietly dispersed.

The British saw the Boston Tea Party as an outrage and they determined not to let it go unpunished. In Parliament William Pitt, now Earl of Chatham, and the eloquent Irish member Edmund Burke warned that punitive measures would lead to revolt. Burke urged the government to let Americans tax themselves, and not worry about whether they were legally required to obey Parliament. But the Burkes and the Pitts were a minority. Other politically influential Englishmen believed, as one expressed it, "that the town of Boston ought to be knocked about their ears and destroyed." Determined to prevent the Americans from ending all parliamentary control, North introduced the

THE BOSTON TEA PARTY

Bostonian John Andrews described the tea controversy in a series of letters to his brother:

November 29th [1773].   Hall and Bruce arriv'd Saturday evening with each an hundred and odd chests of the detested Tea. What will be done with it, can't say: but I tremble for y^e. consequences should y^e. consignees still persist in their obstinacy and not consent to reship it. They have softened down so far as to offer it to the care of Council or the town, till such times as they hear from their friends in England, but am perswaded, from the present dispositions of y^e. people, that no other alternative will do, than to have it immediately sent back to London again. . . . Y^e. bells are ringing for a general muster, and a third vessel is now arriv'd in Nantasket road. Handbills are stuck up, calling upon Friends! Citizens! and Countrymen!

December 1st.   Having just return'd from Fire Club, and am now, in company with the two Miss Masons and Mr. Williams of your place, at Sam. Eliot's,

who has been dining with him at Col^o. Hancock's, and acquaints me that Mr. Palfrey sets off Express for New York and Philadelphia at five o'clock tomorrow morning, to communicate y^e. transactions of this town respecting the tea. . . . The consignees have all taken their residence at the Castle, as they still persist in their refusal to take the tea back. Its not only y^e. town, but the country are unanimous against the landing it, and at the Monday and Tuesday Meetings, they attended to the number of some hundreds from all the neighboring towns within a dozen miles. . . .

December 18th.   However precarious our situation may be, yet *such* is the present calm composure of the people that a stranger would hardly think that ten thousand pounds sterling of the East Indian Company's *tea* was destroy'd the night, or rather evening before last, yet its a serious truth; The affair was transacted with the greatest regularity and despatch. . . . A general muster was assembled, from this and all y^e. neighbouring towns, to the number of five or six thousand, at 10 o'clock

Boston Port Bill. Until Massachusetts had paid for the tea destroyed, a naval force would close Boston Harbor to shipping. Troops withdrawn from the town to Castle William following the Boston Massacre would reenter the city.

Fury in Boston itself was predictable. Messages of sympathy for Boston's plight poured in from every colony. George Washington urged his fellow Virginians to support the Bostonians. We must not "suffer ourselves to be sacrificed by piece meals," he wrote. The Virginia House of Burgesses convened in the Raleigh Tavern in Williamsburg after the Tory governor refused to let it sit at the capitol, and there it called for a continental congress to meet to consider united action. Similar calls came from New York, Providence, and Philadelphia. Everywhere Americans recognized that a crisis had been reached, and in North Carolina groups began to arm and drill in preparation for combat.

The closing of the port of Boston was the first in a series of parliamentary measures of 1774, known collectively as the Coercive or Intolerable Acts. The Administration of Justice Act declared that any royal official sued for carrying out his official duties could have his trial transferred out of unfriendly Massachusetts to Britain, where he would face a more favorable jury. The Massachusetts Government Act struck a severe blow at self-government by taking away from the provincial legislature many of its powers of appointment and giving them to the royal governor. Henceforth the governor, not the assembly, could appoint the council, and juries were to be summoned by sheriffs rather than elected by the town meetings, which only the governor could call.

Another measure passed in 1774, the Quebec Act, was not intended as punishment, but so offended the colonists that it is often included

Indignation over closing the Boston port swept the colonies. The Reverend Joseph Fish of Stonington, Connecticut, wrote to his daughter:

"I don't remember any time, since I lived, so alarming as these, on account of the tyrannical measures which the ministry at home have taken & are designing to take against the colonies. They seem (by accounts sent over) determined to distress us to the last degree, if not to destroy us, unless we submit to the yoke of slavery they have prepared for us."

The Boston town meeting sent a circular letter about the closing of the port to the other colonies, declaring that

"this attack, though made immediately upon us, is doubtless designed for every other colony who will not surrender their sacred rights and liberties into the hands of an infamous ministry. Now therefore is the time when all should be united in opposition to this violation of all the liberties of all."

Thursday morning in the Old South Meeting house, where they pass'd a *unanimous* vote that the *Tea* should go out of the *harbour* that afternoon, and sent a committee with Mr. Rotch to yᵉ. Custom house to *demand* a clearance, which the collector told 'em was not in his power to give, without the duties being first paid. They then sent Mr. Rotch to Milton, to ask a pass from yᵉ. Governor, who sent for answer, that "consistent with the rules of government and his duty to the King he could not grant one without they produc'd a previous clearance from the office."—By the time he return'd with this message the candles were light in [the] house, and upon reading it, such prodigious shouts were made, that induc'd me, while drinking tea at home, to go out and know the cause of it. The house was so crouded I could get no farther than yᵉ. porch, when I found the moderator was just declaring the meeting to be *dissolv'd*, which caused another general shout, out doors and in, and three cheers. What with that, and the consequent noise of breaking up the meeting, you'd thought that the inhabitants of the infernal regions had broke loose. For

my part, I went contentedly home and finish'd my tea, but was soon inform'd what was going forward: but still not crediting it without ocular demonstration, I went and was *satisfied*. They muster'd, I'm told, upon Fort Hill, to the number of about two hundred, and proceeded, two by two, to Griffin's wharf, where Hall, Bruce, and Coffin lay, each with 114 chests of the *ill fated* article on board; the two former with *only* that article, but yᵉ. latter arriv'd at yᵉ. wharf only yᵉ. day before, was freighted with a large quantity of other goods, which they took the *greatest* care not to injure in the least, and before *nine* o'clock in yᵉ. evening, every chest from on board the three vessels was knock'd to pieces and flung over yᵉ. sides. They say the actors were *Indians* from *Narragansett*. Whether they were or not, to a transient observer they appear'd as *such*, being cloath'd in Blankets with the heads muffled, and copper color'd countenances, being each arm'd with a hatchet or axe, and pair pistols, nor was their *dialect* different from what I conceive these geniusses to speak, as their jargon was unintelligible to all but themselves.

among the Intolerable Acts. This law established a permanent government for the conquered province of Canada that provided few of the rights the English colonists enjoyed. It also extended toleration to the predominant religion of Quebec's inhabitants, Roman Catholicism. And the law extended the boundaries of Quebec south to the Ohio River into a region claimed by Virginia, Connecticut, and Massachusetts.

Resistance Turns to Armed Conflict

The First Continental Congress In Carpenter's Hall, in Philadelphia, early in September 1774, the first Continental Congress assembled. Twelve colonies were represented. The popular royal governor had dissuaded Georgians who were trying to pass a resolution to send a delegation. Of the fifty-six delegates, twenty-two were lawyers, and most of the others were planters or merchants. Almost all had been prominent in the affairs of their individual colonies, and many had belonged to the committees of correspondence.

The delegates did not all agree on the best course. Some held it sufficient to petition the King informing him of wrongs done the colonists and asking that he intervene. The Massachusetts delegates, led by John and Sam Adams, along with Christopher Gadsden of South Carolina, and Patrick Henry and Richard Henry Lee of Virginia, favored retaliatory measures such as a new nonimportation agreement and a blunt refusal to pay for the tea dumped at Boston. Still, the delegates quickly demonstrated an emerging sense of continental unity and shared nationality. Patrick Henry, in a sample of his famous oratory, sounded the note. "The distinctions between Virginians, Pennsylvanians, New Yorkers, and New Englanders," he declared, "are no more. I am not a Virginian, but an American." All imperial government, he continued, was at an end. "All Distinctions are thrown down. All America is thrown into one mass." Henry was exaggerating, but the Congress would help to create a new feeling that Americans all shared a common destiny.

It was a radicals' convention. In the midst of the deliberations the delegates received a set of resolutions adopted by a convention recently held in Suffolk County, Massachusetts brought by Paul Revere. These declared that Americans should not obey any of the Coercive Acts, and declared the Quebec Act "dangerous in an extreme degree to the Protestant religion and to the civil rights and liberties of all America." Citizens should "use their utmost diligence to acquaint themselves with the art of war as soon as possible, and do, for that purpose, appear under arms at least once every week." Until redress was obtained, nonimportation of all British goods should be the rule. Over the strong objections of conservatives, the Congress endorsed the "Suffolk Resolves."

When it came to resolutions of their own, the delegates disagreed. On one side were the moderate Joseph Galloway of Pennsylvania and his supporters, who proposed a "Plan of Union" that would establish an overall government for the colonies with a president-general appointed by the King. This official would exercise authority over a grand council selected by the various colonial assemblies. Together the president-

John Singleton Copley's portrait of Paul Revere represents him as a silversmith and craftsman. Revere also cast cannon for the army and designed the state seal still used by Massachusetts.
(*Courtesy, Museum of Fine Arts, Boston*)

general and the grand council would constitute an "inferior branch" of the British Parliament. Radicals in the Congress, believing that this would freeze into law the colonies' political subordination to Britain, tabled it. The radicals' own plan, which was adopted, denounced the Coercive Acts as oppressive and unconstitutional and condemned the various revenue measures Parliament had passed since 1763, the enlargement of the vice-admiralty courts' jurisdiction, the maintaining of a British standing army in America, and the dissolution of colonial assemblies by British authorities. The Congress also adopted a plan known as the Continental Association, a stringent set of regulations virtually cutting off all commercial relations with Britain until American grievances had been redressed. A final resolution called for a second Congress to meet on May 10, 1775, if by that time Britain still refused to yield.

The work of the Congress pleased many colonists. Following adjournment the Pennsylvania Assembly gave the delegates a dinner at the City Tavern, where their work was toasted and praised. Radicals throughout British America congratulated Congress for its efforts. Tories were dismayed and depressed by what had transpired in Philadelphia. Governor William Franklin of New Jersey, Benjamin Franklin's Tory son, noted that the Congress had left Britain "no other alternative than either to consent to what must appear humiliating in the eyes of all Europe, or to compel obedience to her laws by a military force." The Franklins, father and son, became bitter political enemies.

In England itself, high officials were thunderstruck. British merchants once more became a voice for conciliation. So did Pitt and Burke.

Lexington and Concord   In the fall of 1774 in Boston, events moved toward a showdown. For months the army commander there, General Thomas Gage, had been reinforcing the British garrison so that by the end of 1774 there were eleven battalions of redcoats, some 4,000 men, in the city and at nearby Castle William. Patriots, as opponents of parliamentary rule over the colonies were termed, armed and drilled. Outside the city, bands of militia calling themselves Minute Men, ready to "meet at one minute's warning equipped with arms and ammunition," patrolled the countryside and made it dangerous for British troops to leave the city even on official business. Before long, Gage began to feel as though he were under siege and fortified Boston Neck against the time when he might actually be attacked. The Massachusetts Provincial Congress had ordered the stockpiling of arms and ammunition at nearby Concord. Within a few months, the colonists secreted some twenty thousand pounds of musket balls and cartridges, besides a considerable number of tents, axes, spades, and supplies of beef, flour, rice, butter, and rum—all hidden in private houses and barns in Concord. The town's men and women helped to manufacture still more supplies: cartridge boxes, belts, and holsters. A fifteen-year-old girl supervised the young women of the town in manufacturing cartridges. As one Concord resident observed, "the people are ready and determine[d] to defend this Country Inch by Inch."

Relations between Boston patriots and British authorities reached the flash point early in 1775. There was a brawl between butchers and

The poet Ralph Waldo Emerson wrote these verses on the fiftieth anniversary of the Battle of Lexington and Concord:

By the rude bridge that arched the flood,
    Their flag to April's breeze unfurled,
Here once the embattled farmers stood,
    And fired the shot heard round the world.

Following the rout at Lexington,
farmers and Minute Men
surprised the British at the
North Bridge in Concord and
sent them into retreat to Boston.
(Courtesy, Scribner's Archives)

redcoats at the public market. Then British troops tried to confiscate military supplies at Salem, but were turned back by Sons of Liberty. The Massachusetts legislature, in defiance of Gage's orders, was holding meetings at Concord. In mid-April Gage laid a plan to capture the arms that he had heard were stored there and perhaps seize some of the rebellious patriot leaders.

On the evening of April 18, 1775, a force of 700 redcoats set out for Concord. Patriots in Boston quickly learned of the move and dispatched William Dawes and Paul Revere to alert the Minute Men and the patriot leaders that the British were coming. Revere was captured and Dawes turned back, but another rider conveyed the news to the patriots at Concord in time. When the British reached nearby Lexington after marching most of the night, they discovered seventy armed Minute Men lined up on the town commons shivering in the early morning chill. The British commanding officer, Major John Pitcairn, immediately rode toward them shouting: "Ye villains, ye rebels, disperse! Lay down your arms!" At the same time the British light infantry began to run forward to intercept the Americans, who retreated to a stone wall at the edge of the field. Tradition has it that their commanding officer Captain John Parker, said, "Stand your guard. Don't fire unless fired upon. But if they mean to have a war, let it begin here." No one knows which side fired first, but at the wall the Minute Men stopped and fired off a ragged volley, wounding one redcoat and Major Pitcairn's horse. The British replied more effectively, killing eight of the Americans and wounding nine others.

As the British reassembled to move on Concord, the Massachusetts countryside rose in fury. By the time the redcoats arrived at their destination, a large force of armed and angry farmers had collected to intercept them. The British forces entered the town, and the militia took up a position beyond the town's center. In the meantime, Concord's women did their best to conceal the precious stores of military supplies. When the Americans began to advance on their enemy, the British tried to withdraw. At this point the Minute Men fired, killing three and wounding a dozen of the redcoats. Now began a long, dismal, and bloody British retreat from Concord all the way back to the safety of Boston.

The British arrived back in Charlestown in the evening and counted their losses. Despite their contempt for amateur soldiers they had to admit that the colonists' fire was often deadly. Of the 700 men sent to Concord, 73 had been killed, 174 wounded, and 26 reported missing. Only by the sheerest luck had the Americans been prevented from cutting off the whole force and capturing it. The Americans had won a victory against the finest troops of Europe.

The Loyalists   After April 19, 1775, there was no turning back. From that day until July 2, 1776, the Continental Congress, in its desperate efforts to resolve the crisis, was, as John Adams said, caught "between hawk and buzzard." General Gage warned the British government: "These people are now spirited up by a rage and enthusiasm as great as ever People were possessed of, and you must proceed in earnest or give the Business up." Yet in the ensuing months thousands of native-born Americans would become Tories, partisans of the King. Loyalism was to be especially strong among certain groups of Americans. Natives like Thomas Hutchinson who had close ties to the British government were natural loyalists. Anglican ministers who recognized the King as head of the Church of England also tended to take the British side, as did many Anglican laymen, especially in New England, where they formed an unpopular minority. Loyalists were not invariably rich with a large property stake in society. Besides loyalist merchants, officials, and planters, there were also loyalist mechanics, farmers, and small shopkeepers. They too were patriots, with as much right to the title as the rebels had. What claimed their patriotism was not Massachusetts or Rhode Island alone, or British America alone, but the whole British empire including the colonies. By tradition, however, the word "patriot" is reserved to the rebels.

Like the loyalists, the patriot rebels came in different shapes and sizes. Almost all Congregational and many other ministers outside the Church of England chose Congress. In the major port towns—Boston, Newport, New York, Philadelphia, and Charleston—artisans, apprentices, and laborers were rebels. But so were the merchants, especially those who felt threatened by the trade regulations that had been piled on top of the Navigation Acts since 1763. The landed gentry of New York split. Families such as the Delanceys took the King's side; the Schuylers and the Livingstons, equally wealthy and aristocratic, supported Congress. In Virginia and the Carolinas, the patriot leaders were almost all Anglican gentlemen. Many of them, such as George Washington, Henry Laurens, and Thomas Jefferson, were owners of large estates and scores of black slaves.

New England Rallies to Arms   The response of patriot leaders to the events in Massachusetts was prompt and vigorous. In Massachusetts the Provincial Congress, as the illegal colonial legislature was called, authorized the raising of troops and appealed to the other colonies for aid. Before long, several thousand militia from Rhode Island, Connecticut, and New Hampshire, along with contingents of Indians, were pouring into the colony and assembling in a ring around Boston, where Gage's troops were en-

A Philadelphia woman wrote to a British officer:

"I have retrenched every superfluous expense in my table and family. . . . Tea I have not drunk since last Christmas, nor bought a new cap or gown since your defeat at Lexington, and what I never did before, have learnt to knit, and am now making stockings of American wool for my servants, and this way do I throw in my mite to the public good. I know this, that as free I can die but once, but as a slave I shall not be worthy of life. . . . All ranks of men among us are in arms. Nothing is heard now in our streets but the trumpet and drum, and the universal cry is 'Americans, to arms!' "

camped. The American general in charge was Artemus Ward; his subordinates included the talented Nathanael Greene and Israel Putnam.

In some ways the besiegers of Boston were in worse shape than the besieged. The hastily-assembled colonial troops lived without sufficient tents and amidst filth. They were unused to the standards of hygiene necessary where men lived together in masses, and before long dysentery and other diseases invaded the American camp. The British in Boston, on the other hand, seemed to be living off the fat of the land, well housed and well supplied with food and necessities. At the end of May 1775, Gage was joined by three other high-ranking British officers, Sir William Howe, Sir Henry Clinton, and John ("Gentleman Johnny") Burgoyne. Howe took over command from Gage, who remained as civilian governor of the colony.

"Bunker Hill"   Sooner or later, Howe would have had to attack the troops surrounding Boston, but they forced his hand by fortifying Breed's Hill, across the Charles River from Boston and within cannon range of the city. On June 17, 1775, the British navy began to bombard the new fortifications. Confident that the untried amateur soldiers under Colonel William Prescott's command could not stand up against redcoats in a regular battle, Howe and his fellow officers decided to make a direct attack on the entrenched Americans. Troops of grenadiers and light infantry, with packs containing three days' rations, were ferried across the Charles to Charlestown peninsula.

As the British troops landed on the beach, the Americans waited silently. When the redcoats prepared to charge, Prescott gave the order to fire. There was a great crash and a cloud of smoke; scores of Welsh Fusiliers fell. In seconds the light infantry regiment was fleeing in panic, leaving behind its wounded, its dead, and most of its equipment. Meanwhile the tall grenadiers were advancing on Breed's Hill in well-dressed lines. When the redcoats were within twenty yards of the American position a volley rang out, knocking down scores. The grenadiers continued to advance, their bayonets fixed. The Americans, now almost within spitting range, continued to fire away. Finally the grenadiers too broke ranks and fled.

Howe was not finished. Once more he ordered his men against the American position. Once more they were mowed down and retreated. Again Howe ordered his men to attack, this time without their heavy packs. By now the Americans were low in ammunition. Assuming the battle was over, many had disobeyed their officers and had begun to leave for home. Despite heavy casualties, this time the redcoats drove the Americans off the hill and took possession of the Charlestown peninsula. The British had won, but at what a price! Over a thousand redcoat casualties, with over two hundred killed. Almost fifty percent of the British troops engaged were either dead or wounded. As Howe commented: "A dear bought victory, another such would have ruined us."

The battle, misnamed "Bunker Hill," was of vast symbolic importance. To Americans it was a great moral triumph. Combined with Lexington and Concord it had demonstrated that American militia were able to stand up to the best the British could throw against them. In reality, the Americans, with 15,000 men encamped around Boston,

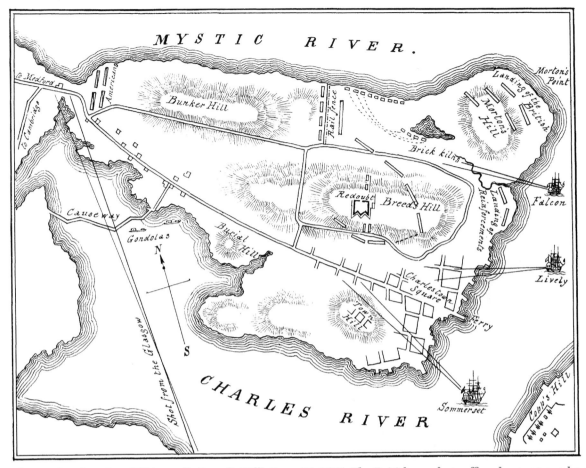

The Battle of Bunker Hill (actually Breed's Hill), June 17, 1775. The British won but suffered a great number of casualties. For the Americans it was a moral victory.

could have done much better with sufficient training. Far too many had been insubordinate. The Americans' staff work and supply services had been poor. American success had been due as much to British errors in using a frontal assault as to their own planning. Still, the Americans had reason to be proud and to look to the future with some hope.

A Continental Army Takes Shape

Washington Takes Command   In early May 1775, the Second Continental Congress had assembled in Philadelphia, as scheduled. Among its first acts was the choice of commander for the whole Continental army, who would take charge of the troops around Boston. Following the advice of John Adams to make a bid for unity by choosing a southerner, Congress on June 15, just days before Breed's Hill, appointed George Washington of Vir-

The Second Continental Congress appointed George Washington commander of the Continental army. A few years earlier he had hoped to get a commission as an officer in the British army. The portrait is by Charles Willson Peale. (*Courtesy, The Pennsylvania Academy of the Fine Arts*)

George Washington's appointment filled him with "inexpressible concern." Other Americans exulted in having a leader at last. By the fall of 1775, babies were being named after him. Phillis Wheatley wrote, "A crown, a mansion, and a throne that shine, / With gold unfading, WASHINGTON! be thine." She sent her poem to General Washington, and he wrote to thank her, adding, "If you should ever come to Cambridge, or near head-quarters, I shall be happy to see a person so favored by the Muses."

ginia. Congress also voted to raise six companies of riflemen from the middle colonies and the South to join the New Englanders at Boston and decided to issue bills of credit to support the accelerating rebellion.

Despite the outbreak of hostilities, Congress resisted a final political break with Britain. A few, among them Sam Adams, favored a bold declaration of American independence. His cousin John, however, urged the delegates to accept the advice of Massachusetts and endorse the formation of new constitutions for each colony to break the tie with England. These independent states, he believed, would ally themselves in a continental league that would be equivalent to a free nation. But even this oblique road to independence did not please most of the delegates, who still hoped for British conciliation.

Washington arrived in the Boston area after Breed's Hill to find the largely New England army a disappointment. They were, the Virginian complained, "an exceedingly nasty and dirty people," excessively concerned with money. Other observers found the troops enterprising, though highly individualistic, and unwilling to submit to discipline or even to call their officers by official titles. The new commander in chief had to turn this ragged collection of farmers and mechanics into an army and to combine it smoothly with the regiments of Virginians, Marylanders, and Pennsylvanians who began to arrive at Cambridge.

In these months of 1775, and virtually all through the war, one of the general's chief problems was simply to keep his force intact. Few Americans considered military service a full-time occupation. Farmers were willing to enlist for a few months, especially in the winter or after the crops had been planted. But when needed at home, or when confronted with long stretches of idleness, they grew restless. Some simply deserted. Others waited until their term of enlistment had ended and, regardless of the military situation, went home.

Early Fighting

Even before Washington arrived to construct a Continental army out of fifteen thousand individualists encamped outside Boston, the war was progressing elsewhere. In May 1775 a force of Massachusetts men and Vermonters under Ethan Allen and Benedict Arnold had attacked and captured the small British garrison at Fort Ticonderoga on Lake Champlain. The Americans acquired valuable military supplies, including a hundred cannon. In August the rebels launched from the captured British post an attack on Canada led by General Philip Schuyler of New York and Richard Montgomery, born in Britain. On November 13, 1775, Montgomery captured Montreal. Meanwhile, Arnold, with one thousand volunteers from Washington's force, set out across Maine heading toward Quebec City. He reached the British fortress in November and was joined by Montgomery and his men. The combined little army attacked the city in a howling snowstorm. In the battle Montgomery was killed and Arnold wounded. A hundred Americans were killed and four hundred captured. With his pitiful remnant Arnold continued to besiege the town all through the winter. In the spring he gave up the siege and returned home.

In Virginia the royal governor, the Earl of Dunmore, had gathered the colony's loyalists together at Norfolk, formed them into a small army, and set them to destroying plantations owned by patriots. In November, Dunmore issued a proclamation establishing martial law and calling on all citizens to support the King. He also offered freedom to all slaves who would desert their patriot masters and join his forces. This proved to be a mistake. Dunmore's little army did attract some runaway slaves, but white Virginians feared nothing more than a slave uprising, and Dunmore's proclamation may have pushed many of the undecided into the patriot camp. When he sallied out of Norfolk with his mixed band of loyalists and blacks, he was defeated. Soon after, he loaded his followers aboard ships and abandoned Norfolk to the Americans. He later returned and set fire to the city.

Peace Proposals   While Americans and Englishmen were sporadically killing one another in the fields and forests of North America, efforts were being made to bring the two sides together. In July 1775 Congress adopted the Olive Branch Petition announcing continued American attachment to the King and asking him to desist from further hostile acts until some scheme of reconciliation had been arranged. It also adopted a "Declaration of the Causes and Necessities of Taking Up Arms." This document did not proclaim independence, but pronounced American determination to refuse submission. Several weeks later, Congress rejected Lord North's proposals of February, by which the British government offered to forgo parliamentary taxes on any colony that would agree to tax itself for defense and to pay its own expenses.

Congress adjourned in August 1775, but reconvened in mid-September with a full representation from all thirteen colonies. In early November, members learned that the King had rejected the Olive Branch Petition and declared the colonies in open rebellion. On December 6 Congress responded to the King's declaration by disavowing American obedience to Parliament, but acknowledging continued allegiance to George III, perceived as the legitimate sovereign of all the British empire. If Congress had gotten its way, Parliament would have legislated for the inhabitants of Great Britain and American legislators for the colonies, both peoples giving homage to the Crown.

Wartime Government   As these proposals and counterproposals flew back and forth across the Atlantic, Americans were moving rapidly toward practical self-government. Congress had a Continental army. It appointed commissioners to deal with the Indian tribes and set up a post office department. It organized a navy. Its most momentous act was to appoint in November 1775 a five-man Committee of Secret Correspondence to negotiate with potential allies abroad. In December the Committee made contact with a French agent, who informed it that France would aid the colonists against the British. The French, of course, were delighted to see the British empire weaken. Soon after, the French Foreign Minister, Comte de Vergennes, consulted his Spanish counterpart regarding joint action to aid the Americans. When the Spanish gave their approval, Vergennes ordered a large amount of munitions to be shipped to the Americans through a "front" company, Hortalez et Companie. In April 1776 Congress opened American ports to the commerce of all nations except Britain.

Common Sense and
The Declaration of Independence

A final wrench to the remaining ties of empire came with the publication of *Common Sense,* a hundred-page pamphlet published early in 1776 by a recently arrived Englishman, Thomas Paine. Written with extraordinary passion and eloquence, *Common Sense* denounced the institution of hereditary kingship. "For all men being originally equals, no *one* by *birth* could have a right to set up his own family in perpetual preference to all others forever," Paine declared. George was a "royal brute," not the generous father of his people, and Americans had no reason to continue to obey him or remain his subjects. George III was in fact not a royal brute, but *Common Sense* was an important document in the modern rejection of the whole system of hereditary rule.

The pamphlet had an electrifying effect. Countless Americans read it as it passed from hand to hand, and were profoundly affected by its message. Washington noted that it was "working a powerful change in the minds of men." After reading it, he himself ceased to toast the King, as he had done till then.

The Declaration of Independence
On April 12, 1776, the North Carolina Convention authorized the colony's delegates in Congress to vote for independence. The Virginia legislature followed soon after. On June 7 Richard Henry Lee, responding to the House of Burgesses, offered a motion in Congress that "these United Colonies are, and of a right ought to be, free and independent states, and that all political connection between them and the state of Britain is, and ought to be, totally dissolved." Despite John Adams's earlier remark that "Every post and every Day rolls in upon Us, Independence like a Torrent," the delegates were not unanimous in support of such a bold move.

Congress responded by appointing to frame a statement of independence a five-man committee consisting of Thomas Jefferson, John Adams, Benjamin Franklin, Roger Sherman, and Robert Livingston. The group chose Jefferson to write a first draft. At thirty-three the tall Virginian was one of the youngest members of Congress. But he was also a man of great charm and eloquence, with a reputation for scholarship.

Jefferson's Declaration of Independence is one of the most eloquent and moving endorsements of human freedom and equality ever composed. With simplicity and directness the document, reprinted along with the Constitution at the end of this book, captures the essence of the ideas that numbers of European political philosophers had articulated, among them the seventeenth-century English Whigs who had overthrown James II and helped establish England's constitutional

COMMON SENSE
by Thomas Paine
Paine's rousing pamphlet circulated by the tens of thousands and galvanized sentiment against England in the spring of 1776.

"The sun never shined on a cause of greater worth. 'Tis not the affair of a city, a county, a province, or a kingdom; but of a continent—of at least one-eighth part of the habitable globe. 'Tis not the concern of a day, a year, or an age; posterity are virtually involved in the contest, and will be more or less affected even to the end of time by the proceedings now. Now is the seedtime of continental union, faith, and honor. The least fracture now will be like a name engraved with the point of a pin on the tender rind of a young oak; the wound would enlarge with the tree, and posterity read it in full grown characters. . . .

Small islands not capable of protecting themselves are the proper objects for government to take under their care; but there is something absurd in supposing a continent to be perpetually governed by an island. In no instance hath nature made the satellite larger than its primary planet; and as England and America, with respect to each other, reverse the common order of nature, it is evident that they belong to different systems. England to Europe: America to itself. . . .

O ye that love mankind! Ye that dare oppose not only the tyranny but the tyrant, stand forth! Every spot of the old world is overrun with oppression. Freedom hath been hunted round the globe. Asia and Africa have long expelled her. Europe regards her like a stranger, and England hath given her warning to depart. O receive the fugitive, and prepare in time an asylum for mankind."

monarchy. The document announces that "all men are created equal" and "endowed by their Creator with certain unalienable Rights," more especially to "Life, Liberty and the pursuit of Happiness." Governments exist only to "secure these rights." When a government becomes "destructive of these ends," it is "the Right of the People to alter or abolish it" and establish a new one that will respect them. The colonists' rights of Englishmen had now transformed themselves into the natural rights of peoples everywhere.

Americans today do not have to be reminded that the framers of the Declaration of Independence did not intend the reference to "the People" to imply that all inhabitants of a country should be active participants in the political life of the nation. The Congress was accustomed to institutions that defined a portion of the population as expressing the will of the whole. Masters were seen as speaking for servants; husbands for their wives. A few months prior to the signing of the Declaration, Abigail Adams had written to her husband, John Adams, that she longed "to hear that you have declared an independency." And, she added, for the new code of laws "which I suppose it will be necessary for you to make I desire you would Remember the Ladies, and be more generous and favourable to them than your ancestors." Abigail Adams was not claiming citizenship or equal political rights for women. She sought only that the lawmakers "not put such unlimited power into the hands of the Husbands." For, she reminded her husband, "all Men would be tyrants if they could." John Adams' wife marvelously adapted the revolutionary vocabulary of her day to women's situation as she understood it. She accepted women's domestic role, but sought to introduce greater freedom for women into that sphere. Should men fail to reduce their own domestic tyranny, she warned, the ladies would surely foment their own "Rebellion." And any notion of the Declaration as a democratic and egalitarian document will have to take account of

Windsor chair, reputed to be the sort used by Thomas Jefferson while he wrote the Declaration of Independence, probably made in New England, mid-eighteenth century. *(Courtesy, Index of American Design)*

The Declaration of Independence by John Trumbull shows, standing at center, left to right, John Adams, Roger Sherman, Robert R. Livingston, Thomas Jefferson, and Benjamin Franklin. *(Courtesy, Yale University Art Gallery)*

An angry New York crowd pulls down a statue of George III in 1776. Patriots had long accepted the conventional belief that the King could do no wrong and had attacked his ministers instead. The change in regard for the King was embodied in the Declaration of Independence, which repudiated George III, accusing him of plotting "an absolute tyranny." *(Courtesy, The New York Public Library, Astor, Lenox, Tilden Foundations)*

Twelve-year-old Jemmy Noyes of Connecticut, visiting New York City, wrote to his grandmother:

"I see four large ships there; one a seventy gun ship; and I saw the King's statue, and he sat on a great horse, both covered over with leaf gold; and the King had one bullet hole through his cheek, and another through his neck, and they talk of running his Majesty up into bullets for he and his horse are made of lead."

the existence of slavery, about which the members in their deliberations showed a flicker of conscience, but little more.

The rest of the Declaration was a detailed indictment of King George III, not the real culprit, which was Parliament. Here Jefferson marshaled virtually every American grievance, both immediate and of long standing, against Britain and defended the actions of the colonists during the years since 1763. All pointed toward one inescapable end: "these United Colonies are, and of Right ought to be, Free and Independent States." "With a firm reliance on the Protection of Divine Providence," the Declaration concluded, "we mutually pledge to each other our Lives, our Fortunes and our sacred Honor."

Adams, Franklin, and the rest of the committee suggested a number of changes, primarily stylistic. Congress as a body, when it received the draft, struck out several phrases and clauses, including an attack on the slave trade. On July 2 Congress voted to accept it. But it is July 4, when members of the Congress signed it, that Americans have chosen to commemorate. The Declaration was read to large gatherings of Americans throughout the self-proclaimed independent country. In Philadelphia John Nixon, head of the city guard, read the document to a large audience in the State House yard. When he finished, the crowd cheered. In New York, the officers of the Continental army, after hearing the Declaration read, all "went to a Publick House to testify to . . . their joy at the happy news of independence." The next day the statue of George III in New York City was "pulled down by the populace," and its 4000 pounds of lead were melted down for musket balls. Bostonians celebrated by removing from the State House wall the plaque bearing the King's coat of arms and burning it.

That the list of accusations in the Declaration of Independence largely exaggerates the actions of the British is to be expected of a document intended to justify a revolution. The document makes out the

King to be the villain. George III, to be sure, had been among the most eager advocates of a policy of forcing the colonists into submission, but it was Parliament that had been the effective agent of repression, and for some time the American rebels had professed their loyalty to the King, rejecting only parliamentary rule. Taken literally the attack on the King, foreshadowed in Paine's *Common Sense,* is absurd. But it is not to be taken literally. In effect, the King was serving as a symbol. In the earlier days of colonial resistance, he had been a symbol of the British nation and institutions, for which the rebels still felt affection. Now he was a symbol of arbitrary power, which the revolution claimed to be overthrowing in defense of liberty. The man George III, confused and muddling through like the rest of the human race, deserved better than to be appointed either symbolic role.

Now there could be no turning back. Victory would mean that the efforts at Philadelphia had not been in vain. Defeat might mean the surrender of lives, fortunes, and sacred honor.

John Adams wrote to his wife Abigail that the adopting of the Declaration would be

"celebrated by succeeding generations as the great anniversary festival. . . . It ought to be solemnized with pomp and parade, with shows, games, sports, guns, bells, bonfires and illuminations, from one end of the continent to the other, from this time forward forevermore."

Suggested Readings

Study of the American Revolution should begin with Bernard Bailyn's classic, *The Ideological Origins of the American Revolution* (1967) and Kenneth Lockridge, *Settlement and Unsettlement in Early America: The Crisis of Political Legitimacy before the Revolution* (1981). Kenneth Silverman, *The Cultural History of the American Revolution* (1976) is a detailed analysis of relationships between politics and the arts. On social history see Oscar and Lilian Handlin, *A Restless People: Americans in Rebellion, 1770–1787* (1982), and Stephanie Grauman Wolf, *As Various as their Land: The Everyday Lives of Eighteenth-Century Americans* (1993). Gary Nash studies the importance of cities in *The Urban Crucible: Social Change, Political Consciousness, and the Origins of the American Revolution* (1979).

Pauline Maier traces the rise of popular hostility of England in *From Resistance to Revolution* (1972). See also Peter Thomas, *Tea Party to Independence: The Third Phase of the American Revolution* (1991). More specialized works include Edmund and Helen Morgan, *The Stamp Act Crisis* (1953), Benjamin Labaree, *The Boston Tea Party* (1964), Hiller Zobel, *The Boston Massacre* (1970), and David Ammerman's *In Common Cause: The American Response to the Coercive Acts of 1774* (1974). David Hackett Fischer's *Paul Revere's Ride* (1994) examines the outbreak of hostilities at Lexington and Concord.

See also Robert Gross, *The Minute Men and Their World*

(1976), Benjamin Quarles, *The Negro in the American Revolution* (1961), Philip Foner, *Blacks in the American Revolution* (1976), Ira Gruber, *The Howe Brothers and the American Revolution* (1972), Charles Royster, *A Revolutionary People at War* (1979), J. A. Henretta, *The Evolution of American Society* (1973), Michael Kammen, *Empire and Interest* (1974), Francis Jennings, *Empire of Fortune* (1988), Edward Countryman, *The American Revolution* (1985), and A. F. Young, ed., *The American Revolution* (1976).

On the Declaration of Independence see Pauline Maier's *American Scripture: Making the Declaration of Independence* (1997) and Gary Wills's *Inventing America: Jefferson's Declaration of Independence* (1978). Other studies include Marc Egnal, *A Mighty Empire: The Origins of the Revolution* (1988), Philip Lason, *George Grenville: A Political Life* (1984), John Phillip Reid, *Constitutional History of the American Revolution: The Authority of Rights* (1986), Peter D. G. Thomas, *The Townshend Duties Crisis: The Second Phase of the American Revolution, 1767–1773* (1987), Richard Bushman, *King and People in Provincial Massachusetts* (1985), Jerrilyn Greene Marston, *King and Congress: The Transfer of Political Legitimacy, 1774–1776* (1987), Fred Anderson, *A People's Army: Massachusetts Soldiers and Society in the Seven Years' War* (1984), Bernard Bailyn and Philip D. Morgan, eds., *Strangers Within the Realm: Cultural Margins of the First British Empire* (1991).

Why Did the Americans Rebel?

Bernard Bailyn

The primary goal of the American Revolution was not the overthrow or even the alteration of the existing social order but the preservation of political liberty, threatened by the apparent corruption of the [British] constitution. . . .

The colonists believed that they saw emerging from the welter of events during the decade after the Stamp Act a pattern whose meaning was unmistakable. They saw in the measures taken by the British government and in actions of officials in the colonies something for which their peculiar inheritance of thought had prepared them only too well, something they had long conceived to be a possibility in view of the known tendencies of history and of the present state of affairs in England. They saw about them, with increasing clarity, not merely mistaken, or even evil, policies violating the principles upon which freedom rested, but what appeared to be evidence of nothing less than a deliberate assault launched surreptitiously by players against liberty both in England and in America. The danger to America, it was believed, was in fact only the small, immediately visible part of the greater whole whose ultimate manifestation would be the destruction of the English constitution, with all the rights and privileges embedded in it.

This belief transformed the meaning of the colonists' struggle, and it added an inner accelerator to the movement of opposition. For once assumed, it could not be easily dispelled: denial only confirmed it, since what conspirators profess is not what they believe; the ostensible is not the real; and the real is deliberately malign.

It was this—the overwhelming evidence, as they saw it, that they were faced with conspirators against liberty determined at all costs to gain ends which their words dissembled—that was signaled to the colonies after 1763, and it was this above all else that in the end propelled them into Revolution.

It was an elevating, transforming vision: a new, fresh, vigorous, and above all morally regenerate people rising from obscurity to defend the battlements of liberty and then in triumph standing forth, heartening and sustaining the cause of freedom everywhere. In the light of such a conception everything about the colonies and their controversy with the mother country took on a new appearance. Provincialism was gone: Americans stood side by side with the heroes of historic battles for freedom and with the few remaining champions of liberty in the present. What were once felt to be defects—isolation, institutional simplicity, primitiveness of manners, multiplicity of religions, weakness in the authority of the state—could now be seen as virtues, not only by Americans themselves but by enlightened spokesmen of reform, renewal, and hope wherever they might be—in London coffeehouses, in Parisian *salons,* in the courts of German princes. The mere existence of the colonists suddenly became philosophy teaching by example.

Bernard Bailyn, *The Ideological Origins of the American Revolution* (Cambridge: Harvard University Press, 1967).

Gary B. Nash

Recent studies of the American Revolution have relied heavily on the role of ideas to explain the advent of the American rebellion against England. The gist of the ideological interpretation of the Revolution is that colonists, inheriting a tradition of protest against arbitrary rule, became convinced in the years after 1763 that the English government meant to impose in America "not merely misgovernment and not merely insensitivity to the reality of life in the British overseas provinces but a deliberate design to destroy the constitutional safeguards of liberty, which only concerted resistance—violent resistance if necessary—could effectively oppose." It was this conspiracy against liberty that "above all else . . . propelled [the colonists] into Revolution."

An important corollary to this argument, which stresses the colonial defense of constitutional rights and liberties, is the notion that the material conditions of life in America were so generally favorable that social and economic factors deserve little consideration as a part of the impetus to revolution. "The outbreak of the Revolution," writes Bernard Bailyn, a leading proponent of the ideological school, "was not the result of social discontent, or of economic disturbances, or of rising misery, or of those mysterious social strains that seem to beguile the imaginations of historians straining to find peculiar predispositions to upheaval." Nor, asserts Bailyn, was there a "transformation of mob behavior or of the lives of the 'inarticulate' in the pre-Revolutionary years that accounts for the disruption of Anglo-American politics."

I do not suggest that we replace an ideological construction with a mechanistic economic interpretation, but argue that a popular ideology, affected by rapidly changing economic conditions in American cities, dynamically interacted with the more abstract Whig ideology borrowed from England. These two ideologies had their primary appeal within different parts of the social structure, were derived from different sensibilities concerning social equity, and thus had somewhat different goals. The Whig ideology, about which we know a great deal through recent studies, was drawn from English sources, had its main appeal within upper levels of colonial society, was limited to a defense of constitutional rights and political liberties, and had little to say about changing social and economic conditions in America or the need for change in the future. The popular ideology, about which we know very little, also had deep roots in English culture, but it resonated most strongly within the middle and lower strata of society and went far beyond constitutional rights to a discussion of the proper distribution of wealth and power in the social system. It was this popular ideology that undergirded the politicization of the artisan and laboring classes in the cities and justified the dynamic role they assumed in the urban political process in the closing decades of the colonial period. . . .

The most generally recognized alteration in eighteenth-century urban social structures is the long-range trend toward a less even distribution of wealth. Tax lists for Boston, Philadelphia, and New York, ranging over nearly a century prior to the Revolution, make this clear. By the early 1770s the top 5 percent of Boston's taxpayers controlled 49 percent of the taxable assets of the community, whereas they had held only 30 percent in 1687. In Philadelphia the top twentieth increased its share of wealth from 33 to 55 percent between 1693 and 1774. . . .

Though city dwellers from the middle and lower ranks could not measure this redistribution of economic resources with statistical precision, they could readily discern the general trend. No one could doubt that upper-class merchants were amassing fortunes, when four wheeled coaches, manned by liveried Negro slaves, appeared in Boston's crooked streets, or when urban mansions, lavishly furnished in imitation of the English aristocracy, rose in Philadelphia and New York. Colonial probate records reveal that personal estates of £5000 sterling were rare in the northern cities before 1730, but by 1750 the wealthiest town dwellers were frequently leaving assets of £20,000 sterling, exclusive of real estate, and sometimes fortunes of more than £50,000 sterling—equivalent in purchasing power to about 2.5 million dollars today. Wealth of this magnitude was not disguised in cities with populations ranging from about 16,000 in Boston to about 25,000 in New York and Philadelphia. . . .

In the third quarter of the eighteenth century poverty struck even harder at Boston's population and then blighted the lives of the New York and Philadelphia laboring classes to a degree unparalleled in the first half of the century. . . . The data on poor relief leave little room for doubt that the third quarter of the eighteenth century was an era of severe economic and social dislocation in the cities, and that by the end of the colonial period a large number of urban dwellers were without property, without opportunity, and, except for public aid, without the means of obtaining the necessities of life.

Reprinted from "Social Change and the Growth of Prerevolutionary Urban Radicalism" by Gary B. Nash, in *The American Revolution: Explorations in the History of American Radicalism,* edited by Alfred F. Young. Copyright © 1976 by Northern Illinois University Press. Used by permission of the publisher.

Josiah Wedgwood (1730–1795), manufacturer of English ceramics, designed this medallion as an antislavery symbol. It appeared on the title page of the 1814 edition of Equiano's *Narrative* and remained the symbol for the abolition movement through the American Civil War. *(Courtesy, Smithsonian Institution)*

146

Revolution and Independence 1776–1787

LIBERTY AND SLAVERY

To those slaves who heard it, the rhetoric of liberty and equality that accompanied the American Revolution must have sounded hollow. What would African slaves have made of Patrick Henry's "Give me liberty, or give me death" or Thomas Jefferson's "All men are created equal"?

Slaves did not write letters to one another or set down their thoughts in diaries, but their actions give ample proof that the extreme irony of the patriot cause was not lost upon them. In 1765 slaves in Charleston, South Carolina, frightened whites by parading and shouting "liberty" in imitation of a recent patriot demonstration against the Stamp Act. In 1773 some slaves in Boston petitioned for their freedom. In 1774 in Georgia's St. Andrew Parish, a small band of slaves conspired to rebel and killed or wounded several whites before being apprehended.

The irony of cries for "liberty" in colonies that held some 500,000 individuals in bondage was not lost upon the British, who seriously debated offering freedom to slaves as a way to retaliate against colonial rebels. News of an emancipation proposal in the British House of Commons reached the colonies in January 1775. The proposal did not carry, but the news of it did—to both slaves and slaveholders. In April 1775 a group of Virginia slaves offered to join that colony's loyalist governor, John Murray, Earl of Dun-

continued

HISTORICAL EVENTS

1775
• First antislavery society formed
• Committee on Indian Affairs established

1776
British send fleet to New York
• Independence is declared
• Continental Congress sends Franklin to France to negotiate alliance

1777
British capture Fort Ticonderoga
• Battle of Saratoga • Articles of Confederation adopted

1778
Franco-American alliance

1779
War at stalemate

1780
Benedict Arnold commits treason
• "Tarleton's Quarter"
• Pennsylvania passes gradual emancipation law

HISTORICAL EVENTS

1781
Cornwallis surrenders at Yorktown
• Articles of Confederation ratified
• paper currency crisis

1783
Treaty of Paris • Massachusetts
abolishes slavery • British West Indies
closed to most American commerce

1784
Treaty of Fort Stanwix

1785
Land Ordinance
(Northwest Territory)

1786
Statute of Religious Freedom
(Virginia)

1787
Constitutional Convention
• Northwest Ordinance

1795
Treaty of Greenville

more, in opposing local patriots. On that occasion he refused their offer and told them to "go about their business." A few months later he had second thoughts.

In November 1775 Lord Dunmore issued a proclamation promising freedom to all "indented servants, Negroes, and others . . . that are able and willing to bear arms," if they would desert their patriot masters and ally themselves with the British cause. By December Governor Dunmore had a regiment of about three hundred slave soldiers in uniforms that bore the slogan "Liberty to Slaves." Other slaves served the British as crewmen and pilots for the many small vessels that plied coastal waters. Slaves also conducted raids on plantations and farms along that coast, taking livestock and other provisions for use aboard British ships.

To American slaves Paul Revere's famous warning, "The British are coming!" carried a far different meaning. In Charleston, many slaves left their masters' households and fled to an island in Charleston Harbor to await the arrival of British ships. Sullivan's Island was not much frequented, since it was the site of the pest house, where diseased passengers off ships from the Caribbean and Africa were quarantined. Now it was a hopeful place, as more and more fugitives stealthily rowed their way to its beaches. In those chill December days, as they camped on the island, the runaways were heartened by the support of South Carolina's loyalist governor.

On December 7, 1775, the South Carolina Council of Safety ordered one of its officers to send two hundred men "this ensuing night" to "apprehend a number of negroes, who are said to have deserted to the enemy." An ominous postscript to this order, added that "The pest house is to be burned, and *every kind of live stock to be driven off or destroyed*." Within the next few days some of the Sullivan's Island blacks found safety aboard the British man-of-war *Scorpion* and other British vessels. Other slaves, assigned to work details in Charleston Harbor, refused to obey their masters, in open defiance of white authority. Finally, before daylight on the morning of December 18, a force of about fifty "patriots" referred to in a report as "Indian Rangers" attacked Sullivan's Island, burned a house, captured four blacks, and killed many others.

Henry Laurens, slave holder, fervent patriot, later president of the Continental Congress, wrote: "It is an awful business notwithstanding it has the sanction of Law, to put even fugitive & Rebellious Slaves to death." But Laurens blamed the British for the deaths, and justified the patriot actions as necessary for "the American Cause" and "the happiness of ages unborn."

The slaves who died at the hands of colonial patriots give a new poignant meaning to Henry's "Give me liberty or give me death." What happened there, moreover, confounds simple explanations of racial, ethnic, and political divisions in the colonies: Americans killing slaves, white soldiers behaving like Indians, British embracing slaves: In the words of a contemporary song, the American Revolution did indeed bring about a "World turned upside down."

The Armies

The King's and Patriot Armies

A soldier of the Revolution who overheard talk in the ranks of the King's troops might have caught the sound of various accents from the British Isles, or American accents, for there were several loyalist regiments among the Crown troops. And it is likely that he would have heard German. In the eighteenth century a nation might rent whole military units from such rulers as were willing to go into the business, and in the course of the war the British rented nearly 30,000 troops from German princes, including the Hessians from the principality of Hesse-Cassel. The regular British army also contained many Germans recruited by contractors. The patriot army, like the troops who were to fight for the Union in the Civil War nearly a century later, was itself a little congress of nations and ethnic groups, as were the colonies themselves. New Englanders, descendants of German and Scotch-Irish immigrants, and southerners of varied ancestry in the British Isles were prominent. The Continental army, like the loyalist forces in Virginia, contained black recruits. About 5,000 blacks, including many freemen from the New England states, fought for American independence.

In Virginia, South Carolina, and Georgia many slaves sided with the British, who promised them freedom. In the course of the war there were deserters from the patriot forces to the King's troops, and from the King's to the patriot, which added to the diversity in both armies.

In the American navy, which preyed on British commerce, the *Bonhomme Richard* can exemplify the diversity of the ethnic and national strains that could collect under a single flag. This ship, the conqueror in 1779 of the British warship *Serapis*, had been supplied by France. It was under the command of John Paul Jones, a Scotsman who had come to America not long before the war. Only a minority on board the *Bonhomme Richard* were clearly definable by residence as American. By their side were seamen from Scotland and Ireland, Scandinavia, Portugal, and France.

The patriot forces contained both local militias and Continental army troops. Congress had no power to conscript troops, and so it had to assign quotas to the states for the Continental army and let each state decide how to fill them. Congress, also lacking the authority to tax, even had to requisition money from the states and hope that they would fulfill their obligations. More effective, perhaps, were the bounties that states offered, which later in the war were supplemented with a draft. A state, in turn, might impose quotas on towns, and they could pay men to enlist. States also raised their own militias, in which discipline was likely to be light. After Washington took command outside Boston, he induced about 10,000 militiamen to join the Continental army. The army of the

A British sentry in full regalia; the colonists wore simpler uniforms or their ordinary clothes.
(Courtesy, The New York Public Library, Astor, Lenox and Tilden Foundations)

Midshipman Augustus Brine,
**1782. The American painter, John
Singleton Copley, painted this
young British seaman.** *(Courtesy,
The Metropolitan Museum of Art)*

Revolution was a foreshadowing of something more modern than the
King's troops: it represented the beginnings of a citizens' army, like
those that have fought in the major wars since the French Revolution.
And like citizens' armies since then, it had to find ways of dealing with
the reluctance of citizens to join.

**The Rebel
Way of
Fighting**

As the patriot troops differed from the Crown forces
in their recruitment, they differed at least somewhat
in methods of fighting. At the beginning of the war
outside Boston, soldiers had been electing their own
officers, and it was some time before the practice was ended. The
Continental army had to instill discipline, which was difficult among
soldiers with no thought of becoming long-term military professionals.
In 1778 Washington put the Baron von Steuben, a former captain in the
Prussian army, in charge of training the troops. He made an army out of
the ragtag Continentals, commanded a division, and became an American citizen after the war. These forces did not remain consistent or
predictable in size. Citizen soldiers, committed more to their families

*General Nathanael Greene remarked of
the militiamen:*

"They are naturally brave and spirited, as the peasantry of any country,
but you cannot expect veterans of a raw
militia from only a few months' service."

and their crops than to army life, might decide to go home to plow, returning to the army if and when they felt like it.

Soldiers so averse to military discipline and the formalities of eighteenth-century battle not unexpectedly became known for fighting as individuals, firing from behind cover rather than in ranks, and taking aim. Some Americans were expert marksmen and used the Pennsylvania rifle, which was more accurate at longer distances than the smooth-bore musket. The colonists' method of fighting from cover had come from fighting the Indians, who also fought as individuals and had never read a military manual. These tactics infuriated the British, who thought the colonists unprofessional or cowardly. But as rifle fire became more deadly, supplemented by explosives, barbed wire, air bombardment, and the increasingly sophisticated weaponry of recent times, the eighteenth-century American practice of firing from cover along with a reliance on the skills of individual soldiers would become standards of warfare. Like the American Civil War of the 1860s, the American Revolution fore-shadowed the course of military practice.

The picture that comes down to us of the American always crouched behind a stone fence and picking off soldiers in the bewildered British ranks may owe much to the Massachusetts farmers at Lexington and Concord. During much of the war, Americans fought on the open field, managing as much of conventional warfare as training could teach them and their inclinations allowed. And in the course of the fighting, the Continental army developed a pride in itself as a seasoned and knowledgeable fighting force. If few of its troops wanted to become permanent professionals, if most of them like citizen soldiers in later wars wanted a quick return to their homes, they were nonetheless more than farmers or artisans who had picked up a gun for a scrap or two with the British. They were now real soldiers of a trained and national army. That meant that they were a major embodiment of the new nation itself.

Women and the Military   The women who accompanied the army in diverse capacities also contributed to its being a people's army, an incorporation of American society. Only officers were provided with quarters that could accommodate their wives, but other women accompanied the army as laundresses, nurses, cooks, provisioners, and camp-followers. Wives might also accompany husbands to the actual field of battle and assist them by such tasks as fetching the water required to keep the cannon functioning. It is not certain that the legendary Molly Pitcher actually existed, but many women did what has been attributed to her: they not only brought their husbands water for the cannon, but then also took over firing it themselves after their husbands had been wounded. Some women disguised themselves as men and fought undetected for long periods. Others capitalized on their femininity to serve successfully as spies and messengers.

Many American women who did not participate in battle or accompany the armies also provided important services that today would be the responsibility of the military authorities. They provided lodging for officers or allowed their homes to be turned into prisons and hospitals, and a vast network of women emerged to make shirts and knit stockings

A Connecticut man would remember:

"I was att my house in bed, between Brake of Day and Sunrise. I hard the Signel of an-larm by the fireing of thre Cannon . . . I turn'd Out and ask'd my wife to git Brakefast as soon as possabel for I must go off. I went Down on the hill . . . Whare the fleet was in fare Site in a line acrost the haber. There was 15 Sale of Ships an other Square rig'd Vesels, besides other Vesels. I came home. My brakefast was redy. After Brakefast . . . My hors Being redy I Slung my Musket & Cartrig Box and mounted with my littel Black Boy to bring the hors Back . . . After I got Under Way my wife Called to me prety loud. I Stopt my hors and ask'd her What She wanted. Her answer was Not to let me hear that you are Shot in the Back."

A lament of one girl a soldier left behind is said to date from the American Revolution.

Here I sit on Buttermilk Hill,
Who could blame me cry me fill?
And every tear would turn a mill;
Johnny has gone for a soldier.

I'd sell my clock, I'd sell my reel,
Likewise I'd sell my spinning wheel
To buy my love a sword of steel;
Johnny has gone for a soldier.

Some women raised money for Washington's army.

Philadelphia, July 4th, 1780
Sir,

The subscription set on foot by the ladies of this City for the use of the soldiery is 200,580 dollars, and £625 6s.8d. in specie, which makes in the whole in paper money 300,634 dollars.

The ladies are anxious for the soldiers to receive the benefit of it, and wait your directions how it can best be disposed of. We expect some considerable additions from the country and have also wrote to the other States in hopes the ladies there will adopt similar plans, to render it more general and beneficial. . . .

E. Reed

for the soldiers. Nothing better illustrates the impact of the war on American society than the extensive participation of women. The war effort fully mobilized the nation.

The King's Way of Fighting The British were not scrupulous in their methods of recruitment. British prisons yielded some recruits for the army, and strict enforcement of the vagrancy laws helped, for enlistment was a way to avoid prison. But harsh British military discipline turned the recruits into a fighting machine that operated according to a set of prescribed rules for battle. Officers would march the troops as close to the enemy as possible. The soldiers, placed in several parallel ranks, one behind the other, would fire in unison, not taking careful aim, for the troops on the other side were also closely packed. The troops might thereupon have time to reload and fire at will, as the British had done on the Plains of Abraham against the French defending Quebec. But reloading was a lengthy process, and in place of a second volley the soldiers might charge with bayonets, which in the eighteenth century were a major weapon. What a European army needed from the bulk of its troops, then, was not literacy, technical or administrative skills, or initiative in the performance of a job. Required instead was the ability to go through the formal operations of an eighteenth-century manual of arms: to stand or kneel in rank and not break under fire, to shoot or to charge at the proper time. The disposition of troops in a battle, one rank behind another, had as one of its objects to prevent the front ranks from fleeing. European discipline produced an army that could endure much enemy fire without breaking. But under sufficiently heavy fire, the best of soldiers could break.

The Fortunes of War

The Critical Battles, 1776–1778 Against the rebels Britain massed an overwhelming force. Only days after Congress proclaimed independence in July 1776 a huge British fleet—a "forest of masts"—sailed into New York harbor: 32,000 soldiers with 11,000 sailors manning thirty major ships of the line and dozens of transports. The commanders, General William Howe and his brother Admiral Richard Howe, aimed at establishing a principal base in New York, isolating New England from the other states, and providing easy communication with Canada. One British force would descend from Canada by way of Lake Champlain and the Hudson River; the main force would strike New York City from the sea. The British fleet's blockade of the coastline was intended to deprive the Americans of both income and supplies from trade. The Howe brothers had brought with them instructions from Lord North to put out offers of peace. The "revolting colonies," said the prime minister, "cannot last long." But he was mistaken, and the peace overtures were ignored.

The Howes' upstate campaign was never effective. The brilliant tactics of Benedict Arnold in his courageous stand against a superior enemy fleet on Lake Champlain delayed a British thrust southward for

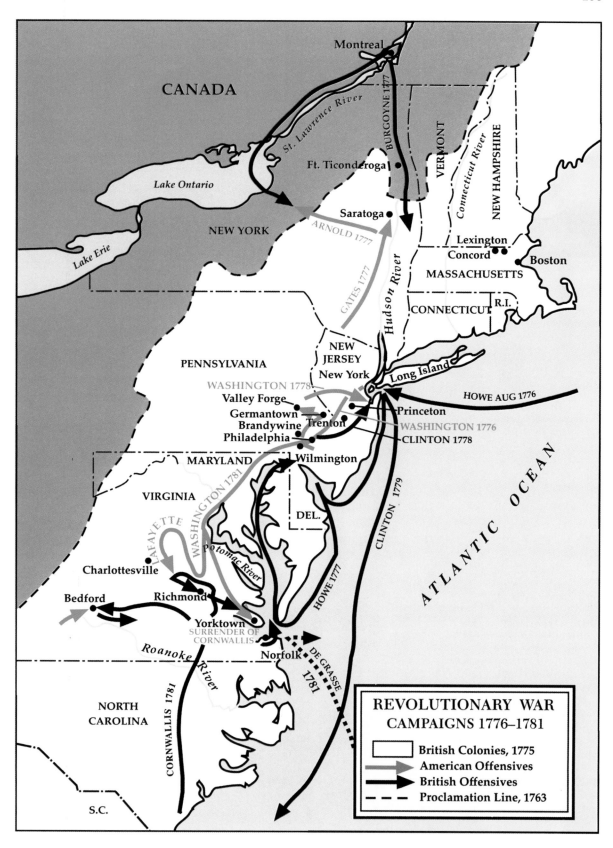

Montreal

CANADA

St. Lawrence River

BURGOYNE 1777

Lake Ontario

Ft. Ticonderoga

VERMONT

NEW HAMPSHIRE

Connecticut River

NEW YORK

Saratoga

ARNOLD 1777

Lexington
Concord

Boston

Lake Erie

GATES 1777

Hudson River

MASSACHUSETTS

CONNECTICUT

R.I.

PENNSYLVANIA

NEW JERSEY

New York

Long Island

WASHINGTON 1778

Valley Forge

HOWE AUG 1776

Germantown

Brandywine

Philadelphia

Trenton

Princeton

WASHINGTON 1776

CLINTON 1778

Wilmington

MARYLAND

WASHINGTON 1781

VIRGINIA

DEL.

CLINTON 1779

ATLANTIC OCEAN

LAFAYETTE

Charlottesville

Potomac River

Bedford

Richmond

HOWE 1777

Yorktown
SURRENDER OF
CORNWALLIS

Norfolk

DE GRASSE 1781

Roanoke River

NORTH
CAROLINA

CORNWALLIS 1781

S.C.

REVOLUTIONARY WAR
CAMPAIGNS 1776–1781

British Colonies, 1775
American Offensives
British Offensives
Proclamation Line, 1763

The Marquis de Lafayette wounded at the Battle of Brandywine Creek. *(Courtesy, Emmet Collection, New York Public Library)*

One of Washington's soldiers was to recall that the crossing of the Delaware River took place on

"as severe a night as I ever saw—the frost was sharp, the current difficult to stem, the ice increasing, the wind high and at eleven it began to snow."

Washington Crossing the Delaware, by Emanuel Leutze. On Christmas night, 1776, General George Washington led his troops across the icy Delaware River, a maneuver that surprised the Hessian troops at Trenton and led to a much-needed American victory. This romantic mid-nineteenth-century painting is, however, filled with historical inaccuracies and unlikely poses: The crossing took place at night; Washington was not standing; the flag shown was not yet in use; and so on. *(Courtesy, The Metropolitan Museum of Art)*

a year. The British strike against New York City, on the other hand, was child's play. Washington unwisely divided his makeshift army, sending about half of his troops to Long Island while the rest stayed on Manhattan. English ships slipped around both islands to block retreat, while Howe's soldiers attacked Brooklyn Heights, inflicting heavy losses. Realizing his mistake, Washington skillfully eluded the blockade, retreating across both islands into New Jersey. It was, Washington lamented, a "disgraceful and dastardly" flight. With the retreating army, now demoralized and in disarray, was volunteer aide-de-camp Thomas Paine, who had written in a widely-distributed pamphlet, "These are the times that try men's souls. The summer soldier and the sunshine patriot will, in this crisis, shrink from the service of his country; but he that stands by it now, deserves the love and thanks of man and woman."

Wishing to negotiate with the revolutionaries, not destroy them, Howe pursued them only as far as the Delaware River. Washington used this pause to regroup his armies, and on Christmas night of 1776 returned to the attack. After a daring military maneuver across the icy Delaware River, his army pounced on a camp of Hessian mercenaries at an outpost in Trenton, New Jersey. The Hessians, who had gone to bed drunk and confident that no army would attack on such a hallowed occasion, were quickly overwhelmed. Nearly 1,000 were captured. A week later Washington struck again, outmaneuvering a British force at Princeton and driving the enemy back to the Hudson before both armies went into hibernation. Washington took up winter quarters in the hills of western New Jersey; Howe diverted himself in New York "in feasting, banquetting, and in the arms of Mrs. Loving. . . ." He had fumbled a chance to end the war quickly.

In 1777 Britain's army renewed its efforts to occupy major coastal cities and isolate New England. In July General Howe embarked from New York with 15,000 men, sailed around to land at the head of Chesapeake Bay, and began fighting his way toward Philadelphia. Washington and his troops scurried overland to meet the British at Brandywine Creek, but could not turn them back and made an orderly retreat. By September 26 Washington had lost a fifth of his total force

and Howe had occupied Philadelphia, forcing Congress to flee to the Pennsylvania interior. On October 4, at the Battle of Germantown, Washington executed a series of intricate maneuvers that placed him in a position to destroy Howe's main encampment, but the American troops became lost in a heavy fog and at one point even fired on one another. Only General Nathanael Greene's skill prevented complete disorder. Humiliated, Washington's ill-clothed and underfed remnant of an army was forced to spend the winter near Valley Forge, Pennsylvania, one of the few iron foundries still in patriot hands.

Saratoga   Colonial leaders had long worried that the British might become "masters of the Hudson River," which would "divide our strength, and enfeeble every effort for our common preservation and security."

The campaign began with a signal British victory by General Burgoyne on July 6, 1777, the capture of Fort Ticonderoga, essential to the lake route to Albany. But then Burgoyne immediately blundered. Deciding that he now had ample time to move his army a mere seventy miles to Albany, he set out through the woods rather than follow Lake George. Hauling fifty-two cannon, his enormous wardrobe, his ample wine cellar, and a female entourage along a route obstructed by hundreds of trees that the Americans had felled, Burgoyne covered only twenty-three miles in twenty-four days. Meanwhile, at Oriskany and Fort Stanwix in the Mohawk Valley, in tough hand-to-hand fighting, the Americans soundly defeated the British army advancing from the west. Then the murder and scalping of a young New York woman, Jane McCrea, by Burgoyne's Indian allies sent the citizens of the upper Hudson Valley into a fury at the British, who had been paying Indians for the scalps of revolutionists.

Short of troops, hungry for supplies, and facing a large and capable Continental army well supported by local militia, Burgoyne was now in serious trouble. Crossing the Hudson he stood at Saratoga, New York, facing General Horatio Gates's army, which held a commanding position behind powerful fortifications built at the direction of a Polish engineer, Tadeusz Kósciuszko. On September 19, Burgoyne threw his troops into action against Gates at Freeman's Farm. The battle sapped British strength while Gates easily reinforced his army. With supplies running low, Burgoyne had to decide whether to fight again or retreat. He fought and on October 7, in the second battle of Saratoga, again suffered heavy losses. A popular topical verse said it all:

> Burgoyne, alas! unknowing future fates,
> Could force his way through woods,
> but not through GATES.

The French Alliance   As early as 1775, the Continental Congress had sent agents to France. Some, like Silas Deane and Arthur Lee, had arranged a trickle of loans and shipments of military supplies. The small Dutch island of St. Eustatius in the Caribbean served as a transit point: French ships unloaded munitions there, and patriots picked them up. Late in 1776, Congress sent Ben-

Private Joseph Martin wrote of eating nothing at Valley Forge for two days

"save half a small pumpkin, which I cooked by placing it upon a rock, the skin side uppermost, and making a fire upon it.... Had there fallen deep snows (and it was the time of year to expect them) or even heavy and long rainstorms, the whole army must inevitably have perished."

The Marquis de Lafayette, the Frenchman who had fought with Washington, observed that

"the unfortunate soldiers... had neither coats, nor hats, nor shirts, nor shoes; their feet and legs froze till they grew black, and it was often necessary to amputate them."

Franklin's unique combination of sophistication and homespun ways won him favor as a diplomat in Paris. *(Courtesy, Scribner's Archives)*

General Washington himself petitioned the Continental Congress in the fall of 1780 after he had been chided for inaction:

"Where are the Men—where are the Provisions—where are the Cloaths— the every thing necessary to warrant the attempt you propose, in an inclement Season? Our numbers, never equal to those of the enemy in new York—our state lines never half compleat in Men, but perfectly so in every species of want, were diminished in the Field so soon as the weather began to grow cold—near 2000 men, on account of Cloaths which I had not to give. . . . It would be well for the Troops if like Chameleons they cd. live upon air—or like the Bear suck their paws for sustenance during the rigour of the approaching season."

jamin Franklin to Paris to negotiate an alliance. But King Louis XVI hesitated. His government was nearly bankrupt; his Spanish allies feared that the example of the Revolution might encourage revolution among their own colonies; the armies of the United States appeared weak. It seemed enough to have the secret trade in military hardware supporting the patriot armies, accomplishing French objectives by tying Britain down in a protracted war. However much Franklin's republican wit and easy charm captivated courtiers at Versailles, diplomatic grace could not by itself gloss over hard realities. For two years, Franklin moved through France, winning many friends for the new nation and establishing his own formidable reputation. But for the moment the King avoided any overt alliance.

Nonetheless, France and Spain did see opportunities. King Louis yearned for revenge against an old enemy, while Spanish courtiers in Madrid feared the mushrooming British empire in the New World. After the Battle of Saratoga, opponents of the war in Britain persuaded Parliament to open peace negotiations, and by early spring 1778 a delegation under the Earl of Carlisle was on its way to the colonies with an offer of limited autonomy within the British empire. Fears that the Americans might accept such terms, along with the victory at Saratoga, finally prompted Louis XVI and his foreign minister to offer Congress a formal alliance. The patriots ratified the bargain on May 4, 1778, only weeks before the Carlisle commissioners arrived in Philadelphia. With the entry of France into the conflict, the American Revolution became a world war.

Dark and Drifting Times

By 1778, the United States could not find a winning strategy; neither could British generals defeat Washington's army or control the countryside. One major difficulty for the British was the sheer vastness of the country. The redcoats fought at the end of a 3,000-mile line of supply; slow-moving ships could not maintain large land armies. Americans, on the other hand, could attack like guerrillas and then easily escape across rivers into forests. Short of occupying the whole country—a physical impossibility—His Majesty's generals could find no way to strike some final blow that would crush the rebellion once and for all. Fighting to bring the rebels back into the empire, some of the British soldiers sympathized with the Americans' cause. As British strategy failed to divide the states or to quell the rebellion, Parliament grew increasingly restless with the war.

American strategy played upon British weakness. Unable to dislodge the redcoats from major seaport cities or confront their superior numbers in pitched battles, Washington adopted a policy of watchful waiting. Patriot forces sometimes conducted guerrilla warfare against isolated British units or their supply columns. Washington hoped to wear down the resolve of the British to continue the war or to force them into a situation in which he could make a decisive strike.

Washington needed time, and yet the new nation found even this passive strategy difficult to execute. Most men shunned enlistment in the Continental army, especially as patriotic fervor subsided after 1776.

Farming required the most work in spring and early fall, precisely those times most favorable for battle. The sense of a common nationhood was as yet half-formed, and state governors maintained tight control over their local militias, sometimes not letting them leave the state. Many Americans, fearful of military authority and centralized power, refused to pay taxes to support Washington's troops, and so the regular army lacked not only soldiers but also adequate arms and equipment. Unable to levy taxes, the Continental Congress printed millions of paper dollars popularly called "continentals." This flood of currency drove up prices mercilessly. After the French alliance Congress, hoping that the French would help pay its bills, printed still more paper money. By 1780 few merchants or farmers would accept "continentals" in payment for supplies. Washington had to resort to impressment—forced sales on credit—to provision his troops.

Stalemate   By 1779 the war had reached a stalemate. Both sides reduced the scale and intensity of the fighting in North America as skirmishes there simply became part of an international war. Now forced to defend as well their possessions in India and the Caribbean, the British withdrew ships and men from America. France, benefiting from England's distress, was slow to aid the patriot forces. For a year after the unsuccessful battle of Monmouth, New Jersey, in June 1778, Washington's beleaguered army had mounted no major offensive.

Civilian morale sagged; unrest mounted in the army. In 1780 General Benedict Arnold, reprimanded for misuse of his powers while he was commander of colonial troops at Philadelphia, began treasonable negotiations with the British to turn over West Point. When his activities were discovered he fled to the British, who made him a brigadier general. Bonuses paid to new recruits outraged some Pennsylvania troops in Washington's army, and on New Year's Day 1781, they mutinied and marched off to seek redress from Congress. Only promises of quick relief persuaded them to return to camp. Three weeks later some New Jersey troops mutinied, and two soldiers were executed.

In the winter of 1778–79 the new British commander in chief in America, General Henry Clinton, lacking sufficient troops to pacify the North, had shifted British operations to the South, where he anticipated aid from the large loyalist population. Events there gave the patriot cause little reason for encouragement. The British took Savannah and Charleston and encouraged the loyalists to make war on their patriot neighbors. In these circumstances the war in the backcountry became uncharacteristically savage. At Waxhaws Creek, South Carolina, in May 1780, Colonel Banastre Tarleton's loyalist troops massacred a Virginia regiment that had surrendered. The term "Tarleton's Quarter" became a rallying cry among southern patriots.

One boost to American morale in these bleak years had been the unexpected naval victory of John Paul Jones's *Bonhomme Richard* over the British warship *Serapis* in September 1779. The story has it that when asked whether he wished to surrender at one point during the battle, the intrepid Jones replied, "I have not yet begun to fight."

Colonel Banastre Tarleton.
(Courtesy, Hugh Cleland Collection)

According to an eyewitness to the Waxhaws Creek massacre:

"Not a man was spared . . . and for fifteen minutes after every man was prostrate [the Tories] went over the ground plunging their bayonets into everyone that exhibited any signs of life, and in some instances, where several had fallen one over the other, these monsters were seen to throw off on the point of the bayonet the uppermost, to come at those beneath."

"A successful cavalry charge exploited by a bayonet attack is bound to be messy," observes one scholar of Tarleton's Quarter.

An American at Yorktown wrote in his diary an account of the final days of the war:

17th.—Had the pleasure of seeing a drummer mount the enemy's parapet, and beat a parley, and immediately an officer, holding up a white handkerchief, made his appearance outside their works. . . . Our batteries ceased. An officer from our lines ran and met the other, and tied the handkerchief over his eyes. The British officer conducted to a house in rear of our lines. Firing ceased totally. . . .

19th.— . . . All is quiet. Articles of capitulation signed; detachments of French and Americans take possession of British forts. . . . I carried the standard of our regiment on this occasion. On entering the fort, Baron Steuben, who accompanied us, took the standard from me and planted it himself. The British army parade and march out with their colors furled; drums beat as if they did not care how. Grounded their arms and returned to town. Much confusion and riot among the British through the day; many of the soldiers were intoxicated . . . our patrols kept busy.

As the British formally surrendered at Yorktown, the band played, among other tunes, the British nursery rhyme "The World Turned Upside Down":

If buttercups buzzed
after the bee;
If boats were on land,
churches on sea;
If ponies rode men,
and grass ate the cow;
If cats should be chased,
into holes by the mouse;
If mammas sold their babies,
to gypsies for half a crown;
If summer were spring
and the other way round;
Then all the world would be
  upside down.

Victory   Then, in the summer of 1781, the war turned in favor of the rebels. Congress centralized the administrative departments and enacted a new financial program under the direction of Robert Morris. Supplies were soon flowing to the army again. Meanwhile French money and manpower finally began to arrive in significant amounts. And on the military front Washington in August 1781 received word that a French fleet was en route to Chesapeake Bay. Washington at last had a chance to strike.

In the Carolinas, harassed by guerrillas and "tired out marching about the country in quest of adventures," General Charles Cornwallis marched his army north toward Virginia for the purpose of cutting rebel communications between North and South. Counting on protection and supplies from the seemingly invincible Royal Navy, he violated one of the cardinal rules of warfare: never let your forces be backed up to terrain where retreat is impossible. In August 1781 Cornwallis made the fatal blunder: he moved his army onto a narrow peninsula between the York and James rivers near Yorktown and encamped there. Soon the French navy was at his back and a combined force of 9,000 Americans and 7,800 French began to besiege him by land. Hopelessly trapped, he surrendered his whole army on October 19, 1781.

Diplomacy and Independence

The defeat at Yorktown was by no means a complete military disaster for the British, since they still held America's major seaports. What Yorktown did accomplish was to dramatize how slender were the possibilities for eventual British victory against the combination of American armies and guerrillas and French power. Another vital consideration was that an end to the fighting in North America would free badly needed fleets and armies to fight against England's enemies in the West Indies and India. Early in 1782, Parliament forced Prime Minister North out of office and demanded negotiations with the United States. Although George III disagreed, many of his subjects thought that a generous peace might conciliate the former colonists, and even draw them back into the British orbit.

The Peacemaking   The Americans, too, were ready to end the war. In the Continental Congress one overworked member complained that "the little leisure we have is not sufficient for the common functions of life & exercise to keep us in health." The Continental Congress was near collapse, and local loyalties and interests were continuing to strain against the national purpose. In Congress, planters worried about "getting home to their plantations at a season in which planters in general have so very much to attend to." One lawyer complained, "I have lost my Clients the benefit of a Circuit and now despair of doing any thing the ensuing Term." Said another, "This trade of patriotism but ill agrees with the profession of a practising Lawyer." One member, however, enjoyed "the company of a number of very fine ladies." Another could talk of nothing but his speculation in western land.

The victory at Yorktown, however welcome, was more lucky circumstance than a triumph of superior military power or skill. Chances for a large territorial settlement and the prospect of better relations with Britain, a dangerous adversary for any nation so exposed to attack from the sea, understandably attracted many Americans. In fact, the Congress authorized its negotiating team, headed by Benjamin Franklin, to accept almost any treaty that included independence and a withdrawal of British troops. With their mutual interests so aligned, the two enemies seemed likely to conclude a quick agreement.

Yet negotiations in Paris dragged on for nearly two years. The Franco-American alliance of 1778 bound the United States not to make a separate peace. In turn, Louis XVI and his minister Vergennes, in order to gain Spanish support, had promised ministers in Madrid much British territory as booty, especially strategic Gibraltar. The Spanish, moreover, wanted to confine the United States to the area east of the Appalachian Mountains. Although the Spanish could expect few concessions from Great Britain, they might hold up indefinitely a settlement between Britain and the United States. America now had more to lose from its friends than from its enemies.

The Treaty of Paris   At last, Franklin broke the diplomatic deadlock by violating the terms of the alliance with France and opening separate negotiations with English agents. The French, themselves weakened by a long and costly conflict, were not much upset. Once started, talks progressed steadily. The series of treaties that ended the war, collectively known as the Treaty of Paris, was signed on September 3, 1783. England granted independence and promised to withdraw all its troops from the colonies. The new nation acquired a huge grant of land: from the Atlantic seacoast to the Mississippi River. Its boundaries in the north with Canada remained vague, and redcoats still occupied forts south of the Great Lakes. The Gulf Coast was ceded to Spain, although both Americans and Englishmen were guaranteed navigation rights on the Mississippi. Britain successfully demanded that "no unlawful impediment" block the collection of prewar debts Americans owed to British merchants. The treaties also pledged the United States to make restitution to loyalists who had suffered financially during the Revolution. British merchants did succeed in closing the Americans out of imperial commerce, a serious loss for the young nation. Despite these concessions and the lack of adequate enforcement procedures, the Americans had benefited handsomely from European rivalries. War and diplomacy created a new nation with boundaries generous enough to ensure future growth and prosperity.

The War at Home

Prosperity and Inflation   Eight years of warfare not only profited many individuals but also invigorated the whole economy. An immense amount of money in circulation raised the price of nearly everything. The Continental Congress and the state governments had spent on the war nearly $200 million in hard money, followed by many more millions in paper currency. British soldiers and

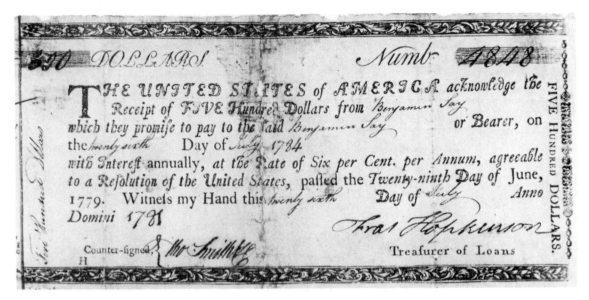

Bonds paying 6% per year were sold to finance the Revolution. The inflation rate was much higher.
(Courtesy, Chase Bank Collection of Moneys of the World, New York)

Head of a Negro, by John Singleton Copley. By 1780, some 500,000 slaves worked the lands of the South.
(Copyright © 1983, Founders Society, Detroit Institute of Art)

purchasing agents poured another $50 million into the economy. All this money created an extraordinary demand for commodities and, of course, persistent inflation resulted. Yet few Americans suffered economically. War stimulated production. The need for uniforms and arms, for example, produced rapid growth in the textile and iron industries. Merchants' inventories and farmers' crops grew in value. Bankers lent at high rates of interest to importers and privateers—goods brought through the British blockade commanded enormous profits. Many state and local governments imposed price and wage controls, a device used since the Middle Ages to control inflation. Congress regulated monopolies and prevented some exports of needed raw materials. More and more local economies were coming together into a broad national market. A nation was slowly unifying.

Despite occasionally rigorous efforts at regulation, the pressures of wartime inflation produced extensive black markets. Shopkeepers and small farmers preferred to deal with Englishmen and private citizens who spent silver and gold coin. An indignant Pennsylvanian angrily refused to sell his grain to one of Washington's agents, saying, "Your money's not worth a damn continental." The phrase caught on. Throughout most of the war, private citizens prospered while the government and army suffered penury and hardship. This paradox so angered Washington that he proposed hanging all profiteers.

Social Change   Major changes occurred in the pattern of land ownership. Probably a quarter of the population was loyal to the British Crown, either openly or secretly. By 1778 all thirteen states had confiscated the property of those who "took refuge with the British tyrant." Some 100,000 already had left the country, most for Canada or England, and their estates were sold for money to support the patriot cause. Much of the confiscated land was bought up by rich speculators or other large landowners, not by tenants and small farmers, who rarely had enough money to buy in places already settled. Instead, many of them and their children looked westward to the mountains and beyond. Even before the war ended, thousands had migrated, going into what were to be Tennessee and Kentucky, into northern New England and northern New York.

Religion   The Revolution also affected religion. Most states disestablished churches, ending the special privileges or civil functions of particular sects. Only Massachusetts and Connecticut still collected taxes to fund a state church; the other states viewed competing religions as equal in the eyes of the law. Tolerance did not extend to atheists, however, and most state legislatures established a religious test for holding public office. Blasphemy remained a crime punishable by imprisonment.

Documents like Thomas Jefferson's Statute of Religious Freedom in Virginia, finally enacted by the Virginia legislature in 1786, granted tolerance for the free practice of religion, not a guarantee of rights for nonbelievers. If narrow by twentieth-century standards, the statute was for its time a model, proclaiming to the rest of the world an example of the nation's new freedom.

Slaves   The Revolution also made for a rhetoric of liberty that stumbled against the reality of human bondage. "How is it," chided the crusty British writer Samuel Johnson, "that we hear the loudest yelps for liberty among the drivers of Negroes?" A group of blacks in Boston announced to the General Court that their race looked for "great things from men who have made such a noble stand against the designs of their *fellow-men* to enslave them." During the war over 5,000 blacks served in the American army and navy. Several states granted freedom to slaves who served in the military. Soon a voluble antislavery movement emerged. Philadelphia Quakers had formed the first antislavery society in 1775. In most northern states, slavery was not a large part of the economy, and patriot leaders struck decisively at the institution.

In 1780 the Pennsylvania legislature passed a gradual emancipation law freeing its slaves; and Massachusetts abolished slavery by court order in 1783. Connecticut and Rhode Island soon passed general abolition laws, and New York and New Jersey passed similar laws. In 1787 Congress passed the Northwest Ordinance, which prohibited slavery in the Ohio Valley, the region that would become Ohio, Indiana, Illinois, Michigan, and Wisconsin. After fierce debate in 1787 the Constitutional Convention permitted outlawing the importation of slaves after 1808. The American Revolution that brought freedom from England won, for northern African Americans, freedom from bondage.

Legal freedom did not mean equality. Most northern whites were racists, and they acted on their fears and convictions. In Ohio, Indiana, and Illinois white settlers from the South segregated free African Americans whenever possible, and black youths were often placed in long-term apprenticeships closely resembling slavery. African-American

In 1781 a Massachusetts judge declared:

"As to the doctrine of slavery and the right of Christians to hold Africans in perpetual servitude, and sell and treat them as we do our horses and cattle, nowhere is it expressly enacted or established. It has been a usage—a usage which took its origins from the practice of some of the European nations, and the regulations of British government respecting the then Colonies, for the benefit of trade and wealth. But whatever sentiments have formerly prevailed in this particular or slid in upon us by the example of others, a different idea has taken place with the people of America, more favorable to the natural rights of mankind, and to that natural, innate desire of Liberty, with which heaven (without regard to color, complexion, or shape of noses . . .) has inspired all the human race. And upon the ground our Constitution of Government, by which the people of this Commonwealth have solemnly bound themselves, sets out with declaring that all men are born free and equal—and that every subject is entitled to liberty and to have it guarded by the laws, as well as life and property—and in short is totally repugnant to the idea of being born slaves."

*The inscription on the Concord grave-
stone of John Jack, a slave who bought
his freedom in the 1760s and died in
1773, reads:*

God wills us free; man wills us slaves.
I will as God wills; God's will be done.
Here lies the body of
JOHN JACK
a native of Africa who died
March 1773 aged about 60 years
Tho' born in a land of slavery,
He was born free.
Tho' he lived in a land of liberty,
  he lived a slave. . . .

adults could not serve on juries or vote, and the immigration of blacks from other states was barred. Between 1807 and 1837 New Jersey, Connecticut, New York, Rhode Island, and Pennsylvania passed laws disfranchising African Americans. And throughout the North, black people were widely discriminated against in the job market.

Indians   Conscience sharpened by the libertarian rhetoric of the Revolution moved white Americans to make some efforts toward the elimination of slavery. Neither conscience nor the language of the Declaration bestowed noticeable benefits on the Indians. Relations between the Indians and the new republic took their character not from the sensibility of the eastern educated gentry, but from the land greed, the fears, and the prejudice of western settlers.

During the war both Britain and the United States vied for Indian support. In 1775 the Continental Congress formed a Committee on Indian Affairs, and commissioners went to different tribes either to win their support or to persuade them to remain neutral during the conflict. Most tribes, however, joined the English cause. During the French and Indian War they had sided with the French instead of the English and subsequently paid a price for their decision. It was to be no different this time. When the war ended in 1783, England recognized the independence of the United States but neglected to put any provisions into the treaty protecting their former Indian allies. Under the Articles of Confederation, the new central government was too weak to control Indian affairs effectively, especially since the states had supreme authority to handle policy within their boundaries. When the Confederation government passed the Northwest Ordinance of 1787, establishing steps by which an area could achieve statehood, it included a clause urging the fair and just treatment of the Indians. But again, land speculators and settlers, now resentful of the aid Indians had given to the British during the Revolution, continued to ignore Indian rights.

For a brief period after the American Revolution many colonists, having defeated the British, could treat as conquered peoples the Indian allies of the redcoats. The government dictated several treaties. In the Treaty of Fort Stanwix of 1784, for example, the Iroquois had to cede lands in western New York and Pennsylvania. During the last decades of the eighteenth century, the Iroquois living in the United States quickly degenerated as a nation, losing most of their remaining lands. Witnessing the destruction of the Iroquois Confederacy, tribes such as the Shawnees, Miamis, Delawares, Ottawas, Wyandots, and Potawatomis formed their own confederacy and informed the United States that the Ohio River was the boundary between their lands and those of the settlers. It was only a matter of time before further hostilities ensued.

By 1790 the tens of thousands of settlers living in Kentucky and the Ohio Valley demanded that the United States send expeditions against the Indians who were attacking their settlements. In 1790 and again in 1792, American expeditionary forces were defeated in their attempts to subdue the confederacy. Finally, in August 1794, General "Mad" Anthony Wayne defeated the confederacy at Fallen Timbers. The Indians signed the Treaty of Greenville in 1795, surrendering to the United

States most of present-day Ohio and Indiana. Settlers poured into the newly available western lands.

The American Revolution had much to offer the world by way of example. But for most Indians, the Revolution and its aftermath were an unmitigated disaster.

Women's Lives   The war also affected the lives, and perhaps the self-image, of women. Many had participated in the war effort, either at the front or on the home front. Many more had become accustomed to discussing politics and military news. Some few, like Mercy Otis Warren, who first wrote anti-British plays and then a history of the Revolution, engaged directly in propaganda. Others, like Abigail Adams, took over the management of farms and businesses about which they had previously known little. In this sense, the war years offered many women an education in independent action.

Few, if any, colonial women translated their revolutionary experience into a demand for political rights or equality with men. But many women must have emerged from those years with greatly increased confidence in their own abilities. Those who had worked together in the Ladies Association that organized a national fund drive to collect money for the American troops had also experienced the power and satisfaction of collective action. That experience would be multiplied in the many women's voluntary associations that emerged in the early nineteenth century.

By and large, women did not gain independence from the Revolution in the same sense that most free men gained it. During the final decades of the eighteenth century single, property-holding women were allowed to vote in New Jersey, but that state soon rescinded this limited suffrage. Few Americans of either gender seriously contemplated political rights for women. Certainly the Revolution did not noticeably improve married women's standing in law in general, or their right to hold property in particular. Yet in one respect the Revolution brought significant improvement in the status of women—the ideal of virtuous "republican motherhood." This suggested that women—republican mothers—deserved a special kind of independence and dignity within the domestic sphere. There they would contribute their special qualities of nurture to the raising of virtuous young republicans to ensure the future of the new nation.

No more in this respect than in any others did the slim advantages gained by free white women extend to black slave women, whose experience looked more like a grim caricature than like an extension of the sanctity and dignity of motherhood.

A version of the concept of republican motherhood was set forth in the commencement oration at Columbia College in 1795:

"Let us then figure to ourselves the accomplished woman, surrounded by a sprightly band, from the babe that imbibes the nutritive fluid, to the generous youth, just ripening into manhood, and the lovely virgin. . . . Let us contemplate the mother distributing the mental nourishment to the fond smiling circle . . . watching the gradual openings of their minds, and studying their various turns of temper. . . . the Genius of Liberty hovers triumphant over the glorious scene."

How Revolutionary?

Historians have argued about whether or not American society became more open, more fostering of upward mobility, during the Revolutionary era. Certainly some older marks of privilege did disappear. Since feudal times European law, seeking to keep intact the property of the upper classes, had enforced the principle of entail, that property could be passed on only within the same family, and the rule of primogeniture, that it could not be divided in inheritance but must go to the eldest son. Such rules had survived in some colonial laws, applying at least in cases in which a landowner had not provided otherwise in a will. These laws were now swept aside as relics of an age of artificial privilege and inequality. In addition, the emigration of thousands of loyalists left many local political offices vacant and created new opportunities.

Yet America remained firmly under the control of an elite that had never had a fixed membership. Revolutionary ardor hardly touched the traditional politics of deference south of Pennsylvania. There the local gentry kept control over tidewater society and government. In Philadelphia, New York, and Boston a coalition of lawyers, merchants, and landowners dominated the cities after the war, much as it had before. The rich held disproportionate power in the Continental Congress. Robert Morris, for example, a merchant and speculator who served in the early 1780s as the nation's chief treasury official, possessed a fortune of $8 million.

The American Revolution and its aftermath, then, presented no scenes of revolutionary crowds pitted against a besieged upper class. What happened instead was an application of the principle, pronounced in the Declaration of Independence, that governments derive "their just Powers from the consent of the governed." Under the new state constitutions drafted during the war, most legislatures welcomed representatives from backcountry areas; the middling ranks of society—small farmers, local businessmen, and artisans—came to occupy office in larger numbers; and bills of rights prefaced many constitutions. Everywhere governors lost power, and elected assemblies gained control of patronage and tax matters. Legislators stood for election each year. In Pennsylvania, a new constitution abolished altogether the legislature's upper house, traditionally the bastion of the wealthy. Pennsylvania's candidates for election were forbidden to give "meat, drink, money, or otherwise" as gifts to voters. New York experimented with the secret ballot instead of voice voting, claiming that the ballot "would tend more to preserve the liberty and equal freedom of the people."

Some less democratic practices lingered. In many states property ownership was still a requirement for voting; high political office might require the ownership of large amounts of land. Upper chambers of most state legislatures could block the demands of the majority, and in South Carolina, Virginia, and Georgia, unfairly apportioned assemblies mocked the popular will. In Georgia, for example, the piedmont—the inland region just east of the mountains—contained three-fourths of the population yet received only one-fourth of the seats in the assembly, which tidewater plantation owners still rigidly dominated. Nonetheless, in all the colonies government officials were elected, lower houses had most of the power, and state officials proved susceptible to public opinion. Many people never before interested in politics had discovered their voice. Individuals of every class now found themselves taking part in a democracy of public discussion and common action—a democratic activity more basic than the formal democracy of the vote.

"Hessian Soldier" andiron, one of a pair; cast iron, painted; late eighteenth century. *(Index of American Design)*

Dress, imported brocaded silk, made in Boston, about 1770. *(Index of American Design)*

Republicanism   The most radical implication of the American Revolution was a concept derived only in part from the Declaration of Independence and expressed only partially in the democratic reforms initiated by the states. This was the idea and creation of a republic.

Republicanism has much to do with liberty, but the meaning of the word should not be confused with popular notions of freedom. It does not mean the liberty to be private, to withdraw property and energies from uses that might serve the public good. That is a later corruption of what eighteenth-century philosophers were thinking. Liberty was perceived as the proud possession of republican citizens virtuous in habits, industrious, generous, quick to engage in public service. The word "republic" had to eighteenth-century revolutionists a noble ring. It recalled the austere city-states of Greece, the stern citizenry of Rome, the stately Roman senators. To be a citizen of a republic was to be an actor in a continuing history, a contributor to the common good. Yet liberty in the service of the public welfare does not mean surrender to the popular will. Free citizens, as republican theorists perceived them, have minds of their own and can stand against the mass emotions of the moment. Virtuous liberty is a necessity for the continuance of a republic. The republic, in turn, has as its purpose the cultivation of liberty and virtue.

Republicanism defined as the participation of free citizens in a collective enterprise was as much an accident as an ideological choice on the part of the leaders of the Revolution. The citizen Continental army that Congress projected and Washington led was a necessity of war. The participation of civilians, male and female, in the war effort seems to have been more the expression of individual conviction and social pressure than the product of some idea of republicanism. Yet the result suggests the deliberately, philosophically republican decree of the French revolutionary leaders of 1793 in the face of invasion of France: "Young men will go into combat. . . . Women will make tents and uniforms and serve in hospitals. . . . Old men will have themselves carried to public places to arouse the courage of warriors and to preach hatred of kings and the unity of the Republic."

A conflict between republican unity and republican liberty was foreshadowed even before the Revolution. The mobs that appeared periodically in resistance to British measures demanded unity and attacked whoever they believed to be in support of British oppression. Against popular passions stood libertarians: Lieutenant Governor Thomas Hutchinson of Massachusetts, the crusty descendant of the dissenter Anne Hutchinson and the opponent of the Revolution; Boston patriots John Adams and Josiah Quincy, who successfully defended in court the British officer accused of responsibility for the Boston Massacre. And in American history ever since, the claims of individual liberty and dissent have clashed with the clamors of conformist popular emotion.

Property and republicanism have had a similarly uneasy relationship. Early in American national history, republican theorists such as Thomas Jefferson expected a wide distribution of property ownership, made possible by the abundance of land, and assumed that holders of

Lantern of pierced tin called a "Paul Revere"; probably made in New England; eighteenth to nineteenth century. *(Index of American Design)*

Dowry chest, Pennsylvania German; inscribed with name of first owner, Jacob Rickert, dated 1782. *(Index of American Design)*

small property would make responsible, public-spirited citizens. Yet property, especially ownership of land, also drew Americans away from one another: physically so in the westward movement, socially in the unwillingness of the owning classes to put their property to public uses. Economic individualism and republican virtue would continue a quarrel that derived from their common grounding in American material, political, and ideological conditions.

Yet another dilemma for American republicanism lay in the belief that virtues most flourish in simple agricultural societies. Republics themselves, those of ancient Greece along with Rome and more recent polities, were city-states, and cities, most notably Boston, were breeding grounds for the American Revolution. Still, the idea persisted that living on the land and working it made for habits of diligence, honesty, and independence. But the energies released in part by the American Revolution would lead to the development of great cities and of industries severed from the land. In time it became necessary for American social critics to learn the ways in which these too can give shape to virtue.

The Articles of Confederation
and the Critical Period

The New Government   The Continental Congress that convened in May 1775 following the battles at Concord and Lexington sat in continuous session until 1787. Members came and went, but during this wrenching and momentous period Congress operated with remarkable effectiveness. While drafting a new form of government, the Articles of Confederation, Congress raised an army and appointed its commander in chief, negotiated with the enemy, authorized a navy, and sent agents and commissioners to France, Spain, Prussia, Austria, and Tuscany. It also issued millions of dollars of paper money.

In June 1776, almost simultaneously with the resolution that led to the Declaration of Independence, Richard Henry Lee proposed a permanent new government to represent all the states. In July, John Dickinson of Pennsylvania, chairman of the committee appointed to draw up the plan of government, submitted his proposals. Dickinson's scheme contained several controversial features. The new Congress was to have broad powers, including the right to establish state boundaries and to dispose of unoccupied western lands. Each state would have one vote, regardless of its population and the number of representatives it actually sent to Congress.

The Dickinson proposals came under immediate attack in open Congress. The large and influential state of Virginia, which claimed much of the trans-Appalachian West, opposed granting the new government sweeping powers over lands. Many of Virginia's most prominent leaders had for years anticipated selling western lands to the farmers whom they expected to spill over the mountains when peace returned. On the other hand, delegates from states such as Maryland and Pennsylvania, owning no western lands as far inland as Virginia claimed, wanted the United States as a whole to acquire the lands toward the Mississippi River. Only in this way, they insisted, could Americans from all parts of the new nation benefit from these millions of fertile acres. The delegates also fought over the voting provision. Large states wanted voting by size of population. The small states supported Dickinson's proposal. By their reasoning, allotting one vote to each state meant that the new government was a league of sovereign states. Apportioning representation to the states on the basis of their population would suggest that the power of the new government flowed directly from the American people, bypassing the states. Some members of Congress feared even the Dickinson document for giving too much power to the central government. This issue would arise again in the debates on the Constitution of 1787, and, in fact, the question of states' rights was to be a perennial problem in American politics.

| **The Articles of Confederation** | For almost a year and a half, amidst the smoke and flames of war, Congress debated the powers of the new government. One New Jersey man thought |

that "Congress have not reserved enough power for themselves." Opponents of the original proposal succeeded in adding to it a provision that Congress could exercise only those powers specifically delegated to it by the states. Another change was a victory for Virginia. Under strong pressure from that land-rich state, the delegates at Philadelphia agreed to drop the provision that Congress would control the new nation's western lands. With these modifications accepted, Congress in November 1777 adopted the Articles of Confederation and sent the new frame of national government to the states for ratification.

Twelve states swiftly ratified the Articles. Maryland, however, held out for the original proposal that Congress control western lands and refused to ratify until it was restored. A number of prominent Virginians, including Thomas Jefferson, had a grander vision of the West than merely as a mammoth, overgrown Virginia. The great interior valley of North America, they believed, should be carved into new, self-governing states, rather than remain colonies of the seaboard. For the good of the whole nation they were willing to surrender their own state's claims. Under their influence, Virginia ceded its western lands to Congress, and in 1781 Maryland relented and the Articles of Confederation finally went into effect. It pledged all the states to "a firm league of friendship" with one another, and committed them to mutual support against attack. It gave to Congress sole power over foreign affairs and over the issues of war and peace. Congress would also deal with the Indians, and the states agreed to surrender to one another all escaped criminals and to give "full faith and credit" to court orders, sentences, and other judicial decisions of sister states.

From the very first, the Articles proved inadequate as a basis for dealing with the difficulties of a new nation. The Confederation amounted to a league of virtually independent sovereign states, not a modern nation. The new government lacked one vital power—the power to tax or to force the states to levy taxes in its behalf. Congress had to depend on contributions from the states. Nor could it regulate trade and commerce among the states. Any attempt to change or modify

Article 2 of The Articles of Confederation and Perpetual Union Between the States *provided:*

"Each state retains its sovereignty, freedom, and independence, and every power, jurisdiction, and right which is not by this confederation expressly delegated to the United States in Congress assembled."

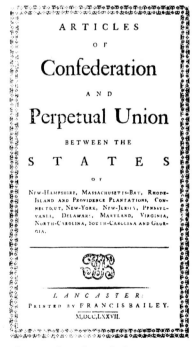

The Articles of Confederation pledged the thirteen states to "a firm league of friendship" with one another but failed to create a strong national government.

The story of Rachel Wells is particularly revealing of the problems faced by the impoverished states:

"To the Honnorabell Congress I rachel do make this Complaint Who am a Widow far advanced in years & Dearly have ocasion of ye Interst for that Cash I Lent the States. I was a Sitisen in ye jersey when I Lent ye State a considerable Sum of Moneys & had I justice dun me it mite be Suficant to suporte me in ye Contrey whear I am now, near burdentown. I Leved hear then . . . but Being . . . so Robd by the Britans & others i went to Phila to try to get a Living . . . & was There in the year 1783 when our assembley was pleasd to pas a Law that No one Should have aney Interest that Livd out of jearsey Stats . . .

Now gentlemen in this Liberty, had it bin advertised that he or She that Moved out of the Stat should Louse his or her Interest you mite have sum plea against me. But I am Innocent Suspected no Trick. I have Don as much to Carrey on the Warr as maney that Sett now at ye healm of government. . . . your asembly Borrowed £300 in gould of me jest as the Warr Comencd & Now I Can Nither git Intrust nor principall Nor Even Security. . . . My dr Sister . . . wrote to me to be thankfull that I had it in my Power to help on the Warr which is well enough but then this is to be Considered that others gits their Intrust & why then a poor old widow to be put of[f]. . . .

God has Spred a plentifull table for us & you gentlemen are ye Carvers for us pray forgit Not the Poor weaklings at the foot of the Tabel ye poor Sogers [soldiers] has got Sum Crumbs That fall from their masters tabel."

the Articles required the agreement of all the states. There were no executive and no national judiciary. Under this instrument of government, however weak, Americans did succeed in bringing the war to a successful conclusion. But the Confederation's authority would be too feeble to garner the fruits of victory and manage demobilization.

Debt Problems

During the months following Yorktown, the strains of nationhood, no longer obscured by military events, became painfully apparent. By early 1783 discontent plagued the army. Officers protested Congress's failure to establish a promised pension system for discharged veterans. In early March a group of officers at Newburgh, New York, threatened a military coup until Congress found the means to provide the officers with five years of full pay in lieu of the pensions.

The rank-and-file soldiers still had not received their pay. Congress simply could not raise the money. In the end, Congress discharged most of the troops without meeting their demands. Most of them rushed back to civilian life with little fuss, but several hundred marched to Philadelphia protesting their shabby treatment. Unable to meet the soldiers' demands and terrified by the angry troops, Congress fled first to Princeton, then to Annapolis, and finally came to rest in New York, which remained the national capital for several years.

Some patriots despaired over the pitiful state of the national government. Congress could pay neither its troops nor its creditors. The war had been financed by a combination of loans, paper money, and, in the case of several states, some taxes. The paper money had seriously depreciated; in 1781 Congress announced that it would not give in exchange to holders of paper currency the hard coin (specie) that in those days was considered to be the only reliable money. Other sizable obligations remained. Congress had borrowed directly from its own citizens, issuing IOU's in exchange for supplies, food, services, and cash. It had also borrowed from Dutch bankers. The states had similar problems. Massachusetts and a few others imposed high taxes to pay their debts; most were content to default like the Confederation government. These unpaid public debts cast a pall over the nation in the years after the war. How could such a country not be an object of scorn in the eyes of the whole world?

Creditors of the new government, whether original holders of the securities issued by Congress or speculators in them, had reason not to respect the new government. They had little hope of ever being paid. Farmers who had supplied commodities to the British West Indies and southern Europe, merchants who had traded with these regions, and all those in the port towns who had relied on this trade for a living saw their economic horizon shrink. Equally aggrieved were craftsmen and artisans in the towns whose businesses and jobs were washed out by a deluge of cheap British goods.

Debtors, too, found times hard and sought to offset the difficulties they encountered. One favorite scheme of debtor groups to counteract the postwar deflation was paper money issued by the states. When paper money is in circulation a unit of money tends to decline in value more quickly than when the only currency is in hard money of gold or silver. That is because the quantity of gold and silver is limited while paper can be printed in any amount a government chooses. Even when the understanding is that the government will give gold or silver to any holder of paper money who demands the exchange, the government can print more paper than it possesses in gold and silver, hoping that it will never be asked to exchange all the paper for metallic coin. The more paper money a government prints, or the greater the public expectation that the government will flood the economy with paper, the less will be the value of any single unit of currency. A paper currency would therefore be to the advantage of debtors, for they would be able to pay their debts with units of money cheaper than those they had borrowed. In Maryland indebted planters supported paper-money schemes, and in Pennsylvania and South Carolina merchants endorsed them. Not only were planters and merchants often in debt themselves, but many believed that the lack of paper money made all business hard to conduct and contributed to the depressed state of the economy.

In a number of states, paper money became in effect a way of confiscating a part of creditors' property. In North Carolina, Georgia, and New Jersey the paper money issues authorized by the state legislatures quickly depreciated, yet creditors were forced to take it at face value. The most notorious case occurred in 1786 when Rhode Island issued an avalanche of paper money. These notes were legal tender, so if any creditor refused to accept them the bills could be deposited with a judge and the debt legally canceled. Many Rhode Island merchants closed their doors rather than accept the notes. Creditors fled the state to escape debtors anxious to pay them in depreciated paper.

Toleware coffee pot from Lebanon, Pennsylvania.
(Index of American Design)

Trouble with Spain   Spain controlled both Florida and the lower reaches of the Mississippi, including the important port of New Orleans. By the end of the Revolution 50,000 American farmers lived on the "Western waters" in Kentucky and Tennessee, and many more Americans were eagerly awaiting the opportunity to cross the mountains to the fertile lands of the Mississippi Valley. If these people were not to remain subsistence farmers, they would need outlets for their wheat, pork, beef, corn, and forest products. The route east over the mountains was too difficult for the shipping of bulky products, but the great river that flowed to the Gulf of Mexico was a cheap and safe natural highway. Raft-like flatboats could be constructed of local lumber and loaded with barrels of pickled beef, pork, and grain to float with the current to New Orleans. There the rafts could be broken up and sold for lumber, and the barrels reloaded on oceangoing vessels to be carried to the Atlantic coast ports, the Caribbean islands, or Europe. The farmer could then buy some horses and return to Kentucky with some cash in his pocket and manufactured goods in his saddlebags. Control of New Orleans, then, gave Spain a strong hand in dealing with the United States.

In 1784 the Spanish government announced that it was closing the Mississippi to American commerce. Now only Spanish subjects could use the river and the port of New Orleans. All others would be arrested.

Broadax, wrought iron, oak handle, eighteenth century.
(Index of American Design)

Settler's wagon; length, over
14 feet; wagon bed, 10½ feet;
wheel diameters, 42 inches
and 33½ inches; about 1800.
(*Index of American Design*)

Westerners threatened to raise ten thousand troops to march on New Orleans. Some listened to British agents who promised protection if they would reunite with Great Britain. George Washington, seriously worried at the prospect of national dismemberment, reported after a long journey through the frontier that "the western settlers . . . stand as it were upon a pivot. The touch of a feather would turn them any way."

The nation's diplomatic weakness was soon confirmed. Negotiations began in 1785 between Spain and the United States over the "right of deposit" at New Orleans—in effect, the right to use the port there for foreign trade. Dour, tight-lipped John Jay, Congress's Secretary for Foreign Affairs, met with the suave and charming Don Diego de Gardoqui, Spain's negotiator. The Spanish emissary knew that the powerless Americans were in no position to threaten Spain, and refused to grant the major American demand, the right of deposit, although he was willing to make minor boundary adjustments along the West Florida border and allow some American trade within the Spanish empire. Congress refused to accept the treaty, and it died. New Orleans remained a locked gate at the mouth of the Mississippi.

Trouble with Britain   The British, who could make more trouble for the new nation than Spain, had no reason to wish the Americans well. In July 1783 the Privy Council issued an order that closed the British West Indies to most American commerce. This order dismayed farmers of the northern states, who had long sent their surplus provisions to Jamaica, Barbados, and the other British islands. It also hurt the New England fishing industry, which had supplied the sugar plantations with dried cod and mackerel, and the merchants of New York, Philadelphia, Salem, and Boston who had carried these goods. The shipping industry employed hundreds of seamen and thousands more in such related occupations as shipbuilding and the making of sail and rope. The British Caribbean planters connived at the smuggling of needed products, but this scarcely made up for the damage to American interests.

The Americans were in no position to retaliate. The British, of course, needed the American market for their manufactured goods, and in the immediate postwar period flooded the United States with cheap products to the distress of American artisans and manufacturers. Paying for imports from Britain also drained gold and silver coin from the nation. Several states, urged on by mass meetings of artisans and craftsmen, imposed duties on foreign goods. But the British found ways of sending their product through adjacent states that had no such taxes. Efforts to erect trade barriers among states created bad feeling between neighbors. Merchants of New London, Connecticut, boycotted New York; New Jersey taxed the New York lighthouse at Sandy Hook.

Under the peace treaty ending the war, the British had granted the United States the territory south of the Great Lakes and north of the Spanish possessions—all the way to the Mississippi River—and had promised to give up their military posts in the Northwest "with all convenient speed." For some time, however, they refused to remove the garrisons. The British did not wish to abandon their Indian allies and were reluctant to surrender the rich fur trade. They justified their delay by citing two provisions of the peace treaty: the promise that the Americans would do nothing to prevent British creditors from collecting millions of pounds in prewar debts, and the assurance that Congress would try to get the states to compensate loyalists for their wartime losses. The states had not yet fulfilled either of these promises, and Congress was powerless to compel compliance.

Barbary Pirates One final confrontation came close to being the most humiliating of all. For many years the deys and pashas of the Barbary Coast states of North Africa, Algiers, Tunis, Tripoli, and Morocco had preyed on European commerce. Most European nations either paid blackmail to these corsairs or provided naval protection for their own commerce. So long as the Americans were dependents of Great Britain, the British navy and treasury had covered them as well as Englishmen. After independence this protection ceased. In 1785 the New England ship *Maria* was captured by Algerians, who stole its merchandise, stripped the crew of all their clothes and possessions, and then sold them into North African slavery. American merchants demanded that Congress respond to such ruthless attacks. But without a navy or the means to create one, the Confederation government could do nothing to overawe the Barbary Pirates. Congress did manage to raise $80,000 to buy exemption from the deys, but this was so little that only the Moroccan leader concluded a treaty. In a few years, under the administration of Thomas Jefferson, the American navy in one of the most assertive acts of the new nation would punish the pirates. Great Britain later crushed them for resuming their attacks.

The Period of the Confederation

Expanding Commerce With the break from England, American merchants, no longer hindered by the Navigation Acts, began direct trade with parts of Europe from which they had been virtually excluded. Soon American vessels were showing up regularly in the harbors of Sweden, Holland, and Denmark, and even faraway Russia.

Still more interesting was the new trade with the Far East. In 1784 Robert Morris and some partners fitted out the 360-ton *Empress of China* with a cargo containing ginseng root, which the Chinese believed increased sexual potency. The vessel sailed for Canton around the Cape of Good Hope. It returned to New York the following year with tea, silk, chinaware, cotton cloth, and other goods that earned a profit for the promoters of almost $40,000. In a few years American ships were rounding Cape Horn, scudding up the Pacific coast to the region north of California, picking up otter skins in the Pacific Northwest, and sailing on to Canton. On one such voyage in 1792, Captain Robert Gray discovered the mighty Columbia River. These voyages provided a much-

Tribute to the Barbary States, 1785–1802

The United States, as a newborn maritime nation, faced the age-old problem of securing safe passage for its merchant ships, and paid tribute to the Barbary States:

Morocco 1786: £5,000 for a treaty guaranteeing "no future presents or tributes"; 1795: the same sum for renewal of the treaty plus consular presents, field-pieces, small arms, and gunpowder; 1802: top gun carriages.

Algeria 1793: $10,000 for relief of prisoners; 1796: nearly $1,000,000 for a treaty—$612,500 in cash, $21,000 annual tribute in naval stores, and $300 in gifts to the Dey. A long delay in payment called for an additional $53,000 in presents and bribes and the promise of a 36-gun ship; 1797: frigate *Crescent* delivered; 1798: the *Hamdullah* and $8,000 in lieu of stores; 1799: the brig *Sophia* and two schooners in lieu of stores.

Tunis 1798: $107,000 for a treaty and one barrel of gunpowder for every salute requested by an American ship; private presents (jewels, small arms, cloth) for the Bey; and public gifts suitable to the occasion; 1800: additional presents amounting to £7,000; 1802: special jewels and clothes for the Bey.

Tripoli 1787: demand (unpaid) for $100,000 yearly for peace or 30,000 guineas for perpetual peace; 1796: $56,486 for a treaty; 1799: $24,000 for presents and other items, in lieu of stores; 1802: $6,500 to ransom the crew of the *Franklin*.

(Courtesy, American Heritage)

needed outlet for American commodities, and at the same time created a taste for Chinese furniture, housewares, and textile patterns, as well as an interest in Chinese civilization.

The Public Lands   The peace treaty of 1783 had left the United States with a princely landed domain. Between the Appalachians and the Mississippi, stretching from Canada in the North to Florida in the South, lay enough unoccupied real estate to provide every free American family with a tract of 750 acres, or over one square mile of land. The Indians, especially the Shawnee, Wyandot, Iroquois, and Miami in the North, and the Cherokee, Choctaw, and Chickasaw to the south, claimed millions of acres as their hunting grounds. Most stood ready to resist any white settlers who would come to occupy their lands. Isolated settlements of French farmers and merchants were still scattered through the region.

The legal rights to this magnificent region were ambiguous. Virginia, with the broadest claims, had ceded its lands to the Confederation government. But other states tried to hold substantial portions of the West, a number of them awarding some of this land to their war veterans. Bit by bit, the states gave up their claims in favor of the nation, retaining in most cases only small parcels. For many years, however, state and federal claims overlapped.

Some easterners who feared the political eclipse of their own part of the country wanted the new region to remain secondary to the older states, with new settlers denied full representation in Congress. Others hoped to see equal states carved out of the region. It was in the interest of the older states to use the public domain as a source of federal revenue. One obvious maneuver was to sell the land at high prices for immediate returns. Large wholesale parcels could be sold to land speculators, who in turn could profit by retail sales to settlers. Against this notion of the uses of the federal lands was a vision of a West of small or moderate farms made easily available to settlers of modest financial means.

The Land Ordinance of 1785 was one of two measures in which the Confederation government laid down its basic policy toward the West and the public domain. It provided first for a careful survey of the land and then its division into townships six miles square, these to be divided into thirty-six sections, each one square mile, or 640 acres. Half the township might be sold as a unit; the other half would be offered on the market only in single sections. Actual sales at auction to the highest bidder started with a minimum price of a dollar an acre. Congress reserved four sections of each 36-section township for later use and kept one to sell for revenue to maintain local schools.

The Land Ordinance did not please everyone. Its minimum price and prescribed plot size meant that a pioneer farmer needed at least $640 to acquire a farm—in those days, a hefty sum. At the same time, the ordinance favored the establishment of family farms over speculation. Congress soon violated its own principles, however, by also selling almost two million acres of land to a group of speculators organized under the name of the Ohio Company, granting them an option on an additional five million—all for well under a dollar an acre.

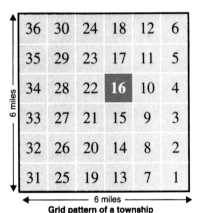

6 miles
Grid pattern of a township
36 sections of 640 acres (1 square mile each)

16 Income of one section reserved for the support of public education

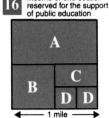

1 mile
A Half-section 320 acres
B Quarter-section 160 acres
C Half-quarter section 80 acres
D Quarter-quarter section 40 acres
Land Ordinance of 1785

The
Northwest
Ordinance

Before long, Congress also reached a decision on the political organization of part of the trans-Appalachian area—the region bounded by Pennsylvania on the east, the Great Lakes to the north, the Mississippi on the west, and on the south the Ohio River. The Northwest Ordinance of 1787 was a milestone in the progress of Americans across the continent. This law, along with the Land Ordinance, was a triumph of statesmanship for the Confederation Congress. Borrowing from an earlier plan proposed by Jefferson, the Ordinance laid out the process by which the Northwest might eventually become a group of self-governing states, equal in all respects to the original thirteen.

The area would be carved into between three and five territories, governed initially by officials appointed by Congress. When a territory acquired a population of 5,000 adult males, it would be allowed to elect an assembly and could send a nonvoting delegate to Congress. Attaining a population of 60,000 free inhabitants would make the territory eligible to apply for admission as a fully equal, self-governing state. The final section of the Ordinance of 1787 reflected the most liberal spirit of the Revolutionary era. All residents of a territory were to enjoy complete freedom of worship, trial by jury, full representation in the territorial assembly in proportion to their numbers, and other fundamental protections to both persons and property. In the whole of the vast region slavery was forbidden.

There remained an important western problem that the Confederation government could not solve: what to do with the Indians. In 1784 Congress had sent five commissioners to meet with the tribes of the Northwest in an effort to open the eastern portion of the region to white settlement. At Fort Stanwix the commissioners got the Iroquois to surrender their claims for a few trinkets. Next, they coerced the Chippewa, Ottawa, Wyandot, Shawnee, and Delaware into giving up most of their Ohio lands. The resentful tribesmen quickly repudiated these agreements and were soon trading blows with the frontiersmen now

Primitive conditions on the American frontier enforced a life of simplicity. The woman in this engraving stands proudly at the door of a hut, described by another pioneer as "a barbarous rectangle of unhewed and unbarked logs." The menacing pine trees hint at the artist's reservations about isolation and difficulties of life in the wilderness. *(Courtesy, Newberry Library)*

pouring into the Ohio country. The government sought to pacify the irate Indians by promising them additional gifts, while at the same time it strengthened the army garrisons in the West.

Daily Life

A lady's dressing table of the era, made in Baltimore. Patriotic touches, like the eagle that surmounts the mirror, are characteristic of post-Revolutionary times. (*Index of American Design*)

Farmers and Planters
Despite the problems of government in the "Critical Period," in the summer of 1787 most ordinary Americans went about their daily affairs without giving too much thought to the concerns of the new nation. The vast majority of the 2.5 million Americans of 1780—say, ninety percent—made their living from the soil. They were by no means all alike. Some 600,000, virtually all living south of Pennsylvania, were black slaves. Another considerable group was made up of white tenants or white servants. A few thousand Americans, most of them in the South, some in the Hudson Valley and a few other spots as well, were owners of great estates or plantations. The largest group, perhaps sixty percent, was made up of free farmers who owned their own land.

Yeoman farmers who owned their hundred to two hundred acres of land outright were especially numerous in New England, Pennsylvania, New Jersey, and the backcountry and mountain areas of the southern states. Those who lived close to cities or were connected to them by good roads or navigable rivers produced crops not only for themselves and their families, but also perhaps for distant markets in the West Indies, the Mediterranean, or Newfoundland. These farmers were by no means rich; the trade provided the means to buy a few luxuries and goods they could not themselves produce. Families were large, and children helped. Their labors created modest comfort and a rough abundance of food, clothing, and shelter.

A few got rich cultivating the soil: successful tobacco growers in Maryland and Virginia, some rice planters in South Carolina and Georgia, New York landlords who grew grain and raised livestock. Along the streams and inlets of the Chesapeake region, in the Carolina and Georgia sea islands and coastal lowlands, and in the Hudson Valley, a traveler could encounter many fine houses. Most of these houses built since the 1740s were of brick with plaster trim, designed in the gracious Georgian style with evenly spaced windows and classical cornices and moldings over windows and doors. With large ballrooms, imported English furniture, and many bedrooms, these structures attested to growing affluence and sophistication.

Merchants and Townspeople
Maritime merchants of the port cities constituted another wealthy class. In Boston the average merchant left $5,000 in real estate and personal property to his heirs at a time when few laborers earned more than fifty cents a day. A few merchants were fabulously rich. Sharing in the prosperity in about equal measure were lawyers and doctors, especially those who practiced in the larger communities. Instead of country homes the urban rich had large townhouses surrounded by gardens. These men and women, like their counterparts in the country, ate

elaborate meals, dressed in silk and fine broadcloth, wore wigs or powdered their hair, and traveled by coach or on horseback.

The towns were busy with the work of shopkeepers, innkeepers, clerks, seamen, laborers, and artisans. A day laborer's wages could keep a young man in modest comfort, but not a married man with a family. Porters, pick-and-shovel workers, and the like could make ends meet only if their wives worked as seamstresses, laundresses, or servants. Skilled craftsmen, on the other hand, had little trouble earning a good living. Many carpenters, blacksmiths, shipwrights, tailors, cordwainers, barrelmakers, masons, printers, and other artisans owned their own shops. Some craftsmen became fairly prosperous. One tailor, for example, had a house and land worth $1,130, a silver pocket watch, silver buckles for his shoes, two gold rings, six silver spoons, and furniture and household goods worth $375.

Pat Lyon at the Forge, a painting by John Neagle. Many skilled craftsmen owned their shops and had little difficulty earning a good living. Lyon, at the time a prosperous man, had once been jailed for debt in the building shown behind him. *(Courtesy, Museum of Fine Arts, Boston)*

Churches   Sunday was a day of rest not only in Congregational New England, but also in the middle states and the South, where there were many Baptists, Methodists, and Presbyterians, as well as Episcopalians. Religious observances were more than a quest for solace in an uncertain world, or traditional rites imposed by community pressure. They were also social events. People dressed up not only for the minister but for one another. And church was one of the few meeting places for young men and women. Many a courtship began in church under the watchful eyes of parents and older brothers and sisters.

Members of the evangelical sects, such as the Baptists, Methodists, and "new light" Presbyterians, found deep emotions in church attendance and did not confine their religious participation to Sundays. Beginning in the 1780s, great revivals periodically swept the backcountry, especially in the South. Many of these were held in churches; others took place at temporary encampments in open places where hundreds of pious people came for several days to listen to eloquent preachers exhort sinners to repent their evil ways, turn to God, and find everlasting salvation. More sedate people despised these camp meetings; they sneered at the "ranting" preachers and expressed horror at the shrieks, jerks, and groans of the listeners caught up in the emotions of the event. Critics also claimed that these camp meetings were opportunities for the nubile young to indulge their awakening sexual appetites. However unseemly or disreputable, the camp meeting provided an important emotional release for rural Americans whose lives otherwise were largely bound up in rounds of monotonous toil.

Urban   The ten percent of Americans who dwelt in substan-
Amusements   tial towns or cities enjoyed more varied lives. Cities
                  were centers of culture. Boston, New York, Philadelphia, and Charleston had theaters where traveling companies performed the works of Shakespeare and other English playwrights. There were subscription concerts in several cities, and in Charleston the St. Cecilia Society, founded in 1762, the oldest musical society in America, imported musicians from Philadelphia and New York. In Boston in 1786 a "Concert of Sacred Music" with seventy performers played to an audience of 2,000. There were no art galleries or museums, but a hand-

ful of distinguished painters—Charles Peale, John Singleton Copley, John Trumbull, and Gilbert Stuart—were the equals of Britain's artists. Battle scenes and portraits by American artists captured the Revolution for posterity. Benjamin West, another outstanding painter American in birth, had lived in England since before the Revolution.

In addition to concerts and plays in the cities, there were dances, horse races, and celebrations of public events. During and after the war the anniversary of the signing of the Declaration of Independence became a general occasion for bonfires, fireworks, and noisy parades. In Philadelphia, news of the treaty of peace set off a surge of revelry so boisterous that prudent citizens feared for the safety of their property.

Then, as today, Americans were susceptible to fads and crazes. A peculiar one of the Confederation period was for balloons, the first of which, inflated with hot air, had recently been launched in France. The

The Constitution, mural by Barry Faulkner, showing James Madison presenting the Constitution to George Washington and the Convention. *(Courtesy, The National Archives, Washington, D.C.)*

idea that the human race could free itself from the force of gravity seized the public's imagination. By midsummer 1784 it was said that nothing attracted attention unless it had the word "balloon" attached to it. Fashionable people wore "balloon" ornaments and a farmer hawking his vegetables in town sold them as "fine balloon string beans."

Prelude to the Constitution

The move to convert the Confederation government into a more effective political instrument had begun when the war ended. In 1783 nationalists devised a scheme to grant Congress the right to collect duties on imported liquors, sugar, tea, coffee, cocoa, molasses, and pepper; each state would collect the duties at its own ports and then

remit them to the Confederation treasury. This plan was submitted as an amendment to the Articles, and so required the agreement of all the states. New York, however, refused to accept it.

As Congress declined to little more than a sleepy debating society, the future of national affairs passed into the hands of men who thought, as Alexander Hamilton of New York put it, "continentally." In early 1785, commissioners from Virginia and Maryland met at Washington's home, Mount Vernon, to discuss common problems concerning navigation of the Potomac River, which separated the two states. So successful was this meeting that it led to calls by Virginia for a larger conference on commercial cooperation to meet at Annapolis the following year. Only twelve delegates from five states turned up at Annapolis, and so consideration of the planned agenda was postponed. Instead the delegates, led by Hamilton, drew up a proposal for a new convention, to meet at Philadelphia in May 1787, to discuss every issue necessary "to render the constitution of the Federal Government adequate to the exigencies of the Union." Congress received this proposal and cautiously endorsed it.

By the time of the Philadelphia meeting, all doubts moderate Americans may have entertained about the need for a stronger central government had been shattered by the farmers of western Massachusetts. One state that took its wartime debt seriously, Massachusetts had imposed heavy taxation on its citizens to meet this obligation. At the same time, farm prices declined. There were efforts to relieve by issues of paper money the distress of farmers who had gotten into debt. But in Massachusetts creditor groups defeated the attempts to issue paper currency. In the Berkshire hills of western Massachusetts, where few farmers had ready cash, many lost their land for non-payment of debts or taxes. The troubles that followed made it look as though anarchy threatened at least a portion of the new republic.

Suggested Readings

A recent study by a master historian is Edmund Morgan's *Inventing the People: The Rise of Popular Sovereignty in England and America* (1988). Also provocative are Michael Kammen, *A Machine that Would Go of Itself: The Constitution in American Culture* (1986) and John P. Diggins, *The Lost Soul of American Politics: Virtue, Self-Interest, and the Foundations of Liberalism* (1984). See also Robert M. Calhoon, *Dominion and Liberty: Ideology in the Anglo-American World, 1660–1801* (1994), and Jack N. Rakove's *Original Meanings: Politics and Ideas in the Making of the Constitution* (1996).

Garry Wills's, *Explaining America: The Federalists* (1981) offers a fresh reading of the work of devising the Constitution. Gordon Wood explores the relationship between political ideology and society in two works, *The Creation of the American Republic* (1969) and *The Radicalism of the American Revolution* (1992). See also Christopher Duncan, *The Anti-Federalists and Early American Political Thought* (1995), Stanley Elkins and Eric McKitrick, *The Age of Federalism* (1993), and Thornton Anderson, *Creating the Constitution: The Convention of 1787 and the First Congress* (1993). In *We the People: The Economic Origins of the Constitution* (1958) and *E Pluribus Unum: The Formation of the American Republic, 1776–1789* (rev., 1979), Forrest McDonald presents the Founding Fathers as statesmen committed to the founding of a secure republic. On the Anti-Federalists see Stephen Boyd, *The Politics of Opposition: Anti-Federalists and the Adoption of the Constitution* (1979).

Jackson Turner Main stresses class and sectional differences in *The Social Structure of Revolutionary America* (1966) and subsequent studies. Other important works are Mary Beth Norton, *Liberty's Daughters: The Revolutionary Experience of American Women* (1980) and Linda Kerber, *Women of the Republic: Intellect and Ideology in Revolutionary America* (1980). A nationalist account of the confederation era is Jack N. Rakove, *The Beginnings of National Politics: An Interpretive History of the Continental Congress* (1979).

See also Robert A. Becker, *Revolution, Reform, and the Politics of American Taxation, 1763–1783* (1980), Ira Berlin and Ronald Hoffman, eds., *Slavery and Freedom in the Age of the American Revolution* (1983), Joy Day Buel and Richard Buel, Jr., *The Way of Duty: A Woman and Her Family in Revolutionary America* (1984), Laurel Thatcher Ulrich's prizewinning *Midwife's Tale* (1990), Jan Lewis, *The Pursuit of Happiness: Family Values in Jefferson's Virginia* (1983), and Michael Kammen, *A Season of Youth: The American Revolution and the Historical Imagination* (1978). Sylvia Frey examines the effects of the American Revolution on African Americans in *Water from the Rock: Black Resistance in a Revolutionary Age* (1991). Indian attitudes are explored in Gregory Dowd, *A Spirited Resistance: The North American Indian Struggle for Unity, 1745–1815* (1992).

How Radical Was the American Revolution?

Forrest McDonald

Revolutions, we customarily think, are born amidst the poor and oppressed. The crowds call for bread and for release of political prisoners whose bodies are broken with torture. In the American Revolution the colonists were indeed reacting in anger, an anger that seems to come from a people brutally abused by vicious masters. The King, wrote Thomas Jefferson in the Declaration of Independence, has "sent hither swarms of Officers to harass our People, and eat out their substance. . . . He has plundered our seas, ravaged our Coasts, burnt our towns, and destroyed the lives of our people." But the slaveholders and merchants who led the American Revolution were in no way the victims either of poverty or of British oppression, nor were the common folk who lived in comfortable and prosperous North America.

It is also customary to expect revolutions to make for violent change: the destruction of a ruling class, the overthrow of political institutions, and even the coming of a revolutionary style of dress and behavior. The French Revolution favored mustaches and for men the trousers (in place of stockings and knee breeches) and short hair that have been standard ever since, and revolutionists addressed one another as Citizen, as Communists would later call one another Comrade. By such measures as these, the American Revolution was no revolution at all. It was instead an attempt by Americans to preserve what they already had.

What the leaders of the Revolution had to preserve was their substance and position. Neither was seriously threatened by the attempts the British government had begun making to rule the colonies more closely, but the taxes and the trade regulations passed by Parliament could make a dent in their fortunes, and they did not care for this. The wealthy revolutionary families talked much about the rights of the people, and they even meant it, but they were not intent on making a revolution that would redistribute land and power downward to the common folk.

Nor did those common folk demand any such thing. The small farmers, the craftsmen, and the frontiersmen who supported the Revolution did not resent the leadership of the powerful, or at any rate not enough to turn against them. As conservatives, well satisfied with their basic condition, common people joined with the wealthy in resisting the efforts of the British to impose change on the colonies.

Britain, the ideological leadership of the Revolution believed, had once been a virtuous agricultural nation, with a balanced government, honest labor on the land and craftsmanship in the cities, and direct honest trade among individuals. It had been, in effect, a society much like that in the British colonies. But Britain, so the argument held, had now sunk into corruption, enslaved to money that brought monopolies, standing armies, and vicious government hungry for tax revenues. Britain had actually given birth to a modern, dynamic, expanding economy that would greatly improve the well-being of its inhabitants. In this sense the American Revolution was a conservative rebellion against the forces of modernism.

The American Revolution, then, was culturally, politically, socially, and economically a conservative movement. But the revolutionists' successful defense of their established ways had an ironic outcome. Their victory brought great change. The new states found themselves unable to deal with their problems, and soon they had to create a central government with far greater powers than any that Parliament had dared to exercise.

Precisely because the impulses to revolution in eighteenth-century America bear little or no resemblance to the impulses that presumably account for modern social protests and revolutions, we have tended to think of the American Revolution as having no social character, as having virtually nothing to do with the society, as having no social causes and no social consequences. . . . Consequently, we have generally described the Revolution as an unusually conservative affair, concerned almost exclusively with politics and constitutional rights, and, in comparison with the social radicalism of the other great revolutions of history, hardly a revolution at all.

If we measure the radicalism of revolutions by the degree of social misery or economic deprivation suffered, or by the number of people killed or manor houses burned, then this conventional emphasis on the conservatism of the American Revolution becomes true enough. But if we measure the radicalism by the amount of social change that actually took place—by transformations in the relationships that bound people to each other—then the American Revolution was not conservative at all; on the contrary: it was as radical and as revolutionary as any in history. . . .

That revolution did more than legally create the United States; it transformed American society. Because the story of America has turned out the way it has, because the United States in the twentieth century has become the great power that it is, it is difficult, if not impossible, to appreciate and recover fully the insignificant and puny origins of the country. In 1760 America was only a collection of disparate colonies huddled along a narrow strip of the Atlantic coast—economically underdeveloped outposts existing on the very edges of the civilized world. The less than two million monarchical subjects who lived in these colonies still took for granted that society was and ought to be a hierarchy of ranks and degrees of dependency and that most people were bound together by personal ties of one sort or another. Yet scarcely fifty years later these insignificant borderland provinces had become a giant, almost continent-wide republic of nearly ten million egalitarian-minded bustling citizens who not only had thrust themselves into the vanguard of history but had fundamentally altered their society and their social relationships. Far from remaining monarchical, hierarchy-ridden subjects on the margin of civilization, Americans had become, almost overnight, the most liberal, the most democratic, the most commercially minded, and the most modern people in the world.

And this astonishing transformation took place without industrialization, without urbanization, without railroads, without the aid of any of the great forces we usually invoke to explain "modernization." It was the Revolution that was crucial to this transformation. It was the Revolution, more than any other single event, that made America into the most liberal, democratic, and modern nation in the world. . . .

The Revolution not only radically changed the personal and social relationships of people, including the position of women, but also destroyed aristocracy as it had been understood in the Western world for at least two millennia. The Revolution brought respectability and even dominance to ordinary people long held in contempt and gave dignity to their menial labor in a manner unprecedented in history and to a degree not equaled elsewhere in the world. The Revolution did not just eliminate monarchy and create republics; it actually reconstituted what Americans meant by public or state power and brought about an entirely new kind of popular politics and a new kind of democratic officeholder. The Revolution not only changed the culture of Americans—making over their art, architecture, and iconography—but even altered their understanding of history, knowledge, and truth. Most important, it made the interests and prosperity of ordinary people—their pursuits of happiness—the goal of society and government. The Revolution did not merely create a political and legal environment conducive to economic expansion; it also released powerful popular entrepreneurial and commercial energies that few realized existed and transformed the economic landscape of the country. In short, the Revolution was the most radical and most far-reaching event in American history.

Reprinted from Gordon S. Wood, *The Radicalism of the American Revolution* (New York: Alfred A. Knopf, 1992).

THE BILL OF RIGHTS

During the debates over the Constitution, some delegates argued for increased protection of individual rights, including freedom of religion, speech, the press, assembly, and petition, and judicial safeguards such as the right to a speedy trial and prohibition of cruel punishments. The Bill of Rights, amendments one through ten, added such provisions to the Constitution in 1791.

Amendment I

Congress shall make no law respecting an establishment of religion, or prohibiting the free exercise thereof; or abridging the freedom of speech, or of the press; or the right of the people peaceably to assemble, and to petition the Government for a redress of grievances.

Amendment II

A well-regulated Militia being necessary to the security of a free State, the right of the people to keep and bear Arms shall not be infringed.

Amendment III

No soldier shall, in time of peace, be quartered in any house without the consent of the Owner, nor in time of war, but in a manner to be prescribed by law.

Amendment IV

The right of the people to be secure in their persons, houses, papers, and effects, against unreasonable searches and seizures, shall not be violated, and no Warrents shall issue but upon probable cause, supported by Oath or affirmation, and particularly describing the place to be searched, and the persons or things to be seized.

Amendment V

No person shall be held to answer for a capital or otherwise infamous crime, unless on a presentment or indictment of a Grand Jury, except in cases arising in the land or naval forces, or in the Militia, when in actual service in time of war or public danger; nor shall any person be subject for the same offense to be twice put in jeopardy of life or limb; nor shall he be compelled in any criminal case to be a witness against himself, nor be deprived of life, liberty, or property, without due process of law; nor shall private property be taken for public use without just compensation.

Amendment VI

In all criminal prosecutions, the accused shall enjoy the right to a speedy and public trial, by an impartial jury of the State and district wherein the crime shall have been committed, which district shall have been previously asertained by law, and to be informed of the nature and cause of the accusation; to be confronted with the witnesses against him; to have compulsory process for obtaining witnesses in his favor, and to have the Assistance of Counsel for his defense.

Amendment VII

In suits at common law, where the value in controversy shall exceed twenty dollars, the right of trial by jury shall be preserved, and no fact tried by a jury shall be otherwise reexamined in any Court of the United States, than according to the Rules of the common law.

Amendment VIII

Excessive bail shall not be required, nor excessive fines be imposed, nor cruel and unusual punishments inflicted.

Amendment IX

The enumeration in the Constitution, of certain rights, shall not be construed to deny or disparage others retained by the people.

Amendment X

The powers not delegated to the United States by the Constitution, nor prohibited by it to the States, are reserved to the States respectively, or to the people.

We the People
1787–1800

THE BILL OF RIGHTS

The Constitutional Convention of 1787 did not provide a bill of rights for the new government. During the ratification struggle the antifederalists, fearful of a stronger central government, asserted that its absence was a purposeful attempt to deprive the American people of their fundamental liberties. It was no such thing.

The antifederalist supporters of the Constitution argued that they were creating a government of limited powers, and that therefore the new government could only exercise powers specifically granted to Congress. Alexander Hamilton asked why "should it be said that the liberty of the press shall not be restrained, when no power is given by which restrictions may be imposed?"

During the ratification debates North Carolina's James Iredell noted, the Crown's "usurpations" of the people's liberties had made England's Bill of Rights necessary. But under the new Constitution such usurpations by the national government were impossible, for the government would be founded on the will of the people rather than that of a monarch. To suggest the necessity of a bill of rights amounted to implying that the people, through their elected representatives, would destroy their own liberties.

Opponents of a written bill of rights also proposed that it might even be dangerous. A complete enumeration of all rights would be impossible, and listing only a few could allow the assumption that Congress had the power to do away with all the unlisted freedoms.

Following the adoption of the Constitution, Madison in a letter

HISTORICAL EVENTS

1786–87
Shays's Rebellion

1787
Constitutional Convention meets in Philadelphia

1788
Jay, Hamilton, and Madison publish The Federalist

1789
Constitution ratified • Washington elected President • Congress drafts the Bill of Rights • French Revolution begins

1790
Rhode Island becomes the last state to ratify the Constitution

1791
Hamilton writes his Reports • Congress approves a national bank and excise tax on alcohol • Bill of Rights adopted

1793
King Louis XVI and Marie Antoinette executed • Citizen Genet solicits U.S. support for France • Washington declares neutrality

continued

HISTORICAL EVENTS

1794
Whiskey Rebellion

1795
Jay Treaty • Pinckney Treaty

1796
First contested presidential election
• John Adams elected President
• Jefferson becomes Vice President

1797
XYZ Affair

to Jefferson, elaborated on his argument that the public could discard any protection of liberty that went against its will, whether or not the protection had been written into law.

But Madison promised his Virginia neighbors that if elected to Congress he would propose a bill of rights. He acknowledged that "political truths declared" in a "solemn manner" would "acquire by degrees the character of fundamental maxims of free Government, and as they become incorporated with the national sentiment, counteract the impulses of interest and passion." Madison included the right of the minority to stand against the majority. In 1789 Congress passed the amendments that, when ratified by the states in 1791, became the Bill of Rights. History has proved Madison's fears to have been quite sensible. Popular majorities will often attempt to subvert the liberty of minorities, and the Bill of Rights has not always been a successful barrier to these encroachments on liberty. Madison was also correct in finally conceding that setting out the liberties of the people in the Constitution would have a value in educating Americans about liberty. The most controversial of the first ten amendments is number two, guaranteeing the right to bear arms. Some constitutional experts argue that the "original intent" of the founders, especially Madison, was to restrict this right to the militias. The issue is a muddle because Madison originally sought clarity in this "right" by inserting it in the Constitution itself.

Shays's Rebellion

On a snowy January afternoon in 1787 at Springfield, Massachusetts, a ragtag army of 1,200 farmers advanced toward the federal arsenal building. They were angry because the state legislature had ignored the petitions of hundreds of debt-ridden farmers whose farms and homes were in danger of foreclosure for failure to pay taxes. At their head was Daniel Shays, a former captain in the Continental army, now a destitute

Paul Revere, the patriot silversmith, made this silver punch bowl to honor the militia for defeating the Massachusetts farmers' rebellion led by Daniel Shays. *(Courtesy, Yale University Art Gallery)*

farmer. Near the arsenal, some 600 militiamen under General William Shepard waited, their cannons trained on Shays and his men. When the farmers came within a hundred yards of the arsenal, the cannons belched fire and smoke, the attackers faltered, and four fell dead. The rest broke ranks and retreated in disarray.

On January 27 General Benjamin Lincoln and a hastily- recruited force of over 4,000 men joined the militia at Springfield and pursued the embattled farmers across western Massachusetts to the village of Petersham. On February 4, this little army surprised the rebels and captured 150 of them. The rest fled, and Shays escaped across the snow-covered hills to Vermont.

Ever after, this episode was known as Shays's Rebellion. Some politicians made much of the unrest in Massachusetts as proof of the weakness of the Articles of Confederation government.

How did it happen that less than a decade after the Revolution, former comrades in arms were aiming guns at each other, and some people feared that the fragile young republic was about to disintegrate? In 1782 the Massachusetts state government, in order to pay off its Revolutionary War debts, had required all taxes to be paid in spe-cie—hard money—instead of depreciating paper money, so that the state could afford to pay off its notes and bonds at their full face value. But for many people, coin was hard to come by. Especially in the four westernmost counties was the tax burdensome. Foreclosures were growing each year with no relief in view and little chance of redress from the legislature, which was controlled by the maritime and mercantile interests of the eastern part of the state.

In the spring, annual elections replaced Governor James Bowdoin with John Hancock, and a new slate of legislators who were mostly sympathetic to the farmers' plight took control. With a "total change of men," said Noah Webster, "there will be, therefore, no further insur-rection, because the Legislature will represent the sentiments of the people." Hancock pardoned Shays; the legislature passed laws offering tax relief and exempting clothing, household items, and tools from seizure for debt. The rebellion was over, but concerns about the stability and order of the young republic remained.

The Constitutional Convention

The delegates from the thirteen states who gathered in 1787 in Inde-pendence Hall were a mixed lot. Several men were prominent national leaders; others disappeared from history after their brief day at the Convention. Together this group from a settlement on the edge of a wilderness were to produce one of the most remarkable political ar-rangements in the history of Western civilization.

The Founding Fathers The presiding officer, George Washington, richly honored as the commander in chief of the Continen-tal forces that had defeated the British and made independence possible, enjoyed enormous prestige throughout the nation. His opening appeal to "raise a standard to which

"I am a plain man, and I get my living by the plow," wrote Jonathan Smith, a farmer unsympathetic to Shays. He spoke to his fellow "plow-joggers": "I have lived in a part of the country where I have known the worth of good govern-ment by the want of it. The black cloud of Shays rebellion rose last winter in my area. It brought on a state of anarchy that led to tyranny.... People, I say, took up arms, and then, if you went to speak to them, you had the musket of death presented to your breast. They would rob you of your property, threaten to burn your houses. . . .

When I saw this Constitution [of the United States] I found that it was a cure for these disorders. I got a copy of it and read it over and over. I had been a member of the convention to form our own state constitution, and had learnt something of the checks and balances of power; and I found them all here. . . .

I don't think the worse of the Con-stitution because lawyers, and men of learning, and moneyed men are fond of it. [They] are all embarked in the same cause with us, and we must all swim or sink together."

The American Star, by Frederick Kemmelmeyer. (*Courtesy, The Metropolitan Museum of Art*)

the wise and the honest can repair" set the tone for the solemn deliberations that followed. Nearly as eminent was Benjamin Franklin, fresh from the triumphs he had won as minister to France and chief negotiator of the peace treaty. Though now eighty-one and somewhat infirm, Franklin could still inspire confidence and rally support. Both men favored a stronger central government. Yet a short and lively Virginian, the thirty-six-year-old James Madison, proved more important at the Convention than either of these two commanding figures. A close friend of Jefferson, a man of wide reading and deep reflection, Madison would be the major architect of the Constitution.

A few of the more able men present at Philadelphia during the spring and summer of 1787—Robert Yates of New York, Luther Martin of Maryland, and George Mason of Virginia, for example—remained defenders of local power against expanded federal authority. Most of the delegates, however, were strong nationalists who wished and expected to remake the federal government into an effective instrument of the national will. Perhaps the Convention's most extreme nationalist was also one of the youngest: New York's Alexander Hamilton, at the age of thirty, had scant use for the states at all and would prefer to see them reduced to little more than administrative units.

All through the Philadelphia summer the fifty-five delegates in Independence Hall argued, negotiated, maneuvered, and deliberated. Nearly all of them lawyers and educated men, they drew on their knowledge of history, especially the experience of the ancient Roman republic. They also culled ideas from the political thinkers of their time, most notably Montesquieu, Harrington, and Blackstone. But ultimately their own common sense, their experience of government, and the interests of their states and their sections guided their decisions. Said John Dickinson, "Experience must be our only guide. Reason may mislead us."

All agreed that the new government must be strong without being oppressive, and the delegates kept striving to balance liberty and order. The Constitution they finally produced reflects a series of compromises between strong government and government limited in the interests of freedom, between national and local authority, and between the interests of the large states and the concerns of the smaller ones. Their debates produced a document that in both strengthening and limiting the powers of government has served the country to this day.

Virginia and New Jersey Plans

As debate opened Edmund Randolph of Virginia presented a proposal by his friend Madison. The Virginia Plan, as it would come to be called, recommended a new national legislature representing not the states, as the Confederation Congress did, but the people. The new body was to have two houses. The numbers that each state would have in both houses was to be proportionate either to its population or to its wealth. The voters of each state would choose directly their representatives to the lower house, and that state's delegation would select its delegates to the upper house. On other matters delegates in both houses were to vote as individuals, not as members of separate delegations. The new Congress could define the powers of the federal government and overrule the states, appoint a national executive, and choose a new national judiciary.

The Virginia Plan came under immediate attack. Many delegates believed that it veered too far toward nationalism, practically obliterating the states as governing units. It also smacked of favoritism: the largest and richest states such as Virginia, Massachusetts, or Pennsylvania would have many more delegates in the new Congress than the smaller or poorer ones such as New Hampshire, Georgia, and Rhode Island.

Opponents of the Virginia Plan countered with a scheme submitted by William Paterson of New Jersey. This New Jersey Plan provided for all the states to have equal representation in a single-chamber legislature. This new Congress would regulate foreign and interstate commerce, levy tariffs on imports, and impose various internal taxes. It would also choose the officers of the executive and judicial branches. All those powers not specified were to remain with the states.

For many weeks, debate swirled around these two proposals. Against Paterson's proposal was the consideration that it would be unjust to allow, say, the voice of a few thousand New Jerseyites to equal the voice of many more Virginians. Randolph's scheme raised another difficulty: who were to be counted as "population"? Should slaves, who could not vote, be considered the equals of free men for purposes of representation? If so, the southern states, with their many slaves, would have many more delegates in proportion to their voting population than the northern states.

A Balanced Government   In a committee charged with seeking a way out of the impasse over representation, the delegates from Connecticut took the lead in proposing what became known as the Connecticut Plan. This compromise that the Convention finally hammered out established today's two-house national legislature. In the lower, the House of Representatives, the people of each state would be directly represented in proportion to population. In the upper, the Senate, each state legislature would elect two members regardless of population. A later arrangement determined that a slave would be treated as three-fifths of a person for the purpose of calculating representation in the House of Representatives. The new Congress was given broad powers over foreign and interstate commerce, permitted to levy taxes directly on citizens, and awarded the sole right to coin money and regulate its value.

The Constitution borrowed from the British model of mixed government. In Great Britain that meant a government of monarch, aristocracy embodied in the House of Lords, and democracy (actually expressed in the votes of a small portion of the British public) represented in the House of Commons. In the American scheme the President was no monarch, but he was supposed to provide the unifying force that in Britain was assigned to the Crown. The Senate would supply, not quite an aristocracy, but at least the wisdom and stability that supposedly resided in an upper class of wealth and social standing. The House of Representatives was intended to convey the will of the democracy.

Political Parties

Students of government have credited American political parties with making the constitutional system work. It is therefore no small irony that the Founding Fathers detested the very idea of political parties and hoped to create a political system in which the "spirit of party" would wither away. Their feelings go back to pre-revolutionary days. As colonists, Americans had come to associate British parties with corruption. Eighteenth-century British parties, in fact, often were corrupt. They were organized by means of family ties and patronage. And the Crown, because it had at its disposal a vast number of political offices, was frequently able to use the "spirit of party" to control Parliament. Colonists, in turn, often blamed their own troubles on these same corrupt parties.

In *The Federalist*, Number 10, Madison wrote that the great diversity of interest groups in the new country would prevent the formation of large parties. In fact, it did not. Diversity did, however, help determine the character of the parties that arose. The need to achieve a majority in the electoral college forced American parties to become broad coalitions that could then appeal to a broad range of interests. So the United States got parties, but they were very different from both the small clusters of individuals that had formed in the eighteenth-century British Parliament and the large but ideologically cohesive parties that developed in nineteenth-century Europe.

Baron de Montesquieu (1689–1775), author of *Spirit of Laws*, was a French philosopher who, distrustful of republics, advocated dividing powers among the executive, legislative, and judicial branches of government. *(Courtesy, Scribner's Archives)*

Along with this arrangement went another that partly overlapped with it, a scheme of checks and balances ensuring that no one part of government would be able to wield unrestrained power. To this purpose the Constitution projected another triad: the executive; Congress as a whole, embracing both senators and representatives; and the judiciary. The President, or executive, would be chosen by a group of "electors" in each state, the electors being in turn selected by any method each state legislature deemed best. The judicial branch, headed by a Supreme Court, would be selected by the President with the approval of the Senate. To ensure the judges' independence from political pressure, the Convention provided that they would serve for life and could not have their salaries reduced. The President, too, was to be independent of Congress. His term of office would last four years regardless of what Congress thought of him, and he could be reelected. Each branch of government—executive, legislative, and judiciary—was empowered to check the others.

Among these was the President's power of veto over laws enacted by Congress. This veto could be overridden by a two-thirds vote in both houses. The President would choose all federal judges, ambassadors, and high officials of executive departments, including what would later come to be called his cabinet. But most of these appointments had to be confirmed by the Senate. The Supreme Court, having jurisdiction over violation of federal laws and over suits between citizens of different states, was also going to exercise its own important brake on the other two branches. Though the Constitution contains no clause giving the Supreme Court and the lower federal courts the power to declare a federal law to be in violation of the Constitution, the Court soon after its establishment was to conclude that by implication it possessed that authority, and it has exercised that implicit power ever since. Congress, in its turn, could put on trial and remove from office for bad conduct both the President and members of the judiciary. The model of mixed government gave Congress its own built-in check.

The Senate, the upper house, its members chosen by state legislatures rather than by the people at large, would supposedly be above the public whim that might sway the House of Representatives. That lower chamber, which by custom has come to be called simply "the House" or "Congress," would in turn be able to resist the aristocratic arrogance that might infect the Senate. Since any measure would have to pass both chambers to become law, each would check the other. To assure protection against excessive taxation, the Convention provided that all money bills would have to originate in the House.

By September 1787 the new Constitution had assumed its essential form. A substantial number of delegates continued to complain that the Constitution conferred too much power on the federal government. At least one delegate, Alexander Hamilton, believed it created too weak a government for the nation's needs. Gouverneur Morris of Pennsylvania wrote a preamble to the document, and, with only three members abstaining (George Mason of Virginia said that he would rather cut off his right hand than sign the new document), the delegates affixed their signatures to the Constitution. Now it awaited the approval of the Confederation Congress—and the people.

Ratification

On September 20, 1787, the Confederation Congress in New York received the Constitution composed in Philadelphia. One of its sharpest critics was the man who had first proposed independence in 1776: Richard Henry Lee of Virginia. Favoring the new strengthened Union was his cousin "Light Horse Harry" Lee, a young ex-cavalry officer and the future father of Robert E. Lee, who in the 1860s would lead an army against that Union. Article 7 of the proposed Constitution provided for a ratification process in which the document was submitted to special state conventions. For over a year, national political discussion would revolve about whether to accept the new Constitution or continue with the Articles.

The Anti-Federalists, the opponents of the Constitution, have been called "men of little faith." Beneath their specific objections to one or another provision of the new constitution lay a deep-seated distrust of all government no matter what form it might take. Governments are dangerous, said the Anti-Federalists, because they are composed of men, and men are corrupted by the exercise of power.

Federalists were themselves men of little faith. They shared with their political opponents the same dour view of human nature. The difference was that they feared government less and people more. Hence they were eager to shield much of the government from direct popular control. Only the House of Representatives would be directly answerable to the people, and then only once every two years. The Senate was to be elected by the state legislatures, the President by an electoral college. The judiciary would be appointed, and would hold office indefinitely. Each branch of the government would balance the others so that no one individual or party could long work its will.

By early 1788, five states, either unanimously or by overwhelming majorities, had ratified the Constitution. Elsewhere, especially in Massachusetts, Virginia, and New York, there was a strong opposition. The *Massachusetts Gazette* observed: "It is impossible for one code of laws to suit Georgia and Massachusetts." In March 1788 the Federalists received a modest setback when Rhode Island rejected the Constitution. Since Rhode Island had refused even to send delegates to the Constitutional Convention in 1787, Federalists did not expect much support there; but the nature of the political struggle was significant. Rhode Island politics during the 1770s and 1780s had been known for its battles between debtors and creditors. The state represented a clear-cut division along economic lines. The merchants and professional men, smelling certain defeat, boycotted the state ratifying convention, and their absence gave the Anti-Federalists a margin of ten to one. But Federalist victories by large margins soon followed in Maryland and South Carolina. On June 21, New Hampshire became the ninth state to ratify and, by the terms of its own ratification provision, the new Constitution was now technically in effect, for nine states had accepted it. Yet two very important states, New York and Virginia, had not yet acted.

In Virginia the formidable Patrick Henry, James Monroe, and George Mason led the Anti-Federalists. Favoring the Constitution were

Amos Singletary, a self-described "poor" person of Massachusetts, put his case against the new Constitution:

"We fought Great Britain—some said for a three-penny tax on tea; but it was not that. It was because they claimed a right to tax us and bind us in all cases whatever. And does not this Constitution do the same?

These lawyers and men of learning and moneyed men, that talk so finely and gloss over matters so smoothly, to make us poor illiterate people swallow down the pill, expect to get into Congress themselves. They expect to be the managers of this Constitution, and get all the power and money into their own hands. And then they will swallow up all us little folks, just as the whale swallowed up Jonah!"

The votes of nine states were needed to ratify the Constitution of the United States. *(Courtesy, American Antiquarian Society)*

Ratification of the Constitution Votes at State Ratifying Conventions		
State	Date	Vote Y/N
Delaware	Dec. 1787	30– 0
Pennsylvania	Dec. 1787	46– 23
New Jersey	Dec. 1787	38– 0
Georgia	Jan. 1788	26– 0
Connecticut	Jan. 1788	128– 40
Massachusetts	Feb. 1788	187–168
Maryland	April 1788	63– 11
South Carolina	May 1788	149– 73
New Hampshire	June 1788	57– 47
Virginia	June 1788	89– 79
New York	July 1788	30– 27
North Carolina	Nov. 1789	194– 77
Rhode Island	May 1790	34– 32

When a president-to-be of another era, John F. Kennedy, was growing up, his father made him and his brothers take the parts of Hamilton, Jefferson, and others, and argue at the dinner table over whether to ratify the Constitution.

James Madison, Edmund Randolph, and, above all, George Washington. The expectation that the state's most revered statesman would be the first President of the Republic made the Federalists difficult to stop. In the end Virginia ratified, but like Massachusetts requested a bill of rights.

The Federalist Papers and The Bill of Rights

Now the struggle shifted to New York. The inclusion of that state, with its great port and strategic mid-continental location, was essential if the Union was to work. But for a while it seemed as if New York would refuse to ratify. The convention that assembled in Poughkeepsie was under the control of the state's stalwart Anti-Federalist governor, George Clinton. Arrayed against Clinton and his supporters, however, were John Jay and the strong-willed Hamilton. Soon these two New York Federalists, joined by James Madison, were engaged in a war of words with their Anti-Federalist opponents. Day after day the *Independent Journal* carried the closely-argued essays in which the three men, writing under the common name "Publius," explained the virtues and necessity of the new Constitution. Dealing both with immediate concerns and universal political values, these eighty-five pieces—in 1788 published under the collective title *The Federalist*—constitute a classic commentary on the nature and purposes of government. Publius's articles, however, did little to change the minds of the Poughkeepsie delegates, most of whom were Anti-Federalists. More important was pressure from New York City, where merchants and artisans threatened that if New York State did not join the Union, New York City would. On July 25, 1788, after an impassioned personal address to the delegates by Hamilton, the state ratified the new frame of government.

Rhode Island and North Carolina were still outside the new Union, but they did not seem essential. One North Carolinian grumbled, "We see plainly that men who come from New England are different from us. They are ignorant of our situation, they do not know the state of our country. They cannot with safety legislate for us." Yet in November 1789 North Carolina officially ratified the Constitution and entered the Union. Reluctant Rhode Island joined at last in 1790.

After setting up electoral procedures, the old Congress operating under the Articles of Confederation quietly passed out of existence. When the body of electors—called the "electoral college"—voted on February 4, 1789, every presidential vote cast went for Washington, with John Adams of Massachusetts receiving the vice presidency. Newly-elected representatives and senators set out for the nation's temporary capital, and on March 4, 1789, the first Congress under the new Constitution assembled in New York City. Federal Hall, the former city hall, was still being remodeled and the new senators and representatives took their seats amidst the carpenters' noise and flying sawdust. The confusion and disorder caused little harm. Only eight senators and thirteen representatives had slogged their way through the muddy roads of spring to take their oaths of office that opening day.

On April 14, 1789, Washington received formal notice of his election. Two days later he wrote in his diary, "About ten o'clock I bade farewell to Mount Vernon . . . and with a mind oppressed with more anxious and painful sensations than I have words to express, set out for New York." There, in the nation's temporary capital, on April 30, he was sworn into office and delivered his first inaugural address. The celebration in New York when Washington came to the city for his presidential inauguration exceeded anything previously held in the young nation. The barge that brought the President-elect across New York harbor from New Jersey was surrounded by large and small vessels of every sort, full of cheering passengers. Washington made his way through streets lined with exuberant citizens. At night the city was illuminated with bonfires, and celebrants crowded the thoroughfares.

The next few months were busy ones. In the fall, Congress drafted a Bill of Rights, the first ten amendments to the Constitution, which the prescribed three-fourths of the states quickly ratified. The first eight amendments placed certain fundamental restraints on the power of the federal government over ordinary citizens. Congress could not limit free speech, interfere with religion, deny to the people the right to keep and bear arms, require the quartering of troops in private homes, or allow homes to be searched by federal authorities without search warrants. Persons accused of federal crimes could not be made to testify against themselves, nor could the federal government deny the citizens trial by jury or deprive them of life, liberty, or property "without due process of law." The central government could not impose excessive bail or "cruel and unusual punishments." Amendment IX ordained that the rights included in the earlier list did not exclude others; Amendment X provided that those powers not given to the federal government or denied the states should belong solely to the states or the people.

Never before had any single document enumerated so clearly and emphatically the rights of private citizens. The Bill of Rights became, accordingly, a landmark in the history of human liberty. But the Bill applied to the federal government only. Most of the states had similar provisions in their own constitutions. But what if a state chose to violate fundamental human rights; would a citizen have any official or agency to turn to? The Thirteenth, Fourteenth, and Fifteenth Amendments, adopted after the Civil War, would begin to address that question, but it was not really to be answered until the civil rights movement of the 1960s, if then.

The Newly Formed Regime

The New Government Friends of the Constitution composed most of Congress. Many members had been present at Philadelphia during the momentous summer of 1787 to write the new frame of government, and the majority hoped to carry out the purposes of the nationalists: to make the United States a going concern and create respect for the republic among the older nations of the world. The framing of the Bill of Rights was in itself one of the most momentous actions of any Congress in the nation's history.

Yet the first deliberations had been nearly farcical. For three weeks the members debated the proper title of address for the President. Vice

President John Adams insisted that without some such title as "His Elective Highness" or "His Excellency," the President might be mistaken for the head of a volunteer fire company. Adams' opponents believed any such title would be "aristocratical," unrepublican. They mocked the pudgy Vice President's serious concern, and took to calling him "His Rotundity."

Washington himself settled the momentous issue of his title. Though protective of his dignity on all occasions, he preferred to avoid "monarchical" trappings. He did travel through the streets in a gilded coach and held "levees," formal receptions for visitors and guests, but he would not accept a title of any sort. He wished to be addressed as "Mr. President"—the same as when he had presided over the Convention of 1787. From the beginning, Washington's commanding presence lent the new government some badly needed stateliness. Besides his title, the first chief executive set other less impressive precedents for the conduct of the presidency. Early in his administration Washington, taking literally his power to "make treaties" with "the advice and consent of the Senate," appeared before the senators to explain an Indian treaty. After an awkward debate a senator proposed referring the treaty to committee. The President, offended by this snub, stormed out, saying that he would "be damned" if he would ever come back. He did return once, but no other President has attempted to discuss treaties personally with the entire Senate.

Meanwhile, Congress had set up three major executive departments, State, War, and Treasury, and appointed a postmaster general. It also passed the Federal Judiciary Act, which specified that the Supreme Court was to consist of a chief justice with five associates. John Jay, the first chief justice, resigned to run for governor of New York in 1795, saying that under "a system so defective, the court would not obtain the energy, weight and dignity which are essential. . . ." At Jefferson's urging the justices discarded the English practice of wearing wigs, which he said made "the English Judges look like rats peeping through bunches of oakum." Congress also established a system of federal courts and created the office of attorney general for the government's chief law officer.

Alexander Hamilton and the Nation's Debts

In response to one of the new government's most pressing concerns, that of providing itself with revenues, Congress passed the nation's first tariff, setting low duties on a host of imported goods. Congress now had the means to pay the army and official salaries, and to begin to meet its debts. By 1789 those debts amounted to about $52 million—$40 million owed to Americans, and $12 million due foreigners. In addition to these obligations of the federal government, there were the state debts still unpaid, amounting to about $25 million.

Few people doubted that the foreign debt must be paid in full. Otherwise, the United States would not earn the respect of foreign powers or be able to borrow abroad again. But what about the domestic debt? Speculators had bought Continental IOU's for a song from those who had actually given the wartime Congress money or supplies to fight

Alexander Hamilton advocated a strong central government. The artist is John Trumbull. *(Courtesy, Yale University Art Gallery)*

the British. Should these speculators alone benefit by the improved credit of the national government, or should the original holders also get something? And what about the state debts? Some southern states had paid portions of these obligations while many northern states had not. If the government were to "assume" or take over these obligations, the residents of the middle states and New England would benefit at the expense of those south of Pennsylvania. Congress turned over to Alexander Hamilton, Washington's secretary of the treasury, the problem of how to handle the debt as well as other pending financial questions.

A young man of thirty-five, Hamilton was a former aide-de-camp to Washington who had married into the prominent Schuyler family of New York. Able, handsome, and well-connected, he had risen high in New York political life after his army service despite his West Indian origin and his illegitimate birth.

Hamilton was a nationalist, lacking the emotional attachment that men like Jefferson and Madison felt for the local community. Like many other veterans of the Continental Army, he recalled bitterly the petty jealousies and selfishness of the states during the Revolutionary War. He had so little respect for the states that at the Constitutional Convention he had proposed their virtual elimination. He prized banking, trade, and manufacturing, and believed that the United States could not afford to remain an agricultural nation, producing raw materials for Europe. Britain, rapidly becoming the industrial workshop of the world, must be the country's example, he claimed. This required a vigorous central government commanding its citizens' loyalty. Hamilton was skeptical of human nature. A branch of the eighteenth-century Enlightenment that included Jefferson believed that human beings were inherently more good than evil, social and political evil being the result largely of evil institutions. Freed of these, mankind would undoubtedly flourish. But Hamilton believed that the people tended to be "ambitious, vindictive, and rapacious."

Congress's problem was Hamilton's opportunity. The new secretary of the treasury seized the occasion to advance some of his fondest political and economic hopes. In three great *Reports* he incorporated into larger plans for American society his solution to several immediate problems.

Hamilton's Reports   The *Report Relative to Public Credit* boldly proposed that the national debt be paid in full through a complicated process known as "funding." Current holders would exchange their IOU's at par for interest-bearing bonds. Hamilton asserted that the public debt would prove a "national blessing." His *Report on a National Bank* early in 1791 explained why. The nation's economic development required stronger currency and banking facilities. Hamilton proposed a new federally chartered banking corporation, drawing its capital both from the Treasury and from private investors. The new "Bank of the United States," governed by privately elected directors and others chosen by the government, would serve both public and private needs. It would stimulate commerce and manufactures by lending money to private businessmen. The bank would as well hold the government's deposits, pay its bills, and accept its receipts. The institu-

Alexander Hamilton wrote:

"A national debt, if it is not excessive, will be to us a national blessing."

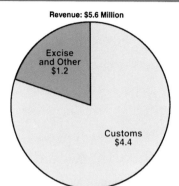

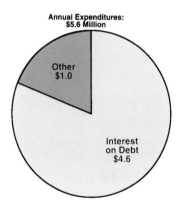

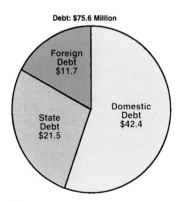

Under Hamilton's plan, over 80 percent of federal revenues went to pay the interest on the national debt. In the 1990s, interest payments consumed less than thirty percent of the federal budget.

James Goodwyn, *American Sleigh Ride.* *(Courtesy, Museum of Fine Arts, Boston)*

Alexander Hamilton had clear ideas and expressed them forcefully:

"All communities divide themselves into the few and the many. The first are the rich and wellborn, the other the mass of the people. . . . The people are turbulent and changing; they seldom judge or determine right. Give therefore to the first class a distinct, permanent share in the government. They will check the unsteadiness of the second. . . ."

tion's most important service was to issue the paper money of the nation. In itself, paper money was considered a cheap, untrustworthy currency, but the Bank's paper would have something solid to back it up. Its holders could, if they so wished, have the government give them in place of it an equivalent amount in the securities that were part of the new funding scheme. And the public's knowledge that the currency would be so exchanged would make for willingness to use it. Hamilton was planning to convert the national debt of a gold-poor country into a powerful engine for mobilizing its economy.

Later in 1791 Hamilton issued the last of the major *Reports,* on manufactures. The secretary acknowledged that agriculture was currently the most important single economic activity, but he saw no conflict between agriculture and industry. The two complemented each other; both together would benefit the nation. Noting the beginnings of the factory system in Britain, Hamilton observed that the new system of manufacture employed every class of people in productive labor, even women and children. Hamilton especially favored the employment of women in factories, believing that in a predominantly agricultural society men would be needed, and would prefer, to work the land. He viewed women as the most readily available pool of wage labor. The United States with its magnificent resources was potentially a great industrial nation, but to compete with other nations would require government aid. To protect "infant industries" until they could compete successfully, the government must impose high tariffs that would raise the price of foreign manufactures. It should also offer premiums for the production of needed goods and for inventions. Above all, the proposed bank must lend capital to entrepreneurs.

Hamilton's *Reports* together outlined an economic revolution. Through the energetic use of the national government, the country might be transformed: bustling cities, humming factories, and busy arteries of communication and transport would erupt from the quiet American landscape of prosperous farms and trackless forests.

Opposition to Hamilton's Nationalism

The Hamiltonian program, so bold in its projections, aroused fierce opposition. Said one observer, "Faction glows within like a coalpit." Hamilton's vision threatened to violate the character of the nation as some Americans saw it, a land of small farms and the simple social relations of the countryside. Many also feared the expansion of federal powers his program required. They imagined that Hamilton's schemes would create an all-powerful centralized government breeding graft and corruption. In the new nation, as in Britain, liberty and republican virtue would then degenerate into tyranny and licentiousness. Especially fearful were the Virginia leaders—James Madison, now a leading member of the House of Representatives, and Thomas Jefferson, Washington's secretary of state. The two Virginians believed that Hamilton and his supporters wanted to create a plutocracy, a government of the rich. Jefferson feared both the rich and the mob; the Hamiltonians, it seemed, feared only the mob.

Hamilton's bill to fund the public debt aroused Madison, who quickly became the leader of the forces arrayed against him. Madison spoke as a southerner, aware that four-fifths of the unpaid securities and state debts were northern. Yet his attack was a principled one. He did not oppose funding in itself, he declared; rather, he believed that Hamilton's scheme unduly benefited speculators. Under Hamilton's plan these people would receive the full face value of their holdings, while original possessors would get nothing. Even now, Madison and his supporters asserted, advance news that the government would assume the state debts had been leaked by people in high places, and speculators were traveling through the South buying up securities from gullible farmers.

For many weeks the funding bill remained blocked. The particular sticking point was the provision that the federal government would assume the payment of the states' debts. Then one morning in July, Jefferson bumped into Hamilton on the steps of the President's house. The secretary of the treasury told the secretary of state that the deadlock in Congress was endangering the Union. Could Jefferson do anything to help? The next day the two cabinet officers met with Madison, and a deal was arranged. The national capital would be moved from New York to Philadelphia. Then, in ten years, it would be permanently located in the South between Virginia and Maryland. ("It is the opinion of all the Eastern states," one northerner protested, "that the climate of the Potomac is not only unhealthy, but destructive to northern constitutions.") In return, Madison and his friends would cease to oppose assumption. The following month the funding measure passed Congress.

The Bank of the United States

Next on the agenda was a national bank. The bill would charter a Bank of the United States for twenty years with a capital of $10 million, one-fifth to be subscribed by the federal government and the remainder by private investors. Philadelphia was to be the bank's home office, but it might establish branches in other cities.

Over the opposition of Madison, Congress passed the bill charter-

BROTHERLY LOVE AMONG THE FOUNDING FATHERS

John Adams on Thomas Jefferson:
"[He has] a mind, soured, yet seeking for popularity, and eaten to a honeycomb with ambition, yet weak, confused, uninformed, and ignorant."

—on Alexander Hamilton:
"This man is stark mad, or I am." "[Consider] the profligacy of his life; his fornications, adulteries and his incests."

—on Benjamin Franklin:
"His whole life has been one continued insult to good manners and to decency. . . . From five complete years of experience of Dr. Franklin . . . I can have no dependence on his word. . . . I wish with all my soul he was out of public service."

Thomas Jefferson on Adams:
"[He is] distrustful, obstinate, excessively vain, and takes no counsel from anyone."

—on Hamilton:
"I will not suffer my retirement to be clouded by the slanders of a man whose history, from the moment at which history can stoop to notice him, is a tissue of machinations against the liberty of the country which not only has received and given him bread, but heaped its honors on his head."

Alexander Hamilton on Jefferson:
"A man of profound ambition and violent passions . . . the most intriguing man in the United States . . . the intriguing incendiary, the aspiring turbulent competitor . . . prone to projects which are incompatible with the principles of stable and systematic government."

—on Adams:
". . . disgusting egotism . . . distempered jealousy . . . ungovernable indiscretion." ". . . vanity without bounds."

Despite Hamilton's grand plans, most American pioneers settled into subsistence farming. One recounted:

"In the early years, there was none but a home market and that was mostly barter—it was so many bushels of wheat for a cow; so many bushels for a yoke of oxen. The price of a common pair of cowhide boots would be $7, payable in wheat at·62 cents per bushel."

ing the Bank and sent it to the President for his signature. Washington was stumped. His fellow Virginian, Madison, had raised doubts about whether the Constitution allowed Congress to charter such a bank. The President asked for the opinions of his cabinet. Both Jefferson and Attorney General Edmund Randolph replied that by no stretch of its meaning did the Constitution authorize a federally chartered bank. Hamilton took the opposite view. In a masterly application of what came to be called the principle of "broad construction" of the Constitution, he argued that since a bank was necessary to the collecting of taxes, the regulating of trade, and other functions explicitly conferred on Congress in that great document, its constitutionality was "implied," even though not specified. Convinced by Hamilton's logic, Washington signed the bill into law.

The Whiskey Rebellion (1794)   Although the federal government now possessed augmented powers under the new Constitution and the prestige that the national hero, George Washington, brought as its President, it was nonetheless a most fragile polity beset by enormous pressures. No one was certain what to expect from a republic. Different American regions, political factions, and ethnic groups had their own interests, and looming over all were the diverging concerns of the rich and the poor, the agrarians and the developing commercial elites, the varying class and economic groups of a sprawling new nation.

The tarring and feathering of an excise officer during the Whiskey Rebellion. *(Courtesy, Brown Brothers)*

The new government's great initiative to unite this variegated republic was Hamilton's financial plan. One cornerstone of that policy was an excise tax on alcoholic beverages. This would provide revenues to fund the national debt and to finance the government—including, many feared, its military capacity.

Whiskey was the cash crop of western Pennsylvania. Readily transportable and salable, corn liquor stored much better than the grain whence it came. Some of it no doubt gurgled and jostled in jugs and barrels swaying across the mountains on the backs of pack animals to slake the thirst of easterners. Westerners, even when they hungered for the word of God, continued to thirst for the "old Monongahela rye," and most of it was consumed in the West. The evangelical religion so strong in western Pennsylvania had not yet come out against drinking.

Though the farmer with a small still paid very little excise tax, westerners did not like it. They objected, as one petition phrased it, to "a duty for drinking our grain more than eating it." They objected to the appointment of excisemen with their right of entering private property and inspecting stills. And they especially objected to the federal court's trying cases against those who refused to pay the exciseman's levy. These trials required expensive and disruptive jaunts across the mountains to federal court at Philadelphia. The West, in 1794 still cut off from the Mississippi trade by the Spanish, and from most trade other than in alcohol by the expense of carrying goods over the mountains, was desperately short of currency. The drain of excise payments, though comparatively slight, was a burden on the region's economy.

The backcountry was not strong on being governed. These western farmers had little faith in anyone's governance but their own. They were soon passing resolutions not merely calling for an end to the tax, but overtly threatening excisemen and even those who cooperated with them by paying the tax. Soon barns began to be fired, gristmills damaged, excisemen attacked. "Tom the Tinker's men," it was claimed, were everywhere "mending" stills. This became the local expression for shooting holes in stills whose owners had paid the tax.

The West was not united on the issue. Battle spread between the small and the large whiskey producers, as the more prosperous distillers began to realize that this specie-draining tax would eventually drive the small producers out of business, leaving the more substantial men with a lucrative monopoly. Wealthy men feared as well that this excise rebellion could ignite into a war against property. In 1794 this almost came true, as the backwoods farmers marched on Pittsburgh, threatening to burn to the ground that symbol of the advance of commercial capitalism. Only adroit maneuverings by several Pittsburgh leaders persuaded the farmers that they ran too large a risk of retribution if they fired the city.

Something had to be done about the sporadic rioting in the West. A finding that the courts had been obstructed in carrying out the excise law provided the federal government with grounds for intervention. Hamilton, eager for a show of force that would establish the authority of the federal government, led the administration in a vast overreaction. Washington himself for a time directed a larger force than he had ever at one time commanded during the Revolution. Disorganized militia,

A local observer wrote of the backcountry habits:

"The use of whiskey was universal. The quality was good, the taste pleasant, its effect agreeable. Storekeepers kept liquor on their counters and sold it in their stores, and the women customers used it as well as the men. Farmers kept barrels of it in their cellars. . . . It was good for fevers, it was good for a decline, it was good for ague, it was good for snake-bites. It made one warm in winter and cool in summer. It was used at all gatherings. Bottles of it were set out on the table at christenings and wakes. . . . Ministers drank it. . . . Rev. Father McGirr's drink was whiskey-punch, of which it is said he could drink with any of his day without giving scandal."

about 13,000 strong, slogged through endless mud during a rainy November in search of a rebellion. Hamilton marched with the army from start to finish but was not away from his desk overly long; the army remained in the West about three weeks before arresting a few men and marching back to Philadelphia for heroes' welcomes. A grand jury in 1795 indicted over thirty men for treason. All of these but two were let free. Both of the others were mentally incompetent, and Washington pardoned them.

Despite the element of comedy within the rebellion, a sense that it had perhaps resulted from a bit too much of the spirits at issue, the episode possesses considerable importance for the political and constitutional development of the United States. A direct result of the insurrection was the forcing out of the last Jeffersonian, Edmund Randolph, who had succeeded Jefferson as secretary of state. Never again, except in moments of wartime emergency and then as a deliberate departure from the norm, would any President strive for a nonpartisan rather than a party government. The events of the rebellion had brought successes for both sides in the quarrel. The precedent of national power that Hamilton and Washington considered necessary for the future success of the American experiment was firmly established: without an armed clash, they had won something they had succeeded in defining as a war. What the farmers failed to achieve by rioting they got from the political activity that followed: in 1802 the new Jeffersonian government repealed the hated excise tax. Americans remained by all accounts one of the hardest-drinking people in the world for two more generations until a new wave of evangelism from the West brought fundamental changes in American values, and popular sentiment for the "old Monongahela rye" gave way to denunciation of Demon rum.

Hamiltonians vs. Jeffersonians
As Congress and the American people debated the Hamiltonian program, two distinct and conflicting positions began to emerge. One had as its principal spokesmen Jefferson and his chief congressional lieutenant, Madison. On the other side were Hamilton and his followers, John Adams, and, increasingly, President Washington himself.

The Jeffersonians favored state over national power and agriculture over industry, trade, and banking. They advocated a limited government and "strict construction" of the Constitution, a refusal to believe that the Constitution granted to any branch of government the slightest particle of power beyond what the words of the document specifically stated. They claimed to have faith in the people and to distrust the rich and powerful. Many were southerners, deeply attached to their local communities, which they did not want to come under the domination of a powerful central government. But the Jeffersonian party would also win support among the farmers of the middle and New England states and the artisans of the towns. Many Baptists and Methodists were of like opinion. Increasingly these citizens called themselves the Democratic Republicans, a label they adopted to contrast their political views with the supposedly more "monarchical" ideas of their Federalist opponents.

The Hamiltonians favored an ever stronger federal government, if necessary at the expense of the states. They believed that the nation's future lay in industry, not in agriculture alone. Generally speaking, they accepted republicanism as best suited to the American genius, but they did not trust majority rule as much as did their opponents, and they hoped to attract the support of the rich and the powerful to the new national government by making their interests coincide with those of the government. The Federalists could count on strong support within the major commercial towns, including such southern ports as Charleston. As defenders of order and stability they could also count on those people who were by temperament conservative. One group that contained many Federalists was the Congregational church in New England, which for a time enjoyed the support of state governments in the region.

The Government Seeks a Foreign Policy

The French Revolution (1789)   No sooner had the new government under the Constitution begun its work in New York than Europe went into a colossal political convulsion. In France, the colonies' ally in the war for independence, the American struggle for liberty had been deeply influential. "Enlightened" men and women recognized a larger significance in the event, and it strengthened their resolve to reform the Bourbon monarchy, custodian of the privilege and inequality that for centuries had shackled the French people. In August 1788 King Louis XVI, faced with a severe financial crisis induced partly by France's recent aid to the American revolutionaries, called into session the Estates General, representative of the clergy, nobility, and middle class, expecting that body to give him the taxes he needed, and then adjourn. But instead groups of reformers quickly took over. In a matter of a few months they had converted the Estates General into a revolutionary body that began to replace the entire old regime and convert the nation into a constitutional monarchy based on respect for human rights and on wide popular political participation. On July 14, 1789, a Paris mob attacked the Bastille, the prison that had become a notorious symbol of oppression, tore down the walls, and freed the prisoners.

The early response in the United States to the electrifying events in France was almost universally favorable. When the Marquis de Lafayette, who had helped lead the early stages of the Revolution, sent Washington the key to the Bastille, the President hung it prominently in the presidential mansion. He later wrote Gouverneur Morris that he hoped the disorders in France would "terminate very much in favor of the rights of man." If such a reserved and inherently conservative man as Washington could applaud the French uprising, the followers of Jefferson were sure to be still more enthusiastic. Some Republicans, in imitation of French egalitarianism, adopted the title "Citizen" or "Citizeness" in place of "Mister" or "Mistress." Others began to abandon knee breeches and adopt the long trousers worn by the Paris artisans and the French radicals. Within a few decades, trousers along with the short hair favored among revolutionary men in France were to become the standard among male Europeans and Americans, whatever their politics.

At first, Republicans considered the French Revolution the beginning of an age. As Jefferson wrote, "the liberty of the whole earth" depended on the contest in France. In time the initial consensus among Americans disintegrated. Increasingly the French radical leaders, called Jacobins, denounced the church and organized religion. In 1791 Louis XVI fled Paris with his family, but was caught and thrown into prison. By this time many enemies of the Revolution, including a large part of the French clergy and nobility, had been either driven from the country or hustled off to jail. Soon after, the revolutionary leaders began a reign of terror against all opponents of their policies, even the moderate reformers. In 1793 a revolutionary tribunal proclaimed a "war of all peoples against all kings." The tribunal then pronounced the death sentence on Louis XVI, and the sentence was promptly carried out. In October his Queen, Marie Antoinette, was also sent to the guillotine. As time passed the excesses of the French revolutionaries shocked many Americans.

France Seeks Aid   Before long, France was at war with Austria, England, Prussia, and Spain. Surrounded as it was with enemies, France sought aid from its friend, the United States. Jefferson thought France's struggle "the most sacred cause that ever man was engaged in" but did not want to go to war. Under the alliance of 1778 the Americans were bound to protect France's West Indies colonies against any enemy. England was certain to use her powerful fleet to blockade and, if possible, take these possessions. The United States now faced the serious prospect of war with Great Britain.

Many Americans would have welcomed such a war. Britain still limited American commerce with her own West Indies possessions. She still occupied western forts on United States soil. She still stirred up the Indians of the Northwest to discourage American settlement west of the mountains. Now that Britain was locked in combat with revolutionary France, she seemed the special enemy of liberty and freedom. And in 1793 the British began to seize American vessels engaged in trade with the French West Indies and to throw their crews into foul dungeons.

Among the followers of Hamilton, however, France represented all that was chaotic, disorderly, irreligious. That country, exclaimed Fisher Ames, was "an open hell, still ringing with agonies and blasphemies, still smoking with sufferings and crimes." Britain the Hamiltonians perceived as a bulwark of sanity and moderation, and they thought her victory in the struggle to be essential for world order. Another consideration weighed heavily in Federalist calculations. The whole Hamiltonian fiscal program depended on international trade, and in 1793 the United States, like the colonies for over a century before, traded primarily with Britain. Any wartime disruption of this trade would dry up revenues, injure the new national government, and thwart the Federalist economic program.

Citizen Genet   Meanwhile, the French Republic had dispatched Citizen Edmond Genet as diplomatic minister to the United States to do what he could to make trouble for Great Britain. Arriving on April 8, 1793, Genet immediately set to work recruiting Americans in his nation's cause. Even before presenting his formal credentials to Washington and Secretary of State Jefferson in Philadelphia, he had commissioned Americans as privateers to prey on British commerce, and opened negotiations with several American frontier leaders to attack Spanish Florida and Louisiana. Despite these highhanded actions, American friends of France cheered Genet as he made a triumphal procession to the capital. "I live in a round of parties," he wrote, "Old Man Washington can't forgive my success."

But Washington, supported by Hamilton and Jefferson, had decided to proclaim American neutrality. On April 22, 1793, the President issued a proclamation declaring the intent of the United States "to pursue a conduct friendly and impartial toward the French and British." Genet learned of this seeming repudiation of the 1778 treaty but, convinced by his recent experience that Americans were fervent partisans of the French, he determined to ignore it. Hinting that the United States might acquire Canada by aiding the French cause, Genet commissioned several land speculators as officers in the French army. Though at first a hero to Jeffersonians, Genet finally offended even the friends of the French Republic. So outrageous were his actions that Jefferson wrote Madison that the French minister would "sink the Republican interest" if the Republicans did not "abandon him." Reprimanded by President Washington and informed that his acts infringed upon American sovereignty, Genet promised to cease his activities, but then he immediately set about arming yet another vessel as a privateer. Warned not to continue, he threatened to appeal to the American people over the head of Washington. The administration decided it had had enough. In August the United States government demanded Genet's recall. Washington informed the Congress that the French envoy's conduct threatened "war abroad and discord and anarchy at home." But in France the Jacobins were in power, and Genet, who did not belong to this group, most certainly would have been beheaded had he been forced to return to France. The administration allowed him to stay in the United States, but refused to deal with him any further. He soon married the daughter of a member of the politically prominent Clinton family and settled into the quiet life of a country gentleman.

Reconciliation with Great Britain   While Americans rioted in the streets for or against Genet, the United States was moving toward a settlement of sorts with Great Britain. Late in 1793 Jefferson resigned as secretary of state. Edmund Randolph, another Virginian, succeeded him. Early in 1794 after learning that the British were building a new fort south of Lake Erie and were attacking United States ships in the West Indies, Washington sent Chief Justice John Jay to England as special envoy. John Adams wrote to Jefferson: "The President has sent Mr. Jay to try if he can to find a way to reconcile our honour with Peace. I have no great Faith in very brilliant

Citizen Genet, who came to America to stir up controversy against Britain, remained to live as a country gentleman in Orange County, New York. *(From the Emmet Collection, Manuscript Division, New York Public Library)*

Success; but hope he may have enough to keep us out of war." Jay, a staunch Federalist, knew that it would be difficult to get an agreement with Great Britain that would be popular. He was right. But Alexander Hamilton, in threatening war against Britain, had prepared the way.

One journalist wrote:

"John Jay, ah, the arch traitor—seize him, drown him, hang him, burn him, flay him alive! Men of America, he betrayed you with a kiss! As soon as he set foot on the soil of England he kissed the Queen's hand . . . and with this kiss betrayed away the rights of man and the liberty of America."

John Jay, by Gilbert Stuart. Jay's Treaty of 1795 settled most of the disputes with Britain left over from the Confederation period, but was very unpopular at home. *(Courtesy, National Gallery of Art, Washington, D.C. Lent by Mrs. Peter Jay)*

The Jay Treaty (1795)   The British made much of the American emissary. He in turn bowed to the Queen and kissed her hand, an act that outraged ardent Republicans. The British, who feared French attacks in Canada, drove a hard bargain. In the agreement that Jay carried back from London, the British promised finally to surrender the military posts they had illegally occupied since 1783. Other disagreements, including disputes over the pre-Revolutionary debts owed Englishmen, a boundary dispute with Canada in the Northwest, and the recent British ship seizures, were referred to arbitration commissions composed of British and American representatives. This device of an arbitration commission was an important diplomatic innovation, and in future years the two countries would make much use of it. Left unsettled were such long-standing American complaints as British incitements of Indians in the West and restrictive trade practices in the British West Indies colonies. On the question of British right to limit neutral trade in wartime, Jay retreated from the original American principle "free ships make free goods"—that a nation at war could not seize the goods carried in a neutral ship trading with the enemy nation— and agreed that the British could seize French or other enemy property found aboard American ships. Jay returned to the United States to find his fellow Americans in no mood to swallow this agreement.

In 1795 Jay's negotiations were greeted everywhere with outrage. One ardent Republican, unable to contain his feelings, inscribed on his fence: "Damn John Jay! damn every one that won't damn John Jay!! damn every one that won't put lights in his windows and sit up all night damning John Jay!!!" When Republicans met in taverns they toasted "A perpetual harvest to America; but clip't wings, lame legs, the pip, and an empty crop to all Jays." Jay himself ruefully remarked that he could have traveled across the nation by the light of his burning effigies.

Hamilton and other Federalists nonetheless marshaled their forces and wrote articles supporting the agreement as the best that could be obtained. Federalist Congressman Fisher Ames argued that if it were not approved the British and Indians would attack the frontier settlements. Washington put his prestige behind the treaty, earning for his efforts the contempt of the Republicans. Jefferson remarked: "Curse on his virtues; they have undone the country." But in June 1795 the Senate by a close vote confirmed the treaty, and the public reelected a Federalist Congress in 1796.

Whatever its inadequacies, the Jay Treaty settled most of the disputes with Britain left over from the Confederation period. But difficulties with Spain remained. Then, in 1795, the Spanish government and the United States signed the Pinckney Treaty. This agreement, coming after Jay's Treaty had neutralized the British, granted the Americans rights of access to the Mississippi River, imposed restraints on the Florida Indians, and provided Americans the right to take their goods through New Orleans for a period of three years. Spain also recognized American boundary claims under the Treaty of 1783, which consisted of the Mississippi River to the west and the 31st parallel to the south. Although the three-year provision implied possible trouble for the future, the nation greeted the Pinckney Treaty with great enthusiasm and the Senate ratified it unanimously. The treaty ended temporarily the threat that western regions of the United States, dependent on unimpeded use of the Mississippi River, might secede from the Union.

The Presidency of John Adams

Political Parties

In 1796 the nation faced its first contested presidential election. By this time American voters had a choice between two distinct parties. As yet, little of the machinery of party politics or campaigns had appeared, but throughout the nation people had begun to call themselves either Federalists or Republicans and their opponents by ruder names. Public men, Jefferson wrote a friend, no longer seemed "to separate political and personal differences. Men who have been intimate all their lives, cross the street to avoid meeting, and turn their heads another way, lest they should be obliged to touch their hats." Name-calling and violence became commonplace, especially in the newly emerging party press. The extreme Federalist William Cobbett described Republicans as "cut-throats who walk in rags and sleep amidst filth and vermin." Some New Yorkers threw stones at Alexander Hamilton. Even Washington himself became the target of vicious remarks: in Virginia his opponents toasted "a speedy death to President Washington."

President John Adams, by E. F. Andrews. Washington's Vice President won a close election in 1796 to become America's second President. *(Courtesy, The New-York Historical Society, New York City)*

By the mid-1790s the two political parties possessed distinct characteristics. The Federalists were centered in the Northeast, where business and commerce were concentrated. Many were well-to-do businessmen who wanted to use the federal government to strengthen the industrial sector of the economy. Federalists favored high tariffs and the national bank. Republicans clustered in the South and West. There were also substantial numbers of working-class Republicans living in the eastern cities. The Republican persuasion favored a weak central government, opposed high tariffs and the national bank, and championed states' rights.

The division of the country into these two opposing political camps disturbed many Americans. The founders of the republic, including the authors of the Constitution, had not envisioned political parties. The voters, they believed, should choose for office the best, most public-spirited men. Partisan organizations appeared to be dangerous instruments of selfish men that impeded, rather than advanced, expression of the general will. Many Americans of the 1790s regarded parties as symptomatic of a disease within the body politic. Even the ambitious men engaged in creating the factions thought that they were, at best, necessary evils. "If I could not go to heaven but with a party," Jefferson once wrote, "I would not go there at all." Such fears were, in part, the legacy of revolutionary thought, particularly the tendency to see an embattled republic surrounded by foreign foes and beset with domestic dangers. These beliefs actually contributed to the party spirit and the frenzied political temper of the 1790s. The distrust of party, the belief that party politics expressed corruption and conspiracy, made Americans of each faction look on the other side as polluting the virtuous republic: and so each faction deepened its own partisan emotion.

Washington's official family felt the strains. Even before his resignation from the Cabinet, Jefferson, the arch-Republican, ceased to talk to Hamilton, the arch-Federalist. In 1795 Hamilton, too, left official life, going back to the practice of law in New York. Neither man, however, abandoned politics. From Monticello, the classical mansion he designed for a hill with a view of the Blue Ridge Mountains, Jefferson continued to advise by letter his friends and political allies in Philadelphia and around the nation. Hamilton also remained active politically and would exert great influence in the administration that followed Washington's.

Washington, no doubt, could have held the presidency for life had he so desired. But he was weary of politics and anxious to return to Mount Vernon; he looked forward, he said, to sitting down to dinner alone with his wife, Martha. He refused to accept a third term, and with the help of Madison and Hamilton he prepared a final address to his fellow citizens. Washington's Farewell Address (never presented orally but printed in a Philadelphia newspaper) devoted more attention to domestic than to foreign matters. The retiring President deplored the state of political conflict that had arisen and warned Americans against disunity, whether sectional or political. He also cautioned the nation to be wary of permanent alliances with foreign nations. He did not advocate isolation from international affairs; he merely recommended that the country be guided by its own essentially modest interests and not become too closely tied to the grander designs of other nations.

As Washington prepared to return to Virginia, political conflict remained fierce. As yet there were no national nominating conventions as we now know them. Instead, both Federalist and Republican leaders merely agreed among themselves on who should run.

The Election of 1796   The choice of the Federalist Party was Vice President John Adams. Less extreme than the "high Federalists" such as Hamilton, he was nevertheless peppery and opinionated as well as learned and public-spirited. Ever since the 1770s Adams had been in the forefront of the struggle for nationhood. Now he considered France the chief threat to his country's peace and order. The Republicans turned to their acknowledged chief, Jefferson. Tall, loose-jointed, red-haired, the former secretary of state was as hostile to the British and as friendly to the French as ever. Britain, he believed, was determined to subjugate the United States economically and he thought that under Hamilton's auspices the British had come to dominate the American government.

Intrigues, maneuverings, libels, and attacks flourished. The Republican press assailed Adams as a monarchist who, if elected, would enslave the American people. The Federalist press accused Jefferson of being a lackey of the French and claimed that as governor of Virginia during the Revolution he had fled his capital in a "cowardly" escape from the British.

In his Farewell Address of September 1796 President Washington denounced partisanship, pleading for the republican ideal of disinterested, independent statesmen as the only safe guide for the nation. He also warned against permanent foreign alliances and cautioned that the Union would be endangered if political parties continued to be characterized "by geographical discriminations—*Northern* and *Southern, Atlantic* and *Western*—whence designing men may endeavor to excite a belief that there is a real difference of local interests and views."

Meanwhile, the new French Minister in the United States, Citizen Adet, was angry at the Federalist administration for coming to terms with the British and he joined the fracas. In November 1796 he published in the American newspapers a set of proclamations announcing that France would suspend diplomatic relations with the United States and come down hard on neutral shipping. The blame for this new policy, he declared, lay with the Federalists' friendship with Britain.

Adams gained seventy-one electoral ballots to Jefferson's sixty-eight, with Thomas Pinckney—an ally of Hamilton—coming in third. Under the then existing provisions of the Constitution, John Adams became the second President of the United States, and Jefferson the Vice President. Two political enemies—a Federalist and a Democratic Republican—were now yoked together. Besides partisan politics President Adams would face a complex set of problems, especially in foreign relations.

Renewed Trouble with Britain
The United States by now had become a major international trader, its ships calling in virtually every port in the world. The reason for this growth was the great European war. As the British Royal Navy swept French and Spanish vessels off the high seas, France and her allies depended increasingly on the most important maritime neutral, the United States, to carry goods to and from their colonies. By 1796 American merchants were bringing in millions of dollars' worth of molasses, rum, sugar, and other products from French and Spanish possessions in the New World, landing them at New York, Baltimore, Charleston, or Philadelphia and then sending them, marked as American exports, to France, Spain, or some other part of continental Europe. They were also pouring into the French and Spanish colonies European goods that Britain's enemies feared to carry on their own vessels.

This wartime trade rained dollars, pounds, doubloons, and gilders on American merchants. Great mansions arose in Salem, Boston, Newburyport, Charleston, and the other centers of foreign trade. Every harbor along the Atlantic coast was dotted with the white sails and black hulls of the brigs, sloops, barges, and full-rigged ships engaged in world trade, while on the shore the streets were crowded with clerks, stevedores, porters, teamsters, and jack-tars hurrying about their business of moving the world's goods and making money.

The British were angry. The good fortune of the United States came at their expense. Not only were the Americans helping their enemies evade the British blockade of Europe and of French and Spanish America, but they were also taking over business formerly handled by British merchants. And the expanding American merchant marine was luring many of Britain's best seamen. Experienced British merchant seamen preferred the high wages and clean ships of the Americans, and were deserting.

For a while after the Jay Treaty, the British left American ships and seamen alone. But then, in 1796, when marine manpower shortages began to hurt, they resorted to impressment. Whenever a British man-of-war stopped an American merchant vessel to inspect her cargo for goods going to France, a British naval officer lined the men up on deck. Back and forth he went, asking each to speak up and identify himself. Anyone with an English, Irish, or Scottish accent could be assumed to be a British subject and removed to serve in the Royal Navy. The *American Daily Advertiser* fumed: "Are our sailors to be maltreated, our ships plundered and our flag defied with impunity?" Some of the sailors taken by the British, wrote one ship captain, "are American born, and have wives and children, whose existence, perhaps, depends on the welfare of a husband in slavery—a father in chains!"

The XYZ Affair   The French were no better. The French Directory, as the ruling body was called between 1795 and 1799, considered the victory of Adams, a sympathizer with Britain, to be an unfriendly act on the part of the American people. In 1797 the French government ordered that every United States citizen captured aboard a British vessel be hanged; if any single item of British make was found aboard an American ship, the vessel was to be confiscated. The French gave the United States minister his walking papers, in effect cutting off diplomatic relations.

Knowing that the United States was ill prepared to go to war, Adams decided to negotiate and appointed three commissioners, Elbridge Gerry, Charles Cotesworth Pinckney, and John Marshall, to go to Paris to seek a settlement. At the same time, the administration asked Congress for money to build naval vessels and expand the army. In October 1797 the three American emissaries arrived in Paris prepared to negotiate with the French foreign minister, Talleyrand. Over several weeks they were forced to talk to three French officials whom they later identified only as X, Y, and Z. The Americans, these gentlemen informed Marshall, Gerry, and Pinckney, would have to apologize for some recent anti-French statements of President Adams; they would need to promise a loan to France; and they must privately pay money to Talleyrand and members of the Directory. The American envoys were not naive about how diplomacy was conducted in Europe, but they refused to pay bribes before the French agreed to a settlement, and broke off the talks. Said Pinckney, "No, no, not a sixpence!" Soon after, the emissaries reported to Adams on what had transpired during their mission.

In 1798 the American government published the entire "XYZ" correspondence. "Millions for defense but not a cent for tribute"— a famous toast to Justice John Marshall on his return from a trip to France in 1795—became a popular slogan. Whatever the worldly American emissaries felt, the American people were shocked by France's seeming contempt for the United States. Overnight all but the most ardent Republicans became anti-French. Congress appropriated money for forty naval vessels, and for trebling the size of the army. Congress also ended commerce with France and ordered the suspension of the Franco-American alliance of 1778. Shortly thereafter, a full though undeclared naval war broke out on the Atlantic, American frigates and French vessels exchanging broadside volleys and French privateers attacking United States merchant vessels within sight of the American coast.

A cartoon indicating the anti-French feeling generated by the XYZ Affair. The three American ministers at left reject the "Paris Monster's" demand for money.

In the undeclared naval war with France, the American frigate *Constellation* captured the French ship *L'Insurgent*, February, 1799. *(Courtesy, The Peabody Museum of Salem)*

Alien and Sedition Acts (1798)   In this time of intense political excitement, Federalists found it impossible to regard their opponents' views as legitimate expressions of dissent. As yet, few Americans fully accepted the legitimacy of a party system and so Federalists (like Republicans) found the opposing party to be treacherous by its very existence. And the French Revolution went so far beyond the American Revolution in attacking traditional social institutions that conservatives saw in it chaos, anarchy, and atheism. In this mood a Congress dominated by the Federalists passed in 1798 four measures, called collectively the Alien and Sedition Acts, designed to curb opposition and prevent internal subversion.

The Naturalization Act extended from five to fourteen years the period of residence required for citizenship. The Alien Act gave the President the power to deport any alien suspected of "treasonable or secret" intentions. The Alien Enemies Act gave him the authority in time of war to arrest or banish from the country any citizen of an enemy power. These three measures were all aimed at foreigners. The Sedition Act was directed at Americans, and especially at opponents of the administration. Under its terms any resident of the United States who sought to prevent the execution of federal law, to stop a federal official from performing his duties, or to start any riot, "insurrection," or "unlawful assembly" could be fined or imprisoned. Anyone convicted of publishing "any false, scandalous and malicious writing" against Con-

The Republican congressman Matthew Lyon of Vermont saw in President Adams

"every consideration of public welfare swallowed up in a continual grasp for power, an unbounded thirst for ridiculous pomp, foolish adulation and selfish avarice; men of real merit daily turned out of office for no other cause but independency of spirit . . . men of firmness, merit, years, abilities and experience discarded in their applications for office, for fear they possess that independence, and men of meanness preferred, for the ease with which they can take up and advocate opinions, the consequences of which they know but little of."

Of the repressive Alien and Sedition Acts passed by the Federalists, a mass meeting in Woodford County, Kentucky, declared:

"That for the servants of the people to tell those who created them that they shall not, at their peril, examine into the conduct of [their] servants for the abuse of power is tyranny!"

gress, the President, or the government could be fined or sentenced to prison for two years. A New Jersey man, watching a salute fired to honor President Adams on a visit there, remarked that he would have liked to see the cannon wadding "lodged in the President's backsides." For that observation he was fined $100.

Using his powers under the Alien and Sedition Acts, Secretary of State Timothy Pickering began a series of prosecutions of Republican newspaper editors and political leaders. The owners of four leading Republican newspapers were indicted and three Republican editors were convicted of violating the Sedition Act. Pickering also charged Matthew Lyon, a Vermont congressman, with libel against President Adams. Lyon is immortalized in American history for spitting in the eye of a Federalist Representative from Connecticut and then being drawn into a brawl with his enemy. The Irish-born Lyon—once an indentured servant and later one of Ethan Allen's Green Mountain Boys who captured Fort Ticonderoga during the Revolution—was convicted, fined a thousand dollars, and hustled off to jail for four months. He was, however, reelected to Congress from his jail cell.

The prosecutions under the Sedition Act damaged Adams and the Federalists badly. Many fair-minded Americans considered the acts violations of the freedom of speech and press guaranteed by the Bill of Rights. Before long, opponents of the measures and the prosecutions were holding meetings throughout the middle states, the South, and the West and sending petitions of protest to Congress. Great rolls of paper containing thousands of names were soon deposited on the desks of the House and Senate clerks.

Kentucky and Virginia Resolutions   No Americans were more disturbed by the Federalist repressions than the leaders of the Republican Party, Jefferson and Madison. Both regarded the Alien and Sedition Acts not only as a violation of freedom, but also as granting excessive power to the federal government over the states. Jefferson and Madison each secretly drafted a set of resolutions against the Federalist laws; friends steered Jefferson's through the Kentucky legislature, and allies took Madison's through Virginia's.

The Kentucky Resolution argued that "when the federal government exercises powers not specifically delegated by the Constitution, each state has equal right to judge for itself . . . of the mode of redress." The Virginia Resolution claimed that when the federal government acts contrary to the Constitution the states "have the right and are in duty bound to interpose for arresting the progress of the evil." Together the Kentucky and Virginia Resolutions stated that the federal government was a compact of states for certain limited purposes. Under the Constitution the national government did not possess the sort of powers it was seeking to exercise under the Alien and Sedition Acts. The two Republican leaders then attacked the Sedition Act as contrary to the Bill of Rights. Neither Kentucky nor Virginia went so far as to nullify the Alien and Sedition Acts, but in 1832 South Carolina would draw on this precedent to nullify a federal tariff.

Adams Compromises with France
Despite his lack of personal popularity, Adams and his party remained in firm control, and the President could have gotten Congress to declare war on France. Instead, in 1799, without consulting the cabinet, Adams announced that he intended to send another mission to France to resume negotiations of outstanding differences.

When the American delegates arrived in Paris, they encountered a changed situation. The leader of France now was First Consul Napoleon Bonaparte. Flushed with new victories, the French were reluctant to grant the Americans the indemnities they wanted for "spoliations" of their commerce. But Napoleon was not entirely unreasonable. He agreed to end the naval war and attacks on American commerce; he also consented to release the United States from its obligations to France under the Treaty of 1778. The American envoys were disappointed but seeing no possibility of better terms accepted this convention of 1800. Many Federalists thought it a cowardly surrender. The President disagreed—the negotiations, he believed, were "the most disinterested, the most determined, and the most successful" of his whole career. But they cost him a second term.

John Adams wrote:

"I desire no other inscription over my gravestone than: 'Here lies John Adams, who took upon himself the responsibility of the peace with France in the year 1800.'"

The Election of 1800

The political campaign of 1800 was one of the most momentous in the nation's history and in the evolution of modern political democracy. For the first time power passed peaceably and constitutionally from one political party to another.

The rhetoric was by no means peaceable. The Republicans attacked the President once again as a friend to Britain, a monarchist, a spendthrift who had burdened the country with enormous debts. Jefferson, the Federalist press charged, was an atheist who placed scientific reason above the teachings of the Bible. Elect him President, Federalists said, and religion would vanish and infidelity flourish. The man was a "voluptuary" who, it was alleged, had fathered children by a slave.

The New Capital
One item in the Republicans' indictment of their opponents was the extravagant cost of the new national capital under construction on the Potomac River. Actually, by the time the government moved from Philadelphia, the federal city was still more a plan than a reality. The scheme drawn up by a Frenchman, Major Pierre L'Enfant, was magnificent in its broad streets, its malls, plazas, and circles; but for the moment it had given place to a more modest and achievable plan. The government had begun construction of the President's house in 1792, and shortly thereafter the Capitol began to rise. The third building to appear was a tavern.

The first government officials arrived from Philadelphia in June 1800. On November 1, President Adams and his family moved into the president's house. The new city was little more than a paper community. Besides the Capitol, the tavern, and the President's house (it would not be called the White House until the early 1900s), Washington consisted of some boarding houses, a few huts for construction workers, and not

Abigail Adams confided to a friend her impressions of her journey in 1800 to the new capital in Washington, D.C.:

"I arrived here on Sunday last, and without meeting with any accident worth noticing, except losing ourselves when we left Baltimore, and going eight or nine miles on the Frederick road, by which means we were obliged to go the other eight through woods, where we wandered two hours without finding a guide, or the path. Fortunately, a straggling black came up with us, and we engaged him as a guide, to extricate us out of our difficulty; but woods are all you see, from Baltimore until you reach [Washington]. . . ."

Pierre L'Enfant's plan for the city of Washington. The basic plan with its circles and broad converging streets was retained. (*Courtesy, Stokes Collection, The New York Public Library*)

John and Abigail Adams were the first presidential couple to occupy the new "President's Palace," as the executive mansion was called. In late 1800, just three months before Adams would vacate it for Jefferson, they moved in. Only six rooms in the mansion were finished, but they had to move in because a 1790 law stated that Philadelphia would be the seat of government for only ten years. In a letter to her daughter, Abigail described her feelings about the new lodgings:

"The house is on a grand and superb scale, requiring about 30 servants to attend and keep the apartments in proper order, and perform the ordinary business of the house and stables. . . .

The lighting of the apartments from the kitchen to parlors and chambers is a tax indeed and the fires we are obliged to secure us from daily agues is another cheerful comfort. To assist us in this great castle, and render less assistance necessary, bells are wholly wanting, not one single one being hung in the whole house, and promises are all you can obtain. This is so great an inconvenience that I know not what to do. . . .

If they will put me up some bells, and let me have wood enough to keep the fires, I deign to be pleased. I could content myself almost anywhere for three months; but surrounded with forests, can you believe that wood is not to be had. . . . We have not the least fence, yard or other convenience without; and the great unfurnished audience room I make a drying-room of to hang up the clothes in."

much else. Streets had been laid out, but these muddy or dusty tracks were lined, not with residences or stores, but with virgin forest. Even the President's new home was only half complete.

Aaron Burr   Under the existing provisions of the Constitution, the electors who would place a President and Vice President in this raw new city did not vote separately for each office. Every elector cast two ballots, and the person with the highest vote total was declared President while the runner-up became Vice President. The Republican caucus in Congress had designated Jefferson as the party's presidential and Aaron Burr as its vice-presidential candidate, but in the actual voting all the Republican electors voted for both equally. When the votes were counted, therefore, Jefferson and Burr were tied for first place. This situation threw the choice of President into the House of Representatives, where the members of each state would cast a single collective vote and for election a candidate needed the vote of a majority of states.

The Federalists did not control enough states to reelect President Adams, but they could deny the presidency to anyone else. It was not likely that they would block a choice, since that would paralyze the nation, but they were capable of excluding Jefferson and substituting Burr. And the Federalists found Burr preferable to Jefferson. The New Yorker was an aristocrat, a friend of banks and Hamiltonian funding, and a believer in a strong executive. He also had the reputation of being corrupt, ambitious, cynical, and unscrupulous, but under the circumstances that was to the good: he could be counted on to make whatever arrangements with the Federalists they desired. The choice of Burr would also be sure to upset and confound the Republicans.

Some Federalist leaders nonetheless recoiled from this choice. Hamilton despised Burr, who he believed would "employ the rogues of all parties to overrule the good men of all parties." Jefferson, though in Hamilton's view "tinctured with fanaticism nor even mindful of truth," had some "pretension to character." Hamilton advised voting for the Virginian if he would give the Federalists guarantees that he would uphold the Federalist fiscal system, remove no Federalist from office except those of Cabinet rank, sustain the army and navy intact, and maintain the principles of neutrality in foreign affairs established by the two Federalist Presidents. Burr was meanwhile refusing to treat directly with the Federalists, since that would have outraged his fellow Republicans and lost him any scrap of their support.

In the end, Jefferson gave the Federalists some indirect assurances and he was declared elected. The nation could now resume as a going political concern.

The Revolution of 1800	Jefferson's election has been called the "revolution of 1800." The apprehensive Federalists would not have disagreed. Not only had they lost the presi-

dency; they had also been swept from power in Congress. There was still hope: the judiciary might be saved. Hours before leaving office President Adams appointed a flock of Federalists to new judgeships and other legal posts created by the Judiciary Act of 1801. These "midnight judges" might be able to stop the Republicans from upsetting the economic and political arrangements of the country. Adams separately appointed John Marshall to be chief justice of the United States. The President did not rank this appointment as one of the great contributions of his administration, yet it would turn out to be the most significant of all.

A Slave Plot

While Federalists and Democratic Republicans fought their political battles in the election of 1800, in Jefferson's own Virginia another kind of battle was almost joined. In Richmond a slave blacksmith named Gabriel Prosser and his brother, Martin, a slave preacher, organized a slave uprising that came to be known as Gabriel's Rebellion. Inspired by the rhetoric of the American and French revolutions and the ongoing political discourse in the United States about rights and liberty, Gabriel plotted with slaves in outlying plantations to march on Richmond and kill all the whites except some Quakers and Methodists who were known to harbor antislavery views. But the uprising never took place: on the designated night a fierce rainstorm washed out the unpaved roads leading into Richmond, and the would-be rebels scattered, their momentum gone.

Suggested Readings

On George Washington see Richard Brookhiser's *Reinventing George Washington* (1996). See also James Thomas Flexner, *Washington: The Indispensable Man* (1974) and Marcus Cunliffe's *George Washington: Man and Monument* (1958). Forrest McDonald's *Alexander Hamilton* (1979) and Richard Beeman's *Patrick Henry* (1982) offer views of a staunch Federalist and an equally adamant Anti-Federalist. On the background of the Constitution see David Szatmary's *Shays's Rebellion: The Making of an Agrarian Insurrection* (1980), Jay Fliegalman, *Prodigals and Pilgrims: The American Revolution Against Patriarchal Authority, 1750–1800* (1982), and Richard Beeman, Stephen Botein, and Edward C. Carter, eds., *Beyond Confederation: Origins of the Constitution and American National Identity* (1987).

Lance Banning, *The Jeffersonian Persuasion* (1978) traces Republican thought in the 1790s. Banning explores James Madison's role in the shaping of the new nation in *The Sacred Fire of Liberty: James Madison and the Founding of the Federal Republic* (1995). Morton J. Horowitz in *The Transformation of American Law, 1780–1860* (1977) examines the process by which law, having been rigid in the eighteenth century, became more flexible in the nineteenth.

Alexander DeConde is standard on *The Quasi-War: Politics and Diplomacy of the Undeclared War with France, 1797–1802* (1966). Like everything else that Richard Hofstadter wrote, *The Idea of a Party System* (1973) is illuminating and graceful. On the slave uprising in Virginia see Douglas Egerton, *Gabriel's Rebellion: The Virginia Slave Conspiracies of 1800 and 1802* (1993).

See also Joseph J. Ellis, *After the Revolution: Profiles of Early American Culture* (1979), Reginald Horsman, *The Frontier in the Formative Years, 1783–1815* (1970), Ralph Adams Brown, *The Presidency of John Adams* (1975), Richard H. Kohn, *Eagle and Sword: The Federalists and the Creation of a Military Establishment in America, 1783–1802* (1975), and John F. Hoadley, *Origins of American Political Parties, 1789–1803* (1986). Lorraine Smith Payle and Thomas L. Payle, *The Learning of Liberty: The Educational Ideas of the Founding Fathers* (1993), explores early efforts to promote civic virtue in a democratic republic. Jack P. Greene, *The Intellectual Construction of America, Exceptionalism and Identity from 1492 to 1800* (1993) examines European and American views of America's unique role as a land of opportunity and democracy.

☆ ☆ ☆ **POINTS OF VIEW** ☆ ☆ ☆

What Did Women Gain from the Revolution?

Elizabeth Fox-Genovese

Was the American Revolution, whether conservative or radical for men, a revolution at all for women?

When Abigail Adams wrote to her husband that he should "remember the ladies," she was asking that the domestic powers of husbands be reduced and, above all, that they cease behaving like tyrants within the household. But she was not asking that women be allowed to participate in government. During the second half of the eighteenth century advanced advocates of women's rights were insisting on women's capacity for an essentially female excellence, not asking that women be recognized as functionally interchangeable with men.

In effect, the American Revolution strengthened gender as a form of social classification. Previously women had been able to relate to the polity, or at least the public area, as delegates of families on occasion when family and class membership superseded gender membership. After the Revolution they related to the polity as women first and members of families or classes second. This intensification of gender as a form of social classification has led historians to argue that women actually lost opportunities as a result of the Revolution. Others contend that women gained through their heightened identification with other women, through the emergence of a recognizable "woman's sphere" within which they forged tight bonds of sisterhood. But the question remains: if the Revolution did not result in women's inclusion in the polity, if the new republic did not welcome women as citizens, what did the revolutionary times specifically offer women?

The change amounted to an improvement in the view of women specifically as women: the view of what it meant to be a woman. Earlier seen as potentially dangerous and deviant, as possible witches or probable shrews, women were suddenly seen as the mothers of citizens of the republic. Previously obliged to labor under the direction of the male heads of their households, they now were granted governance of the home. The ties that bound women to their gender tightened, but their gender gained status. The belief that women had a particular feminine sensibility legitimated their demands for education, though an education different from that for men. The conviction that they were capable of superior moral purity and had special insights into the human condition legitimated their concern with social problems, as long as they did not take those concerns into the political sphere. The respect and self-respect that they had won legitimated their quest for excellence within their own sphere.

The record then leaves us with a paradox. The most important results of the Revolution were political and resolutely excluded women. The indirect results were social and ideological and attempted to circumscribe and control women. But in contributing to a clearer definition of women as women, these results also undercut the time-honored vision of women as inferior or lesser men. By proposing that women should aspire to excellence in their own sphere, they allowed that women *could* be excellent. Once that possibility had been granted, it remained only a matter of time until women would begin to claim that they could be excellent in roles previously ascribed to men.

Before, during, and after the Revolution, American women were experiencing important demographic changes that ultimately contributed to their socioeconomic subordination in the modern world. These demographic factors were of such an evolutionary nature, however, that few seem to have been directly affected by the Revolution itself, save for the temporary disruption of the nuclearity of family life, as men left home to participate in political or military activities, and for the lowering of sexual and moral standards that normally accompany wars. . . .

By 1750, at least northern colonial America could no longer be considered a "paradise on earth for women," where every free, white female could marry and where a stable, parental dominated marriage system or family of orientation (birth) prevailed. It was in the throes of a "demographic crisis. . . ." In addition to facing the possibility of not being able to marry, or remarry, in the case of widows, by the time of the Revolution women had been gradually adjusting to changing courtship and marriage patterns, loosened sexual mores, smaller family size, and (among the wealthier, better educated) to more permissive theories from foreign authors about child raising, romantic love, and sex-stereotyped definitions of feminity. All of these demographic alterations were part of the process of family modernization—that is, the evolution from the family of orientation to the family of procreation. This transition was most pronounced in the late eighteenth and early nineteenth centuries, and is therefore coincidentally connected but not substantially affected by the Revolution.

[E]xcept for the actual years in which the war was fought, colonial women found more and more of their traditional familial duties and responsibilities syphoned off as the economy became more commercially specialized and as other social institutions such as schools became more commonplace. Only women living in the most isolated frontier areas escaped this experience of declining importance and function within the family unit, and their position was far from enviable because of the physical and mental harshness of frontier life. . . .

Even the best educated women could not realize that they were demographically on their way toward modernization within the family of procreation that offered them the "cult of true womanhood" in place of collective validation and a sense of individual worth. Nor could they be expected to have anticipated other "double standard" limitations associated with this new family pattern, such as increased vicarious fulfillment through their husbands or male children and the psychic burden of the permissive child-centered household that epitomized individualism.

Reprinted from *The American Revolution: Explorations in the History of American Radicalism*, ed. Alfred F. Young (De Kalb: Northern Illinois University Press, 1976), 82, 83, 84, 88.

Thomas Jefferson, inaugurated as third President of the United States in March 1801. *(Portrait by Rembrandt Peale, 1800, White House Collection)*

Independence Confirmed 1800-1816

THOMAS JEFFERSON AND SALLY HEMINGS

The peculiar institution could lead to complicated civil and sexual relations. Some slave owners acknowledged their offspring, even provided for their education. Harriet Jacobs, author of well-known reminiscences of slave life, tells of one white man who treated her not as property but as a lover—a story well this side of horror.

Slavery, then, was never a system about which any one specific set of behavior could be predicted. In essence, slavery meant simply that one person was the property of another. But since that "property" was a human being, the system could not reduce itself to the simple and definable ways of a farmer's working of the land or a banker's management of financial capital. Instead, any number of manners in which human beings connect to one another could come of it: cruelty, the arrogance of mastership, exploitation such as a capitalist could impose on a hired worker, sexual union, even at times friendship or love. And at the turn of the nineteenth century, slavery had not so firmly fixed itself in the South as it later would.

In illustration of the troubled conscience of the most articulate southerners, Thomas Jefferson comes quickly to mind. He was the major composer of the Declaration of Independence, a great document in the modern creed of liberty and equality, and he expressed his discomfort over slavery. But like George Washing-

continued

HISTORICAL EVENTS

1801
Spain cedes Louisiana to France
• Barbary Pirates declare war

1803
Marbury v. Madison
• Louisiana Purchase

1804
Lewis and Clark expedition begins
• American navy blockades coast of Tripoli (Algeria)

1806
Berlin Decree

1807
Embargo Act

1809
Embargo Act repealed
• Non-Intercourse Act

1810
Macon's Bill No. 2

1811
Battle at Tippecanoe Creek

1812
War of 1812 • campaigns against Canada fail

215

HISTORICAL EVENTS

1813
Battle of the Thames • British
capture Fort Niagara and Buffalo
• Battle of Lake Erie

1814
British burn Washington but are
turned back at Baltimore
• Treaty of Ghent

1814–15
Battle of New Orleans

1816
James Monroe elected President
• Second Bank of the United States

ton, he was a slave owner. An old story about Jefferson, founded in the primitive hatreds of the nation's early politics and culminating in the cold realms of present-day science, raises further questions about Jefferson's relations with the slave system.

In 1802 a Federalist newspaper published an account of a black woman who had given birth to a "litter" of Jefferson's children. Combining gutter-level racism with seething hostility to the President, the article referred to her as a "wench" (a common term for slave women) and "slut" whose natural home might be the pigsty. The woman so maligned was Sally Hemings, daughter of Jefferson's father-in-law and a slave of Jefferson. When he was American minister to France, she had traveled there with one of his daughters. Though under French law she became free, she went back with him to the United States. Four of her children lived to maturity, and all of them became free: two were runaways, and Jefferson's will freed the two youngest sons. Soon after his death, Sally too became free.

The circumstances would suggest at least a friendship between Jefferson and Sally Hemings, and some neighborhood rumor held them to be lovers. In 1873 Sally's son Madison Hemings, then living in Ohio, told a journalist of his mother's informing him that he and his siblings were Jefferson's children. Sally, the account went, had returned with Jefferson from France on his promise to free all the children the two might have together.

Among historians it became customary to reject the story of Sally Hemings. In 1997, however, Annette Gordon-Reed published an argument questioning the scholarly grounds of the dismissal. A year later a journal published the results of DNA testing that compared with the male chromosome of a descendant of Jefferson's paternal grandfather the male chromosome of a descendant of Easton Hemings, one of Sally's offspring. The test established with a high degree of probability that Easton Hemings had been in the line of some male Jefferson. While the finding cannot indicate whether the Jefferson was Thomas, it combines with other evidence to throw very heavy weight on the side of the traditional rumor.

Whether Sally Hemings was Jefferson's mistress or simply a favored servant, her relations with him complicate the figure of Jefferson and bear on the character of the slave system itself. Suppose his special treatment of her and her children—he freed few of his slaves—came of a sexual liaison. That would indicate an ability on his part to break partly with a common pattern of connections between male owner and female servant as object of lust. Certainly in the later days of the institution, it would not be unusual to use defenseless slave women and then treat the owner's offspring merely as slaves, to be worked or sold. Is it possible that Jefferson, whatever his relationship with Sally Hemings, made amends to her and her children for a guilt at slavery that he could not translate into a public attack on it? The detail of the transactions between Sally Hemings and Thomas Jefferson will remain mysterious, representing an unrecoverable multiplicity of daily encounters of slaves and slavemasters dictated by the waywardness of human nature.

President Thomas Jefferson

The Inauguration At noon on a blustery March day in 1801, Jefferson took the oath of office and became the third President of the United States. He had come to Washington the previous November and had spent the winter at Conrad and McMunn's boardinghouse, where for $15 a week he dined and roomed unostentatiously. The inauguration ceremonies were brief and austere, as befitted a party that made a point of republican simplicity. Jefferson's expensive velvet suit failed to arrive, and he walked in plain garb to the still uncompleted Capitol.

In the crowded Senate chamber, Jefferson swore to defend the Constitution and faithfully discharge the duties of his office. Then he delivered his inaugural address, pledging freedom of religion and the press. He endorsed the encouragement of agriculture, and of commerce as its handmaid. The federal government, the new President declared, must conduct its business economically and attempt to pay off its debts. The state governments were "the surest bulwarks against anti-republican tendencies." But besides making these predictable Republican pronouncements, Jefferson sought to calm the fears of Federalists. The nation, he declared, must avoid "entangling alliances": this was a signal that the Republicans would accept the recent termination of the 1778 French alliance. They would also avoid extreme partisanship. Now that the great contest of 1800 was over, all Americans "will, of course, arrange themselves under the will of the law, and unite in common efforts for the common good." Minority rights would be protected, and no one would suffer persecution: "We are all Republicans, we are all Federalists. . . . Let us, then, with courage and confidence pursue our own Federal and Republican principles, our attachment to union and representative government."

So softly did the fresh-minted chief executive speak that few in the crowded room could hear what he said. But printed copies of the speech were available, and ushers distributed these to the assembled dignitaries. That evening, the President returned to Conrad and McMunn's to dine as usual. When he entered the dining room, a lady among the paying guests offered him a chair. Jefferson declined and went to his usual place at the foot of the table, far from the warming fire. A simpler age of American manners had begun.

Yet republican plainness, as Jefferson understood it, meant something quite opposite to the affected bluntness and democracy of style, and the crude appeals to popular emotions, that have been a temptation among American politicians. Jefferson was a gentleman. Graciousness,

"I have this morning witnessed one of the most interesting scenes a free people can ever witness," a Philadelphia woman wrote to her sister-in-law. "The changes of administration, which in every government and in every age have most generally been epochs of confusion, villainy and bloodshed, in this our happy country take place without any species of distraction, or disorder."

Thomas Jefferson struck a strong note of conciliation in his First Inaugural Address:

"We are all Republicans—we are all Federalists. If there be any among us who would wish to dissolve this Union or to change its republican form, let them stand undisturbed as monuments of the safety with which error of opinion may be tolerated where reason is left free to combat it."

Thomas Jefferson's home, Monticello, near Charlottesville, Virginia. *(Courtesy, Virginia State Travel Service)*

an unwillingness to draw attention to himself, a refusal to make overly much of his social and governmental rank belonged to a sophisticated gentleman's behavior. The republic Jefferson sought was not a mobocracy but a nation of citizens raised upward in learning, independence, and virtue. Reflective of what a republican citizen—an extraordinary one, to be sure—might do in private life was Jefferson's most striking achievement: his home Monticello, built near Charlottesville, Virginia.

Monticello   The mind of the new President put scientific curiosity and political vision to a large project. In Monticello, his country estate, his restless intelligence applied itself to specific problems in invention. Monticello is an early instance of the tinkering and practical science that Americans were to think of as a mark of the American character.

Jefferson had begun building his "little mountain" home near Charlottesville in 1768 on land that his father had owned. The site overlooks the sunset and the Blue Ridge Mountains in the west and the Virginia plains to the east, vistas that had intrigued Jefferson since childhood. Unable to find a competent architect in the colonies, the resourceful Virginian studied more than a few books, drew his own plans, and supervised most of the forty-one years of construction. Laid out as an Italian villa, Monticello also has a Greek portico, a Roman dome, and colonial detail. But Jefferson relied principally upon Andrea Palladio, the architect who had created the Georgian style in England. Taken together, Monticello's diverse design did much to launch the classical revival in architecture, which swept the United States during the early nineteenth century.

Graceful use, not merely symmetrical display, dictated the general layout of the thirty-five-room manor. Most colonial estates grouped carriage house, kitchen, stable, laundry, and smokehouse in separate buildings removed from the main house. For convenience and efficiency, Jefferson moved these functional areas indoors, connected to the living quarters. He built them under terraces that flank Monticello on either side and open away from the inside. This innovation was soon copied throughout the South. Between the two basements were separate storage rooms for wine, beer, hard cider, and rum.

Monticello is noted for its gadgetry. A pair of glass doors between the main hall and a drawing room opens simultaneously when only one is pushed—Jefferson had installed a series of gears under the floor, much like a modern bicycle-pedal system. Jefferson connected the weathervane on the roof of Monticello to a dial on the ceiling of the portico so he could read the wind without going outside. A pulley arrangement carried a used bottle of wine to the cellar and retrieved a cooled one. The kitchen drew from a pond stocked with fish to be caught fresh for the dinner table.

Style, contraptions, and even its history mark Monticello as uniquely American. In 1781 a platoon of British soldiers raided the house in hopes of capturing its owner, then governor of Virginia; Jefferson narrowly escaped up the mountainside. After a life of political and diplomatic service to the nation, he would retire from the presidency in 1809 and return to the just-completed house. Despite spiraling debts, aggravated by the costs of Monticello's upkeep, loans from friends enabled Jefferson to live in the house until his death on July 4, 1826.

Among Jefferson's opinions:

"There is a natural aristocracy among men. The grounds of these are virtue and talents."

"The selfish spirit of commerce . . . knows no country, and feels no passion or principle but that of gain."

"Government, even in its best state, is a necessary evil; in its worst state, an intolerable one."

"I have sworn upon the altar of God eternal hostility against every tyranny over the mind of man."

Limited Government   Jefferson simplified the government. He and his treasury secretary Albert Gallatin opposed any rise in the federal debt, and they managed to cut military spending to a third of what it had been under the Federalists. The army was reduced to just 3,000 regulars and 172 officers. The five frigates built during Adams's administration were all rendered inactive; in their place the Jeffersonians created a navy of gunboats fit only for coastal service. The President also closed the American legations in Holland and Prussia. The new administration could not abolish the Bank of the United States before its charter expired in 1811, but under Gallatin the government sold its Bank stock at a profit and ceased to take on any further banking role.

If government as Jefferson conceived of it had little business regulating finances, and little use for a large military establishment, it certainly had no taste for enforcing political loyalty. He allowed the Sedition Act to lapse; there would be no more criminal prosecutions for attacking the government.

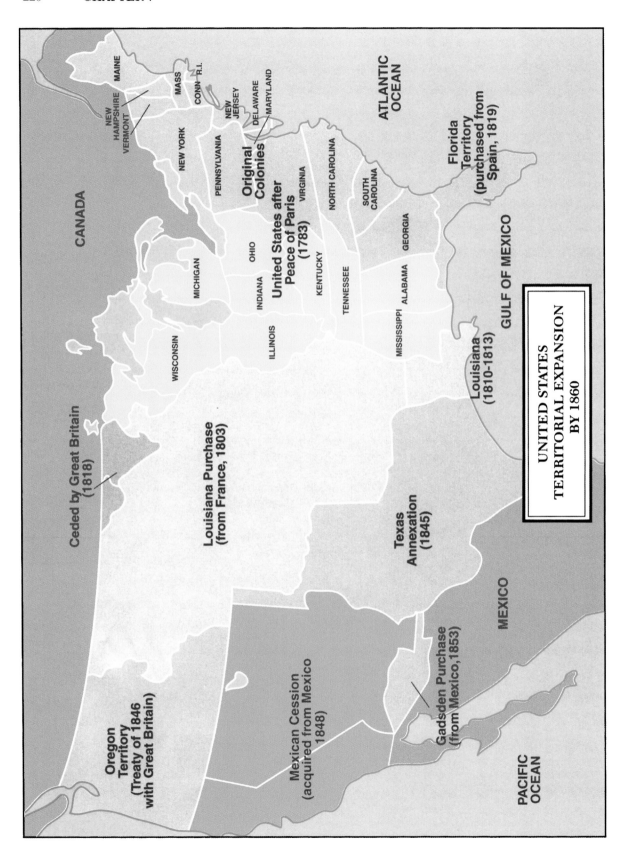

UNITED STATES
TERRITORIAL EXPANSION
BY 1860

Jefferson's republic would have a virtuous simplicity. He would have shuddered at the size and scope of twentieth-century governments; but he would have shuddered also at twentieth-century business or twentieth-century cities. He advocated the very sort of limited government that Hamilton in *The Federalist* had warned against: "a government at a distance and out of sight." The national government, Jefferson declared in his first message to Congress, was "charged with the external and mutual relations only of these states." It was the states that had "principal care of our persons, our property, and our reputation." The national government had become "too complicated, too expensive"; offices and officers had "multiplied unnecessarily and sometimes injuriously to the service they were meant to promote." As means to his goal, Jefferson's administration sought economy, a limit to federal powers, and decentralization. It is curious that the Federalists, less egalitarian than Jefferson, actually had a concept that comes closer to the reality of modern democratic societies. They had planned for a more active economy than Jefferson seems to have envisioned, and their government policies would draw the country's labor and resources more closely together and put them more vigorously to work for the increase of prosperity.

Marbury v. Madison (1803)

Far more significant in its ultimate result was the Jefferson Administration's attempt to undo the effects of the 1801 Judiciary Act. Under that measure Adams, just before leaving office, had appointed a flock of Federalist judges and law officials with lifetime tenure; his purpose had clearly been to retain Federalist control in at least one branch of government and, as the Republicans saw it, prevent the new administration from carrying out the will of the people. Hoping to frustrate this goal, Jefferson's secretary of state Madison refused to deliver several newly appointed officials their commissions. William Marbury sued the secretary, charging that his action was illegal under the Judiciary Act of 1789. By the provisions of that measure, Marbury's lawyers argued, the Supreme Court could compel a federal official to issue a commission whether he wished to or not.

In 1803 the case came before the United States Supreme Court, Chief Justice John Marshall presiding. Marshall was a Virginian, but not of the political stamp of his fellow Virginians Jefferson and Madison. A Federalist, he deplored the Republican preference for a small national government. He also wanted a strong Supreme Court. Yet Marshall and the Court held, in *Marbury v. Madison,* that the Court could not compel Madison to deliver a commission to Marbury, since that portion of the Judiciary Act of 1789 that would have made Madison issue the commission was unconstitutional and therefore unenforceable. The Supreme Court, it seems, was surrendering a little power that it might have claimed and exercised. But it was doing so at great gain. *Marbury v. Madison* immeasurably strengthened the Supreme Court, for it announced and won wide acceptance of the principle of judicial review: that the Court could decide whether a piece of federal legislation was constitutional. Although the idea of judicial review had been asserted

As Chief Justice of the United States, John Marshall wrote decisions that helped strengthen the federal government. *(Portrait by J. W. Jarvis, Courtesy, Richard Coke Marshall Collection, Frick Art Reference Library)*

A sentence in the decision the Supreme Court issued in *Marbury v. Madison* (1803) declares: "It is a proposition too plain to be contested that the Court controls any legislative act repugnant to it: A legislative act contrary to the Constitution is not law."

before *Marbury v. Madison,* that case provided the first occasion for the Supreme Court to define and exercise the right.

The Louisiana Purchase (1803)   In 1803 the United States acquired the province of Louisiana from France and thereby almost doubled in size. Louisiana was a gigantic wedge of territory stretching from the Gulf of Mexico in the South to somewhere in the present-day Dakotas in the North, and from the Mississippi in the East to the Rocky Mountains in the West. Its exact boundaries were unclear, its richness and strategic value unquestioned.

Spain had owned the province until ceding it to France in 1801 with the promise that it not be given to a third party. Tentative reports of the transfer alarmed Jefferson. The President looked forward to an "empire for liberty" consisting of American farmlands stretching over

THE LEWIS AND CLARK EXPEDITION

Thomas Jefferson wrote eloquently of independence, religious liberty, the education of a free people. So had others; but Jefferson's words inspired a new nation, a bill of rights, a system of education. The expedition of Meriwether Lewis and William Clark from 1804 to 1806, exploring the Missouri River, the Rocky Mountains, and the Columbia River basin, was a bold Jeffersonian vision become a great historical event.

Like Christopher Columbus, Jefferson saw the westward passage as a way to the riches of the East. Commerce might move "possibly with single portage, from the Western ocean . . . to the Atlantic." To this old dream Jefferson added the prospect of more immediate riches: the "great supplies of furs and pelts" that were then flowing chiefly into English, not American, coffers. It meant even more to Jefferson that much of the West could become a vast, peaceful garden filling with the sturdy yeomen he expected to be the embodiments of republican virtue. The West could also be a garden for Indians weaned from their hunting ways by the advance of trade that would "place within their reach those things which will contribute more to their domestic comfort than the possession of extensive, but uncultivated wilds." The more rugged West of the great rivers and mountains would exhibit treasures of natural history. Mammoths, Jefferson suspected, might still roam the lands farther west. Perhaps the llama ranged this far north. For years, Jefferson had encouraged all who would listen to explore the great West for science, for country, for riches.

Except for slightly underestimating the number of men who would be needed (thirty to fifty in various stages of the expedition), and with no idea that an Indian woman, her infant son, and a giant Newfoundland dog named Scammon would go along as well, Jefferson got exactly the expedition and the results he had envisioned. Seven men kept diaries; almost every moment they were taking detailed field notes and reworking them into coherent accounts, complete with drawings, maps, and lexicons for Thomas Jefferson and the world.

Meriwether Lewis and William Clark, like Jefferson, were amateurs. Though both were soldiers, neither had been a professional military man. Lewis sought the counsel of the nation's most distinguished physician, Dr. Benjamin Rush of Philadelphia, who supplied him with a little information and a large supply of "Rush's Thunderbolts," his famous, violently purgative pills, which Lewis and Clark used for all ailments.

The expedition went from St. Louis to the mouth of the Columbia River and back, through incredibly difficult country, with elementary equipment. The first leg, up the Missouri with a winter's stop in an Indian village, was brutally hard work: poling, pulling, and portaging a string of boats up a huge river whose powerful current undermined banks at each bend, created mudslides, and sent vast jams of tree trunks cascading downriver to knock over the expedition's boats. The second leg, over the mountaintops through high barren badlands, was the hardest part of all. The trip down the Columbia River system was least eventful. The way west would not be direct or easy: the hope three centuries old of finding a direct northwest passage had to be forgotten, at least for a time.

Lewis and Clark studied dozens of Indian tribes, arranging trade agreements, asserting the government's influence, presenting gifts, recording manners and customs, seeking geographical information. Lewis and Clark also identified 300 new plant and animal species or subspecies, collecting bones, fossils, and seeds. The homely much of North America. So long as weak Spain controlled the sparsely settled province, Jefferson could afford to wait until it dropped into the American lap. But if powerful France now possessed it, who knew whether the United States would ever be able to acquire it? Besides, Louisiana included the port of New Orleans. Whoever controlled this port controlled the trade and commercial outlet for much of the western United States. Hoping to prevent consummation of the arrangement between Spain and France or at least to acquire some port on the Gulf Coast, Jefferson dispatched Robert Livingston to Paris.

The French meanwhile were beginning to lose interest in the territory. For a time Napoleon had hoped to fit Louisiana into a great French colonial empire that would also include the valuable Caribbean sugar island of Hispaniola. He first had to recapture the western part of Hispaniola from the blacks who in the 1790s had risen up against French masters there and established the Republic of Haiti. Napoleon sent an

names they gave the new species—since neither man knew Latin—have not survived in the naturalist literature; but creatures like *Salmo clarkii*, the beautiful cutthroat trout named for Clark, and *Asyndesmus lesis*, Lewis's woodpecker, attest to the ichthyologists' and ornithologists' appreciation of their works.

The rigors of the journey produced much illness and hardship, yet only one man lost his life—from a ruptured appendix that in those days would have killed him even had he been in Philadelphia. The only serious injury was to Lewis himself, when one of his own men accidentally shot him in the backside. (Lewis made few mistakes: going hunting for food with a one-eyed sergeant was one of them.) There were only one or two small scrapes with Indians, although it took diplomacy and carefully manned swivel guns, small portable cannons, to prevent a few rough encounters from becoming dangerous. Clark's slave, York, the one black member of the expedition, was the wonder of dozens of Indian tribes. The Indians would pay to touch his hair or run their fingers over his skin to see whether the dark color would come off. One of the interpreters persuaded Lewis to allow him to take his Indian wife, Sacajawea, and their two-month-old baby on the roughest part of the trip from the upper Missouri over the mountains to the Pacific. Apparently, her knowledge of the Shoshonean dialects led the captain to agree. When they met up with the mountain Indians, the first party of braves they encountered had as its chief her brother, whom she had not seen since she had been abducted from his hunting party as a small child. No novelist could have gotten away with such an unlikely plot.

Jefferson had made to Congress his proposal for the expedition before Talleyrand offered to sell the United States the Louisiana Territory; the President had planned to grasp the trade of the West with stations on territory both unknown and unowned. By the time the

expedition set out from St. Louis, Louisiana was United States territory. But the Oregon country beyond the Great Divide was not. It belonged perhaps to Great Britain or maybe to Spain. Yet Lewis, once back at St. Louis, wrote of "possessions" west of the mountains, and Jefferson himself by January 1807 was referring to "our country, from the Missisipi [sic] to the Pacific." Lewis and Clark's expedition would, in the end, make Jefferson's largest vision—a continental United States—the future.

Lewis and Clark filled their journals with drawings and descriptions of plants and animals, such as this report on the white salmon trout.
(Courtesy, Library of Congress)

William Wordsworth, the English poet, wrote of Toussaint L'Ouverture's consignment to a dungeon by the French:

There's not a breathing of the common
  wind
That will forget thee; thou hast great
  allies;
Thy friends are exhultations, agonies,
And love, and man's unconquerable
  mind.

Toussaint L'Ouverture proclaims the constitution for the republic of Haiti. *(Courtesy, Library of Congress)*

army of thirty thousand men, headed by his brother-in-law, to subdue the Haitians under their brilliant leader Toussaint L'Ouverture. The task was impossible. Eventually the French captured L'Ouverture by treachery, but not before their army had been virtually wiped out by a combination of enemy action and tropical disease. Napoleon decided to abandon his dream of a restored French empire in the New World.

When he arrived in Paris, Livingston confronted this new situation. France no longer cared much about Louisiana; and Napoleon, now rearming to invade archenemy Britain, was certain that he could not keep it from falling into British hands. On the American side, the situation had also changed. In October 1802 Spain, still in legal possession of New Orleans, decided to deny once more to citizens of the United States the access to the port that the Pinckney Treaty of 1795 had temporarily granted.

Jefferson now dispatched James Monroe to France with new orders. He should try to get New Orleans from the French, or at least to acquire from Spain part of the Gulf Coast panhandle of West Florida. Either would give the United States an outlet for southern trade. Two days after Monroe joined Livingston in the French capital, they learned a prodigious piece of news: Napoleon would sell not only New Orleans but all of Louisiana. The price: 60 million francs, and up to 20 million francs in settlement of all American claims against France for the "spoliations" of the 1790s. The offer flabbergasted the envoys. They were not authorized to negotiate such an arrangement, but it was far too good to turn down, and they eagerly accepted. In short order, the signed document was on its way to Washington for Congress and the President to confirm.

It may seem surprising that any American should have questioned such an extraordinary bargain, but many did. One prominent Federalist denounced the purchase as "a miserable calamitous business"—the new nation would now be so gigantic that it would fall apart. Some Federalists were unhappy that the United States had promised to grant citizenship to all the French and Spanish inhabitants of Louisiana. Federalists like Timothy Pickering were sincere opponents of slavery, concerned that the new territory would allow for extension of slaveholding. Even Jefferson worried that by buying Louisiana he had exceeded the authority of the federal government under the Constitution, and for a while he supported a constitutional amendment authorizing the purchase. In the end neither side's scruples could compete with the reality of the most successful land deal in history. On October 20, 1803, the Senate confirmed the treaty, and two months later the United States took formal possession of the province. For a total of $15 million the United States had acquired a region almost equal in area to the whole of western Europe.

Burr Again   Burr was a complex man. Witty, charming, and intelligent, he was also ambitious and devious. This son of a Presbyterian minister, this grandson of Jonathan Edwards, this former theology student became a notorious womanizer. In 1804 at Weehawken, New Jersey, he killed Alexander Hamilton in a duel that was the culmination of long-standing animosity between the two men.

A year later, Burr, according to the adventurer James Wilkinson, was scheming to detach Louisiana from the United States, join it with Texas and other parts of Spanish Mexico, and create a new nation. But Wilkinson decided in the end that it was more profitable to stay in Spain's employ than to continue with this chancy venture. In November 1806 he wrote to Jefferson, warning that Burr intended to detach the West from the United States.

Jefferson ordered the arrest of Burr, who quickly set out for Pensacola in Spanish Florida, probably intending to escape to Europe. But he was captured and brought to Richmond, Virginia, and tried for treason, Wilkinson serving as an important witness against him. The prosecution produced much damaging evidence against Burr. But the former Vice President had the support of the presiding judge, Chief Justice Marshall; when the jury returned the verdict of "not proved," Marshall changed it to "not guilty."

The government refused to drop the matter. Soon after, it obtained Burr's indictment on another treason charge. This time Marshall granted him bail pending trial and rather than face another legal battle, Burr fled to Europe. He remained abroad for four years, and then returned to live a scandalous life in New York City. In his seventies he

Aaron Burr's schemes to detach the West from the United States led to indictments for treason, charges which he managed to escape. *(Courtesy, The New-York Historical Society)*

fathered two illegitimate children, and at the age of eighty he was sued for divorce on the grounds of adultery.

The Dawn of a Century

The People   In the twenty-five years since the opening gun of the Revolution the country's population had grown from about 2.5 to 5.3 million. The nation's white population remained overwhelmingly British in origin and Protestant in religion. Germans were found in eastern Pennsylvania, in the Shenandoah Valley, and along the Mohawk River in New York. The Hudson Valley contained many Dutchmen. Scattered here and there, primarily in the towns, were small enclaves of Jews and Huguenot French, as well as a handful of Irish Catholics. The largest non-British group was black, over a million, almost all south of Pennsylvania and the overwhelming majority slaves. But the Revolution and difficulties of postwar readjustment had discouraged the slave trade as well as immigration.

Americans were a young people. Half the population was under seventeen years old. Households were large; almost one-fourth of all families had seven or more people living under one roof. This placed a heavy burden on families, and especially on women, who spent many of their best, most vigorous years bearing and rearing children.

The United States in 1801 was a nation of farms and villages. Only 300,000 Americans lived in communities of even 2,500 people—fewer than seven percent of the total.

The Cities   Of these the largest and most gracious was Philadelphia, with almost 70,000 inhabitants. Penn's town was also the most modern. Most American city dwellers drew their water from wells or bought it from vendors. They relied on hogs to consume the garbage dumped on the street. They were forced to tramp roads sometimes ankle deep in either dust or mud, depending on the season. Not so Philadelphians: the city of Brotherly Love, after cholera and yellow fever epidemics in the 1790s, piped its water from the Schuylkill River and its streets, paved with cobblestones, were regularly cleaned.

Boston, with 25,000 inhabitants, had fallen behind New York and Baltimore in population since colonial days. Nevertheless, it remained the commercial, financial, and intellectual capital of New England. With its narrow streets and crowded wharves, it had not much changed since the 1770s. The city government was still the same as in the seventeenth century: its affairs were in the hands of "selectmen" chosen at the town meeting. Although Boston's elite was no longer composed of stern Puritan gentlemen, the Federalist merchants, ministers, and lawyers who now formed the town's upper crust retained much of the old Puritan granite character and respect for learning.

Two hundred miles to the south and west of Boston was New York, on Manhattan Island. Even more than Boston and Philadelphia, New York thrived on commerce; most of its 60,000 inhabitants were crowded into the southeastern corner of the island, adjacent to the docks and warehouses. The rich resources of New York port—its accessibility in winter, its many landing spots, its deep water—would soon catapult the city into becoming the nation's most populous.

Baltimore was a comparatively new city. The outlet for much of the Chesapeake tobacco crop, it also tapped the farm produce of the Pennsylvania backcountry through the Susquehanna River. Charleston, the capital of South Carolina, may have been the most colorful of all. It was both a major port and a summer resort where rice planters from the malaria-ridden coastal lowlands went during the fever season to protect their health. Built in brick and stone, the city was ruled by a planter and merchant elite who combined republican principles with the aristocratic arts of good living, polite letters, fine manners, and elegant hospitality. These avowed republicans could not live without slaves. Of the 18,000 people who packed the little port, 6,000 were blacks; they helped keep its streets clean, its markets stocked, and its wharves busy.

Any observer of Charleston between 1790 and 1800 would have noticed a particularly promising development: a new crop, cotton, was being loaded aboard ships in the harbor by black stevedores. With the perfection of the cotton gin by the Connecticut Yankee Eli Whitney, green-seed cotton had become a profitable crop in the interior of the Carolinas and Georgia. The South's one major Atlantic port was feeling the invigorating economic effects of the thousands of bales it shipped to Liverpool and Glasgow to feed the new textile factories of Great Britain.

The small town of Pittsburgh was situated where the Allegheny and Monongahela rivers join to form the great Ohio River. With about two thousand inhabitants in 1800, it had become a supplier of manufactured goods to the burgeoning West, producing iron, glass, and textiles, along with vessels for the river trade. As early as 1800 an English visitor reported the town covered with a pall of smoke from the numerous coal fires that fueled the iron foundries and glassworks.

Outside the new United States other settlements that would eventually become cities in the new nation were slowly gaining population. St. Augustine, Florida, founded by the Spanish in 1585, would be an American town by 1819. New Orleans, settled by the French in 1718, had 10,000 people when Jefferson purchased Louisiana in 1803. In Texas, San Antonio, also dating back to 1718, had over 1,200 people by 1800, and Santa Fe, New Mexico, along with San Diego and San Francisco in California, were small trading villages.

The Farms   A typical American yeoman and his family worked hard for what they had. Animals had to be fed and watered, their stables cleaned. Plowing in the spring, weeding and cultivating in summer, and harvesting in fall all required heavy labor. The women cooked, cleaned, spun, made preserves, and took care of flocks of young children. Clearing new land on the frontier required the backbreaking labor of girdling trees, clearing underbrush, and breaking virgin sod. The pioneer farmer of Vermont, western New York, or the newly opened Ohio or Alabama country was lucky if he could add more than four or five usable acres to his farm a year. Even then it took many years before the frontier farmer's land was fully cleared of stumps and he could plow a straight furrow. Meanwhile, his family lived in a primitive one-room log house with an attic above used for sleeping.

His farm, said a Maryland yeoman of Jeffersonian times,

"gave me and my family a good living on the produce of it; and left me, one year with another, one hundred and fifty dollars, for I have never spent more than ten dollars a year, which was for salt, nails, and the like. Nothing to wear, eat, or drink was purchased, as my farm provided all. With this saving, I put money to interest, bought cattle, fatted and sold them, and made great profit."

Some young men left the farm to attend school. A student in Philadelphia wrote a letter to his parents in Allegheny County:

"I now take up my pen to write, but what to say I know not, sinking into debt and no prospect of making any thing to relieve myself. I continue to teach a gentleman's sons the Greek and Latin languages, for which I receive one hundred dollars per year, but this is far from being sufficient to answer my demands. . . . Last summer I bought two pair of nanking pantaloons and a light vest, the whole amounting to $7.60, and this is all I have got since I left home. If I should leave this place, one thing will be in my favour, that is I shall not be burthened with clothes. . . ."

This symbol of the Philadelphia Society for Promoting Agriculture illustrates Republican agrarianism. The yeoman farmer is shown ploughing his field under the approving gaze of the figure of Columbia.

Techniques of planting and harvesting had not advanced much beyond medieval practices. American plows in 1800 were heavy wooden contraptions pulled by oxen or mules. Farmers still used the scythe to harvest grain and threshed it with a hand flail made of two sticks joined by a leather thong.

Yet the yeoman family enjoyed a rough abundance. Since the soil was rich, the American farm family ate well and produced more than it consumed. Travelers through the nation's rural regions remarked on signs of prosperity. One Englishman reported of the Connecticut countryside during Jefferson's presidency that it "had the appearance of wealth, numerous broods of poultry straying about, with sheep and cattle grazing in great numbers in the fields." Travelers who accepted the hospitality of local yeomen, rather than brave the fare of notoriously bad country inns, reported on the abundance of everything served. Breakfast tables were loaded down with boiled fish, beefsteak, ham sausages, hot breads, and cheese.

Isolation   The typical farm family was an isolated social unit. Except in southern New England, where the imprint of the old town system of colonial days remained, the rural American lived in a house widely separated by fields and virgin forest from his nearest neighbor. Communication benefited from an improvement in postal service and roads. In the 1790s there were seventy-five post offices in the entire nation, connected by 1,875 miles of post roads. But by the War of 1812 the nation had 2,610 post offices and over 39,000 miles of roads. The steepness of postal rates (8 cents per letter, 12½ cents for a letter sent over 100 miles) still worked to isolate much of the rural population.

Farm women suffered acutely from the isolation of their lives. Many lacked the close network of female kin and friends from which New England women drew comfort and companionship. One lonely woman in Ohio lamented: "'Tis strange to us to see company. I expect the sun may rise and set a hundred times before I shall see another human that does not belong to the family." Ribbons and mirrors remained rare; cookstoves and shoes might have to be ordered from New England. And although husbands and wives frequently worked as close collaborators in daily life—bringing in the harvest, or even delivering children—the lines between male and female spheres remained tightly drawn. When men would get together to raise a house, the women cooked for the large throng.

A way out of the desolateness was newspapers. One traveler noted how a small New Hampshire town hungered for news: "It was entertaining to see the eagerness of the people on our arrival to get a sight of the last newspaper from Boston. They flocked to the post-office and the inn, and formed a variety of groups round those who were fortunate to possess themselves of a paper." But in rural New England a traveler in the early 1800s observed that "there is scarcely a poor owner of a miserable log hut, who lives on the border of the stage road, but has a newspaper left at his door." In 1801 there were 200 newspapers in the nation; by the 1830s there would be more than 1,200.

For a portion of the rural population, relief might come by way of books. Almanacs, a staple of the farm homestead, urged farmers to buy and read books. The farmer, one author claimed, sees "his barns, granaries, and cellars, all well filled by his own industry and frugality; his farm affording him all the comforts and necessaries of life, enables him to spend the long and tedious winter evenings with his family round a good fire and a clean hearth, where he may read THEOLOGY, GEOGRAPHY, HISTORY, &C. and edify and entertain them...." The *Farmer's Almanack* paid tribute to another almanac-writer, Benjamin Franklin, recommending "The Life of Dr. Franklin" (published in 1794) "for the amusement of winter evenings."

When rural Americans did gather with neighbors and friends, it was often to engage in rough-and-tumble sports that could turn brutal. Wrestling included kicking, biting, punching, and eye-gouging. "I saw more than one man who wanted an eye," noted an easterner as he crossed the border into Kentucky. Country people, especially on the frontier, "baited" bulls and bears—that is, set large dogs to attack them while rooting for either attacker or defender—or they bet on the outcome of cockfights. Whether at taverns or at religious camp meetings, at dances and hoedowns or in the home, Americans consumed vast quantities of whiskey, rum, and brandy. Women drank punch or toddies made of these.

It would take years of steady cultivation of the land, good roads, and growth of towns before the rudeness of the country lessened along with its isolation.

France and England Once More

Foreign Entanglements   Thomas Jefferson had been in office for only a few months when foreign policy demanded his attention. Ever since 1789 the United States had followed the British practice of paying tribute to the Barbary States: Algiers, Morocco, Tripoli, and Tunis. In return, the Barbary Pirates, as many Americans preferred to call them, agreed to allow American merchant vessels to have free access to the Mediterranean ports of North Africa. But in May 1801 the Pasha of Tripoli substantially increased his tribute demands and unilaterally declared war on the United States. Jefferson decided to take a stand. He sent a small naval fleet to the Mediterranean late in 1803, and early in 1804 the fleet destroyed an American ship that Tripoli had captured and converted to its own use. The American navy then blockaded the Tripoli coast. After more than a year, Tripoli acquiesced and signed a treaty ending the war.

In the early 1800s England and France ended their long, exhausting war. It now looked as if the American people would be spared the ordeal they had faced ever since war between the world's two most powerful nations erupted in 1793. No longer would American commerce be the defenseless prey both of the Royal Navy and of French revenue cutters and port officials. But peace lasted only fourteen months. By May 1803 Britain was once more at war with France. Once again, the United States found itself caught between the British hammer and the French anvil.

The Royal Navy immediately resumed its practice of impressing seamen aboard American vessels, claiming that they were deserters from the British fleet. Outside American harbors, British ships waited for American merchant vessels, stopped them, sent an officer aboard, and took crewmen. Britain also reversed its former policy and refused any longer to allow Americans the "broken voyage," a practice by which they had transported French goods under the protection of American neutrality by shipping them through American ports. Britain's primary purpose was not to injure United States commerce but to frustrate the French war effort.

Responding to the British blockade of the continent of Europe, dominated by France, Napoleon issued in 1806 the Berlin Decree, ordering the seizure of any vessel carrying British goods. The following year he directed French privateers to stop all ships, including neutral ones, suspected of carrying enemy cargo. The Berlin Decree set off a round of British countermeasures, followed by still further French retaliation. It began to seem that no American ship would be able to leave port or approach European shores without facing confiscation.

The American response to these indignities and harassments was mixed. Since Britain was now violating American sovereign rights even more flagrantly than France, Britain was the object of an enraged American patriotism. Continuing problems with the Indian tribes in the Northwest increased anger against the British. Not all Americans, however, agreed that strong measures were called for. Especially in the Atlantic ports, many citizens were willing to accept harassment. For despite it, American commerce was flourishing in a war-stricken world. So pressing was the need for shipping space that ocean freight rates shot upward. Insurance costs were also high and there was always the risk of confiscation, but profits were unprecedented. Between 1803 and 1807 American exports, much of them in tropical goods from the French and Spanish New World colonies, leaped from $56 million to $108 million, and the American merchant marine grew from 950,000 tons to almost 1.3 million. Why not accept the situation, asked the merchants of Boston, Salem, Providence, New York, Philadelphia, and other ports.

Pressures for War   Still, even the most materialistic citizens could forget their immediate interests in the heat of anger at some indignity committed by the British or French. One such incident took place in the early summer of 1807.

On June 22, the *Chesapeake*, a brand-new Navy frigate commanded by Commodore James Barron, left Norfolk, Virginia, for a Mediterranean cruise. Aboard were several deserters from the Royal Navy. When the *Chesapeake* was only a few miles at sea, it was overtaken by H.M.S. *Leopard*, part of the British squadron patrolling off Hampton Roads. The British captain ordered Barron to heave to and allow a naval party to board to look for deserters. This was the first time the British had attempted impressment of an American man-of-war, and Barron refused. But most of the *Chesapeake's* guns were not yet mounted, and the ship could not defend itself. After repeated murderous broadsides from the *Leopard*, Barron struck his colors; the British removed four

The attack on the U.S.S. *Chesapeake* by H.M.S. *Leopard* on June 22, 1807, set off a furor among Americans, but Jefferson avoided armed conflict through diplomacy and passage of the Embargo Act. *(Courtesy, The Mariners Museum, Newport News, Virginia)*

deserters and departed. The *Chesapeake* limped back to port with three dead, eighteen wounded, and a tale certain to inflame every American patriot.

Americans demanded war against Britain. "The country," Jefferson noted, "had never been in such a state of excitement since the battle of Lexington." But the President, although he could undoubtedly have obtained a declaration of war from Congress, wished to avoid armed conflict. He was not a pacifist, but he deplored the expensive armies and navies war required. In accordance with his distaste for a large military, Jefferson had so reduced American forces that war was virtually out of the question. And the United States, he believed, still had at its disposal some powerful unused weapons short of war.

Diplomatic pressure was one of these, and Jefferson immediately dispatched a message to Britain demanding disavowal of the attack, reparations for lives lost and damage inflicted, and an end to the impressment policy. He also ordered all British ships out of United States territorial waters and stepped up preparations for defense in case the British forced the nation's hand. The British response to American diplomatic demands was unsatisfactory. Jefferson now invoked his last peaceable weapon. American trade, the President believed, was essential to both the major belligerents. Both needed American wheat, provisions, and lumber, and the French relied on the United States to carry their Caribbean products. During the imperial crisis before 1775, Americans had forced Britain to back down by boycotting British goods. In all likelihood, Jefferson thought, they would yield to commercial pressure if it were applied firmly.

The Embargo and Non-Intercourse Acts   Under the President's prodding, Congress passed the Embargo Act of 1807. The law prohibited American commercial ships from sailing for foreign ports. The Embargo Act was temporarily popular in the South and the West. But to the trading centers of the Northeast it seemed a disaster. Almost overnight the glittering

John Lambert, a stevedore, wrote of the effects of the embargo on the wharves of New York City:

"When I arrived at New York in November [1807], the port was filled with shipping, and the wharfs were crowded with commodities of every description. Bales of cotton, wool, and merchandise; barrels of potash, rice, flour, and salt provisions; hogsheads of sugar, chests of tea, puncheons of rum, and pipes of wine. . . . All was noise and bustle . . . But on my return . . . the following April, what a contrast was presented to my view! . . . The coffee-house slip, the wharfs and quays along South street, presented no longer the bustle and activity that had prevailed there five months before. The port, indeed, was full of shipping; but they were dismantled and laid up. Their decks were cleared, their hatches fastened down, and scarcely a sailor was to be found on board. Not a box, bale, cask, barrel or package, was to be seen upon the wharfs."

trade bubble that had lasted since 1793 burst. Ships rode at anchor, their sails furled, while worms riddled their wooden hulls. Waterfront streets once busy stood emptied of their milling crowds of seamen, teamsters, tavern-keepers, and stevedores.

Overall, the embargo did not have much effect on the European belligerents. It hurt British workingmen and French colonists, but the ruling classes in both Britain and France were scarcely affected. British manufacturers, meanwhile, could continue to send their goods in their own vessels to compete with American products in the United States. "It was," wrote a critic, "as if a flea had tried to stop a dogfight by threatening suicide."

In demanding the subordination of economic self-interest to peace, Jefferson had overestimated the patience and patriotism of his fellow citizens. So loud became the domestic outcry against the Embargo Act that Congress in 1809 replaced it with the Non-Intercourse Act, permitting exports to every nation except England and France. These two offenders could now neither buy from the United States nor sell to her. If either of the two powers reversed its hostile policies toward the United States, this country could resume trade with it. The man who would administer the new law was not Jefferson but his successor, James Madison.

James Madison, inaugurated as President in 1809, faced growing pressure from the "War Hawks" and others to act against Britain and finally declared war in June 1812. *(Portrait by Gilbert Stuart, Courtesy, Bowdoin College Museum of Fine Arts, Brunswick, Maine)*

John Randolph of Roanoke. *(Courtesy, Scribner's Archives)*

James Madison Takes Over

No one else had been so instrumental as Madison in fostering and shaping the federal Constitution. After the inauguration of the national government, it had been Madison who led the forces against Hamilton and, in alliance with his good friend Jefferson, helped to create the Republican Party. In 1801 Jefferson selected him as his secretary of state and he served with distinction in that office.

Many Republicans viewed Madison as Jefferson's natural successor—but not all. Opposed to him was a group of militant Republicans called the "Tertium Quids," who considered both Jefferson and Madison to be too friendly to Federalist principles. The leading voice of the Quids was John Randolph of Roanoke, an eloquent defender of lost causes and an irresponsible verbal brawler. The Quids tried to deny Madison the nomination, but with Jefferson's support the party caucus in Congress endorsed him. The Federalists were now the minority party, and Madison in 1808 easily defeated their candidate, Charles Cotesworth Pinckney of XYZ fame.

Physically, the new President was not a commanding figure. Small and wizened, he spoke in a barely audible voice and often seemed bored. The First Lady, the former Dolley Todd, helped to offset her husband's dour demeanor. Buxom, pink-cheeked, and charming, Mrs. Madison was a vivacious hostess whose parties and receptions seemed to the social set a vast improvement over the widowed Jefferson's bachelor dinners. Washington was still a city of magnificent intentions, as an early observer of its raw, unfilled spaces called it; the presidential mansion was still not complete. But at least the capital now had a social focus it had lacked before.

The new Non-Intercourse Act created difficulties for Madison. Ships leaving American ports were not supposed to touch at French or British ports, but it quickly became clear that there was no way of guaranteeing they would obey the law. The British, in particular, scorned it; it promised to cause them little harm, and they could see little reason to settle the pending *Chesapeake* claims or satisfy American commercial demands. The British minister in Washington, David Erskine, was friendly to the United States and wanted to placate the Americans. He told Madison that the British intended to modify their harsh policy toward American trade. On this basis, the President issued a proclamation reopening trade with Great Britain while retaining the restrictions on France. Soon after, British Foreign Secretary Canning learned of his minister's indiscretion and disavowed it. The President thereupon reimposed the Non-Intercourse arrangement on Britain.

Macon's Bill No. 2   Dissatisfaction with the Non-Intercourse Act forced Congress into a new tack against the belligerents. In May 1810 it passed Macon's Bill No. 2. This measure was one of the most devious in American history. It allowed the President to reopen trade immediately with both Britain and France. In the event that either of the two warring powers modified its trade policies toward the United States before March 1811, the President might reimpose the trade prohibition upon the other. In effect, the United States was offering to ally itself economically against whichever nation was the slower in according it its commercial rights.

An embarrassing and costly blunder was soon forthcoming. In August 1810, when Napoleon learned of the terms of Macon's Bill, he instructed his foreign minister, Duc de Cadore, to inform the Americans that his commercial decrees would be revoked as of November 1, provided that the United States invoke nonintercourse against the British. (Napoleon had larceny in his heart: even as he issued these instructions he prepared to seize any American vessels that might appear near France.) Cadore took the liberty of informing the United States that the French decrees had actually been canceled. Once again, as in his optimistic reaction to Erskine's assurances, Madison responded without checking. He reopened trade with France and declared that trade with Britain would be closed the following February, unless Britain should revoke its Orders in Council before that time. The British replied by once again stationing their warships outside New York harbor and stepping up their campaign of impressing seamen on American ships. Vessels that eluded British capture were confiscated by Napoleon as soon as they reached France.

The War Hawks   Among the victors in the 1810 elections to Congress was a group of young men, most of them from the West and South, who were unwilling to temporize. Labeled War Hawks, the aggressive youngsters were led by Henry Clay of Kentucky, a young congressman with a rare eloquence and an unusual charm. Although this was his first term in the House of Representatives, the magnetic Clay was elected Speaker. He quickly placed young men of like mind in key House posts. Peter Porter of western New York became chairman of the Foreign Relations Committee, where he had the support of such fellow War Hawks as John C. Calhoun of South Carolina, Felix Grundy of Tennessee, and Joseph Desha of Kentucky.

The War Hawks thundered against the indignities inflicted by the British. England's "aggression, and her injuries and insults to us," proclaimed Henry Clay, were "atrocious"—far more so than those of France. Besides, British assaults on American shipping were responsible for the weakness of crop prices in the West since they interfered with sales of these crops abroad. The British practice of taking seamen from American ships and impressing them into the service of the Royal Navy constituted a violation of national sovereignty. The War Hawks also blamed British agents for instigating Indian uprisings. The Kentucky *Gazette* complained that the British could wield "greater influence with [the Indians] of late than American justice and benevolence."

Western Indians   For some time, in fact, the government had been carrying on military campaigns against western Indians. The real explanation for the renewed violence on the western frontier, however, was the increase in white settlement. By 1810 there were approximately 875,000 settlers in Ohio, Kentucky, Tennessee, Indiana, Illinois, and Missouri. Tecumseh, the Shawnee chief, and his brother The Prophet were concerned about the rising tide of settlement and forged an alliance of several regional tribes. The Indians wanted to present a united force to block the expansion of American settlement. Aware that relations between Great Britain and the United States were reaching the breaking point, Tecumseh also hoped to secure British support.

In 1811 Governor William Henry Harrison led a strong militia force against the Indians and defeated a multitribe force at Tippecanoe Creek. At the time Tecumseh was working his way through several southern tribes, attempting to recruit them into the coalition. Harrison went on to attack and destroy Tecumseh's main camp at Prophetstown. When

To his braves, Tecumseh said:

"Since the days when the white race first came in contact with the red men, there has been a continual series of aggressions. The hunting grounds are fast disappearing, and they are driving the red men farther and farther to the west. The mere presence of the white men is a source of evil. . . . The only hope . . . is a war of extermination against the paleface. They seize your land; they corrupt your women. . . . Back whence they came, upon a trail of blood, they must be driven!"

Tecumseh saving white prisoners. Despite his martial intentions, he was known for his revulsion at senseless cruelty. (*Courtesy, Henry E. Huntington Library and Art Gallery*)

Harrison discovered a cache of British weapons at Prophetstown, and released the news to government officials and the press, protest swept throughout the United States. Feelings were most intense, however, in the West. The War Hawks were especially vocal in denouncing the British. When the War of 1812 broke out, General Harrison was determined to kill Tecumseh and destroy his confederacy. In October 1813 at the Battle of the Thames, he succeeded in both goals.

Land Hunger The War Hawks had even more than the common American appetite for land. For years the United States had disputed with Spain the boundary of West Florida. That narrow province stretched westward along the Gulf coast from the main Florida peninsula, cutting off much of the American Southwest from the sea. Spain, now an ally of England, held the province loosely. If war broke out, it could certainly be wrenched easily from her feeble hands. And there was Canada. One congressman declared that "the Author of Nature has marked our limits in the south, by the Gulf of Mexico; and on the north, by the regions of eternal frost."

While the War Hawks and their supporters naturally thought of attacking and taking the exposed colonies of both Spain and England, conquest was not their chief purpose. They were nationalists and patriots who remembered the Revolution and hated British arrogance, yearning to avenge the humiliations Britain had recently inflicted. For twenty years, they argued, Britain had refused to treat the United States as a sovereign nation. The effort to preserve peace at any price was making the American republic once more a British colony.

The Coming of War Madison, concerned especially with maintaining American agricultural markets in Europe, was soon adopting a tougher policy toward England. In 1811 he asked Congress to vote money to build up the army and navy. In the spring of that year, the U.S.S. *President* encountered the British sloop of war *Little Belt*. Although the results were actually inconclusive—the powerful *President* gave the *Little Belt* a drubbing, but failed to sink the weaker British vessel—Americans considered the results ample revenge for the *Chesapeake* attack of four years before.

For months in early 1812 the prospect of war hovered while both the chief executive and Congress dithered. The Republicans had by now come to assume that war was inevitable, but when it came to voting money in preparation for it, their fear of extravagance got in the way of their common sense. Little had been done to authorize the building of new ships, and appropriations for the army remained inadequate. How the country intended to defend its commerce, and pursue an aggressive policy toward Florida and Canada, nobody made clear.

In the end, war came by mistake. Early in 1812, the British government finally decided to modify its commercial policies. On June 23 it announced that the notorious Orders in Council that had so offended the United States would be lifted. It was too late. Before the news arrived, Madison impatiently had asked for a declaration of war. On June 4, the House voted in favor by 79 to 49; two weeks later the Senate followed, 19 to 13. The vote revealed a disunited nation. If the

"What are we not to lose by peace?" Clay asked. His answer: "Commerce, character, a nation's best treasure, honor! I prefer," orated Clay, "the troubled ocean of war, demanded by the honor and independence of this country, with all its calamities and desolation, to the tranquil and putrescent pool of ignominious peace."

Henry Clay. *(Courtesy, Scribner's Archives)*

way congressmen voted is taken as indicative, southern New England, as well as much of New York, New Jersey, and Maryland, opposed the war. Would they continue to resist once the fighting had begun?

The War of 1812

"Mr. Madison's War"

By almost any measure, the War of 1812 was mismanaged, and for three years the Americans lumbered from one encounter to another.

The country presented a logistical nightmare. To move troops and supplies over such enormous distances would be next to impossible. Roads were few and poor. The steamboat had been introduced on the Hudson in 1807, but steamboat travel on the Mississippi and the Great Lakes was in its infancy. The armed forces were unready. Only 7,000 men were immediately available for service, and most of these were scattered in small frontier posts. The state militias were a potential pool of manpower, but most militiamen were poorly trained and led. The best of the state forces were those of New England. But the Yankee governors refused to allow their soldiers to be called into federal service unless their own states were threatened with invasion.

And the country was disunited. Many Federalists thought the war a mistake. It was "Mr. Madison's war," a Republican venture, not a national one. Particularly in New England, the bastion of Federalism, the war seemed likely to produce a commercial disaster. Inevitably, Yankees said, theirs would be the commerce swept off the seas by the Royal Navy. Strong leadership might have overcome many of these difficulties, but Madison was a better philosopher and congressional manager than war leader. And almost all the high military officers were elderly gentlemen who had not commanded troops against a trained European army since the Revolution.

Canadian Campaigns

Oblivious to these weaknesses, the United States began the fighting with an invasion of Canada led by General William Hull, commanding 2,000 regulars. Launched from Detroit, far to the west of Canada's chief population centers, the invasion was seriously misconceived. It required extended supply lines, and to protect these long lines the troops of the United States had to control Lake Erie. But without much of a naval force on the lake they could not do so.

Nevertheless, the campaign at first seemed to be succeeding. Hull crossed the Detroit River into Canada unopposed. He immediately issued a proclamation that if the Canadian militia remained at home they had nothing to fear from the American republic. In a matter of days half of them had deserted the British and returned to their farms. The British now expected an immediate attack across the river from Detroit on Fort Malden, which was garrisoned by only a few hundred regulars, some Indians, and the remaining militia. But the invaders delayed. By the time Hull's forces mounted their guns against the British, the United States garrison at Michilimackinac to the east had surrendered. Certain that his supply lines were now endangered, Hull withdrew across the river

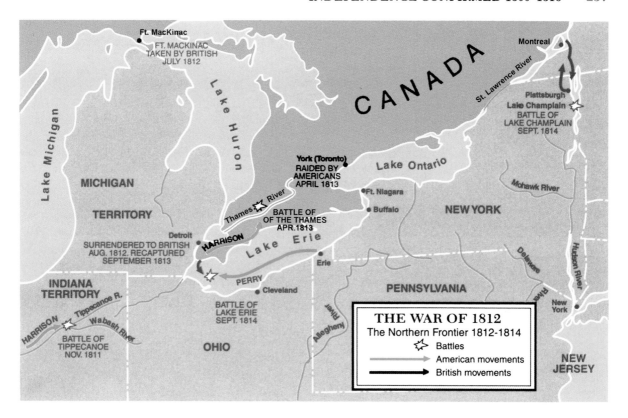

Ft. MacKinac
FT. MACKINAC
TAKEN BY BRITISH
JULY 1812

Montreal

CANADA

St. Lawrence River

Plattsburgh
Lake Champlain
BATTLE OF
LAKE CHAMPLAIN
SEPT. 1814

Lake Huron

Lake Michigan

York (Toronto)
RAIDED BY
AMERICANS
APRIL 1813

Lake Ontario

Mohawk River

MICHIGAN

TERRITORY

Thames River

BATTLE OF
OF THE THAMES
APR. 1813

Ft. Niagara

Buffalo

NEW YORK

Detroit
SURRENDERED TO BRITISH
AUG. 1812. RECAPTURED
SEPTEMBER 1813

HARRISON

Lake Erie

Erie

Delaware River

Hudson River

INDIANA
TERRITORY

Tippecanoe R.

HARRISON

Wabash River

BATTLE OF
TIPPECANOE
NOV. 1811

PERRY

Cleveland

BATTLE OF
LAKE ERIE
SEPT. 1814

OHIO

Allegheny River

PENNSYLVANIA

New
York

NEW
JERSEY

THE WAR OF 1812
The Northern Frontier 1812-1814
✬ Battles
→ American movements
→ British movements

and locked himself up in Detroit. On August 17 he surrendered to the British commander. Prospects of taking Canada now appeared bleak. If the invasion prong in the West, where the people were enthusiastic supporters of the war, had failed, what could be expected in the hostile East?

From New York, a part of that state's militia crossed the Niagara River to attack the British and Canadian forces. They scored some early successes, but then were pinned down. They could have been rescued and the operation saved, but the remaining New York militia refused to cross the Niagara. Without reinforcements, 900 United States troops were captured at Queenston Heights.

The third prong of the invasion was no more successful than the first two. This attack, aimed at Montreal, was at least strategically sound. That city was the heart of British power in North America, and its capture would have been a disaster to England. But the United States delayed its operations and gave the British many months to prepare. By the time the militia moved northward against a well-entrenched enemy, the autumn was far advanced. The ill-equipped troops slogged their way through mud and drenching cold rain, sleeping without tents on the soggy ground with dripping blankets. When the troops reached the Canadian border, many refused to cross. After fighting a few skirmishes, their commander ordered a retreat to Plattsburgh, New York. There the militia made camp amid mud and snow; many contracted pneumonia. "The very woods," an army surgeon reported, "[ring] with coughing and

A sailor related the fate of one American privateer, cruising the ocean for prey:

"On the 25th of January, 1814, being just one month after we sailed from Portsmouth, at 5 o'clock in the morning, the word was passed from the lookout above, 'Sail, oh!' We bore away, and made sail for the strange vessel. She was a large man-of-war brig, and by her model and rig, we judged her to be an English one. We speedily hauled upon the wind and made all sail, endeavoring to show the enemy a clear pair of heels; . . . . We felicitated ourselves for some time with the hope of escape, but it was a delusive hope. . . . The chaser still gained upon us. We were in the neighborhood of Porto Rico, and we still hoped to keep clear of the brig until darkness came on, and under its cover to escape into the harbor. We lightened our schooner by throwing overboard all our guns, most of our provisions and water, all our small arms, irons, caboose, &c. We sawed down our plank shires, started out the wedges of our masts, and kept our sails continually wet. But all would not do, for at 5 P.M. the brig had neared us sufficiently to commence firing on us with her bow-guns. The brig kept up a steady fire upon us till 7 o'clock; but as we were low in the water, they did not often strike us. At 7 o'clock, all hope of escape departed from the captain. He mounted up into the main rigging, and hailing the brig, announced our surrender."

groaning." Shortly afterward the invasion force dispersed. Eighteen-twelve ended with Canada still firmly in British hands and the morale of the United States in the cellar.

The Naval War   The naval war on the Atlantic Ocean was going better. Although the British far outmanned and outgunned the Americans at sea, they were also stretched thin, and suffered from overconfidence. The Americans, they were certain, could not match the Royal Navy in battle or do serious damage to their merchant shipping. They were wrong. Many American merchant captains had secured letters of marque commissioning their vessels as privateers. Over the next two and a half years, these ships attacked British commerce in the West Indies, off the east coast of the United States, and even in the waters around the British Isles. While many privateers were captured, others took rich prizes. The success of the small American navy, though less significant in material terms, was important for national morale. The American frigates proved to be remarkably effective in single-ship combat.

In August 1812 the U.S.S. *Constitution,* commanded by Isaac Hull, sighted the British frigate *Guerrière* in the mid-North Atlantic. The *Guerrière* was a slightly smaller vessel with a lighter broadside; part of her crew, moreover, consisted of impressed Americans who had to be allowed to go below rather than fight their own countrymen. The British captain tried evasive maneuvers, but Hull was able to bring his ship within fifty yards of the enemy. For two hours he poured deadly broadsides into the British ship, leaving it a wreck. The *Guerrière* struck her colors. Both sides had fought well and bravely, but the performance of the inexperienced Americans was exceptional. American sailors had fought with greater spirit than American infantry. This victory was the first of several such single-ship combats that helped redeem the honor of American arms. Several weeks later the *United States,* under Stephen Decatur, encountered H.M.S. *Macedonian* and in a bloody battle sank her. At the end of the year the *Constitution* defeated H.M.S. *Java* in a two-hour engagement. Chagrined by their losses, the British began to

Constitution **and** ***Java.*** *(Courtesy, New-York Historical Society)*

reinforce their squadron off North America. Bit by bit its blockade of the American Atlantic coast became tighter and more effective, confirming all the fears of Northeasterners that war would destroy American commerce. The Americans soon lost control of their own coasts and shortly would be unable to repel British troop landings when they came.

Further Defeats in Canada   Another major attack on Canada came in 1813. In April, 8,500 troops gathered at the eastern end of Lake Ontario under the command of Henry Dearborn. On April 25, 1,700 men of this force sailed off to attack the Canadians at the western end of the lake, and two days later they arrived before York (now Toronto). The town was defended by only 800 soldiers and some Indians. The British had prepared a surprise in the form of a giant underground mine jammed with high explosives, but the mine went off at the wrong time, killing as many British as United States troops. Dismayed and outnumbered, the British commander now withdrew. After occupying York for four days, the invaders from the south looted it and burned the parliament buildings—acts for which their country would pay dearly the following year. They then departed for the mouth of the Niagara to attack Fort George. This time the aging Dearborn was too exhausted to lead the expedition, and he turned his command over to the vigorous Winfield Scott. Soon to join the expedition was an equally aggressive young naval officer, twenty-seven-year-old Oliver Hazard Perry.

The strengthened naval force was transported across Lake Ontario, and completed a difficult amphibious landing before Fort George. The troops, led by Scott and Perry, scrambled ashore with their heavy equipment and secured a foothold while still more men followed. Supported by the guns of the flotilla, the invasion force drove off the British counterattack. The British commander now withdrew from Fort George and retreated. Scott was all for pursuing the enemy and destroying his army completely, but was overruled by his superior in the Niagara theater of operations. When the troops of the United States were finally allowed to set off after the defeated British, Scott remained behind. The results were disastrous. The British commander surprised the invaders in their sleep, captured their leaders, and drove them back.

The British had now regained the initiative, and advanced with a supplement of Indians. The Indian auxiliaries fell upon a number of soldiers from the broken invasion force, who held them off until a party of British regulars approached under a flag of truce. Lieutenant James Fitzgibbon, the young British officer in charge, told the commander of the beleaguered unit that he was being closely followed by the main British army of 1,500 regulars and 700 Indians. The defenders, Fitzgibbon argued, could not possibly withstand the attack of this force, and in all likelihood the British would not then be able to restrain the bloodthirsty Indians; the wise course would be to surrender now and prevent a massacre. The defenders laid down their arms and waited for the main British party to arrive. It never did. A unit of 500 men had surrendered to a force only half its size. The setback on the Niagara frontier was matched by a major defeat before Montreal. Advancing on the Canadian city, the forces from the United States ran into stiff opposition and abandoned the invasion. Soon afterward, the British captured Fort Niagara. They also took Buffalo and burned the city to the ground.

The Battle of Lake Erie   In July 1813 six British warships arrived by way of the Saint Lawrence River at Lake Erie, and Captain Perry, commanding the hastily-built American fleet there, sent an urgent plea for men: "Think of my situation: the enemy in sight, the vessels under my command more than sufficient, and ready to make sail. . . ." But when the men came, he complained that they were "a motley set, blacks, soldiers, and boys. . . ." His commanding officer wrote back: "I regret that you are not pleased with the men sent you . . . , a part of them are not surpassed by any men we have in the fleet; and I have yet to learn that the color of the skin, or the cut and trimmings of the coat, can affect a man's qualifications or usefulness." On September 10, 1813, Perry and his crew, about one-fourth of whom were black, defeated the British fleet in a bloody three-hour battle. On the back of an envelope, Perry scrawled a now-famous message to General Harrison: "We have met the enemy and they are ours." Lake Erie was now in the hands of the United States, and the British were forced to abandon Detroit. A month later, Harrison overtook a retreating party of British and Indians and at the Battle of the Thames in Canada defeated them decisively. The chieftain Tecumseh was one of those who fell on the British side. Soon afterward, Tecumseh's federation of tribes collapsed and most of Britain's Indian allies deserted her cause.

These victories and the notable performance of the American navy notwithstanding, the British established a clear superiority in the Atlantic and in American coastal waters. The Royal Navy could with impunity sail up the Chesapeake Bay, attack merchant ships, and bombard strategic towns and military positions, amplifying the desperate plight of the United States and the Madison Administration's blunders. Hard-pressed New England was riddled with disloyalty. Yankees had not wanted war and felt little inducement to support it now that it was proving so expensive. Hoping to rescue something from the calamity, they became the chief suppliers of commodities to the British army in Canada. Madison sought to cut off this dangerous trade and induced Congress to pass an embargo bill in December 1813 restricting all exports from the United States. The effects were disastrous. American

Oliver Hazard Perry's dispatch to General Harrison on his victory at Lake Erie reflected the pride of the Americans on finally winning a naval battle.

exports plummeted and prices increased sharply. The Treasury found that it could not borrow the money it needed for military operations, and was forced to the edge of bankruptcy. In April 1814 Congress repealed this embargo.

Meanwhile the gloomy military situation promised to get worse. In the spring of 1814, Napoleon's empire collapsed and the conqueror of Europe went into exile on the island of Elba. Until then, the British had been conducting a series of holding operations in America on both land and sea. Now, with France out of the war, all the vast resources of the Royal Navy and the seasoned veterans of the European fighting would be free to teach the pesky Americans a lesson. In early May, the first detachments of British troops began to arrive in Quebec from Europe. Their mission, as explained in orders to the British commandant in Canada, Sir George Prevost, would be to drive the troops of the American republic out of Canada and recover the American Northwest, and thereby to secure Canada's safety. Winfield Scott leading the United States troops attacked first. At Chippewa and Lundy's Lane, his troops fought gallantly against many of the same seasoned British and Canadian forces who had earlier won at Detroit. The campaign ended in a draw if not a British victory, but temporarily British goals in the Northwest had been frustrated.

British Offensives   The British soon resumed the offensive. In late summer they set out for Plattsburgh, New York, near Lake Champlain. The British plan, as during the Revolution, was to split the United States in two along the line of Lake Champlain and the Hudson Valley. By September Prevost's army was at Plattsburgh's gates. There the American commander was the scrappy John Wool. Though outnumbered almost three to one, Wool put up such a fight along the approaches to Plattsburgh that Prevost paused and called on Captain George Downie, in command of the British fleet on the lake, to come to his aid. Together the navy and army would pound the Americans into submission and advance on New York City to complete their mission.

It was not to be. Standing between Prevost and the fulfillment of his scheme was the United States naval squadron commanded by Captain Thomas Macdonough. Macdonough's little fleet on Lake Champlain consisted of four moderate-sized vessels and ten tiny gunboats, but in firepower it just about matched Downie's squadron.

Downie attacked the Americans. His first shot hit the deck of Macdonough's flagship, the *Saratoga,* and destroyed the coop of the sailors' champion gamecock. The bird was unhurt and immediately flew to a gun carriage where, its feathers ruffled, it crowed defiance at the enemy. The men laughed and cheered; it seemed a good omen. For over two hours the opposing fleets poured ammunition into each other. Macdonough himself was knocked unconscious three times. At last the British surrendered. Macdonough brought the defeated British officers aboard the *Saratoga,* complimented them on their bravery, and refused to accept their swords. And a signal victory it was. When Prevost learned of Macdonough's triumph, he decided he could not continue; with the enemy in command on the water, his flanks were exposed. Instead of resuming the assault, he marched his men back to Canada. Another invasion threat was over.

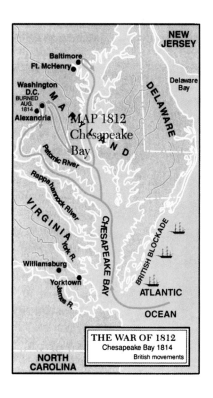

The Burning of Washington A second British invasion prong was meeting with greater success. On August 19, 1814, Sir George Cockburn landed with 4,000 men between Baltimore and Washington, and set out for the nation's capital. A hastily organized defense force of militia, sailors, and a few regulars sought to stop the British just outside the capital at Bladensburg, but the inexperienced Americans could not hold against seasoned veterans and many fell into British hands. Later that afternoon, after learning of the defeat, Madison and his Cabinet left the city to avoid capture. His wife, the resourceful Dolley, had already removed the sterling silver and other valuables from the presidential mansion. At 8 p.m. the British entered the city. At the President's house British officers ate the formal dinner Madison had abandoned. The next morning British soldiers burned the public buildings, including the President's house, the Capitol, the Treasury, and the War Office. The following day they left the smoldering capital, having avenged the burning of York.

In early September the British, arriving by land and sea, moved on Baltimore. They broke through the Americans' first line of defense and drew to within a mile and a half of the city. At this point the British commander decided to call on the British flotilla offshore to bombard the city, to help soften it up for his final assault. All through the day and night of September 13 the British fired rockets, big guns, and mortars at Forts McHenry and Covington, but could not silence them. At daybreak the American flag still flew over Fort McHenry. Watching the attack was a Baltimore lawyer, Francis Scott Key. Deeply moved by the sight of the flag, he wrote a poem, "The Star Spangled Banner." Soon set to the melody of a popular English drinking song, the piece was to be adapted as the national anthem in 1931, well over a century later. The British failure to reduce the harbor defenses discouraged further action, and they withdrew. The city was safe.

Baltimore's escape was, of course, a welcome event, but it could not wipe out the memory of Washington's capture and the general

---

A British soldier recalled the "beautiful spectacle" of the burning of Washington:

The blazing of houses, ships, and stores, the report of exploding magazines, and the crash of falling roofs [informed him and his troops] as they proceeded, of what was going forward. You can conceive nothing finer than the sight which met them as they drew near to the town.

The sky was brilliantly illumined by the different conflagrations; and a dark red light was thrown upon the road, sufficient to permit each man to view distinctly his comrade's face. A storm began and the flashes of lightning seemed to vie in brilliancy, with the flames which

burst from the roofs of burning houses, while the thunder drowned the noise of crumbling walls, and was only interrupted by the occasional roar of cannon, and of large depots of gunpowder, as they one by one exploded.

The President [James Madison] had hurried back to his own house, that he might prepare a feast for the entertainment of his officers, when they should return victorious. For the truth of these details, I will not be answerable; but this much I know, that the feast was actually prepared, though, instead of being devoured by American officers, it went to satisfy the less delicate appetites of a party of English soldiers. When the detachment, sent out to destroy Mr. Madison's house, entered his dining parlour, they found a dinner-table spread, and

In August 1814, the British captured and burned the city of Washington, including the President's house, the Capitol, the Treasury, and the War Office. *(Courtesy, The New-York Historical Society)*

ineptness of the American war effort. In the wake of the Chesapeake invasions defeatism swept the nation.

The fall and winter of 1814–15 was also a time of political crisis. Massachusetts elected representatives to meet with delegates from other New England states at Hartford, Connecticut, to consider defense problems and to discuss the possibility of revising the federal Constitution. Behind this action were the profound disgust of New Englanders with the war and their feeling that their section was suffering unduly. At Hartford the militants intended to consider either seceding from the war or seceding from the Union itself, but by the time the convention met in December they were outnumbered. New Hampshire and Vermont refused to send delegations at all; and the delegates from Connecticut and Rhode Island proved to be more moderate than anyone

covers laid for forty guests. Several kinds of wine, in handsome cut-glass decanters, were cooling on the sideboard; plate holders stood by the fire-place, filled with dishes and plates; knives, forks, and spoons, were arranged for immediate use; in short, every thing was ready for the entertainment of a ceremonious party. Such were the arrangements in the dining room; whilst in the kitchen were others answerable to them in every respect. Spits, loaded with joints of various sorts, turned before the fire; pots, sauce-pans, and other culinary utensils, stood upon the grate; and all other requisites for an elegant and substantial repast, were exactly in a state which indicated that they had been lately and precipitately abandoned.

You will readily imagine, that these preparations were beheld, by a party of hungry soldiers, with no indifferent eye. An elegant dinner, even though considerably over-dressed, was a luxury to which few of them, at least for some time back, had been accustomed; and which, after the dangers and fatigues of the day, appeared peculiarly inviting. They sat down to it, therefore, not indeed in the most orderly manner, but with countenances which would not have disgraced a party of aldermen at a civic feast; and having satisfied their appetites with fewer complaints than would have probably escaped their rival *gourmands*, and partaken pretty freely of the wines, they finished by setting fire to the house which had so liberally entertained them.

Francis Scott Key's "The Star-Spangled Banner": detail written during the War of 1812.

had expected. The Convention did not call for dissolution of the Union. It urged amendments to the Constitution that would reduce the power of the West and the South and require that non-intercourse acts, admission of new states, and declarations of war all receive a two-thirds vote of Congress. But the resolutions in the end amounted to little more than a protest.

The Treaty of Ghent

As early as November 1813 the British and American governments, partly at the urging of the Russian Tsar, had agreed to meet to discuss peace terms. Neither government was happy about the war both had sought to avoid; now, even while fighting continued, they began to arrange for its end.

Negotiations conducted at Ghent in Belgium moved slowly. The British hoped that before long their armies would occupy large stretches of the United States and they could use this territory as leverage for extracting favorable terms. Perhaps they might even get their long-held wish to create an Indian state in the Northwest, cutting off the United States from the interior of the continent. The American negotiators, Henry Clay, John Quincy Adams, and Albert Gallatin, rejected any scheme to slice up their country and insisted on the abandonment of the impressment of sailors from American ships. At first, neither side would budge.

During the last half of 1814, however, the British began to realize that, though they could win victories, they could not count on totally defeating the stubborn Americans. Then, too, Britain and Russia began to clash at the Congress of Vienna called to sort out the complex affairs of Europe after Napoleon's defeat. Under the circumstances, war with the United States now seemed an unimportant sideshow that should be ended as soon as possible. The Americans, too, were anxious to bring matters to a conclusion, and they abandoned their demand for an explicit condemnation of impressment.

On Christmas eve, 1814, the commissioners at Ghent finally signed a peace treaty. This agreement merely restored the situation as it had existed before the war. Commissioners from both nations would meet to settle a dispute over the boundary between the United States and Canada, a dispute that had resulted from imperfections in the geographical knowledge available in 1783. The war had been nearly pointless. It would not be the last such in American history.

The Battle of New Orleans

Yet the war went on. News of the Treaty of Ghent did not reach the United States for many weeks, and by that time hundreds of men had died in unnecessary battles. The greatest of these was the Battle of New Orleans, which created a national hero, helped destroy what remained of the Federalist Party, and restored the nation's battered self-respect. The hero was General Andrew Jackson of Tennessee, a roughhewn, self-made planter, lawyer, and soldier.

General Andrew Jackson Born in South Carolina, Jackson had gone to Tennessee when that future state was still the western district of North Carolina. He had served his adopted state in Congress and as a judge. In 1813–14 he led the Tennessee militia against the Creek Indians in Mississippi Territory following the massacre of 250 whites at Fort Mims. At Horseshoe Bend, Jackson surprised the Creeks and defeated them in a fierce battle. For his services the government made him a major general in the army and commander of the Seventh Military District with headquarters at Mobile.

While at Mobile, Jackson learned that the British, as part of their final push to crush the Americans, intended to attack New Orleans with another army of European veterans. Though weak with fatigue and dysentery, Jackson hurried to the city to prepare its defenses. A flood of directives—to obstruct the roads and bayous leading to the city, to build fortifications, and to strengthen the existing ones—flowed from his headquarters. Militia and volunteers from Kentucky, Tennessee, and Mississippi made up the core of Jackson's army, and he recruited additional troops from among the people of French or Spanish origin and black freemen of New Orleans. To the army paymaster who questioned equal pay for the black troops Jackson wrote: "Be pleased to keep to yourself your opinions upon the policy of making payments of the troops with the necessary muster rolls without inquiring whether the troops are white, black or tea." Jackson also agreed to accept the services of a group of river pirates led by Jean Laffite, a colorful rogue in trouble with the governor of Louisiana.

On the morning of December 23, 1814, British troops newly arrived from the West Indies began to disembark fifteen miles southeast of New Orleans, after a cold trip across Lake Borgne in open boats. Jackson quickly learned of the landings. A more cautious general might have waited to see whether this was the main attack or a mere feint. But Jackson immediately turned to his officers and declared: "Gentlemen, the British are below; we must fight them tonight!" With 2,000 men he advanced on the British force of some 1,600 that was waiting for further reinforcements before advancing against the city. Jackson achieved

To the governor of Louisiana General Jackson wrote:

"Our country has been invaded. . . . She wants Soldiers to fight her battles. The free men of colour in your city are inured to the Southern climate and would make excellent Soldiers. They will not remain quiet spectators of the interesting contest. They must be for, or against us—distrust them, and you make them your enemies, place confidence in them, and you engage them by every dear and honorable tie to the interest of the country who extends to them equal rights and priviledges with white men."

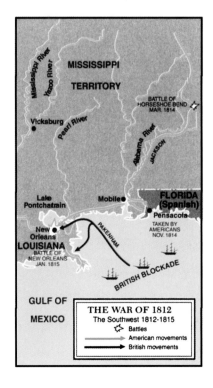

complete surprise and gave the enemy a serious shellacking. The British line held, however, and Jackson withdrew to a position between the river and a swamp.

Here, just as the commissioners were signing the peace treaty at Ghent, Jackson and his men prepared to face the British assault behind breastworks of cotton bales and earth. Both sides were being reinforced. All night long, American raiders made sorties against the British, doing little harm, but keeping their opponents from getting any sleep. The next morning, with the battlefield enveloped in ground fog, the British advanced on Jackson's men hidden behind their breastworks. For a while they made headway against the firearms and artillery to their front, but shelling on their flank by the U.S.S. *Louisiana* from the river proved more than flesh could bear, and the advance stopped.

For the next three days the two armies confronted each other across a field strewn with dead and dying. On the morning of December 31, the British attacked again and the battle became an artillery duel, Laffite's pirates with their big guns doing especially effective work. For almost five hours the cannon boomed, until the discouraged British suspended their attack. Once more both sides brought up reinforcements. When the British commander, Sir Edward Pakenham, was ready to resume the attempt to reach New Orleans, he had close to 10,000 men to Jackson's 5,000.

On the morning of January 8, 1815, Pakenham asked his veterans for the last time to brave the American defenses. Once more, the attack failed. As the redcoats trudged across the ground in front of the American position, their ranks were shredded by grapeshot and arms fire. Some reached the American lines, but then a counterattack threw them back. Many British officers were hit, and Pakenham himself died on the field.

Victory after Defeat   The victory was astounding. Over 2,000 British troops had died or been wounded against American casualties of twenty-one. Soon after the smoke cleared, Jackson and his jubilant staff passed along the lines of cheering troops to the stirring strains of "Hail Columbia" played by the army band. It was a glorious moment for the young nation.

A mismanaged war that had humiliated Americans now became a matter of great national pride. Overnight new confidence suffused the nation. Americans had taken on the greatest power in the world, and in the end had defeated the best it could throw at them. No longer would the nations of Europe treat the United States with the contempt they had been showing. American nationalists managed the incredible feat of puffing a disastrous war into an epic victory.

The war had momentous political consequences. The Federalists had bet on the wrong side. If not for New Orleans and the exhilaration that made a bungled national enterprise seem a triumph, Federalist opposition to the war might have been rewarded with public favor, but Jackson's victory made suspect the patriotism of every Federalist who had praised England and attacked the administration. In the presidential contest of 1816, the Republican James Monroe overwhelmed the Federalist candidate, Rufus King of New York, carrying every state in

An ecstatic American newspaper writer could hardly contain himself in his dispatch describing the Battle of New Orleans:

"Glory be to GOD, that the barbarians have been defeated and that at Orleans the intended plunderers have found their grave!—Glory to *Jackson*, *Carroll* and *Coffee*, and the hardy and gallant *Tennesseeans*, *Kentuckians* and *Louisianians* who 'seized opportunity by the forelock' to 'demonstrate' what freemen can do in defence of their altars and firesides. Glory to the *militia*, that the 'soldiers of *Wellington*,' the boastful conquerors of the legions of *France*, have shrunk from the *liberty-directed* bullets of the high-souled sons of the west! Sons of freedom—saviors of *Orleans*—benefactors of your country and avengers of its wrongs, all hail! Hail glorious people—worthy, thrice worthy, to enjoy the blessings which heaven in bounteous profusion has heaped on your country! Never may its luxuriant soil be trodden unrevenged by insolent foreigners in arms!

Who would not be an American? Long live the republic! All hail! last asylum of oppressed humanity! Peace is signed in the arms of victory!"

the Union except Massachusetts, Connecticut, and Delaware. Thereafter, although they continued to muster some isolated support, the Federalists were finished.

Meanwhile, a strange thing happened: the Republicans became Federalists. In his annual message in 1815, Madison asked Congress to pass a protective tariff, charter a second Bank of the United States, and appropriate funds for the construction of roads and canals—"internal improvements," as they came to be known. Led by Clay, Calhoun, and other nationalists, Congress obliged. In 1816 it passed a tariff affording at least modest protection to American industry, and established the Second Bank of the United States with an even larger capitalization than that of the first. Madison, having changed his mind, vetoed the bill for internal improvements on the grounds that federal funding of them was of dubious constitutionality; but his successors thought differently and thereafter federal subsidies would help the nation overcome its vast distances.

Finally, there was Andrew Jackson. New Orleans had created the nation's first folk hero since George Washington. Congress struck a gold medal in Jackson's honor and confirmed his rank of major general with the munificent salary of $2,400 a year. Before long, a biographer was busy writing a life of the general for an eager public. At this point Jackson might have chosen a life of ease at the Hermitage, his plantation near Nashville, amidst the plaudits of his fellow citizens. His future took a different course. Before many months had passed, Americans would hear from him again.

Suggested Readings

Studies of the years 1800 to 1816 includes Joyce Appleby, *Liberalism and Republicanism in the Historical Imagination* (1992), Drew McCoy, *The Last of the Fathers: James Madison and the Republican Legacy* (1989), Pierre Berton, *The Invasion of Canada* (1980), (1987), J. C. A. Stagg, *Mr. Madison's War: Politics, Diplomacy, and Warfare in the Early Republic, 1783–1830* (1983), and James P. Ronda, *Lewis and Clark Among the Indians* (1984). See also John Logan Allen, *Passage Through the Garden: Lewis and Clark and the Image of the American Northwest* (1968). Alexander DeConde surveys *This Affair of The War of 1812* (1969). On the War of 1812 see also Donald R. Hickey, *The War of 1812: A Forgotten Conflict* (1989), Clifford L. Egan, *Neither Peace nor War: Franco-American Relations, 1803–1812* (1983), Burton Spivak, *Jefferson's English Crisis: Commerce, the Embargo, and the Republican Revolution* (1979), and Robert A. Rutland, *Madison's Alternatives, Jeffersonian Republicans and the Coming of War, 1805–1812* (1975).

Dumas Malone presents *Jefferson and His Times* (1948–1981) in six volumes. Merrill Peterson's is a one-volume biography, *Thomas Jefferson and the New Nation* (1970). Forrest McDonald's *The Presidency of Thomas Jefferson* (1976) complements Fawn M. Brodie's *Thomas Jefferson: An Intimate History* (1974). Gore Vidal's *Burr: A Novel* (1973) presents the controversial Aaron as a gentleman and portrays the vulgarities and hypocrisies of the society that surrounded him. Also sympathetic is Milton Lomask's biography, *Aaron Burr* (1983).

Useful on politics are Noble E. Cunningham, Jr., *The Process of Government under Jefferson* (1978), Marshall Smelser, *The Democratic Republic, 1800–1815* (1968), David Hackett Fischer, *The Evolution of American Conservatism* (1965), and James M. Banner, *To The Hartford Convention: The Federalists and the Origins of Party Politics in Massachusetts, 1789–1815* (1970).

On the women at the Lowell Mills see Thomas Dublin, *Women at Work: The Transformation of Work and Community in Lowell, Massachusetts, 1826–1860* (1979). Two rewarding studies of other women's experiences in this period are Nancy Cott's *The Bonds of Womanhood: "Woman's Sphere" in New England, 1780–1835* (1977) and Suzanne Lebsock's *The Free Women of St. Petersburg: Status and Culture in a Southern Town, 1784–1860* (1984). For an interpretation of child-rearing practices see Philip Greven, *The Protestant Temperament: Patterns of Child-Rearing, Religious Experience, and the Self in Early America* (1982).

How Republican Were the Jeffersonian Republicans?

Drew McCoy

Many years after his first election to the presidency, Thomas Jefferson commented that "the revolution of 1800" was "as real a revolution in the principles of our government as that of 1776 was in its form." Jefferson was undoubtedly using the term "revolution" not in the modern sense of a radical creation of a new order, but in the traditional sense of a return to first principles, of a restoration of original values and ideals that had been overturned or repudiated. For him, the election of 1800 was a revolution because it marked a turning back to the true republican spirit of 1776. Jefferson was excited by the prospect of the first implementation of the principles of America's republican revolution in the national government created by the Constitution of 1787, since in his eyes a minority faction . . . had captured control of that government almost immediately after its establishment. From Jefferson's perspective, indeed, the Federalists had done more than threaten to corrupt American government by mimicking the English "court" model. Just as frightening was their apparent desire to mold the young republic's political economy along English lines, a desire reflected both in their call for the extensive development of government-subsidized manufacturing enterprises and in their attempt to stimulate a highly commercialized economy anchored to such premature and speculative ventures as an overextended carrying trade. Jefferson's fundamental goal in 1801 was to end this threatened "Anglicization" of both American government and society. In so doing he would restore the basis for the development of a truly republican political economy, one that would be patterned after Benjamin Franklin's vision of a predominantly agricultural empire that would expand across space, rather than develop through time.

Within the Jeffersonian framework of assumptions and beliefs, three essential conditions were necessary to create and sustain such a republican political economy: a national government free from any taint of corruption, an unobstructed access to an ample supply of open land, and a relatively liberal international commercial order that would offer adequate foreign markets for America's flourishing agricultural surplus. The history of the 1790s had demonstrated all too well to the Jeffersonians the predominant danger to a republican political economy of corruption emanating from the federal government. They were especially troubled by the deleterious political, social, and moral repercussions of the Federalists' financial system, which they regarded as the primary vehicle of corruption both in the political system and in the country at large. Although Jefferson concluded rather soon after his election that his administration could not safely dismantle Hamilton's entire system with a few swift strokes, he was committed to doing everything possible to control that system's effects and gradually reduce its pernicious influence. Extinguishing the national debt as rapidly as possible, reducing government expenditures (especially on the military), and repealing the Federalist battery of direct and excise taxes became primary goals of the Jeffersonians in power. . . .

In itself, the electoral revolution of 1800 promised to remove the primary threat to a republican political economy posed by the machinations of a corrupt administration. But the Jeffersonians also had to secure the other necessary guarantors of republicanism: landed and commercial expansion. Although the pressure of population growth on the supply of land in the United States had never been a problem of the same immediate magnitude as political corruption, the social and economic dislocations of the 1780s had prompted some concern with this matter. Through the Louisiana Purchase of 1803, undoubtedly the greatest achievement of his presidency, Jefferson appeared to eliminate this problem for generations, if not for centuries, to come. But the third and thorniest problem, in the form of long-standing restrictions on American commerce, proved far more frustrating. . . .

Drew McCoy, *The Elusive Republic: Political Economy in Jeffersonian America* (Chapel Hill: The University of North Carolina Press, 1980).

I believe that the new European demand for American grains—the crops produced by most farm families from Virginia through Maryland, Pennsylvania, Delaware, New Jersey, New York, and up the Connecticut River Valley—created an unusually favorable opportunity for ordinary men to produce for the Atlantic trade world. Far from being viewed apprehensively, this prospect during the thirty years following the adoption of the Constitution undergirded Jefferson's optimism about America's future as a progressive, prosperous, democratic nation. Indeed, this anticipated participation in an expanding international commerce in foodstuffs created the material base for a new social vision owing little conceptually or practically to antiquity, the Renaissance, or the mercantilists of eighteenth-century England. From this perspective, the battle between the Jeffersonians and Federalists appears not as a conflict between the patrons of agrarian self-sufficiency and the proponents of modern commerce, but rather as a struggle between two different elaborations of capitalistic development in America. Jefferson becomes, not the heroic loser in a battle against modernity, but the conspicuous winner in a contest over how the government should serve its citizens in the first generation of the nation's territorial expansion.

Anyone searching for the word *yeoman* in the writings of the 1790s will be disappointed. The absence of the word *yeoman* is negative evidence only. The error in current scholarly usage, however, is not lexical, but conceptual; it points Jefferson and his party in the wrong direction. Despite Jefferson's repeated assertions that his party was animated by bold new expectations for the human condition, the agrarian myth makes him a traditional, republican visionary, socially radical perhaps, but economically conservative. The assumed contradiction between democratic aspirations and economic romanticism explains why his plans were doomed to failure in competition with the hard-headed realism of an Alexander Hamilton. . . .

Viewed retrospectively by historians living in an industrial age, Jefferson's enthusiasm for agriculture has long been misinterpreted as an attachment to the past. So dazzling were the technological triumphs of railroad building and steam power that the age of the marvelous machines came to appear as the great divide in human history. . . .

Two interpretative tendencies have followed from this point of view. One has been to treat proponents of agricultural development as conservative and to construe as progressive those who favored manufacturing and banking. The contrast between Jefferson cast as an agrarian romantic and Hamilton as the far-seeing capitalist comes readily to mind. The other retrospective bias has been the characterization of industrialization as an end toward which prior economic changes were inexorably moving. Both classical economic and Marxist theory have contributed to this determinism, which recasts historical events as parts of a process, as stages in a sequential morphology. Under this influence the actual human encounter with time is reversed; instead of interpreting social change as the result of particular responses to a knowable past, the decisions men and women made are examined in relation to future developments unknown to them. The situation in America at the end of the eighteenth century is exemplary.

Joyce Appleby, *Liberalism and Republicanism in the Historical Imagination* (Cambridge, MA: Harvard University Press, 1992), pp. 257–58, 259, 260–61.

The Erie Canal at Rochester, New York. Cities prospered all along the canal, which extended from Buffalo on Lake Erie, to Albany on the Hudson, opening an economical transportation system from the Great Lakes to the Atlantic. *(Courtesy, New-York Historical Society, New York City)*

Sinews of Nationhood

THE ERIE CANAL

Pushed through the New York legislature in 1817 by Governor De Witt Clinton's powerful political machine, the Erie Canal project has been called "the most decisive single event in the history of American transportation." Beginning at Albany on the Hudson, the finished canal wound 363 miles through the Mohawk River Valley to Buffalo, on Lake Erie. Along the way eighty-three locks lifted the boats up and down the 650-foot elevation, and eighteen stone aqueducts carried the canal over rivers and streams. The Great Western Canal—one of its more formal names—was but four feet deep and forty feet wide, later deepened to seven feet and widened to seventy.

The Erie Canal was an immediate success. Before its opening, the cost of hauling grain across the Appalachian foothills to New York City had been three times the market value of wheat, six times that of corn, ten times that of oats. Overnight these stifling transportation costs disappeared, as horses pulled hundred-ton barges loaded with freight along "Clinton's Big Ditch" at rates as low as a cent a ton-mile. At the canal's Albany terminus steamboats took over for the comparatively swift and economical trip down the Hudson to New York City. By 1825, when the Erie was completed, toll revenues already exceeded a half million dollars a year. Soon the canal's entire $7 million cost had been recovered, and state officials ordered the canal widened to accommodate the increased traffic. Towns all along the route from Buffalo to New York City prospered, none more than New York, which became the transportation gateway to the West and the nation's largest port.

HISTORICAL EVENTS

1807
Fulton invents the steamboat

1810
Fletcher v. Peck

1811
Charter of the first Bank of the United States expires

1814–15
Hartford Convention

1816
James Monroe elected President • Tariff of 1816 • Second Bank of the United States is chartered

1819
Panic of 1819 • *Dartmouth College v. Woodward* • *McCulloch v. Maryland*

1820
James Monroe reelected President

1821
Cohens v. Virginia

1823
Biddle becomes president of the Bank of the United States

1824
Gibbons v. Ogden

251

Governor De Witt Clinton of New York predicted:

"As an organ of communication between the Hudson, the Mississippi, the St. Lawrence, the great lakes of the north and west, and their tributary rivers, [the canal] will create the greatest inland trade ever witnessed. The most fertile and extensive regions of America will avail themselves of its facilities for a market. All their surplus . . . will concentrate in the city of New York. . . That city will, in the course of time, become the granary of the world, the emporium of commerce, the seat of manufactures, the focus of great moneyed operations. . . . And before the revolution of a century, the whole island of Manhattan, covered with habitations and replenished with a dense population, will constitute one vast city."

Once opened in 1825, the Erie became an essential part of a tourist's itinerary: "The canal is in everybody's mouth," one traveler rather awkwardly expressed it. The bustle and activity, the remarkable circumstances of its construction, its overwhelming success and national importance made it an eighth wonder of the world. Mule teams on the towpath zipped the fast passenger boats (called packets) along at the canal speed limit of four miles an hour, while freighters made but one and a half to two miles per hour, and log rafts annoyed everyone with their slowness.

"Commending my soul to God," remarked a first-time rider boarding at Rochester, "and asking His defense from danger, I stepped on board the canalboat and was soon flying towards Utica." Long trips by water had always been dangerous, and the idea of taking a trip of over 300 miles in complete safety was fascinating. Mock-heroic epics of the dangers of a storm at sea became a standard bit of Erie folklore: the ship pitching, the captain barking orders, the endless verses celebrating each maritime danger.

Buffalo was the tame end of the canal. At the other end, in Watervliet near Albany, the notorious "side-cut" area with its twenty-nine saloons in two blocks with names like The Black Rag and The Tub of Blood, its fights, its large-scale vice, and an occasional body floating in the canal gained the district the title "The Barbary Coast of the East."

The Erie traveler saw a splendid microcosm of a young nation.

SHOOTING PIGEONS

by James Fenimore Cooper

Not too many miles south of the route of the Erie Canal the environmental splendors of the United States were already under attack. James Fenimore Cooper (1789–1851), born in upstate New York, wrote the Leather-stocking Tales, *a series of five novels about life on the American frontier. The series takes its name from its hero, a woodsman who is variously called Natty Bumppo, Deerslayer, Hawkeye, Pathfinder, Leather-stocking, and the "trapper."*

This excerpt, taken from Pioneers *(1823), describes a pigeon hunt. The passage furnishes one of the earliest lessons in environmentalism to be found in American literature. Cooper perceived the limits of the seemingly inexhaustible American landscape.*

If the heavens were alive with pigeons, the whole village seemed equally in motion with men, women, and children. Every species of fire-arms, from the French ducking-gun with a barrel near six feet in length, to the common horseman's pistol, was to be seen in the hands of the men and boys; while bows and arrows, some made of the simple stick of a walnut sapling, and others in a rude imitation of the ancient cross-bows, were carried by many of the latter.

The houses and the signs of life apparent in the village, drove the alarmed birds from the direct line of their flight, toward the mountains, along the sides and near the bases of which they were glancing in dense masses, equally wonderful by the rapidity of their motion, and their incredible numbers. . . .

Across the inclined plane which fell from the steep ascent of the mountain to the banks of the Susquehanna, ran the highway, on either side of which a clearing of many acres had been made at a very early day. Over those clearings, and up the eastern mountain, and along the dangerous path that was cut into its side, the different individuals posted themselves, and in a few moments that attack commenced.

The men and women who made the canal work, "part water, part sand, part wind . . . but all canawler," were a colorful lot. The tough Irish workers who had dug the ditch now crewed the boats. The pompous captains, the fierce lock-keepers in endless battle with the crews, the floating showboats, saloons, general stores, and vice dens were famous among travelers, as were the legendary cooks: one "with a bosom like a boxcar," another who "stood six feet in her socks; her hand was like an elephant's ear, her breath would open locks."

These boats to Buffalo allowed remarkable freedom for travelers to see the countryside when they were not ducking under the famous low bridges. Even on the packets, a passenger could walk the towpath alongside the boat for exercise. On the slower boats, poor travelers could step ashore and forage for their food, picking berries and hunting rabbits. And the scenes were grand: bustling ports, ingenious locks and romantic swamps, rivers, and streams, and magnificent aqueducts; curious bridges of water allowed ships to pass over such picturesque obstacles. Sometimes the canal cut straight through primeval forests with no hint of man's work but the calm swath of canal and towpath. Charles Dickens has left a vivid recollection. The "exquisite beauty of the opening day, when light came glancing off from everything; the gliding on at night so noiselessly, past frowning hills sullen with dark trees and sometimes angry in one red, burning spot high up, where unseen men lay crouching round a fire; the shining out of the

The Erie as an Engineering Project

The canals were the first projects that required modern engineering skills. If their walls were not of a needed thickness, for example, they would leak, the water level would fall, and the boats would be unable to move. This is, in fact, what happened with several of the country's early canals.

The Erie presented enormous technical challenges. Gratings had to be measured exactly, new kinds of locks designed and built, and all constructed to last for generations. The rule of thumb would not suffice. So the first generation of American engineers learned their profession on the job. For the next thirty years, the graduates of the Erie Canal would build the nation's canals, railroads, and machines.

In this sense the Erie had an enormous impact on American economic and cultural development quite apart from the improvement in transportation and shipping it brought. The Erie not only opened the West, but also provided the opportunity for Americans to learn the skills that rapid industrialization would require.

Among the sportsmen was the tall, gaunt form of Leather-stocking, walking over the field, with his rifle hanging on his arm, his dogs at his heels; the latter now scenting the dead or wounded birds, that were beginning to tumble from the flocks, and then crouching under the legs of their master, as if they participated in his feelings at this wasteful and unsportsmanlike execution.

The reports of the fire-arms became rapid, whole volleys rising from the plain, as flocks of more than ordinary numbers darted over the opening, shadowing the field like a cloud; and then the light smoke of a single piece would issue from among the leafless bushes on the mountain, as death was hurled on the retreat of the affrighted birds, who were rising from a volley, in a vain effort to escape. Arrows, and missiles of every kind, were in the midst of the flocks; and so numerous were the birds, and so low did they take their flight, that even long poles, in the hands of those on the sides of the mountain, were used to strike them to the earth. . . .

Among the relics of the old military excursions, that occasionally are discovered throughout the different districts of the western part of New-York, there had

been found . . . a small swivel, which would carry a ball of a pound weight. . . . This miniature cannon had been released from the rust, and being mounted on little wheels, was now in a state for actual service. For several years it was the sole organ for extraordinary rejoicings used in those mountains. On the mornings of the Fourths of July, it would be heard ringing among the hills. . . .

"An't the woods his work as well as the pigeons? Use, but don't waste. Wasn't the woods made for the beasts and birds to harbor in? And when man wanted their flesh, their skins, or their feathers, there's the place to seek them. But I'll go to the hut with my own game, for I wouldn't touch one of the harmless things that cover the ground here, looking up with their eyes on me, as if they only wanted tongues to say their thoughts."

With this sentiment in his mouth, Leather-stocking threw his rifle over his arm, and followed by his dogs, stepped across the clearing with great caution, taking care not to tread on one of the wounded birds in his path. He soon entered the bushes on the margin of the lake, and was hid from view.

bright stars undisturbed by any noise of wheels or steam or any other sound than the limpid rippling of the water as the boat went on; all these were pure delights."

A New Society

Tocqueville observes in his optimistic Democracy in America:

"No novelty in the United States struck me more vividly during my stay there than the equality of conditions. In America men are nearer equality than in any other country in the world. . . . Wealth . . . is within reach of all. . . . In Europe to say of someone that he rose from nothing is a disgrace and a reproach. It is the opposite here. . . . The whole society seems to have turned into one middle class."

When the French nobleman Alexis de Tocqueville began his tour of the United States in 1831, he imagined that he was looking into the very face of the modern democratic future. His *Democracy in America*, published here in translation in the late 1830s, described a nation of exploding energies, of individualists throwing lifetimes of force and work into the pursuit of achievement. Certainly many immigrants complained about the "go along steam-boat" pace of life in the United States. James Dawson Burn, a British immigrant, wrote that "work, work, work is the everlasting routine of everyday life." Americans were "savagely wild in devouring their work."

At first skeptical about democracy, Tocqueville nevertheless liked much of what he saw. He was respectfully surprised that American society had managed to enjoy so much liberty amid an equality that he had thought to be an enemy to liberty. And yet he found American individualism flawed. The haste to succeed prevented the slow cultivation of excellence, and the individual American, lacking smaller communities and classes with which to identify, was pitifully submissive to public opinion.

Tocqueville's analysis of early nineteenth-century American individualism does not take adequate account of powerful elements of community and cooperation in neighborhoods, in churches, in voluntary associations and activities. And in describing the American mentality as one of submission to public opinion, he was writing too early to see the full flowering of an American literature of private visions and of brooding inquiry into the depths of the soul. Nathaniel Hawthorne, Edgar Allan Poe, Herman Melville, and other seers into the secret heart might have revealed to Tocqueville a side of the American mind that was not bustlingly aggressive but darkly introspective. Tocqueville's portrayal of the energetic American, free to chase after wealth, did not fit the case of Americans condemned to drudgery, struggle, and isolation on farms, or pressed down into the poverty of the growing cities. And of course, as he knew, it did not apply to the black slaves. But Tocqueville offers a starting point for understanding a society that was, by and large, bursting with energy and hope, and committed to democracy, with its conflicting urges toward freedom and toward conformity.

The Transportation Revolution

In 1808, when Secretary of the Treasury Albert Gallatin proposed his ambitious system of internal improvements at federal expense, it took a New Yorker three days to travel to Boston, ten days to reach Charleston, and nearly six weeks to journey west to St. Louis. The movement of bulky or heavy goods over long distances by land was prohibitively expensive:

it cost more to drag a ton of iron overland a few miles than to bring it across the ocean. Farmers and merchants still depended mainly on waterways to move their crops and merchandise. Coastwise shipping was inexpensive but slow. Inland areas were peculiarly dependent upon river transportation. But this was strictly a one-way affair—downstream. The flatboats that floated down to New Orleans with western produce had to be broken up for lumber, and the boatmen left to get home as best they could. Sectional jealousies and constitutional squabbles prevented the passage of Gallatin's and Clay's plans for internal improvements. Transportation remained haphazard and wasteful. Nonetheless, the fragmented American republic slowly linked itself into a connected whole.

Turnpikes   Early American roads were little more than broad, stump-filled paths through the forest. Impassable in wet weather, they were adequate only for local needs. A system of through routes, bringing together the chief commercial centers, was desperately needed. In the 1790s private corporations had begun building turnpikes along the most important routes of travel. These companies financed construction mainly by the sale of stock to investors, and sought profits by collecting tolls from people using the roads. The best turnpikes had a firm stone foundation overlaid with gravel, drainage ditches for run-off, and substantial stone or wooden bridges. The extreme difficulty of moving men and material during the War of 1812 stimulated a boom in turnpike construction. By 1825 these roads crisscrossed New England and the mid-Atlantic states; Pennsylvania alone had about 2,400 miles of toll road. In the West and South, where private capital was scarce, state and local governments often financed the turnpikes. The greatest of them all, the National Road, was built by the federal government. Begun in 1811, it ultimately stretched from Cum-

Leila T. Bahmah, *Geese in Flight* (ca. 1850). The absorbing theme of this painting is movement both man-made and in nature: the geese, the smoke and steam of the riverboat and locomotive, the galloping horse. *(Courtesy, National Gallery of Art)*

Robert Fulton. *(Courtesy, Library of Congress)*

Steamboats were also hazardous. One account of 1851 noted:

"Our steamboats very far exceed in number those of any other country, and the navigation of most of our rivers is dangerous in the extreme. The frequency of explosions upon our Western boats is owing in a great measure to their employing high pressure boilers and engines. The steam is generated with great rapidity by this mode, yet as long as the boat is in motion all is safe, but let a boat under a full head stop suddenly and there is always a danger of explosion; so much so indeed, that old stagers will generally be seen hurrying to the stern as soon as the engineer's bell is heard to command 'stop her. . . .' With regard to the frequent losses of boats by fire, these are too often the result of the manner in which they are built and freighted. The cabin is entirely above the deck, built of the lightest material, and always as dry as tinder, from the constant heat beneath. It only wants a full load of cotton to complete the danger. When a boat is fully freighted with

(continued on p. 257)

berland, Maryland, to Vandalia, Illinois. Travelers on this great western highway encountered a stream of people on foot, on horseback, in stagecoaches, on one-horse wagons, and driving lumbering teamster wagons.

Few of these turnpikes ever showed a profit to their owners. Maintenance was a constant drain. The public devoted considerable ingenuity to outwitting toll collectors: short roads popularly known as "shunpikes" frequently circled around the toll gates. The turnpikes, although popular with travelers, failed to provide economical long-distance freight transportation. Even where tolls were low, it was not profitable for heavy wagons with six- and eight-horse teams to make long hauls over them. Many of the turnpike companies had failed even before the emergence of competition from canals and railroads.

Steamboats   Men had been experimenting worldwide for years with the application of steam power to water transportation, but it remained for Robert Fulton, a young American engineer, to perfect an efficient design. His steamboat, the *North River* (or *Clermont*), equipped with an English-built engine and paddle wheels, averaged five miles per hour on its first voyage up New York's Hudson River in 1807. Spectators on shore watched in astonishment as it overtook the sluggish sailing vessels and "passed them as if they had been at anchor." Fulton and his partner, Robert R. Livingston, tried to keep exclusive control over their invention, but steam navigation was too important to be monopolized. By the time the Supreme Court, in *Gibbons v. Ogden* (1824), formally annulled the Fulton-Livingston monopoly in New York, steamboats had been introduced on every major river in the country.

The years from 1820 to 1850 were the age of the steamboat, the first economical inland transportation for both freight and people. On eastern rivers, harbors, and bays, steamboats served primarily as passenger vessels. They were designed for speed and comfort, with razor bows, long narrow hulls, giant paddle wheels amidships, and elegantly furnished cabins. Even larger boats plied the Great Lakes, carrying thousands of immigrants west to Detroit and Chicago. But it was in the fertile valley of the Mississippi that steamboats had their greatest importance. Ingenious shipbuilders quickly adapted them to navigate the western rivers even at low water. Hulls were made broad and shallow, engines and cabins placed on deck, and paddle wheels moved to the stern. Western rivermen boasted that all they needed for successful navigation was a heavy dew. Some of their boats could operate in water as shallow as thirty inches. These ungainly boats brought the West firmly into the national economy.

The new steamboats at last made it economical to ship the bulky exports of the interior to market. Receipts of produce at New Orleans jumped from $12 million in 1820–21 to $197 million in 1850–51. There larger ships took on the grain and cotton for destinations on the east coast or in Europe. On their return upstream the steamboats carried consumer goods formerly hauled overland at enormous cost.

The boats were not what Americans of the 1990s would consider fast. One helmsman wrote home to his family: "They can run from New

(continued from p. 256)

this article she appears like a moving
mass of cotton bales, no part of her hull
being visible except the paddle-boxes.

Around the bows and upon the
guards the bales are piled as high as the
'hurricane deck.' They almost touch the
boilers, which are exposed and unpro-
tected upon the forward deck, and generally surrounded by huge piles of
wood, not unfrequently in absolute contact with them. A tier of cotton often
adorns the hurricane deck itself, and
needs but a spark from the smoke-pipe
to convert the boat into a fiery furnace,
from which the chance of escape is small
indeed."

Orleans to Pitsburgh in 16 and 18 days which is 25 hundred miles. They
can go down in 8 and 10 days. They can carry 200 passengers each." The
correspondent added: "Thare are a grate many fish caught in this river.
Catfish which way from 10 to 100 pound. Thare are steam packets that
carry from 100 to 700 tuns burden each."

Canals   Knowing the success of the early English canals,
landlocked Americans had talked for years of link-
ing the nation's navigable rivers and lakes with artificial waterways. A
major obstacle was the inability of private capital to supply the large
sums—$25,000 a mile or more—necessary for canal construction. By
1816 only about a hundred miles of canals had been constructed in the
United States, most less than two miles long. None had returned a profit
to their owners. Then came the Erie Canal.

The success of the Erie touched off a nationwide boom in canal
building. Several eastern states, jealous of New York's position, tried to
tap the western market with canals of their own. Pennsylvania's Main
Line system over the Allegheny Mountains required a portage railroad—a stairstep of inclined planes by which cable cars carried the canal
boats up one side of the highest ridges and down the other. In the West,
Ohio and Indiana raced to link the waters of Lake Erie and the Ohio
River. Indiana's contribution, the Wabash and Erie Canal, was over 450
miles long. By 1840, when the boom collapsed, the American people
had constructed over 3,300 miles of canals, at a total cost of $125 million.
State governments provided most of this huge capitalization, selling
bonds against anticipated revenues. Few states or bondholders recovered even a fraction of their investment. Many of the canals were poorly
planned and constructed; maintenance costs were high; ice or low water
closed them at certain seasons. Nevertheless, these costly ditches greatly
stimulated the economy. They offered the first economical means of
transferring eastward the bulky products of the West.

Peter Cooper's "Tom Thumb," the first locomotive made in America, racing with a horse-car on the Baltimore and Ohio line, 1830. *(Courtesy, New York Public Library)*

Railroads   The nation soon had cheaper, faster, more dependable and profitable overland transportation. Americans had taken an early interest in another English development, the railroad. Construction of a few small tramways began in the United States during the 1820s, and in 1828 the first major railroad, the Baltimore and Ohio, was chartered. Many early railroads ran only short distances, being designed to serve mainly as feeders into nearby rivers and canals, but major eastern cities like Boston and Baltimore, which lacked adequate water connections, promoted longer lines. Merchants of Charleston, South Carolina, anxious to divert upcountry cotton shipments to their wharves, built a railroad to Hamburg on the lower Savannah River. When completed in 1833, it extended 136 miles and was the longest railroad in the world. In these years ingenious American inventors made a number of important technical improvements in the design of locomotives and roadbeds. By 1840 the nation's total railway mileage equaled that of canals, and many lines were competing successfully with canal companies for business.

Railroads, like other forms of transportation, received public aid. Between 1830 and 1843 the national government lowered tariff duties on railroad iron. State legislatures—once again taking the lead in public assistance—granted tax incentives, required newly chartered banks to invest in railroad stock, extended large grants, and sometimes operated lines directly. Added to the foreign capital that American railroads attracted, government help provided strong impetus to private companies. Almost 9,000 miles of track were laid in the 1840s and 22,000 more in the next decade. At the beginning of the Civil War railroads overshadowed all other forms of long-distance transportation in the country.

Corporations

To finance the more extensive of the manufacturing and transportation enterprises of the astonishing economy that was emerging early in the nineteenth century, society had a ready and time-honored institution, the corporation. The word comes from the Latin *corpus,* for "body," and corporations or bodies of various sorts had been a major form of organization in the European past. The members of the company that colonized Massachusetts Bay and later governed it constituted a corporation. An economic corporation was a body of investors chartered in Britain by the Crown and in the United States by a state—there was no federal equivalent—to engage in an undertaking that the chartering authority held to be at least in part for the common good. The grant would set the terms of the project, which might be as small as a bridge or as large as a railroad, and it would give the investors certain rights and protections.

Corporations so construed were entirely in accord with the original concept of a republic. The members of the corporations aimed, of course, to get money, power, or both. But they were also bringing their initiative and intelligence to an enterprise for the public welfare, and acting under directions set by the state. Yet as corporations in the course of the nineteenth century became increasingly an instrument of quick and big money, even the concept of a stockholder as being, in a sense, a quasi-public official as well as a public benefactor was to fade. Here was one of many ways in which a republic of virtue came into danger of becoming a republic of acquisition.

Sources of Northern Labor

The transportation revolution, making the movement of goods vastly easier and cheaper, opened up a large new potential market for manufactured products. Corporations made possible the bigger manufacturing concerns along with large transportation projects. But where would the workers come from to produce these goods?

Since colonial times, labor had been in short supply. Cheap land was so available that people could work their own land instead of hiring out their labor. In 1800 only ten percent of the white labor force were people who sold their services. The rest of the workforce were farmers, self-employed artisans and mechanics, and independent tradesmen.

Early manufacturers experimented with various ways of overcoming this acute labor scarcity. One was the "domestic" or "putting-out" system. Entrepreneurs furnished raw materials to people who worked in their own homes, making cloth, shoes, and wearing apparel; the entrepreneurs then collected and marketed the finished product. At a time when most people lived in the countryside, this system, though cumbersome, allowed manufacturers to tap a tremendous pool of part-time labor, especially women and children. Other businessmen tried to centralize production, hiring whole families whom they housed in tenements adjacent to their mills. But as factories grew larger, requiring a labor force of hundreds, even thousands, factory owners turned increasingly to the Waltham system.

The Waltham System   This system was the brainchild of Francis Cabot Lowell, an early textile manufacturer in Waltham, Massachusetts. Eager to recruit young women from New England farms to work in his mill at East Chelmsford, Massachusetts. Lowell built dormitories nearby to house them. In order to counteract the widespread reputation of mills as places of loose morals, he placed these dormitories in charge of respectable widows who maintained rigid rules of conduct. The factory girls typically had to be in their rooms by 10 p.m., to attend church regularly, and to save part of their earnings. A few mills sponsored evening classes and libraries for their workers.

Lowell's plan was an immediate success and East Chelmsford was renamed Lowell in his honor. Many young women welcomed the chance to get away from the farm for a few years and to earn a little money of their own. In the 1820s and 1830s they flocked by the thousands to New England mill towns like Lowell, Chicopee, and Manchester. Visitors to the textile factories usually praised the Waltham system. After a tour in 1834, Davy Crockett described Lowell's "mile of gals" as "well-dressed, lively, and genteel" and happy in their work.

In time, though, the economics of profit took over. The workers

"Susan," a Lowell worker, wrote home of the difficulties of the work itself:

"It makes my feet ache and swell to stand so much. . . . The girls almost all say that when they have worked here a year or two they have to procure shoes a size or two larger than before they came. The right hand, which is the one used in starting and stopping the loom, becomes larger than the left; but in other respects the factory is not detrimental to a young girl's appearance."

Penhallow, Printer, Wyman's Exchange, 28 Merrimack St.

opposed a series of attempts by the mill owners to increase the amount of work—"speed up" and "stretch out"—and reduce the pay. A group of the more experienced workers founded the Lowell Female Reform Association, essentially one of the first labor unions in the United States. Ultimately, their two large strikes and their appeal to the Massachusetts state legislature failed to accomplish their goals. The rapid increase in the immigration of destitute Irish during the 1840s permitted the owners to turn to a new and more dependent supply of labor.

Lowell himself, as befitted an upper-class New Englander, had intended his plan to be not merely a moneymaker for himself but a contribution to the social good. In this sense, the Lowell mills were a forerunner of the reformist schemes in education, care of the mentally ill, abolition of slavery, and other goals that Yankees of social station would later be sponsoring. That Lowell was concerned for the financial independence and the intellectual development of young women makes him something of a deviant among early nineteenth-century American men as they have often been portrayed. Lowell's approach, to be sure, was paternalistic; but genteel reformers could be equally paternalistic toward the male recipients of their benevolence. And in their own way, the Lowell mill girls constituted something of an elite labor force. When they struck they claimed the rights of direct heiresses of the Revolution, daughters of the Sons of Liberty. The events at Lowell in fact had much to do with the status of women in the early nineteenth century.

Inventions   Improved transportation unified the national economy, mass immigration provided the necessary labor force, and corporations nurtured its larger undertakings. Only one additional ingredient was yet required for the American economy to take off—a native technology capable of sustaining mass production.

Here again, the nation was at first heavily dependent on Britain. When Robert Fulton designed his steamboat, he had the engine made in England, for no one in the United States could produce such a complex piece of machinery. Why did Americans turn to technological innovation? It has been suggested that Britain's restriction on the export of textile machinery and on the emigration of skilled mechanics unwittingly forced Americans to become inventive. Or that the shortage of labor compelled Americans to devise labor-saving machinery. But in colonial times, Britain had not exported textile machines, and later Americans borrowed some British technology shaping it to their needs.

Neither the absence of machinery nor the absence of a large labor force compelled Americans to become technologically progressive. Certain facts of American society and culture, however, may explain why modern technology, once Americans did begin to take to it, grew so much more rapidly here than elsewhere. The new nation had a sense of its newness, an awareness of itself as an invention, and this self-image could have invited Americans to engage in technical experimentation. Perhaps also the nation's natural wealth and the spread of prosperity among its citizens enticed Americans to see how the bounty at their disposal could be made even richer through technology. And the inventiveness that flowered amid this freedom and this promise was not for the sake of material gain alone: intellectual curiosity and an urge to

One very articulate worker at Lowell, Harriet Robinson, remembered:

"At this date woman had no property rights. A widow could be left without her share of her husband's property. . . . A woman was not supposed to be capable of spending her own or of using other people's money. In Massachusetts, before 1840, a woman could not legally be treasurer of her own sewing-society, unless some man were responsible for her.

The law took no cognizance of woman as a money-spender. She was a ward, an appendage, a relict. Thus it happened, that if a woman did not choose to marry, or, when left a widow, to re-marry, she had no choice but to enter one of the few employments open to her, or to become a burden on the charity of some relative.

In almost every New England home could be found one or more of these women, sometimes welcome, more often unwelcome, and leading joyless, and in many instances unsatisfactory, lives. The cotton-factory was a great opening to these lonely and dependent women. From a condition approaching pauperism they were at once placed above want; they could earn money, and spend it as they pleased; and could gratify their tastes and desires without restraint, and without rendering an account to anybody. . . ."

invent were then powerful motives, as they have been in other times of technological and scientific experimentation.

During the first half of the nineteenth century, inventions for manufacturing and agriculture multiplied. Besides developing the automated grist mill, Oliver Evans pioneered in the design of the high-pressure steam engine, a distinct improvement over the British engines of Newcomen and Watt. Norbert Rillieux, a free black, invented a multiple-effect evaporator to process the sugar cane grown in his native Louisiana. The endless fields stimulated significant improvements in farm machinery. Before Cyrus McCormick invented his reaper in 1831 a man with a sickle could cut approximately one acre of wheat in a day; with a reaper he could harvest ten to twelve. In 1837 John Deere perfected a steel plow capable of turning the tough prairie sod of Iowa and Illinois. In 1860 the United States Patent Office issued 4,589 new patents, a five hundred percent increase over patents granted in 1820.

While inventions transformed basic industries and with them much of American life, other ingenious tinkerers sought to increase the comforts of the home: the steam radiator for home heating; an immensely important ice-making machine; condensed milk and concentrated coffee (which came in a cube, light, and with sugar), both invented by Gail Borden in the 1850s; the paper window shade; hundreds of different kinds of new stoves and lamps; thousands of household gadgets. A comfortable, efficient home sheltering a happy and sturdy family was an implicit part of the American democratic ideal, and technology rushed to further it.

Interchange-able Parts   Along with inventions came a specifically American development: mass production employing interchangeable parts. This concept had originated in Europe, but Eli Whitney, an American son of a three-hundred-pound Scots peddler, first put it into practice. An outstanding inventor best known for his cotton gin, a device for extracting seeds from raw cotton that transformed southern agriculture, Whitney struck upon an idea for producing great numbers of muskets quickly. A factory making muskets would not make each one separately from parts constructed for it alone, but would make every component part in great quantity and then assemble the parts into identical muskets. "In short," Whitney wrote federal officials in 1798, "the tools which I contemplate are similar to an engraving on copper plate from which may be taken a great number of impressions exactly alike."

Eli Whitney. *(Courtesy, Library of Congress)*

This was a bold proposal at a time when gunsmiths still made muskets one at a time, filing and fitting the individual pieces to mate them into a working mechanism. The government, then fearful of war with France, and highly respectful of Whitney's talents, accepted his audacious offer to manufacture ten thousand muskets in twenty-eight months. Whitney badly underestimated the difficulties of tooling up for this kind of operation; he was several years late in delivering the promised muskets. Gradually, however, his uniformity system gained acceptance, and it was applied in dozens of industries. The spread of interchangeable parts made it possible for owners of damaged objects

Technological Developments, 1790–1860
(Dates refer to patent or first successful use)

Year	Inventor	Contribution	Importance / Description
1793	Eli Whitney	Cotton gin	Simplified process of separating fiber from seeds; made cotton a profitable staple of southern agriculture
1798	Eli Whitney	Jig for guiding tools	Facilitated manufacture of interchangeable parts
1802	Oliver Evans	Steam engine	First American steam engine
1807	Robert Fulton	Steamboat	*North River* (or *Clermont*), first successful American steamboat based on earlier invention of John Fiten
1813	Richard B. Chenaworth	Cast-iron plow	First iron plow made in three separate pieces, making possible replacement of parts
1830	Peter Cooper	Railroad locomotive	First steam locomotive built in United States
1831	Cyrus McCormick	Reaper	Mechanized harvesting
1836	Samuel Colt	Revolver	First repeating pistol
1837	John Deere	Steel plow	Steel surface made farming easier on rich prairies
1839	Charles Goodyear	Vulcanization of rubber	Made rubber free of sticking and melting in hot weather
1842	Crawford W. Long	First administered ether in surgery	Reduced pain and risk of shock during operations
1844	Samuel F. B. Morse	Telegraph	Long-distance communication made instantaneous
1846	Elias Howe	Sewing machine	Practical machine for automatic sewing
1846	Norbert Rillieux	Vacuum evaporator	Improved method of removing water from sugar cane; revolutionized sugar industry and later other industrial processes
1847	Richard M. Hoe	Rotary press	Printed an entire sheet in one motion
1851	William Kelly	"Air-boiling process"	Improved method of converting iron into steel; similar to later Bessemer process
1853	Elisha G. Otis	Passenger elevator	When electrified, stimulated development of skyscrapers
1859	Edwin L. Drake	First American oil well	Initiated United States oil industry
1859	George M. Pullman	Pullman car	First sleeping car for long-distance travel

to send away to a factory for the needed part, confident that the new one would precisely substitute for the old. Americans proved especially adept at designing and building the lathes, borers, and calipers necessary for the precision manufacture of parts for clocks, watches, and sewing machines.

Industrialism and the Republic

Manufacturing on a mass scale altered American expectations. From colonial days the material environment had been permanent. Most people lived in the same houses, used the same furniture, employed the same implements, wore the same clothes, and viewed the same scene from youth to old age. Variety was the privilege of the rich. With the growth of manufactures all this changed. The material surroundings of the average American became diversified in ways undreamed of before. Americans were learning to live in a perpetually changing environment. Their surroundings increasingly taught them that the physical world of buildings, vehicles, implements of work could change again and again, as the older, stable, agricultural environments had once taught people that the world never changes much.

The industrial order that began with Whitney and Lowell, with steamboats and the Erie Canal, was in spirit both the extension and the overturning of the republic of Washington and Jefferson. What occurred, in essence if not in words, was the transformation of the republican concept of virtue.

For all the radical newness of the early republic, Americans who thought of such matters were likely to equate proper conduct with the maintenance of good and established republican practices. These would include well-ordered families, intelligently tended crops, proud and independent crafts, honest businesses and professions, dignified governance. The yeoman doubtless wished to learn how to increase the yield of his land, the craftsman to perfect his skill. But the point of a good life was conscientiously to work the land or the shop, to train children in citizenship, and otherwise to ensure the continuance of the good life that settlers and revolutionists had planted in the new continent. The very idea of a republic was backward-looking, to the ancient polities of Greece and Rome.

Perhaps the forward-looking ways first clearly revealed themselves in Methodism and the revival movements that preceded by some years the flourishing of the new inventions and industries. These invited a moment of radical conversion, a receptivity to divine grace that could involve overwhelming emotions of repentance and joy and, if it occurred at a revival meeting, violent motions of the body. The outcome, however, as at least some evangelical Christians conceived it was to be a lifetime of attention to work and the other virtues. Methodists, freewill Baptists, and other nineteenth-century sectarians expected more than their Puritan ancestors that the redeemed human will can achieve greater and greater goodness, an increasing conquest of sinful impulses. An extension of this was to assume that society can improve in response to reformist programs. The physical world itself, it was meanwhile becoming apparent, could be increasingly subdued by industrious individuals, coaxing greater productive efficiency from it as they achieved victories over their wayward urges.

Evangelical religion, though countless Americans remained outside it, contributed to supplementing the original republican idea of virtue with strenuous mastery of self. Of comparable importance was the effect of invention itself. The demonstration that steam engines and textile machines could order the physical world made some Americans perceive that achievement as an important continuing task for the nation. Others saw it as a means to quick wealth.

At the same time that industrialization progressed in company with a revised view of morality, it threatened the whole republican project of good citizenship. The individual, set free to seek moral self-improvement or to corner some portion of the growing material wealth of the country, was at increased liberty to pursue personal aggrandizement. And so that fine old institution the corporation, understood to be a band of respectable gentlemen taking on a project in the public interest, came to be quite unashamedly an instrument of swift personal profit. Even in that form, to be sure, corporations would do a great amount of good, along with much harm, in their financing and organizing of invention and productivity. But that very fact reinforced the belief, which early in the nineteenth century had become economic orthodoxy, that self-interest is the best engine of economic progress.

The effect of industrialization on the common American varied, of course, from one individual to another. Through much of the nineteenth century, a great amount of production and maintenance remained in the hands of individual artisans and craftsmen: blacksmiths, cobblers, carpenters. Many such labors continue today, in shops aided by machinery on a small scale or undertaken by skilled hired hands. Probably most Americans of English, Scottish, or other old American lineage continued to live out as much of the old republican existence as could survive. As for those Americans, a very large portion of them immigrants or second-generation citizens, who worked in factories, debate continues over whether industrialization degraded them and robbed them of skills or required new kinds of thinking and adaptation. Yet industrialization seemed to require the spread of one particular skill, that of literacy. That became essential as old sedate ways of passing on practical knowledge gave way to the necessity of reading instructions, job advertisements, and whatever other information the individual might need to negotiate increasingly mechanized surroundings.

A Resurgent Nationalism

At the end of the War of 1812, no federal official would have foreseen the enormous role that national and state government was going to take in the process of industrialization. Political events, however, were taking the federal government in a direction eventually beneficial to industry and innovation. In essence, the federal establishment was learning to do what Hamilton had wished of it: to become an active partner in economic growth. It was to provide further sinews of nationhood.

What happened to the Federalists once their party disintegrated?

Some remained in office, especially in Connecticut and Massachusetts. Others, like John Quincy Adams, went to the Republicans and continued in public life. Still others folded their tents and stole away, a few reappearing in sulky memoirs.

Among the most interesting of the Federalists are those who sought nongovernmental means of furthering their social and political goals. Clyde Griffen has written a fascinating account of this last group who became *Their Brother's Keeper* by establishing a series of benevolent societies. Their societies, like the American Bible Society, the American Tract Society, and the American Anti-Slavery Society, formed a "benevolent empire." The goal was to shore up the social order, temper the excesses of democracy, and raise the moral tone of the nation. The societies, which quickly became very large, encouraged people to observe the Sabbath, avoid drunkenness and unseemly language, attend church regularly, and practice the other traditional Christian virtues. They organized Sunday Schools, financed ministers in the developing West, distributed millions of pamphlets and tracts, and otherwise sought to raise the moral tone of society.

The Decline of the Federalist Party

By the end of the War of 1812 the Federalist Party of George Washington, Alexander Hamilton, and John Adams had crumbled before the assaults of Jeffersonian Republicans who championed the yeoman farmers and denounced the monied interests of the Northeast. But it was not their look of elitism that doomed the Federalists. During the war, many Federalists openly opposed the military effort, and their opposition resulted in the Hartford Convention of 1814–15, when Federalist delegates from the New England states protested the war and even hinted at secession. The Hartford Convention was held in secret, and when news of the meetings reached the press, Democrats roundly criticized Federalists for disloyalty and conspiracy. Andrew Jackson's great victory at New Orleans occurred during the deliberations of the Hartford Convention, which embarrassed the Federalists. In the election of 1816, James Monroe defeated Rufus King by 183 electoral votes to 34. The Federalist Party then disappeared.

Era of Good Feelings

After many years of political bickering, an interlude of one-party politics followed the war. However divisive the War of 1812 had been, its ending brought a general sentiment of patriotism along with an awareness of weaknesses that had made the conduct of the war so difficult. A consensus grew in favor of some unified political solution to the nation's problems. For a time it was common for voters to call themselves Jeffersonian Republicans, and politics became no more than a contest of personalities within a politics of national harmony. To a people brought up with an eighteenth-century view of political parties as self-serving, divisive instruments, this actually seemed healthy. The "demon of party," a newspaper editor noted in 1817, had been exorcised for good.

Like his Virginia predecessors, James Monroe had spent his life serving his country. At eighteen he had been wounded in the Revolutionary War. He later served as minister to France, governor of Virginia, minister to England, and secretary of state. (From 1813 to 1815 he frequently doubled as secretary of war.) Monroe when he became President was nearing sixty years. Dignified in appearance, cautious in manner, he provided a link with the heroic past. At a time when most men wore trousers, he still dressed in old-fashioned knee breeches and silk stockings. On ceremonial occasions he wore a faded Revolutionary uniform—fitting garb for the last Revolutionary War veteran in the White House.

President Monroe's Grand Tour

As President, Monroe sought to create "a union of parties in support of our republican government." His choice of Cabinet members reflected this goal: he tried to pick Republicans from every section of the country. Secretary of State John Quincy Adams was a New Englander. Georgian William H. Crawford stayed on in the Treasury Department. Unable to find a westerner for secretary of war, Monroe finally picked young John C. Calhoun of South Carolina. Restrained by their loyalty to the President, these political rivals served Monroe well. He also worked hard to gain the confidence of prominent Federalists. Harrison Gray Otis was deeply touched when the "Old Sachem" not only invited him to the White House for dinner, but "drank a glass of wine with me to make friends."

In pursuit of national unity, Monroe set out shortly after his election on a tour of the northern and eastern states. Paying his own travel costs, he followed the seaboard north to Portland, Maine, then headed westward, going as far as Detroit—a three-and-one-half month journey by carriage and steamboat. It was a triumphal procession. Everywhere crowds gathered to honor this "last of the Revolutionary farmers." The high point came at Boston, where over forty thousand turned out to welcome the President. At a public dinner, local Federalists and Republicans sat down together for the first time in years. Monroe's visit, a staunch Federalist editor reported, had established an "Era of Good Feelings." Newspapers throughout the country soon picked up the phrase. For a time, despite bickering on the state and local levels, it seemed appropriate. In 1820 Monroe was reelected without opposition; only one negative vote in the electoral college prevented his election from being, like Washington's, unanimous.

James Monroe, elected in 1816, sought to unify the states and parties, and establish an "Era of Good Feelings." *(Portrait by Gilbert Stuart, Courtesy, The Metropolitan Museum of Art, Bequest of Seth Low, 1929)*

Government and the Economy

Monroe's presidency was also a time of economic nationalism. Instructed perhaps by the War of 1812 that the country could not get by with the limited central government that the Jeffersonian Republicans had once favored, President Madison in 1815 had recommended an energetic governmental program for the nurturing of the economy. Congress responded by rechartering a national bank, voting funds for internal improvements, and enacting a protective tariff. "Our two great parties," said the retired President John Adams, "have crossed over the valley and taken possession of each other's mountain."

Transportation—"Let us conquer space" During the War of 1812, the nation's transportation network had proved no more adequate to wartime demands than its banking system. With coastal shipping choked off by the British blockade and canals still in their infancy, the burden fell almost entirely on the roads. In a few places in the East turnpikes had been built, but they deteriorated quickly under heavy use. Most roads were hardly more than broad country paths through the forest, filled with ruts and stumps, turning to mud during rain.

Recognition that the country needed a better transportation system was one element in the governmental and economic nationalism to which President Madison turned from his earlier philosophy of limited government. He called for a system of roads and canals "executed under national authority." He recommended a constitutional amendment that would eliminate continuing doubts over the federal government's authority to finance such projects. Representative John C. Calhoun of South Carolina, then a vigorous young nationalist, brushed aside constitutional objections. Sheer size and poor communication, he warned the House—in words that would later haunt him—exposed the country to that "greatest of all calamities," disunion. "Let us, then, bind the Republic together with a perfect system of roads and canals. Let us conquer space." Calhoun proposed setting aside, as a fund for internal improvements, the government's share of the profits from the new Bank of the United States. In 1817 Congress narrowly approved Calhoun's plan, only to have Madison, then about to leave the White House, veto it on constitutional grounds. The states and private enterprise would have to finance most internal improvements. That very year New York began construction of the Erie Canal.

The Tariff of 1816   Before 1807 Americans had imported most manufactured goods from Europe, but Jefferson's embargo and the war had stimulated the growth of domestic industries. In New England and the Carolinas, mills were spinning and weaving cotton; a new iron industry flourished at Pittsburgh; Kentuckians began making local hemp into bagging. But when the war ended, British manufacturers moved quickly to crush these new rivals. In 1816 they dumped vast quantities of goods on the American market at cut-rate prices, in order, a spokesman explained, "to stifle in the cradle those rising manufacturers in the United States, which war had forced into existence, contrary to the natural course of things." To protect these new industries, President Madison proposed increased tariff duties on competing imports, which would push up their price. Congress was receptive, since nearly every section of the country had an interest to be protected. Southerners, who had the least to gain, supported higher duties on political and patriotic grounds. The Tariff of 1816 placed a duty of twenty-five percent on woolen, iron, and cotton products coming into the United States. Congress imposed rates as high as thirty percent on a variety of paper, leather, and textile products. A

The American Economy		
	1815 (1820*)	**1860**
U.S. Population	8,419,000*	31,513,000
Northeast	50.4 percent*	36.5
South	30.4	25.6
West	19.2	37.8
Annual Immigration	8,385	153,640
Miles of Railroads	23	30,626
Cotton Production (bales)	209,000	3,841,000
Lumber Production (board feet)	600,000,000	8,000,000,000
Soft Coal Production (tons)	253,000	9,057,000
Comparative GNP per capita	67.6	137.0

subsequent Tariff of 1818 increased the tariff rate on iron and extended the duty on cotton until 1826. Within a few years, a series of threatening events would cause many southerners to reexamine their jubilant support of economic nationalism.

The Second Bank of the United States   When the charter of the first Bank of the United States expired in 1811, the state banks had gone wild. The number increased from eighty-eight to over two hundred. In making loans and paying debts, they issued huge quantities of banknotes, which thereupon circulated as regular currency. A banknote was, in effect, a piece of paper carrying a bank's promise that upon request the bank would give to the bearer of the note an amount of money in specie (gold or silver) equal in value to the sum printed on the note. A holder of a banknote for, say, $1.00 could believe that while the note was not itself a real dollar, it was virtually an equivalent since it could be exchanged for a specie dollar: and so storekeepers and other merchants were willing to accept banknotes from customers.

As long as there was plenty of reliable specie in the banks—enough to cover a comfortable portion if not all of the banknotes in circulation in case many holders of notes got hungry for metallic money—the notes were a useful currency. A bank's ability to issue them allowed it to make more loans, pay more debts, and in general nourish more business than it could have done if its activities had been restricted to what its holdings in specie alone could accomplish. But if the banknotes got far out of proportion to the specie on which they were supposed to be based, the public would cease to trust them as currency, they would depreciate in value, and business would suffer from the uncertainty. And that is what happened as the state banks multiplied and carried out their transactions with no national bank to steady them. The mass of confusing, depreciated paper money worried businessmen and pleased counterfeiters. The lack of a national currency such as a Bank of the United States could have issued made it difficult to carry on business among different parts of the country.

Then wartime borrowing overwhelmed this shaky system. By the summer of 1814 every bank outside of New England had suspended the practice of paying specie to holders of notes who demanded it. The country's credit practically vanished. And after the war the federal government, to accommodate settlers in the West, offered for sale vast tracts of public land. The government's terms were generous: the minimum purchase was 160 acres, and the purchaser had four years to complete payment. Much of the land was purchased with credit supplied by state banks. Land sales, then, were inviting more bad currency into circulation.

In response to the crisis in banking, Congress in 1816 chartered a second Bank of the United States, with headquarters at Philadelphia. It was capitalized at $35 million, of which the government put up $5 million. The President was to appoint five "government directors," and the domestic stockholders would elect the other members of the twenty-five member board: foreign stockholders were not allowed to vote. The Bank was to serve as a repository of government funds and could establish branches as the directors saw fit. It could issue its own banknotes and thereby provide a more stable paper currency than the state banks were issuing. And it had the informal power to regulate the activities of state banks. A decision to be cautious in lending to them, or to refuse weak notes in payment of debts owed to the national Bank, could force the state banks to act more cautiously themselves. That, at any rate, is how it was supposed to operate.

The Panic of 1819 and the Bank

By 1820 the good feelings of the postwar years had begun to wear thin. As the memory of war faded and the Republican Party, lacking the discipline of electoral competition, declined as a national organization, the various sections of the country began looking to their own interests. Among the reasons for the end of the harmony of the postwar years was a resurgence of jealousies among the sections. A revival of slavery would set slave owners to quarreling with opponents of the institution and its expansion into the western territories. Another agent in disrupting the smooth politics of the time was the Panic of 1819, a financial collapse of the greatest magnitude the nation had yet known. The panic was the result of a buoyant but unhealthy expansion of the American economy during the years immediately after the wars, an expansion that economic dislocations in Europe had encouraged.

In 1816 and 1817 Europe had suffered widespread crop failures. These created a large and high-priced market for American rice, corn, wheat, and meat. British cotton textile manufacturers, moreover, having done without American cotton for three years, had accumulated a great backlog of demand for it. The price of cotton, having fluctuated around fifteen cents a pound before the war, now rose to twenty-five and thirty cents.

Americans responded to this boom in typical American fashion. On the one hand, they grossly overexpanded production, especially of cotton: in the years 1816–19 annual production of cotton more than doubled over that of 1814. The production of other American staples likewise increased rapidly, though not so spectacularly as that of cotton. Americans by the thousands also succumbed in these prosperous times to what had been, since colonial days, practically a national disease: speculation in land.

Speculation and Collapse Instead of paying attention first to farming the fields they already possessed and profiting from the inflation in crop prices while they could, vast numbers of people put every spare cent into land. To accommodate demand, the federal government after the war threw vast tracts of public land on the market. Auctions at the district land offices attracted eager crowds, including squatters hoping to buy the lots they had already occupied and speculators seeking choice tracts for resale at inflated prices. In spite of efforts by speculators to stifle competitive bidding, prices at the sales frequently soared well above the minimum $2 an acre. In the spring of 1818, fertile bottom land near Huntsville, Alabama, brought $70 to $78

A Scotsman traveling in the Ohio Valley described the bank boom:

"The recent history of banking in these western States, is probably unrivalled. Such a system of knavery could only be developed in a country where avarice and credulity are prominent features of character. About four years ago, the passion for acquiring unearned gains rose to a great height; banking institutions were created in abundance. The designing amongst lawyers, doctors, tavern-keepers, farmers, grocers, shoemakers, tailors, &c. entered into the project, and subscribed for stock. . . . To deposit much capital was out of their power; nor was it any part of their plan. Their main object was to extract it from the community. A common provision in charters stipulated that the property of each partner was not liable, in security, to a greater amount than the sum he had subscribed. This exempted the banks from the natural inconveniences that might be occasioned by the insolvencies and elopements of members. When it was found, that a few of them could not redeem their bills, the faith of the people was shaken. A run on the paper shops commenced. . . ."

an acre. Total annual sales of public land rose from less than $3 million in 1815 to over $13 million in 1818. Much of this land was purchased with credit supplied by the steadily increasing numbers of state banks, of which Hezekiah Niles wrote in 1816, "Wherever there is a church, a blacksmith's shop and a tavern seems a proper site for one of them."

A Scapegoat: The Bank of the United States   The new Bank of the United States not only made little effort at first to check this speculation, but itself was a major source of credit expansion. For a while it exchanged Bank stock for IOUs instead of specie. Supervision over Bank branches was notoriously lax. Those in the South and West greatly overexpanded their loans and their issues of banknotes. The officers of the Baltimore branch engaged in embezzlement. By 1818 the Bank had loaned out over $41 million. Some of it was invested in canals, turnpikes, and farm improvements; much more, however, went for speculative ventures in urban real estate, cotton futures, and western land. Indebtedness mounted, but as long as prices and rents increased, farmers and speculators would hope to meet their obligations.

Suddenly the economy collapsed. The return of good harvests abroad in the fall of 1818 cut demand for American grain. At the same time, British manufacturers finally reduced their imports of American cotton: prices for the South's great staple dropped by over one half in 1819. Planters and farmers who had borrowed heavily to expand production could not repay their loans.

This reversal left the Bank of the United States in desperate straits. Its liabilities exceeded its specie reserves by a ratio of ten to one, double the limit allowed by law. The Bank then called in the loans of state banks, which forced them in turn to call in their loans. A wave of bank failures followed, most of them in the South and West; money disappeared and credit dried up, and economic distress spread throughout the country. Speculators who had purchased public land were stuck with it. Agricultural prices sank. Merchants sold their stock at high losses or declared bankruptcy. In Philadelphia County alone, over 1,800 people went to prison for debt during 1819. Thousands were thrown out of work: in Pittsburgh, thirty percent of the population went back to the country. A traveler remarked on "great numbers of strangers lately camped in the open field near Baltimore, depending on the contributions of the charitable for subsistence." Americans for the first time confronted a nationwide depression, remembered as the Panic of 1819.

The economic crisis provoked a heated debate over both the causes of the depression and appropriate measures of relief. Stephen Girard, a Philadelphia financier, blamed the state banks, which "with their fictitious capital have acted imprudently." The state banks, anxious to conceal their own shortcomings, criticized the national Bank. Many, including President James Monroe, lamented the postwar spirit of extravagance and speculation, and called for a return to republican ways. Advocates of a protective tariff pointed to the nation's dependence on European trade, and urged Americans to produce more of the manufactured goods they consumed. Congress rejected a higher tariff and a bill to abolish federal imprisonment for debt, but did agree in 1821 to

Senator Daniel Webster of New Hampshire spoke in the Senate in support of banks:

"There are persons who constantly clamor. They complain of oppression, speculation, and pernicious influence of wealth. They cry out loudly against all banks and corporations, and a means by which small capitalists become united in order to produce important and beneficial results. They carry on mad hostility against all established institutions. They would close the fountain of industry and dry all streams."

allow people who had purchased public lands on credit additional time to pay. Real debtor relief came mainly from the states. Several passed stay laws delaying foreclosure for debt. Cities set up soup kitchens, and churches collected funds for the relief of paupers.

Out of the confused debate on the depression, the Bank of the United States emerged as the chief scapegoat. Charges of fraud and mismanagement abounded. The old southern agrarians, Thomas Jefferson among them, condemned the Bank and the federal government for creating a "paper bubble" and hoped the shock of depression would restore the country to its sound, paper-free past. These critics likened the Bank to a monster, foreclosing everything in its path.

"I know towns, yea cities," charged one westerner: "where this bank already appears as an engrossing proprietor. All the flourishing cities of the West are mortgaged to this money power . . . they are in the jaws of a monster! A lump of butter in the mouth of a dog! One gulp, one swallow, and all is gone!"

Many of these accusations were unfair. Fraud and mismanagement there had been, but the Bank was not responsible for fluctuations in the world market or for the public's compulsion for speculation. If the Bank had been inconsistent in dealing with the state banks, so had politicians and the public. But these considerations made little impression on a people mired in debt and depression. The economy recovered in the early 1820s, but by this time the reputation of the Bank among some constituencies had deteriorated beyond repair. Yet the recovery would owe much to the Bank and its new president, Nicholas Biddle.

Nicholas Biddle Brings Order

Biddle, a wealthy Philadelphian, took over the Bank in 1823 and immediately set about putting its affairs in order. Born into a wealthy Philadelphia family, Biddle had displayed a precocious versatility from the start. After graduation from Princeton at the age of fifteen, he traveled widely, served in the diplomatic corps, and wrote a classic account of the Lewis and Clark expedition. Impressed with his knowledge of banking, President Monroe appointed him a director of the Bank; four years later, at the age of thirty-seven, he became its president. The choice was a good one. Biddle understood banking and the function of the Bank in the American economy at a time when few others did. One reform was to increase the BUS's specie reserve, the amount of hard currency it kept on hand. This policy effectively meant that the paper money issued by the Bank was "as good as gold." Biddle also reformed the BUS's policies with respect to the notes issued by other banks. Most state-chartered banks had little specie reserve for their notes. When those notes were presented to the BUS for redemption, as they routinely were, Biddle could either demand payment in specie from the bank of issue or refrain from doing so. This was an enormously important power because it enabled Biddle and the other BUS directors to control how much currency was in circulation. That was critical for the simple reason that there was far too little gold and silver available to support a growing economy. The nation's gross national product, the total amount of goods and services produced, was perhaps fifty times greater than the amount of gold and silver. Without paper money the economy would have come to a halt. Too much of it, of course, would further weaken the economy. And it was Biddle's bank that largely determined how much money would circulate.

For the most part Biddle exercised these enormous powers wisely, and after a shaky start the bank prospered. But the Bank's private

Nicholas Biddle, president, beginning in 1823, of the Second Bank of the United States. *(Courtesy, The National Portrait Gallery)*

ownership remained a source of suspicion. Another potential problem was Biddle's practice of making loans on especially favorable terms to important politicians and newspaper editors. The Bank had many enemies, and charges of corruption would dog its career throughout Biddle's tenure in office.

Nationalism and the Supreme Court

Between 1810 and 1824, the Supreme Court, in a series of important cases decided under Chief Justice John Marshall, provided a legal and judicial equivalent to the political and economic nationalism that swept the country during and after the War of 1812. The decisions expanded the constitutional authority of the federal government in ways that complemented its increasing political and economic power. The Court declared the primacy of the federal government over the states and strengthened federal control over interstate commerce. It also reduced the power of state governments over corporations, and protected private contracts against state regulation. These rulings, in weakening the authority of the states, indirectly added to that of the nation.

Leading Constitutional Decisions Marshall's commitment to the sanctity of contracts was revealed in 1810 when the court handed down its decision in *Fletcher v. Peck*. In 1795 the Georgia legislature had sold thirty-five million acres along the Yazoo River to four land companies for $500,000. The deal was riddled with corruption complete with bribes and kickbacks to the legislators, and during the next legislative session, a new group of legislators rescinded the land grants, claiming that they were corrupt, fraudulent, and therefore invalid. When the case reached the Supreme Court, Marshall wrote the majority opinion, declaring unconstitutional the law to rescind the sales. Marshall argued that the law violated the section of the Constitution prohibiting the states from invalidating contracts.

In *Dartmouth College v. Woodward* (1819) the Court ruled that the Constitution protected charters of incorporation from legislative interference. Dartmouth College had been granted a charter in 1769 by King George III. In 1816 the New Hampshire legislature, in an effort to make the college more democratic, tried to replace the self-governing trustees with a board appointed by the state governor. The trustees retained Daniel Webster, a Dartmouth alumnus and eloquent orator, to fight their case. Webster's theatrics ("It is . . . a small school," he plaintively told the Justices, "and yet there are those who love it.") and his arguments proved effective. Dartmouth's charter, wrote Marshall, was a contractual relationship between the Crown and the College. The state of New Hampshire was a continuation of the Crown; the obligations of contract remained unchanged. So long as the trustees did not abuse their powers, the state could not interfere without violating the contract clause of the Constitution. Coming at a time when private corporations were rapidly gaining favor in transportation, finance, and manufacturing, this defense of contracts made it more difficult for the states to control corporate activity.

The act of the New Hampshire legislature put the Dartmouth campus in an uproar. One student wrote:

"Such a state of [affairs] necessarily discomposes the mind, and unfits it for steady and quiet reflection. . . . You may easily suppose that it is impossible to sit down cooly & composedly [to] books, when you are alarmed every minute by a report, that the library is in danger or that a mob is about collecting or that we are all about to [be] fined & imprisoned."

"Let the end be legitimate," wrote Chief Justice Marshall enunciating the doctrine of implied powers in *McCullough v. Maryland* (1899): "let it be within the scope of the Constitution, and all means which are appropriate, which are plainly adapted to that end, which are not prohibited, but consistent with the letter and spirit of the Constitution, are constitutional."

In *McCulloch v. Maryland* (1819) the Court confirmed the broad construction of the Constitution that Alexander Hamilton had defended thirty years before during arguments over the first Bank of the United States. Several states, Maryland among them, had placed high taxes on the Bank's branches within their borders. The cashier of the Baltimore branch, James McCulloch, refused to pay the tax and Maryland brought suit. In his opinion, Marshall upheld the constitutionality of the Bank. The creation of such an institution, he admitted, was not among the powers listed in the Constitution. But Congress also possessed "incidental or implied powers." He found that the financial powers of the national legislature gave it the implied power to charter a national bank that would aid Congress in exercising its authority over finance. Maryland's tax, which attempted to destroy a lawful agency of the federal government, was therefore unconstitutional: "the power to tax . . . is the power to destroy." Champions of states' rights denounced this opinion, which would stretch the Constitution beyond its literal statements and have it implicitly grant large powers to the federal government.

Marshall's opinion two years later in *Cohens v. Virginia* further distressed states' rights advocates. At issue here was the right of a state to limit appeals to the United States Supreme Court from its own courts. The Cohens had been convicted of selling lottery tickets under a Virginia law that prohibited appeals from such a conviction. Asserting that the case involved a "federal question," they turned to the Supreme Court for relief. Counsel for Virginia denied the Court's right of judicial review, claiming that the state's legitimate authority was under attack. The Chief Justice disagreed. He maintained that Virginia had surrendered some of her powers when she joined the Union. The right of the Supreme Court to review cases involving "federal questions" was absolutely essential if the operation of the Constitution was to be uniform throughout the country. Otherwise, the federal government would be prostrate "at the feet of every state in the Union." This opinion, added to that in *Marbury v. Madison*, solidly fixed the Supreme Court as the final arbiter of all constitutional questions.

Gibbons v. Ogden (1824), Marshall's last great decision, gave force to the clause of the Constitution that had empowered Congress "to regulate commerce with foreign nations, and among the several states." Early in the nineteenth century a number of states had begun awarding monopolies to the operators of the new steamboats. In 1808 New York gave Robert Fulton and Robert Livingston an exclusive right to operate steamboats on the state's waters. It also awarded Aaron Ogden an exclusive franchise to run steamboats on the Hudson River between New York and New Jersey. When Thomas Gibbons began a rival service on this route, Ogden brought suit to restrain his competitor. The New York courts upheld the monopoly. Gibbons appealed to the Supreme Court. Once again Marshall championed federal supremacy. A narrow construction of the Constitution, he declared at the outset, "would cripple the government, and render it unequal to the objects for which it is declared to be instituted, and to which the powers given, as fairly understood, render it competent." New York's law was unconstitutional because it conflicted with a 1793 act of Congress regulating the coastwise trade. Congress's power to regulate commerce, "like all others vested in Congress, is complete in itself, may be exercised to its utmost extent, and acknowledges no limitations, other than those prescribed in the Constitution."

A few years later Marshall could not prevent the removal of the Cherokee Indians from Georgia. He also ducked a case involving the rights of free blacks. Yet his nationalism ultimately helped to free the slaves. For over thirty years Marshall had argued that the United States was a consolidated nation rather than merely a compact of sovereign states. In 1861, when Abraham Lincoln called for troops, thousands of young men took up arms to defend the national Union Marshall's decisions had done so much to define. And consigning slavery to economic and social obsolescence was the industrial system that, under the protection of the federal government, had both extended and transformed the classical republicanism of the Jeffersonians.

Suggested Readings

On the transportation revolution see David Hawke, *Nuts and Bolts of the Past: History of American Technology, 1776–1860* (1988), David J. Jeremy, *Transatlantic Industrial Revolution: The Diffusion of Textile Technology Between Britain and America, 1790–1830* (1981), Thomas Dublin, *Farm to Factory: Women's Letters, 1830–1860* (1981), Barbara Tucker, *Samuel Slater and the Origins of the American Textile Industry, 1790–1860* (1984), and Thomas C. Cochran, *Frontiers of Change: Early Industrialism in America* (1981). On canals see Peter Way, *Common Labour: Workers and the Digging of North American Canals, 1780–1860* (1993) and Ronald E. Shaw, *Canals for a Nation: The Canal Era in the United States, 1790–1860* (1990).

Other studies of economic development are Charles Sellers, *The Market Revolution: Jacksonian America, 1815–1846* (1991), Stuart Bruchey's *Roots of Economic Growth, 1607–1861: An Essay in Social Causation* (1968), Thomas C. Cochran's *200 Years of American Business* (1977), and George Rogers Taylor's *The Transportation Revolution, 1815–1860* (1951). The economic changes under way in the pre–Civil War era are covered in Cochran's *Frontiers of Change* (1981) and Paul Gates's *The Farmer's Age: Agriculture, 1815–1860* (1960). A recent study is Stuart Bruchey, *Enterprise: The Dynamic Economy of a Free People* (1990).

See also David A. Hounshell, *From the American System to Mass Production, 1800–1932: The Development of Manufacturing Technology in the United States* (1984). Anthony Wallace's *Rockdale: The Growth of an American Village in the Early Industrial Revolution* (1977) is an important study of an early textile community near Philadelphia.

The classic work on the United States of the 1830s is Alexis de Tocqueville's *Democracy in America* (1835), which remains one of the most perceptive studies of American society. Bray Hammand's *Banks and Politics in America from the Revolution to the Civil War* (1957) admires the Bank of the United States, and admiring of Biddle is T. P. Govan, *Nicholas Biddle* (1959). See also Peter Temin, *The Jacksonian Economy* (1969) and J. M. McFaul, *The Politics of Jacksonian Finance* (1972).

On John Marshall's Supreme Court decisions, see G. Edward White, *The Marshall Court and Cultural Change, 1815–1860* (1991), R. K. Nemya, *The Supreme Court Under Marshall and Taney* (1968), Richard E. Ellis, *The Jeffersonian Crisis: Courts and Politics in the Early Republic* (1971), F. M. Stites, *John Marshall: Defender of the Constitution* (1981), and John A. Garraty, *Quarrels that Have Shaped the Constitution* (1987).

American Living Standards in an Industrializing Economy

Sean Wilentz

In 1845, the New York *Daily Tribune* prepared a series of reports on the condition of labor in New York. What the *Tribune* reporters found shocked them, and they groped for explanations—especially to account for the outrageous underbidding and exploitation that riddled the city's largest trades. A few years later, after he had read the works of the greatest urban journalists of the age, a *Tribune* correspondent named George Foster had found the right term: it was "sweating," "the accursed system. . . ." It arose in its purest forms in the consumer finishing trades, and most notoriously in the production of clothing.

From the cutting rooms (out of sight of the customers), the head cutter or piece master distributed the cut cloth to the outworkers and contractors, and it was here that the worst depredations of sweating began. A variety of outwork schemes existed. While most contractors were small masters unable to maintain their own shops, or journeymen looking for the surest road to independence, some cutters and in-shop journeymen also managed to subcontract a portion of their work on the sly. Some firms dealt directly with outworkers. In all cases, the system invited brutal competition and a successive lowering of outwork piece rates. At every level of the contracting network, profits came from the difference between the rates the contractors and subcontractors received and the money they paid out for overhead and labor. Two factors turned these arrangements into a matrix of unremitting exploitation: first, the successive bidding by the contractors for manufacturers' orders (as well as the competition between manufacturers) depressed the contractors' income; second, the reliance of the entire trade on credit buying by retailers and country dealers prompted postponement of payment to contractors until finished work was done—and, hence, chronic shortages of cash. The result: contractors steadily reduced the rates they paid their hands and often avoided paying them at all for as long as possible. To middle-class reformers, the great villain of the system was the contractor himself, the "sweater," the "remorseless sharper and shaver," who in his endless search for profits fed greedily on the labor of poor women and degraded journeymen. But the contractors and garret bosses had little choice in the matter, as they tried to underbid their competitors and survive on a wafer-thin margin of credit. "If they were all the purest of philanthropists," the *Tribune* admitted in 1845, "they could not raise the wages of their seamstresses to anything like a living price." Hounded by their creditors, haunted by the specter of late payment and bankruptcy, the contractors and garret masters lived an existence in which concern for one's workers was a liability and in which callousness (and, in some recorded cases, outright cruelty) became a way of life. . . .

The sufferings of the outwork and garret-shop hands—the vast majority of clothing-trade workers—taxed the imaginations of even the most sentimental American Victorians; if the reformers' accounts sometimes reduced a complex situation to a moral fable, they in no way falsified the clothing workers' conditions. All pretensions to craft vanished in the outwork system; with the availability of so much cheap wage labor, formal apprenticing and a regular price book had disappeared by 1845. At any given moment in the 1830s and 1840s, the underbidding in the contracting network could depress outwork and garret-shop piece rates so low that stitchers had to work up to sixteen hours a day to maintain the meanest of living standards: in 1850, some of the largest southern-trade clothing firms in the Second Ward paid their *male* workers, on the average, well below subsistence wages. Housing was difficult to come by and could amount to no more than a cellar dwelling or a two-room flat, shared with two or more families; single men crammed into outwork boardinghouses. During slack seasons or a bad turn in trade, the clothing workers struggled harder to make ends meet, with a combination of odd jobs, charity relief, and the starchiest kinds of cheap food.

Sean Wilentz, *Chants Democratic: New York City and the Rise of the American Working Class, 1788–1850* (New York: Oxford University Press, 1984).

[A] prosperous American economy was a precondition for large-scale immigration. Henry Price, a cabinetmaker, recalled in his diary his reasons for leaving England: "I never had enough to spend on to supply what I conceve to be sufficient for the supply of the legitimate Wants of My family." . . .

Although the tight labor market kept wages high, the true cost of labor was low because the pace of work was so fast and regular. American manufacturers were aware of this. "The French weaver," the *United States Economist and Dry Goods Reporter* told its readers, "lives very cheap, but he works very slowly. American labor costs more, but is more productive." . . .

The compensation for such hard work was the ability to live at a standard higher than in Europe. Indeed, male and supplementary female workers, both native and foreign, discovered for one of the first times in history that common people might live comfortably. . . .

Even more remarkable was the American *diet*. Its quality and availability had an impact on the standard of living of the common people that can only be called revolutionary. . . .

The prospect of improved diet seems to have been the most important factor in encouraging immigration. "Hunger brought me . . . here [and] hunger is the cause of European immigration to this country," wrote Henry Brokmeyer, a German immigrant who worked in New York in the 1850s as a tanner and shoemaker. Ole Helland wrote back to Norway in 1836, "I have such good service with board and bed that you would not believe it. Yes, I often think of you when I go to a prepared table with much expensive food before me." In 1844 Robert Williams wrote, "the chief farmers of Wales would be amazed to see the tables of the poor spread with dishes at every meal."

Grain was the staple food in Europe and meat a luxury rarely indulged in. By contrast, meat was virtually the staple of the American workingman's diet: of the $12 million in sales of produce in the city in 1841, 39 percent was spent on meat, 25 percent on grain, 22 percent on dairy products, and 10 percent on vegetables. Of the meat sold, 53 percent was beef, 22 percent pork. The huge amount of uncleared land in the Midwest suitable for grazing kept beef and pork prices low, and high wages made meat easily affordable. In New York meat was "beef-steaks (cut from the ribs), mutton chops, fish, fried potatoes, boiled potatoes, huckleberries and sugar . . . fresh butter, [and] new bread" three times a day. . . . Bread in the New World was almost always wheaten. "Not one in a hundred" New Yorkers had even heard of eating oat bread. In addition, it was always first-class wheat bread.

John Harold recorded in his diary his astonishment at New York boardinghouse fare. The day began with "Beef Steaks, fish, hash, ginger cakes, buckwheat cakes etc such a profusion as I never saw before at the breakfast tables," and dinner was "a greater profusion than breakfast." . . .

Generally, physicians were impressed with the health of city residents. The physician Benjamin McCready, though warning of overcrowded housing, was relieved that in 1837 the city was free of the "disease and deformity which . . . could only be found in the over-grown towns of Europe. . . ."

Workers did not live luxuriously, but most workers' apartments were decently furnished. Many homes had frame beds, comfortable chairs, and bookcases. William Thomson, a Scottish weaver, noted that American workers "have rocking arm chairs that are a real luxury." Most amazing to immigrants was the presence of rugs in workingmen's apartments. Burn noted in 1865 that the floors "even [of] the poor classes of the people are covered with bits of carpet." Large carpet factories, such as the Higgins Company in Ward 22, produced rugs at modest prices. . . .

William McLurg no doubt spoke for many when he wrote to his parents, "there is nothing I regret so much as not coming here . . . sooner."

Richard B. Stott, *Workers in the Metropolis: Class, Ethnicity, and Youth in Antebellum New York City* (Ithaca: Cornell University Press, 1990).

John Gast's rendition of **Manifest Destiny** shows Indians and wild animals skulking off before the advance of westward expansion embodied in Columbia's stringing telegraph wires across the continent. *(Courtesy, Library of Congress, ca. 1862)*

Sectionalism and Party 1816–1828

THE WESTWARD MOVEMENT

For almost 200 years American society had grown in the corridor between the Atlantic Ocean and the Appalachian range. Mountains, Indian tribes, and conflict among European powers had discouraged Americans from pushing into the West. Even those who crossed some of the eastern mountains found the inviting valleys angling south through Pennsylvania, Virginia, and the Carolinas far more tempting than scaling the next ridges toward an uncertain domicile in the western plains. Then, after about 1795, with the Revolution won, the Indian tribes dispersed, and the price of good eastern land mounting, a vast folk migration began. Only briefly interrupted by wars and depressions, it relentlessly populated the continent. The land seemed suddenly and permanently to have tilted, shaking its human burden westward in a long rough tumble toward the Pacific.

The return of peace on the frontier after the War of 1812 and rising prices worldwide for agricultural products quickened the migration. In 1810 only one American in seven lived west of the Appalachians; in 1820 it was one in four. Before the land fever subsided, five new states had entered the Union—Indiana in 1816, Mississippi in 1817, Illinois in 1818, Alabama in 1819, and in 1821 Missouri—and they made the West a new force to be reckoned with in national affairs.

Settlers traveled by wagon, flatboat, horse, even on foot. The road west was often scarcely a road at all, but a slightly widened

continued

HISTORICAL EVENTS

1787
Northwest Ordinance prohibits slavery in the Northwest Territory

1793
Whitney perfects the cotton gin

1803
South Carolina reopens its foreign slave trade

1808
Constitution ban on importation of slaves takes effect

1811
Astor establishes fur-trading post in Oregon • Henry Clay becomes Speaker of the House

1814
Revolutions begin in Central and South America

1816
Monroe elected President

1817
John Quincy Adams becomes secretary of state • Rush-Bagot agreement

279

HISTORICAL EVENTS

1818
Treaty of 1818 with Britain • Jackson advances with his troops into Florida

1819
The Tallmadge Amendment is debated • Adams-Onis Treaty

1820
Missouri Compromise

1822
Monroe vetoes funds for the Cumberland Road • Vesey Conspiracy • U.S. formally recognizes Mexico, Colombia, Chile, Peru, and the provinces of Río de la Plata

1823
Monroe Doctrine

1824
John Quincy Adams elected President • Bolívar proposes Pan-American conference

1828
Andrew Jackson elected President

New Englanders traveled west singing:

Come all ye Yankee farmers who wish to
    change your lot,
Who've spunk enough to travel beyond
    your native spot,
And leave behind the village where Ma
    and Pa do stay,
Come follow me and settle in Michi-
    gania.

But others who had been there chanted:

Don't go to Michigan, that land of ills;
The word means ague, fever, and chills.

trail full of ruts and stumps so that for a passenger in the unsprung wagons "the pain of riding exceeded the fatigue of walking." Americans of the early nineteenth century were hungry for internal improvements, for turnpikes, canals, and finally railroads.

Often, in the stretches that were to be one day a land of motels, fast-food stands, and gas stations, the travelers perceived all around them nothing but a forest of tall hardwood trees, dark, sinister, and gloomy. Settlers gloated over the mighty fires that followed a boisterous log-rolling, when perhaps hundreds of trees, felled after backbreaking labor, vanished into smoke, fire, and ash.

Yet the farmers preferred the forests to the prairies, endless meadows of tall grass sweeping across northern Indiana and Illinois and beyond. Settlers, much as they might curse the trees they had to girdle, cut, and burn, hard as they might work to let in sunshine so that crops could grow, believed that hardwood forests indicated fertile soil. The prairies (actually richer soil where thick grass strangled other vegetation) evoked, as one traveler noted, "a certain indescribable sensation of loneliness." Rich as prairie soil was, settlers discovered that to farm this land meant first to break the thick, heavy sod. In the early part of the century, when plows were still small and primitive, it was muscle-wrenching labor.

In addition to doing backbreaking agricultural labor, a man with implements no more sophisticated than an axe and chisel would make "gates, carts, barrows, plow frames, ox yokes, wooden shovels, hay forks, troughs, benches, woodhorses, tool handles, stirring paddles, rakes, mortars, flails, cradles for mowing, swingling knives, flax brakes, and many other articles." More talented woodworkers could make their own wagons and furniture as well. And of course everyone, with neighbors helping to raise the logs, built his own house. Women worked equally hard or harder, raising vegetables and herbs, making soap, butter, and other household articles, and carrying out every step of the manufacture of clothing, from spinning to sewing. This labor, combined with housekeeping and childbearing, tolled heavily. Many women appeared old at thirty, and men widowed two and three times were common. Clouds of flies and mosquitoes, drafty walls, primitive sanitation, and animal waste around cabins were more hazardous to life than the better-known dangers of hostile Indians and prairie fires.

The reward was often worth the travail. At the end of the journey and the settlement lay independence and wealth as nineteenth-century Americans understood it: the ownership of productive agricultural land. The true pioneer stage passed rapidly; mills, towns, canals, newspapers, churches, cloth imported from the East, hardware, glass, even pianos eased and elevated the crude life of the frontier, and families rapidly moved from the backwoods to the front pews.

But for a moment, and only for a moment, the frontier was just what legend says it was. A vivid frontier imagination spoke in words attributed to Davy Crockett of western Tennessee. "I'm fresh from the backwoods," he is said to have boasted, "half alligator, a little touched with the snapping turtle; can wade the Mississippi, leap the Ohio, ride upon a streak of lightning . . . hug a bear too close for comfort. . . ."

A Resurgent Sectionalism

The expansion of the country and its economy made for clashing interests among regions. These soon expressed themselves in disputes over the tariff, internal improvements, and land policy.

The Tariff   The South produced cotton for export, obtaining manufactured goods from the North and West as well as from Europe. The tariff pushed up the retail price of European products in this country and thereby allowed northern manufacturers to raise their prices, too, or forced foreign products out of the American market. Compelled to purchase at higher prices, southern planters feared also that Europe would retaliate against American tariffs by putting high duties on southern agricultural goods. Southerners quickly regretted their support for the Tariff of 1816. The disastrous decline in cotton prices after 1819, which cut the planters' purchasing power, made the tariff still more burdensome. In 1820 southerners in Congress barely defeated a bid to raise import duties again.

Internal Improvements   Sharp sectional jealousies thwarted plans for a national system of internal improvements. New England did not favor building roads that, by connecting rival ports with the West, would injure Boston. New York and Pennsylvania longed for the national government to construct such routes; but finally, having lost extravagant sums put into their own roads and canals, they abandoned their enthusiasm for federal projects. Southern support for federal improvements faded rapidly. Such expenditures, increasing the need for revenue, would justify the hated tariff, and federal internal improvements implied a broad construction of the Constitution that could ultimately interfere with sectional interests. Only the West consistently demanded a federal system of internal improvements. A shortage of capital and a vast expanse of territory made that section perpetually hungry for government assistance.

Several times Congress responded by appropriating funds for western roads, but a series of presidential vetoes blocked these expenditures. The most prominent of those vetoes came from President James Monroe in 1822. Congress had passed legislation to pay for completion of the Cumberland Road, also known as the National Road, to link Cum-

Timothy Flint, a missionary in the Ohio Valley in the 1820s, wrote:

"The backwoodsman of the West, as I have seen him, is generally an amiable and virtuous man. His general motive for coming here is to . . . have plenty of rich land. . . . His manners are rough. He wears, it may be, a long beard. He carries a knife or a dirk in his bosom and when in the woods has a rifle on his back and a pack of dogs at his heels. An Atlantic stranger would recoil from an encounter with him. But his rifle and his dogs are among his chief means of support and profit. Remember that he still . . . meets bears and panthers."

One observer caught the flavor of raw western politics:

"I have just witnessed a strange thing—a Kentucky election—and am disposed to give you an account of it. An election in Kentucky lasts three days, and during that period whisky and apple toddy flow through our cities and villages like the Euphrates through ancient Babylon. I must do Lexington the justice to say that matters were conducted here with tolerable propriety; but in Frankfort, a place which I had the curiosity to visit on the last day of the election, Jacksonism and drunkenness stalked triumphant—'an unclean pair of lubberly giants.' A number of runners, each with a whisky bottle poking its long neck from his pocket, were busily employed bribing voters, and each party kept half a dozen bullies under pay, genuine specimens of Kentucky alligatorism, to flog every poor fellow who should attempt to vote illegally. A half a hundred of mortar would scarcely fill up the chinks of the skulls that were broken on that occasion. I barely escaped myself."

berland, Maryland, with Wheeling on the Ohio River in present-day West Virginia. Monroe believed that the bill was unconstitutional, that Congress did not have the authority to finance such a road. He claimed that a national system of internal improvements could not be undertaken until an appropriate constitutional amendment had been ratified. His veto forced state governments and private corporations in the Northwest to join in financing an extensive network of turnpikes and canals.

Public Land Policy

Public land policy also divided the sections. The West craved cheap land but land sales were a major source of federal revenues, and the seaboard states favored high prices. Northern manufacturers also hoped that such prices would discourage their workingmen from going west. Though the worn-out cotton lands of the older slave states could not compete with the virgin soil of the Southwest, southeasterners usually voted for cheap land, perhaps seeing the West as a field for the expansion of a slave system to which they were becoming culturally and politically loyal. In

A PIRATE SLAVE SHIP IS BOARDED

The conditions described aboard this slaver are typical. The importation of slaves from outside the United States had ended in 1808, but slave traders continued to sell their human cargoes in the Caribbean and Latin America until the 1830s.

On Friday, May 22, [1829] . . . a midshipman entered the cabin and said in a hurried manner that a sail was visible to the northwest on the larboard quarter. We immediately all rushed on deck, glasses were called for and set, and we distinctly saw a large ship of three masts, apparently crossing our course. It was the general opinion that she was either a large slaver or a pirate, or probably both. . . .

At twelve o'clock we were entirely within gunshot, and one of our long bow guns was again fired at her. It struck the water alongside, and then, for the first time, she showed a disposition to stop. While we were preparing a second she hove to, and in a short time we were alongside her.

The first object that struck us was an enormous gun, turning on a swivel, on deck—the constant appendage of a pirate; and the next were large kettles for cooking, on the bows—the usual apparatus of a slaver. Our boat was now hoisted out, and I went on board with the officers. When we mounted her decks we found her full of slaves. She was called the *Veloz*, commanded by Captain José Barbosa, bound to Bahia. She was a very broad-decked ship, with a mainmast, schooner rigged, and behind her

foremast was that large, formidable gun, which turned on a broad circle of iron, on deck, and which enabled her to act as a pirate if her slaving speculation failed. She had taken in, on the coast of Africa, 336 males and 226 females, making in all 562, and had been out seventeen days, during which she had thrown overboard 55. The slaves were all inclosed under grated hatchways between decks. The space was so low that they sat between each other's legs and [were] stowed so close together that there was no possibility of their lying down or at all changing their position by night or day. As they belonged to and were shipped on account of different individuals, they were all branded like sheep with the owner's marks of different forms. These were impressed under their breasts or on their arms, and, as the mate informed me with perfect indifference "burnt with the red-hot iron." Over the hatchway stood a ferocious-looking fellow with a scourge of many twisted thongs in his hand, who was the slave driver of the ship, and whenever he heard the slightest noise below, he shook it over them and seemed eager to exercise it. . . .

But the circumstance which struck us most forcibly was how it was possible for such a number of human beings to exist, packed up and wedged together as tight as they could cram, in low cells three feet high, the greater part of which, except that immediately under the grated hatchways, was shut out from light or air, and this when the thermometer, exposed to the open sky, was standing in the shade, on our deck, at 89dg. The space

1820 Congress reduced the minimum purchasable tract from 160 to 80 acres and the price from $2 to $1.25 an acre. An act of 1830 gave special rights to the squatter who occupied public land he did not own; he could later purchase his tract prior to public sale at the minimum price, regardless of its market value.

The Revival of Slavery   In the North the libertarian ideology of the American Revolution, along with the larger drift of the eighteenth century toward rationalism and humanitarianism, had led numbers of people to believe slavery was in decline. Beginning with Pennsylvania in 1780, the northern states provided for the abolition of slavery. Federal legislation ended the importation of slaves as of 1808. The South's depressed economy in the years after the American Revolution reinforced the moral objection to slavery. Soil exhaustion and a glutted world market injured Virginia's and Maryland's tobacco economy. Many planters switched to wheat, a crop that required fewer slaves to cultivate.

between decks was divided into two compartments 3 feet 3 inches high; the size of one was 16 feet by 18 and of the other 40 by 21; into the first were crammed the women and girls, into the second the men and boys: 226 fellow creatures were thus thrust into one space 288 feet square and 336 into another space 800 feet square, giving to the whole an average of 23 inches and to each of the women not more than 13 inches. We also found manacles and fetters of different kinds, but it appears that they had all been taken off before we boarded.

The heat of these horrid places was so great and the odor so offensive that it was quite impossible to enter them, even had there been room. They were measured as above when the slaves had left them. The officers insisted that the poor suffering creatures should be admitted on deck to get air and water. This was opposed by the mate of the slaver, who, from a feeling that they deserved it, declared they would murder them all. The officers, however, persisted, and the poor beings were all turned up together. It is possible to conceive the effect of this eruption—517 fellow creatures of all ages and sexes, some children, some adults, some old men and women, all in a state of total nudity, scrambling out together to taste the luxury of a little fresh air and water. They came swarming up like bees from the aperture of a hive till the whole deck was crowded to suffocation from stem to stern, so that it was impossible to imagine where they could all have come from or how they could have been stowed away. On looking into the places where they had been crammed, there were found some children next the sides of the ship, in the places most remote from light and air; they were

lying nearly in a torpid state after the rest had turned out. The little creatures seemed indifferent as to life or death, and when they were carried on deck, many of them could not stand.

After enjoying for a short time the unusual luxury of air, some water was brought; it was then that the extent of their sufferings was exposed in a fearful manner. They all rushed like maniacs towards it. No entreaties or threats or blows could restrain them; they shrieked and struggled and fought with one another for a drop of this precious liquid, as if they grew rabid at the sight of it.

It was not surprising that they should have endured much sickness and loss of life in their short passage. They had sailed from the coast of Africa on the 7th of May and had been out but seventeen days, and they had thrown overboard no less than fifty-five, who had died of dysentery and other complaints in that space of time, though they had left the coast in good health. Indeed, many of the survivors were seen lying about the decks in the last stage of emaciation and in a state of filth and misery not to be looked at. . . .

While expressing my horror at what I saw and exclaiming against the state of this vessel for conveying human beings. I was informed by my friends, who had passed so long a time on the coast of Africa and visited so many ships, that this was one of the best they had seen. The height sometimes between decks was only eighteen inches, so that the unfortunate beings could not turn round or even on their sides, the elevation being less than the breadth of their shoulders; and here they are usually chained to the decks by the neck and legs. . . .

Eli Whitney's cotton gin created a cotton boom in the South—and a doubling of the number of slaves by 1820. *(Courtesy, The Smithsonian Institute)*

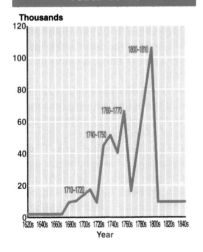

Importation of slaves into America by decade, 1620s–1840s

Cotton Gins   But southern planters were anxiously experimenting with new crops, especially cotton. Samuel Crompton's spinning-mule, James Hargreave's spinning-jenny, and Richard Arkwright's spinning-frame and water-frame, as well as other innovations in manufacturing, had dramatically lowered the cost of spinning and weaving cotton fiber into cloth, stimulating a worldwide demand for cotton goods. The appetites of English manufacturers for raw cotton became insatiable. As early as 1786 planters in lowland South Carolina and Georgia began to experiment with growing the silky, long-fibered sea-island cotton. It proved much superior to the short-staple upland variety that had been produced in small quantities for many years. When the cotton bolls were passed between two close-set rollers, the smooth black seeds of the sea-island variety popped right out; the same roller gin crushed the sticky green seeds of the upland variety, making it unmarketable. But sea-island cotton would grow only in the warm, humid lowlands of the coast. Large-scale cotton cultivation awaited a successful process to remove the seeds from short-staple cotton.

Eli Whitney   A Connecticut Yankee came to the South's rescue. In 1793 young Eli Whitney, fresh out of Yale and unemployed, came South to work as a tutor. On the way he stopped to see his friend Phineas Miller, the overseer at Mulberry Grove near Savannah, the plantation of Catherine Greene, widow of General Nathanael Greene. There he turned to inventing a machine to clean the cotton of its seed. In just six months he had perfected his "absurdly simple contrivance." The cotton was fed into a hopper. A toothed roller caught the fibers of the cotton boll and pulled them through a slotted iron guard, its slits wide enough to admit the teeth and the cotton fibers caught on them, but too narrow to let the seeds through. A revolving brush then swept the cotton from the roller's teeth. One man could operate a small gin; larger ones could operate by horse or water power. Whitney and his friend quickly formed a partnership to manufacture their gins. "It makes the labor fifty times less," the inventor observed proudly, "without throwing any class of people out of business."

Whitney's statement hid a cruel fact. The agricultural depression, by throwing slaves out of work, might ultimately have ended slavery. The cotton gin fastened slavery on the South. Rival manufacturers and local artisans quickly copied Whitney's design. Cotton cultivation spread rapidly through upland South Carolina and Georgia. By 1820 the United States was producing 335,000 bales of cotton (a bale weighed about 500 pounds), as opposed to 10,000 bales in 1793. The opening of the rich Black Belt of Alabama and Mississippi after the War of 1812 pushed the crop above one million bales by 1835. The cotton boom created an unprecedented demand for slaves. In 1803 South Carolina reopened its foreign slave trade. Before the federal ban went into effect in 1808, nearly 40,000 Africans had entered Charleston. Between 1790 and 1820 the slave population of the South more than doubled, from 657,000 to more than 1,509,000. Such a massive growth would have enormous political and social repercussions.

The career of Eli Whitney held another irony for the South. This imaginative inventor went from the cotton gin to the manufacture of arms, and in that line he was instrumental in developing the principle of interchangeable parts. The principle was a major contribution to the industrial revolution. And industrialism, so it can be argued, met the South on the battlefields of the Civil War, defeating the slavery that the cotton gin had revived.

The Question of Slavery: The Tallmadge Amendment   Saturday, February 13, 1819, was a dull day in Washington. The Senate was not meeting and the House was occupied with a proposal to reduce the number of officers in the army. Late in the day the representatives took up a routine bill for Missouri statehood. Without warning, James Tallmadge, Jr., of New York offered an amendment to prohibit the further introduction of slavery into Missouri and gradually to emancipate slave children born there. An "interesting and pretty wide debate" on Tallmadge's amendment began at once. For the next two and a half years the question of slavery in Missouri—which Thomas Jefferson likened to "a fire bell in the night"—paralyzed Congress. "This momentous question, . . ." the seventy-six-year-old ex-President wrote, "awakened and filled me with terror. I considered it at once as the knell of the Union."

Prior to 1819 new states had entered the Union without much controversy over slavery. The Northwest Ordinance had prohibited slavery in the territory north of the Ohio River. North Carolina and Georgia ceded to the federal government most of the area south of the Ohio, with the stipulation that slavery should be permitted. Before 1820 new slave and free states entered in equal numbers: Louisiana, Mississippi, and Alabama balanced Ohio, Indiana, and Illinois. In 1819 there were eleven slave and eleven free states. The admission of Missouri threatened to upset this delicate balance.

New Englanders had watched with dismay the march of settlement westward; some hoped to preserve their section's influence by checking the expansion of slavery into new territory, and thereby making it their economic and political ally. Federalists had long attributed the triumph of Jefferson's Republican Party to "slave representation." They charged that the Constitution's "three-fifths" clause, allowing three-fifths of the slave population of a state to be counted in granting it House seats, gave the South a disproportionate influence in national politics. Advocates of the tariff and internal improvements looked increasingly on slaveholders as the opponents of their special interests. But at bottom the opposition of slavery was before long to join two quite differing ideas: the conviction that human bondage violated the ethos of the Revolution and the republic; and, especially as time passed, the nineteenth-century humanitarian impulse to abolish or mitigate suffering by means of social reform.

Federalist leaders such as Senator Rufus King of New York aimed at reinvigorating their party with an appeal against slavery's expansion. They allied with a faction of northern Republicans under Governor De Witt Clinton of New York, who resented the southern leadership of the party. Antislavery activists like former Chief Justice John Jay added their support. The House passed Tallmadge's amendment during 1819, but the Senate rejected it. Congress adjourned without reaching an agree-

Soon northerners would spread accounts, many of them true, of cruel slave owners. Stories like this one gradually awakened the moral sense of the nation:

"I now entered on my fifteenth year—a sad epoch in the life of a slave girl. My master began to whisper foul words in my ear. Young as I was, I could not remain ignorant of their import. I tried to treat them with indifference or contempt. . . . He was a crafty man, and resorted to many means to accomplish his purposes. . . . He peopled my young mind with unclean images, such as only a vile monster could think of. I turned from him with disgust and hatred. But he was my master. I was compelled to live under the same roof with him— where I saw a man forty years my senior daily violating the most sacred commandments of nature. He told me I was his property; that I must be subject to his will in all things. My soul revolted against the mean tyranny. But where could I turn for protection? No matter whether the slave girl be as black as ebony or as fair as her mistress. In either case, there is no shadow of law to protect her from insult, from violence, or even from death; all these are inflicted by fiends who bear the shape of men. The mistress, who ought to protect the helpless victim, has no other feelings towards her but those of jealousy and rage. The degradation, the wrongs, the vices, that grow out of slavery, are more than I can describe."

One northerner observed:

"I believe some years ago there was an openness in the minds of the people, in which they saw the iniquity of slavery, but I believe since the discussion of the Missouri question in Congress, the prejudices of slaveholders have increased against the advocates of liberty. . . ."

ment, and Missouri remained a territory. For the time, congressional politics was taking on a distinct sectional alignment, pitting North against South as morality, politics, and self-interest intersected.

The Missouri Compromise   In due course a compromise emerged. Massachusetts had agreed to the creation of a new state, Maine, out of her northern counties, provided Congress acted by March 4, 1820. The free states hoped to admit Maine before the deadline. The Senate decided to tie Maine to Missouri. It added to the Maine statehood bill then before Congress a section admitting Missouri without restrictions on slavery. In order to make this bill more acceptable to the northern-dominated House, Senator Jesse B. Thomas of Illinois offered his famous amendment prohibiting slavery "forever" in the rest of the Louisiana Purchase territory north of latitude 36° 30′—the southern boundary of Missouri. In this form the Maine-Missouri bill went to the House, where, after much wrangling, Speaker Henry Clay secured its passage on March 2. On the key question of excluding slavery in Missouri the vote was extremely close—the motion lost by 90 to 87, with four northern congressmen absent. The vote was traumatic for southerners, who increasingly drew into themselves and lived in a closed society.

Denmark Vesey   In the summer of 1822 the white South was shaken by the discovery of an apparent conspiracy led by Denmark Vesey, a free black carpenter who had closely followed the Missouri debates. It was said that he had recruited hundreds of slaves in Charleston, South Carolina, to rise up at midnight, kill whites, and fire the city. A slave revealed the plot to authorities only a few days before the apparent time of the uprising, and a special court sentenced thirty-five blacks to death. The executions were a public spectacle: at a mass hanging on July 26 several of the condemned twisted in an "agony of strangulation." Afterward, the authorities left the bodies dangling for hours as an example to other blacks.

Slaves and slaveholders everywhere trembled. The court report noted Vesey's careful reading of the Missouri debates. The involvement of so many trusted family servants was especially disturbing to whites. The South Carolina governor had often left his family in the care of Rolla, his beloved personal slave. Yet Rolla was listed among the archconspirators.

Southern lawmakers moved at once to prevent a repetition of the Denmark Vesey slave conspiracy. They tightened their slave codes and outlawed the distribution of antislavery propaganda. Southerners resisted all further discussion of slavery in the federal Congress. The South Carolina legislature forbade the entry of free blacks into the state. Free black seamen who violated the law were jailed until their ships left port. When the British government protested these detentions and a federal judge ruled the law unconstitutional, the South Carolina Senate defiantly replied that "the duty of the state to guard against insubordination or insurrection" was "paramount to all *laws*, all *treaties*, all *constitutions*. It arises from the supreme and permanent law of nature, the law of self-preservation; and will never by this state be renounced, compromised, controlled or participated with any power whatever." Neighboring states quickly passed similar statutes. Henceforth, the South bristled at every criticism of what came to be called its "peculiar institution."

In the period that followed the angry arguments over Missouri, and in reaction to the Vesey conspiracy, criticism of slavery virtually ceased in the South. Proslavery theorists—South Carolina's John C. Calhoun among them—who might earlier have labeled slavery a "necessary evil," began to defend it as a "positive good." Blacks, they contended, could not prosper as freedmen, and the South would be abandoned without black labor to work the cotton fields and rice swamps. Protected by benevolent masters from the burdens of sickness, unemployment, and old age, the slaves, they claimed, were better off than industrial workers in the North or in Europe.

Viewing the growing intransigence of the South on slavery as well as the hardening antislavery feeling in the North, politicians resolved to mute the slavery issue in the future. For a time they succeeded. The division of the Louisiana Purchase territory into slave and free soil removed the question of slavery expansion from national politics for twenty-five years. But beginning in 1846, with the acquisition of new territory, the furious political struggle over slavery was to revive. Just as John Quincy Adams had predicted, the Missouri Controversy turned out to be "a mere preamble—a title-page to a great tragic volume."

John Quincy Adams and American Continentalism

For the United States, a fortunate feature of the Louisiana Purchase was that no one knew the exact boundaries. When Robert Livingston, one of the American negotiators, pressed the French minister Talleyrand on this point, he replied: "I can give you no direction; you have made a noble bargain for yourselves, and I suppose you will make the most of it." John Quincy Adams, President Monroe's secretary of state, did just that. In important boundary treaties Adams expanded the nation's frontiers into a continental realm.

Few men have been better equipped to guide American diplomacy than John Quincy Adams. In 1778, at age eleven, he had accompanied his father, John Adams, to France. By the time he was thirty he had served as American minister to the Netherlands and to Prussia. Then, in 1801, Massachusetts elected him to the United States Senate as a Federalist. To the distress of his party, Adams proceeded to side frequently with the rival Jeffersonians. When he voted for the hated Embargo, the state legislature, dominated by the Federalists, evicted the "scoundrel" from his seat. Under President Madison he acted as American minister to Russia and to England, and helped negotiate the Treaty of Ghent. In 1817 Monroe named him secretary of state.

Adams took great pride in his country's military and diplomatic victories during these years. The law of nature had intended "our proper dominion to be the continent of North America." It was our national mission to expand westward to the Pacific and north and south as well.

As secretary of state under Monroe, John Quincy Adams negotiated treaties in seeking to build an "American Continental Empire." This photograph, suggesting his bulldog tenacity and moral commitment, is an interesting daguerreotype of Adams taken when he served in the House of Representatives later in his life. *(Stuart and Sully Portrait, Courtesy, Fogg Art Museum, Harvard University)*

Adams disliked European colonialism, with its commercial monopolies and its pretentious claims to "fragments of territory . . . fifteen hundred miles beyond the sea, worthless and burdensome to their owners. . . ." As secretary of state, Adams deliberately sought to make an "American Continental Empire."

One step toward it was taken in 1817. By a mutual agreement between the United States and Great Britain, both nations signed notes limiting their naval forces on the Great Lakes. This arrangement, known as the Rush-Bagot agreement, was formalized by acting Secretary of State Richard Rush and the British minister Charles Bagot.

The Treaty of 1818 with Britain But controversy still lingered with Britain over the northwest boundary. The treaty of 1783 had described the boundary line as running from the north-westernmost point of the Lake of the Woods due west to the Mississippi River—an impossible line, since the Mississippi actually arises 150 miles south of the Lake of the Woods. The Louisiana Purchase had compounded the error by creating a northern boundary running all the way to the Rocky Mountains. Britain had repeatedly sought to set the boundary far enough south for Canadian access to the Mississippi.

West of the Louisiana Purchase was land inviting territorial dispute. In 1792, when he discovered the Columbia River, Captain Robert Gray had first claimed the Oregon country for the United States. The explorations of Lewis and Clark fired American interest in the area; John Jacob Astor's company established a fur-trading post there in 1811. The United States, Great Britain, Spain, and Russia each had claims in this region. During the War of 1812 British forces seized Astor's post, which they renamed Fort George. Britain retained this fort until 1818, when Lord Castlereagh, the foreign secretary, ordered it returned to the United States. Castlereagh intended this gesture as looking to a reconciliation between Britain and the United States. Britain, absorbed by events in Europe, dared not risk a further quarrel with the United States. The War of 1812, moreover, had shown how exposed was Canada's position—only military blundering on the part of the United States had saved it. Canada had become a hostage for Anglo-American peace.

Castlereagh next invited the United States to send commissioners to London for the purpose of settling all the differences between the two countries. At these negotiations the American envoys, acting under Adams's instructions, secured important gains for the United States. The Treaty of 1818—which one expert has called the most important treaty in the history of relations between Canada and the United States—granted the republic permanent rights to fish off the coasts of Newfoundland and Labrador. On the northwest boundary the United States refused to budge, and Britain agreed to draw it at 49° north latitude as far as the Rocky Mountains. Adams's stubbornness had saved for the United States a strip of land more valuable than he could have realized: it contains the rich Mesabi iron range of northern Michigan and Minnesota. West of the Rockies, neither side would yield its claim. As a stopgap, both agreed to joint occupation of the Oregon country, a compromise that lasted until the 1840s.

The Treaty of 1819 with Spain

Adams inherited another set of problems with Spain. The Spanish government had never accepted the American claim that west Florida was part of the Louisiana Purchase, nor had the border between Louisiana and Texas ever been determined. Beyond Texas, the western boundary of the Louisiana Purchase remained undefined. Spain still hoped to salvage part of this vast area, and to retain its own claim to the Oregon country.

The United States had tried for years to acquire the strategic area of West Florida, which stood out on the map like a pistol barrel pointing at New Orleans, the vital outlet for the Mississippi River. Spain's grasp on the whole of Florida gradually loosened after the War of 1812. The Napoleonic conflict in Europe and revolutions in Spanish America had exhausted its strength. When President Monroe ordered troops to occupy Amelia Island, Spain in 1817 decided to offer Florida to the United States in return for a favorable boundary west of the Mississippi and a pledge not to recognize the provinces of Spanish America that had revolted.

The two sides were still far apart in negotiations at Washington

William Sidney Mount, _Early American Farmhouse._ (*Courtesy, Metropolitan Museum of Art*)

when General Andrew Jackson took matters into his own hands. Old Hickory had been sent to the Florida frontier with orders to adopt all "necessary measures" to halt Indian raids into the United States. Jackson, interpreting his orders broadly, advanced into Florida in 1818 with 3,000 soldiers, pushed back the Seminole Indians, and seized the towns of St. Marks and Pensacola. For good measure, he tried and executed two British subjects who had been inciting the Indians. Jackson's acts embarrassed the Monroe Administration. Secretary of War John Calhoun wanted Jackson court-martialed, but Adams defended Jackson's conduct. The secretary of state urged that the occupation of the towns continue until Spain should send a force sufficient to pacify the Indians. Monroe agreed, and Spain received an ultimatum: either place a force in Florida adequate to maintain order or cede it to the United States.

These bold strokes got the negotiations moving. After weeks of hard bargaining, the two sides agreed, and Adams and the Spanish minister, Luis de Onis, signed the Adams-Onis treaty of 1819. Spain ceded Florida to the United States. Nothing was said about the recognition of the rebellious Spanish colonies. In return for fixing the Texas boundary at the Sabine River, Adams secured a magnificent transcontinental settlement from Spain, including title to all Spanish territory north of latitude 42° between the Continental Divide and the Pacific Ocean, which would include much of the present Northwest. Adams reckoned that the four nay votes on the treaty in the Senate included two Clay men, one enemy of Jackson, and one suffering from "some maggot in his brain." With this treaty Adams had at last achieved his "Continental Empire" and a place in history as a brilliant secretary of state.

The Monroe Doctrine

The boldest assertion of nationalism in this period came from President James Monroe. His annual message in December 1823 laid down two important principles: that "the American continents, by the free and independent condition which they have assumed and maintain, are henceforth not to be considered as subjects for future colonization by any European power"; and that the United States would consider any attempt by the European powers "to extend their political system to any portion of this hemisphere as dangerous to our peace and safety." In later years these two maxims, known as "non-colonization" and "non-interference," came to be called together the Monroe Doctrine. No other presidential statement, with the possible exception of Washington's Farewell Address warning against "entangling alliances," has won such acceptance from the American people. On the hundredth anniversary of Monroe's message, Mary Baker Eddy, the founder of Christian Science, spoke for millions when she said: "I believe in the Monroe Doctrine, in our Constitution, and in the laws of God."

From the first, Americans had sought refuge in the New World in order to escape the Old. Out of the Revolutionary experience inevitably flowed the belief that the New World should where possible and in its self-interest try to isolate itself from the alliances, the quarrels, and the

A French newspaper derided President Monroe for assuming in the Monroe Doctrine

"the tone of a powerful monarch, whose armies and fleets are ready to march. . . . Mr. Monroe is the temporary President of a Republic situated on the east coast of North America. This republic is bounded on the south by the possessions of the King of Spain, and on the north by those of the King of England. Its independence was only recognized forty years ago; by what right then would the two Americas today be under its immediate sway from Hudson's Bay to Cape Horn?"

colonizing schemes of the European powers. Washington gave this idea its classic expression in his Farewell Address, and Jefferson echoed it in his warning against subordinating American affairs to those of Europe. In 1823 Monroe and Secretary of State John Quincy Adams shaped these broad beliefs into an official statement.

Russia and Spain   Adams had for years sought an excuse to forbid further European colonization in the Western Hemisphere. Russia unexpectedly gave him the opportunity. Russian explorers had long before laid claim to the northwest coast of America. By 1812 the Russian-American Company extended its trading operations southward to within only a few miles of San Francisco. Suddenly, in 1821, Tsar Alexander I issued an imperial decree conferring upon this company exclusive trading rights down to 51° north latitude and forbidding all foreign vessels to come near the coast. In July 1823 Adams flatly told the Russian minister at Washington that the United States would assert the principle "that the American continents are no longer subjects for *any* new European colonial establishments." Here was the genesis of the Monroe Doctrine; President Monroe inserted almost these very words into his annual message six months later.

The warning against European interference within the hemisphere attacked a fundamental threat to interests of the United States. Spain's colonies in Central and South America had been struggling for independence for some time. When Spain tried to regain her American provinces by force, full-scale war broke out. For six years, beginning in 1814, the revolutionists, led by Simón Bolívar and José de San Martín, liberated one colony after another. The United States sympathized with these heroic struggles and granted belligerent status to the rebellious colonies, enabling them to buy supplies in this country. But Monroe, and especially Adams, hesitated to recognize the new revolutionary governments until Britain did. The British government twice refused invitations from the Monroe Administration to do this jointly. Finally, the United States decided to act alone, extending formal recognition in 1822 to Mexico, Colombia, Chile, Peru, and the provinces of Río de la Plata, present-day Argentina. Having taken this bold step, the administration was alarmed at the prospect of intervention.

Great Britain shared this concern, for the Spanish-American revolts had opened a whole continent to British trade. When in 1823 rumors of possible intervention by other European powers reached George Canning, the British foreign secretary, he decided to seek the cooperation of the United States in opposing such a scheme. Canning proposed a treaty or exchange of notes between the two countries expressing joint opposition to any attempt to restore Spain's lost colonies by force; he still refused, however, to agree to immediate British recognition of the former colonies.

Monroe almost accepted Canning's offer. Former Presidents Jefferson and Madison both advised acceptance, as did all the Cabinet— except the secretary of state. "It would be more candid as well as more dignified," Adams argued, "to avow our principles explicitly . . . , than to come in as a cock-boat in the wake of the British man-of-war." At this point in 1823 Monroe drafted the famous declaration in his annual message opposing further intervention by the European powers in the Western Hemisphere. At Adams's insistence Monroe inserted a statement claiming that his country had no intention to interfere "in the wars of the European powers in matters relating to themselves." And Adams publicly admitted that it was the power of the British navy that had enabled the United States to throw down its audacious challenge to the rest of Europe.

Americans cheered the President's message. Europeans labeled it "blustering," "haughty," "arrogant." It had little effect on the actions of the continental powers. Russia, a major object of the non-colonization clause, had already decided to limit its territorial claims in North America to the area north of latitude 54° 40′. Late in 1823 Canning, tired of waiting for American agreement on a joint statement, had served an ultimatum on France. During the next twenty years Britain and France both violated the Doctrine with impunity. Not until the late nineteenth century, when the United States had become a major power, did the Old World respect the new hemisphere. Yet Monroe's message had an important future. Against an Old World order founded on a doctrine asserting the absolute rights of sovereigns and empires, Monroe championed a new order founded on the right of peoples to determine their own destiny. Only later, by a series of corollaries, did Monroe's successors turn his Doctrine into an instrument for meddling by the United States in Latin American affairs.

The Election of 1824

From 1796 to 1816 meetings of the congressional members of each party had nominated their own presidential candidates. In 1820, when President Monroe ran unopposed, the Republicans did not even bother with a caucus nomination. By 1824 that party, lacking an organized opposition, had dissolved into a series of warring factions.

The "Old Republicans," of the caucus devoted to states' rights and economy, pushed William H. Crawford of Georgia as their candidate for President. Others attacked the caucus as undemocratic. Crawford is an obscure figure today, but to his contemporaries he was a "plain *giant* of a man." Like many young men of his day, he had turned a successful law practice into a distinguished career. He married a wealthy heiress, spent a few years in the state legislature, and then went to Washington as a senator. Crawford later served as minister to France and secretary of war, and had, since 1816, been secretary of the treasury. He used this last post to pack government offices with his supporters. In 1823, just when his position seemed impregnable, illness struck him. Medical experts bled him twenty-three times within three weeks. Crawford never fully recovered, but his partisans continued to put his name forward.

As an alternative to the congressional caucus, the other candidates accepted nominations from state legislatures and public meetings. Several New England states endorsed John Quincy Adams, Monroe's capable secretary of state. South Carolina had supported John C. Calhoun, but he dropped out when Pennsylvania Republicans failed to

William H. Crawford of Georgia, who might have become President. *(Courtesy, Scribners Archives)*

nominate him. The young Carolinian would instead accept the vice-presidential spot. Besides these candidates were Henry Clay, one of the most dynamic politicians in American history, and Andrew Jackson, among the most charismatic.

Henry Clay and Andrew Jackson   Henry Clay had been charting a course toward the White House for a decade. Born in Virginia, he had migrated to Kentucky, where he became a highly successful criminal lawyer—so successful, according to legend, that no person who hired Clay to defend him was ever hanged. After a stint in the state legislature he went on to Congress, a perfect environment then for a man with his quick mind, engaging personality, and fondness for drinking and gambling. In 1811 his colleagues made him Speaker of the House. After the war Clay became a vigorous advocate of internal improvements, a national bank, and a protective tariff. He hoped that this program, which he called the American System, would win support in every part of the country. This was, for practical purposes, the nation's first campaign platform. Clay had anticipated rising sectional jealousies. "I will be opposed," he wrote before the election, "because I think that the interests of all parts of the Union should be taken care of. . . ."

Clay's rival for the western vote was Andrew Jackson, a latecomer to the race. Jackson's victories over the Creek Indians at Horseshoe Bend and the British at New Orleans had made him a national hero. "I cannot believe that killing 2,500 Englishmen at New Orleans qualifies for the various, difficult and complicated duties of the Chief Magistracy," said Clay. Jackson's arrogant conduct during the Seminole campaign in 1818 only increased his popularity. In spite of brief terms in both houses of Congress, Old Hickory was not associated in the public mind with the grimy politics of Washington; he was a "plain farmer," his backers claimed, fresh from the people. In the uncertain politics of the time, his lack of experience in public affairs probably worked to his advantage. While the other candidates discussed the tariff or internal improvements, the Jackson people, observed John Quincy Adams resentfully, had only to shout "8th of January and the Battle of New Orleans" to win votes.

The Questioned Election of 1824   The Constitution had granted to the legislature of each state the authority to decide on a method for selecting presidential electors, the small group of people who actually vote for the President. By 1824 it had become common for states to choose these electors by popular vote. That November, the popular ballots cast for electors committed to Jackson added to 43 percent of the nationwide total. Electors for Adams, his nearest rival, garnered 31 percent. But none of the candidates had a clear majority in the electoral college; there were 99 votes for Jackson, 84 for Adams, 41 for Crawford, and 37 for Clay. As the Constitution provides, the House of Representatives was required to select the chief executive from among the three men with the largest number of electoral votes. Each state would cast one ballot, determined by majority vote of its delegation.

Everyone now looked to Clay, whose fourth-place finish had eliminated him from the contest. As Speaker he had enormous influence in the House, and the managers and friends of the three candidates besieged him with arguments and deals. Clay carefully considered their words and his own political fortunes before making up his mind. He easily eliminated Crawford; the Georgian was physically unfit to assume the burden of the presidency. Clay was inclined to dismiss Jackson as a "military chieftain" with no moral, intellectual, or other attributes worth the name. And the general was a dangerous rival for the western vote; it was to Clay's future political advantage to exclude him from the contest. This left John Quincy Adams. The two men had quarreled in the past, but Adams was unquestionably qualified for the presidency, and he shared Clay's faith in a strong national government. After consulting with friends, Clay threw all his support behind the secretary of state. By a bare majority, John Quincy Adams was elected President.

At first Jackson took the news of his defeat gracefully. Then, three days after the election, Adams announced his intention to appoint Clay to be secretary of state. The warm and impulsive Clay contrasted to the dour Adams. Working together in Belgium on the treaty to end the War of 1812, Adams had written in his diary: "Just before rising I heard Mr. Clay's company retiring. . . . I had left him . . . at cards. They parted as I was about to rise." But the appointment was made, and the cry of "corrupt bargain" went up at once. "So you see," wrote Jackson bitterly, "the *Judas* of the West has closed the contract and will receive the thirty pieces of silver." Had there been a deal? No evidence, then or later, has clarified the matter. Adams insisted that the Kentuckian was the best man for the job. Politically, the appointment drove the Jacksonians and the Calhoun men into immediate opposition to the newly elected administration. Jackson, heretofore a hesitant candidate, set out for Tennessee in full cry: "The people have been cheated," he charged. "The corruptions and intrigues at Washington [have] defeated the will of the people." The campaign of 1828 was under way before John Quincy Adams had settled into the President's house in 1824.

The Second President Adams

John Quincy Adams, a biographer once remarked, "was not among America's more lovable figures." By his own description, he was reserved, stubborn, and independent. "It is a question," an observer wondered, "whether he ever laughed in his life." A reporter at the Ghent peace conference termed him "a bulldog among spaniels." When he was secretary of state, these qualities served Adams well; once he was President, they quickly became his undoing.

Instead of seeking to overcome his liabilities by building a political machine in the federal bureaucracy and developing a popular program, Adams in the interest of conciliation appointed to his Cabinet political opponents and retained outspoken critics in government offices. Above all, he scorned public opinion. The great object of government, Adams believed, was to improve the condition of mankind. It was the President's duty to give direction to the national government, and the peo-

The House of Representatives, 1821. As provided in the Constitution, the House elected John Quincy Adams President in 1824 after none of the four candidates had received a majority in the electoral college. *(Courtesy, Library of Congress)*

ple's to follow. Even when proposing a popular measure, Adams made no effort to dramatize it. Rather than make a straightforward statement urging Congress to pass a federal bankruptcy law, he recommended "the amelioration in some form or modification of the diversified and often oppressive codes relating to insolvency." In 1828 the Jacksonians would revive a withering popular campaign slogan: "John Quincy Adams who can write and Andrew Jackson who can fight."

Adams had an articulate nationalistic program. Now that the nation's independence had been secured and her borders enlarged, he would strengthen the country internally with a nationally planned and financed system of roads and canals, a national university, a naval academy, astronomical observatories along with expeditions to map the country, both supported by the government, and a department of the interior to regulate the use of natural resources. Adams expected to finance this program by selling public lands. But it was not the right time for a nationalist President, particularly one lacking the political skill to rally support. Westerners wanted free or cheap public land, not sales at high prices for revenue. Southerners increasingly feared that a powerful federal government would interfere with slavery. The Old Republicans accused the President of trying to revive the Federalist policies of his father. "The cub," John Randolph remarked, "is a greater bear than the old one." The Jacksonian press derided Adams's proposals: his reference to astronomical observatories as "light-houses of the skies" became a national joke. Congress rejected every one of the President's recommendations.

At every turn, Adams's integrity and his belief in national authority landed him in trouble. In 1825, for example, he refused to enforce a fraudulent treaty dispossessing the Creek Indians of their tribal lands in Georgia. Governor George Troup of Georgia, anxious to open these rich cotton lands to settlement, sent surveyors into the Indian country anyway. A confrontation between the United States and Georgia threatened. A new treaty averted a clash: the Creeks agreed to cede all their lands and move west. Adams's stand had been honorable, the more so in being unpopular. Southerners condemned his challenge to state authority; westerners objected to it for defending Indians.

The failure of Adams's domestic program had profound consequences for the country. A vast system of roads and canals, coming at a time when the forces of sectionalism were gaining strength, might have tied the nation together and in such manner as to resist the later disintegration of the Union. Instead, as Adams predicted, "the clanking chain of the slave" was riveted "into perpetuity," and "the invaluable inheritance of the public lands" was wasted "in boundless bribery to the West."

The Panama Congress

Adams's presidency was never to reward with success the skills and brilliance he brought to it. His chief effort in foreign policy went no farther than his domestic programs.

In 1824, Simón Bolívar, the "Liberator" of Spanish America, proposed a conference to be held in Panama. He hoped to bind the former Spanish colonies into a confederation to protect the hemisphere against Europe's Quadruple Alliance. Mexico and Colombia, rebuffed in earlier efforts to obtain individual treaties of alliance with the United States, added the republic of the North to the list of participants. All hoped to bring the United States into a hemispheric alliance that would make the Monroe Doctrine Pan-American. Their invitations reached Washington early in 1825, just as John Quincy Adams was entering the White House.

Secretary of State Henry Clay welcomed the idea of an inter-American conference. He had ardently supported the cause of Latin American independence. Clay envisioned a cooperative system of republics, led by the United States, standing against the despotism of the Old World. Adams himself, as Monroe's secretary of state, had rejected all proposals for collective security with the Latin American republics. At Clay's urging, however, he asked Congress to confirm the appointment of two delegates to the Panama meeting. It was the time, he decided, to extend "the most cordial feelings of fraternal friendship" to our sister republics. Adams hoped to advance throughout the hemisphere fundamental principles of commercial reciprocity, neutral rights, freedom of the seas, and resistance to European colonization.

The President's request met unexpected opposition in Congress. Led by Vice President Calhoun and supporters of Andrew Jackson, the faction within the Republican Party that was to call itself the Democrats attacked the administration. It accused Adams and Clay of seeking to fasten the United States to a hemispheric alliance. Southerners had a

Bolívar, who won independence for much of South America from Spain, wrote,

"A state too extensive in itself . . . ultimately falls into decay. Its free government is transformed into a tyranny; it . . . finally degenerates into despotism."

further objection to the Panama meeting. Delegates from Haiti were expected, and the question might arise of recognizing the black republic, whose slaves under the leadership of Toussaint L'Ouverture had won their indepedence from France and their colonial masters. Haiti was the second republic in the western hemisphere, founded in 1804. Recognition warned a Georgia senator, would "strengthen and invigorate" the determination of black revolutionaries, whose hands still reeked "in the blood" of their murdered masters, "to spread the doctrines of insurrection" to the United States.

Adams defended his proposal. Times and circumstances, he argued, had changed since Washington's day; the United States had trebled its territory, population, and wealth and must act with a breadth of vision befitting a great nation, said this devoted nationalist. After months of debate and delay, Congress finally approved the President's choice of delegates and appropriated funds for the mission. Adams had scored a major triumph—the only one of his presidency.

But the triumph was empty. One of the delegates from the United States died on his way to the conference; the other arrived too late. The meeting itself was a fiasco. Only four Latin American nations sent representatives. They signed a treaty of mutual defense and alliance, and quickly adjourned from fever-ridden Panama City, planning to meet again in Mexico early in 1827. By that time Bolívar had lost interest in the idea of a hemispheric confederation, and the conference never reconvened.

At home, the issue of Haiti quickened the sectional controversy that had flared in the debates over the Missouri Compromise. Southerners once again envisioned the federal government as moving against their "peculiar institution." Adams's proposal gave his political enemies their first opportunity to attack the President and his secretary of state. Once again John Quincy Adams was ahead of his time; the American people in 1826 were looking west, not south. Not for another fifty years would the United States take an interest in the concept of Pan-Americanism.

His administration a failure in both domestic and foreign affairs, Adams gave up all hope of reelection. His subsequent career was notable of an American President. In 1830 he was elected to the House of Representatives. "No election or appointment conferred upon me ever gave me so much pleasure," said Congressman Adams. A spokesman for the antislavery forces and a model of integrity, he served until his death in 1848 at the age of eighty-one.

Andrew Jackson and the Election of 1828

A national hero since the Battle of New Orleans in 1815, Andrew Jackson would put his stamp on American politics and give his name to an age. Jackson had been born in 1767 in the Waxhaws, a wooded frontier area on the border between North and South Carolina. During the Revolution he lost both brothers and his widowed mother. For a time he seemed destined to be "the most roaring, rollicking, game-cocking, horse-racing, card-playing, mischievous fellow" in the neighborhood. Then, fired with ambition, he began reading law. In 1788, after completing his studies, he moved to Tennessee to take a position of public prosecutor.

This developing country was the ideal place for an eager young attorney. Jackson speculated avidly in land, slaves, and horses. As a public prosecutor, he usually sided with the creditors, executing numerous writs against debtors. In 1796 he was elected to Congress from Tennessee. Albert Gallatin would remember him as "a tall, lanky, uncouth-looking personage . . . [hair] down his back tied with an eel skin . . . manners of a rough backwoodsman." After three years in Washington he returned to Tennessee, where he served as a superior court judge, once again siding with the land barons. Near Nashville he acquired a fine plantation, the Hermitage, and many slaves. Although success had polished his rough edges, Jackson never lost his "roaring, rollicking" character; he was wounded three times in duels.

When in 1814 the theater of war with the British shifted south, a desperate national government called on this victor against the Creeks to save New Orleans. His famous victory over "the conquerors of Europe" electrified the country. He was the nation's savior, its greatest hero since George Washington. His rough handling of the Florida Indians and their British allies in 1818 was wildly popular on the frontier.

Jackson lost heavily in the Panic of 1819. In its wake a group of his wealthy friends, alarmed by the growing demand for debtor relief in Tennessee, decided to use Jackson's immense popularity to protect their assets. They began touting him as the "people's candidate" for President—this man who had recently brought suit against 129 people who owed him money. His candidacy caught fire. For what people believed about Jackson was perhaps more important than the facts.

Though Jackson was a large landowner and by some standards an aristocrat, he did have perhaps more democratic sentiments than any previous President. He had a westerner's inherent distrust of entrenched status and dictatorial government. In his youth he had been of fairly moderate means. And so if Jackson did not come to the presidency with any clearly articulated beliefs, he did have styles and tastes that accorded with popular policies other politicians devised.

The Second Party System   In the 1820's a second two-party system was forming, in which each of the parties would appeal more directly for wide popular support than had the old Federalists and Republicans. They would in time set up extensive local organizations for winning an electorate and holding its loyalty. The new party system rested in part on legal changes that broadened the popular base of government: the gradual removal of qualifications for voting, and the trend among the states toward popular election of public officials and presidential electors in place of the earlier practice of leaving the choice to state legislatures. The new party system was a way of capturing this larger voting public.

In choosing John Quincy Adams over Jackson in 1824, the House of Representatives had unwittingly ushered in the new era of partisan politics. In the next four years the followers of Adams and Clay, working for federal policies that would actively promote the nation's economy, began to call themselves National Republicans; their opponents went by the name Democratic Republicans, soon shortened to Democrats. Because the House had selected Adams over General Jackson—recipient of the greater number of popular and electoral votes—under circumstances that suggested to many people the existence of a "corrupt bargain," Jackson became an even stronger political figure than before. He captured the imagination of the public and infused new glamour into national politics.

After his defeat, Jackson allied with Senator Martin Van Buren of New York, a highly skilled political manager, to create the new Democratic Party. At its core were the original Jackson men, those who had supported him in 1824. They were joined after the election by the followers of John C. Calhoun, whose own path to the presidency the alliance between Adams and Clay had blocked. Between 1826 and 1828, Van Buren brought into the party the southern Republicans who had formerly supported Crawford. United in their opposition to the policies of Adams and Clay that gave the federal government a larger role in organizing the economy, the new coalition worked in Congress to block the administration's programs.

Election of 1828   The election of 1828 was a landmark in American politics. For the first time in nearly twenty years two vigorous parties contested for the presidency. Responding to this stimulus, the voters turned out in unprecedented numbers to elect Andrew Jackson President of the United States.

Jackson had begun by building the necessary organization to boost him into the presidency. Most states had adopted the system, still in use today, that gives all the state's electoral votes to the presidential candidate who wins the state's popular vote. Since winning a majority of the popular vote brought so rich a reward, parties wanted a state machinery that could mobilize voters throughout the state. Van Buren thoroughly organized the Democratic Party, establishing central committees in Washington and Nashville. These committees worked closely with influential state leaders, who in turn organized Hickory Clubs at the local level. A string of newspapers favorable to Old Hickory appeared across the country. Jackson remained at home in Tennessee, posing as the innocent victim of a "corrupt bargain." Yet he supervised every detail of the campaign. In order to hold together his fragile coalition, he avoided taking a stand on issues. When asked for his position on the tariff, Jackson replied ambiguously that he favored a "middle and just course." When Van Buren quoted Jackson's comment on the tariff at a New York rally, one man in the audience cheered the remark and then asked his neighbor: "On which side of the tariff question was it?" Meantime, Adams steadfastly refused to electioneer in his own behalf. Too late, his friends tried to erect an organization similar to that of the Democrats.

In 1828, as in 1824, more was made of personalities than of issues. The campaign itself was unbelievably dirty. No charge was too base. Jackson was portrayed as a frontier ruffian, a gambler, the son of "a

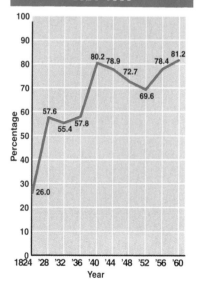

Voter Participation in Presidential Elections 1824–1860

COMMON PROSTITUTE." A "coffin hand-bill" charged the general with the cold-blooded murder of six militiamen during the Creek Campaign of 1814. A rhymester wrote:

All six militia men were shot;
And O! it seems to me
A dreadful deed—a bloody act
of needless cruelty.

Jacksonians replied that the six were deserters who had been executed after a proper court-martial. Jackson's wife Rachel was not spared. The two had met while Rachel was separated from her first husband. In 1791, believing that her husband had obtained a divorce, she married Jackson. Not until some time later did the couple learn that the divorce had not become final. The earlier marriage was formally dissolved in September 1793, after which Rachel and Andrew recited their wedding vows a second time. Rumors of this technical adultery circulated for years. But when his beloved Rachel, sick and shamed by

The Verdict of the People, by George Caleb Bingham. Americans of the 1830s widely linked Andrew Jackson with the rise of the common man, though the number of elective offices had been increasing for decades. *(Courtesy, Collection of the Boatmen's National Bank of St. Louis)*

the "wormwood and gall" of ugly publicity, died suddenly in December 1828, Jackson blamed his political opponents. "May God Almighty forgive her murderers," he cried at her funeral, "as I know she forgave them. I never can." And he never did.

Jacksonians countered with some mudslinging of their own. It was said that President Adams, while minister to Russia, had procured an American girl for Tsar Alexander I. Adams's wife was reported to have had premarital relations with her husband. Stories of the president's "aristocratic" receptions at the White House and his use of public funds to buy "gambling devices" (actually a chess set and a billiard table) circulated widely.

Jackson's victory in November 1828 was a triumph both for the Old Hero and for the Democrats' fresh style of political appeal. Over three times as many voters turned out as in 1824. The general received fifty-six percent of the popular vote, a margin unequaled in any other presidential election during the nineteenth century. Jackson the southwesterner, to all appearances a reflection of the democratic way of the West and a spokesman for inland interests however ill-defined, swept the South and West. Adams carried his native New England along with Delaware and New Jersey, and shared with his rival New York and Maryland, which had not instituted the system of awarding the state's entire electoral vote to the popular winner. Exuberant Jacksonians hailed the election results as a revolution, a triumph of "democracy" over "aristocracy." The following January, after burying his wife, a broken-hearted Andrew Jackson set out for Washington.

The Spoils System
Arriving in Washington, Jackson found the government offices filled with bureaucrats, many of them supporters of the men who had slandered his beloved Rachel. As an astute politician, Jackson recognized the value of rewarding his partisans with government jobs. He agreed with his New York lieutenant, William Marcy, that "to the victors belong the spoils." And Jackson firmly believed that no one had "any more intrinsic right to official station than another." Men who held office too long were "apt to acquire a habit of looking with indifference upon the public interests, and of tolerating conduct from which an unpracticed man would revolt." In his first annual message, Jackson therefore recommended that appointments be limited to four years. Congress balked, but Jackson "rotated" officeholders anyway, insisting: "The duties of all public officers are, or at least admit of being made, so plain and simple that men of intelligence may readily qualify themselves for their performance." In eight years Jackson replaced about twenty percent of the government's employees, sometimes with due cause. Jefferson had removed roughly the same proportion. But it was the Jacksonians who fixed firmly upon American politics the spoils system and rotation in office as expressions of a system of parties shaped to capture and represent popular wishes. For example, when the Jacksonian Democrats lost to a new party, the Whigs, in the election of 1840, Democrats lost their government jobs, which were filled by members of the new party. The process would become an American political tradition through most of the nineteenth century.

The Rise of the Common Man?

For years many history books pictured Jackson as the champion of frontier democracy, battling the forces of privilege and corruption. During his presidency the common man won the right to vote and took politics out of the hands of the elite. Socially and economically, too, the Jacksonian era brought greater equality. With Jackson's election, according to one historian, "a new day dawned in American history. The democratic philosophy of Thomas Jefferson became a reality."

Recent studies have substantially modified this view. Historians now realize that the political power of the common man had been increasing for decades. Even in colonial times, the franchise had been quite open in some places. The Revolutionary ideology and the fierce political contests of the Jeffersonian era brought still greater participation in politics. The new western states adopted constitutions that gave the vote to all adult white males and made most public offices elective. Many of the older states, concerned about the loss of population to the West, followed their example. By Jackson's time only two states, Delaware and South Carolina, still left to their legislatures the selection of presidential electors. The Jacksonians shrewdly developed techniques to win this broader electorate. But the most notable political innovation of the Jackson period, the national convention, initially a democratic way of capturing popular sentiment, was invented not by Democrats but by the Anti-Masonic Party in 1831. The Anti-Masons were a short-lived party opposing the fraternal order of Freemasonry, which had aroused suspicion with its secrets and its tight loyalties.

Foreign visitors such as the French writer Alexis de Tocqueville and the English writers Frances Trollope and Charles Dickens wrote with amazement of America's egalitarian social conditions. Recent historians have thought differently. Two million blacks were held as slaves. For most women, free blacks, Irish-Catholic immigrants, and many others, social and economic equality did not exist. Such important economic developments as the rise of the factory system and the transportation revolution were not affected much by Jackson's presidency. Many studies of social mobility indicate an increasingly less egalitarian society, urban elites growing in wealth while industrialism and mass immigration created new lower classes.

And yet people at the time believed that Jackson's eminence was linked to the "rise of the common man." Millions of Americans—for diverse and often conflicting reasons—could readily identify with him. It was a "Go Ahead" era, remarked one observer; "the whole continent presents a scene of *scrambling* and roars with greedy hurry." And some saw in Jackson the egalitarian spirit of the nation; he was a child of the frontier, self-made, independent, and democratic. They gloried in his success and hoped to imitate it. As a big loser in the Panic of 1819, this pursuer of his own debtors appealed to hard-pressed debtors in the West and South. His opposition to the older entrenched banking system got him support from businessmen who wanted banks that would extend credit more freely. Others, looking back romantically to what they thought of as a simpler agrarian society, perceived Jackson as a simple and noble embodiment of that earlier time.

Parties and the Republic

In their opposition to political parties, what the first republicans had feared were not the nationwide institutions that today go by the name. In the eighteenth century, these did not exist, though the Federalists and the Jeffersonian Republicans foreshadowed them. "Party," in the thinking of early Americans, referred to groups of politicians in pursuit of some narrow objective. The parties that took form in the 1820s under the superintendence of such political artisans as Martin Van Buren were essentially new. Both in sustaining eighteenth-century republicanism and departing from it, that new party system was equivalent to what was also happening in economics, industry, and civic life.

The contribution that the new structured parties made to the republican principles of an earlier time is simply stated. It drew to the polls a larger percentage of the population than had before voted. Neither the possession nor the exercise of the vote had been so important to traditional republicans as has sometimes been thought. The practice of farming or a trade, the raising of a family, perhaps even the public expression of an opinion: these were more solid expressions of republican civic responsibility than the mere casting of a ballot. But voting is at least the simplest gesture of citizenship. To that extent the new party politics, which presented issues to voters, mobilized them, and got them to the polls, extending the implications of the republic of 1776.

The parties emergent during the 1820s, however, also had a place in the alteration of the old republican concept of personal and civic virtue. They signified what in reality had been the case from the beginning: that American politics were to be not a stately, ritualistic maintainance of a status quo but a ceaseless forging and winning of reformist programs. In this they resembled the industrial enterprises intended to transform the physical world, and the reform movements, soon to appear in abundance, that aimed to transform social relations and, in some cases, the human soul.

Suggested Readings

On politics, see Mary M. W. Hargreaves, *The Presidency of John Quincy Adams* (1985) and Ralph Ketcham, *Presidents Above Party: The First American Presidency, 1789–1829* (1984). On the fateful beginnings of slavery as a political issue see Randolph B. Campbell, *An Empire for Slavery: The Peculiar Institution in Texas, 1821–1825* (1989) and Robert McColley, *Slavery and Jeffersonian Virginia* (1964).

On the changing history of the American West see Richard White, *"It's Your Misfortune and None of My Own": A History of the American West* (1991), Patricia Nelson Limerick, *The Legacy of Conquest: The Unbroken Past of the American West* (1987), Julie R. Jeffrey, *Frontier Women: The Trans-Mississippi West, 1840–1880* (1979), Annette Kolodny's *The Land Before Her: Fantasy and Experience on the American Frontiers* (1984), and June Nmias, *White Captives: Gender and Ethnicity on the American Frontier* (1993). See also *The History of the Westward Movement* (1978) by Frederick W. Merk and Ray Allen Billington's *Westward Expansion* (rev. 1974). See also Malcolm J.

Rohrbough, *The Land Office Business: The Settlement and Administration of American Public Lands, 1789–1837* (1968) and John Mack Faragher, *Sugar Creek: Life on the Illinois Prairie* (1986).

On population shifts, there are Richard H. Easterlin, *Population, Labor Force, and Long Swings in Economic Growth* (1968) and Robert Riegal and R. G. Athearn, *America Moves West* (1964).

On other issues of this period see Ernest R. May, *The Making of the Monroe Doctrine* (1975), Harry Ammon, *James Monroe: The Quest for National Identity* (1971), George Dangerfield, *The Awakening of American Nationalism* (1965), Glover Moore, *The Missouri Compromise* (1953), Richard Wade, *The Urban Frontier* (1964), Stuart Blumin, *The Emergence of the Middle Class: Social Experience in the American City* (1989), and David Roediger, *The Wages of Whiteness: Race and the Making of the American Working Class* (1991).

North vs. South: A Clash of Cultures?

Edward Pessen

Several historians have recently argued that the Old South, though influenced by modern capitalism, belonged (as do early modern India and Saudi Arabia, among others) to the category of "premodern" societies that have been the economic and political dependencies of the dynamic industrial world that exploits them. The antebellum South's banking, commercial, and credit institutions did not in this view manifest the section's own capitalistic development so much as they served to facilitate the South's exploitation by the "capitalistic world market." . . .

[But] capitalism is not a rigid system governed by uniform economic practices, let alone inflexible definitions. The economy of the antebellum United States, like capitalistic economies in Victorian England and other nations, was composed of diverse elements, each playing a part in a geographical and functional division of labor within the larger society. Southern planters had the attitudes and goals and were guided by the classic practices of capitalistic businessmen. The antiurbanism and antimaterialism that [Eugene D.] Genovese has attributed to the great planters is unconvincing because they are thinly documented and contradicted by much other evidence. Some people, including planters themselves, may have likened the planter class to a seigneurial aristocracy. Unlike the lords of the textbook manor, however, Southern planters depended heavily on outside trade, participated enthusiastically in a money economy, and sought continuously to expand their operations and their capital. . . .

The Southern economy did differ in important respects from the Northern, developing special interests of its own. Yet, far from being in any sense members of a colony or dependency of the North, the Southern upper classes enjoyed close ties with the Northern capitalists who were, in a sense, their business partners. The South was an integral component of a wealthy and dynamic national economy, no part of which conformed perfectly to a textbook definition of pure capitalism. In part because of the central place in that economy of its great export crop, cotton, the South from the 1820s to the 1860s exerted a degree of influence over the nation's domestic and foreign policies that was barely equalled by the antebellum North. The South's political system of republicanism and limited democracy, like its hierarchical social structure, conformed closely to the prevailing arrangements in the North, as they also did to the classic features of a capitalistic order.

The antebellum North and South were far more alike than the conventional scholarly wisdom has led us to believe. Beguiled by the charming version of Northern society and politics composed by Tocqueville, the young Marx, and other influential antebellum commentators, historians have until recently believed that the Northern social structure was far more egalitarian and offered far greater opportunity for upward social movement than did its Southern counterpart and that white men of humble position had far more power in the Old North than they did in the Old South. In disclosing that the reality of the antebellum North fell far short of the egalitarian ideal, modern studies of social structure sharply narrow the gulf between the antebellum North and South. Without being replicas of one another, both sections were relatively rich, powerful, aggressive, and assertive communities, socially stratified and governed by equally—and disconcertingly—oligarchic internal arrangements. That they were drawn into the most terrible of all American wars may have been due, as is often the case when great powers fight, as much to their similarities as to their differences. The war owed more, I believe, to the inevitably opposed but similarly selfish interests—or perceived interests—of North and South than to differences in their cultures and institutions.

Late in the Civil War, William King of Cobb County, Georgia, reported that invading Union officers had told him, "We are one people, [with] the same language, habits, and religion, and ought to be one people." The officers might have added that on the spiritual plane Southerners shared with Northerners many ideals and aspirations and had contributed heavily to those historical experiences the memory and symbols of which tie a people together as a nation. For all of their distinctiveness, the Old South and North were complementary elements in an American society that was everywhere primarily rural, capitalistic, materialistic, and socially stratified, racially, ethnically, and religiously heterogeneous, and stridently chauvinistic and expansionist—a society whose practice fell far short of, when it was not totally in conflict with, its lofty theory.

Reprinted by permission from "How Different from Each Other Were the Antebellum North and South?" *American Historical Review,* 86 (December 1980).

The Jacksonian Era 1828–1840

THE TRAIL OF TEARS

Early in 1837 about six hundred Cherokee Indians were removed by United States government policy from their home in the southeastern United States to land in present-day Oklahoma under the Treaty of New Echota (1836). Along with them on their journey through Kentucky, Illinois, Missouri, and Arkansas went oxen, horses, and slaves. Had this been the general story of the Cherokee migration, its path would not be known today as the Trail of Tears. But it is not the whole story.

The second wave of Indians had a wretched time of it. Traveling much of the way by water, they were subject to a range of sicknesses. The mass of the Cherokee population in the East, preferring to remain in old Cherokee country, was meanwhile victimized by a policy so harsh that even some of the soldiers assigned to carrying it out were unhappy at their task. General Winfield Scott, whose historical misfortune it is to have been associated with the removal itself, showed in various kindnesses to his charges his own discomfort at their plight.

Soldiers, some of them acting with a brutality that Scott had warned them against, seized some thirteen thousand Indians, plucking families from their cabins, and put them in stockades where for months they endured overcrowding, illness, and the psychological pains of uprooting. Then in separate groups army escorts accompanied them westward in 1838. They had scarcely

HISTORICAL EVENTS

1828
Tariff of 1828 • Calhoun writes
Exposition and Protest

1829
Senator Foote proposes limiting sale
of public lands

1830
Jackson vetoes bill for interstate
turnpike • Indian Removal Act

1831
Cherokee Nation v. Georgia
• first nationwide presidential
nominating convention

1832
Tariff of 1832 • Bad Axe Massacre
• *Worcester v. Georgia* • Charter
of the Second Bank of the United
States • Jackson reelected

1833
Force Bill • Compromise Tariff

1836
Specie Circular • government
deposits in state banks • Martin Van
Buren elected President

continued

HISTORICAL EVENTS

1837
Panic of 1837 • *Charles River Bridge v. Warren Bridge*

1838
Trail of Tears

1840
Independent Treasury Bill • William Henry Harrison elected President

1841
Bankruptcy Act of 1841

One survivor remembered of "The Trail of Tears":

"One each day, and all are gone. Looks like maybe all be dead before we get to new Indian country, but always we keep marching on. Women cry and make sad wails. Children cry, and many men cry, and all look sad when friends die, but they say nothing and just put heads down and keep on go toward west. . . . She [his mother] speak no more; we bury her and go on."

One spokesman argued in the Indians' behalf:

"Do the obligations of justice change with the color of the skin? As the tide of our population has rolled on, we have added purchase to purchase [of Indian lands]. The confiding Indian listened to our professions of friendship: we called him brother, and he believed us. Millions after millions he has yielded to our importunity, until we have acquired more than can be cultivated in centuries—and yet we crave more. We have crowded the tribes upon a few miserable acres on our southern frontier; it is all that is left to them of their once boundless forests: and still, like the horse-leech, our cupidity cries, 'give! give!' "

enough supplies to carry them through. Sickness followed the migrants during a brutally cold winter. Of all the Cherokee who were subject to removal, about three to four thousand died in stockades or on the trail.

How did such inequalities in conditions come to the Cherokee people? The Cherokee had originally lived in a roughly egalitarian society. Law and coercion in a European sense were entirely absent, and women were not excluded from positions of leadership, including war councils. The Cherokee lived for war. A white account reports that when the English in 1730 urged them to make peace with the Tuscarora, the Cherokee replied that then they would merely have to make war on someone else. Frontiersmen found the Cherokee prone to savagery and bloodlust; the Indians found the frontiersmen insatiably land-hungry. Both judgments got it right.

The new American government faced genuine dilemmas after winning independence. Committed to a respect for the individual and communal rights of everyone except slaves, and recognizing that frontiersmen were no better for the welfare of Indians than Indians had been for the safety of the white frontier, the government reasoned that removal to a land of their own might be good for the tribes. Besides, whites kept encroaching on Cherokee and other Indian lands, and the government had to recognize that for practical purposes the old tribal territories were shrinking. Americans of that age believed that land and other resources should be so worked as to support as many people as possible. Southern states, moreover, were not eager to accept Indians as citizens. From Jefferson's time onward the government had been urging the Indian tribes to sell their lands and migrate westward.

In a string of dealings, Washington won land cessions from the Cherokee Nation, typically in exchange for relief from debts. Thereafter the government urged the Cherokee and other Indians to move west. At the same time it was contradictorily advocating that they adopt in their present locations the ways of white agriculture and industry. Missionaries would set up schools for young people of both genders, teaching them farming and industrial techniques. The Cherokee Nation made major progress against illiteracy, aided by the Indian alphabet devised by the famous Sequoyah.

In 1829 Andrew Jackson, who had commanded Cherokee troops during the War of 1812 but was known to be no friend to their claims, became President. At the end of the year Georgia passed a series of laws seizing part of Cherokee territory. Much of American public sentiment was now recoiling from the policy of Jackson and Georgia. In *Worcester v. Georgia*, the Supreme Court in 1832 in effect found Georgia to be illegally superseding federal jurisdiction over the Cherokee. The case seemed to be a victory for the Nation, but President Jackson's unwillingness to force Georgia to cease interfering with Cherokee affairs made it irrelevant. A well-known but unverifiable story is that the President remarked, "John Marshall has made his decision. Now let him enforce it."

In the next few years, unanimity within the Nation shattered. What happened is that the transformation from a simple tribal existence to a more energetic pursuit of farming, the crafts, and lawmaking brought with it the visions, the arguments, and the divisions of modern society. In its past already distant by the 1830s, the tribe had relied on a single activity, that of making war. Now the Cherokee had a class structure based in wealth and indirectly in race: mixed bloods, whose white ancestors had passed on their property and education, had the best opportunities. A number of prosperous mixed bloods were declaring their support of emigration. The simplest explanation is that the Indian supporters of removal believed it was in the interest of all Cherokee to submit to inevitability and get the best possible deal from the government. One point is certain: Whatever their larger motives, the advocates of removal brought about a fraudulent arrangement. Presenting themselves—without tribal wish or authorization—as the representatives of the Cherokee Nation, they effected with the federal government the agreement for removal.

Sequoyah (1770?–1843) devised the Cherokee written alphabet in the early nineteenth century. (*Courtesy, Library of Congress*)

Removal of Indians

The Indian Removal Act (1830)

For some time, white Americans had been considering the idea of removing eastern Indians to the West. President Thomas Jefferson had supported such a scheme, and the establishment of an "Indian country" beyond the Mississippi River was one reason for the Louisiana Purchase of 1803. While greed for land was a primary consideration, "removal" was not merely a malicious assault on Indian land titles. Many people, including President Andrew Jackson himself, believed that the removal policy was the only way of saving Indians from extermination. As long as they remained on land coveted by white settlers, their lives were in danger, and as long as they even lived in relatively close proximity to white communities, they would be ravaged by disease, alcoholism, and poverty. Removal would insulate them from the worst features of white civilization. An assimilationist rhetoric also supported the idea of removal. Protestant missionary groups interested in proselytizing and "civilizing" the Indians believed that if the Indians were living in relatively secure places, the opportunities to teach them the virtues of Christianity, agriculture, and the nuclear family life would improve greatly. So while white settlers were clamoring for removal in order to

General Scott threatened:

"The full moon of May is already on the wane, and before another has passed away, every Cherokee man, woman, and child must be in motion to join their brethren in the far west. . . . My troops already occupy many positions in the country that you are to abandon; thousands and thousands are approaching from every quarter, to render resistance and escape alike hopeless. Will you, then, by resistance, compel us to resort to arms? God forbid! Or will you, by flight, seek to hide yourselves in mountains and forests, and thus oblige us to hunt you down? I am an old warrior, and have been present at many a scene of slaughter; but spare me, I beseech you, the horror of witnessing the destruction of the Cherokees."

free up valuable land for settlement, Protestant churches were supporting those demands for humane reasons. Still other whites opposed removal altogether.

Since Jefferson's time the government had been forcing the Indian tribes to sell their lands and migrate westward. In 1830 the President urged Congress to set apart "an ample district west of the Mississippi" for their permanent use. Here the "aborigines" might learn "the arts of civilization" and form "an interesting commonwealth, destined to perpetuate the race and to attest the humanity and justice of this government." Senators such as Theodore Frelinghuysen of New Jersey courageously defended the right that Indians possessed by "immemorial possession, as the original tenants of the soil," but the Indian Removal Act passed anyway. The Act provided for the relocation of most tribes in the eastern United States to reservations west of the Mississippi River. Some tribes, particularly the remnants of the Iroquois Confederacy, were allowed to remain on reservations in the East. But the rest of the Indians were not so fortunate. In the following years many Indian nations, recognizing the futility of resistance, signed over their lands and moved west, some of them prodded by the federal army.

Resistance and Resignation   Although disunited and demoralized by defeat, some Indians did not passively acquiesce in the march westward. In Illinois portions of the Sauk and Fox tribes, led by Chief Black Hawk, refused to leave their rich ancestral lands. Black Hawk initially hoped that, if his people remained peaceful, they would be permitted to keep their farming communities and live alongside the incoming whites. But land hunger on the part of whites and incessant military pressure finally forced Black Hawk into war. It was a one-sided fight. In the final battle of the Black Hawk War, the Bad Axe Massacre of 1832, regular troops and militiamen killed between 400 and 500 Indian men, women, and children. In the South, the Seminole War that lasted from 1835 to 1838 was even bloodier. Many Seminole tribesmen, led by Chief Osceola, refused to leave Florida. Accompanied by runaway blacks, they retreated into the swamps. Jackson sent troops, but the Indians conducted a skillful guerrilla war in the impenetrable Everglades. It took several years and $14 million even partially to subdue Osceola's warriors.

Other Trails of Tears   The Choctaws, who like the Chickasaws and the Cherokees were a settled people skilled in agriculture, were forced out of Mississippi in the dead of winter, "thinly clad and without moccasins." In 1838 the government forcibly removed the Potawatomis from Indiana. They began the trek west "under a blazing noonday sun, amidst clouds of dust, marching in a line, surrounded by soldiers who were hurrying their steps. Next came the baggage wagons, in which numerous invalids, children, and women, too weak to walk, were crammed." Dozens died along this "Trail of Death." The resettlement of these farming Indians west of the Mississippi River created bitter resentment among the Plains tribes who hunted there. The government was soon forced to send troops to the West to separate the warring peoples.

Andrew Jackson's Inaugural

In the winter of 1828–29 Washington, D.C., was a cheerless place. The weather was dreadful: "snow storm after snow storm—the river frozen up, and the poor suffering the extremity of cold and hunger," wrote Margaret Bayard Smith, a resident who has left us the most vivid account of Washington in the winter of Jackson's inauguration. Even the supporters of the victorious Andrew Jackson were subdued. With their leader in mourning over the recent death of his wife, Rachel, Democrats avoided putting on too boisterous a display of pleasure over their triumph.

Jackson decreed a sober and dignified inauguration: he would have no military parades, no pre-inaugural festivities. Like Jefferson, he would walk to the Capitol to take the oath, then proceed to the presidential mansion on horseback. Margaret Smith approved Jackson's "avoidance of all parade—it is *true* greatness, which needs not the aid of ornament and pomp," but wished that "the good old gentleman might indulge himself with a carriage." But some 20,000 people of every class and from every section of the country flooded into the capital to witness the inauguration of the "people's President." It was "like the inundation of the northern barbarians into Rome," wrote one haughty Washingtonian, "save that the tumultuous tide came in from [all points] of the compass."

The sun finally shone on March 4, and tens of thousands of citizens gathered for the oath-taking. The spectacle reflected the fondest hopes of ardent Democrats. People "without distinction of rank" stood "silent, orderly and tranquil" to glimpse Jackson—who could be picked out from the crowd around him because he alone wore no hat—a servant of the sovereign people: "There, there, that is he." "Which?" "He with the white head." "Ah, there is the old man and his gray hair, there is the old veteran, there is Jackson."

Jackson, in a low voice that only a handful of the massed thousands could have heard, delivered his inaugural address, which John Quincy Adams described as "short, written with some eloquence, and remarkable chiefly for a significant threat of reform." Then, in a scramble of people that suggested to some the mobs of the French Revolution, but to a modern observer would seem reasonably orderly, farmers, politicians, women, children, carts, wagons, horses, and carriages followed the silver-haired hero down Pennsylvania Avenue to the official reception. Once there they jammed inside hoping to pump the President's hand and share his offering of ice cream, cake, lemonade, and orange punch that had been intended only for the eligible social elite of Washington.

It was a physical impossibility. Ladies fainted from the press; in the grab for refreshments glasses and china broke, people's clothing got ripped, fights broke out; strong men had to cordon off the frail President to prevent injury by exuberant well-wishers. To thin the crowd inside the house, alert servants began carrying tubs of rum punch onto the lawn. The event passed off with nothing worse than mudprints on the furniture (anything to catch a glimpse of Old Hickory) and broken plates and cups. It was not a party anyone would want to repeat, but neither

Asher Durand conveys Andrew Jackson's willfulness by giving attention to his angular nose and jaw; even his swept-back hair stands at attention. (*Courtesy, Historical Pictures Service, Chicago*)

A Washingtonian wrote this account of Jackson's inaugural party:

"The *Majesty of the People* had disappeared, and a rabble, a mob, of boys, negros, women, children, scrambling, fighting, romping. What a pity, what a pity! No arrangements had been made, no police officers placed on duty and the whole house had been inundated by the rabble mob. We came too late. The President, after having been *literally* nearly pressed to death and almost suffocated and torn to pieces by the people in their eagerness to shake hands with Old Hickory, had retreated through the back way or south front and had escaped to his lodgings at Gadsby's. Cut glass and china to the amount of several thousand dollars had been broken in the struggle to get the refreshments, punch and other articles carried out in tubs and buckets, but had it been in hogsheads it would have been insufficient. . . . Ladies fainted, men were seen with bloody noses and such a scene of confusion took place as is impossible to describe,— those who got in could not get out by the door again, but had to scramble out of windows."

was it the opening scene of a social revolution. The product of happenstance, of poor planning, the inaugural party spoke as much of the American people's instinctive good-natured sense of order as it did of their new sense that the President's home and the President now belonged to them.

The character of the newly elected representative of the people illustrates the elusive nature of American democracy. Of humble origins, Jackson was nonetheless by this time clearly a member of the patrician class: a slaveholder, a commander of troops, the master of a large and gracious estate. Even his simple manners, which had the politically useful look of democracy, could as easily present itself as the plain direct demeanor appropriate to a military aristocracy. Americans have thought themselves committed to democracy. They have also wisely or absentmindedly neglected to establish any rigorous test of what properly constitutes a democracy or its leadership.

Van Buren vs. Calhoun

John C. Calhoun. As Vice President, Calhoun worked against Jackson, especially during the controversy over a state's right to nullify a federal law that infringed on its sovereignty. *(Courtesy, Collection of the Corcoran Gallery of Art)*

The coalition that elected Andrew Jackson in 1828 was a makeshft. Immediately after the election a struggle broke out between two of its major figures, Martin Van Buren and John C. Calhoun. The clash between these two intensely ambitious men was inevitable.

Usually dressed in black, Calhoun with his great eyes glowing looked as though his face were consumed by inner fires. Having already suffered one setback in his quest for the presidency, Calhoun accepted another vice-presidential term in 1828, with the firm expectation of succeeding Jackson in 1832.

In Martin Van Buren, Calhoun met his equal. This shrewd New Yorker was one of the nation's first professional politicians. Starting as a lawyer in his hometown of Kinderhook, Van Buren had climbed the political ladder rung by rung: county surrogate, state senator, state attorney general, United States senator. He fashioned a powerful political machine in New York, known as the Albany Regency, which dispensed patronage, subsidized friendly newspapers, ran campaigns, and set the party line. Van Buren usually worked invisibly, trying to mold a consensus toward his own ends. Whenever possible, he avoided controversial commitments. He had managed "to be on circuit" in 1820 when a meeting was called at Albany to endorse the prohibition of slavery in Missouri; he was accompanying "a friend on a visit to the Congressional Cemetery" during a key vote on the tariff in 1827. Enemies considered Van Buren devious, opportunistic, hypocritical; admirers nicknamed him the Red Fox and the Little Magician.

In 1828 Van Buren helped to bring the Old Republicans into the Jackson camp and worked tirelessly for the general's election. Jackson rewarded Van Buren's efforts by making him secretary of state. Otherwise, the new Cabinet was undistinguished. Jackson had no intention of calling on it for advice or of allowing powerful figures like Calhoun to undermine his own power. Instead, he relied on an informal circle of political cronies, who came to be called the Kitchen Cabinet. Besides old Tennessee friends like Major William B. Lewis, who actually roomed at the White House, this group included several newspaper editors and, before long, even Van Buren, who took up horsemanship in order to accompany the President on his morning rides.

The Peggy Eaton Affair   Calhoun fretted over these signs of Van Buren's growing influence. The Vice President had hoped to control the Cabinet appointments, and especially to make a South Carolinian secretary of war. But Jackson appointed to that position another old Tennessee friend, John H. Eaton. Calhoun was humiliated, and to reassert his power, he set out to force Eaton from the Cabinet. An opportunity soon appeared. The secretary of war had recently married the notorious Peggy O'Neale Timberlake, a Washington tavern-keeper's daughter with a dubious reputation. Eaton had lived with her while she was married to John Timberlake, a navy officer, and it was said that he even used his influence to have Timberlake sent to sea. After Timberlake's death, Eaton married Peggy with Jackson's blessing. Washington society hummed with scandal. An English diplomat described one of Mrs. Eaton's antagonists in the "Ladies' War" as having "worn the enamel off of her teeth by the slander of her tongue." The other Cabinet wives, led by the aristocratic Mrs. Calhoun, refused to receive Peggy socially.

The President, recalling the slander heaped on his own wife, was sympathetic to the Eatons. "I tell you," roared the Old General, "I had rather have live vermin on my back than the tongue of one of these Washington women on my reputation." Jackson had a tendency to personalize issues, to make them death struggles with a hated foe. Calhoun, he announced, was trying "to weaken me . . . and open the way to his preferment on my ruin." He summoned a special Cabinet meeting to examine the evidence, then pronounced Peggy "chaste as a virgin," and demanded that she be treated with respect. When most of the Cabinet refused, further meetings were suspended. Only Van Buren, long a widower, accepted Mrs. Eaton as a respectable lady.

This petty struggle dragged on into 1831. Finally, to break the deadlock, Van Buren and Eaton offered their resignations. This calculated gesture gave Jackson a chance to reorganize his Cabinet. He asked the other secretaries to resign and replaced them with loyal followers. As a reward, Jackson nominated the faithful Van Buren to be minister to Great Britain. In December, when Congress reconvened, Calhoun plotted revenge. A tie vote in the Senate allowed him, as Vice President, to cast the deciding vote, and he gleefully spiked Van Buren's nomination. "It will kill him dead, sir, kill him dead," Calhoun gloated. "He will never kick, sir, never kick." But others agreed with Missouri Senator Thomas Hart Benton, who replied, "You have broken a minister, and elected a vice-president."

Benton was right. The President had suspected for some time that it was Calhoun who had urged Monroe's Cabinet in 1818 to censure Jackson's Florida raid. During the Peggy Eaton controversy Calhoun's old enemy, William H. Crawford, provided proof of Calhoun's complicity. Hastily, the Vice President published a pamphlet disclosing the feuds within the administration. When Jackson saw it, his well-known

The British traveler Harriet Martineau would describe the gaunt Calhoun as

"the cast-iron man, who looks as if he had never been born and never could be extinguished. . . . His mind has long since lost all power of communicating with any other. I know of no man who lives in such utter intellectual solitude. He meets men, and harangues them by the fireside as in the Senate; he is wrought like a piece of machinery."

temper flared. "They have cut their own throats," he said of Calhoun and his allies. Van Buren's triumph was complete. He would be Jackson's successor.

Jackson and States' Rights

For years Van Buren had worked to build a political alliance between North and South, stressing principles of laissez-faire and states' rights. He sought particularly to avoid conflicts over the slavery issue, fearing the rise of an antislavery party in the North, and to find a compromise on the tariff. Pennsylvania Democrats desired a protective tariff—a tariff high enough that it would protect American manufactured goods by pushing the price of imported goods beyond the level at which they could compete—while southern party voters demanded free trade. Van Buren's efforts to reconcile the two sections marked his early career, as opposition to southern slavery would define him later.

Calhoun, who also advocated states' rights and limited government, had as much taste for confrontation as did Van Buren for compromise. The South Carolinian, increasingly the champion of southern rights, believed that only a party dominated by southerners could protect the South. During Jackson's first term, he and his followers worked in Congress to create an alliance between South and West based on a program of cheap land for the West and a tariff kept low in the interest of the South. The political maneuvering soon provoked a great national debate on the nature of the federal Union.

Those who argued for states' rights denounced Jackson as "King Andrew" who stomped on the rights of the states. *(Courtesy, Hugh Cleland Collection)*

Public Lands   Late in 1829 Senator Samuel A. Foote of Connecticut proposed a resolution of inquiry into limiting the sale of public lands. Senator Benton of Missouri promptly denounced Foote's resolution as a plot by eastern manufacturers to prevent their workers from migrating to the West. Robert Y. Hayne, a debonair young senator from South Carolina, supported Benton and spoke vigorously in favor of a cheap land policy. Continued large revenues from land sales, he warned, would be used to create a powerful and tyrannical government; they would be "a fund for corruption—fatal to the sovereignty and independence of the states. . . ."

Webster vs.   Daniel Webster of Massachusetts rose to answer
Hayne   both Benton and Hayne. The New Englander was one of the great orators and constitutional lawyers of the day. Deliberately goading Hayne, Webster claimed that the South Carolinian's appeals to state sovereignty were equivalent to preaching disunion. In January 1830 Hayne, with Calhoun's coaching, rose to the challenge. He vigorously defended the right of a state to nullify a federal law that violated "the sovereignty and independence of the states." New Englanders, he reminded Webster pointedly, had been "not unwilling to adopt" this same doctrine at Hartford in 1814, "when they believed themselves to be the victims of unconstitutional legislation."

The next day, before a packed gallery, Webster answered Hayne. The people, Webster contended, and not the states, had formed the

Constitution. They, and not the individual states, were sovereign. If each of the states could defy the laws of Congress at will, the Union would be a mere "rope of sand." The Union was "a copious fountain of national, social, and personal happiness," and the individual states and sections should subordinate their selfish interests to the common good. Webster closed with a moving appeal, memorized by later generations of school children: "Liberty *and* Union, now and forever, one and inseparable!"

Jackson vs. Calhoun   Webster had voiced the feelings of a generation of Americans who believed that "while the Union lasts we have high, exciting, gratifying prospects spread out before us—for us and our children." Did Andrew Jackson share this vision? The President's answer came a few weeks later, at a Jefferson Day dinner. The exponents of nullification planned to use the celebration to advertise their views. Jackson, forewarned of their intentions, had prepared his toast in advance. When his turn came, the President, glaring at Calhoun, raised his glass and declared: "Our Federal Union—it must and shall be preserved." The boisterous crowd stood in deathly silence. The diminutive Van Buren had climbed onto a chair so as not to miss a moment of his triumph. Calhoun, his hand trembling so "that a little of the amber fluid trickled down the side" of his glass, replied: "The Union—next to our liberties most dear." There was no mistaking the President's words; despite his sympathy for states' rights, he would not countenance nullification. Calhoun was further discredited. Westerners scurried to the banner of Jackson and Van Buren.

Jackson, the most politically powerful champion of the federal Union, tried to balance the powers of the federal government and the rights of the states. In 1830, anxious to reassure the strict constructionists in the party, he vetoed a bill providing federal aid for the construction of a turnpike from Maysville to Lexington, Kentucky. This road lay entirely within a single state, and Jackson doubted the constitutionality of federally funding projects of a "purely local character." But well-publicized vetoes like this were the exception; at other times Jackson approved substantial amounts of federal aid for building roads and canals. During his presidency, appropriations for this purpose averaged over $1.3 million annually, nearly double that under Adams.

A Conflict of Interests

South Carolina and Nullification   South Carolina had once been rich. The mucky swamps of its low country were ideally suited for growing rice. After the invention of Whitney's gin, the Carolina upcountry became a major cultivator of cotton and for a time the little state produced half the nation's crop. Rejoicing in prosperity, South Carolinians shared fully in the nationalistic fervor of the early republic. Native sons like the Pinckneys, Calhoun, and Cheves served ably in the nation's councils.

Abruptly in 1819, the state's economic fortunes slid into decline. Falling world prices for cotton, coupled with increased competition from the newer states to the Southwest that could produce it more cheaply, wrecked the South Carolina cotton planters' economy. Their worn-out soils could not stand against the fertile lands of Alabama and Mississippi. Facing ruin, South Carolinians migrated westward by the thousands.

The Tariff   Those who remained increasingly fixed their frustration and anger on the protective tariff. When Congress began raising duties to protective levels, they objected angrily. Resentful at being deprived of the cheaper prices that foreign manufactured goods would have carried without the tariffs, South Carolinians also warned that foreign governments might retaliate by imposing high tariffs on American exports, such as cotton. In 1830 Congressman George McDuffie of South Carolina charged that higher prices ultimately cost the southern planter the equivalent of forty out of every one hundred bales of cotton produced. McDuffie and others exaggerated the tariff's pernicious effect on their economy, but protective duties were not in the interest of South Carolina.

In 1824 representatives from the manufacturing, grain, and wool states had pushed through a bill increasing duties on a wide variety of items. Flushed with victory, protectionists held a grand convention at Harrisburg, Pennsylvania, to map out a campaign for still higher duties. In the 1828 session of Congress, northern protectionists resorted to a trading of votes and programs that goes by the term logrolling. They persuaded members representing Missouri lead miners, Kentucky hemp raisers, Vermont wool growers, and Louisiana sugar planters to support higher rates on manufactured articles in exchange for protective duties on their own constituents' products.

Nullification   Recoiling from this "Tariff of Abominations," southerners threatened to boycott goods from the tariff states. Some began dressing in clothes of homespun, scorning northern broadcloth. Immediately after the tariff bill passed, the South Carolina delegation in Congress met at the home of Senator Robert Y. Hayne to plot resistance. In the fall of 1828 Vice President Calhoun set to work writing his famous *Exposition and Protest* developing the doctrine of nullification, which held that a state could prevent the exercise of a federal law within its borders.

By now Calhoun was revealing himself to be a relentlessly combative political philosopher, single-minded in his commitment to the doctrine of state sovereignty. Must South Carolina submit to the federal government? No, Calhoun insisted, and here, rather than on the tariff issue itself, his argument had its most ominous implications.

Prior to the formation of the Constitution, Calhoun observed, the states had been independent and sovereign. They had created the federal government and endowed it with strictly limited powers. A state therefore had the "right" to "interpose" its original sovereignty against the "despotism of the many," the sheer weight of a national majority. Thus a state could call a state convention and nullify any act of Congress that exceeded the authority granted by the Constitution.

Under the Constitution, Calhoun argued, Congress might tax for

---

By 1832 nullifiers like George McDuffie were spoiling for a fight. "South Carolina," he told Congress in a typical speech

"is oppressed (a thump). A tyrant majority sucks her life blood from her (a dreadful thump). Yes sir (a pause), yes, sir, a tyrant (a thump) majority unappeasable (horrid scream), has persecuted and persecutes us (a stamp on the floor). We appeal to them (low and quick), but we appeal in vain (loud and quick). We turn to our brethren of the North (low, with a shaking of the head), and pray them to protect us (a thump), but we t-u-r-n in v-a-i-n (prolonged, and a thump). They heap coals of fire on our heads (with immense rapidity)—they give us burden on burden; they tax us more and more (very rapid, slam-bang, slam—a hideous noise). We turn to our brethren of the South (slow with a solemn, thoughtful air). We work with them; we fight with them; we vote with them; we petition with them (common voice and manner); but the tyrant majority has no ears, no eyes, no form (quick), deaf (long pause), sightless (pause), inexorable (slow, slow). Despairing (a thump), we resort to the rights (a pause) which God (a pause) and nature [have] given us (thump, thump, thump). . . ."

purposes of raising revenue, but not to protect domestic industry against foreign competition. The Tariff of 1828 was therefore "unconstitutional, unequal, and oppressive." It made southerners "the serfs of the system—out of whose labor is raised, not only the money paid into the Treasury, but the funds out of which are drawn the rich rewards of the manufacturer and his associates in interest." A state, said Calhoun, could legitimately nullify the tariff.

Racial Fears   In 1828 Calhoun's remedy seemed too drastic for many Carolinians who still turned hopefully to Jackson. In the meantime, the nullifiers worked to strengthen their cause. They were aided by a deepening of racial fear in South Carolina, a state where in some areas slaves outnumbered whites by a ratio of eight to one. Denmark Vesey's revolt in their own state in 1822 and a rebellion in Virginia led by Nat Turner in 1831 left white southerners fearful for their property and lives. They blamed these events on the small but noisy antislavery movement. The bitter Missouri controversy had awakened slaveholders everywhere to the potential threat that the federal government posed to their peculiar institution. And so even those whites who had not suffered by the fall in cotton prices embraced the doctrine of nullification as offering a constitutional protection against the growing antislavery movement.

The Ordinance of Nullification   By 1832 Jackson and his party, faced with an impending election, were determined to reform the Tariff of Abominations. John Quincy Adams, newly elected to the House of Representatives and already the chair of the Committee on Manufacturing, would help. Adams realized that the tariff was a sectional rather than a party issue and accepted the political necessity of moderating the rates. So he cooperated with the administration in framing a bill that essentially repealed the increases of 1828 and restored the rates of the tariff of 1824. Jackson happily signed a lower tariff that provided a real measure of protection to northern manufacturers and also met the legitimate complaints of the South, or so he thought. John C. Calhoun did not agree. He had resigned as Vice President to lead the anti-protection battle in the Senate and was determined to press the issue even after the tariff of 1832 was passed.

In October, after a hard-fought contest, the nullification party elected an overwhelming majority to the South Carolina legislature. The governor immediately called the legislature into session, whereupon it authorized a state convention and a special election of delegates. On November 19, 1832, 136 nullifiers and 26 unionists met at Columbia, the state capital. The convention passed an Ordinance of Nullification declaring the tariffs of 1828 and 1832 unconstitutional, and null and void in South Carolina. The collection of duties by the federal government after February 1, 1833, was forbidden, unless Congress lowered the tariff to twelve percent. Any attempt by Washington to coerce the state, warned the Ordinance, would be "inconsistent with the longer continuance of South Carolina in the Union." The legislature, at its regular session in December, took steps to implement the Ordinance and appropriated money to buy arms and raise an army.

John C. Calhoun wrote:

"I never use the word 'nation' in speaking of the United States. I always use the word 'union' or 'confederacy.' We are not a nation, but a union, a confederacy of equal and sovereign states. . . ."

The Nullification Crisis threatened to tear the Union apart. This 1833 cartoon supporting Jackson portrays the South Carolina resolution as leading to civil war and despotism. *(Courtesy, The New York Public Library, Astor, Lenox and Tilden Foundations)*

The nullifiers soon discovered that they had penned themselves in. At home, a band of unionists prepared to resist their fellow Carolinians by force: both sides were soon drilling volunteers across the state. Neighboring slave states sympathized with South Carolina, but condemned her "reckless precipitancy." President Jackson was determined to uphold national authority. He reinforced federal installations in Charleston harbor and ordered General Winfield Scott to take charge of military preparations. The President's famous Nullification Proclamation of December 10, 1832—written by a southerner, Edward Livingston, of Louisiana—squarely repudiated the doctrine. American nationhood, Jackson asserted, had existed before the states; the Constitution only made more workable a preexisting Union. Under these circumstances, "to say that any state may at pleasure secede from the Union is to say that the United States is not a nation." The power of nullification was *"incompatible with the existence of the Union, contra-dicted expressly by the letter of the Constitution, unauthorized by its spirit, inconsistent with every principle on which it was founded, and destructive of the great object for which it was formed."* Disunion by armed force, Jackson concluded, was *"treason,"* in the face of which he, as President, could not "avoid the performance of his duty." On a trip to New York City, greeted enthusiastically by a corps of state militia, Jackson announced *"Nullification will never take root* HERE."

The Compromise Tariff of 1833   At the same time that he confronted the nullifiers, Jackson reached out to them. He urged Congress further to lower the tariff, limiting protection to articles essential to the nation's defense. In order to avoid a premature clash of arms, he removed federal troops from the Charleston Citadel to the forts in the harbor. Yet he also secured a Force Bill from Congress early in 1833, authorizing the collection of import duties from ships offshore and reaffirming his power to call up the state militias and to use the army and navy. Old Hickory had completely outmaneuvered the Carolina radicals. As the "Fatal First" of February approached, they prudently decided to delay enforcing nullification until Congress completed its deliberations on the tariff. Early in March 1833, Congress passed a compromise tariff, which provided that rates on protected articles would be lowered in gradual stages to twenty percent in mid-1842. Even though the new rates were eight percent higher than what the nullification ordinance had demanded, South Carolinians accepted the compromise figure with relief. The convention promptly rescinded the Ordinance of Nullification; then, as a symbolic gesture, it declared the Force Bill null and void.

South Carolina had lost. The passage of the compromise tariff was a signal triumph for nationalism. Nullification as a principle had been thoroughly discredited. In the process, South Carolinians had learned an unforgettable lesson: successful resistance to northern "tyranny" demanded the cooperation of the other slave states.

The Second Bank of the United States

Andrew Jackson brought with him to the White House a westerner's instinctive dislike of monopolies and entrenched privilege, and a vague distrust of banks and paper money. Beyond this, however, he had few ideas about economics; political needs shaped his tariff and internal improvement policies. But in his first message to Congress he sharply criticized the Bank of the United States for its failure to establish "a uniform and sound currency." He urged the lawmakers to consider carefully "the constitutionality and expediency" of renewing the Bank's charter at its expiration in 1836. Though his direct responsibility was to private stockholders, Nicholas Biddle's chief concern as the head of the Second Bank of the United States seemed to be the welfare of the country as a whole. He liked to boast that the institution was "the balance wheel of the banking system."

Troubles of the Bank Biddle's very success proved his undoing. Some people sincerely questioned the constitutionality or the wisdom of making an essentially private bank the depository of the public funds. Many still blamed the Bank for the Panic of 1819. Advocates of cheap money, most of them state bankers and speculators, objected to the Bank because it restrained the state banks from issuing notes as freely as they wished. At the other extreme partisans of hard money, believing that specie was the only safe currency, condemned all note-issuing banks—the National Bank among them—as instruments of speculation. Advocates of hard money were now employing the populistic rhetoric, spiced with denunciations of privileged wealth, that more often in American history, as in the case of Shays's Rebellion, has been the rhetoric of champions of cheap or paper currency. Banknotes, wrote one critic, formed "the foundation of *artificial* inequality of wealth, and, thereby, of *artificial* inequality of power."

The source of Jackson's own hostility to the Bank remains uncertain. He did not act in response to popular demand or on behalf of state banks. In spite of his well-known suspicion of banks and paper money, Old Hickory had kept his own money in the Bank's Washington and Nashville branches for years. Most likely, his antagonism stemmed from the uncontrolled political power of the Bank and its identification with unfriendly eastern interests. He readily believed the reports that some of the branches had worked against his election in 1828, and reached the conclusion that the Bank was a "hydra of corruption—dangerous to our liberties by its corrupting influence everywhere." He must, he decided, strip the "Monster" of its malign power. Once engaged in the contest, Jackson quickly turned the dispute into another death struggle between himself and a loathesome foe.

For a time Biddle tried to placate Jackson, but with no success. He then turned to the President's enemies for support. He extended generous loans to Clay, Webster, and other influential politicians and newspaper editors. In 1832 he reluctantly acquiesced in their plan to seek a recharter well in advance of the expiration date. It was an election year, and the Bank's friends reasoned that Jackson would hesitate before vetoing a recharter bill. If he did veto it, they would have a good issue in the presidential campaign.

The Bank War

The bill renewing the Bank's charter cleared Congress in July 1832, with nearly a third of the Democratic representatives voting in favor. Jackson was enraged. "The Bank," he told Van Buren, "is trying to kill me, *but I will kill it!*" Jackson was, he said, "as firm as the Rocky Mountain. . . . Providence has a power over me, but frail mortals . . . can have none." He sent the bill back to Congress with a blistering veto message in which he denounced the Bank as "not only unnecessary, but dangerous to the government and country." It enjoyed a virtual "monopoly of foreign and domestic exchange"; it threatened the rights of the states and the liberties of the people; it discriminated against the West. Refusing to be guided by the opinion of the Supreme Court in the *McCulloch* case,

Jackson declared the Bank unconstitutional: "The opinion of the judges has no more authority over Congress than the opinion of Congress has over the judges, and on that point the President is independent of both." One fourth of the Bank's stock was held by foreigners, the veto message observed; the country needed a *"purely American"* institution. Jackson closed with an impassioned attack on the renewal bill as an attempt by "the rich and powerful" to "bend the acts of government to their selfish purposes" and pledged to resist "the advancement of the few at the expense of the many."

Jackson vs. the Bank   The veto message was superb propaganda but poor economics. A developing country like the United States needed a stable currency to encourage foreign investment, not wildcat banking to drive it away. The Bank was not a monopoly. In 1830 it made about one-fifth of the nation's bank loans and had barely one-third of the total bank deposits and specie reserves held by American banks. In his message Jackson completely ignored the important services the Bank provided and offered no effective substitute for them.

At first, Jackson's enemies rejoiced over the message. Biddle compared the President to "a chained panther biting the bars of his cage" and called the veto "a manifesto of anarchy." But in November 1832 Jackson, with Van Buren as his running mate, overwhelmed the National Republican candidate, Henry Clay, by a margin of five to one in the electoral college.

Jackson took his decisive victory as a mandate to destroy the Bank even before its charter expired. As soon as the nullification crisis passed,

Anonymous, *Stage Coach*, nineteenth century. *(Courtesy, Museum of Fine Arts, Boston)*

he set out to remove the government deposits from the bank and place them in selected state banks. By law, it was the secretary of the treasury who had to give the actual order for removing them. When he refused, Jackson "promoted" him to the State Department and named a new treasury secretary. This official, too, refused to do Jackson's bidding, citing the "irresponsible" policies of the state banks. The President then replaced him with Roger B. Taney, formerly the attorney general. The faithful Taney continued drawing on the government's funds in the Bank to meet current expenses, but he began depositing the incoming receipts in certain state banks. These banks were supposedly chosen for their fiscal soundness, but political considerations were not overlooked. Prior to 1836 over seventy-five percent of the officers in these banks were Democrats. The administration's critics nicknamed them "pet banks."

As the government's deposits dwindled, Biddle began calling in loans and curtailing the issuing of new notes. In the beginning this contraction was thoroughly justifiable, since the federal deposits had given the notes much of their reliability. But Biddle soon succumbed to opportunistic motives. He continued the contraction into the spring of 1834, in the hope of producing a short recession that would force a recharter of the Bank. "Nothing but the evidence of suffering," he reasoned, would "produce any effect in Congress." As interest rates climbed and credit dried up, the business community begged for relief. All over the country supporters of the Bank organized meetings and flooded Congress with petitions. A Cincinnati man tried a more direct approach: "Damn your—soul," he wrote Jackson, "remove them deposits back again, and recharter the bank or you will certainly be shot in less than two weeks and that by myself!!!"

The Bank Closes Its Doors   Old Hickory refused to budge. Told of rumors that a mob threatened to "lay siege to the Capitol until the deposits were restored," he promised to hang the ringleaders "as high as Haman." When a delegation of businessmen visited him seeking relief, he replied coldly: "Go to the Monster, go to Biddle. . . . Biddle has all the money!" In the end Jackson had his way. Biddle was forced to let credit flow more freely, and the economy quickly recovered.

The chief result of the so-called "Biddle depression" was a marked decrease in the Bank's popularity. In 1836, when the old federal charter expired, the Bank received a new one from the state of Pennsylvania. In 1841, after a series of financial reverses, it closed its doors forever. Biddle died three years later, a broken man. Jackson had destroyed the Bank in the name of sound money and "those habits of economy and simplicity which are so congenial to the character of republicans." But in so doing he removed the most effective restraint on "the stock-jobbers, brokers, and gamblers" he professed to despise. Aided by the government deposits, the "pets" flooded the country with paper banknotes. An orgy of speculation and inflation followed. Belatedly, between 1834 and 1836, Jackson tried to drive paper money from circulation. He directed the deposit banks not to issue or receive notes worth less than $10. Land officers were instructed not to take small notes in payment for public lands. Jackson secured a law preventing deposit banks from issuing bills valued at under $20. Finally, in 1836, Jackson issued the Specie Circular, which prohibited the purchase of public lands in anything but coin. He acted too late. In 1837 bad money helped to plunge the country into its worst depression to date. Jackson had accused the Second Bank of being beyond federal control, but so were the state banks in which he had deposited federal revenues.

Boom and Bust

On March 4, 1837, Andrew Jackson turned over the presidency to Martin Van Buren. As the Old Hero left the Capitol, the crowds cheered him lustily. For once, remarked Thomas Hart Benton, "the rising was eclipsed by the setting sun." Even as Van Buren delivered his inaugural message, depression was clouding the country again.

Since the early 1820s the American economy had grown steadily. Demand for American agricultural products seemed insatiable: exports of cotton alone increased from 92 million pounds in 1818 to 300 million pounds in 1830. Moving these bulky products to market required the expenditure of immense sums on transportation projects of all kinds. Construction of turnpikes and bridges continued in most parts of the country, and steamboat building became an important industry. The success of the Erie Canal in New York State brought a time of canal building, even while more than three thousand miles of railroad were completed in the same period. And the construction boom went far beyond internal improvements: the rapid settlement of the West and the growth of urban areas created a great demand for new homes, barns, stores, and public buildings. Manufacturing industries, particularly cotton textiles, iron, and machinery, also grew rapidly.

Martin Van Buren of New York was one of the country's first professional politicians. His loyalty to the President won him the chance to succeed Jackson in that office. *(Courtesy, Scribner's Archives)*

The United States had long had a vigorous entrepreneurial tradition. Fathers in Boston during Jacksonian times guided sons on daily walks to the wharves, banks, and counting houses a few blocks from home. Eight-year-old Frank Appleton reported to his bank-president father that he had "laid out 1 cent for 8 marbles and one cent for 2 allies." As teenagers, William and Amos Lawrence kept strict accounts, heeding their parents' advice to record *"every cent* you receive, and *every cent you expend."* Western farms were now becoming more intent on making money by selling part of their crops than on raising produce for their own consumption. And westerners and southerners often opposed entrenched financial interests that prevented them from getting ahead.

Speculative Fever   But by the middle 1830s healthy growth was giving way to feverish speculation. Investors, most of them British, bought enormous quantities of stock in state-owned canal companies and other public works of increasingly doubtful utility and profitability. With labor and materials in short supply, these new construction projects merely drove up wages and prices. Sales of public land—mainly to speculators—rose from only $2,300,000 in 1830 to almost $25,000,000 in 1836. As speculators snapped up everything in sight, urban land values also soared. When Chicago was incorporated in 1833, optimists were already buying and selling lots twenty miles from

Lake Michigan. All over the West and South, farmers and planters plunged heavily into debt for land and slaves, sometimes borrowing at rates as high as thirty percent. The number of state banks rose from 330 in 1830 to 788 in 1837. Many were purely speculative ventures, deliberately located "out where the wildcats howled" on the assumption that there they could avoid holders of their notes seeking redemption in specie. Lax state laws permitted these "wildcat banks," as they were called, to issue banknotes without maintaining adequate specie reserves to back them up. The note circulation of state banks soared from $61 million in 1830 to $149 million in 1837.

The Panic of 1837

In 1837 the boom collapsed. The Specie Circular requiring all payments for public lands in gold or silver led banks in the West to draw heavily on eastern banks for coin. In the midst of this specie drain a recession in Britain depressed cotton prices, and British investors called in their loans. On May 10 New York banks suspended specie payments. Other banks followed. Prices fell and credit tightened: for speculators the only question, an observer wrote, "was as to the means of escape, and nearest and best route to Texas."

The depression that stretched from 1839 to 1843 was one of the severest in American history. Prices fell by as much as one-half in some places; real estate values and stocks declined even more drastically. The collapse of prices set off a wave of bankruptcies. Under the federal Bankruptcy Act of 1841, some 28,000 debtors freed themselves of nearly a half-billion dollars of debt. Rural areas were hardest hit, but they at least were self-sustaining. In the cities unemployment brought widespread distress.

Mobs in New York looted the flour stores in 1837 and similar violence flared elsewhere. Once again municipalities and charitable agencies set up soup kitchens and unemployment offices. Casting about for a more permanent solution to urban unemployment, the journalist Horace Greeley advised the unemployed to "go to the Great West, anything rather than remain here." Public land sales had plunged by 1842 to less than six percent of their 1836 peak. With land sales and tariff receipts declining, the federal government, which had been out of debt since 1835, began running a new deficit. The states, which had contracted nearly $200 million of debts, were especially hard-pressed. By 1842 eight of them had defaulted, and three had even repudiated part of their debt, thereby ruining American credit with European investors for years to come.

One faction in the Democratic Party favored banks and paper money, wanting the federal government to maintain some active role in managing the economy. Radicals, on the other hand, clung resolutely to hard money and would have the government do little in the economy except discourage banks from issuing paper notes. Van Buren decided to stick with Jackson's policies. He refused to repeal the Specie Circular. Calling Congress into special session, he blamed the depression on "excessive issues of bank paper" and "reckless speculation." Concerned about the growing strain on the federal Treasury, he asked Congress to authorize the borrowing of $10 million for current expenses. And he specifically recommended passage of a law permitting the federal government to keep its receipts in its own Treasury vaults, which would sever all connections with the nation's banks. Beyond this Van Buren refused to go. It was not the place of government, he insisted, to relieve economic distress. The framers of the Constitution had "wisely judged that the less government interfered with private pursuits the better for the general prosperity." Many of the states made at least some effort to relieve hunger and unemployment.

In spite of protests against leaving the people to survive on their own, most of Van Buren's program became law in 1837. The President's opponents concentrated their fire on the Independent Treasury Bill. This proposal would require customs collectors, postmasters, and other government receivers of funds to hold their receipts until ordered to pay them out. It would also direct the secretary of the treasury to withdraw the government's deposits from the "pet" banks and to place them in special subtreasuries. Opponents charged that the bill would curtail loans and credit, thereby stifling recovery. Van Buren's supporters countered that it would keep the government independent and the currency safe and check unwise expansion of bank notes. A coalition blocked the scheme until 1840, when it finally passed Congress. But the Democratic Party was now presiding over a depression, and that is never a good position for a party in power to occupy.

The Democrats vs. the Whigs

By the end of Andrew Jackson's second term in 1837, the Democratic Party had changed significantly. Gone was the diverse political coalition that had elected the Old Hero in 1828; its leadership now adhered to a fairly definite body of ideas. Government, the Jacksonians believed, should restrict its intervention in the economy to eliminating special privilege and monopoly, leaving a fair field for individual competition. Like Adam Smith, whose *Wealth of Nations* (1776) many of them had read, they believed that the power of the marketplace would best regulate the economy and distribute wealth equitably. Fearing that the rich would use the government for personal advantage, the Jacksonians advocated universal political freedom (for white men) and majority rule. Although recognizing the supremacy of the Union, Jacksonians respected states' rights, holding that federal authority should be kept within narrow bounds.

The party in the late 1830s and 1840s was much influenced by the Locofocos, a powerful Democratic splinter group in New York. These dissidents—who took their name from a type of friction match they had used to light candles when rival Democrats tried to disrupt one of their meetings by turning off the gas lights—opposed monopoly in any form. They denounced banks and corporations, demanding a return to hard money and the abolition of laws allowing limited liability for stockholders. They advocated free trade, labor unions, free public education, and abolition of imprisonment for debt.

Chief Justice Roger Taney. A former secretary of the treasury under Jackson, Taney succeeded John Marshall in 1836. *(Courtesy, Library of Congress)*

Chief Justice Roger Taney   The decisions of the Supreme Court in the late 1830s reflected Democratic thinking. During his two terms, Jackson appointed seven associate justices. And when Chief Justice John Marshall died in 1835, the President named Roger B. Taney (pronounced "tawny") to succeed him. Under Taney's leadership the Court showed a less rigid respect for private property rights as against the rights of popular majorities, and had more regard for states' rights.

In the *Charles River Bridge* case of 1837 the Court again took up the question posed in the 1819 *Dartmouth College* case of whether a state could alter an agreement with a private corporation. The Massachusetts legislature had incorporated the Charles River Bridge Company to operate a toll bridge under a long-term contract. Later it authorized another corporation to build a bridge over the Charles River at a point nearby that would in twenty years become toll free. The older company sought an injunction, contending that the second charter constituted a breach of contract. Taney sided with Massachusetts. The great object of government, he declared, was "to promote the happiness and prosperity of the community." In a collision between the rights of private property and those of the community, the rights of the people came first. The Court could not consent, Taney said, to take away from the states "any portion of that power over their own internal police and improvement, which is so necessary to their well being and prosperity." Denounced by conservatives as a blow to business and the sanctity of contract, the decision was in fact liberating. The young American economy would have been greatly handicapped if established companies had been able to maintain monopolies and choke off competition. Taney's opinion opened the way for a host of developments in industry and transportation.

Two years later, in *Bank of Augusta v. Earle,* the Court enlarged state powers again. Here Taney rejected the claim of a Georgia bank that under the federal Constitution a corporation, like a citizen, could automatically enter another state and engage in business there. Though in the absence of positive legislation a company might do business in another state, said Taney, that state had the power to exclude the corporation if it wished. In the wake of this decision, many states enacted regulatory laws for outside corporations. On the whole, they were socially beneficial, since there was as yet virtually no federal regulation of interstate commerce.

Rising Opposition to the Jacksonians   The Democratic appeals for strict economy, equal rights, and the abolition of government favors appealed to popular sentiments. By the late 1830s there was some truth in Jackson's claim that his party represented the "farmers, mechanics, and laborers." It especially attracted people who resented the privileges that established bankers and tariff-protected businessmen enjoyed; people who had been affected adversely by changing patterns of transportation and trade; ordinary people who had been hurt by currency fluctuations and unstable commodity prices. Others supported the Democrats for special reasons. Many southern planters looked to them to protect slavery and southern rights from government interference. Businessmen engaged in international trade favored Jackson's call for a lower tariff. The Democratic Party early recognized and encouraged the aspirations of immigrants, particularly Irish Catholics, who flocked to the party. Opponents of evangelical Protestantism, with its righteous moralizing and aggressive crusading, found refreshing the rough-and-tumble egalitarianism of the Democrats. The party attracted freethinkers and intellectuals. Many Democratic voters just plain liked Jackson.

Yet Jackson's policies and political success provoked growing opposition. Initially, Old Hickory's opponents lacked cohesion, and political alliances were unsettled. In time they would gather into a party that could compete with the Democrats in the tapping of popular emotions.

One of the first of the forces to oppose Jackson was the Anti-Masonic Party, which after 1826 had gained strong support in New England, New York, and Pennsylvania. Originally a protest movement against the supposedly despotic political and economic power of Masonry, it soon turned into a general protest against inequality and immorality. As a powerful religious and democratic movement, it attracted ambitious young politicians—William Seward, Thaddeus Stevens, Horace Greeley, and Millard Fillmore—who welded it into an effective political party. Because Andrew Jackson was a Mason, and because his party was in power, these leaders made the Democrats the chief target of attack. In 1831 the Anti-Masons held at Baltimore the first nationwide presidential nominating convention in the country, choosing William Wirt as their presidential candidate. He won just seven electoral votes in 1832, splitting the anti-Jackson vote with Henry Clay, the National Republican candidate. After that election, leaders of these two groups began organizing a political force alternative to the Democrats.

The Anti-Masons were joined by a motley assortment of former Jacksonians. Jackson's firm rebuke to nullification drove many southern states' righters into opposition. Then the bank war caused many to desert the President. The selection of the New Yorker Martin Van Buren as Jackson's successor awakened hostility in the South and West. Even John C. Calhoun cooperated for a time with nationalists like Clay and Webster in opposing administration measures in Congress.

The Whigs   In 1834 a newspaper gave the anti-Jackson coalition the title "Whigs." That name had been in use for earlier British opponents of policies of the monarchy, and for rebel colonists in the period of the American Revolution; it was now supposed to define the opponents of the tyrannical "King Andrew."

Use of the name "Whig" by opponents of Jackson and Jacksonianism became widespread in 1834, but the actual formation of a Whig Party varied in time from state to state. It was organized first in the New England and mid-Atlantic states, later in the West and South. The lack of an effective national organization and conflicts in ideology among the coalitionists hindered the Whigs in 1836. Unable to agree on a common platform or a single presidential candidate, they adopted the strategy of running strong regional candidates in the hope of throwing the election into the House of Representatives. In the South, the Whigs' choice was

Hugh Lawson White, a Tennesseean who, like many southern Jacksonians, distrusted Van Buren on the tariff and slavery. In the East, they ran Daniel Webster. The candidate in the West was General William Henry Harrison of Ohio, a former governor of Indiana Territory and the hero of the Battle of Tippecanoe. Among them the three Whigs piled up 124 electoral votes, but Van Buren, with Jackson's prestige behind him, had 170, enough to win the election.

The Nature of the Growing Whig Party   During the next four years the Whigs slowly gathered strength and developed a more coherent political philosophy. As the Panic of 1837 worsened, people throughout the country flocked to the new banner, convinced that Van Buren's hard-money policies were somehow responsible for their woes. The Whigs' ambitious economic nationalism attracted new adherents in the South, even while it drove Calhoun and the extreme states' righters back to the Democrats.

The Whigs brought democratic manners and sentiments to an essentially Hamiltonian concept of government and economics. They believed that it was a chief function of government to promote, actively and positively, the national economy. They advocated a national banking system, internal improvements at federal expense, and a protective tariff for industry. As they saw it, a wise government working alongside capital and labor would harmonize the interests of every class and section.

There was also a strong strain of evangelical Protestantism in Whiggery, which gave rise to moral and humanitarian reform. Many Whigs still hoped "to Christianize America through politics." They frequently criticized Jackson's Indian policy; and numbers of northern Whigs opposed slavery. Reformist activities among Whigs came in part from the more well-to-do element in the party, who like upper-class federalists before them took seriously the responsibility of the favored class to give moral direction to society.

The Whigs attracted a substantial following among all classes of society. Many northern merchants, bankers, and industrialists found the Whig philosophy appealing; so did large cotton, tobacco, and sugar planters and their urban business associates in the South. Many farmers, hungry for internal improvements, voted Whig. The party was popular among Protestants and native-born Americans concerned about the influx of immigrants, particularly Irish and German Catholics. Workingmen in industries hurt by foreign imports, or fearful of immigrant competition for jobs, supported the Whig ticket. With broad support throughout the country, the Whigs looked forward eagerly to the election of 1840.

The Election of 1840

In 1840 the second national party system came of age. The Democratic organization now faced a Whig Party just as skillfully devised for the winning of a large electorate. The Whigs now proceeded to beat the party of Jackson at its own game.

The Democratic convention had little choice but to renominate

Van Buren. The Democratic platform endorsed the Independent Treasury and condemned federally sponsored internal improvements, a national bank, and protective tariffs.

The early front runner for the Whig nomination was Henry Clay. The veteran senator from Kentucky had been the chief spokesman for Whiggery and master of the opposition to Jackson in Congress. The new professional politicians in the Whig Party, however, had a different strategy in mind. Men like Thurlow Weed of New York wanted a candidate with "availability"—someone inoffensive who could appeal to a broad spectrum of the electorate. Clay was too closely identified with the Bank of the United States, and had too many enemies. The Whigs especially wanted a military hero. Their convention passed over Clay and chose William Henry Harrison, whose rout of Tecumseh's outnumbered Indians at Tippecanoe in 1811 had made him a national figure. In an attempt to balance the ticket geographically, the Whigs selected as Harrison's running mate John Tyler of Virginia, a states' rights strict constructionist. Because there were divergent views within the party on national issues, the Whigs adjourned without drafting a platform.

The Log Cabin Campaign

Born on a Virginia plantation in 1773, the son of a signer of the Declaration of Independence, Harrison had begun his career in the Old Northwest, first as an army officer, then as governor of Indiana Territory. Later, "Tippecanoe," as commander in the Northwest during the War of 1812, had won the important Battle of the Thames, finally driving the British and their Indian allies off the soil of the United States. Following the war, Harrison spent much time on his farm in Ohio, and also served briefly as a United States senator and as minister to Colombia. Thereafter, however, his career languished and he was serving as a county clerk in 1836 when the Whigs tapped him as one of their presidential candidates. His strong showing at the polls—he got over half the Whig vote—kept him in public view until 1840.

At first, the Democrats professed joy at the Whigs's decision to run "Granny" Harrison (he was sixty-seven) instead of Clay. But when a Democratic newspaper, sneering at Harrison's presumed lack of sophistication, suggested that he would be content with a barrel of hard cider, a log cabin, and a pension of $2,000 a year, the Whigs seized on the remark. Mounting an elaborate campaign, they cast Harrison in Jackson's image and portrayed the Whigs as the friends of the people.

In their songs and speeches Whig orators glorified Harrison as a plain, virtuous farmer whose cabin door (he actually owned three thousand acres and lived in a substantial home) was always open to strangers. "Matty" Van Buren, by contrast, was pictured as a bloated aristocrat, squandering the public funds on lavish White House entertainments in the midst of a depression. Why, thundered one Whig orator, this *"democratic peacock"* had even installed a bathtub at a cost of "thousands of the people's dollars." Davy Crockett observed that "it would be difficult to say, from personal appearance, whether he was man or woman. . . . Aunt Matty was the perlitest cretur among the wimmen."

The Whigs held parades and rallies, with floats, flags, bands, and endless replicas of log cabins. They paraded fake Indians, to remind the

One gem from the musical political campaign of 1840 purported to give a biography of Van Buren:

Who never did a noble deed?
Who of the people took no heed?
Who is the worst of tyrant's breed?
    Van Buren!

Who, while but a little boy,
Was counted crafty, cunning, sly,
Who with the wily fox could vie?
    Van Buren!

Who, when an urchin, young at school,
Would of each classmate make a tool,
In cheating, who the roost would rule?
    Van Buren!

Who like the wily serpent clings,
Who like the pois'nous adder stings,
Who is more base than basest Kings?
    Van Buren!

Who rules us with an iron rod,
Who moves at Satan's beck and nod,
Who heeds not man, who heeds not God?
    Van Buren!

Who would his friend, his country sell,
Do other deeds too base to tell,
Deserves the lowest place in Hell?
    Van Buren!

A political cartoon captured the colorful nature of the 1840 presidential campaign.
(Courtesy, Hugh Cleland Collection)

A Democrat, after witnessing the spectacle of 10,000 Whigs celebrating Harrison Day in Cleveland on September 10, 1840, recoiled with disgust:

"I have seen vast assemblages collected together at great labor and cost, not to respond to any principle, or listen to any argument but to drown the voice of reason in shouts of revelry, and lead captive the feelings of the people in a senseless excitement. Hurrah for the newly found hero, annunciations of his poverty or his residence in a Log Cabin and love of hard cider, the hauling of miniature log hen coops and canoes, gourds, shells, and cider barrels through the streets, the rolling of balls, and a display of different colored banners with unmeaning mottos, doggerel, rhymes, and vulgar pictures.

The drinking of hard cider . . . and imitating the cries of birds and the howl of wild beasts with other mummery and mockery, are disgraceful to the country. It is saying to the people, you are too ignorant for self government, and is a down right insult to the good understanding of the American freeman."

voters of Harrison's record of Indian fighting. Another reminder was their catchy campaign slogan, "Tippecanoe and Tyler Too!" Barrels of cider were everywhere, with sweet cider for the drys and hard for the wets. The E.C. Booz Company of Philadelphia packaged its Old Cabin whiskey in log-cabin-shaped bottles, and "booze" entered the language as a synonym for hard liquor. Wealthy Whigs dressed in homespun and boasted of their humble upbringing. The party distributed a campaign newspaper, the *Log Cabin,* and countless songbooks in the first musical campaign of American history.

The Whig campaign theme, then, made use of the democratic, populistic posturing that had served the Democrats so well. But it was not merely posturing and strategy. The Hamiltonian program for economic development, a clear antecedent to the program of the Whigs, had seemed aristocratic, but that was partly because of the character of its Federalist architects. The idea of a federal government actively managing a single national economy in the interest of the common good is at bottom entirely democratic, and to that the politics of the twentieth century will attest. The economic nationalism and the populism of the Whigs went together genuinely as well as strategically, and foreshadowed a continuing if rocky alliance of Hamiltonianism and democracy.

The Democrats tried to counter hard cider with hard money, commending the virtues of the newly established Independent Treasury. No one listened. Attracted by the ballyhoo and angry over the depression, voters swarmed to the vigorous young party. Nearly eighty percent of the eligible electorate went to the polls. Harrison won a clear-cut victory, carrying nineteen out of twenty-six states and fifty-three percent of the two-party vote. Nearly unnoticed in the hullabaloo was the Liberty Party, whose meager 6,225 votes represented an early stirring of antislavery politics in the North.

The election of 1840 established a new pattern in American politics. For the first time a President had been saddled with responsibility for hard times and turned out of office. The carnival atmosphere of the campaign inaugurated a tradition that has to some extent persisted in American presidential elections. The public had adopted politics as its favorite spectator sport, and the presidential campaign as its most important national ritual. For the rest of the nineteenth century, about eighty percent of the electorate turned out to vote in most presidential contests.

World Affairs in the Jacksonian Era

During the age of Jackson, Americans were preoccupied with redefining their political philosophies, coming to terms with the meaning of democracy and realigning their political parties. Presidents Andrew Jackson and Martin Van Buren had little to think about in foreign policy. But the nation did face some delicate situations.

French Affairs   During the Napoleonic era, French naval vessels had periodically boarded and seized American merchant ships carrying goods to and from Great Britain. The United States at the time demanded compensation, but when the War of 1812 broke out and France was in effect an American ally, those demands receded. In the years afterward the United States raised the issue, reminding France of the claims, but in turn the French began arguing that the United States had violated the rights of some French citizens in Louisiana. Diplomatic teams from both countries negotiated the differences, and in July 1830 a treaty was signed. France agreed to pay twenty-five million francs in six annual installments, beginning in 1834, and the United States agreed to a payment of 1.5 million francs to compensate French citizens in Louisiana.

In 1834, France over the vehement protests of the Jackson Administration unilaterally decided to postpone the payments. In December 1834 the President threatened to seize property under French ownership in the United States in lieu of the payments, and he spoke threateningly of naval action. Eventually, Great Britain took the role of mediator in the dispute. France made in the spring of 1836 a single payment of seventeen million francs and completed the compensation during the next two years.

Amistad Incident   One diplomatic incident during Van Buren's presidency involved slavery, the issue that would not lie still. In 1839 off the coast of Cuba a Spanish ship carrying slaves from Africa and bearing the ill-fitting name *Amistad*—"friendship"—fell to a mutiny by its black captives, who were suffering under vile conditions. When it entered the territory of the United States, the navy in Long Island Sound seized their brave leader Cinqué along

Cinqué was an African chief who aboard a slave ship organized a mutiny that killed most of the Spanish crew. Spain had signed a treaty, however, agreeing not to take part in the slave trade. Cinqué and his cohorts wound up in a Connecticut jail after entering Long Island Sound. Defended by seventy-three-year-old John Quincy Adams, then a congressman, Cinqué was released in 1841. *(Courtesy, National Portrait Galley).*

with the mutineers and took them to New Haven, Connecticut. The Spanish insisted on their return, and Van Buren's administration wished to send them back. Their case went through the court system, finally reaching the Supreme Court. Before that body Congressman John Quincy Adams pled their cause, and in 1841 they were freed. They went home to Africa.

In the *Amistad* affair and throughout the later years of his life, Adams was a major opponent of the institution of slavery. In 1848, he fell sick on the floor of the House of Representatives while protesting an honor to be paid to officers in the Mexican War, dying soon after. Antislavery forces had detested that war for its injustice to Mexico and its possible opening of conquered territory to plantation slavery. Conscience soon put Van Buren in the antislavery ranks. In 1848 he ran for the presidency as the candidate of the Free Soil Party, which argued for banning slavery from the western tertitories, governed directly by the federal government.

The Jacksonian Legacy   The Jacksonian era, which includes the campaigning of the Whigs who were victorious in 1840, firmly established the political system that has prevailed ever since. The significance of the change does not lie primarily in the extended importance of the popular vote or in the increased rowdiness of popular politics. Of greater moment was the

George Caleb Bingham, *Raftsmen Playing Cards,* 1847. *(Courtesy, The Saint Louis Art Museum)*

appearance of parties that, far more broadly than the old Federalists and Jeffersonians, could articulate fairly complex national policies and present them to the public. In 1840, to be sure, the Whigs did little explaining: cider and log cabins are not issues that bear largely on the future of the republic. But the emergence of nationwide parties that, however divided internally, represented clear interests and beliefs went parallel to the industrial revolution in marking the demise of the staid old republicanism of the Founders. Together with the inventions, the factories and railways, the westward expansion of one-crop commercial agriculture, and the other quickened activities of the time, they signified that from then onward the country was to be a project worked and reworked by the restless will of its people.

Suggested Readings

On the Jacksonian Era see Daniel Feller, *The Jacksonian Promise: America, 1815–1840* (1995), Harry Watson, *Liberty and Power: The Politics of Jacksonian America* (1990), and Arthur Schlesinger, Jr.'s classic on Jacksonian democracy, *The Age of Jackson* (1945). See also Lawrence Kohl, *The Politics of Individualism: Parties and the American Character in the Jackson Era* (1989), Merrill D. Peterson, *The Great Triumvirate: Webster, Clay, and Calhoun* (1987), Richard E. Ellis, *The Union at Risk: Jacksonian Democracy, States' Rights, and the Nullification Crisis* (1987), Daniel B. Cole, *Martin Van Buren and the American Political System* (1984), and Edward Pessen, *Riches, Class, and Power before the Civil War* (1973). See also Pessen's *Jacksonian America* (rev. 1978) and Marvin Meyer's *The Jacksonian Persuasion* (1957). Richard P. McCormick describes *The Second Party System* (1966). On Jackson, Robert V. Remini's three-volume biography of *Andrew Jackson* (1977, 1984, and 1987) is definitive. David B. Cole, *The Presidency of Andrew Jackson* (1993) is a fine one-volume biography. Michael Paul

Rogin's *Fathers and Children: Andrew Jackson and the Subjugation of the American Indian* (1975) is intriguing and debatable history and psychohistory. Compare William G. McLaughlin, *Cherokee Renascence in the New Republic* (1980) and Michael D. Green, *The Politics of Indian Removal* (1982). Lee Benson's *The Concept of Jacksonian Democracy: New York as a Test Case* (1961) remains provocative.

See also John Niven, *John C. Calhoun and the Price of Union* (1988), Richard Hofstadter, *The Idea of a Party System: The Rise of Legitimate Opposition in the United States, 1780–1840* (1970), Harry L. Watson, *Liberty and Power: The Politics of Jacksonian America* (1990), John Niven, *Martin Van Buren: The Romantic Age of American Politics* (1983), Daniel W. Howe, *The Political Culture of the American Whigs* (1979), Thomas Brown, *Politics and Statesmanship: Essays on the American Whig Party* (1985), and Irving H. Bartlett, *John Calhoun: A Biography* (1993).

Why Did Jackson Remove the Indians?

Michael Paul Rogin

America clearly began not with primal innocence and consent but with acts of force and fraud. Indians were here first, and it was their land upon which Americans contracted, squabbled, and reasoned with one another. Stripping away history did not permit beginning without sin; it simply exposed the sin at the beginning of it all. The dispossession of the Indians, moreover, did not happen once and for all in the beginning. America was continually beginning again on the frontier, and as it expanded across the continent, it killed, removed, and drove into extinction one tribe after another.

The years spanned by Andrew Jackson's life were the great years of American expansion. Born on the frontier, Jackson joined the movement west as a young man. In the years of his maturity and old age, from Jefferson's Presidency to the Mexican War, expansion across the continent was the central fact of American politics. Two-thirds of the American population of 3.9 million lived within fifty miles of the ocean in 1790. In the next half-century 4.5 million Americans crossed the Appalachians, one of the great migrations in world history. The western states contained less than three percent of the U.S. population in 1790, twenty-eight percent in 1830. In two decades the west would become the most populous region of the country.

Indians inhabited in 1790 almost all the territory west of the original thirteen states. If America were to expand and take possession of the continent, they would have to be dispossessed. Indians had not mattered so much, in the history of Europeans in the English new world, since the colonial settlements. They would never matter so much again. Indian removal was Andrew Jackson's major policy aim in the quarter-century before he became President. His Indian wars and treaties were principally responsible for dispossessing the southern Indians during those years. His presidential Indian removal finished the job. . . . Historians, however, have failed to place Indians at the center of Jackson's life. They have interpreted the Age of Jackson from every perspective but Indian destruction, the one from which it actually developed historically.

Indian dispossession, as experienced by the whites who justified it and carried it out, belongs to the pathology of human development. Indians remained, in the white fantasy, in the earliest period of childhood, unseparated from "the exuberant bosom of the common mother." They were at once symbols of a lost childhood bliss and, as bad children, repositories of murderous, negative fantasies. . . . Replacing Indians upon the land, whites reunited themselves with nature. The rhetoric of Manifest Destiny pictured America as a "young and growing country"; it expanded through "swallowing territory," "just as an animal eats to grow." Savagery would inevitably "be swallowed by" civilization. . . .

Expansion, whites agreed, inevitably devoured Indians; only paternal governmental supervision could save the tribes from extinction. Paternalism, however, met white needs better than Indian ones. . . . In their paternalism toward Indians, white policy-makers indulged primitive longings to wield total power.

Indian dispossession is part of the history of American capitalism. Jackson and other political figures, freeing Indian land for the commodity economy, initiated a market revolution. They cleared the obstacles to free market relations, politically and by force, before the market could act on its own. The state and private instruments of violence massively assaulted tribal structures. They acquired the resources under Indian control for capitalist development. Force and fraud characterize American-Indian relations throughout our history, but their scope and timing give the Age of Jackson its significance.

Michael Paul Rogin, *Fathers and Children: Andrew Jackson and the Subjugation of the American Indian* (New York: Alfred A. Knopf, 1975), 3–4, 9, 10, 12, 13. Reprinted by permission.

The draft treaty [of 1835] provided that the Nation cede and relinquish to the United States their rights and titles "to all lands owned, claimed and possessed" by the Cherokees, including lands reserved for a school fund, east of the Mississippi River, in return for which they would receive $5 million. This amount, in the opinion of one modern historian, represented "unprecedented federal generosity." A program of removal was also provided, along with scheduled payments for subsistence, claims and spoliations, blankets, kettles, rifles, and the like. After due notice, the treaty was to be submitted to the Cherokee National Council assembled at New Echota, Georgia, for their approval, and for the approval of the President with the advice and consent of the Senate. . . .

The treaty plucked from the Cherokees an enormous domain of choice land in western North Carolina, northern Georgia, northeastern Alabama, and eastern Tennessee, comprising approximately 7 million acres. It was an acquisition of staggering proportions. Small wonder American newspapermen gloated over it and reckoned the spectacular benefits for the country. Cherokees were aghast at the loss of their country and pledged to fight it at New Echota. Some of them appealed to Jackson for better terms. They assured him that the treaty could never win approval. They predicted death for those who had signed the document in the name of the Cherokee Nation, and they reminded Jackson of the many services they had provided him personally, going back to the Creek War in 1813. They said they were sure he would heed their supplications and do justice to his "red children."

As always, Jackson accorded Cherokee delegations marked deference when they visited him at the White House to make this appeal. He treated them as dignitaries of a foreign nation, although he would never acknowledge anything remotely resembling independence or sovereignty. And, as usual, he gave them one of his famous "talks," a talk usually distributed among the Cherokee people and published in the newspapers. . . . "Most of your people are uneducated, and are liable to be brought into collision at all times with your white neighbors. Your young men are acquiring habits of intoxication. With strong passions, and without those habits of restraint which our laws inculcate and render necessary, they are frequently driven to excesses which must eventually terminate in their ruin. The game has disappeared among you, and you must depend upon agriculture, and the mechanic arts, for support. And, yet, a large portion of your people have acquired little or no property in the soil itself, or in any article of personal property which can be useful to them. How, under these circumstances, can you live in the country you now occupy? Your condition must become worse and worse, and you will ultimately disappear, as so many tribes have done before you."

On December 28, what came to be called the Treaty of New Echota—it basically repeated the provisions of the "draft treaty" approved in March—was brought to the assembled Cherokees. The committee of twenty announced its acceptance of the terms of the treaty. A vote was taken and the treaty approved by the count of 79 to 7. This incredibly low number represented few Cherokees, certainly not the elected government of the Nation and certainly not the thousands of Indians who should have participated in the ratifying process. No matter. The treaty was approved and signed.

It was chicanery, pure and simple. The ratifying process was a fraud, an act approaching highway robbery. Nonetheless, it produced a removal treaty, and the power of the Cherokee Nation was broken at last.

The removal of the American Indian was one of the most significant and tragic acts of the Jackson administration. It was accomplished in total violation not only of American principles of justice and law but of Jackson's own strict code of honor. . . .

Andrew Jackson left office bowed down by the stupefying misery involved in removal, but he left knowing he had accomplished his goal and that thousands of Indians had found what he considered a safe haven west of the Mississippi River. He left believing he had saved the Indians from inevitable doom. And, indeed, he had.

Robert V. Remini, *Andrew Jackson and the Course of American Democracy, 1833–1845,* III (New York: Harper & Row, 1984), 296–7, 298, 300, 314. Reprinted by permission.

Elizabeth Cady Stanton. *(Courtesy, American Antiquarian Society)*

Lucretia Mott. *(Courtesy, Library of Congress)*

Stanton and Amelia Bloomer shown wearing the daring loose "bloomers"—long full Turkish trousers of black broadcloth with a short skirt and Spanish cloak. *(Seneca Falls Lily)*

An Age of Reform

THE WOMEN'S DECLARATION OF SENTIMENTS, 1848

The World Anti-Slavery Convention, held in London in 1840, was an important event in the women's rights movement as well as in the antislavery movement. American women, who had gained their first access to public platforms in antislavery activity, were horrified when their idols, the heroes of Great Britain's successful abolition of slavery in the empire, refused to allow them to be seated as delegates to the conference. Lucretia Mott, who had long exercised a public role both in Quaker and in antislavery affairs, was particularly incensed. Her straightforward anger, her willingness to argue with the men, and especially her preaching in a Unitarian Church in London "opened to me a new world of thoughts," Elizabeth Cady Stanton would recall. "As Mrs. Mott and I walked away arm in arm, commenting on the incidents of the day, we resolved to hold a convention as soon as we returned home, and form a society to advocate the rights of women."

Eight years elapsed before this resolve bore fruit in the Seneca Falls Woman's Rights Convention. The barriers had been many. Elizabeth Cady Stanton was newly married in 1840, and in the subsequent eight years she settled in three different locations, bore three children, and assumed all the other cares of a busy middle-class household. She needed further maturation and confidence to move on to a public stage. Lucretia Mott was unusual in having had so many opportunities, largely because of her Quaker environment, to speak in public and organize meetings. Her more cautious friend worked for a New York State law that would give married women control of their inherited wealth, but

HISTORICAL EVENTS

1817
American Colonization Society founded

1820
Washington Irving publishes "Rip Van Winkle" and "The Legend of Sleepy Hollow"

1821
Prison built in Auburn, New York, featuring solitary confinement at night and group labor by day

1823
James Fenimore Cooper begins the "Leatherstocking Tales"

1830
Joseph Smith publishes *Book of Mormon*

1831
The *Liberator* established in Boston
• Nat Turner revolt in Virginia

1833
Legal emancipation of British West Indian slaves

1839
Mormons migrate to Illinois and establish city of Nauvoo
• Theodore Weld, Angelina Weld, and Sarah Grimké publish *American Slavery as It Is*

continued

HISTORICAL EVENTS

1840
World Anti-Slavery Convention
• William Henry Harrison elected
President • anti-Mormon and
anti-immigrant sentiment grows

1841
Dorr's Rebellion

1848
Women's Declaration of Sentiments

1850
Nathaniel Hawthorne's
The Scarlet Letter

1851
Maine's prohibition statute
• Nathaniel Hawthorne's *The House
of the Seven Gables* • Herman
Melville's *Moby Dick*

1854
Garrison burns a copy of the
Constitution

1855
Walt Whitman's *Leaves of Grass*

she remained quite timid, fearing the social disapproval that might befall women who spoke in public on any subject, more particularly women's rights. Finally in 1848, Lucretia Mott having planned a visit to relatives in the Seneca Falls area, the two women made a last minute decision to hold a small local convention on July 19–20, which they advertised only in the Seneca Falls newspaper.

The results were a surprise to the organizers, the participants, and particularly the press and pulpit whose subsequent attacks gave the conference much of its historical importance. Three hundred people—including forty men—attended this meeting. Overwhelmed by the response, the women had Lucretia's husband James preside. In two days of orderly meetings, the Convention heard a series of well-prepared speeches, adopted a Declaration of Sentiments and a set of resolutions, and planned a set of further meetings that flowered into one of the major reform movements of American history.

What made the Seneca Falls Convention special and powerful was its Declaration of Sentiments. Written by Elizabeth Cady Stanton and modeled after Jefferson's Declaration of Independence, the document aligned women's rights with American ideology, challenging the nation to be true to its tradition.

DECLARATION OF SENTIMENTS (1848)

When, in the course of human events, it becomes necessary for one portion of the family of man to assume among the people of the earth a position different from that which they have hitherto occupied, but one to which the laws of nature and of nature's God entitle them, a decent respect to the opinions of mankind requires that they should declare the causes that impel them to such a course.

We hold these truths to be self-evident: that all men and women are created equal; that they are endowed by their Creator with certain inalienable rights; that among these are life, liberty, and the pursuit of happiness; that to secure these rights governments are instituted, deriving their just powers from the consent of the governed. Whenever any form of government becomes destructive of these ends, it is the right of those who suffer from it to refuse allegiance to it, and to insist upon the institution of a new government, laying its foundation on such principles, and organizing its powers in such form, as to them shall seem most likely to effect their happiness. Prudence, indeed, will dictate that governments long established should not be changed for light and transient causes; and accordingly all experience hath shown that

mankind are more disposed to suffer, while evils are sufferable, than to right themselves by abolishing the forms to which they were accustomed. But when a long train of abuses and usurpations, pursuing invariably the same object evinces a design to reduce them under absolute despotism, it is their duty to throw off such government, and to provide new guards for their future security. Such has been the patient sufferance of the women under this government, and such is now the necessity which constrains them to demand the equal station to which they are entitled.

The history of mankind is a history of repeated injuries and usurpations on the part of man toward woman, having in direct object the establishment of an absolute tyranny over her. To prove this, let facts be submitted to a candid world.

He has compelled her to submit to laws, in the formation of which she had no voice.

He has withheld from her rights which are given to the most ignorant and degraded men—both natives and foreigners.

Having deprived her of this first right of a citizen, the elective franchise, thereby leaving her without repre-

In the 1840s farmers and craftsmen, inventors and factory workers, were pressing form and efficiency upon the physical world. Evangelical Protestantism and the growing public school system were working to bring greater order to American minds and souls. A new party system was claiming to design programs for the better management of the American economy. Amidst these efforts, the women's rights movement along with innumerable other reform efforts of its time represented a large determination to perfect the republic of the Founders and, if possible, the world beyond the nation's borders.

Political and Economic Radicalism

During the second quarter of the nineteenth century, new social forces broke in upon the American villages, farms, and regions that had once existed in near isolation, practicing slow, traditional ways of work and life. Poverty, disease, and illiteracy became more concentrated and apparent as cities grew. The transportation revolution broke down barriers of distance and isolation, uprooting established communities and existing markets. Increasing reliance on machines turned independent craftsmen and sturdy farmers into wage earners. The tempo of life had speeded up. An English watchmaker who emigrated to New

---

sentation in the halls of legislation, he has oppressed her on all sides.

He has made her, if married, in the eye of the law, civilly dead.

He has taken from her all right in property, even to the wages she earns.

He has made her, morally, an irresponsible being, as she can commit many crimes with impunity, provided they be done in the presence of her husband. In the covenant of marriage, she is compelled to promise obedience to her husband, he becoming, to all intents and purposes, her master—the law giving him power to deprive her of her liberty, and to administer chastisement.

He has so framed the laws of divorce, as to what shall be the proper causes, and in case of separation, to whom the guardianship of the children shall be given, as to be wholly regardless of the happiness of women—the law, in all cases, going upon a false supposition of the supremacy of man, and giving all power into his hands.

After depriving her of all rights as a married woman, if single, and the owner of property, he has taxed her to support a government which recognizes her only when her property can be made profitable to it.

He has monopolized nearly all the profitable employ-

ments, and from those she is permitted to follow, she receives but a scanty remuneration. He closes against her all the avenues to wealth and distinction which he considers most honorable to himself. As a teacher of theology, medicine, or law, she is not known.

He has denied her the facilities for obtaining a thorough education, all colleges being closed against her.

He allows her in Church, as well as State, but a subordinate position, claiming Apostolic authority for her exclusion from the ministry, and, with some exceptions, from any public participation in the affairs of the Church.

He has created a false public sentiment by giving to the world a different code of morals for men and women, by which moral delinquencies which exclude women from society, are not only tolerated, but deemed of little account in man.

He has usurped the prerogative of Jehovah himself, claiming it as his right to assign for her a sphere of action, when that belongs to her conscience and to her God.

He has endeavored, in every way that he could, to destroy her confidence in her own powers, to lessen her self-respect, and to make her willing to lead a dependent and abject life.

A British mechanic wrote of his observations in the United States during the late 1830s:

"Mechanics work harder, and labour in most occupations is greater, generally speaking, than in any other part of the world. Everything, in fact, connected with trade or business seems to proceed at a sort of railroad pace; all move at the very top speed—at a kind of high pressure rate: 'go along steam-boat' is the familiar expression of one to the other; sex and age offer no difference—the impulse is common to all."

York in 1832 wrote in his diary: "My employers have brought me so much work that I have scarce anytime for reading." An Irish moulder was shocked by his first visit to an American foundry: "I peered into the semi-darkness and saw men, bare-headed and almost nude racing back and forth, handling between trips small wooden hammers most dextrously. I asked . . . a bystander what was going on inside, and was told it was a foundry. The information made me gasp. I had never seen a foundry like it. Mechanics, and for that matter all others in the old country never worked so exhausting a way as these men did. . . . The American moulders seemed desirous of doing all the work required as if it were the last day of their lives."

During the first half of the nineteenth century a few Americans questioned the very foundations of capitalism. Some turned to religious or social experiments designed to reform society. A large number aimed at correcting specific problems. Reformers disagreed on goals and methods. But they shared frustration at disorder in society, apprehension about loss of consensus and community, and fear that morality was declining. These pessimistic motives for reform combined with an optimistic motive: a faith in the ultimate perfectibility of the world in general and American society in particular. A vigorous and many-sided movement for reform gained energy in the 1830s and continued to the Civil War.

The Early Labor Movement	The American labor movement had its origins in the economic upheavals of the Jacksonian era. In dozens of cities, craftsmen and artisans organized associa-

tions and sponsored strikes for better hours and wages. A few citywide federated unions and one national federation—the National Trades' Union—existed until hostile judges and the economic cataclysm of 1837 dragged them under. Labor also entered politics. In the early 1830s, for example, New York City workingmen organized politically to seek improved working conditions, free public education, abolition of imprisonment for debt, and an end to chartered banks and other monopolies. Most of their demands were eminently practical; some of their leaders were not.

The writer and social critic George Henry Evans had another remedy for unemployment and poverty: "Let us . . . emancipate the white laborer, *by restoring his natural right to the soil.*" As early as 1834, Evans advocated free land grants to actual settlers and a limitation on the holdings of any one person. Adopting the motto "Vote yourself a farm," he tried for years to convince eastern workingmen that their happiness and independence could be found only in agriculture. In 1862, six years after Evans's death, Congress passed the Homestead Act, offering free grants of western land. Workingmen did not have the capital, the knowledge, or the desire to go west and take up farming; and so the Homestead Act did not succeed in making independence and prosperity available to the whole nation. But the Act, an important component of the new Republican Party's scheme for nurturing the economy under governmental leadership, was a nineteenth-century foreshadowing of more daring twentieth-century social reforms.

Labor agitation and similar efforts were addressing, without quite recognizing the fact, a problem inherent in the American political, social, and economic system. Freeing work and property of traditional restrictions allowed for accumulations of land and other property. Unrestricted freedom also invited a competitiveness that militated against the cooperative civic ethic that had been another component of traditional republicanism and mocked the spirit of charity preached by American religion. Ever since, American reformers have striven to resolve the contradictions.

Voting Rights   Among the powerful social and political forces that the spirit of Jacksonian democracy unleashed in the United States, none was more compelling than the question of voting rights. Real democracy, of course, was still a long way in the future. The debates over voting rights during the Jacksonian era included no serious discussion of extending political rights to women or minorities. At the time of the Civil War, free African Americans would have the vote only in New Hampshire, Maine, Massachusetts, and Vermont. The only issue at hand was whether all adult white males should be able to vote. In 1800, only Vermont, New Hampshire, and Kentucky allowed all adult white men to vote. Every other state had either property or taxpaying requirements.

But as the rhetoric of democracy became increasingly popular in the early 1800s, the property and taxpaying requirements for voting began to fall. Conservatives still made their arguments, and some farmers worried that extending the right to vote to urban workers would only give more power to their employers. But other people were arguing that voting was a God-given right and should not be confined to elites. Between 1800 and 1840 state after state dropped the property requirement for voting. By 1840 only Louisiana, Rhode Island, and Virginia still had restrictive requirements.

The Rhode Island restrictions led to Dorr's Rebellion in 1841. At the time less than half of Rhode Island's white males could vote. Thomas W. Dorr, a Democrat and a lawyer, campaigned for relaxation of the property requirements, and when the governor and legislature refused to respond, he organized his own convention to write a new state constitution and abolish the property requirements. The governor called out the state militia to break up the convention, and in response Dorr and some of his followers attacked the militia's arsenal in Providence. Dorr was arrested, convicted of treason, and sentenced to life in prison. But by that time he was a folk hero to many people in the state, and in 1842 the governor gave him a pardon. In 1843 Rhode Island adopted a new state constitution that substantially broadened the right to vote.

Thomas W. Dorr led a popular rebellion in Rhode Island in 1841 to extend the franchise. *(Courtesy, Library of Congress)*

An Egalitarian Culture   The growing faith in the common people, the suspicion of political, social, and economic elites, had its reflection in the dress and demeanor of politicians. Earlier in the century, for example, national politicians had proudly worn powdered wigs, silk suits and stockings with knee breeches, polished shoes with buckles, and ruffled shirts, while other American men, even of conservative persuasion, were adopting the long trousers and short hair popularized by the French Revolution. Even after the disappearance of details of prerevolutionary dress, politicians continued to cultivate a look not of equality but of wealth, breeding, and refinement. All that changed with Andrew Jackson. Politicians began to brag about their common roots, about making it by their own effort. Silk was out, and cotton and woolen fibers were in. The Whig campaign of 1840 marked how far the styles of democracy had gone.

European travelers in the United States were quick to point out how the spirit of democracy was affecting other American institutions. By the late 1830s, most hotels in the United States had abandoned first-class accommodations and room service. All rooms were the same size with the same appointments, and guests ate their meals in family style around a large table. Some hotels refused to take advance reservations by mail, advertising themselves as first-come, first-serve establishments. Many domestic steamships, stagecoaches, and railroads also abandoned services that divided people into classes, catering to the well-to-do.

During the 1830s and 1840s a reaction also took place against professionalism. By that time the nation was well into the beginnings of the industrial revolution, and the importance of job skills, education, and technical expertise was increasingly clear. As society and the economy became more complicated, the educational requirements for engineers, accountants, physicians, and attorneys also became more complex. But those changes came at a time when it was a fashion to be suspicious of any elites—political, economic, or professional. When doctors tried to secure legislation in the 1840s requiring minimal educational requirements before an individual could practice medicine, they encountered stiff resistance in state legislatures where faith healers, naturopaths, and herbal practitioners joined with Jacksonians to defeat the measures. When the representatives of large banks tried to secure legislation requiring new state banks to have at least a defined amount of capital, they encountered similar resistance.

Religious Movements

The Second Great Awakening

In the 1820s and 1830s Americans experienced a second Great Awakening of religious enthusiasm. This religious resurgence reflected distinctly American values and attitudes. Its intensely democratic message stressed individual free will and immediate salvation; it breathed optimism; it brought religion to the people in language they could understand. Relying on the excitement of revival meetings, a wide variety of evangelical sects sought to turn the masses toward spiritual regeneration. Evangelists like Charles Grandison Finney rejected the harsh traditional Calvinist view of original sin and predestination and preached that any good Christian could attain eternal salvation. Their teachings generally involved a literal interpretation of the Bible. Many emphasized the Second Coming of Christ and believed that God's Kingdom would establish itself on earth. The common people appreciated sermons devoid of "literary quibbles and philosophical speculations." As one hymn put it to music, every person wanted to "see bright angels stand waiting to receive me."

The Second Great Awakening has been called "a women's awakening." Men certainly responded to the religious enthusiasm, but women far outnumbered them among converts and played a decisive part in leading men either back to established churches, or into new ones. Historians have shown that male conversions frequently followed the conversion of one or more female members of the family. Mothers often proved especially influential in converting their sons and husbands. But the most characteristic converts were adolescent girls. An affirmation, or reaffirmation, of religious belief and commitment seems to have offered young women a powerful sense of identity and purpose.

A belief distinctive to some participants in the Second Great Awakening was perfectionism, the idea that human beings could not merely achieve salvation, but overcome sin altogether. Perfectionism's scriptural basis lay in the New Testament account of Jesus' telling his disciples that they are to "be perfect, even as your Heavenly Father is perfect." Charles Finney, the most successful of the revivalists of the day, read this text literally. Jesus does not tell his followers to try to be perfect, Finney reasoned. He tells them to be perfect. Since he does so, Finney argued, he must have also supplied the means for them to do so. Like the first Great Awakening of a century before, the new evangelicalism was more than a religious movement. And the spirit of perfectionism animated the many reform movements of the era.

Religious enthusiasm rapidly increased the membership of most Protestant denominations, Methodists and Baptists increasing the fastest. But new sects also arose. Each new prophet, interpreter, or mystic found followers willing to join in anticipating the literal fulfillment of even the most outlandish prophecies. For a time the poor farming district of upstate New York burned with religious emotions. "Enthusiastic" sects, sects cultivating emotion, flourished in this "burned-over district," as it was called: whatever the original derivation of the phrase, it came to signify a region seared by fires of religious enthusiasm.

The Age of Finney

Historians, long preoccupied with politics, have characterized the period between the "Era of Good Feelings" and the onset of the Civil War as the Age of Jackson. An equally strong case can be made for calling it the Age of Finney—after the leading revivalist of the day, Charles Grandison Finney. Finney was the George Whitefield of the nineteenth century. His revivals had the same spectacular success. And his methods were equally sensational. Finney, for example, often prayed for sinners by name.

Finney's preaching reflected the general concern for order. Like the upper-class reformers who generously supported his work, he saw religion as a bulwark of the social order. And he encouraged his converts to join established churches. But Finney also preached the primacy of the individual conscience. He told his listeners that conversion would mark a radical change in their lives. They should, he urged, reexamine the whole pattern of their lives. Finney always left it for his converts to determine the direction of their new lives for themselves. He did not attempt to channel the enthusiasm he unleashed. And so Finney's revivals, despite the conservative cast of much of his preaching, could produce radicals of various stripes.

The Shakers and the Mormons   The Shaker faith, brought to this country by Ann Lee in 1774, received that name from one of its most distinctive practices, a sacred dance during which the members "shook" their bodies free of sin through their fingertips. "Mother Ann," as she was called, believed that she had received direct revelations from God and, since she preached millennialism—that is, the imminent coming of the millennium, the period of Christ's rule on earth—she saw no need for the Shakers to have children. The members therefore practiced celibacy. After reaching a membership of some six thousand in the 1830s, the Shakers gradually died out. Their furniture and housing arrangements, which were simplicity itself, are their best-remembered achievements.

By far the most important of the religious communitarians were the Mormons. Mormonism strikingly elaborated the new theology of free will, direct revelation, universal salvation, the expectation of Christ's imminent return, and the establishment of a millennial Kingdom.

In 1830, at the age of twenty-five, Joseph Smith of Palmyra, New

Shaker Society Meeting. During worship members were sometimes "seized with a mighty trembling, with violent agitations of the body, running and walking on the floor, with singing, shouting, and leaping for joy." *(Courtesy, American Antiquarian Society)*

The Mormon monument, a forty-foot shaft capped by a statue of the angel Moroni, stands atop Hill Gumorah, a glacial rise in northwestern New York State. Here, in 1823, Joseph Smith said he found the golden plates he translated into the *Book of Mormon. (Courtesy, American Heritage)*

York, published the *Book of Mormon.* He had transcribed it, he claimed, from gold plates that had lain undisturbed in a nearby hillside for more than a thousand years. The angel Moroni directed him to the spot where the plates were buried. Using two magic "seeing stones" fixed in silver bows, Smith translated the ancient script into a readable text. The book was a curious mixture of Old Testament theology, popular history, and social beliefs of the times.

Although Mormonism borrowed freely from the convictions and practices of evangelical Protestantism, it offered a simple alternative to the confusing proliferation of Christian sects. By extending salvation to all adherents and clerical status to each adult white male, and by stressing the sanctity of secular accomplishments and the need for a community of "saints" (the church's official name was and is "The Church of Jesus Christ of Latter-day Saints"), the new faith tapped the energies and talents of the unsuccessful and the neglected. In Joseph Smith, a prophet who was believed to receive revelations directly from God, Mormonism provided theological truths and authoritarian leadership to whoever craved practical and spiritual guidance.

After converting a small group of relatives and friends, Smith moved his flock to Ohio and then to Missouri in an attempt to establish a commonwealth of believers. In each place, nonbelievers persecuted the Mormons and drove them from their lands. In 1839 Smith led his followers to Illinois. After securing political authority from state officials, he founded a city, called Nauvoo, which became a self-sufficient religious community. The success of Nauvoo, which grew to fifteen thousand inhabitants by 1844, as well as its voting power in state elections, brought the envy and hostility of outsiders. Smith's increasingly eccentric behavior (he declared himself a candidate for President in 1844) also generated unfavorable publicity. When a disgruntled Mormon confirmed that Smith and other members of the church's elite practiced polygamy, state officials arrested him and his brother. Soon after their confinement at Carthage, a mob of disbanded militia murdered them both.

"A New Zion"   When the harassment and violence continued, Brigham Young, Smith's successor to the presidency of the church, led the Mormons on the long difficult exodus from Illinois to uninhabited Mexican territory beyond the Rocky Mountains. Under Young's stern but effective leadership, the Mormons established a thriving agricultural community near the Great Salt Lake. By 1877, the year of Young's death, the commonwealth numbered some 350 settlements with a total population of 140,000.

Organized like a medieval kingdom, the church collected from each individual an annual tithe in goods, labor, or money, and channeled this surplus into projects that benefited everyone. Banning or discouraging the use of tea, coffee, tobacco, liquor, fashionable clothing, and elegant furniture, the church curtailed wasteful spending and assured the development of an industrious community. This mixture of collectivism and private enterprise saved the community from the worst evils of uncontrolled capitalism and prevented Utah from becoming dependent on imports from the industrial East.

Although the Mormons wished to be self-sufficient and independent, they also considered themselves Americans and asked for Utah's admission to the Union. Congress, however, balked at the Mormon practice of polygamy, which the new Republican Party of Abraham Lincoln had linked to slavery. In fact, only a small percentage of the community participated in this patriarchal institution; but the American public thought that Brigham Young's twenty-seven wives and fifty-six children were typical. In 1890 the church formally renounced polygamy, and Congress admitted Utah to the Union in 1896.

Millennialism   Some Americans looked to the fulfillment in their own time of the New Testament prophecy of Christ's Second Coming. The foremost exponent of millennialism was William Miller, a hardworking farmer in upstate New York who became caught up in a revival shortly after the War of 1812 and spent the rest of his life pondering religious questions. A literal interpretation of the Bible led him to a graphic belief in the Second Coming or Advent, which he calculated would occur in about 1843.

Aided by the widespread economic distress of the late 1830s, Miller made crowds of converts throughout New England with his vivid sermons depicting the glory of the Advent, the joy of those who would be saved, the suffering of the unrepentant. In a single year he gave 627 hour-and-a-half lectures before eager audiences, often of a thousand or more. Ministerial disciples with a knack for publicity spread Miller's views over an even wider area.

Miller hesitated to give his frantic followers a definite date, promising only that deliverance would come soon, in God's appointed time. As 1843—the Last Year—passed, March of 1844 came to be accepted as the crucial month. Finally, when nothing happened, a weary and discouraged Miller frankly admitted his mistake, explaining that he had done his best. But his lieutenants were not yet ready to quit. They chose October 22, 1844, as the new "Advent Day" and talked Miller into accepting it. Excitement mounted higher than before as extensive preparations were made to enter God's Kingdom. The faithful made

Priscilla Evans, though pregnant, walked with a handcart made of hickory from Iowa to Utah. Her account reveals the religious and economic motives that drove the Mormons across the continent to the Great Salt Lake.

"We began our journey [from Iowa City to Utah] of one thousand miles on foot with a handcart for each family, some families consisting of man and wife, and some quite large families. There were five mule teams to haul the tents and surplus flour. Each handcart had one hundred pounds of flour, that was to be divided and [more got] from the wagons as required. At first we had a little coffee and bacon, but that was soon gone and we had no use for any cooking utensils but a frying pan. The flour was self-raising and we took water and baked a little cake; that was all we had to eat.

After months of travelling we were put on half rations and at one time, before help came, we were out of flour for two days. We washed out the flour sacks to make a little gravy. . . .

No one rode in the wagons. Strong men would help the weaker ones, until they themselves were worn out, and some died from the struggle and want of food, and were buried along the wayside. It was heart rending for parents to move on and leave their loved ones to such a fate, as they were so helpless, and had no material for coffins. Children and young folks, too, had to move on and leave father or mother or both. . . .

We were much more fortunate than those who came later, as they had snow and freezing weather. Many lost limbs, and many froze to death. . . .

We reached Salt Lake City on October 2, 1856, tired, weary, with bleeding feet, our clothing worn out and so weak we were nearly starved, but thankful to our Heavenly Father for bringing us to Zion. . . ."

William Miller spoke lines like these throughout the 1830s:

"Ah! what means that noise? Can it be thunder? Too long—too loud and shrill—more like a thousand trumpets sounding an onset. It shakes the earth. . . . See how it reels. How dreadful! How strange! The very clouds are bright with glory. . . . See, the heavens do shake, the vivid clouds, so full of fire, are driven apart by this last blast, and rolling up themselves, stand back aghast—And O, my soul, what do I see? A great white throne, and One upon it. . . . Before him are thousands and thousands and thousands of wingèd seraphim, ready to do his will. The last trumpet sounds—the earth now heaves a throb for the last time, and in this last great throe her bowels burst, and from her sprang a thousand thousand, and ten thousand times ten thousand immortal beings into active life. . . . I saw them pass through the long vista of the parted cloud, and stand before the throne. . . . The air now became stagnated with heat; while the dismal howlings of those human beings who were left upon the earth, and the horrid yells of the damned spirits . . . filled my soul with horror not easily described."

themselves white "ascension robes" and neglected nearly all secular business. Voting in the fall elections was very light in some districts. On the night of October 21, Millerites gathered on hilltops to meet the new world together. No provisions were made for eating or sleeping, and many suffered as the night and the next day and then another night passed; thunderstorms added to their terror. Some claimed to have seen a jeweled crown in the sky, and there were meteor showers that night. In western New York, an earthquake intensified the expectation. A few Adventists committed suicide—one man leaped over Niagara Falls. The day of the "Great Delusion" effectively ended that movement, although Adventist sects continue to flourish.

The Fox Sisters   Various forms of spiritualism, or attempts to contact the spirit world, were another manifestation of the desire to break down all barriers between this world and the next. Mesmerism, electro-biology, clairvoyance, phrenology, magnetism—each had its following.

New York farmer John Fox had two remarkable young daughters, Maggie and Katie. Wherever they went in their home, mysterious rapping sounds were heard. Eventually the girls and their mother worked out a system of communication with the presumably other-worldly source of the rappings. Soon the neighbors flocked in to observe these conversations with the spirit world. The Fox home in the year 1848 set off a mania of spiritualist excitement. With an older sister acting as manager, the Fox girls began holding exhibitions—at the insistence of the spirits, of course—and quickly developed into professional fee-charging media.

With the wide publicity given the Fox sisters, media rapidly appeared all over the country, and spiritualist circles developed in nearly every town and village. They refined their techniques as they went along; the Foxes' managing sister, for instance, discovered that total darkness could produce many more manifestations of the spirits' presence. Table-moving, spirit-writing, and cold, ghostly hands soon supplemented the mystic rappings, and within a few years all the now-familiar paraphernalia of spiritualism were in use. The spiritualist excitement filled for thousands of people a need to become more comfortable with the mysteries of death and immortality. A number of intellectuals saw in spiritualism a replacement for traditional Christianity—a proof of the existence of a supernatural world for a scientific age that could not accept revelation resting only on faith. Even when the Fox sisters some years later admitted that their whole career had been a fraud (the rappings had from the first been produced by the joints of their toes), many spiritualists remained undeterred.

Methodism   The most powerful evangelical movement, more orthodox than these other religions of excitement, had begun in the eighteenth century. John Wesley had led within the Church of England a revival movement that after his death produced a separate denomination, the Methodist church. Methodists believed in free will. In its early days especially, Methodism had a strong element of emotional revivalism; but it also preached a rigorous piety and a morality of self-discipline, industry, thrift, and good works. Methodism was powerfully attractive, in Great Britain to the working classes and to the poor, and in this country to people on the frontier. In both nations it had something to do with the bringing of an ordered moral life to previously disordered sections of society. While the Methodist church did have an organization, in its first period it did not stress the role of bishops or of a highly trained ministry. That made it possible for Methodism here to develop a distinctive and effective system in which preachers, many with little, if any, formal religious education, would travel about on the frontier, bringing a sustaining Methodism to the families and communities at which they stopped.

Each preacher worked a "circuit" or route that covered a particular area. Francis Asbury, who had come to this country in 1771 and was influential in the beginnings of Methodism here, was an early and influential traveling preacher. The typical circuit rider went by horseback, depended on friendly settlers for food and shelter, and was much a part of the frontier environment: the evangelist Peter Cartwright could thrash a rowdy who tried to disrupt a Methodist meeting. Cartwright would hold his revivals outside in a grove because the local church could not hold the crowds he attracted.

The Methodists divided their territory into regions, each holding an annual conference that heard reports, appointed new preachers, and assigned circuits. As the frontier became heavily populated, large circuits—some had been hundreds of miles long—were replaced by smaller ones, and by about the middle of the nineteenth century these had given way to settled parishes. By that time the Methodist church was one of the largest Protestant denominations in the country.

Secular Communitarianism

Dozens of experimental communities built upon a trust in human perfectibility sprouted up in the nineteenth century. Some of them later succumbed to selfishness, quarrels, or loss of interest.

New Harmony   Robert Owen was a famous English socialist whose model factory town at New Lanark, Scotland, inspired many American utopians. In 1824 he organized his own communal experiment at New Harmony, Indiana, collecting a mixed group of followers whom he intended to transform into a prosperous, self-governing community. Practicing cooperation and common ownership of property, Owen hoped to eliminate selfishness and want. Quarrels and dissatisfaction finally forced Owen to abandon his misnamed experiment. Such experiments, his son Robert Dale Owen later concluded, were bound to fail in a country where cheap land and high wages fostered individualism and discouraged cooperative action.

Nashoba   The Owens's friend, feminist reformer Fanny Wright, tried her own utopian experiment in 1824 in Tennessee. Spending her inheritance, she established a community

Of his own conversion at a camp meeting, the Methodist minister Peter Cartwright recalled:

"The people crowded to this meeting from far and near. They came in their large wagons, with victuals mostly prepared. The women slept in the wagons, and the men under them. Many stayed on the ground night and day for a number of nights and days together. Others were provided for among the neighbors around. The power of God was wonderfully displayed; scores of sinners fell under the preaching, like men slain in mighty battle; Christians shouted aloud for joy.

To this meeting I repaired, a guilty, wretched sinner. On the Saturday evening of said meeting, I went, with weeping multitudes, and bowed before the stand, and earnestly prayed for mercy. In the midst of a solemn struggle of soul, an impression was made on my mind, as though a voice said to me, 'Thy sins are all forgiven thee.' Divine light flashed all round me, unspeakable joy sprung up in my soul. I rose to my feet, opened my eyes, and it really seemed as if I was in heaven; the trees, the leaves on them, and everything seemed, and I really thought were, praising God."

called Nashoba, where selected slaves would work the land, earn enough money to buy their freedom, and then be relocated outside the United States. But Fanny Wright also advocated free love and sexual equality in Nashoba, and her project had few outside supporters. She finally settled a few of the slaves in Haiti, but financial problems and public disapproval ended Wright's dream of emancipating America's blacks. She later moved to New York and took up the cause of urban working-men. Working with Robert Dale Owen, she edited a newspaper and recommended such radical notions as state guardianship of all children. In the 1840s she became an enthusiastic supporter of the women's rights movement.

Brook Farm   Brook Farm, a New England community, existed for a few years in the 1840s. Most of its members, such as Margaret Fuller, Nathaniel Hawthorne, and its founder George Ripley, were New England intellectuals; and it was influenced by Transcendentalism, a moral and spiritual doctrine to which numbers of New England writers and social critics adhered. Transcendentalism was an American variant of the idealist philosophy which teaches that the world of material objects as we see them is really no more than an expression of mind or consciousness. Transcendentalists believed that since it is mind rather than the objective and physical world that is the ultimate reality, the mind ought to draw into itself and cultivate its own powers. Transcendentalist intellectuals such as Ralph Waldo Emerson opposed slavery and other institutions that they perceived as getting in the way of individual and collective perfection. Emerson's *Essays* (1844) emphasized self-reliance and originality, perhaps a semi-solitary life close to nature. Brook Farm aimed at combining manual and intellectual work; this, its members hoped, would develop and enrich the inner self. Brook Farm—much of it destroyed by a major fire—is remembered for the high and not always practical intellectuality of its life, though residents did operate a successful experimental school.

The Oneida Community   John Humphrey Noyes, whose social ideas rested on perfectionism, founded a community at Oneida in upstate New York. Residents operated thriving manufactures, but the community was better known for its sexual arrangements. Wishing to substitute cooperativeness for competitive individualism, Noyes prohibited "special love" and instead established "complex marriage," a system in which every member resident was considered married to every other of the opposite sex. Like the Shakers, the communitarians at Oneida were seeking to control sexuality. They wished to break down the idea that any woman "belonged" to any man or that any child was the exclusive "property" of the biological parents. So while the Shakers practiced strict abstinence, Noyes and his followers engaged in what they called "sexual communion." This involved sexual intercourse in which the male refrained from climax, unless the community had previously decided on the desirability of the woman's becoming pregnant.

Sexual communion involved the regular rotation of sexual partners.

The sharp line between men's and women's spheres did not exist at the Oneida community, as this photo of a pea-shelling bee in the 1850s shows. *(Courtesy, Oneida Ltd. Silversmiths)*

And it entailed the use of communal nurseries to raise children. Women had sexual equality with the men and shared in the work; the entire community had responsibility for the children. The community had a prosperous and successful existence, derived from making Oneida silverplate and carrying on other successful business enterprises. Later in the century it abandoned complex marriage in the face of attacks from moral critics.

Social Reform

Some shared an optimistic conviction that the United States was still a growing society, not yet set in its ways, and therefore malleable to the reformers' efforts. Some prison reformers, for example, thought that new penitentiaries would all but eradicate crime. Others came to reform out of a deep pessimism. They believed that American society was in an advanced state of collapse and that only the most radical reform could halt the decay they saw all about them.

At the top of their list of danger signals was the decline, as pessimistic reformers saw it, of religion in American public life. Actually, Americans in the Jacksonian era were much more likely to belong to a church and to attend it faithfully than their parents and grandparents of the Revolutionary era had been. But as people followed the frontier westward, they left their churches behind and many feared that the Ohio and Mississippi Valleys would develop as pagan enclaves. Or worse. Protestants worried that the Catholic presence in St. Louis, a holdover from the French exploration of the Mississippi, might presage the loss of the interior of the continent to Romanism, as Catholicism was often called. Many Americans were leaving their homes not for the frontier but for the rapidly growing cities. Some, like Rochester, New York, were brand new boom towns. Others, like New York City, were already well established. No longer was the church the essential institution it had been, and still was, in village life. No longer did the pastor exert personal influence over everyone's public behavior. In the cities houses of prostitution operated seven days a week. Taverns served all comers. And the city's anonymity weakened old forms of social control, such as neighbors' disapproval of certain kinds of behavior. Large-scale immigration, especially of Irish and German Catholics, seemed further to endanger the old reign of Protestant morality.

Still another danger sign was the crime that accompanied urban growth. Packs of young toughs roamed the streets and made travel after dark a risky undertaking. As disturbing as crime was the growth of a highly visible underclass of the propertyless and homeless. Middle- and upper-class Americans were horrified to discover young children, often called street arabs, sleeping in alleyways, begging for food, and selling themselves into prostitution.

In the first half of the nineteenth century, reformers of all sorts set themselves the task of shoring up the social order, as pessimists thought, or to perfect what optimists believed to be an already progressive society. Such organizations as the Bible Society, the American Tract

Society, and the Home Missionary Society worked to instill religious principles in the population or portions of it; meanwhile, revivalists like Charles G. Finney preached to crowds. Other reformers worked for education, women's rights, improvement of prisons, care of the insane, temperance in drinking, total abstinence from drink, or the abolition of war. The best known of the reform movements, of course, were those opposed to slavery. Some opponents of slavery wished to colonize former slaves in Africa; some wanted to keep slavery from being permitted in the western territory; others, the most militant, called for abolition of slavery in the South. For all its varieties and conflicts of objectives, much of the reformist activity in the United States was of a single mind in its restless morality, its conviction that the world can be improved.

Personal experience motivated such reformers as southern abolitionists Angelina and Sarah Grimké, of a South Carolina slaveholding family, and the black abolitionist Frederick Douglass. Thomas Gallaudet's work for the deaf led to the founding of the American Asylum, a free school for the deaf in Hartford, Connecticut. Numbers of reformers, especially members of the Bible societies and the American Tract Society, came from a social elite. Fearing that disorder would grow worse unless the masses were inculcated with proper values, they took it upon themselves to serve as the moral stewards of the nation. "The gospel is the most economical police on earth," said a leader of the Home Missionary Society. The religious enthusiasm of the 1830s inspired such men as the antislavery activist Theodore Dwight Weld and the temperance advocate Neal Dow. And the prevalent belief in moral perfectionism sharpened the conviction of many reformers. Samuel Gridley Howe, a doctor, toured the country with a blind and deaf girl, Laura Bridgman, in order to prove that such people were not mentally deficient. The abolitionist editor William Lloyd Garrison, for example, became so committed to moral purity that he publicly burned a copy of the Constitution, symbolically dissociating himself from a document contaminated by slavery.

One former drinker confessed:

"I began Backsliding to the drinking of Eggnog. I went to a house-raising never thinking Satan would tempt me But they had the curse of the nation there and they took sugar, milk, and Eggs and stirred into the whiskey and begged me to Drink of it and I was green enough to submit and drank too much I crawled away and lay down, trying to hide the Disgrace. Poor old mother wept bitter tears when she heard of my Downfall and begged me to repent But all to no purpose for I was young and stubborn. I kept going on from bad to worse. Drinking fighting gambling playing the fiddle for dances and a great many other things."

Temperance   From colonial days Americans had been heavy drinkers. When Thomas Jefferson returned from France in 1789, he brought back over three hundred bottles of wine. New Englanders settled for rum, which the Puritans and later generations distilled from West Indian molasses. Before the advent of canals and railroads, farmers often sent their corn to market distilled in a jug or barrel: whiskey cost less than corn to ship over long distances and found a ready market. In many places it was safer to drink than water. An early nineteenth-century traveler in Ohio found the use of ardent spirits near universal: "A house could not be raised, a field of wheat cut down, nor could there be a log rolling, a husking, a quilting, a wedding, a sheepwashing, or a funeral without the aid of alcohol." Concerned particularly over the harm that drink could do to the family, reformers mounted a determined attack on it.

The temperance crusade was one of the most successful reforms. Using techniques borrowed from religious revivals and mass politics, temperance workers distributed leaflets, held "cold water parades," and

The DRUNKARD'S PROGRESS,

OR THE DIRECT ROAD TO POVERTY WRETCHEDNESS & RUIN.

Designed and Published by J.W.Barber, *New Haven. Com. Sept. 1826.*

Woe unto them that rise up early in the morning that they may follow Strong Drink . . . Isa. 5 C. 11v.

Woe unto them that are mighty to drink wine, and men of strength to mingle Strong Drink . . . Isaiah 5 C.22v.

Who hath woe? Who hath sorrow? Who hath contentions? Who hath wounds without cause? . . . They that tarry long at the wine. Prov. 23

The drunkard shall come to poverty. Proverbs. 23. Chap. 21 v. The wages of Sin is Death *Romans. 6. Chap. 23 v*

The MORNING DRAM.

The Beginning of Sorrow, Neglect of Business, Idleness, Languor, Loss of Appetite, Dulness and Heaviness, a love of Strong Drink increasing.

The GROG SHOP.

Bad Company, Profaneness, Cursing and Swearing, Quarreling & Fighting, Gambling, Obscenity, Ridicule and Hatred of Religion. The Gate of Hell.

The CONFIRMED DRUNKARD.

Beastly Intoxication, Loss of Character, Loss of Natural Affection, Family Suffering, Brutality, Misery, Disease, Mortgages, Sheriffs, Writs &c.

CONCLUDING SCENE.

Poverty, Wretchedness, a Curse and Burden upon Society, Want, Beggary, Pauperism, Death.

An 1826 caricature depicting the evils of drink. *(Courtesy, The New-York Historical Society)*

organized lecture circuits of reformed drunkards who made emotional appeals for converts to sign temperance pledges.

In the late 1830s a million people belonged to temperance societies. Timothy Shay Arthur's lurid account of the evils of drink, *Ten Nights in a Bar-room, and What I Saw There* (1845), ranked just behind *Uncle Tom's Cabin* as a best-seller of the 1850s. A book of etiquette of the period instructed a lady to write to a young man fond of liquor: "Under ordinary circumstances, I would be delighted to go to the opera with you. I regret to add, however, that I have undoubted evidence that you are becoming addicted to the use of the wine-cup. With an earnest prayer for your reformation, ere it be too late, I beg you to consider our intimacy at an end." The growing numbers of immigrants, the Germans bringing their tradition of beer and the Irish their taste for hard liquor, gave temperance crusaders further concern, and gave to the temperance cause an element of anti-Catholicism and hostility to immigrants. Many women's rights activists also joined the cause. Feminists argued that women, as the victims of the behavior of drunken men, were the chief sufferers.

Slowly, moral appeals gave way to political action. Under the leadership of Neal Dow, Maine in 1851 passed the nation's first state-wide prohibition statute. In the next decade over a dozen states followed Maine's lead, although not all of these measures remained on the books.

The temperance agitation of those times and later is remembered

"Signing the Pledge."
A temperance society lithograph of
1846. *(Courtesy, Library of Congress)*

Alcohol Consumption per Capita, 1820–1850

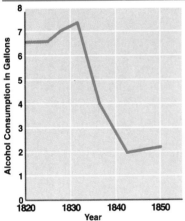

Whatever the underlying causes for the dramatic fall in alcohol consumption during the 1830s, the untiring efforts of temperance reformers must have had some effect.

for its passion and its moral absolutism. Yet within the temperance movement were advocates not of total abstinence from alcohol but of moderation in its use, accompanied perhaps by a decision to refrain from hard liquor. Some of the evils they denounced were real. Drunkenness on the frontier, and in the growing cities with their individuals uprooted from traditional communities and thrown into urban crowds and poverty, was a destroyer of families and lives. In the course of the nineteenth century, restraint in the use of alcohol appears to have spread. That may be attributable to orderly conduct inculcated by public schooling, and to the diffusion throughout society of middle-class modes of behavior. But surely some credit should go to the temperance crusade itself.

Public   For much of American history, formal education had
Education   been the province of families who could afford to pay
                           for it. The Puritans, of course, had been exceptions
to that rule, but for the most part, until the early nineteenth century, education was a private affair. Jacksonians wanted to remove education from the control of social and economic elites.

Like temperance, educational reform appealed both to Americans who believed that moral decay was spreading throughout the land and to others who more cheerfully thought that their age was a time of universal progress. Horace Mann, the first Massachusetts superintendent of education, warned that "the unrestrained passions of men are not only homicidal, but suicidal; and a community without a conscience would soon extinguish itself." Universal education, entailing moral guidance and firm discipline, must become the responsibility of the state and receive public financing. Mann and his supporters in the common school movement argued that leaving education in the hands of families, or preserving it as a luxury of the elite, threatened the nation's political and economic stability. The schools would also prepare Americans for the exercise of intelligent, informed citizenship.

In 1800 there were no public school systems outside New England; by 1850 every state had at least some public elementary and secondary schools. Northern states surpassed southern in the percentage of white children enrolled. Several states made appropriations for schools to educate the deaf and the blind. Public schools required a new, more practical curriculum in place of the traditional, classical learning designed for an elite. The study of Greek and Latin along with classical authors would be of limited value for future generations of farmers and mechanics. McGuffey's *Reader* and Webster's *Speller,* whose short lessons simultaneously taught useful skills and proper moral habits, became standard classroom texts, and teachers added exercises in geography, American history, and science. Gradually, the look of the classroom changed—maps, globes, and blackboards all made their first appearance.

Institutions of higher education also proliferated. New kinds of schools opened: technical schools such as Rensselaer Polytechnic Institute in New York; state universities in most western states; hundreds of denominational colleges; and some "colleges"—more correctly, advanced academies and seminaries—for women. Women's education presented a special problem and challenge to the reform movement. Since the end of the eighteenth century, sentiment had grown among both men and women in favor of education for women. But few of those who sought to educate women wanted to train them for the professions or otherwise give them a schooling identical to men's. Women were to be educated for enlightened republican motherhood, and to be suitable companions to educated husbands. Female educators such as Emma Willard, founder of Troy Seminary, and Mary Lyon, who founded Mount Holyoke Seminary, justified women's schooling with the claim that educated women would enhance the home. But increasingly, some female educators, notably Catharine Beecher—daughter of Lyman Beecher and sister of Harriet Beecher Stowe—also stressed the importance of educating women as primary school teachers, especially single women who would have to earn their livings. The teaching profession, by the middle of the century distinctly moving toward feminization, was viewed as an appropriate extension of women's primary domestic role.

Throughout higher education the content of schooling changed. Older universities modified their curricula, reducing the heavy dose of theology and the classics in favor of modern languages, political economy, and the sciences. Several added professional programs in law, medicine, or engineering. A number of western colleges adopted the unusual concept of student self-help through manual labor. Founded by radical reformers, these schools, such as Oberlin in Ohio (also, in 1837, the first to be coeducational) and Knox in Illinois, became centers of both educational experimentation and antislavery activism.

In taking over from the family the primary obligation for schooling, the state was doing what it was coming to do also for other dependent members of society. Formerly, responsibility for them, too, had gone to the family or to local authorities; but as an increasing density of popula-

In a republic," Horace Mann wrote "ignorance is a crime."

"If we do not prepare children to become good citizens—if we do not develop their capacities, if we do not enrich their minds with knowledge, imbue their hearts with the love of truth and duty, and a reverence for all things sacred and holy, then our republic must go down to destruction, as others have gone before it; and mankind must sweep through another vast cycle of sin and suffering, before the dawn of a better era. . . ."

tion intensified social problems, reformers began seeking better solutions. To the Christian cult of perfectionism these humanitarians added a growing belief in the power of environment to shape human character. The result, in the words of one historian, was "the discovery of the asylum."

Reform of Prisons and Asylums

At the urging of reformers, most states rewrote their colonial penal codes, abolishing imprisonment for debt and restricting the application of the death penalty to murderers. For lesser offenses, imprisonment took the place of such brutal corporal punishments as whipping, dunking, and branding. To house and rehabilitate prisoners, the states began to build modern prisons. (Connecticut had formerly housed felons in an abandoned copper mine.) New York, with the construction of its prison at Auburn in 1821, inaugurated the system of individual confinement by night and group labor by day. Under the theory that isolation would promote moral reflection (in fact it often promoted suicide), Pennsylvania in 1829 established a penitentiary that provided for strict solitary confinement of prisoners at all times. Alexis de Tocqueville concluded that while the Pennsylvania system made "the deepest impression on the soul of the convict," the Auburn system was "more conformable to the habits of man in society, and on this account effects a greater number of reformations." States also created special correctional facilities for juveniles, and for minor criminals such as drunks and vagrants.

Before 1840, victims of mental illness had been cared for privately—in locked rooms, cages, or outhouses—or else confined to jails and poorhouses. A Massachusetts schoolteacher, Dorothea Dix, undertook an investigation of the problem in her native state. Armed with the facts, she prepared a memorial to the legislature. Pledging to "tell what I have seen," she described graphically "the *present* state of insane persons confined within the Commonwealth, in *cages, closets, cellars, stalls, pens! chained, naked, beaten with rods, and lashed into obedience!*" The lawmakers, shocked by her descriptions, voted funds in 1843 to enlarge the state hospital for the insane. During the next decade Miss Dix traveled over thirty thousand miles in behalf of her cause. As a result, nearly every state made some provision for the care and treatment of the indigent insane. Some members of the health care services were also coming to believe that asylums, besides easing the suffering of the mentally ill, could provide an environment in which patients could regain their sanity.

The Science of Reform

The concept of the penitentiary and the asylum, along with the extension of the public school system, shared half explicit assumptions. One of them, reflected also in religious perfectionism and those temperance advocates who called for voluntary abstinence or moderation, was that human will and intelligence can be brought to master the rest of the wayward personality. Criminals can be conditioned to overcome their deviant impulses, the insane to recover lucidity, schoolchildren to acquire or-

Dorothea Dix's crusade on behalf of victims of mental illness led most states to make provisions for the indigent insane. *(Courtesy, Library of Congress)*

derly thought and conduct. Beyond this was a notion that there is a right method for improving the state of individuals and society. Even as assertive democrats were denying that scientific professions have the right to establish standards for admission, fields of social expertise were beginning to emerge. A people increasingly aware that method could trap steam and command threads to weave themselves into fabrics could scarcely doubt that method might also bring health to society and its members.

Women's Sphere The career of Dorothea Dix illustrates nicely the general plight of free women in the mid-nineteenth century. Intelligent, educated, and an expert in her field, she was obliged, in the interests of maintaining a "womanly dignity," to work quietly, rarely speaking in public herself. The only professions open to upper-class and middle-class women at that time were those of teacher, missionary, and writer; women of other classes worked in factories or as laundresses, seamstresses, or servants.

In other ways, society was defining for middle-class women a life of privacy and domesticity. From the beginning of the nineteenth century, but especially following 1820 and particularly in the Northeast, home was becoming separate from income-earning work. A major reason was that the development of commerce and cities, along with the march of modern industry, created workplaces physically as well as socially distant from dwellings. Men went out to work; women, or a large proportion of them, stayed home. This separation of home from "work" reinforced the nineteenth-century ideals of domesticity and true womanhood, which suggested that human life is divided into a public male sphere of labor and a private female sphere of nurture and morality. In the home under a woman's governance a "man . . . seeks refuge . . . where some of his finest sympathies, tastes, and moral and religious feelings are formed and nourished," so declared a New Hampshire minister in 1827.

Public opinion and economic circumstance were embodied in the law, which regarded women as perpetual minors. Married women had almost no rights over their property or children and could not sue in their own name. They could not even sign contracts. Divorces were rarely granted. The Civil War diarist Mary Chesnut wrote: "there is no slave . . . like a wife."

Women and Reform After the Seneca Falls Convention of 1848, all this could have discouraged women from joining reform movements, which aggressively entered the public sphere that tradition claimed to be the domain of males; and many women undoubtedly drew that lesson. But the idea central to the nineteenth-century exclusion of women from public life, the belief that they possessed a superior intuition into morality and a superior urge to nurture the sick and helpless, was to provide in time an argument for their entrance into the public sphere. If morality is the special province of women, they must have important things to say about issues that were

This letter of 1837 expresses the Congregationalist clergy's reaction to speeches in favor of abolitionism. The document indicates the degree of authority felt and exercised by the clergy at that time, and their concern over the public role of women who were making speeches at antislavery conventions.

"We invite your attention to the dangers which at present seem to threaten the female character with wide-spread and permanent injury.

The appropriate duties and influence of woman are clearly stated in the New Testament. Those duties and that influence are unobtrusive and private, but the source of mighty power. When the mild, dependent, softening influence of woman upon the sternness of man's opinions is fully exercised, society feels the effects of it in a thousand forms. The power of woman is in her dependence, flowing from the consciousness of that weakness which God has given her for her protection, and which keeps her in those departments of life that form the character of individuals and of the nation. We appreciate the unostentatious prayers and efforts of woman in advancing the cause of religion at home and abroad; in Sabbath-schools; in leading religious inquirers to the pastors for instruction; and in all such associated effort as becomes the modesty of her sex. . . .

But when she assumes the place and tone of man as a public reformer. . . , we put ourselves in self-defence against her; she yields the power which God has given her for protection, and her character becomes unnatural. We cannot, therefore, but regret the mistaken conduct of those who encourage females to bear an obtrusive and ostentatious part in measures of reform, and countenance any of that sex who so far forget themselves as to itinerate in the character of public lecturers and teachers."

ELIZABETH BLACKWELL

Elizabeth Blackwell was the first woman in the United States to receive a medical degree, awarded to her by Geneva Medical College in 1849. She had applied for admission to Harvard, Yale, and other schools only to be rejected. Then she was accepted by a little known institution in upstate New York. She was overjoyed to receive a letter stating:

"Resolved that one of the radical principles of a Republican Government is the universal education of both sexes; that to every branch of scientific education the door should be open equally to all; that the application of Elizabeth Blackwell to become a member of our class meets with our entire approbation."

Classmates gave these accounts:

"Elizabeth Blackwell was a determined young lady and took the train and stage to the village on Seneca Lake. Her first step was to find a room in a boarding house, but many landladies were afraid to rent a room to a female planning to become a doctor. What would the other boarders say? Finally Elizabeth persuaded a tough-minded Scotswoman to accept her. Her fellow boarders were shocked. Some ignored her; others gave her a frozen glance.

She then went to the college where the dean was astonished to see her; he had never expected that she would actually appear. He told her that in order to matriculate she needed the approval of the faculty and student body. Furthermore she would need the unanimous approval of the students who had never voted unanimously in the history of the college.

Great was the excitement and hilarity of the students who treated the matter as a joke. Some shouted: 'Down with the men.' Others called for trousers for all students. When the student chairman put the motion to admit Elizabeth to the college, the assembly shouted 'Yes.' One weak voice in the corner said 'No.' At once his neighbors surrounded him, shoved him to the floor, and pounded on his shoulders. He finally whispered 'Yes.'

The dean wrote a letter to Miss Blackwell welcoming

This portrait, by Elizabeth Glaser of Maryland in about 1830, epitomizes the "cult of true womanhood." The doll-like woman seems unsuited for anything more demanding than fanning herself. *(Courtesy, Scribner's Archives)*

at once public and moral, such as the dangers of alcohol, or matters concerning the protection of the weak and the ill.

Women engaged in a long struggle to assert their right to speak in public, to organize, and eventually to vote on behalf of moral issues. They made slow but solid progress. In their effort they relied particularly upon the bonds and networks that they had established with other women—the bonds of sisterhood. These female networks supported a wide variety of female associations providing charity to the needy, raising funds for the education of ministers, combating slavery, working for various moral reforms that included temperance and the elimination of prostitution, and giving support to mothers seeking to set their children on the right path. Although many reform associations, such as those contributing to the abolitionist and the temperance movements, remained firmly under male leadership throughout the first half of the nineteenth century, female reformers supplied much of the dedication.

Women's Rights

The cause of women's rights soon became a movement in itself. Lucy Stone, an antislavery and women's rights activist who retained her maiden name after marriage, refused to pay taxes since she was not represented in the government. Some women rejected their long, immobilizing skirts in favor of the less constricting "Bloomer" costume. It consisted of a tunic that fell to mid-calf worn over a pair of ample bloomers that covered the legs and were gathered tightly at the ankle. In its time and place, it earned the women who wore it ridicule, hostility, and a show-her to the student body. The students signed it with mixed feelings. Many thought that she would not accept or would never stay because of the hostile greeting. Dean James Hadley, however, offered to conduct her to her first class and he urged the students to treat her with respect. Although she had to suffer some pranks and horseplay, she soon showed her ability. In 1849 she graduated at the head of her class."

Another observer described the commencement exercises to a friend:

"We sat in the Second tier [the gallery]. About half past ten or eleven the procession entered the building. The Lioness of the day, Miss Blackwell, met them at the door and entered with the Medical Students—*without* hat or shawl. She wore a black silk dress and cape-lace collar and cuffs and her reddishly inclined hair was very nicely braided. She sat in the front side pew with old Mrs. Waller until she received her Diploma. . . . Take it altogether—*the ladies* carried the day! There was scarcely a coat—excepting the Students'—visible! Nothing but a vast expanse of woman's [sic] bonnets and curious eyes. The noise on the 'Singers' bench' completed, President Hale made a brief Address to the graduating class, then donned the velvet cap and seated himself in the large chair. . . . He called up the graduates. Four at a time they came on the stage. The Doctor spoke. They *looked* Knowing. One of them grasped the bundle of sheepskins, all four bowed and vanished. Last of all came 'Domina Blackwell'. She ascended the steps. The President touched his cap and rose. You might have heard a pin drop. He handed her the diploma and bowed, evidently expecting she would bow also and retreat. Not so, however! She seemed embarrassed and after an effort, said to the Dr.—'I thank you Sir. It shall be the effort of my life, by God's blessing, to shed honor on this Diploma'—then bowed, blushed scarlet, left the stage and took her seat in the front pew among the Graduates amid the Enthusiastic applause of all present. . . ."

Dr. Elizabeth Blackwell founded the New York Infirmary for Women and Children where she trained women to become doctors.

ering of rotten eggs and tomatoes. Even those most determined advocates of women's rights, Susan B. Anthony and Elizabeth Cady Stanton, eventually gave up the mode of dress with heartfelt relief. The Bloomer costume was an attempt to break through social convention and constriction. Other reforms aimed at protecting women against the harms to which they were distinctively subject.

Woman reformers proved especially active in defense of the personal rights of other women whom they perceived as oppressed or exploited by the familial and sexual demands of men. Susan B. Anthony helped a woman kidnap her child from her husband's custody—idealization of motherhood notwithstanding, fathers usually got custody of children. Other women worked for temperance to protect women from the beatings and domestic violence of drunken husbands. Objecting to the double standard that allowed men to have sex outside marriage while denying it to women, a group of New York women started a society to reform the city's prostitutes.

Numbers of middle-class women who took up feminist causes had begun by becoming involved in other social reforms. As women extended their interests outside the home, met together, assumed leadership, and became adept at public speaking, they soon came to recognize the status in which women were kept. "In striving to strike the [black man's] irons off, we found most surely, that *we* were manacled ourselves," wrote Abby Kelley, a women's rights leader. But if the antislavery cause helped launch the women's rights movement, it also contributed to a temporary demise. Even many sympathetic men aban-

Angelina Emily Grimké, originally from South Carolina, was both an abolitionist and a crusader for women's rights. She wrote succinctly that

"[I]t is a woman's right to have a voice in all the laws and regulations by which she is governed, whether in Church or State. . . . The present arrangements of society, on these points are a *violation of human rights, a rank usurpation of power,* a violent seizure and confiscation of what is sacredly and inalienably hers."

Sojourner Truth. In her bag
she often carried copies of the
narrative of her life to sell.
*(Courtesy, State University College,
New Paltz, N.Y.)*

doned feminist causes when they threatened to divert or divide the antislavery crusade.

One especially striking feminist was a former slave, Sojourner Truth. Born Isabella in New York in 1797, she stood at a stunning six feet. A domestic servant for many years following New York's emancipation law of 1827 and illiterate until her death, she was a commanding orator in the cause of both abolition and women's rights.

Reaction   Women's rights advocates encountered stiff resistance from conservative groups. Industrialization, the reform movements, and the rise of a democratic political culture were rapidly altering American society, and most people wanted to preserve at least some of the old ways. They decided to keep their homes as they supposedly had always been, and that meant confining women to domestic careers as wives and mothers. The "Cult of Domesticity," or "True Womanhood," was a powerful force. Popular magazines talked incessantly about the elevated status of women: they raised the sons who would become the next generation's leaders, they kept men's sexual passions in line, and their purity, chastity, and compassion preserved virtue and gentility in a rapidly changing world. A popular poem of the 1840s, very much in the spirit of "True Womanhood," is a repudiation of the women's rights movement. The only "rights" that women embrace, the poet explains, are

> The right to love whom others scorn,
> The right to comfort and to mourn,
> The right to shed new joy on earth,
> The right to feel the soul's high birth.

Many years after the event, an Ohio feminist, who had presided over the 1851 women's rights convention, recorded this inspiring talk of Sojourner Truth:

Every eye was fixed on this almost Amazon form, which stood nearly six feet high, head erect, and eyes piercing the upper air like one in a dream. At her first word there was a profound hush. She spoke in deep tones, which, though not loud, reached every ear in the house, and away through the throng at the doors and windows.

"Wall, chilern, whar dar is so much racket dar must be somethin' out o' kilter. I tink dat 'twixt de niggers of de Souf and de womin at de Norf, all talkin' 'bout rights, de white men will be in a fix pretty soon. But what's all dis here talkin' 'bout?

Dat man ober dar say dat womin needs to be helped into carriages, and lifted ober ditches, and to hab de best place everywhar. Nobody eber helps me into carriages, or ober mud-puddles, or gibs me any best place!" And raising herself to her full height, and her voice to a pitch like rolling thunder, she asked, "And a'n't I a woman? Look at me! Look at my arm! (and she bared her right arm to the shoulder, showing her tremendous muscular power). I have ploughed, and planted, and gathered into barns, and no man could head me! And a'n't I a woman? I could work as much and eat as much as a man—when I could get it—and bear de lash as well! And a'n't I a woman? I have borne thirteen chilern, and seen 'em mos' all sold off to slavery, and when I cried out with my mother's grief, none but Jesus heard me! And a'n't I a woman? . . .

Den dat little man in black dar, he say women can't have as much rights as men, 'cause Christ wan't a woman! Whar did your Christ come from?" Rolling thunder couldn't have stilled that crowd, as did those deep, wonderful tones, as she stood there with outstretched arms and eyes of fire. Raising her voice still louder, she repeated, "Whar did your Christ come from? From God and a woman! Man had nothin' to do wid Him." Oh, what a rebuke that was to that little man.

The Dark Side of Reform

The reform movements were not unmixed blessings for the United States. The reformers, in their passion for eliminating evil, sometimes defined evil in a way that had vicious consequences.

Hostility to Catholicism and Mormonism   The conviction that American society has special democratic and moral traditions to preserve and protect has led more than once to movements to rid the country of something or somebody. A case in point is the rapid growth of anti-Catholic sentiment after 1830. Before then American Catholics had been too few in number to attract much attention. Over the next thirty years, mass immigration, especially from Ireland and Germany, swelled the Catholic proportion of the total population from one in fifty to one in ten. Many native-born Protestants believed that the newcomers posed a direct threat to the nation's democratic heritage. In part this conviction grew out of their understanding of history.

The American Revolution, in their eyes, was an extension of the Protestant Reformation, particularly of Luther's doctrine of the primacy of individual conscience. The Reformation, many thought, had been a struggle for liberty against an oppressive, autocratic perversion of true

Some native-born Protestant Americans despised immigrant Catholics, as illustrated in this lithograph of a Philadelphia riot in 1844 between Catholics and non-Catholics. This sentiment led to the founding of the American Party in the 1850s. *(Courtesy, Library of Congress)*

Christianity. Their own Revolution had carried the struggle into the political domain. So the rapid increase in the Catholic population caused many to worry for the nation's commitment to a republican form of government. Such prominent men as Lyman Beecher, the celebrated preacher, and the inventor Samuel F. B. Morse warned against "papal puppets working to inflame and divide the nation, break the bond of our union, and throw down our free institutions." American bishops and other Catholic clergy aggressively campaigned in New York City and Lowell, Massachusetts, and elsewhere for public funds for parochial schools, an issue that especially inflamed Protestants. Militant Protestants formed societies aimed at converting "Papists" to Christianity (these had little success) and stoutly resisted all attempts at suggestions of public aid to parochial schools (sometimes with success, sometimes not). Some antislavery activists were hostile to Catholicism, holding it to be, like slavery, an affront to republican freedom.

Anti-Catholicism, however, did not spring simply from devoted concern for the purity of the Revolutionary tradition. It also sprang from distaste for the immigrants themselves. The Irish were stereotyped as drunken brutes. One woman recalled seeing the "poor fellows, strung along the canal, stupid from drink . . . they are for the most part covered with mud, where they have rolled when drunk." The German-American practice of bringing beer even to such innocent activities as Sunday picnics affronted Protestant sensibilities. Protestant nativists also drew upon centuries of anti-Catholic propaganda. Zealots composed and circulated fictitious stories of convent life replete with sex orgies among nuns and priests.

Mormons, like Catholics, came into conflict with many traditional Protestants. Wherever they had settled, Mormons voted as a bloc, following the dictates of their leaders, Joseph Smith and later Brigham Young. In their loyalty to their community and its leaders, the Mormons closed ranks and often enjoyed political power far greater than numbers alone would provide. The practice of polygamy was also an outrage to nineteenth-century Protestantism. It contradicted the Bible, the laws of the land, and the cult of true womanhood. In the 1840s Mormons were victims of harassment and violence.

The Anti-Immigrant Crusade

The attacks on Catholics and Mormons were part of a larger, ethnocentric fear of immigrants. While the influx of millions of Irish immigrants in the 1830s and 1840s swelled the numbers of Catholics in the United States, the Mormon Church had attracted thousands of immigrant converts from the British Isles and Scandinavia. The fear on the part of native-born Protestants was not only of alien religions, but also of immigration in itself as a threat to democratic values and the fundamentals of Anglo-American culture.

For some time, a nativist movement had been prominent in American society and politics. In 1843 the American Republican Party called for limiting the right to vote to native-born American Protestants. In April 1844 nativists established the American Republican Association at Philadelphia. Its anti-immigrant rhetoric led to rioting in Philadelphia and the deaths of twenty people. The next year the group became known as the American Party. By the early 1850s it would be known as the "Know-Nothing Party," after a popular perception of its members as secretive, refusing to acknowledge that they knew anything about the movement.

The Arts

During Jacksonian times and just after, the United States at last achieved cultural independence of Europe in literature, painting, and architecture. The newly popular lyceums and public lectures furnished native talent with an audience. In 1860 knowledgeable Europeans would no longer ask, as one English literary wit had in 1820, "In the four quarters of the globe, who reads an American book? Or goes to an American play? Or looks at an American picture or statue?"

Speaking at Harvard in 1837, the transcendentalist philosopher Ralph Waldo Emerson attacked "the timid, imitative, and tame" in American creative life. Americans, he asserted, must learn to work with their own hands and speak with their own minds. And they were doing so.

American painters abandoned the formal, classical style of the eighteenth century. Influenced by the romantic movement and nationalism, they experimented with more individualistic, democratic, emotional styles of painting. Genre painters like William Sidney Mount and George Caleb Bingham took their studios outdoors to capture revealing incidents of American life. Bingham's "Stump Speaker" and "Country Elections" are miniature essays on Jacksonian politics. Nature painters like Thomas Cole glorified the spectacular qualities of the American landscape. Cole was a leader of the so-called Hudson River School, those painters who captured especially the magnificent Hudson River Valley with its deep woods, its jagged rocks, its sweeping vistas.

American architects also turned from eighteenth-century styles of European origin. Their search for a pure, simple, democratic architecture led naturally to the Greek Revival, inspired by the buildings of ancient Greece. Among the best examples of this style are Benjamin Latrobe's Bank of the United States at Philadelphia and Robert Mills's Treasury Building at Washington. Responding to the individualistic and romantic impulses of the age, American architects later adopted a variety of styles. By 1850 Philadelphia had an Egyptian jail, a Greek bank, medieval cottages, and Moorish churches, while New York boasted a synagogue with a Gothic tower.

William Sidney Mount, *The Banjo Player.* *(Courtesy, Museums at Stony Brook)*

William Sidney Mount, *Dancing On the Barn Floor.* *(Courtesy, Museums at Stony Brook)*

American Literature   American writers and poets too were influenced by the forces of nationalism. Breaking with the rigid neoclassical writing of the eighteenth century, they sought a literature that was expressive, imaginative, intuitive.

Much of American literature made use of native settings. Washington Irving drew on the history of his native New York in stories such as "Rip Van Winkle" and "The Legend of Sleepy Hollow" (1820). In a series of novels known as the "Leatherstocking Tales" (1823–41), James Fenimore Cooper's frontiersman is a noble figure. Not at all so are the vulgar common folks whom the patrician Cooper censured for their translation of democracy into pushy assertiveness.

Yet American literature, born of a nation that appeared so boisterously cheerful, was distinguishable for a character of brooding introspection, an exploration into the deepest human motives and the mind's most wayward fantasies. This surely was owing in part to the American religious preoccupation with the inner life. It may also be that American republicanism, in cutting the individual loose from the political and social institutions of older cultures, made novelists curious about the private, inward experience of the individual adrift. Edgar Allan Poe, examining the resources of the imagination with something of the experimental care that other Americans were addressing to the workings of the physical world, labored to awaken in his readers sensations of mystery and eeriness. Ralph Waldo Emerson composed carefully wrought essays and was a great orator. Nathaniel Hawthorne brought intensity, depth, and craftsmanship to the American novel. In works like *The Scarlet Letter* (1850) and *The House of the Seven Gables* (1851) he probed the souls of American Puritans. Hawthorne looked into dark

---

Ralph Waldo Emerson's most famous essay was "Self Reliance":

Trust thyself; every heart vibrates to that iron string. To believe your own thought, to believe that what is true for you in your private heart is true for all men—that is genius. In every work of genius we recognize our own rejected thoughts; they come back to us with a certain alienated majesty. Great works of art have no more affecting lesson for us than this. They teach us to abide by our spontaneous impression with good-humored inflexibility, then most when the whole cry of voices is on the other side. Else tomorrow a stranger will say with masterly good sense precisely what we have thought and felt all the time, and we shall be forced to take with shame our own opinion from another.

Whoso would be a man, must be a nonconformist. He who would gather immortal palms must not be hindered by the name of goodness, but must explore if it be goodness. Nothing is at last sacred but the integrity of our own mind. Absolve you to yourself, and you shall have the suffrage of the world.

What I must do is all that concerns me, not what the people think. This rule, equally arduous in actual and in intellectual life, may serve for the whole distinction between greatness and meanness. It is the harder because you will always find those who think they know what is your duty better than you know it. It is easy in the world to live after the world's opinion; it is easy in solitude to live after our own; but the great man is he who in the midst of the crowd keeps with perfect sweetness the independence of solitude.

The other terror that scares us from self-trust is our consistency. A foolish consistency is the hobgoblin of little minds, adored by little statesmen and philosophers and divines. With consistency a great soul has simply nothing to do. If you would be a man speak what you think today in words as hard as cannon balls, and tomorrow speak what tomorrow thinks in hard words again. . . .

Ralph Waldo Emerson. *(Library of Congress)*

motives and somber emotions, but looked as well for the innocence and freshness that human nature could contain. Herman Melville aspired to be a "thought-diver." His *Moby Dick* (1851), with its driven Captain Ahab searching for the great white whale, symbolized the human quest for the mysterious forces of the universe.

Walt Whitman celebrated every democratic American impulse. He called for a poetry that was one with the spirit of the times and with the country's culture, incarnating its "geography and national life and rivers and lakes." Whitman's *Leaves of Grass* (1855) sings of American labor, land, place names, and crowds.

Popular Writing and Diversions Then, as now, the mass of Americans preferred a different sort of literature. The development of more efficient printing techniques sent inexpensive books and newspapers into wide circulation. The most prolific type of fiction was the sentimental domestic novel. Filled with scenes of domestic joy and sorrow, these novels preached conventional morality and pictured church, home, and family as anchors against life's trials. Novels like Mrs. E. D. E. N. Southworth's *Retribution* and Mary Jane Holmes's *Tempest and Sunshine* were best-sellers for years. Another form of popular culture was the humorous essay, which dated from Benjamin Franklin's *Poor Richard*. It gained new popularity in the 1830s with Seba Smith's *Jack Downing Papers*. Downing was a cracker-box philosopher who commented on current events and poked gentle fun at American foibles. Smith soon had dozens of imitators, among them James Russell Lowell's Hosea Bigelow, Charles F. Browne's Artemus Ward, and Johnson Hooper's Simon Slugs. Plays, minstrel shows, lectures, and public speaking also provided entertainment and education.

The cult of patriotism grew in the early nineteenth century. Holidays were increasingly devoted to skyrocketing oratory, parades, and patriotic enthusiasms. Monuments and statues appeared by the hundreds, and biographies of American heroes sold by the tens of thousands. And along with the cult of patriotism flourished a variety of popular symbols.

Americans had already adopted a native bird, the eagle. For holidays they chose Washington's Birthday and the Fourth of July. "Uncle Sam," a creation of the War of 1812, soon displaced "Yankee Doodle" as the national prototype. Although not adopted officially as the national anthem until 1931, Francis Scott Key's "Star-Spangled Banner" gradually replaced "My Country 'Tis of Thee." No token of nationalism became more important than the American flag. Originally created in 1777, the stars and stripes had remained chiefly a naval flag until 1834, when the army adopted it as well.

Along with symbols, Americans needed heroes. They turned to the Revolutionary War for material. By Jackson's day the important figures in the war—Ethan Allen and his Green Mountain Boys, the martyred Nathan Hale, and Generals Anthony Wayne and Nathanael Greene—were celebrated in song and prose. After the Battle of New Orleans, Andrew Jackson himself became an instant hero. Above all other national heroes was George Washington. Even before his death

Nathaniel Hawthorne. He and the other writers of the period—Poe, Emerson, Melville, Whitman, Thoreau—created a literature that was uniquely American and attracted international attention. *(Courtesy, Essex Institute, Salem, Massachusetts)*

Herman Melville wrote of Hawthorne:

"This great power of blackness in him derives its force from its appeal to that Calvinistic sense of innate depravity and original sin from whose visitation, in some shape or other, no deeply thinking mind is always and wholly free."

Abolitionism: Religious Movement or Psychic Aberration?

Abolitionism was a remarkably dangerous trade. Elijah Lovejoy had his printing press thrown in a river, and subsequently lost his life as a mob sought to seize a second. Other abolitionists also confronted angry mobs. Most escaped with their lives, but not without suffering harrowing ordeals. Terrifying as they were, some abolitionists seemed to court these dangers. Theodore Dwight Weld was wont to ride into hostile towns, announce an abolitionist meeting, and then attempt to convert the angry crowd.

This seeking of danger has led some historians to suspect that many abolitionists suffered from a martyr complex. This explanation may hold for one or another individual, but it is hazardous to psychoanalyze historical figures. And psychoanalysis deals with the individual psyche. It is misleading to speak of whole groups such as the abolitionists as if they shared a single mental life.

We still need to explain the extraordinary fortitude of the abolitionists. One explanation concentrates on the element of religious revivalism in the antislavery movement. Weld was a convert of the evangelist Charles Finney, as were many other abolitionists. They adopted the movement against slavery as a vocation, a form of ministry; it was their calling, the work they were intended to do. And, like the early Christians they so often modeled themselves after, they were even willing to suffer martyrdom. Not all abolitionists, of course, were evangelical converts; some, like William Lloyd Garrison, had no formal connection with any church. Yet Garrison too was an intensely religious person. He too regarded slavery as a sin. There is, in brief, much evidence to suggest that abolitionism is better understood as a religious movement than as a psychic aberration.

Washington had attained in the estimation of his countrymen a place above politics and above criticism. Much of the responsibility for the adulation of Washington should go to Mason Locke Weems. In 1800 this itinerant book salesman and evangelist published his *Life of Washington*. Partly fabricated (the cherry tree story started here), the book fulfilled the American public's need for heroes.

"We were taught every day and in every way," according to the recollections of one nineteenth-century American, "that ours was the freest, the happiest, and soon to be the greatest and most powerful country in the world. . . . We read it in our books and newspapers, heard it in sermons, speeches, and orations, thanked God for it in our prayers, and devoutly believed it always." Not even the cult of patriotism, however, could quiet the issue of slavery, the great contradiction to American patriotic pride in freedom.

The Antislavery Crusade

The roots of the antislavery movement in the United States stretched back to the eighteenth century. Confronted by the powerful forces of rationalism and revolution, many Americans had condemned slavery as incompatible with the egalitarianism of the Declaration of Independence. In 1787 Congress excluded slavery from the area it was organizing north of the Ohio River as the Northwest Territory. That same year the delegates to the Constitutional Convention agreed to a compromise permitting Congress to abolish the African slave trade in 1808. In the meantime, a number of northern states abolished slavery within their own borders, and abolition societies multiplied even in a few southern states.

Many Americans opposed to slavery rejected the idea of its immediate eradication in the South, fearing serious constitutional, economic, and social difficulties. Some favored a policy of gradual emancipation, to be followed by deportation. With the support of such influential men as Henry Clay and John Marshall, these gradualists in 1817 founded the American Colonization Society. The Society worked to resettle emancipated American blacks in Africa, particularly in the new country of Liberia on the coast of West Africa. "We are *natives* of this country," one protested; "we only ask that we be treated as well as *foreigners*." Their opposition gradually undermined the Society's efforts. In 1829 a free black named David Walker published "An Appeal to Blacks," calling for emancipation. The year after this work was published, Walker died under mysterious circumstances.

The Abolition Movement   During the early 1830s a small but vocal band of activists began calling for the total and immediate abolition of slavery. Abolitionism became an integral part of the reform ferment of the Jackson era. Slavery, abolitionists believed, was both a national and an individual sin; Americans could not wait for time or circumstance to eradicate it. These abolitionists viewed gradual emancipation and colonization as dead ends. Any large-scale

deportation of blacks would have raised both enormous practical obstacles and grave moral difficulties. And southern opposition to gradual emancipation, which stiffened after the invention of the cotton gin, indicated that the opponents of slavery had little to lose by adopting a more radical stance. The British abolitionist movement in winning in 1833 legal emancipation of British West Indian slaves gave new hope to advocates of immediate emancipation in the United States. The president of Harvard, Edward Everett, registered the intensity of these militants' feelings when he responded to criticism of his having allowed a black student to take the entrance test: "If this boy passes the examination he will be admitted; and if the white students choose to withdraw, all the income of the college will be devoted to his education."

Everett was a good representative of the eastern intellectual wing of the antislavery movement. Very many abolitionists were of a different character, drawing their inspiration from revivalistic religion. Their religion put the matter as bluntly as Everett but in a different vocabulary. Slavery is wrong; being a good Christian means rejecting and resisting it. When enough individuals embrace God's way, the larger society can be purged of evils such as slavery. Slaveholders meanwhile had only to recognize their complicity in sin and renounce it. It was by using the techniques of moral suasion—appealing to the American conscience rather than employing legal coercion—that abolitionists, so they thought, would end human bondage in the United States.

Garrison and Weld   One person led to abolitionism by perfectionist beliefs was the young William Lloyd Garrison. He had embraced a number of reform causes in the 1820s and worked with the famous Quaker abolitionist Benjamin Lundy before establishing his own antislavery newspaper, the *Liberator,* at Boston in 1831. Garrison preached the cause of immediate abolition with no compensation to slaveholders: "I *will be* as harsh as truth, and

Accounts of slaves sold and families broken made a powerful argument for abolition. Elwood Harvey, an observer at a sale of slaves, recounted the event:

"[In 1846] we attended a sale of land and other property, near Petersburg, Virginia, and unexpectedly saw slaves sold at public auction. The slaves were told they would not be sold, and were collected in front of the quarters, gazing on the assembled multitude. The land being sold, the auctioneer's loud voice was heard, 'Bring up the *niggers!*' A shade of astonishment and affright passed over their faces, as they stared first at each other, and then at the crowd of purchasers, whose attention was now directed to them. . . .

During the sale, the quarters resounded with cries and lamentations that made my heart ache. A woman was next called by name. She gave her infant one wild embrace before leaving it with an old woman, and hastened mechanically to obey the call; but stopped, threw her arms aloft, screamed, and was unable to move.

One of my companions touched my shoulder and said, 'Come, let us leave here; I can bear no more.' We left the ground. The man who drove our carriage from Petersburg had two sons who belonged to the estate—small boys. He obtained a promise that they should not be sold. Asked if they were his only children, he answered: 'All that's left of eight.' Three others had been sold to the South, and he would never see or hear from them again."

as uncompromising as justice. . . . I will not equivocate—I will not excuse—I will not retreat a single inch—AND I WILL BE HEARD." In his moral purity, he denounced the churches as "cages of unclean birds" for tolerating slavery. Northerners at first dismissed Garrison as a fanatic. But the Nat Turner revolt of 1831 made his name familiar throughout the nation, as nervous slaveholders connected the "incendiary publications" of Garrison, and others with the bloody events in Southampton County, Virginia, in which fifty-seven whites were killed. The Georgia Senate offered a $1,000 reward for Garrison's arrest and conviction. Newspapers throughout the country began reprinting his fiery editorials, and the stern Massachusetts editor soon became the very personification of abolition. On July 4, 1854, Garrison burned a copy of the Constitution, proclaiming "So perish all compromises with tyranny."

Some of Garrison's contemporaries, and a few later historians, considered Theodore Dwight Weld an even more important figure. Intense religious convictions about the evils of slavery had driven Weld, like Garrison, into the movement. After being converted by the evangelist Finney, he devoted his life to the cause of moral reform. In 1834, while a student at Cincinnati's Lane Theological Seminary, he organized debates on the slavery question. After eighteen nights of discussion, the students endorsed immediatism—immediate abolition—and rejected colonization. When their antislavery activities aroused opposition among Lane's trustees, Weld and forty others left to attend Oberlin College near Cleveland. Securing funds from two wealthy New York City reformers, Arthur and Lewis Tappan, the Lane rebels made Oberlin a center of abolitionist activity. By employing the techniques and rhetoric of the religious revival, they converted to abolitionism thousands throughout the Old Northwest and nearby areas of New York and Pennsylvania. Weld also joined with his southern wife, Angelina, and her sister, Sarah Grimké, to write *American Slavery as It Is* (1839). This popular tract, a compilation of southern newspaper accounts revealing the cruelties of slavery, offered documentary evidence to support the abolitionists' moral outrage. "Slaves," it declared,

> are often hunted with bloodhounds and shot down like beasts, or torn in pieces by dogs . . . they are often suspended by the arms and whipped and beaten till they faint, . . . and sometimes till they die; . . . they are maimed, mutilated and burned to death over slow fires. All these things, and more, and worse, we shall PROVE.

The treatment of slaves of course reflected the qualities of their masters. Some were kind. Frederick Douglass was "astonished" at the "goodness" of his mistress, Sophia Auld, "a woman of the kindest heart and finest feelings," who taught him how to read. Others were cruel. But that was not the point. The details of slave life were incidental to the violence that the institution of slavery in itself did to the nation's boast of freedom. So in time, the country's reformist energies converged upon the great, divisive, threatening question of slavery.

Suggested Readings

On the women's movement a good beginning is Elizabeth Cady Stanton's autobiography, *Eighty Years and More, Reminiscences, 1815–1897* (1898). Other studies are Barbara J. Berg, *The Remembered Gates: Origins of Feminism—Women and the City, 1800–1860* (1977). See also Blanche Glassman Hersh, *The Slavery of Sex: Feminists and Abolitionists in America* (1978), Ellen Carol DuBois, *Feminism and Suffrage* (1979), Donna Dickson, *Margaret Fuller: Writing a Woman's Life* (1993), Nancy Woloch, *Women and the American Experience* (1984), Mary P. Ryan, *Cradle of the Middle Class, The Family in Oneida County, New York, 1790–1865* (1981), Barbara Welter, *Godey's Lady's Book: The Women Who Wrote It and the Women Who Read It* (1989), and Christine Stansell, *City of Women: Sex and Class in New York, 1789–1860* (1980). On Sojourner Truth see Carlton Mabee, *Sojourner Truth: Slave, Prophet, Legend* (1993) and Nell Irvin Painter, *Sojourner Truth: A Life, A Symbol* (1996). See also Shirley Yee, *Black Women Abolitionists: A Study in Activism* (1992).

On antebellum reforms see Steven Mintz, *Moralists and Modernizers: American Pre–Civil War Reformers* (1995) and B. G. Walter's *American Reformers, 1815–1860* (1978). See also *The Discovery of the Asylum: Social Order and Disorder in the New Republic* (1971) by David S. Rothman. On religion see William G. McLoughlin, *Revivals, Awakenings, and Reform* (1978) and *Modern Revivalism: Charles Grandison Finney to Billy Graham* (1959), Lawrence Foster, *Woman, Family and Utopia: Communal Experiments of the Shakers, the Oneida Community and the Mormons* (1991), Michael Barkun, *Crucible of the Millenium: The Burned-over District of New York in the 1840s* (1966), Marvin S. Hill, *Quest for Refuge: The Mormon Flight from American Pluralism* (1989), Kenneth H. Winn, *Exiles in a Land of Liberty, 1830–1946* (1989), and Richard Rabinowitz, *The Spiritual Self in Everyday Life: The Transformation of Personal Religious Experience in Nineteenth-Century New England* (1989). See also Paul E. Johnson, *A Shopkeeper's Millennium: Society and Revivals in Rochester, New York, 1815–1837* (1978) and John Boles, *The Great Revival in the South* (1972). Herbert Hovenkamp, *Science and Religion in America, 1800–1860* (1978) is a useful survey of the relation of religious to scientific thought in the early republic.

A recent study of alternative lifestyles is Richard Francis, *Transcendental Utopias: Individual and Community at Brook Farm, Fruitlands, and Walden* (1997). See also Louis J. Kern, *An Ordered Love: Sex Roles and Sexuality: Three American Communal Experiments of the Nineteenth Century* (1981).

On the antislavery movement, there are James B. Stewart's *Holy Warriors: The Abolitionists and American Slavery* (1976), Robert H. Abzug, *Passionate Liberator, Theodore Dwight Weld and the Dilemna of Reform* (1980), Benjamin Quarles, *Black Abolitionists: The Negro in the Free States 1790* (1969), John L. Thomas, *The Liberator: William Lloyd Garrison* (1963), and Leonard L. Richands, *"Gentlemen of Property and Standing": Anti-Abolition Mobs in Jacksonian America* (1970).

See also Louis Gerteis, *Morality and Unity in American Antislavery Reform* (1987), Bertram Wyatt-Brown, *Lewis Tappan and the Evangelical War Against Slavery* (1959), Gerda Lerner, *The Grimké Sisters from South Carolina: Pioneers for Women's Rights and Abolition* (1967), and Blanche Hersh, *The Slavery of Sex: Female Abolitionists in Nineteenth-Century America* (1978).

Women in the Antebellum South: Plantation vs. City

Catherine Clinton

Rachel O'Conner of Louisiana was a woman planter of indefatigable energy. She chronicled her activities in a steady stream of correspondence to relatives. In November of 1823, she reported to her brother: "I have seventy bales of Cotton Prep'd and hauling them as fast as possible to the river to ship for N. Orleans—I answered my dear little Niece's last letter on saturday which I am afraid she cannot read easily. It rained and they were preparing cotton and I had to stop very often to get whatever they wanted which put me out of sorts." When her sister-in-law requested directions for planting leeks, Rachel O'Conner sent her a detailed set of instructions testifying to her planting expertise. She wrote to her brother David frequently about the trials of plantation business, bemoaning faulty machinery and the falling price of cotton. Many women kept detailed business records to safeguard themselves in the complex process of plantation management.

Such management, either in a husband's absence or during widowhood, was problematic for reasons that had nothing to do with a woman's personal experience or expertise. Wives who took little or no interest in farming accounts often regretted their neglect after their husband's death, and were forced to call upon male relatives for assistance. But even a mistress who demonstrated a clear ability to manage her plantation as a discrete economic unit and make it pay was not permitted by law to handle personal or business affairs in the public sphere. Women's inadequacies, real or perceived, were a direct result of the "sheltering" system that designated women as dependents, under the protection—and at the mercy—of men. While this sytem failed to keep women from exercising authority and demonstrating capability in daily routines, it effectively shackled them in any external dealing beyond plantation boundaries. Ready to make full use of her talents as household manager and domestic laborer, the society—ruled by males in the legislature and in the courts—deprived the plantation mistress of her own legal identity.

As a result, women rightly felt vulnerable in the world of legal finance. They held no power before the law, which provided for man's total control over woman: her property, her behavior, her very person. This was a logical development in an extended patriarchy, built upon racial and sexual differentiation and bolstered by a hierarchy of fixed roles and duties.

Moral and legal arguments quickly developed to guarantee a husband's domination of his wife, including, of course, the critical issue of reproduction. Women often referred to a girl's marrying as "resigning her liberty." One Virginia matron confessed to her journal: "Our mother Eve when she transgress'd was told her husband should rule over her—then how dare any of her daughters to dispute the point. . . ."

All women in southern society recognized the important financial and legal handicap under which they lived, and most accepted the limitations imposed by society as unalterable. Women did not resist as much as resent dependency. The psychological tensions—exacerbated by the enormous strain of physical chores—created depression, melancholy, and a whole range of debilities for women. . . . These women did not inhabit mythical estates, but rather productive working plantations: the routine was grueling, life was harsh. No wonder they complained of being themselves enslaved. The plantation mistress found herself trapped within a system over which she had no control, one from which she had no means of escape. Cotton was King, white men ruled, and both white women and slaves served the same master.

Catherine Clinton, *The Plantation Mistress: Woman's World in the Old South* (New York: Pantheon Books, 1982), pp. 33–4, 35. Reprinted with permission.

Suzanne Lebsock

Women in Petersburg [a Virginia city, in the early nineteenth century] experienced increasing autonomy, autonomy in the sense of freedom from utter dependence on particular men. Relatively speaking, fewer women were married, more women found work for wages, and more married women acquired separate estates, that is, property that their husbands could not touch.

When we explore how this new autonomy was acquired and what changes it inspired in turn, the line curves in intriguing ways. To cite the clearest example, women acquired separate estates, not because anyone thought women deserved more independence, but because of the nineteenth century's sudden panics and severe economic depressions. A separate estate was a means of keeping property in the family when times were hard and families stood to lose everything because of the husband's indebtedness. It did not take organized feminism to bring about positive change in the status of women. . . .

In the new century . . . the more prominent form of public activity by far was organization, initially for the benefit of the female poor and subsequently for the spread of the gospel. Such organizations were mushrooming all over the country, of course, and historians have rightly identified them as essential to the changing status and developing consciousness of nineteenth-century women. To what ends they were essential, however, is the subject of some controversy, a controversy that is part of the larger argument over the value of women's separate "sphere." Most scholars would agree that the growth of organized benevolence brought women a number of short-term benefits—an area for activity outside the home, a heightened sense of personal usefulness, a deeper appreciation of the needs and abilities of other women, and a chance to develop leadership and organizing skills and to participate in democratic decision making. . . .

"Woman's sphere" was never a fixed space. True enough, the nineteenth century's basic ideology of male and female spheres was already ossified by 1820; women were endlessly told that they belonged in the home while their men braved the crueler worlds of commerce, politics, and war. But this left a considerable quantity of social space unaccounted for. Rigid as nineteenth-century Americans were in defining sex roles, with voluntary associations they left themselves room for invention, maneuver, and experimentation.

Was it coincidence that men took over so many of women's causes in the 1850s? The assumption of voluntary poor relief as a male responsibility, the take-over of the female orphan asylum, the formation of women's auxiliaries, the injunction against women speaking in public, the use of the husband's name to identify the married woman—the motives behind these new moves cannot be assigned with any confidence. . . . The effect was to erase, in symbol and in organizational structure, the appearance of autonomous action by women in the public sphere. This did not entail crushing female assertiveness or achievement wherever it arose. Rather it meant that women's roles were to be relational, that women were to act and achieve through men.

For the women of Petersburg, the story of the antebellum period was not one of linear progress or decline; in organizational terms, it was neither a permanent retreat into a separate sphere nor a steady march from the confines of the home to the riskier and more varied regions the nineteenth century called "the world." Instead, there was a trade of sorts. Women were experiencing growing autonomy in their personal lives. For this, they apparently paid a price; in their public lives, they lost both the symbols and structure of autonomy. The consolation, if there was one, was that the men who co-opted their causes had no choice but to adopt some of their values.

Suzanne Lebsock, *The Free Women of Petersburg: Status and Culture in a Southern Town, 1784–1860* (New York: W. W. Norton & Company, 1984), pp. xv–xvi, 196, 198–99, 236. Reprinted with permission.

Caricature of Davy Crockett. The celebrated Tennessee frontiersman fought for Texas independence.
(Courtesy, American Antiquarian Society)

Westward Expansion: The 1840s

THE BATTLE OF THE ALAMO

In the 1830s, no place in North America had a larger reputation for wild living than Texas. Men tired of society could move to the edges of settlement in their states or go west to the territories, or they could go to Texas. The history of Texas justified this reputation. For nearly three centuries it had belonged to Spain, but hundreds of miles of deserts and mountains separated Texas from the other Spanish lands in Mexico and California, and fierce Plains Indians—mainly Comanches and Apaches—did not take kindly to life at Spanish missions. The land Mexico inherited with its independence from Spain lay long ungoverned.

When Mexico became independent in 1821, Texas was joined to its state of Coahuila, with a promise that when its population was large enough, it would become a separate Mexican state. The newly-established Mexican government planned to develop Texas by encouraging settlers from the United States, provided they became at least nominal Catholics and Mexican citizens. The plan worked too well. By 1831 approximately 20,000 settlers had poured in. Heads of families could, for a modest fee, have 4,428 acres for grazing land and 177 acres for farming. Soon the Mexicans began to fear this potentially rich province slipping from them. So they banned further immigration, raised tariffs, restricted trade, and reinforced their military presence. They did so with reason. Numbers of immigrants from the United States swearing loyalty to their new Mexican country apparently did not mean it, or meant it only indifferently.

HISTORICAL EVENTS

1821
Mexico wins independence from Spain

1833
American Antislavery Society is formed

1834
Santa Anna declares himself president of Mexico

1835
"Gag" rule approved by the House of Representatives

1836
Santa Anna begins his siege of the Alamo (February) • the Alamo falls to Santa Anna (March) • Texans declare independence from Mexico • General Sam Houston defeats Santa Anna

1842
Commonwealth v. Hunt • *Prigg v. Pennsylvania* • Tyler proposes annexation of Texas

1844
James Knox Polk elected President

continued

HISTORICAL EVENTS

1845
Texas becomes a state • John O'Sullivan espouses "Manifest Destiny" • Polk orders troops to Texas

1846
General Taylor advances to the Rio Grande • War against Mexico begins • Santa Fe occupied by U.S. troops • the Wilmot Proviso • Oregon Treaty

1847
U.S. troops capture Monterrey, Saltillo, Vera Cruz, and Mexico City

1848
Gold discovered in California • Zachary Taylor elected President • Treaty of Guadalupe Hidalgo ends Mexican War

The situation was further complicated by unstable Mexican politics. Antonio López de Santa Anna, a Mexican general, was challenging his own government. The Texans, led by Stephen F. Austin, who had brought 300 families in 1825, petitioned for separate statehood. Then in 1834 Santa Anna proclaimed himself president of Mexico forever and sent its Congress home. Said Austin: "War is our only recourse." Once Santa Anna took control in Mexico City and moved to garrison his northern province, the Texans were ready to fight.

Jim Bowie, a legendary figure of the tough southwest frontier, having recently turned from land speculation, slave trading, and brawling with the aid of his famous eight-and-one-half-inch-long knife, is said to have declared: "We will rather die in these ditches than give up [the mission known as the Alamo] to the enemy." Located in present-day San Antonio, the Alamo desperately needed reinforcements. It got a few, powerful in legend. William Barret Travis, an advocate of war and now a colonel in the rag-tag Texas army, arrived with thirty of his soldiers to add to Bowie's volunteers. When Bowie fell ill with pneumonia, Travis took command of the beleaguered fort. Davy Crockett arrived from Tennessee with twelve men. Then as now he was the epitome of the American frontiersman, the teller and subject of tall tales. Following his legend right into the West, by some instinct he wound up at the place that would transform his essentially comic career into real and towering heroism. Eventually thirty-two more volunteers arrived from the nearby town of Gonzales. And so it was that, all told, 187 men including nine Tejanos, or Hispanic Texans, garrisoned the old mission, when on February 23, 1836, Santa Anna's army of 4,000 began its siege.

On February 24 Travis wrote a letter addressed "To the People of Texas and All Americans in the world." The enemy, he declared, "has demanded a surrender at discretion, otherwise, the garrison are to be put to the sword, if the fort is taken—I have answered the demand with a cannon shot, & our flag still waves proudly from the walls—*I shall never surrender or retreat.*"

With Mexican guns tightly ringing the fort, the Alamo's defenders finally abandoned their hopes of further reinforcements. Tradition has it that Travis called the men together, explained their probable fate, and offered a chance to leave to those who wished it. Drawing a line in the dust with his sword, he stepped across it and asked who would join him and who would leave. All but one man—who got through the Mexican lines and lived to tell the tale—crossed the line. Bowie, from his sickbed, asked to be carried across. On March 3 Travis wrote a final letter, correctly predicting that "The victory will cost the enemy so dear that it will be worse for him than defeat." Unknown to Travis and the others inside the Alamo, a convention meeting March 2 at a tiny settlement called Washington-on-the-Brazos had declared independence from Mexico. Texas had become a nation.

As the Mexican troops advanced on the Alamo, Santa Anna's buglers played the dreaded "El Degüello," a tune that everyone knew. It meant "no quarter: death to all enemies."

The first assault with scaling ladders was repulsed with dreadful carnage. A second wave was more successful, actually getting ladders onto the walls, only to be driven off by rifle butts, tomahawks, and Bowie knives. Then came the third assault, and there were simply not enough Texans, enough cannon, or enough wall left. Taking astonishing losses—one regiment lost 670 of 800 men—the Mexican soldiers advanced with a courage to match that of their adversaries. Abandoning the central plaza of the Alamo, the defenders retreated to the smaller rooms, to kill and then to die in hand-to-hand battle. Among the few survivors of the Alamo were some Tejano women and children, family members of men who had joined the Anglo-Texans to fight for Texas, and a black man who was Travis's slave. A handful of the Alamo's defenders were taken prisoner and executed, though the exact circumstances of their deaths are disputed.

There is no question about the result of the battle: Santa Anna's "victory" cost him the war. He had lost at least 1,600 of his best troops, with many more wounded. He had lost not only the weeks it took to besiege the fortress, but the weeks his army needed afterward to recover. That delay gave General Sam Houston a chance to build an army.

Santa Anna and Houston met April 21 at the San Jacinto River where it forms an elbow at an intersection with a bayou. Houston burned his bridges behind him so that neither his army nor Santa Anna's could retreat. The Texans, shouting as their battlecry

General Sam Houston. *(Courtesy, Hugh Cleland Collection)*

The Battle at the Alamo, 1836. The Mexican "victory" cost Santa Anna 1,600 of his best troops and helped Texas win its war of independence. *(Courtesy, Scribner's Archives)*

"Remember the Alamo!" destroyed the Mexican army in an afternoon and captured the general, ending the threat of further hostilities. Texas was an independent nation, the Lone Star Republic, until 1845, when it was admitted to the Union as the twenty-eighth state.

The Nation in 1840

In 1840 the future of the young American republic seemed rich with promise. In fifty years the population had increased by over four hundred percent, while the land area had more than doubled. As each region found what it could best manufacture or grow and as transportation improved, the different sections became more interdependent in the making of a richer economy. With two national parties competing for office in every part of the country, the political system worked not to divide the country but to bind it together, which would have puzzled the nation's earliest leaders in their fear of party. The vast majority of Americans remained English in speech, Protestant in religion, lower middle-class in social status, agricultural in occupation. This common ground, together with the experience of two wars against Britain, made for a shared national loyalty. Each July 4, Americans in every part of the country gathered for elaborate ceremonies glorifying the Union. Alexis de Tocqueville was deeply impressed by one such celebration at Albany, with its dramatic reading of the Declaration of Independence and its parade of Revolutionary veterans "preserved like precious relics, and whom all the citizens honor. . . ."

And yet, even as patriotism and economic interdependence strengthened the Union, the slavery question was becoming entangled with the issue of territorial expansion, and that combination gradually eclipsed all other issues. Unable to settle the question peacefully, by 1861 Americans would resort to arms.

Immigration

Immigration is the single most consistent public event in United States history. During the colonial period, settlers poured in from England, Scotland, Northern Ireland, Germany, and Holland, and after the American Revolution and the Napoleonic wars that stream of settlers became a flood. Nothing had prepared the country for the mass immigration that took place in the first half of the nineteenth century. After 1815, especially beginning in the 1840s, newcomers came in endless waves for a variety of economic and political reasons. Between 1815 and 1860 nearly five million immigrants entered the country—more than the entire population of the United States in 1790. Over ninety percent of the immigrants came from England, Scotland, Wales, Ireland, Germany, Norway, Sweden, and Denmark. Their arrival transformed the political, social, and economic landscape of the United States, as waves of immigration later in the century from eastern and southern Europe would again alter the country's character.

European Background The primary reason so many Europeans came to the United States was economic. The smallpox vaccine, the introduction of the American potato into the diets of poor people throughout Europe, and the lack of protracted warfare all combined to reduce death rates in Europe. Europe's population increased from 140 million people in 1750 to more than 260 million in 1850. The pressure of population, combined with technological changes in Europe and prosperity in the land beyond the ocean, made for one of the greatest migrations in history.

As population grew in Europe, farm sizes dwindled and many younger sons and laborers realized they would never be able to own their own land. At the same time, improvements in American wheat production, combined with faster and more reliable ocean transportation, made cheap American wheat competitive in European markets. World grain prices and the incomes of millions of small European farmers fell. These changes took place gradually over the course of many years, and just as gradually increasing numbers of European farmers began to travel during the winter months to such cities as Bergen, Amsterdam, Christiana, Copenhagen, Hamburg, Bremen, Antwerp, Vienna, or Prague in search of work. Many immigrants had been migrant workers long before they made the move to the United States. Just as opportunities in agriculture were eroding, factory production in Europe was displacing many independent artisans. They found themselves working longer hours for less money in order to compete with mass-produced goods from American, English, and German factories. Worried about their economic futures, they were intrigued by the advertisements of American railroads hungry for workers, steamship companies seeking passengers, and new states and territories eager to attract settlers.

In considerable part, this immigration was not of the most impoverished Europeans. Few chronically unemployed workers and peasants laboring on large landed estates emigrated. Imagination and at least some economic resources were necessary prerequisites to the risky and difficult act of migrating to a new continent. It was status-conscious workers and small farmers, poor but not the poorest of Europe's poor, who came to live in the new lands.

Immigration, 1840–1860	
Belgium	20,000
England	420,000
France	180,000
Germany	1,500,000
Ireland	2,900,000
Italy	15,000
Netherlands	20,000
Poland	5,000
Scandinavia	30,000
Scotland	40,000
Switzerland	30,000
Wales	15,000

The Migration from the British Isles People from the British Isles had constituted the vast majority of immigrants during the colonial period, and that continued to be true during the years before the Civil War. Between 1815 and 1860, approximately 2,775,000 people from Great Britain settled in the United States. More than 750,000 were from England, Scotland, and Wales, while about two million were from Ireland. Another 350,000 Canadians crossed the border into the United States before the Civil War.

Most of the immigrants from England, Scotland, and Wales were Protestant—Anglican, Methodist, Baptist, and Presbyterian. By 1830 Great Britain was the most advanced industrial nation in the world, and perhaps half of these immigrants were skilled workers. They carried their skills with them and settled where they could earn high wages—textile mills, blast furnaces, forges, factories, and iron, coal, copper, and tin mines. Many of the British immigrants who did not get skilled jobs in the new industries of the United States found farms of their own. One English immigrant writing home said: "I *own* here a far better estate than I *rented* in England, and am already more attached to the soil . . . We are in a good country, are in no danger of perishing for want of society, and have abundant means of supplying every other want." The British Protestants were welcome. They shared culture, religion, and language with Americans, and they brought skills with them. The Irish Catholic immigrant received quite another reception.

Irish Immigrants Ireland was poor, and in 1845 that poverty assumed cataclysmic proportions when a mysterious fungus destroyed most of the Irish potato crop. The potato, carried several centuries earlier from the New World to Europe, was the staple of the peasant masses, and they could not survive without it. Similar famines struck the island in 1846 and again in 1847, and in the process more than one million Irish peasants died of starvation. Another two million between 1845 and 1860 escaped by heading for the United States. Most of the Irish arrived here poor, illiterate, and unskilled.

Unlike large numbers of the other immigrants, the Irish stayed in the urban centers of the industrial Northeast. Irish ghettos appeared in Boston, New York, Philadelphia, and Baltimore because the immigrants picked the cheapest housing available and took the first jobs they could find. In the cities they were highly visible. The Irish immigrants were Roman Catholics—devout Catholics who, in spite of their poverty, managed to build churches, parochial schools, monasteries, and convents. The influx of so many Catholics frightened many American Protestants. Religious animosities were intense in the nineteenth century, and more than a few Americans worried about rumors of Catholic conspiracies, led by popes and priests, to take over the country. During the late 1840s and throughout the 1850s, a wave of antagonism to Irish and to Catholics swept through the United States, and Irish Catholics often found themselves victims of discrimination and violence.

It was not uncommon for Irish workers to find themselves trapped in the lowest-paying factory jobs, victimized by their lack of skills and the greed of their employers. During the 1840s they rapidly began to replace native farmers' daughters in New England textile and shoe factories. By now whatever paternalism on the Lowell model might have made factory employment more humane was clearly and permanently absent.

German and Scandinavian Immigrants More than 1,500,000 German-speaking immigrants settled in the United States between 1815 and 1860. Most came from the Lutheran regions of what is today northwestern Germany. During the colonial period, most Germans had settled in Pennsylvania and Maryland, but beginning in the 1830s Germans headed for the upper Midwest. So many German immigrants settled there that the region became known as the "German triangle"—the region bounded by Cincinnati, Ohio, to the east, St. Louis, Missouri, to the west, and Milwaukee, Wisconsin, to the north. The Germans were not treated as well as the British immi-

"I regard people just as I regard my machinery," a manufacturer explained in 1855:

"So long as they can do my work for what I choose to pay them, I keep them, getting out of them all I can. What they do or how they fare outside my wall I don't know, nor do I consider it my business to know. They must look out for themselves as I do for myself. When my machines get old and useless, I reject them and get new, and these people are part of my machinery."

grants or as badly as the Irish Catholics. The Lutheran religion that at least a plurality of them professed did not pose much of a threat to other Protestants, but they seemed insulated and clannish. They spoke a strange language and were extremely loyal to it, and they tended to vote in ethnic blocs, a practice that would give them political power disproportionate to their numbers. During the 1850s anti-immigrant propaganda and political action victimized the Germans. The presence among them of substantial numbers of Roman Catholics added to the hostility.

Approximately 400,000 immigrants came to the United States from Sweden, Norway, and Denmark. The predominant religion among them as among the Germans was Lutheran, and they too headed to the Midwest, settling to the north and west of the German triangle. Most of the Scandinavian immigrants became farmers in Illinois, Wisconsin, Iowa, or Minnesota. Because they were white Protestants and because they settled in rural areas far from population centers, the Scandinavians did not become the victims of sustained anti-immigrant prejudice in the United States. By the second generation they were marrying outside their own ethnic group and rapidly assimilating.

Chinese Immigrants   One of the smallest group of immigrants in numbers, but among the most visible, were the more than 300,000 Chinese who came to the United States between 1849 and 1880. Like the European immigrants, they faced population pressures at home, and when news reached China of the discovery of gold in California in 1848, thousands came across the Pacific Ocean to make their fortune. Most of them were from the coastal area

---

The German immigrant John Sturm, in an autobiographical fragment, recounts his family's crossing of the Atlantic in 1847. It was an easier voyage than was typical for the time. Usually there were several deaths on a crossing.

When we set out from home, we went to Mannheim in a wagon, then to Mainz and Koln on the Rhine in a steamboat and then to Antwerp, a seaport, where we lay over several days until a ship was ready.

Our baggage was supposed to be in Koln when we got there, but it was not there. My father looked around for it for several days, but he did not find it. We were told it must have been sent to Antwerp and we would find it there. But to our misfortune and almost to our utter despair, everything was lost.

In Antwerp we waited several days until our ship was ready to go to sea. My father bought food again for use on the ship, because what we had brought from home was all lost. Before we boarded ship, my father hunted for our baggage again, but in vain. So we had nothing but the clothes on our backs. When the ship was ready to go, we had to go along.

The ship was a three-master, the "Carolina." We had many a stormy day. There were many of us on the ship. There was only one kitchen for all the people to cook in, for the passengers had to cook, each family for itself. So it happened that each family had a chance to cook only once in two or three days. We had little interest in eating, anyway, as most of the people were sea-sick and had no appetite.

The ship heaved and rolled almost all the time so that we had to hold on to something. Many people never came up on deck at all during the entire journey. The trunks and boxes had to be tied fast so they wouldn't be thrown about. Some of the children were happy and gay, but most of them were not.

One day a pirate ship came toward us and everyone had to come on deck, no doubt to show how many able-bodied men we had.

The sailors had their own kitchen and their own cook. Peas cooked with bacon and beans were their main foods. We also had bacon and black bread, which we almost had to split with an ax. Here a dog would hardly eat it. Some had white bread, which was more appetizing than the black. But in spite of all this, we survived. One child died on the ship. It was buried at sea.

of southwestern China, and most of them settled along the Pacific coast, especially in California. The Chinese panned for gold until the easiest finds played out, and then they went to work for commercial mines, construction companies, and railroads.

The Chinese immigrants were unlike the other people coming to the United States. They were racially different from Europeans, and they were Buddhists and Confucians. Unlike most of the other immigrants, the Chinese were known as "birds of passage"—immigrants who did not intend to stay in the United States. The vast majority of them were men who simply wanted to earn a reasonable sum of money, return to China, and purchase land for their families. They were willing to live and work in the United States for many years in order to achieve that objective. They worked hard and lived on a shoestring; it was the only way of making the money they needed to return home in style. Their ethnic distinctiveness and the competition they posed to American workers destined the Chinese immigrants to have a hard time. Discrimination against the Chinese increased steadily in the 1850s and after the Civil War exploded into full racism.

The Land and the People: The Northeast and Mid–Atlantic

Between 1820 and 1860 manufacturing grew rapidly in the New England and mid-Atlantic states. Both sections boasted readily available capital and labor and superior transportation. Turnpikes, rivers, the Erie Canal, and safe harbors provided good access to raw materials and markets. Commerce and agriculture, particularly dairy and truck farming, remained important in the region, but southern New England and the Hudson and Delaware river valleys began to resemble the most industrialized areas of Great Britain in their economy and social structure.

White southerners could be as shocked at the condition of northern "free" labor as some northerners were at slavery. Free labor, wrote George Fitzhugh of Virginia,

"is more cruel, in leaving the laborer to take care of himself and family out of the pittance which skill or capital have allowed him to retain. When the day's labor is ended, he is free, but he is overburdened with the cares of family and household, which make his freedom an empty and delusive mockery. . . . The Negro slave is free, too, when the labors of the day are over, and free in mind as well as body; for the master provides food, raiment, house, fuel, and everything else necessary for the physical well-being of himself and family."

Factory Life   The conditions of labor changed fundamentally after 1820, as independent craftsmen, many men, women, and children from farms, and masses of immigrants became wage earners. The widespread adoption of steam power in the 1840s freed factories from their dependence on rural free-flowing streams for their power, and allowed them to be placed near cities. Henceforth workers were completely divorced from the land. The influx of immigrant labor worsened wages and working conditions in many industries. Most workers had no protection against long hours, occupational hazards, illness, or unemployment. Apprentice girls could have particularly trying assignments; the best that Lydia Noyes could say to her friend Mary was "we are not required to work before light or after nine at night." The limited attempts at unionization in this period failed in the face of public hostility and periodic panics that so depressed the economy as to make it impossible for workers on strike to survive. Not until 1842, in the case of *Commonwealth v. Hunt,* did the Massachusetts Supreme Court uphold the legality of trade unions.

Cities Industrialism, immigration, and the expanding transportation system brought a more rapid growth of cities than has occurred at any other time in American history, before or since. In 1820 only 6.1 percent of the population lived in urban areas, places, as the census bureau would define them, of 2,500 or more inhabitants. On the other hand, Pittsburgh in the same year was so heavily industrialized that, according to one traveler, "It is surrounded . . . with a dense black smoke which, bursting forth in volume from the foundries, forges, glasshouses, and the chimneys of all the factories and houses, falls in flakes of soot upon the dwellings and persons of the inhabitants. It is, therefore, the dirtiest town in the United States." By 1860 close to 20 percent of the people were city dwellers. On the eve of the Civil War there were fifteen cities (nine of them in the Northeast) with populations in excess of 50,000. Philadelphia exceeded 500,000 and New York passed 1,000,000.

The cities were hopelessly ill-equipped to deal with these numbers of people. Municipal water and sewage systems were in their infancy. Pigs roamed city streets, the only effective street cleaners. Housing was always in short supply. Many people lived in tiny apartments; often a whole family, and perhaps a few boarders, were crowded into the same room. The poorest lived in unfinished cellars. In 1849 a Boston doctor found "one cellar . . . occupied nightly as a sleeping-apartment for thirty-nine persons. In another, the tide had risen so high that it was necessary to approach the bedside of a patient by means of a plank which was laid from one stool to another; while the dead body of an infant was actually sailing about the room in its coffin."

Cities festered in filth, overcrowding, and poverty. Cholera epidemics in 1832 and 1849 killed thousands. Fires were an everyday occurrence, sometimes leveling whole sections of cities. Crime, ranging from prostitution to burglary and murder, flourished everywhere, even on New York City's Broadway, where according to one contemporary "whores and blackguards made up about two-thirds of the throng." In response the business and middle classes created or expanded such institutions as the police force. Slowly, grudgingly, but inevitably cities ran up debts to finance water and sewer systems, street lights, schools, and parks.

Cities alternately repelled and fascinated Americans. Moralists condemned them as sinful. Native Protestants shuddered at the rapid growth of ethnic ghettos, where immigrants retained their old customs, languages, and Catholic religion. Americans now confronted contrasts between wealth and poverty that their republic in its origins had never imagined. Still, people came to the cities in ever-increasing numbers—to visit, to work, to seek their fortunes.

A canal boat helmsman wrote in 1834:

"I am at present stearing the canal boat 'Emigrant' which runs from Cincinnati to Dayton which is 65 mils. I went to Santlewes [St. Louis] last sumer and staed thare one month. The collary [cholera] was thare very bad and in Cincinnati. Thare was not many cases on the canal but in town thare ware 80 and 100 of a day."

The Land and the People: The West

Farming Between 1820 and 1860 the American economy grew more and more specialized regionally. While manufacturing expanded in the Northeast and the South continued to cultivate staple crops for agriculture, the West turned increasingly to commercial agriculture. The growth of industry, and the resulting rise

At the beginning of the nineteenth century eastern and European travelers were amazed at the fertility of western farms. One visitor to the Ohio River Valley in 1818 wrote:

"I believe I saw more peaches and apples rotting on the ground than would sink the British fleet. I was at plantations in Ohio where they no more knew the number of their hogs than myself. . . . And they have such flocks of turkies, geese, ducks, and hens, as would surprise you. . . . The poorest family has a cow or two and some sheep . . . and adorns the table three times a day like a wedding dinner—tea, coffee, beef, fowls, pigs, eggs, pickles, good bread; and their favorite beverage is whiskey, or peach brandy."

of cities in the Northeast and in Europe, created a steadily expanding market for farm products. The upper Mississippi and Ohio valleys, with their fertile soil and vast tracts of public land, were in an ideal position to meet this need, especially after canals and railroads made it possible to ship directly eastward large quantities of meat and grain.

With every decade the centers of production for wheat, corn, cattle, hogs, and sheep shifted westward, as settlers opened the prairies to cultivation. Many of these newcomers had abandoned the thin soils of New England for places like Indiana and Michigan, where wheat yields were several times greater per acre. Farmers from the upper South flocked into the southern counties of Ohio, Illinois, and Indiana and gave that region a distinctively southern character. Sizable numbers of English, German, and Scandinavian immigrants migrated west, fanning out through the rich farmlands of Iowa, Illinois, Minnesota, and Wisconsin. On the eve of the Civil War the population of the West, which had numbered less than one million in 1820, exceeded nine million.

Farms were small—about 200 acres on the average. Most farmers owned their own land, relying for labor on their families, on hired help, and increasingly on machines. Wheat was the cash crop; and mechanical drills, harvesters, and threshers permitted an enormous increase in production throughout the period.

In the 1840s and 1850s wheat dominated farming in the upper Mississippi Valley almost as completely as cotton dominated agriculture in the lower South. Wheat and flour became important export items in the fifties. Western farmers also grew much corn and oats, but primarily as feed for livestock. The demands of eastern cities and southern planters assured a ready market and good prices for the beef, pork, and mutton of the prairies. Before railroads came to the Ohio Valley, cattle were driven overland to market; most hogs were slaughtered and packed locally. Frequently they were "stuck," or cut in the throat—often the pioneer woman's job. Then women and children took out and washed the various innards, saving the bladder to inflate and use as a football. So much pork was processed at Cincinnati that the city became known for a time as "Porkopolis." Later, increasing numbers of livestock were shipped east by rail to city markets for slaughter.

Europeans were shocked that Americans bolted their food or gorged themselves on anything within reach, as this English drawing indicates. Such habits reflected both the indifferent preparation of food and the frenetic tempo of American life.
(Courtesy, Scribner's Archives)

Cities   While the Midwest remained primarily agrarian, the region's cities grew swiftly. Older communities like St. Louis, Cincinnati, and Louisville all expanded rapidly. Even more spectacular was the progress of new cities like Milwaukee, Indianapolis, and especially Chicago. In 1833 Chicago consisted "of about 150 wood houses . . . ," wrote one resident. "This is already a place of considerable trade, supplying salt, tea, coffee, sugar, and clothing to a large tract of country to the south and west." The Windy City had barely 17,000 people when Cyrus McCormick moved his farm machinery factory there in 1847: thirteen years later the population numbered 109,000. Yet the city remained a raw and uncomfortable place. Its mud was the subject for endless tales. Signs read "No Bottom," "Road to China," or "Man Lost." A story told of a man who sees a hat in the mud. Picking it up, he discovers a man's face underneath. "Say, stranger, you're stuck in the mud! Can I give you a hand to pull you out?" "Oh, no, thanks," replies the face, "I'm riding a good horse. He's got me out of the worst spots." These western cities served principally as extensions of the rural economy, processing, shipping, and marketing agricultural products. Their mills and packing houses led the country in 1850 in the production of lumber, flour and meal, liquor and meat. Factories in these cities made ever more complex machines that made farming more efficient.

The expansion of urban markets had a powerful effect on sectional alignments. Between 1820 and 1860, western farmers came increasingly to depend on eastern cities to purchase their produce, while the industrial Northeast, in turn, found a growing market for its manufactures in the western states. An economic bond was being forged between the two sections that would undermine the old alliance between the West and the South.

The Farther West   The Indian Removal Act of 1830 made for the eventual settlement west of the Mississippi River of almost 100,000 Indians. Life there was hard for them. The land and climate were unfamiliar. They found farming more difficult and were not as adept at hunting the buffalo as the Plains Indians, who resented the newcomers and resisted their settlement. Comanches, Pawnees, Osages, and other western tribes, aware that government protection of the new tribes was minimal, regularly raided them and stole their livestock. Poverty, disease, and despair became the heritage of the relocated Indians in the 1840s and 1850s.

And no sooner had the Indians been relocated west of the Mississippi River than new waves of white settlers began arriving there as well. By the 1850s settlers were pouring into the Far West, even into land west of the Mississippi River that had so recently been reserved "forever" for the Indians. The mining frontier in California and the intermountain West, the Mormon colonies in the Great Basin, and the glowing reports of excellent farmland attracted hundreds of thousands of settlers into the western territories.

By the end of the 1850s, Governor Isaac I. Stevens of Washington Territory had negotiated fraudulent treaties with such tribes as the Nez Percé, Cayuse, Yakima, Spokane, and Walla Walla. The tribes ceded millions of acres of land and moved to reservations. On the west side of the Mississippi River, government agents in the 1850s had to make way for new hordes of settlers coming into Kansas, Nebraska, and Iowa. They developed a policy of moving tribes to new reservations, including Indians recently arrived from the East. In California, the gold rush brought tens of thousands of miners who, when the gold became more difficult to find, settled on Indian land and became farmers. Between 1849 and 1860, the Indian population of California declined from more than 100,000 to less than 30,000. By 1860 there were only 15,000 Indians still alive in California.

The Land and the People: The South

The antebellum southern economy was surprisingly diverse. Cotton was the most prominent yield, but corn was actually the South's most widely grown crop. Many planters in Virginia and Maryland, their soil exhausted after prolonged tobacco cultivation, shifted to raising wheat or cattle. Rice grew in the swampy low country of South Carolina and Georgia. Southern Louisiana produced another exotic crop, sugar.

Cotton, the South's major cash crop, was cultivated throughout the lower South. The center of cotton production moved steadily westward after 1820, the inevitable result of overplanting and soil exhaustion. Just before the Civil War over a fourth of the 4.3 million bales grown in the United States came from Arkansas, Louisiana, and Texas, all states west of the Mississippi River.

In Texas, or the Lone Star Republic as it was known from 1836 until it entered the Union in 1845, the towns of Galveston, on the Gulf Coast, and Houston, on the banks of Buffalo Bayou, became major ports and trading centers. San Antonio was a center for stagecoaches and freight wagon trains heading westward for California. Texas towns were small—Galveston, the largest in 1850, had a population of five thousand—and rough-hewn, with few urban amenities until after the Civil War. Cattle ranching was widespread, and would eventually give rise to the cowboy culture that set Texas apart from other states. Texas was also different in its cultural diversity. Only about half of its people in 1850 were Anglo-Americans. The rest were Mexican, other Europeans, Indians, and African Americans. Slaves made up over twenty-seven percent of the population.

Contrary to popular myth, the South was not inhabited solely by rich planters, poor whites, and enslaved blacks. In 1860 the bulk of the South's 5.5 million whites lived on small farms not unlike those in the North. These yeoman farmers raised most of the same crops as did the planters: only rice and sugar were confined to the larger growers. Even families living far in the backlands might be living in a rough plenty, keeping unfenced cattle and raising their own subsistence crops.

The Whites   The actual number of planters was small. The federal census of 1860—defining a planter as a person owning at least twenty slaves—counted 46,274. Most of these owned up to fifty slaves and 500 to 800 acres. They were hardworking businessmen with field work to supervise, laborers to oversee, books to balance. And their wives seldom conformed to the southern-belle stereotype. Man-

One visitor to South Carolina observed that the state's inland people were no match for Yankee peddlers:

"As the value of the lands and the wealth of the inhabitants decrease, while you journey toward the back country, so also does the intelligence of the people. I never met in my whole life with so many white persons who could not read nor write, who had never taken a newspaper, who had never travelled fifty miles from home, or who had never been to the house of God, or heard a sentence read from his Holy Word, as I found in a single season in South Carolina. Many of them could not discern between the right hand and the left.

What wonder then that the hosts of Yankee peddlers until driven out by the sumptuary laws, fattened upon the land! 'What do you think I gave for that?' asked an ignorant planter in Sumpter district, while pointing to a Connecticut wooden clock which stood upon a shelf in the corner of the room. 'I don't know,' was my answer, 'twenty dollars, or very likely twenty-five!' The man was astonished. 'Stranger' said he, 'I gave one hundred and forty-four dollars for that clock, and thought I got it cheap at that! Let me tell you how it was. We had always used sun-dials hereabout, till twelve or fourteen years ago, when a man came along with clocks to sell. I thought at first I wouldn't buy one, but after haggling about the price for a while, he agreed to take sixteen dollars less than what he asked, for his selling price was one hundred and sixty dollars. I concluded to strike a bargain.'

In fact, during those years when wealth flowed in an uninterrupted stream through every channel of industry, the farms and plantations of the South became the legitimate plunder of Yankee shrewdness. It was no meeting of Greek with Greek in the contest of wits, but a perfect inrush of shrewd, disciplined tacticians in the art of knavery."

aging a large household required energy and intelligence, not merely graceful manners. Home was more likely to be a modest frame cottage than a Tara or a Mount Vernon. At the apex of southern society were the large planters. Although few in number—only 1,700 people owned as many as a hundred slaves in 1850—these planter aristocrats cast a giant shadow over the region. Their wealth gave them considerable social and political influence. Living in palatial mansions or elegant townhouses, surrounded by vast fields and liveried servants, they were the few authentic representatives of the South of myth and romance.

Plantation kitchen. *(Courtesy, Hugh Cleland Collection)*

In spite of this diversity, the white South possessed a distinctive flavor. The great majority of southern whites were Protestant and of British ancestry. The economy was colonial: southerners raised staple crops for export and imported finished goods. Before the Revolution the South had traded mainly with England, but in the first half of the nineteenth century southern trade, lacking local capital for financing merchant shipping, came increasingly under the control of northerners, and particularly under the dominance of the port of New York. Above all, there was slavery, a uniquely southern institution that exerted a powerful influence over the region.

Although the number of great planters was small, slaveholding was remarkably widespread throughout the white South. According to one estimate, fewer than forty percent of the farmers in the Cotton South in 1850 owned no slaves. By 1860 this number increased to almost half, largely because the rapidly increasing cost of purchasing a slave priced many small farmers out of the market. But the important point is that on the eve of the Civil War a large proportion of white farmers in the cotton-growing portions of the region were themselves slaveholders. And this understates the whites' stake in the South's peculiar institution. Some who did not own slaves rented them. Others served as overseers on plantations, usually in the hope that several successive good harvests would earn them enough to buy a small farm and slaves of their own. Still other white southerners had sold their own slaves, prompted to do so by the windfall profits they could realize. All of these non-slaveholders had as pervasive ties to the institution of slavery as did the planters themselves. Further, the presence of millions of blacks gave whites of all classes a common determination to keep the white race dominant, and an unearned pride in race gave the whites a psychological bond.

The Slaves Slaves worked everywhere in the antebellum South: as common laborers, skilled craftsmen, and servants; in factories, mines, and foundries; on riverboats, wharves, and railroads; in hotels, stores, and private homes. A Charleston census of 1848 listed forty-six occupations that employed slaves. Most, of course, worked as field hands. Over half belonged to planters who owned twenty or more slaves. These large units were especially common in the newer states of the lower South, where the work was harder and the conditions more brutal than in the older slave states.

On farms of less than ten slaves, the slaves usually worked alongside their masters, who directly supervised their labor. Male slaves frequently performed the same tasks as the farmer and female slaves the same tasks as his wife, though in the busiest seasons all slaves were likely

A slave family in the cotton fields of Georgia. *(Courtesy, New-York Historical Society)*

to work in the fields together. On plantations slaves were organized in two ways. Rice planters preferred the task system, allotting individual slaves a particular task for the day. Cotton and tobacco planters favored the gang system, dividing the slaves into work parties under the supervision of an overseer or trusted black driver. The plantation routine followed the seasons in a monotonous cycle. Both men and women worked in the fields, plowing and planting in the spring, weeding in the summer, harvesting in the fall. In winter and in slack times, they dug ditches, repaired fences, and sawed wood. Although masters of large plantations usually worked their female slaves as hard as their male slaves, and assigned them to most tasks in the fields, they frequently observed gender distinctions in the organization of labor. Masters rarely assigned supervisory positions in field work to female slaves. The young and the elderly tended livestock or cared for the small children. Field hands labored from sunrise to sunset, with a rest at midday. Most had Sunday off and received a week's vacation at Christmas. For many slaves these holidays, with their occasional feasts, dances, and visits to neighboring plantations, provided relief from the hardship of their daily lives. And in religious meetings the slaves created an invisible church. On Sunday nights they would go into the woods to sing and pray.

Most slaves lived in rude cabins. Some masters encouraged their bondsmen to marry and live as families; others left the matter to the slaves or assigned them arbitrarily to a mate. The owner provided food, clothing, and medical care. The typical slave's ration consisted of cornmeal, fatback, and molasses; but many slaves varied this boring and unhealthful diet by raising their own vegetables or fishing.

Was Slavery Household servants and city slaves enjoyed a some-
Profitable? what easier life than field hands. And many slave-
holders hired out their bondsmen as servants, laborers, and mechanics, sometimes for extended periods. This practice of hiring out was especially common in the upper South and in the cities, where there was frequently a surplus of slaves. Many hired slaves became quasi-free, but the practice of hiring out normally brought more advantages to male than to female slaves. Female slaves might be hired out as house servants, especially as cooks, cleaners, or nursemaids. Their position did not give them much excuse for free movement in society. Slave women, much like free white women, tended to be confined within households. Masters almost never offered slave women training in such skilled crafts as carpentry or blacksmithing. But the slave men who held those positions received an unusual opportunity to learn to read, to accumulate some money of their own, and, above all, to have an excuse to circulate fairly freely in society. The pool of slave craftsmen provided runaways and participants in revolts in disproportionate numbers. Women were less likely than men to run away or to engage directly in revolts.

Slaves had little motivation to work hard. Although some worked willingly for kindly masters, others delighted in "first-rate tricks to dodge work." In an attempt to make their slaves work efficiently, planters combined close supervision with a system of incentives: praise, additional rations, extra holidays. But many masters found it necessary to resort to whipping, deprivation of privileges, and other punishments. "The only principle that can maintain slavery," one comment went, "is the principle of fear." Those who found distasteful the employment of a lash—and there were many—might see their plantation go to ruin. Yet punishment too severe could bring the injury or loss of a prime male or fertile female, and no owner would want that. And of course there were cases of affection or respect. Some owners allowed their slaves to acquire property or taught them to read and write.

Slave men lacked many of the powers that free men could draw upon to maintain their control of women, notably the legal powers assigned to husbands and property owners. Yet slave women, as women, remained vulnerable to particular hardships such as sexual exploitation on the part of white men and separation from their children. Slave women's ability to bear children also afforded them some marginal advantages. Since masters were eager to increase the numbers of their slaves through reproduction, they were likely to accord women who claimed to be pregnant some release from work. But overall, slave women benefited not at all from the idealization of womanhood that whites cultivated for themselves.

Was slavery profitable to the planters? Not all the evidence is in. Investments in new plantations in the lower South consistently yielded

A former slave, Moses Roper, wrote in the 1840s to a sympathetic white man about the brutal treatment suffered by some slaves.

"It happened where I was then living, at Greenville, in the county of the same name, in South Carolina. This slave was a preacher in the state of Georgia. His master told him if he continued his preaching to his fellow-slaves, he would for the next offense give him 500 lashes. George (for that was the name of the slave) disregarded his master's threat, and continued to preach to them. Upon his master having discovered the fact, George, being dreadfully alarmed lest the threatened punishment should be carried into effect, fled across the Savannah River, and took shelter in the barn of a Mr. Garrison, about seven miles from Greenville. There he was discovered by Mr. G., who shot at him with a rifle, on his attempting to run away, without effect. He was then pursued by Mr. G., who endeavoured to knock him down with the butt end of the piece, unsuccessfully. George wrenched the rifle out of his hands, and struck his pursuer with it. By this time several persons were collected, George was secured, and put into Greenville jail. The facts having transpired, through the newspaper, his master came to Greenville to claim him as his property, but consented, upon being required to do so, to receive 550 dollars as his value, with which he returned home. Shortly after this, George was burnt alive within one mile of the court-house at Greenville, in the presence of an immense assemblage of slaves, which had been gathered together to witness the horrid spectacle from a district of twenty miles in extent.

Take another case in the Village of Liberty Hill . . . Henry, failing to accomplish the task given to him to do on a Saturday, and fearing the punishment of a hundred lashes, with which he had been threatened, finished it on Sunday morning. His labour on the Sabbath was discovered by his master, and on the following day his master, as he said, "for violating the Sabbath," tied him to a tree, and flogged him with his own hand, at intervals from eight in the morning until five o'clock in the evening. About six o'clock two white men, in the employ of Mr. Bell, pitying his wretched condition, untied him, and assisted him home on a horse, a distance of about a mile. He was at this time in a state of great suffering and exhaustion. A short time after they had place him in the kitchen they heard him groan heavily; Bell also heard him, and said, "I will go out and see what is the matter with the nigger." He went, and found him breathing his last, the victim of his brutal treatment.

This case was brought to trial; my then master, Mr. Gooch, was on the jury. The evidence of the two white men was taken, and Bell was adjudged to pay the value of the slave he had destroyed. This he was unable to do, and a Mr. Connighim, a wealthy and extensive planter in the neighbourhood, paid it for him, on condition of Bell's becoming a drive on one of his estates. To this arrangement he consented, and the matter was settled."

A southern senator later asserted:

"You dare not make war on cotton. Cotton is King."

a return upon capital sufficient to attract outside funds, an indication that a well-managed cotton plantation on good soil was at least as profitable as alternative forms of investment. Slaveholders in the less productive regions of the upper South exported their surplus slaves profitably to the Cotton Belt. None of this, however, demonstrates that the slave system itself added to the efficiency and productivity of cotton planting. In the United States and abroad, masses of workers clothed themselves in this strong but comfortable fiber, and textile mills hungered for it. In those early days of large-scale cotton production, a free black labor force might have moved as swiftly as marketed slaves in response to the regional fortunes of cotton production. Still, slavery allowed plantation owners to keep their workers at lowest subsistence level, and thereby to benefit as individuals. For the South as a whole slavery was probably an economic liability. Four million blacks were kept in the strictest poverty, when as free property owners they could have provided a rich market for the products of southern agriculture and industry, and as free workers they could have constituted a versatile and energetic workforce. Slavery caused white southerners to concentrate their resources in staple agriculture at the expense of industry and transportation. And, of course, it stifled the intellectual and creative energies of generations of black Americans.

Race Control Slavery was more than a labor system; it was also a means of race control. The southern states enacted elaborate slave codes touching virtually all of black life. Slave marriages and divorces had no legal validity. Slaves were forbidden to leave their plantations without a pass, to be out after curfew, to congregate in groups unless a white man was present, to carry arms, or to strike a white person. They could not own property or testify in court against whites. Punishment for most crimes was left to the master, who was given immunity from prosecution should a slave die under "moderate" correction. Death was the penalty for rebellion or plotting to rebel. To enforce these codes, the white males mounted regular patrols, which traveled the neighborhood at night in search of arms or runaways. Members were chosen at militia muster and all members of the community—slaveholders and non-slaveholders alike—were supposed to take their turn.

Enslaved blacks faced the constant task of adjusting to the condition of bondage. Rebellion was rare; outright resistance was suicidal. When Nat Turner, a slave preacher, led a band of armed followers through Southampton County, Virginia, in 1831, killing fifty-seven men, women, and children, terrified whites retaliated by slaughtering at least one hundred blacks. The South was on edge for months afterward. No one knew when this black fury, like some smoldering volcano, would erupt again. Individual acts of resistance, such as arson, running away, or even suicide, were not uncommon. Instead of confronting their masters directly, blacks developed various stratagems of accommodation and subtle resistance. They became particularly adept at malingering, breaking tools, and otherwise obstructing the workings of a system in which they were not free participants.

The black family may have been a more cohesive unit than historians and sociologists once believed. If plantation records contain instances of the breakup of families through sale, these same sources reveal many others in which they remained intact over several generations. And even when spouses and children were sent to other areas, black people retained a powerful sense of family. After emancipation, thousands of blacks wandered across the South in search of relatives and loved ones.

A treasury of folklore demonstrates the extent to which slaves retained a sense of identity. Slaves blended African and New World materials into their own culture. Black spirituals were a form of religious music unique in sound and feeling but expressive of profoundly Christian themes of sorrow and hope. Spirituals could also be a commentary on the system in which the slave was imprisoned. One song, ostensibly about Biblical Samson, expressed the wish that "if I had my way, I'd tear this building down."

And in their quarters, conducting prayer meetings of their own, often in defiance of the law, the slaves created forms of preaching, of worship, of social union that would give structure to black society not only under slavery but in the dangerous century of freedom that followed emancipation. The participation of black southern churches in the great civil rights movement of the 1950s and 60s is in its way the culmination and triumph of those humble and at times furtive gatherings.

"Field hollers" and work songs combated the boredom of mindless field labor and provided the coordination and timing essential to people working under close and difficult conditions:

Massa in the great house, counting out his money,
Oh, shuck that corn and throw it in the barn.
Mistis in the parlor, eating bread and honey.
Oh, shuck that corn and throw it in the barn.

The South Closes Ranks

The rise of militant abolitionism, coupled with the Nat Turner uprising, stimulated another round of soul-searching among southern whites. In 1831–32 the Virginia House of Delegates began a lengthy debate on a plan for the gradual emancipation and deportation of all slaves. The proposal was at last defeated, and this defeat marked a turning point. Thereafter, few white southerners would deny that slavery was sanctioned by the Bible and the laws of nature, or that it provided a harmonious solution to the South's racial dilemma and offered beneficent schooling to the black race.

To shore up their "peculiar institution," as it was often called, southern legislatures enacted tougher slave codes and further curtailed the liberties of free blacks. In many states it was illegal to teach slaves to read and write, and in some they were not allowed to work as typesetters or printers. The repression touched whites as well. Slave-state lawmakers forbade the publication or distribution of antislavery propaganda—sometimes under penalty of death. Public pressure silenced other critics of slavery: several prominent university professors left the South. The antislavery societies that had existed throughout the region quickly disappeared.

The increasingly insistent abolitionist rhetoric of the 1830s and 1840s convinced many southerners that the North was really trying to destroy slavery outright. The debate between gradual and immediate abolition meant nothing to southerners, because the end of slavery in any fashion would doom their way of life. In response to northern attacks on slavery, southerners stopped apologizing for the institution, and

CASH!

All persons that have SLAVES to dispose of, will do well by giving me a call, as I will give the

HIGHEST PRICE FOR

Men, Women, &

CHILDREN.

Any person that wishes to sell, will call at Hill's tavern, or at Shannon Hill for me, and any information they want will be promptly attended to.

Thomas Griggs.

Charlestown, May 7, 1835.

PRINTED AT THE FREE PRESS OFFICE, CHARLESTOWN.

southern writers like William Harper, Thomas R. Drew, and James H. Hammond launched an assertive argument for it.

One line of defense claimed to find evidence from the Old Testament that black people were descendents of Ham, the cursed son of Noah, destined for the role of servants. A secular version of that argument held that Africans were biologically different from Europeans, designed for lives of servitude under white owners whose biology dictated responsible and benevolent mastery. Pseudoscientific investigations in aid of this thesis were popular among spokesmen for slavery.

Southern polemicists argued that slavery provided the economic prosperity of the South and the economic foundation for the rise of southern civilization. Many people in the southern planter class came to view themselves as aristocratic. Some claimed descent from the Cavalier aristocracy of Great Britain. Southern society, as they perceived it, was genteel, cultured, and paternalistic.

Finally, the defenders of slavery offered a scathing critique of northern society. They blasted the hypocrisy of northerners who criticized slavery while ignoring the poverty and suffering of their own working classes. Southerners argued that capitalism in the North was a brutal institution that exploited poor people in the name of profits, and they pointed to the plight of factory workers and the urban homeless. Slavery, on the other hand, was an institution in which the slave owners took care of their workers from the cradle to the grave. Slave owners, so southern authors contended, provided their slaves with the blessings of living in a cultured, Christian civilization, and the slaves lived lives of loyalty and tranquility. George Fitzhugh held the organic bond between slaves and owners to be an expression of the harmony and oneness that prevails throughout biological nature. Freedom, by this argument, severs workers from employers and sends cracks and ruptures throughout the human community that should be an instance of the unity of nature.

The "Gag" Rule   Southerners also sought to stifle criticism from outside. Backed by a war chest of over $30,000, abolitionists embarked in 1835 on a campaign to send hundreds of thousands of antislavery pamphlets to all parts of the country. A mob of South Carolinians seized the materials from the Charleston post office and in a huge bonfire burned them, along with effigies of Arthur Tappan and William Lloyd Garrison. Afterward, Postmaster General Amos Kendall, with President Jackson's approval, authorized southern postmasters to censor the mails and stop the flow of antislavery material into the South. Southern politicians urged the House of Representatives not to receive petitions demanding the abolition of slavery in the states or the District of Columbia. Formerly Congress had accepted such memorials and then rejected them as "inexpedient." Following angry debate, the House now approved a modified "gag" rule; henceforth it would receive antislavery petitions but automatically table them without formal consideration. Whatever might be the technical status of the gag rule, it looked very much like a violation of the First Amendment right of the people to petition the government. Former President John Quincy Adams, now a Massachusetts congressman, led the battle to vindicate the historic right of

In January 1848 one new resident in Kentucky observed an increasingly closed society:

"The man with whom I board (a slave holder) says that all questions that involve the subject of slavery ought not to be discussed in Ky. And I have heard him say that slavery was an evil, yet he says it ought not to be debated in Ky. for it makes the Negroes uneasy & has a tendency to make them try to escape (which by the way) a great many do. . . . A minister to go into the pulpit and preach Anti slavery doctrine, as some do in the East, would be in danger of his life, it would not be allowed—Aye, in our boasted land of *Liberty* one has not the privelege of expressing his opinions—Shame on such actions! Call not this the land where Liberty's broad shield shines over all, while one sixth of her sons & daughters toil & bleed beneath the lash, 'tis a disgrace to the Union—Our Eagle is no longer an emblem of protection, but of Despotism, Tyranny, & Oppression. It lives by plunder, it feasts on innocence—& drinks the life blood of its victims. Does not the present war with Mexico show it. It tears her *limbs* from her body & then because she writhes & offers some resistance, she strikes her beak to its very vitals. I have said more than I intended but not half what I feel."

petition. Year after year "Old Man Eloquent," though never an advocate of immediatism, fought to get petitions discussed before the House of Representatives, winning thousands to the antislavery cause in the process. In 1844 Adams finally secured repeal of the gag rule. He served in Congress until 1848 when he suffered a stroke in the House and died two days later at the age of eighty-one.

Repressive tactics rebounded against slaveholders. The gag rules, mob attacks, the censorship of mails, and other violations of civil liberties created a reaction that broadened the antislavery movement's appeal. Abolitionists charged that a vast slave power conspiracy was threatening the liberty of northern whites as well as southern blacks. Slaveholders and their northern allies, those "gentlemen of property and standing," despised freedom in general, for whites as for blacks. That claim, speaking to the pride of white Americans in their own freedom, would become in time a main component of the antislavery movement.

The Antislavery Spectrum

The place of black people in American life became the central political issue in the United States during the 1840s and 1850s. The question of whether, and if so how, the slaves should be freed was only part of the controversy. Free blacks in the North and the South also wanted to know whether they would ever be accepted as equals and enjoy the same civil liberties given to whites under the Constitution.

Northern Blacks   The quarter of a million blacks who lived in the free states had only a threadbare kind of freedom. In most places they could not vote, hold office, or testify in court. They were confined to menial jobs and wretched housing. Everywhere law and public opinion combined to exclude or segregate them: in railroad coaches, schools, restaurants, theaters, churches, even cemeteries. Most northerners, including some who condemned slavery, viewed this not as a departure from democratic principles, but as a natural and legitimate response to the black presence.

Excluded from the dominant political and social institutions, northern blacks found in the abolitionist crusade their first opportunity to have a major role in American public life. Their subscriptions kept Garrison's newspaper alive, and Boston blacks protected him from violence. Escaped slaves like Frederick Douglass lectured and wrote of their experiences. Harriet Tubman, an escapee who made nineteen trips into slave country to bring out runaways, had a price of $40,000 on her head. Initially the protégés of white abolitionists, blacks gradually asserted their independence. They founded newspapers and rights organizations of their own and established vigilance committees in northern cities that protected black fugitives from slave-catchers.

As they struggled to influence popular opinion, abolitionists promoted one broad organization: the American Antislavery Society, founded in 1833. Garrison, Weld, the Tappan brothers, and the Grimké sisters all belonged to the Society, which claimed as many as thirteen hundred local chapters. Under Weld's direction, the Society's members

Illustrations of the American Anti-Slavery Almanac for **1840.**

"*Our Peculiar Domestic Institutions.*"

Northern Hospitality—New-York nine months law. [The Slave steps out of the Slave State, and his chains fall. A Free State, with another chain, stands ready to re-enslave him.]

Burning of McIntosh at St. Louis, in April, 1836.

Showing how slavery improves the condition of the female sex.

The Negro Pew, or "Free" Seats for black Christians. | *Mayor of New-York refusing a Carman's license to a colored Man.*

Servility of the Northern States in arresting and returning fugitive Slaves.

Selling a Mother from her Child.

Hunting Slaves with dogs and guns. A Slave drowned by the dogs.

"*Poor things, ' they can't take care of themselves.' "*

Mothers with young Children at work in the field.

A Woman chained to a Girl, and a Man in irons at work in the field.

Branding Slaves.

Cutting up a Slave in Kentucky.

Paid.   *Unpaid.*

One of the publications of the abolitionist crusade. An integral part of the reform sentiment that began in the 1830s, the movement emphasized moral suasion rather than legal coercion.
(Courtesy, Library of Congress)

bombarded Congress with petitions opposing slavery in the District of Columbia and urging an end to the interstate slave trade. The petition campaign attracted widespread support after southern congressmen obtained their "gag" rule. American abolitionists also sought closer ties with British reformers, and in 1840 many attended the World Anti-Slavery Convention in London. Yet the antislavery movement had deep internal divisions. Personality clashes, doctrinal conflicts among different religious denominations, and fundamental differences over strategy splintered the movement.

Tactical Disagreements   The split over strategy and tactics involved conflicting interpretations of American society and the role of abolitionism in American life. Shocked by mob violence against abolitionists, Garrisonians concluded that American society was sick. Slavery was one of the symptoms of moral decay, but there were others—militarism, expansionism, the oppression of women and the poor. Only a total reformation of the nation's ethical values would suffice. Abolitionists, Garrison maintained, must "revolutionize the public sentiment" by an expanded campaign of moral suasion; having done this, they would accomplish the overthrow of slavery. Garrison's opponents in the antislavery movement believed that efforts to link the movement too closely with other causes risked alienating people who had been converted by the campaign against postal censorship or angered by southern violations of the civil liberties of whites. "Garrisonian fanaticism," so they feared, endangered the future of abolitionism.

Slavery in the Territories

Although Americans had been debating the issue of slavery ever since the Missouri controversy stretching from 1818 to 1820, the debate did not begin to destabilize the political system until the 1840s. The issue that eventually disrupted the Union and brought on the Civil War was the question of whether slavery should be permitted to expand out of its base in the South to the new territories of the West. For a variety of deeply-held political, economic, and social reasons, most southerners supported expansion of slavery westward. A great many northerners, though shunning abolitionism as radical and impractical, opposed that expansion.

The Liberty Party   The "Log Cabin and Hard Cider" campaign of 1840 expressed the nation's new fascination with mass politics, and many antislavery leaders wanted to get involved. Even in these times before the conflict with Mexico and the consequent acquisition of land heated the controversy, the success of the petition drives and other quasi-political activities offered some hope that electoral politics would be responsive to antislavery sentiment. A group of abolitionists formed the Liberty Party in 1840. As their presidential candidate, they selected James G. Birney, a slaveholder turned abolitionist, and they framed a platform attacking slavery. Lost in the hoopla of the contest between the Whig Harrison and the Democrat Van Buren, the Liberty Party attracted little attention. Birney, in London for the World Anti-Slavery Convention, did not even campaign. In the next presidential election Birney polled about 65,000 votes. An improvement over 1840, this still represented only 32 out of every 1,000 votes cast in the North. Garrison and his followers consistently opposed the Liberty Party experiment. Political organizations, they argued, implied acceptance of the legitimacy of the existing system, which they held to be morally diseased at its root. Retaining his faith in perfectionism and therefore rejecting participation in the unclean institutions of law and politics, Garrison refused even to vote.

But abolitionists, even Garrison, were more than simple idealists or frustrated politicians. Most were hard-headed reformers who recognized the need for many types of nonviolent action. They tried unsuccessfully to organize a boycott of the products of slave labor. They worked to impel churches to denounce slavery. A few helped slaves escape on the celebrated "underground railroad."

Slavery in the West   In 1840, the antislavery movement was still struggling for a foothold in American politics. Abolitionist sentiment was vague, sporadic, and moralistic; the slavery interest was concentrated, practical, and testily defensive. Moral suasion had utterly failed to convert southerners, who feared not only a loss of property but a loss of racial mastery. Countless northerners found the abolition movement radical and disruptive. The vast majority of northern whites discriminated against free blacks and were content to leave slavery alone where it existed. Most northerners probably opposed, or sooner or later would come to oppose, slavery in the abstract, but few favored immediate emancipation. They feared that the free states would be overrun with emancipated blacks. Slavery also had powerful allies among northern businessmen dependent on the success of southern crops. The churches, too, wrestled with the problem of slavery. By the end of the 1840s the Presbyterians, the Methodists, and the Baptists, unable to reach a consensus on slavery at their national meetings, had split into northern and southern organizations.

The Constitution itself discouraged abolitionists. Both sides in the slavery controversy recognized that the Constitution perceived slaves as property and that the federal government could not abolish slavery in the states. This was a decision for the people of the states themselves to make. The southern states were happy to uphold a Constitution and a Union that protected slavery. For decades, moreover, Americans had agreed to an informal division of territory into free and slave soil. The Northwest Ordinance of 1787 had prohibited slavery north of the Ohio River. South of the Ohio, North Carolina and Georgia had ceded western lands to the national government on the specific condition that slavery should be permitted in the states that would eventually be formed from these lands. The Missouri Compromise line of 1820 divided the vast Louisiana Purchase into slave and free soil. These arrangements covered all the existing United States territory, leaving nothing after 1820 for argument in Congress. Abolitionists were left to battle over such narrow issues as the gag rule and the status of slavery

One Quaker recalled the workings of the underground railroad:

"In the winter of 1826–27 fugitives began to come to our house. The roads were always in running order, and the connections were good, the conductors active and zealous, and there was no lack of passengers. Seldom a week passed without our receiving passengers by this mysterious road. We knew not what night or what hour of the night we would be roused from slumber by a gentle rap at the door. Outside in the cold or rain there would be a two-horse wagon loaded with fugitives, perhaps the greater part of them women and children. When they were all safely inside and the door fastened, I would cover the windows, strike a light, and build a good fire. By this time my wife would be up and preparing victuals. The companies varied in number, from two or three fugitives to seventeen.

The pursuit was often very close, and we had to resort to various stratagems in order to elude the pursuers. Sometimes a company of fugitives were scattered and secreted in the neighborhood until the hunters had given up the chase. At other times their route was changed and they were hurried forward with all speed. It was a continual excitement and anxiety to us, but the work was its own reward."

Newspapers commonly ran notices like this one:

THIRTY DOLLARS REWARD

Ran away last night, from the subscriber, living on the waters of Little Pipe-Creek, near Westminster Town, Maryland, a tall, well-made, and active country born Negro Man, named PETER, about 30 years of age, 5 feet 8 or 10 inches high, wears the wool on the top of his head commonly platted, and when loose is very long and bushy, but will likely have it cut short; there remains the mark of a burn near the wrist, on the back part of one of his hands, believed to be the right, which he received when young, has a down look when spoken to, but is a handsome erect figure with smaller features, than is common for a Negro of his age, and speaks German nearly as well as English. He was brought up by me to plantation work chiefly, of which he is very capable, but can do a little at blacksmith, shoemaking and carpenters work, and has some knowledge of making gun barrels—he had on and took with him a fur hat about half worn; a home made soili'd lincey doublet of a yellowish color, a swansdown jacket, with yellow flannel backs and lining, a pair of torn linnen trousers, which he wears very high, and a pair of common half worn shoes, but as he is an artful and active fellow, and has money, it is expected that he will soon exchange them. He also plays on the fiddle and fife tolerably well. Whoever takes up said Negro, and brings him home, shall receive if 15 miles from home 5 dollars; if 30 miles 10 dollars; if 60 miles 20 dollars; if 100 miles or upward, the above reward and 10 dollars if lodged in any goal and notice given me thereof by a letter, directed to the Post Office, at Westminster, Frederick County, Maryland.

DAVID SHRIVER

in the District of Columbia, issues over which Congress had undisputed authority.

In one vast area, however, the federal government did hold power over slavery. The Constitution authorized the Congress to make "all needful rules and regulations" respecting the territories. Suddenly in the late 1840s the issue of slavery in the territories came alive. Congress had to deal with slavery in the regions acquired after the Mexican War. The government, which could not constitutionally interfere with slavery in the states, could determine the status of slavery in the territories. Abolitionists, therefore, now had an issue on which they could make a concrete demand of Congress: keep slavery out of the new territories. And because many northerners had economic or political reasons for wanting slavery kept out of the new domain, abolitionists could appeal to self-interest as well as to conscience. Beginning in the late 1840s the antislavery movement fixed upon the territorial issue, and for the next fifteen years this question dominated national politics as no issue before or since.

For a variety of reasons, northerners opposed the expansion of slavery into the territories. Some northerners fought it because they believed that slavery was evil; others opposed it because they had some thought of moving into the new territories and did not want the land monopolized by a slave economy. Many northern businessmen feared that senators and representatives from new slave states would vote in Congress against tariffs, banking, legislation, and internal improvements. Northern workers believed that the expansion of slavery would eliminate jobs and depress wages.

Most southerners, on the other hand, were passionately committed to the expansion of slavery into the western territories. Cotton and tobacco cultivation eventually exhausted the land, forcing slave owners to move to new land farther west. If Congress passed legislation confining slavery to the South, slave owners believed, they would face eventual bankruptcy and, worse yet, would have to free their slaves. Southerners also argued that it was their right to take their slaves out west. The right to possess and keep private property, they claimed as conservatives have claimed ever since, is fundamental; and they considered their slaves to be their property. Finally, many southerners believed it imperative for new slave states to come into the Union. Only then could they maintain their dominance of the United States Senate and protect themselves from legislation in Congress hostile to the South.

Fugitive Slaves

Late in 1841 an American slave ship, the *Creole,* set out from Hampton Roads, Virginia, planning to carry a large cargo of slaves to New Orleans. Off the Atlantic coast of Florida, the slaves mutinied and took control of the ship. They killed one crew member in the process and then sailed the ship to Nassau in the Bahama Islands. The Bahamas were a British colony, and Great Britain had legally abolished slavery in 1833. The United States demanded the return of the ship and all of the slaves, but Great Britain refused. Instead, the British freed all of the slaves except those directly responsible for killing the crew member. In the midst of the controversy, Congressman Joshua Giddings, a Whig from Ohio, introduced a series of antislavery resolutions in March 1842. The resolutions condemned slavery and the slave trade. They did not pass in the House of Representatives, but their introduction inspired dozens of southerners to praise the virtues of slavery on the floor of Congress. Meanwhile, another issue involving fugitives from slavery was further inflaming southern feelings.

The Fugitive Slave Act of 1793 had provided for the use of federal marshals to assist in the capture of slaves who had escaped into free states. But as the slavery issue became more and more controversial in the early nineteenth century, some of the free states refused to provide any assistance in arresting, detaining, and extraditing escaped slaves. Beginning in 1820, a number of northern states, including Pennsylvania, New York, Connecticut, Massachusetts, Vermont, and Ohio, passed what they called "personal liberty laws" to protect the former slaves and impede the enforcement of the Fugitive Slave Act of 1793.

The passage of the personal liberty laws outraged southern slave owners. The matter, to be sure, did pose a constitutional dilemma for them. Ever since Thomas Jefferson and James Madison wrote the Virginia and Kentucky Resolutions in 1799, the South had insisted on the supremacy of states' rights as opposed to the authority of the federal government. That had been the position of Calhoun and South Carolina during the nullification crises. But on the question of runaway slaves, southerners found themselves calling for the federal government to interfere with state prerogatives. They demanded enforcement of the Fugitive Slave Act of 1793 and repeal of the personal liberty laws. Pennsylvania in 1826 had passed its personal liberty law, which banned the seizure and extradition of fugitive slaves. The Pennsylvania statute was challenged by an owner who demanded the return of his escaped slave. Although the Supreme Court in *Prigg v. Pennsylvania* (1842) held the state law unconstitutional, it also proclaimed that enforcement of the Fugitive Slave Act of 1793 was exclusively a federal responsibility and that state governments were not obliged to provide any assistance. The decision led to a series of new personal liberty laws in northern states. The legislation prohibited the use of any state resources—personnel, jails, or courts—in assisting federal authorities in the return of escaped slaves. Without at least some state assistance, the national government was unable to return the vast majority of escaped slaves. The conviction deepened in the South that much of the North was prepared to express its contempt of the slave system legislatively.

Whigs, Democrats, and Westward Expansion

John Tyler: Another Southern President   In March 1841 jubilant Whigs flooded Washington, hungry for government offices. The crush of office-seekers proved tiring for the elderly and infirm William Henry Harrison. A cold contracted while he was doing the presidential grocery shopping soon developed into pneumonia, and on April 4—just a month after the inauguration—he died. Two days later Vice President John Tyler, summoned

President John Tyler. *(Courtesy, Hugh Cleland Collection)*

hastily from his Virginia plantation, took the presidential oath. Since Harrison was the first President to die in office, questions arose over whether Tyler was actually President or merely the Vice President assuming the duties and responsibilities of the presidency. Tyler simply took on the title of President and thereby settled the matter.

Lean and hawk-nosed, with a Virginian's pride and a streak of obstinacy, the fifty-one-year-old Tyler entered the White House with a distinguished career in Virginia politics behind him. He had started in politics as a states' rights Democrat, and he and the Whigs were mismatched from the start. The new President resisted domination by Clay and Webster, the acknowledged leaders of the party. He had no sympathy for the Whigs' economic nationalism. In September, when he vetoed Clay's bill to reestablish a national bank, the entire Harrison Cabinet resigned except Secretary of State Webster. He stayed on to conduct negotiations with Great Britain over various problems, especially the disputed northeastern boundary between Maine and New Brunswick.

Tempers had flared between the United States and Great Britain in 1837 when a small steamer, the *Caroline*, was burned by the British when it was caught ferrying supplies to a group of Canadian nationalists on the Niagara River. Two years later Alexander McLeod, a Canadian deputy sheriff, was arrested in New York State for murder in connection with the *Caroline* incident. McLeod was released only after border skirmishes and talk of war with Britain filled the newspapers. In 1842, the secretary of state managed to conclude the Webster-Ashburton Treaty, which settled the bloodless "Aroostook War" over lumbering rights along the Maine boundary and other problems by compromise, and set an example for the friendly resolution of future disputes between Britain and the United States and between this country and Canada. Shortly after the treaty was signed, Webster too left the Cabinet. That resignation completed the break between Tyler and the Whigs, who henceforth referred to the President as "His Accidency."

Tyler appointed a new Cabinet heavy with southern Democrats, and began searching for issues that would win him reelection. For the North he signed the Tariff of 1842, restoring protective duties to roughly the level of 1832. To soothe southern resentment over the tariff, Tyler offered a daring proposal—the annexation of Texas, an area that since 1836 had been an independent nation known as the Lone Star Republic. Annexation was a policy sure to anger the Mexican republic, which was losing its control over the whole of its vast western lands.

Annexation of Texas   During the Texan war of independence, the United States had adopted a distinctly unneutral attitude. Money was raised for supplies, and many volunteers swelled the ranks of the Texan army. After independence, much of the public on both sides of the border between Texas and the United States favored annexation. But since Mexico refused to acknowledge Texan independence, annexation might provoke war. Politicians also feared that incorporating new slave territory into the Union would aggravate the rising antislavery sentiment in the North. President Jackson waited until his last day in office before recognizing the new Texan republic. His successor, Martin Van Buren, carefully avoided the question of annexation. Texas drifted for several years, developing ever closer ties with Great Britain.

The movement for annexation revived in 1842. Facing an empty treasury and renewed hostilities with Mexico, Sam Houston as President of Texas made overtures to Washington and found an enthusiastic ally in John Tyler. Annexation was politically expedient, and, like other slaveholders, Tyler was convinced that continued expansion was vital to the slave economy and the southern way of life. After the unsympathetic Webster resigned as secretary of state, Tyler appointed a fellow Virginian, Abel P. Upshur, and ordered him to seek a treaty of annexation.

The move was well timed: the country dreamed of continental empire. Southerners feared that Britain, which had abolished slavery in its possessions in 1833, was working to abolish slavery in Texas. Northern commercial interests sought control by the United States of valuable Pacific coast ports as trading centers, and annexation of Texas would shorten the distance to the Pacific. Secretary Upshur, confident that the Senate would approve a treaty, negotiated with Texan representatives. After Upshur's death the new secretary of state, John C. Calhoun, completed the arrangements for annexation and submitted the treaty to the Senate.

James Polk: Expansionist   The Senate, however, delayed action until after the 1844 party nominating conventions, at which Texas suddenly emerged as a major political issue. Both leading candidates, Henry Clay and Martin Van Buren, came out against annexation. The Whigs, passing over President Tyler, nominated Clay; the Democrats bypassed Van Buren in favor of an avowed expansionist, James Knox Polk. This political maneuvering and Calhoun's defense of annexation as a proslavery measure doomed the treaty. A combination of Whigs and disappointed Van Buren Democrats killed it. Tyler refused to surrender; he sent a message to the House of Representatives three days later proposing to annex Texas by other means.

Tyler, before leaving the White House, had forced the issue of expansion to the center of American politics. Democrats hoped to preserve sectional harmony within their party by promising both the "re-annexation" of Texas and the "re-occupation" of Oregon to the very northerly latitude of 54° 40′. Whigs and Democrats again clamored for votes. In Lowell, Massachusetts: "The Whig Party of this city have got a large flag stretched across one of our streets. The Democratic Party not to be outdone [obtained] a large hickory tree surmounted with a flag staff, making the whole length upwards of 100 feet." The Oregon occupation slogan "Fifty-four forty or fight" became popular among expansionists.

Too late, Clay sensed the public mood and endorsed annexation of Texas "upon just and fair terms." That November, Polk won a narrow victory in the presidential election. President Tyler interpreted Polk's victory as a mandate for annexation of Texas. Just before he left office in March 1845, the President got Congress to admit Texas to the Union by a joint resolution, which required only a majority vote in each house, while a treaty would have required approval by two-thirds of the Senate. When Polk entered the White House, annexation was a settled question.

The Oregon Question

Another of Polk's major objectives was the solution of the Oregon boundary question. Formidable mountain barriers had retarded settlement in the Pacific Northwest until the 1830s, when traders and missionaries began publicizing the area. By 1845 some 5,000 Americans had migrated there, settling mainly in the fertile Willamette Valley in Oregon. Throughout his campaign, Polk promised to assert American control over all the Oregon Territory, which the United States and Great Britain had occupied jointly since 1818. Once in power, however, Polk began a search for compromise with Britain.

The British government at first rejected the American idea of putting the line at the 49th parallel, which would place the Columbia River wholly in the hands of the United States. Polk then called upon Congress for authority to give the required one year's notice terminating joint occupation. The United States, he announced, would look John Bull "straight in the eye." Congress consented. Polk served the expected notice in April 1846; on both sides of the Atlantic, people talked of war. One newspaper declared: *"Oregon is ours*, and we will keep it, at the price, if need be, of every drop of the nation's blood."

Neither country really wanted a fight. Britain had all but abandoned to the advancing wave of settlers the land between the Columbia River and the 49th parallel. Polk, anticipating war with Mexico at any moment, could no longer afford a quarrel with Britain. He therefore welcomed a British offer to divide Oregon at the 49th parallel. The Senate approved this arrangement. Northwestern Democrats charged that Polk and his southern Democratic allies, having acquired Texas, had reneged on their promise to acquire "all of Oregon or none." Their residual bitterness combined with antislavery sentiment to strengthen opposition to Polk's conduct of the Mexican War.

Polk's other objective, acquiring California, was not so easily accomplished. Mexico had no intention of selling the province. In March 1845, in protest over the decision of the United States to annex Texas, the proud Latin republic had broken diplomatic relations with the United States. And a controversy had arisen over the question of just what had been annexed. Texans asserted that their republic stretched as far south as the Rio Grande; Mexico insisted that the province's boundary stopped at the Nueces River. Mexico probably had the better case. Polk nevertheless claimed all the disputed area for the United States and used his nation's demands on the Texas boundary to press Mexico to a settlement on California.

The Mexican Settlements

After Mexico won its independence in 1821, the Spanish outposts to the North remained in their customary isolation from the South. They enjoyed much self-sufficiency, and they were receptive to the manufactures that traders from the United States were able to furnish. By 1824 wagons and pack animals were hauling tools, textiles, and weapons over the Santa Fe Trail, forged by William Becknell in the early 1820s. In the 1830s English-speaking Americans and even Europeans began to drift into California. Some traversed the California trail and competed as

"Give up Oregon?" asked one senator:

"History, speaking from the sepulchre of the sainted dead, forbids it. The shades of Washington, of Adams, of Henry, and of their immortal compeers, forbid it. The still small voice of Camden and Concord forbids it. The holy blood that fell in torrents in the parched fields of Monmouth, and Camden, and the Brandywine, forbids it. . . . In the name of the past, in the name of the unborn millions whose proud fortune it will be to direct the destinies of free America— I protest here, in the face of Heaven and all men, against any dismemberment of our territory—the surrender of our principle—the sacrifice of our honor!"

successful ranchers alongside the Spanish. The Swiss John Sutter, who would discover gold in California in 1849, settled in Monterey.

| Young America | As the United States pressed westward, the expansionist urge acquired an explicit ideology. It was associated with the phrase "manifest destiny." In |

Young America   As the United States pressed westward, the expansionist urge acquired an explicit ideology. It was associated with the phrase "manifest destiny." In 1845 John L. O'Sullivan, editor of an expansionist newspaper entitled *The United States Magazine and Democratic Review*, spoke of "our manifest destiny to overspread the continent allotted by Providence for the free development of our yearly multiplying millions." Late in 1845 during the debate over the Oregon Treaty, the New York *Morning News* picked up on the phrase, and by 1846 newspapers made "Manifest Destiny" familiar throughout the United States. Manifest Destiny came to mean that the institutions and values of the United States were destined to spread across the continent, from the Atlantic to the Pacific. Nature and God intended this to take place, and the government should assist in bringing it about, even if it meant war.

Closely associated with Manifest Destiny was the Young America movement. Its leading exponent was George N. Sanders, who wrote regularly for the *Democratic Review*. The advocates of Young America believed that the United States had a special mission that would eventually envelop the entire world. Young America was a global extension of Jacksonian democracy and Manifest Destiny. Its adherents called for the United States to embrace all of North America, not only from the Atlantic to the Pacific but from the Isthmus of Panama to the Arctic. They also wanted the United States to provide assistance to revolutionary movements everywhere. When the revolutions of 1848 erupted throughout Europe, the advocates of Young America wished for the United States to get involved and provide political and economic support to the insurgents. As it turned out, the Young America movement was ahead of its time, but it did generate at least some of the energy that fueled politics during the 1840s and led to expansion into the Spanish Southwest and the British Northwest.

Of the annexation of Texas, the expansionist editor John L. O'Sullivan wrote:

"Texas has been absorbed into the Union in the inevitable fulfillment of the general law which is rolling our population westward; the connexion of which with that ratio of growth in population which is destined within a hundred years to swell our numbers to the enormous population of *two hundred and fifty millions* (if not more), is too evident to leave us in doubt of the manifest design of Providence in regard to the occupation of this continent. It was disintegrated from Mexico in the natural course of events, by a process perfectly legitimate on its own part, blameless on ours; and in which all the censures due to wrong, perfidy, and folly, rest on Mexico alone. And possessed as it was by a population which was in truth but a colonial detachment from our own, . . . their incorporation into the Union was not only inevitable, but the most natural, right and proper thing in the world—and it is only astonishing that there should be any among ourselves to say it nay."

The Mexican War

The Coming of War   In July 1845, Polk ordered General Zachary Taylor, with nearly 4,000 troops, to take up a position south of the Nueces River. Taylor halted at Corpus Christi, where he remained for several months. At about the same time, the President issued secret orders to naval officers in the Pacific to occupy the California ports in the event of war with Mexico. He worked actively to encourage a revolution among settlers in the manner of the Texas uprising. Just in case the dissatisfied settlers from the United States needed any help, the President sent Colonel John C. Frémont and a scientific expedition to California, on which the engineering equipment included a heavy stock of arms.

His weapons now primed and ready, Polk sent John Slidell, a Louisiana politician, to Mexico in November 1845 to negotiate. The

President, refusing to compromise on the Rio Grande River boundary that would bite into territory claimed by Mexico, offered only to assume payment of claims by citizens of the United States against the Mexican government in return for accepting that river as marking the frontier between the two republics. He also authorized Slidell to purchase all or part of Upper California and New Mexico. When two successive Mexican governments refused to risk public disfavor by receiving him, Slidell withdrew. "Be assured," he wrote to the secretary of state, "that nothing is to be done with these people until they shall have been chastised." Polk had reached the same conclusion. In January 1846 he sent General Taylor's army to the Rio Grande. In late March Taylor and his men took up a fortified position opposite the Mexican city of Matamoros; naval units then blockaded the mouth of the river. For several weeks, nothing happened.

On May 9 Polk decided to ask Congress for a declaration of war against Mexico for failing to pay the claims due citizens of the United States and refusing to receive Slidell. News arrived that very evening of a skirmish with Mexican forces on the north bank of the Rio Grande. Polk at once revised his war message. Mexico, he told Congress, had "invaded our territory and shed American blood upon American soil." Congress, not fully aware of the President's maneuvering, voted overwhelmingly for war. Thousands of volunteers enthusiastically answered the call.

Polk and his Cabinet agreed at the outset that the United States must acquire both New Mexico and Upper California (the present state, as distinct from Lower California, still part of Mexico) and secure the Rio Grande boundary. New Mexico and California took but six months to conquer. During the summer of 1846 Colonel Stephen W. Kearny's

One soldier stationed near Matamoros wrote home:

"We had just moved our camp into a corn field newly ploughed, the soil an adhesive clay, and by the time I had in some measure secured my baggage . . . the water was some inches deep, or rather there was a soft adhesive mortar bed, about ankle deep, over the whole camp. The rain and gale were still at their worst, when I began looking about to see the state of the nation. In every direction the tents were overthrown and their contents scattered in the mud. My own company had almost entirely disappeared, a few despairing wretches, groping about in the mud for their arms, were all that were left. The fires were extinguished and desolation reigned throughout the camp."

ESSAY ON CIVIL DISOBEDIENCE (1846)

by Henry David Thoreau

Thoreau was ardently opposed to both slavery and the Mexican War.

How does it become a man to behave toward this American government to-day? I answer, that he cannot without disgrace be associated with it. I cannot for an instant recognize that political organization as my government which is the slave's government also.

All men recognize the right of revolution: that is, the right to refuse allegiance to, and to resist, the government, when its tyranny or its inefficiency are great and unendurable. But almost all say that such is not the case now. But such was the case, they think, in the Revolution of '75. If one were to tell me that this was a bad government because it taxed certain foreign commodities brought to its ports, it is most probable that I should not make an ado about it, for I can do without them.

When a sixth of the population of a nation which has undertaken to be the refuge of liberty are slaves, and a whole country is unjustly overrun and conquered by a foreign army, and subjected to military law, I think that it is not too soon for honest men to rebel and revolutionize. What makes this duty the more urgent is the fact that the country so overrun is not our own, but ours is the invading army.

If the injustice is part of the necessary friction of the machine of government, let it go, let it go, perchance it will wear smooth,—certainly the machine will wear out; if the injustice has a spring, or a pulley, or a rope, or a crank, exclusively for itself, then perhaps you may consider whether the remedy will not be worse than the evil; but if it is of such a nature that it requires you to be the agent of injustice to another, then, I say, break the law. Let your life be a counter friction to stop the machine. What I have to do is to see, at any rate, that I do not lend myself to the wrong which I condemn.

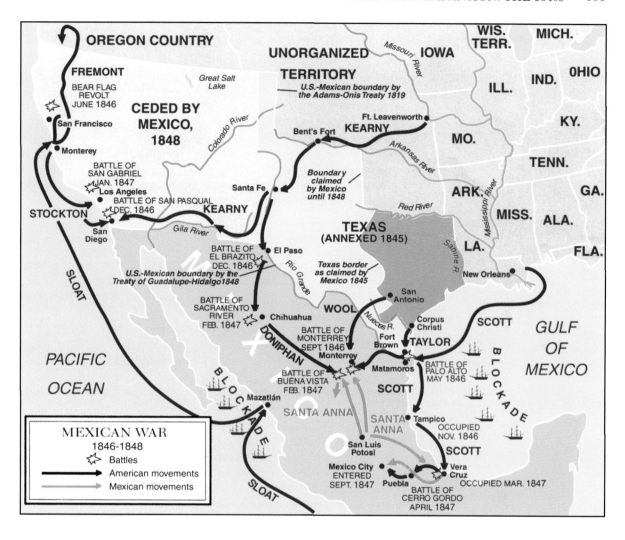

Army of the West (actually just sixteen hundred men) marched from Fort Leavenworth, Kansas, to Santa Fe, and occupied it without opposition. Kearny then proceeded with part of his force to aid the navy in the conquest of California. A column of Missouri volunteers under Colonel A. W. Doniphan descended the Rio Grande to El Paso, marched from there into the interior, and in March 1847 occupied Chihuahua.

Beyond the capture of Upper California and New Mexico, Polk's objectives were unclear. Apparently he hoped that an advance into Mexico would force General Santa Anna into a quick settlement. So Taylor at once pushed the Mexicans back across the Rio Grande and occupied Matamoros. In September, Taylor captured the Mexican stronghold of Monterrey and moved on to Saltillo and Victoria. The following February he repulsed Santa Anna at Buena Vista. Old Rough and Ready's victories and Doniphan's occupation of Chihuahua secured their country's possession of Mexico's northern territories. In the meantime, Polk had decided to bring the stubborn Santa Anna to terms with a strike at Mexico City itself.

At another camp, on the Rio Grande, a volunteer in the Mexican War reported:

"The water here unless well-qualified with brandy has a very peculiar effect on one . . . it opens the bowels. . . . Gen. Scott came to see us the other day. He complimented Major Sumner very warmly on our improvement and especially on the extraordinary vigilance of our scouts—who, as he said, were peering at him from behind every bush as he approached the camp. To those aware of the disease prevalent here, the mistake of the General is ludicrous."

Senator Thomas Corwin of Ohio, a
Whig, also spoke out against the war:

"How is it that my country is involved
in this war? I looked to the President's
account of it, and he tells me it was a
war for the defense of territory of the
United States. . . . I know that the people of the United States neither sought
nor forced Mexico into this war, and I
know that the President of the United
States . . . did seek that war, and that he
forced war upon Mexico."

Polk, hating the Whigs even more than the Mexicans, picked
General Winfield Scott to lead the campaign instead of Zachary Taylor,
who was already being pushed as a Whig presidential candidate. Landing at Vera Cruz in March 1847, Scott took the city with few casualties
on his side. The loss of life among Mexicans at Vera Cruz, by their own
report, was 1,100, mostly by the explosion of shells, while only thirteen
United States soldiers died. Scott then pushed inland through the
mountains, routing Santa Anna at the pass of Cerro Gordo, after a party
of engineers under Captain Robert E. Lee had hacked a path through
ravines and underbrush to surround the Mexicans. On September 13,
Scott's army stormed the fortress of Chapultepec guarding Mexico City.
The capital fell the next day.

**The
Treaty of
Guadalupe
Hidalgo
(1848)**
Whigs meanwhile were capturing a widespread
domestic opposition to "Mr. Polk's War." Whig politicians—among them a young Illinois congressman
named Abraham Lincoln—accused the President of
provoking Mexico into war as an excuse for expansion.

In December 1847 Lincoln introduced resolutions requesting Polk
to inform Congress as to the "exact spot" where the first "blood of our
citizens was shed." He declared "that the war with Mexico was unnecessarily and unconstitutionally commenced by the President." Later
Lincoln praised a speech by Congressman Alexander Stephens of Georgia, who said that "the principle of waging war against a neighboring
people to compel them to sell their country, is not only dishonorable,
but disgraceful and infamous." In the Senate, Illinois Democrat Stephen
Douglas spoke up for the President, quoting Frederick the Great's
maxim, "Take possession first and negotiate afterward." A new senator
from Mississippi, Jefferson Davis, who had fought at Buena Vista, said
that Mexico was held "by title of conquest." If the United States could
not agree, said Davis, then "let the sections part."

Outside Congress, other voices of opposition were heard. James
Russell Lowell accused the President of wanting "bigger pens to cram
with slaves." The American Peace Society grew in membership. Henry
David Thoreau counseled civil disobedience and spent a night in jail for
refusing to pay taxes to a government that supported the war. Some
critics of the war even longed for the defeat of the United States. As
Scott's army approached Mexico City, William Lloyd Garrison thundered in the *Liberator:* "We only hope that, if blood has had to flow,
that it has been that of the Americans, and that the next news we shall
hear will be that General Scott and his army are in the hands of the
Mexicans. . . ."

Especially in the West and in the border states feelings about
slavery and the Mexican War were smouldering on both sides of the
issue. At the same time "Continental Democrats," party members of
extreme expansionist persuasion, were urging the President to take all
of Mexico. Polk had previously dispatched Nicholas P. Trist to Mexico
as a peace negotiator, and although in late 1847 he called Trist home,
the emissary ignored Polk's order and stayed to sign the Treaty of
Guadalupe Hidalgo on February 2, 1848. The United States gained the

Rio Grande boundary, New Mexico, and California in return for an agreement to assume the claims of its citizens against the Mexican government, and to pay $15 million to Mexico.

The ratification in 1848 of the Treaty of Guadalupe Hidalgo turned over to the United States approximately 80,000 Mexicans whose citizenship and property rights the treaty supposedly guaranteed along with their religious freedom. Mexicans residing within the United States gradually saw their property and influence dwindle as they faced increasing pressure from the flood of Anglo Americans. The California Land Law of 1851 required that they submit proof of their land ownership. The cost of doing so in taxes, legal fees, and battles with squatters, in combination with the rainfall conditions that made incomes uncertain, gradually took away their land. Violence broke out in northern California in the 1850s and 1860s, and some Mexican Americans, called *Californios,* resorted to banditry. *Bandidos* who roamed California spawned legends. In southern California, in the 1870s and 1880s, the *Californios* lost more land to the railroads, which nonetheless provided jobs for Hispanics. In New Mexico, the *ricos,* wealthy Mexican landowners and merchants, took an important part in the creation of the territorial government. While remaining largely separate from the Anglo Americans, they retained substantial influence after the Civil War. In Texas, as the cattle industry grew enormously in response to the demand for beef that increased with the country's population, the Spanish and Anglo cultures would blend after the war into now familiar cowboy traditions. But many inhabitants of Mexican birth or ancestry continued to experience discrimination.

A Mexican historian has observed: "To explain then in a few words the true origin of the war, it is sufficient to say that the insatiable ambition of the United States, favored by our weakness, caused it." For an apparently small price the United States had rounded out its continental domain, acquiring the present states of California, Nevada, Utah, New Mexico, and Arizona. Soon, however, the cost would prove enormous: the problem of organizing this vast new territory reopened the explosive issue of slavery expansion, ultimately splitting in two the new transcontinental republic.

Crisis at Midcentury When Congress adopted the Missouri Compromise in 1820 it had also adopted the rule that all territories above 36° 30′ would be closed to slavery while all below this line would be open to it. This formula had worked for a quarter of a century, in large measure because both northerners and southerners believed it fairly divided the national domain. The war with Mexico changed this. Most of the land acquired fell below the line. And California, easily the most valuable of the new territories even before the discovery of gold triggered the famous rush of 1849, would have been divided into two with the compromise line. Meanwhile the Polk Administration's diplomatic settlement of the Oregon boundary with Britain, although probably the best arrangement the United States could have gotten short of war, also rankled northerners who saw the Mexican War as a conspiracy to advance the power of the slave states.

With this in mind a member of President Polk's own party, a

In 1859 Juan Cortina, the "Robin Hood of Texas," launched an armed rebellion to protest the wholesale loss of land by native Tejano farmers to Anglos. He battled United States soldiers and Texas Rangers until the summer of 1860, when he escaped across the border into Mexico. He issued a manifesto to all Mexican Americans in South Texas on November 23, 1859:

"Mexicans! Many of you have been robbed of your property, incarcerated, chased, murdered, and hunted like wild beasts. . . . [J]ustice had fled from this world, leaving you to the caprice of your oppressors, who become each day more furious toward you. . . . Mexicans! My part is taken; the voice of revelation whispers to me that to me is entrusted the work of breaking the chains of your slavery, and that the Lord will enable me, with powerful arm, to fight against our enemies. . . . On my part, I am ready to offer myself as a sacrifice."

first-term congressman from Pennsylvania named David Wilmot, introduced his famous proviso in August of 1846 to a military appropriations bill. The Wilmot Proviso would have prohibited slavery from ever being introduced into lands acquired from Mexico. The House, with both northern Whigs and northern Democrats voting in favor, adopted the Proviso. The Senate, where southerners were more powerful, rejected it. Congress was now splitting not so much between Whigs and Democrats as between northerners and southerners. The question of slavery was taking over politics. Senator Thomas Hart Benton compared it to the Biblical plague of frogs: "You could not look upon the table but there were frogs, you could not sit down at the banquet but there were frogs, you could not go to the bridal couch and lift the sheets but there were frogs!" So it was with the slavery question, "forever on the table, on the nuptial couch, everywhere!"

Sooner or later, Congress would have to act to organize the new territories. And each time a bill concerning them came up in the House, that chamber attached the Wilmot Proviso to it guaranteeing its defeat in the Senate. Calhoun, leader of the militant proslavery forces, determined to force an outcome satisfactory to the South and drew up his own set of resolutions that not only rejected the Wilmot Proviso but declared that Congress had no power to bar slavery in any territory. This meant that, in Calhoun's view, even the Missouri Compromise line was an unconstitutional measure although he was willing to continue to abide by it as a practical matter. Calhoun's resolutions rallied the South. In the midst of this acrimonious and inconclusive struggle the election of 1848 was fought.

James Buchanan, a Pennsylvanian with strong southern ties, sought to settle the debate by extending the Missouri Compromise line to the Pacific. Buchanan's main Democratic challenger, Michigan Senator Lewis Cass, had originally supported the Wilmot Proviso, but quickly realized that he could never hope for any southern support unless he took a more conciliatory line. This he found in a concept he called popular sovereignty. Instead of Congress's deciding the question of slavery in the territories, Cass declared, the voters living there should choose for themselves whether they wanted slavery. This proposal had the merit, from Cass's point of view, of appearing to favor both sections. Southerners could take heart that it did not bar slavery from any of the territories while northerners could find comfort that few slaveholders would be foolish enough to move into the territories and risk their valuable property until slavery had already been adopted.

The Democrats decided on Cass and popular sovereignty. A group of disgruntled New York Democrats, angry over Cass's role in preventing the nomination of their own Martin Van Buren in 1844, formed the Free Soil Party with the Little Magician as their standard bearer. They demanded "free soil, free speech, free labor and free men." They were joined by the so-called "Conscience Whigs," northerners who could not support their own party's nominee, Zachary Taylor, the hero of the Mexican War they had opposed and the owner of a Louisiana plantation. Also joining the Free Soilers were the remnants of the old Liberty Party. The key to Taylor's victory may have been that his position on slavery in the territories was even vaguer than Cass's. If the Michigan sena-

James Buchanan. *(Courtesy, Library of Congress)*

tor's popular sovereignty doctrine blurred the question, Taylor simply ducked it altogether. His southern supporters used the fact of his being a slaveholder to reassure that section that he was safe on the issue. At the same time his northern backers, including such stalwarts as Abraham Lincoln, were promising that, if elected, Taylor would accept the Wilmot Proviso. Taylor himself said nothing. So the election of 1848 ended without any clear resolution of the slavery question.

The Gold Rush and the 49'ers vastly sped up settlement and contributed to the reputation nearby San Francisco was acquiring for gambling, drinking, and prostitution. Most claims soon petered out, and miners either became wage workers or chased the get-rich-quick rainbow to another site. Others coming to California established trading enterprises in San Diego and elsewhere.

One letter sent home measured the gold fever in California in 1849:

"People are arriving and departing daily and hourly. I have no doubt 400 people have already arrived from Oregon. They usually camp for a day or so near us, look about, swear at the high prices and disappear in the grand vortex. . . . It is impossible to get at anything like truth, but that the amount of gold in these mountains exceeds any previous calculation I have no doubt. . . ."

A miner complained to his wife:

"I do not like to be apacking a thousand dollars about in my coat pockets for it has toar my pockets and puld the Coat to peaces."

Suggested Readings

William H. Freehling's *The Road to Disunion: Secessionists at Bay, 1776–1854* (1991) is a good overview of the developing political tensions in the antebellum years. Sectionalism is the theme of William Brock's *Parties and Political Conscience: America Dilemmas, 1840–1850* (1979). Other political works are Paul Bergeron, *The Presidency of James K. Polk* (1987), Steve Stowe, *Intimacy and Power in the Old South: Rituals in the Lives of the Planters* (1987), Norma Peterson, *The Presidencies of William Henry Harrison and John Tyler* (1989), Daniel W. Howe, *The Political Culture of the American Whigs* (1980), Jack Bauer, *Zachary Taylor* (1985), and Gavin Wright, *The Political Economy of the Cotton South* (1978). See also Holman Hamilton, *Prologue to Conflict: The Crisis and Compromise of 1850* (1964) and Merrill Peterson, *The Great Triumvirate: Webster, Clay, and Calhoun* (1987).

Eugene D. Genovese's *Roll, Jordan, Roll: The World the Slaves Made* (1974) has become a classic. Genovese's *The World the Slaveholders Made* (1969) elaborates on the class structure of southern society. Herbert G. Gutman in *The Black Family in Slavery and Freedom, 1750–1925* (1976) challenges theories that speak of the disorganization of the black slave family. Other studies of the domestic side of slavery are Drew Gilpin Faust's *Mothers of Invention:*

Women of the Slaveholding South in the Civil War (1996), Janet Cornelius, *When I Can Read My Title Clear: Literacy, Slavery, and Religion in the Antebellum South* (1991), Elizabeth Fox-Genovese's *Within the Plantation Household: Black and White Women of the Old South* (1989), and Catherine Clinton's *The Plantation Mistress: Women's Work in the Old South* (1982). George M. Fredrickson examines the sources of racist ideas in *The Black Image in the White Mind* (1971).

On the Mexican War see John S. D. Eisenhower, *So Far From God: The U.S. War with Mexico 1846–1848* (1989), Jack Bauer's *The Mexican American War* (1974), David Pletcher, *The Diplomacy of Annexation: Texas, Oregon, and the Mexican War* (1973), and Robert W. Johannsen, *To the Halls of Montezuma: The Mexican War in the American Imagination* (1985). Gene M. Brack's *Mexico Views Manifest Destiny, 1821–1846* (1975) presents the Mexican viewpoint. See also Richard Griswold del Castillo, *The Treaty of Guadaloupe Hidalgo: A Legacy of Conflict* (1990) and *Occupied America: A History of Chicanos* (1988) by Rudolfo Acuna. Andrew Rolle's *John Charles Frémont: Character As Destiny* (1991) is a study of a soldier's position on the West. Frederick Merk, *Manifest Destiny and Mission in American History* (1965) is the classic account of westward expansion.

What Caused the Mexican War?

John S. D. Eisenhower

Overshadowed by the cataclysmic Civil War only thirteen years later, the Mexican War has been practically forgotten in the United States. Through the years, despite our growing interest in Mexico, it is rarely mentioned. And when the subject comes up, it nearly always deals with the questionable manner in which it came about. More specifically, was the United States right in sending Zachary Taylor to the Rio Grande in early 1846, thus provoking war with Mexico? Opinions vary.

Ulysses S. Grant, for one, was certain that the United States was wrong. He did, in fact, call the Mexican War "the most unjust war ever waged by a stronger against a weaker nation. . . . an instance of a republic following the bad example of European monarchies. . . ." And without a doubt, the preponderance of American opinion has agreed with Grant that the United States treated Mexico unjustly.

Actually, the issue is not simple, and opinions on it are colored by its role in accelerating the growth of animosity between the Northern and Southern states of the Union which eventually led to the Civil War. The North feared the expansion of slave territory. Thus the facts regarding the conflict that extended the borders of the continental United States from the Rio Grande to the Pacific have been submerged in the slavery issue. . . .

Contrary to common understanding, the war with Mexico was supported with enthusiasm by most of the population for at least the first year, by the end of which the necessary armies were recruited and supplied. Volunteers flocked to the colors to rescue "Old Rough and Ready," Zachary Taylor, from the menace of the Mexicans on the Rio Grande. And as the result of his remarkable series of victories, that same "Zack" Taylor was later elected president, an honor rendered only to victorious generals in popular wars. Boredom and impatience set in among the American population toward the end of the war, but moral disapproval was confined largely to a few New Englanders and some New England settlers in the Midwest.

The fact is that Mexico stood in the way of the American dream of Manifest Destiny. Although that dramatic, pious term was of relatively recent coinage in 1845, the idea of expansion westward to the Pacific had long been in the American mind. As far back as his first inaugural address in 1801, President Thomas Jefferson referred to a vast territory that would provide "room enough for our descendents to the thousandth and ten thousandth generation." And Jefferson did much to make that dream a reality by purchasing the great Louisiana territory from Emperor Napoleon of France and sending exploratory expeditions to the West, first under Zebulon Pike, later under Lewis and Clark.

To the student of today the fate of Mexico is sad, for the Mexicans were victims of both their history and Yankee expansionism. But that sadness need not be exacerbated by excessive shame for the conduct of the United States, because Mexico's disorganization, corruption, and weakness created a power vacuum that would inevitably have been filled by some predator—if not the United States, then Britain, less likely France, and even, remotely, Russia. American haste to occupy California, for example, was prompted more by fear of British action than by concern of what Mexico would do. After all, the United States and Britain were threatening war over the Oregon territory just north of California. Mexico's weakness stemmed from nearly three centuries of autocratic Spanish rule and from its own devastating war of independence, not from the actions of the United States.

John S. D. Eisenhower, *So Far From God: The U.S. War with Mexico, 1846–1848* (New York: Random House, 1989), pp. xvii–xi. Reprinted by permission.

Mexicans realized . . . that American expansion threatened their territorial integrity. Ambivalence gave way to outright, near-unanimous hostility after 1836, for the struggle over Texas appeared to be nothing but thinly veiled American aggression. . . .

It was as though the United States had set out, purposefully and diabolically, to become an object of hatred in Mexico. Three hundred years of Anglo-Spanish rivalry virtually guaranteed tense relations between the two countries. From Spain, Mexico also inherited fear that the ambitious and rapidly expanding United States threatened the territorial possessions of all who stood in the way of its aggrandizement. Relations nevertheless began rather smoothly, due in large part to prompt American recognition of Mexican independence. And the selection of the able Joel Poinsett as first American minister to Mexico seemed to promise further amity. But Poinsett carried instructions to seek a treaty of limits that would recover Texas, its claim to which the United States had surrendered to Spain in 1819, and to obtain a reciprocal agreement concerning fugitive slaves. Poinsett failed at both, succeeding only in establishing in Mexican minds a direct relationship between American expansion and the institution of slavery, toward which Mexicans felt a genuine loathing. . . .

Given the deportment of American diplomats and the expansionist policies of the American government and people, it did not take long for Mexicans to discern the similarity of American attitudes toward blacks, Indians, and Mexicans. The American, they knew, justified the despoliation of Indians by insisting that the Anglo-Saxon race could make better use of their lands. Americans used precisely the same argument in justifying their craving for Mexican territory. Perhaps the most volatile single issue in the conflict of cultures that divided the two nations was religion. Mexicans were as scornful of American Protestantism as Americans were of Mexican Catholicism. But American Protestantism nurtured also the "work ethic," which exaggerated the supercilious attitudes of Americans toward Mexico and her people. Americans in Mexico frequently observed that Mexicans did not realize that time was money; that Texas under Mexican rule was worthless, but American enterprise caused it to flourish; that Mexican mines produced a fraction of what Americans would take from them; and that Mexicans were simply lazy. The Mexican, then, was no more entitled to his territorial possessions than was the Indian. Over the years Mexicans had become increasingly aware that many Americans, especially those who most vociferously advocated Southwestern expansion, looked upon Mexicans as inferior beings. This had frightening implications, for Americans had respect for neither the rights nor the culture of those whom they considered inferior. They had been merciless in their treatment of the Indian and had reduced blacks to a brutal form of servitude. Mexicans were perceptive enough to recognize that a similar fate threatened them should they fall under American domination.

American racism alone did not cause the Mexican War, of course. Mexico after all did not provide a model of enlightened humanitarianism toward her own Indians, and in their attitudes toward the United States Mexicans appeared in their own way ethnocentric. With the exception of liberals, who tended to be anticlerical, Mexicans scorned American Protestantism. The American frontiersman, viewed in the United States then as now as a noble precursor of civilization, was regarded by Mexicans as a barbaric, shiftless wretch who smoothed the way for the more sophisticated, but shrewdly manipulative, land-hungry, profit-seeking, and more dangerous Americans who followed. Such additional factors as domestic political conditions, the extended incitement of opinion over Texas, and genuine concern for the national honor help to explain Mexican attitudes on the eve of war. Still, without advocating Mexican fear of American racism as a substitute for other causes of the war, many Mexicans seemed genuinely to fear cultural extinction at the hands of Americans, and that fear helps explain why "Manifest Destiny" appeared so threatening to Mexico that she fought a war for which she was dubiously prepared rather than accede peacefully to American territorial ambitions. "Manifest Destiny" was itself an ethnocentric notion.

Reprinted from Gene M. Brack, *Mexico Views Manifest Destiny, 1821–1846* (Albuquerque: University of New Mexico Press, 1975), 169, 170, 181, 182.

This frontispiece of an edition of *Uncle Tom's Cabin* pictures the slave Eliza escaping to freedom over the ice floes in the Ohio River. *(Courtesy, The New-York Historical Society)*

Impending Crisis: The 1850s

UNCLE TOM'S CABIN (1852)

In 1826, when Harriet Beecher was fifteen years old, she had already read much of her father's theological library. She would recall with fondness her pious childhood in Massachusetts and Cincinnati and her admiration for her "God-like" father, Lyman Beecher. In Harriet's youth her father became president of Lane Theological Seminary, and she married a young teacher there, Calvin Stowe. Stowe encouraged his wife's first writings for literary magazines, and she supported him during his long encounter with hallucinations and an inability to work. In 1850, Bowdoin College offered her husband a professorship. Within a few months of Harriet's arrival in Maine she began to turn her moral attention to matters of a worldly nature. After a chance reading of a southern slave-dealing newspaper, American black slavery arrested her with "an icy hand." Mrs. Stowe began a considerable research into the institution of chattel labor, reading southern defenses of slavery as well as the attacks on it by Theodore Weld and Frederick Douglass.

The Fugitive Slave Law of 1850 angered her into action, and she wrote *Uncle Tom's Cabin* in serial form in 1851. Mrs. Stowe later described the novel as having been "dictated" to her from a source outside of herself. One measure of the novel's power was the number of imitations it generated. More than fifty novels about slavery appeared after *Uncle Tom's Cabin* was published, some thirty of which were intent on portraying the institution as

continued

HISTORICAL EVENTS

1846
Treaty with Colombia

1849
Harriet Tubman escapes from slavery

1850
Compromise of 1850 • Fugitive Slave Law • Clayton-Bulwer Treaty

1852
Harriet Beecher Stowe publishes *Uncle Tom's Cabin* • Whig Convention splits over slavery

1853
Gadsden Treaty

1854
Ostend Manifesto • Kansas-Nebraska Act • the Republican and "Know-Nothing" Parties are formed

1855
Kansas has two rival governments and internal fighting begins

1856
James Buchanan elected President

HISTORICAL EVENTS

1857
Federal troops restore order to
Kansas • *Dred Scott* decision
• Lecompton Constitution accepted
by Buchanan • Hinton Helper
publishes *The Impending Crisis of
the South*

1858
Lincoln-Douglas debates

1859
John Brown's raid

1860
John Brown executed • Democratic
Party splits in two factions
• Constitutional Union Party formed
• Abraham Lincoln elected
President

*One southern reviewer wrote in ardent
denial:*

"We have said that Uncle Tom's
Cabin is a fiction. It is a fiction throughout; a fiction in form; a fiction in its facts;
a fiction in its representations and col-
oring; a fiction in its statements; a fiction
in its sentiments; a fiction in its morals;
a fiction in its religion; a fiction in its
inferences; a fiction equally with regard
to the subjects it is designed to expound,
and with respect to the manner of their
exposition. It is a fiction, not for the sake
of more effectually communicating
truth; but for the purpose of more effectually disseminating a slander. It is a
fictitious or fanciful representation for
the sake of producing fictitious or false
impressions. Fiction is its form and
falsehood is its end."

beneficial. None of these captured Mrs. Stowe's great audience. Sales in book form set publishing records: 300,000 copies the first year, a million in seven years. Adapted for the stage, the story quickly became the nation's most popular play. By 1861, millions of northerners had thrilled over Eliza's dramatic escape and wept for Tom's fortitude under the lash.

The first part of the story is about George Harris and Eliza, his wife, slaves so near white that they can pass while escaping from slavery. Mistreated by his master, George disguises himself as a gentleman traveler and quits Kentucky with the help of a sympa-thetic white southerner. Eliza overhears that the slave foreman, a robust, kindly figure named Tom, is to be sold by his master, and she and her son Harry take flight to join George in Canada. With Harry in her arms Eliza escapes from the slave traders—the stage versions have her leaping melodramatically from ice floe to ice floe—across the Ohio River, to the northern underground rail-road. Tom the slave is sold to a New Orleans family and makes friends with the saintly Little Eva, who dies of tuberculosis in a scene that has wrung tears from generations of readers. In the end Tom is sold to Simon Legree, a savage drunk who flogs him. Tom dies, like Christ, forgiving his killers.

Mrs. Stowe cut right to the heart of the matter: it was not fundamentally people who were evil, but the system under which they lived. Given absolute power over their slaves, few masters could resist the temptation to use it. Slavery often dragged down even good masters when circumstances occurred beyond their control. At its worst (Simon Legree's domain) the peculiar insti-tution brutalized everyone—black and white. It is difficult to measure the exact impact of *Uncle Tom's Cabin,* but after its appearance the northern attitude toward slavery would never be quite the same. There was truth in the remark with which Presi-dent Lincoln allegedly greeted Mrs. Stowe when she visited the White House during the Civil War: "So you're the little lady who wrote the book that made the great war."

Mrs. Stowe was not pursuing slavery with a bludgeon. Her instrument was as delicate as a surgeon's knife, and she operated on the national psyche. The slave was commercial property, and the business of slavery passed through northern as well as south-ern hands. The trade in human beings, a constant assault on the black family, tore against the fabric of a society woven of Christi-anity and the family. Mrs. Stowe possessed a firm sense of the uneasiness that many Americans felt over the disrupting tenden-cies of commerce. Instead of making the slaveowning South a direct contrast with the "free" society of the North, she made it a grotesque extension and intensification of that world. Men "alive to nothing but trade and profit—cool, and unhesitating, and unrelenting as death and the grave roamed the American earth, building things and disrupting and destroying lives." Under slavery, men of commerce could take their avarice to its final meaning: trade in human flesh. Mrs. Stowe originally and correctly subtitled her book *The Man That Was a Thing,* a commodity to be traded on the market. Northerners understood her picture of slavery because it reached the guilt they felt about their own society.

Southerners knew this too: their many replies to *Uncle Tom's Cabin* aimed ineffectual blows at northern commercial society.

The Compromise of 1850

It was a warring Congress that met in December 1849. It took three weeks and fifty-nine ballots to elect a Speaker of the House. Californians, tired of waiting for Congress, held a convention at Monterey and drafted a state constitution prohibiting slavery: some of them simply did not want whites to have to compete with black labor. Without waiting for congressional approval, California chose a governor and legislature. California now had to seek formal admission to statehood.

On this Congress could not agree. The new President, Zachary Taylor, decided to intervene in the imbroglio. Although a southerner, Taylor opposed the expansion of slave territory. Like Polk, he considered California and the Southwest unsuitable for slavery. The President therefore recommended to Congress that California and New Mexico be admitted directly to statehood, bypassing the territorial stage. The residents could then decide the slavery question for themselves without embarrassment to Congress. Southerners, seeing that California had already prohibited slavery and expecting New Mexico to do the same, realized that Taylor's plan was as effective as Wilmot's Proviso in keeping slavery out of this area. When they protested, the old soldier drew a firm line, threatening to use force if necessary to preserve the Union.

Taylor, southerners decided, had betrayed them. California would be the first in what they feared were to be many new free states admitted to the Union. Free and slave states had been equal in number, and therefore North and South had enjoyed equal representation in the Senate. Now the South was about to lose that precarious equality. Northerners would make war upon slavery—an institution, southern spokesmen insisted, "upon which is staked our property, our social organization and our peace and safety." When a call went out in October 1849 for the southern states to send delegates to a convention at Nashville the following June to consider secession, most of these states accepted.

The intensity of southern sentiments revealed itself late in 1849 when sixty-nine congressmen and senators from the South convened a special caucus in Washington, D.C. Calhoun, who emerged as leader of the caucus, accused the North of committing numerous "acts of aggression" against the South. According to Calhoun, and the forty-eight congressmen who eventually signed the caucus petition, the North was out to destroy the southern way of life. As proof he cited the individual laws prohibiting slavery in various territories and the problems southerners were having in recapturing fugitive slaves living in the North. Calhoun insisted that the only way out of the impasse was to restore to southerners their Fifth Amendment property rights, which he interpreted as meaning that slave owners should be able to take their slaves anywhere in the United States and should be afforded adequate legal assistance in repossessing escaped slaves.

Senator Daniel Webster of New Hampshire, urged both North and South to avoid extreme positions on slavery. *(Courtesy, Scribner's Archives)*

Daniel Webster made this memorable plea for Union:

"When my eyes shall be turned to behold for the last time the sun in heaven, may I not see him shining on the broken and dishonored fragments of a once glorious Union; on States disevered, discordant, belligerent; on a land rent with civil feuds, or drenched, it may be, in fraternal blood. . . . Liberty and Union, now and forever, one and inseparable."

Clay, Calhoun, and Webster

At this moment, with disunion threatening, an aged Senator Henry Clay offered a compromise that he hoped would settle for good the territorial crisis and other disputed issues between the sections. Clay's plan, introduced in Congress in January 1850, contained five key provisions: immediate admission of free California; organization of the rest of the area acquired from Mexico into two territories, Utah and New Mexico, without restriction on slavery, the matter to be decided by their own constitutions; assumption of the Texan national debt by the federal government; abolition of the slave trade in the District of Columbia; and a tough new fugitive slave law.

The debate on Clay's compromise was the grand twilight for the generation of statesmen who had guided the nation's destinies since 1812. Twice before, in 1820 and 1833, stirring appeals to love of Union, flag, and Constitution had soothed sectional tensions. During the winter and spring of 1850, Senate veterans tried to revive this tested formula. Day after day, packed galleries followed their speeches.

Clay took the floor first, urging the North not to demand the principle of the Wilmot Proviso—nature would as effectively exclude slavery—and to honor the constitutional obligation to return fugitive slaves. He reminded the South of the many benefits she enjoyed in the Union. The Great Pacificator closed his two-day oration with an appeal to both sides to pause at the edge of the cliff, before leaping "into the yawning abyss below." Clay expressed the hope that, should disunion occur, he would not live to see it.

Clay's compromises did not go far enough to satisfy John C. Calhoun. The Old Nullifier, his body wracked by tuberculosis, sat defiantly wrapped in a black shawl while his speech was read for him. Northern agitation on the slavery issue, he said, had "snapped" many of the "cords which bind these states together in one common Union. . . ." The North, moreover, had taken advantage of tariffs and other federal favors to outstrip the South in population and power. Without an equality of votes in the Senate, the fragile equilibrium between the sections was doomed. Without such equality the South was defenseless and could not stay in the Union. Calhoun demanded that the North not only grant slaveholders equal rights in the territories but pass constitutional guarantees giving the South equal power in the government. The only alternative for the South was to secede from the Union. Calhoun would die in less than a month. After his speech, the state of Mississippi called for a convention of southern states "to devise and adopt some mode of resistance to northern aggression."

Daniel Webster spoke on March 7, displaying an eloquence remi-

'CONQUERING PREJUDICE,'
or
"Fulfilling a Constitutional duty with alacrity."

"My God! My Child! Will no one help! Is there no mercy!"

"Any man can perform an agreeable duty, it is not every one that can perform a disagreeable duty."

"By Heaven! he exceeds my most sanguine expectation—he marks his way so clearly & treads so loyally in the track of the Constitution.. It is more than great, it combine I feel a great sense of relief."

New Englanders severely criticized Senator Daniel Webster for his support of the fugitive slave bill that became part of the Compromise of 1850. In this lithograph he is the central figure. "He exceeds my most sanguine expectation," cries the slave catcher running beside him. *(Courtesy, Scribner's Archives)*

niscent of his brilliant reply to Hayne two decades before. He pleaded with both sections to show tolerance for the sake of Union. He criticized the abolitionists' ethical absolutism and deplored the agitation over slavery in the territories. The law of nature precluded a slave economy there, he asserted, and no legislation was needed to reenact God's will. He took sharp issue with Calhoun's talk of "peaceable secession": "There can be no such thing as a peaceable secession. Peaceable secession is an utter impossibility." A thousand physical and social ties bound the sections together. Disunion, Webster warned the South pointedly, "must produce such a war as I will not describe, *in its twofold character*"—a

As a northern Democrat and senator from Illinois, Stephen A. Douglas skillfully engineered the Compromise of 1850. *(Courtesy, Scribner's Archives)*

hint at the prospect of slave revolts. Much to the anger of abolitionists, who criticized it savagely, Webster's Seventh of March speech did much to rally northern support for compromise.

For all his skill, Clay had miscalculated. Patriotic appeals for Union could not overcome sectional bitterness in 1850. When Clay's package of compromise measures came to a vote, opponents of the individual measures defeated it. His bill and his health in ruins, Clay withdrew into retirement.

Stephen A. Five feet four and thirty-four years old, Stephen A.
Douglas Douglas assumed Clay's place in steering the compromise through Congress. This brash, hard-driving senator from Illinois devised a new strategy. He introduced Clay's measures separately, relying on sectional blocs and a few swing votes to form majorities for each. Two events immeasurably aided his efforts that hot summer. The unexpected death on July 9 of President Taylor put in the presidency Millard Fillmore, who supported the compromise measures. And Texas bondholders—who, along with New England bankers they owed money, stood to gain handsomely if the federal government purchased their depreciated securities for giving up some territory to New Mexico—lobbied for the legislation.

Douglas's strategy worked. The individual bills, one observer remarked, resembled "cats and dogs that had been tied together by their tails for months, scratching and biting." Upon being released "every one of them ran off to his own hole and was quiet." The North won admission of free California and a ban on the slave trade in Washington. The South had a more stringent fugitive slave law and a promise that there would be no congressional prohibition of slavery in the New Mexico and Utah territories. The federal government assumed the Texas debt.

The Compromise of 1850 was only a short-lived armistice. The South had lost its majority in the Senate: this was a major defeat. The abolitionists found the Fugitive Slave Act appalling, and it was. But attempts to enforce it only inflamed northerners, giving the antislavery movement splendid propaganda and greater public support. Yet the compromise received an enthusiastic welcome. Celebrations were held in many cities. In Washington, word went out that it was the duty of every patriot to get drunk. Before the next morning dawned, many citizens, including Senators Foote, Douglas, and Webster, had proved their patriotism. To many Americans, it now seemed that the slavery question had at last been settled. But in the South there were still 3,204,000 slaves worth over one and one half billion dollars—a property many southerners were determined to protect at any cost.

Events soon revealed that the Compromise had settled nothing at all. Deliberate ambiguities embedded in it raised questions instead of comfortably obscuring them. The Utah and New Mexico territories had been organized without congressional restriction on slavery. The Compromise said only that they would be admitted to statehood with or without slavery, as their constitutions prescribed "at the time of their admission." But could the people of these territories now restrict slavery as long as the new lands remained in a territorial status? Opponents of slavery believed that even in the period before they attained statehood, the people of Utah and New Mexico would have the right to decide whether to exclude the practice. Southerners, convinced that slaveholding like any other conventional form of property should be permitted unless prohibited by a state of the Union, insisted that as long as the new lands remained territories, slavery must not be restricted. The critical question of slavery in the territories had merely been evaded. There had been no compromise in 1850, only a fragile truce.

The Fugitive Slave Law

President Fillmore, in signing the Compromise of 1850, called it the "final settlement." But its weakest link, the Fugitive Slave Law, soon caused the slavery issue to flare anew. The Constitution itself had contained a clause providing for the return of "any person held to service or labor in one state" who escaped to another. The new legislation had been passed in response to southern complaints that a law passed by Congress in 1793 lacked the strength to be enforced, putting slaveholders to great personal expense and failing to provide for assistance from federal officers. The new law of 1850 remedied these defects, and did

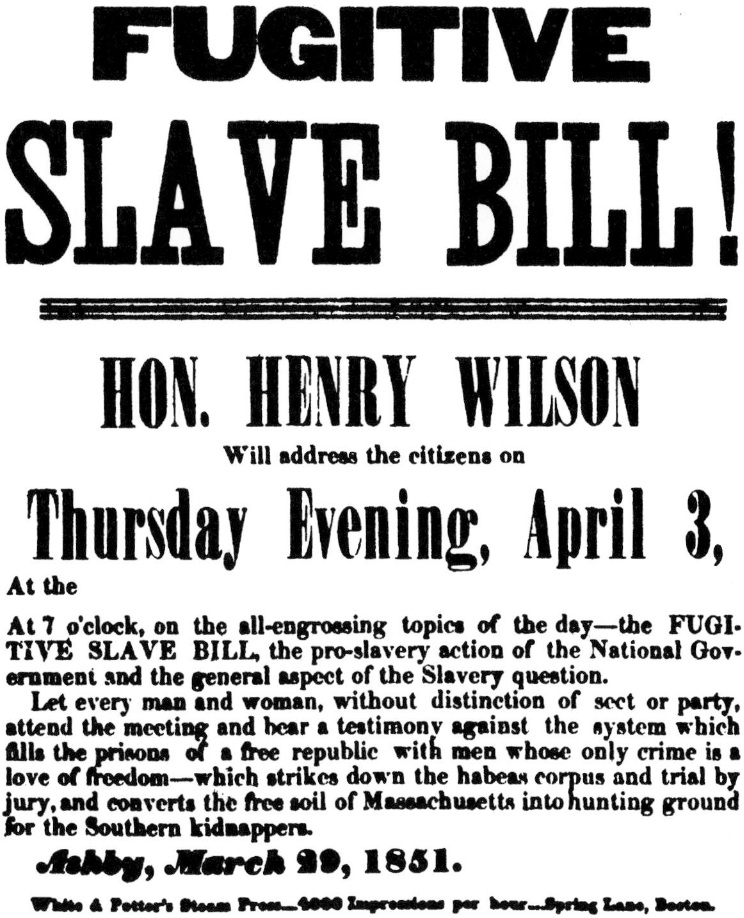

FUGITIVE SLAVE BILL!

HON. HENRY WILSON

Will address the citizens on

Thursday Evening, April 3,

At the

At 7 o'clock, on the all-engrossing topics of the day—the FUGITIVE SLAVE BILL, the pro-slavery action of the National Government and the general aspect of the Slavery question.

Let every man and woman, without distinction of sect or party, attend the meeting and bear a testimony against the system which fills the prisons of a free republic with men whose only crime is a love of freedom—which strikes down the habeas corpus and trial by jury, and converts the free soil of Massachusetts into hunting ground for the Southern kidnappers.

Ashby, March 29, 1851.

White & Potter's Steam Press—4000 Impressions per hour—Spring Lane, Boston.

more. It created special commissioners to deal with fugitive-slave cases. These commissioners had only to be convinced of a fugitive slave's identity before granting the owner authority to seize the runaway. They were empowered to call on federal marshals to enforce the law, and to compensate slaveholders who had incurred undue expense. Anyone who aided fugitives or obstructed their arrest was subject to fine and imprisonment. The new law even required that all citizens were expected to assist officials in apprehending runaways. That cast northerners as slave catchers. Here was a slaveholder's dream. But to many northerners it was an outrage. Especially offensive were the sections denying accused fugitive slaves the right to a jury trial, or even to testify in their own behalf.

Here was not a complicated, constitutional issue pitting federal against local rule in the territories. Here was concrete oppression on northern soil before northern eyes. Northerners had before them the spectacle of fugitive slaves, handcuffed and guarded, and read of cases of mistaken identity in the kidnapping of free blacks. The fugitive slave question drew together the splintered antislavery movement. Garrisonians, free-soilers, Whigs, Democrats, blacks: all could agree on it.

Enforcement of the Fugitive Slave Law sparked several well-publicized acts of resistance. In 1851 a mob of blacks in Boston burst into a courtroom during the extradition hearing of a fugitive slave named Shadrach. While the crowd struggled with the police, two husky blacks grabbed the startled Shadrach and carried him out of the building. Shadrach was soon spirited off to Canada. Later that same year, black and white abolitionists successfully resisted enforcement of the law at Syracuse, New York, and Christiana, Pennsylvania. In Indiana, agents tore one man away from his wife and children and returned him to a slave owner who showed that the former slave had run away nineteen years before.

In over eighty percent of the cases brought under the law, slaveholders successfully recovered their property. But spectacular rescues like that of Shadrach confirmed southerners in their conviction that the Fugitive Slave Law could not be enforced north of the Mason-Dixon Line. As a result, few southerners made use of the new law. Instead the South nursed its feeling that the North had failed to fulfill an essential part of the compromise. A Tennessee man warned that if the new legislation were not enforced, southern moderates would be overwhelmed by *"fire-eaters."*

Harriet Tubman

No one recorded the birthday of Harriet Ross, one of eleven children born to a slave family on the eastern shore of Maryland. But the child who would become Harriet Tubman was probably born in 1820 or 1821. She never spent a day in school and never learned to read or write. Her childhood in any sense that we would understand the term ended at the age of five or six. Then her master attempted unsuccessfully to apprentice her to a weaver. Various efforts to make her useful about the master's house also proved unsuccessful, and Harriet became a runaway for the

An antislavery writer, Thomas Wentworth Higginson, boasted of Harriet Tubman in 1859:

"We have had the greatest heroine of the age here, Harriet Tubman, a black woman, and a fugitive slave, who had been back eight times secretly and brought out in all sixty slaves with her, including all her own family, besides aiding many more in other ways to escape. Her tales of adventure are beyond anything in fiction and her ingenuity and generalship are extraordinary. . . . The Slaves call her Moses. She has had a reward of twelve thousand dollars offered for her in Maryland and will probably be burned alive whenever she is caught, which she probably will be, first or last, as she is going again."

Herself an escaped slave, Harriet Tubman returned to the South and, risking great danger, repeatedly led groups like the one pictured here north to freedom. *(Courtesy, Sophia Smith Collection, Smith College)*

first time at age seven. She stayed away four days, hiding in a pigsty and scrapping with the pigs for garbage to eat, until hunger drove her back to the inevitable whipping. Eventually she was sent to the fields, where she became a powerful worker, a match for most of the men. A serious head injury in her early teens left her with a permanent disability which caused her to fall asleep involuntarily for brief periods, even at the height of danger. Her rebellious temperament, combined with this odd malady, set her apart from others in her youth, and she absorbed a brand of millennial slave Christianity. Marriage to a free black, John Tubman, further aroused her questionings about slavery and freedom, but the difficulty of escape and concern for her parents and husband held her back until 1849, when the death of her owner led her to fear being sold into the deep South. Harriet headed north, traveling by night, and with help from some sympathetic whites made her way to Pennsylvania.

And so she did, earning money as best she could to finance such desperate ventures. Joining with the loose network of free blacks and Quakers—out of whose limited activities post-Civil War legend created the "Underground Railroad," complete with "switching station," "conductors," and "brakemen"—and traveling without benefit of maps or signs, she brought back from Maryland first her relatives, then other slaves, and finally her aged parents. Even in December 1860, with political turmoil over slavery at its height, Harriet made her last trip south before the war, returning with seven slaves, one of them an infant

"I had crossed the line [into northern territory]," Harriet Tubman recalled.

"I was *free*; but there was no one to welcome me to the land of freedom. . . . My home, after all, was down in Maryland; because my father, my mother, my brothers, my sisters, and friends were there. But I was free and *they should be free!* I would make a home in the North and bring them there!"

Other former slaves, such as John P. Parker, worked as "conductors" on the Underground Railroad. Parker dedicated his life to helping slaves cross the Ohio River from Kentucky to Ohio. He remembered:

"I heard the cry of hounds. The patrol had worked faster than I thought. Leaping into the boat to tear up a seat to use as a paddle, I stumbled over the oars, which I had found missing in the dark. With a halloo, I piled the crowd in the boat, only to find it so small it would not carry all of us. Two men were left on the bank."

child who had to be drugged with paregoric to keep its cries from giving away their hiding places. Accounts credit her with aiding in the escape of more than five hundred slaves.

Harriet headed south again during wartime, now to serve as a nurse, a scout, and even a spy for the Union army in South Carolina.

Harriet Tubman outlived the entire generation of antislavery heroes with whom she had worked, becoming a legendary reminder of the age of runaway slaves and abolitionists. Her home in Auburn, New York, became a place of pilgrimage. Black leaders like Booker T. Washington would visit Harriet and then view John Brown's grave in the Adirondacks. Woman suffrage leaders came as well; this had become one of her causes in the postwar years. She founded a Home for the Aged and Indigent in Auburn on land abutting her house, moving to it herself in 1911 when she became too infirm to live alone. She died in 1913 and received, fittingly enough, a soldier's burial, with the local post of the Union army veterans' association, the Grand Army of the Republic, presenting the honors.

Manifest Destiny Revisited

In his inaugural address a new President, Franklin Pierce, would call for further expansion. "My administration," he boldly proclaimed in 1853, "will not be controlled by any timid forebodings of evil from expansion." The direction of any more expansion, of course, would have to be to the south. After the Oregon Treaty of 1846, most policymakers in the United States knew that dreams of expanding north into Canada were unrealistic. Canada was a stable country that Great Britain had no intention of surrendering without a fight. Territories to the south, in the Caribbean, Central America, and Mexico, were more likely candidates for annexation. Mexico, Spain, and the tiny countries there would be hardpressed to defend their territory.

But expansion into Mexico and the Caribbean raised the hostility of abolitionists, free-soilers, businessmen, and workers in the North. Slavery was deeply ensconced in the sugar plantations of Cuba, Hispaniola, and Puerto Rico, and few people doubted the ability of southerners to transplant cotton cultivation to Mexico. Opponents realized that plantation production of crops like coffee, indigo, cacao, and a variety of fruit products was possible in Central America. President Franklin Pierce's ambitious attempts to push the spirit of Manifest Destiny south toward the equator encountered stiff opposition in the North.

The Gadsden Purchase   True to his word, Pierce dispatched James Gadsden of South Carolina to Mexico with instructions to purchase additional territory. At the very least, Gadsden was to acquire the Gila River region, which lay along the proposed southern railroad route to the Pacific. In addition, he might offer up to $50 million for the northern provinces of Mexico. The Mexican government refused to sell anything more than the Gila River region. Even this small triumph for Gadsden was too much for the

Senate; northern senators, suspecting a southern plot to expand the domain of slavery, accepted the Gadsden Treaty only after 9,000 square miles, one-sixth of the total, had been cut from the purchase. For the first time in its history, the United States had refused to accept land ceded to it. Despite this minor setback, the hapless Pierce embarked upon a new imperialist venture. This time the object was Cuba, owned by the Spanish.

The Ostend Manifesto   For a time in the 1850s, some Cubans flirted with the notion of annexation by the United States. During the early part of the century the social and economic relationship between Cuba and the mainland had grown stronger. By the 1840s Cuba's foreign trade with the United States exceeded its trade with Spain, and increasing numbers of Cubans were travelling to the United States on business and vacations. Cuban slaveowners worried that independence from Spain would deprive them of the military means to defend themselves against a slave uprising. They were also concerned that the increasingly powerful antislavery movement in Great Britain might eventually force Spain to abolish slavery in Cuba. Annexation by the United States, where slavery was firmly entrenched, would solve both problems. Cuban slaveowners would be rid of Spain but they would still have a powerful military force capable of maintaining the existing social order. The annexationists tried unsuccessfully to sponsor uprisings in Cuba against the Spanish.

Cuban annexationists were encouraged by expansionist sentiments in the United States. When the Mexican War ended in 1848, President James K. Polk offered to pay Spain $100 million for Cuba, but the offer was refused. Many Cubans living in the United States tried to promote annexation. Cristobal Madán, a prominent Cuban sugar planter, founded the *Consejo de Gobierno Cubano* in New York. Madán's wife was the sister of John O'Sullivan, the New York journalist who originated the phrase "Manifest Destiny." The *Consejo* published its own newspaper, *La Verdad*, and lobbied throughout the United States for annexation. The advocates of territorial expansion had joined hands with the champions of Cuban annexation. Some of the more vociferous advocates of annexation added violence to their campaign. Late in the 1840s and early in the 1850s, Narciso López launched against Cuba a series of "filibustering" expeditions, referring to small-scale private military operations. He enjoyed the financial support of the *Consejo*, and, with small armies composed mostly of southerners, he invaded Cuba in 1848, 1849, and 1851 and tried to inspire insurrection. The expeditions all failed to bring the desired uprising, and at Bahía Honda in 1851 López was captured and executed.

During 1853 the Pierce Administration lent support to John A. Quitman of Mississippi and others who proposed to "liberate" Cuba by force. When Quitman backed off, Pierce instructed the American minister in Madrid, Pierre Soulé, to offer Spain as much as $130 million for Cuba. But Spain indignantly rejected the American offer. Soulé then arranged a meeting at Ostend, Belgium, in October 1854, with the American ministers to London and Paris, to consider further action regarding Cuba. Their recommendations to Washington, known as the

A New Orleans newspaper reflected popular feeling:

"The North Americans *will* spread out far beyond their present bounds. They *will* encroach again and again upon their neighbors. New territories *will* be planted, declare their independence, and be annexed! We have New Mexico and California! We *will* have old Mexico and Cuba! The isthmus cannot arrest—nor even the Saint Lawrence!! Time has all of this in her womb."

In a lighter vein . . .

PERSONAL.

BILLY RED WHISKERS.—I AM DYING TO SEE YOU. The disappointment was too great. Come immediately.   381.

CLARENCE, MEET ME ON BOARD STEAMBOAT, PIER No. 3, Tuesday, at 4½ o'clock.   KATE.

FEARS OF FOUL PLAY.—A SUITABLE REWARD will be paid for any information concerning a young lad by the name of Evan Peters, who left my store on Saturday, about 10 o'clock, to go to the corner of Forty-first street and Third avenue, and to Sixty-fifth street and Second avenue, since which time he has not been heard of. He went to the places with parcels, and then collected some bills. He had on, when he left the store, a straw hat, linen coat and light-colored pants. He is about sixteen years of age, small, thin face, and is light complexioned. Any information given me will be thankfully received and appreciated by his afflicted parents.   F. B. BALDWIN, Nos. 70 and 72 Bowery.

INFORMATION WANTED.—OF JAMES HURLEY, A BEgar maker, formerly of Springfield, Mass., but more recently of New York and Baltimore. Any information concerning him will be thankfully received by his sister, Mary Hurley, No. 7 Boyleston street, Springfield, Mass.

IF THE YOUNG LADY WHO SHOWED A GENTLEMAN a large breastpin daguerreotype at a Bowery concert hall, Sunday evening last, will address De Mott, Herald office, she can renew the acquaintance.

J. Y. JOHNSON WOULD LIKE TO HEAR FROM R. B. He was away from the city July 17. Letter just received.

MISSING.—A YOUNG GIRL, ABOUT 18 YEARS OF age, slender figure, 5 feet 3 inches in height, very fair hair and complexion, prominent nose, long neck, rather small, bluelsh gray eyes, rather round shoulders, pleasing manner and address, a native of Canada, left her home, Staten Island, on the 15th day of June last, and has not since been heard of. Any person giving information that will restore her to her afflicted parents will be rewarded. Address box 3,697 Post office, New York, or to Sergeant Young, Detective Police department, New York.

RECEIVED LETTER.—ALL RIGHT. NOT COMING. Don't see it.   EMMA.

THE YOUNG MAN WHO LEFT HIS HOME ON FRIDAY morning, and who separated from his cousin at the corner of Fulton street and Broadway, at the hour of six o'clock P. M., is most heartily urged and solicited by his friends to return to his home immediately.

VINNIE—I SHALL EXPECT YOU TUESDAY, AT 7 o'clock, without fail.   F. P.

W. G.—COME TO ME OR WRITE BEFORE I AM left penniless by your ptr, E T.   M. G. Western papers please copy.

Z. —IF YOU HAVE ANY PITY, LET ME HEAR FROM you. I have been in great trouble.   Z.

MATRIMONIAL.

A YOUNG MAN OF 23, OF GOOD CHARACTER, good health, buoyant temperament, and very fond of music, wishes to open a correspondence with an American lady, with a view to matrimony. She must not be over 22 years of age, of a loving disposition, amiable, well informed and good looking. Money of minor importance. Communications confidential.   Address Albert Elmore, station D Post office, New York.

TO LEASE—A HEART, HAVING ALL THE MODERN improvements and a most desirable location. Immediate possession given to a perpetual lessee. For particulars address Norman, station B, Post office, N. Y.

The "personal" column in the *New York Herald* was extremely popular.

"Ostend Manifesto," soon found their way into print, to the great embarrassment of the Pierce Administration. Particularly damaging was the statement that, should Spain refuse renewed offers to purchase Cuba, the United States would "by every law, human and Divine, be . . . justified in wresting it from Spain." Both American and European critics denounced the Manifesto. It was "a robber doctrine," "a highwayman's plea." The administration promptly repudiated the Manifesto, whereupon Soulé resigned amidst bitter recriminations. Manifest Destiny had suffered by its association with slavery. Renewed expansion would have to await the return of sectional peace.

The Filibusterers

The filibusterers against Cuba were among a number of paramilitary expeditions coming out of the United States in the 1850s. The most notorious of the filibusterers was William Walker, who had grandiose dreams for himself. In 1853 he led a private army in an unsuccessful invasion of Lower California and barely escaped with his life. Two years later he learned of the desire of the Accessory Transit Company of New York to secure territory in Central America for construction of a transoceanic canal. With the company's financial backing, and with a civil war under way in Nicaragua, Walker launched a new filibustering expedition in 1855. He succeeded temporarily in setting himself up as dictator of Nicaragua. When President Franklin Pierce agreed to receive Walker's diplomatic representative, Walker interpreted it as official recognition, and a few weeks later he issued a proclamation opening up Nicaragua to slavery. Antislavery forces denounced this as one more act of the expansionist slaveocracy. Walker remained in power for another year until Cornelius Vanderbilt, the new head of the Accessory Transit Company, decided he was unstable and ousted him. Walker attacked Nicaragua with a new expedition in 1857 but failed. The United States Navy captured him but let him go with a warning to cease his filibustering campaigns. In 1860 Walker attacked Honduras with a private army, but this time he was captured and executed.

Although most southerners had little to do with the filibustering escapades against Cuba, Mexico, and Nicaragua in the 1850s, northerners accurately saw in them the hand of the enemy. That President Franklin Pierce had tried to purchase Cuba and the originally huge Gadsden region, combined with his initial reception of Walker as head of state in Nicaragua, confirmed northern suspicions that the federal government was trying to expand the base of slave operations.

Paths to the Pacific

The settlement of the Oregon boundary controversy and the acquisition of California made the United States a Pacific power. American commerce quickly expanded across the great ocean. In 1844 Caleb Cushing, the first American minister to China, negotiated a treaty granting Americans special trade privileges in that country. A decade later, Commodore Matthew Perry gained a diplomatic and commercial toehold in Japan. The United States sought unsuccessfully in 1854 to annex the Hawaiian Islands, already a cultural outpost of the United States. Forward-looking Americans proclaimed the dawn of a great commercial era in the Pacific.

HUCKLEBERRY FINN

by Samuel Clemens (Mark Twain). Huck talks about his feelings towards the slave Jim.

. . . I about made up my mind to pray, and see if I couldn't try to quit being the kind of a boy I was and be better. So I kneeled down. But the words wouldn't come. Why wouldn't they? . . . I was trying to make my mouth say I would do the right thing and the clean thing, and go and write to that nigger's owner and tell where he was; but deep down in me I knowed it was a lie, and He knowed it. You can't pray a lie—I found out.

So I was full of trouble, full as I could be; and didn't know what to do. At last I had an idea; and I says, I'll go and write the letter—and then see if I can pray. Why, it was astonishing, the way I felt as light as a feather right straight off, and my troubles all gone. So I got a piece of paper and a pencil, all glad and excited, and set down and wrote:

Miss Watson, your runaway nigger Jim is down here two mile below Pikesville, and Mr. Phelps had got him and he will give him up for the reward if you send.

I felt good and all washed clean of sin for the first time

I had ever felt so in my life, and I knowed I could pray now. But I didn't do it straight off, but laid the paper down and set there thinking— thinking how good it was all this happened so, and how near I come to being lost and going to hell. And went on thinking. And got to thinking over our trip down the river; and I see Jim before me all the time: in the day and in the night-time, sometimes moonlight, sometimes storms, and we a-floating along, talking and singing and laughing. But somehow I couldn't seem to strike no places to harden me against him, but only the other kind. I'd see him standing my watch on top of his'n, 'stead of calling me, so I could go on sleeping. . . . and at last I struck the time I saved him by telling the men we had small-pox aboard, and he was so grateful, and said I was the best friend old Jim ever had in the world, and the only one he's got now; and then I happened to look around and see that paper.

It was a close place. I took it up, and held it in my hand. I was a-trembling, because I's got to decide, forever, betwixt two things, and I knowed it. I studied a minute, sort of holding my breath, and then says to myself: "All right, then, I'll go to hell"—and tore it up.

For shortening the route from Atlantic ports to the Orient and improving communications between the two American coasts, the United States began considering a canal that would link the two oceans. An 1846 treaty with Colombia granted citizens of the United States the right of transit across the Isthmus of Panama, in return for recognition of Colombian sovereignty there. Efforts to control the alternative canal route through Nicaragua aroused protests from Britain, which had bases of its own in the vicinity. In 1850 the two sides compromised their differences in the Clayton-Bulwer Treaty. Each party agreed not to seek exclusive control over the proposed isthmian canal or to colonize the surrounding area. In spite of this official enthusiasm, capitalists showed little interest in the idea of building a canal. Travel across the isthmus remained a primitive affair until 1855, when a railroad replaced mule-back and coach as the chief means of transportation.

More attractive was the idea of a transcontinental railroad. Asa Whitney, a New York merchant who had made a fortune in the China trade, labored throughout the 1840s to persuade Congress to finance construction of a railroad from Lake Michigan to the mouth of the Columbia River. This route, although mountainous, had the advantage of passing north of Mexican California. The Treaty of Guadalupe-Hidalgo brought California into the United States, but a new obstacle—sectional rivalry—soon appeared. The South favored a southern route for the railroad, running from New Orleans to California via Texas and the Gila River Valley. The North preferred either Whitney's northern route or a central way, extending from Chicago or St. Louis by way of

Samuel Clemens (*Courtesy, Scribner's Archives*)

South Pass to San Francisco. Unable to agree on any one route, Congress in 1853 authorized surveys of all three.

This delay was intolerable to Stephen A. Douglas of Illinois, the foremost advocate of a central route. As chairman of the Senate Committee on Territories, Douglas had pioneered in opening the Mississippi Valley to settlement. A Pacific railroad would help his concept of a great West become a reality. Personal considerations also motivated Douglas. His home town of Chicago, where he had heavy real estate investments, would be the probable eastern terminus of a central railroad. But the land known as Nebraska west of Iowa and Missouri was still unorganized Indian country. Until the region had territorial government, it could not be surveyed and opened for settlement. In this respect, advocates of a southern route had a real advantage: all the area along their route had already been made into states or territories.

The Kansas-Nebraska Act

Senator Douglas late in 1853 had to find some way to induce southerners in Congress to vote for a bill organizing Nebraska. Southerners had no motive to support a measure that cleared the path for a rival railroad route to the Pacific. And they had absolutely no reason to vote to create what would become another free territory. As part of the Louisiana Purchase, Nebraska had been made "forever" free by the Missouri Compromise of 1820. Senator David Atchison of Missouri spoke for many southerners when he vowed that he would "sink in hell" before handing Nebraska over to the free-soilers. Douglas therefore decided that he would have to make a concession to the South.

Popular Sovereignty The Illinois Senator offered the repeal of the Missouri Compromise line excluding slavery north of 36° 30′ latitude. His territorial bill, introduced in Congress in January 1854, would create two territories—Kansas and Nebraska. It would specifically repeal the Missouri Compromise restriction on slavery. In its place, Douglas substituted the principle of popular sovereignty, as it was called. The people of the two territories were free "to form and regulate their domestic institutions in their own way." Thus, to enlist southern support for his railroad, Douglas held out the bait of making Kansas and Nebraska slave states by the operation of popular sovereignty.

As Douglas himself had predicted, the idea of repealing the Missouri Compromise line raised "a hell of a storm." Northerners regarded the Act of 1820 as an inviolable pledge of freedom. Repeal was part of a slaveholder's plot to make free territory into "a dreary region of despotism, inhabited by masters and slaves." In Congress, many northern Democrats joined their Whig colleagues in opposition. Objections came not only from abolitionists but from moderates who, having accepted the Compromise of 1850, had now lost all confidence in the good faith of the South. Douglas and his co-conspirators, wrote Horace Greeley in the *New York Tribune,* had made "more abolitionists than Garrison . . . could have made in half a century." Slavery, Douglas insisted in response, was an outmoded institution, unsuited by climate and geography to the plains of Kansas. Popular sovereignty would just as effectively bar slavery as would exclusion. After three months of fierce debate Douglas, with the support of President Franklin Pierce, carried his bill.

Passage of the Kansas-Nebraska Act shredded what little had remained of the uneasy truce of 1850. It turned Kansas into a battle-ground and ruptured the Democratic Party. By using the scheme of popular sovereignty to open free soil to slavery, Douglas discredited what until then had been an effective instrument for compromise. Rarely in American history had so much been risked for so little. The next year—1855—when Douglas introduced his long-awaited Pacific Railroad bill in Congress, his enemies had their revenge by killing it. At Douglas's death in 1861 his great Pacific railroad, on which he had expended so much energy and prestige, was still bottled up in Congress, a victim of the sectional conflict he had helped to revive.

"Bleeding Kansas"

With the passage of the Kansas-Nebraska Act, the slavery contest moved from the halls of Congress to the plains of Kansas. Both sections attached great importance to the decision over slavery there. Southerners hoped to make Kansas a slave state and thereby to restore to the South the equality of representation in the Senate that the region had lost when California was admitted as a free state. Slavery expansion also had great symbolic importance to southerners. By denying the South's right to expand, the North seemed to be denying southern equality. Southerners reasoned that if they could not take their slaves into the common territories, they would no longer be the equal of northern citizens. Opponents of slavery of course wished to prevent its extension into Kansas. Resistance to the expansion of slavery also had a more unsavory side. Many northerners, especially in the Midwest, were determined to preserve the rich prairie soils for the white race. Here, said David Wilmot, "the sons of toil, of my own race and color, can live without the disgrace which association with Negro slavery brings upon free labor." Such attitudes increasingly entered the antislavery movement, and conditioned the public views even of moral opponents of slavery like Abraham Lincoln. The demand for free soil, then, greatly broadened the antislavery movement's appeal at the same time that it diluted the morality of the movement.

Border War   From the beginning, the contest in Kansas over slavery was mainly the work of outsiders. In the North, groups like the New England Emigrant Aid Company, founded in 1854, subsidized the migration of free-state settlers to Kansas. To protect them, the Company sent new breech-loading rifles known popularly as "Beecher's Bibles," after Harriet's ministerial brother, Henry Ward Beecher, who proclaimed them a greater moral agency in Kansas than the Bible. Bands of Missouri border ruffians regularly

A southerner first observed in letters written home to his sister:

"The Missourians . . . are very sanguine about Kansas being a slave state & I have heard some of them say it *shall* be. Everyone seems bent on the Almighty Dollar, and as a general thing that seems to be their only thought."

Later he wrote:

"I fear, Sister, that coming here will do no good at last, as I begin to think that this will be made a Free State at last. 'Tis true we have elected Proslavery men to draft a state constitution, but I feel pretty certain, if it is put to the vote of the people, it will be rejected, as I feel pretty confident they have a majority here at this time. The South has ceased all efforts, while the North is redoubling her exertions."

Thomas Henry Tibbles was sixteen years old when he fought briefly with John Brown in "Bleeding Kansas."

This Platte County, into which John Brown had invited me, was thickly settled. Though most of the houses were built of logs, there were a few fine frame residences. Also, behind these residences, there were always "nigger quarters," ramshackle stables, and loom-houses where Negro women wove the jeans and linsey-woolsey which formed the outer clothing of the whole population. The planters' wealth was made up of fine horses, "likely niggers," and a rich soil which produced immense crops of corn and hemp. Though many of the owners of this countryside could neither read nor write, they were proud and rich. How long John Brown had been secretly lingering there near his chosen rendezvous, or how many men he had with him, I never knew.

Night settled down dark and moonless. Clouds hung low in the west. I had difficulty in making my way to the appointed place, but there I found Brown. . . . [He] directed our group to go to a certain cabin belonging to a certain house and get the slaves who were expecting us. We all were to take them to the [Missouri] River by a road he described. Then the rest of our group were to take these Negroes over the river in skiffs that would be found at a designated place. . . . Brown said there was a regular road in front of the house where we were to get the Negroes, but that, as it was guarded by the planters' patrol, our party was to enter the farm from the rear and approach the slave quarters through a cornfield. He bade me go alone a mile up the direct front road to watch for the patrol and keep our main party informed of any danger from that source.

When I objected to dismounting and separating myself from my horse, Brown told me with a metallic ring in his voice: "You will obey orders." Doubtless if there had been more light, I should have seen a peculiar gleam in his eye. Anyone who had anything to do with Brown in Kansas learned that it was death, after one joined his band, to disobey any order he issued.

I went with his men as he had ordered. Because the night was so very dark, we had difficulty in finding the right place. I took my post in the bend, while the other men crept up through the cornfield. Just then the wind blew furiously and the rain poured down. I could see nothing except when lightning flashed now and then.

crossed into neighboring Kansas to aid the proslavery cause. In March 1855, at the first election for a territorial legislature, their votes helped to give the proslavery party a majority. This assembly immediately enacted a slave code for the territory. Free-state settlers, refusing to recognize this legislature, elected one of their own. By late 1855, Kansas had two rival governments, neither of which would recognize the other's laws or participate in its elections.

Orderly government was impossible, and militants on both sides of the slavery question carried on a private war of their own. After proslavery men raided the free-state stronghold of Lawrence, the fanatical John Brown and seven followers (four of them his sons) retaliated at Pottawatomie Creek by bursting in on five sympathizers with slavery, slashing and hacking them to death with broadswords. When one of his men urged caution, Brown responded that it was "nothing but the word of cowardice." Many settlers had to take sides in self-defense. The recently established telegraph system, which now made possible swift reports of faraway events, brought the warfare in Kansas extensive press coverage. The antislavery press pictured the sack of Lawrence as an orgy of destruction and killing. In reality, it was a rather tame affair; only one person was killed, and he was a proslavery man struck on the head by a falling brick.

Early in 1857 federal troops restored order to Kansas, and the free- and slave-state parties each promptly fell to internal quarreling. Before the year was out, a visitor to Kansas reported that "speculations run high

Without warning someone threw his arms around me from behind, pinioning my elbows to my sides. Instantly two more men leaped upon me, but before they could clap a hand over my mouth, I uttered the loudest yell that had ever come of me. It was the only warning I could give my associates.

My captors tied my hands and feet; they put a rope around my neck and dragged me along the ground by it for some distance. Then they lifted me to my feet, threw the rope end over the limb of a tree. Just at that moment pistols flashed. Two of the men who had been holding the rope dropped to the ground; the other ran away. My "gang," who had succeeded in creeping up through the cornfield and bringing away two Negro men and one woman, had then overheard the rather loud talk of the patrol at my "hanging bee." Thanks to the black night and the rain, they had stolen up to us unnoticed.

They soon had me on my feet and helped me to find Old Titus and mount him.

Long before daylight it became obvious that the entire district was out on the warpath. Certainly John Brown's "nigger stealing" raid into Platte County had started a tremendous uproar. By now, however, probably all the rest of Brown's men were safely back across the river, and here was I, at sixteen, left alone to fight the whole county.

Just as day broke, I reached a dim lane that led toward the river. From sounds behind me I knew that not much over a mile away a large party was on my trail. . . . I leaped a fence into a cornfield—but they had seen me. I have never heard a more fiendish yell than they loosed then and there.

I plunged across the cornfield and finally reached the bottom lands of the river, which were covered in some places with grass as high as a man on horseback and in others with a dense growth of willows. My pursuers evidently had wholly lost my trail. My only way of escape was to swim to Missouri River with its rapid current, its rushing, mud-colored water, and its treacherous quicksands. After much thought I decided to take the risk. I led Old Titus down to the bank. I took hold of his tail and swam behind him; thus I not only relieved him of my weight, but was able to steer him wherever I wished. We landed [safely in Illinois] in a wild and desolate spot.

[here], politics seldom named, *money* now seems to be the question." The territory remained deeply divided, with each side retaining its own government.

The struggle in Kansas forced the slavery issue back into Congress. (The intent of instituting popular sovereignty had been to get the slavery question out of that body.) In 1856 the House of Representatives sent a fact-finding committee to Kansas. Meantime, Congress endlessly debated the Kansas question amid steadily rising tempers. Passion spilled into violence on the floor of the Senate. Senator Charles Sumner of Massachusetts delivered a violent antislavery speech entitled "The Crime Against Kansas." In it he made several personal references to Senator Andrew P. Butler of South Carolina. Butler's nephew, Representative Preston S. Brooks of South Carolina, decided to avenge these insults to an elderly kinsman. Brooks stole up behind Sumner at his Senate desk during a recess and beat him severely over the head with a cane.

The attack, northerners believed, was another example of the domineering insolence of slaveholders. The injured Sumner became a martyr of the antislavery cause. Southerners, although many privately disapproved, publicly applauded Brooks's action and showered him with canes inscribed with slogans like "Use Knock-down Arguments." When Brooks resigned from Congress, his Carolina constituents reelected him. This incident, and the controversy over Bleeding Kansas, further polarized a country already divided.

Political Cataclysm

Before 1850 the country's political system had been a bond of union. In both the Whig and the Democratic parties, strong northern and southern wings had worked together in their mutual interest, especially in presidential elections. The dependence of each wing on the other served to override the potentially divisive effect of issues like slavery. Party loyalty was intense. William Pitt Fessenden, a Whig stalwart, declared that he "would vote for a dog, if he was the candidate of my party." The Compromise of 1850 and the Kansas-Nebraska Act drastically altered the system, destroyed one party, disrupted another, and created a new one. A once unifying political system had become sectionalized.

FILLING IN THE CONTINENT

These excerpts from a letter of Lucia Loraine Williams show that parts of the United States were far removed from the slavery controversy of the 1850s:

September 16, 1851

Dear Mother,

We have been living in Oregon about two weeks, all of us except little John, and him we left twelve miles this side of Green River. He was killed instantly by falling from a wagon and the wheels running over his head.

After passing the desert and Green River [in present-day Wyoming] we came to a place of feed and laid by a day for the purpose of recruiting [resting] our teams. On the morning of 29 June we started on. John rode on the wagon driven by Edwin Fellows. We had not proceeded more than 2 miles before word came for us to turn back—we did so but found him dead. The oxen had taken fright from a horse that had been tied behind the wagon preceding this, owned by a young man that Mr. Williams had told a few minutes before to leave, and [the runaway team had] turned off the road. Two other teams ran also.

John was sitting in the back of the wagon, but as soon as the cattle commenced to run he went to the front and caught hold of the driver who held him as long as he could, but he was frightened and did not possess presence of mind enough to give him a little send which perhaps would have saved him.

Poor little fellow! We could do nothing for him, he was beyond our reach and O! How suddenly!

One half hour before we had left him in health as lively as a lark, and then to find him so breathless so soon was awful. I cannot describe to you our feelings.

We buried him there by the roadside, on the right side of the road, about 1/2 mile before we crossed the Fon-

tonelle, a little stream. We had his grave covered with stones to protect it from wild beasts, and a board with his name and age. If any of our friends come through I wish that they would find his grave and if it needs, repair it.

[The letter proceeds to give excerpts from a diary of the trip.]

NEBRASKA

21 May—We had one of the worst storms that I ever read of. It beggars all description—thunder, lightning, hail, rain and wind. Hailstones so large that they knocked a horse onto his knees. The driver got out and held the oxen by the heads for they showed a disposition to run. Most of our things were completely soaked, so the next day we stopped and dried up.

On the 23rd we came to a creek that overflowed its banks, Elm Creek. The water was some 20 feet deep but not very wide. They fell a tree over the creek and packed the loading [across on foot], put our wagons into the water with a rope attached to the tongue, and swam them across.

June 1—Passed the Sioux village. Their wigwams are made of buffalo skins (the Pawnees' were mud). They seemed to be a much wealthier tribe than any that we [had] yet seen. The squaws were in antelope skins ornamented with beads; the men were also clothed with skins or blankets. They owned a great many ponies. On one of the wigwams were several scalps hung out to dry—taken from the Pawnees. They were friendly.

I saw some beautiful bluffs, apparently not more than 1/2 mile off, and wished to visit them. W consented to go with me but said that it was further than I anticipated. We walked 4 miles, I should judge, crossing chasms and

The Decline of the Whig Party

It was the Whigs who felt the strain of slavery first. They had never been as strong organizationally as the Democrats, and they drew their strength in the North from Yankee Protestants whose sense of moral stewardship made them especially sympathetic to the antislavery cause. The abolitionist and Free Soil movements made many converts among these "conscience Whigs." At the 1852 Whig Convention the dispute over slavery broke wide open. The two sides even disagreed over the choice of a minister to lead the opening prayer. President Fillmore, the favorite of southern Whigs, had supported the Compromise of 1850, and so northern Whigs opposed him. The northerners backed instead another Mexican War hero, the Virginian General Winfield Scott, and Scott was finally chosen after fifty-three ballots: a southerner whose

---

bluffs before we reached the road and after all did not ascend the one we set out for. Camped by the Platte. No wood [to burn], but buffalo chips, which we have used for a long time.

WYOMING

On the 7th we arrived at Fort Laramie, and on the 8th commenced crossing the black hills. Some of them were steep. Laramie Peak to the left covered with snow.

9 June—Crossed the red hills and camped by a lake.

17 June—Traveled over 20 miles and camped by the Devils Hole, or Gate. In the morning two young ladies and myself visited it. The rocks on each side were perpendicular, 400 feet high, and the narrowest place was about 3 feet, where [the] Sweetwater came tumbling through. The road leading to it was crooked and thorny, but we found all kinds of beautiful flowers blooming beside the rocks; it was the most sublime spectacle that I ever witnessed

19 June—[Could] see the Rocky Mountains [at] a distance of some 60 miles. The tops were covered with snow, and from there they looked like fleecy clouds. Camped near two snowbanks in a beautiful valley.

IDAHO

2 July—[During the] night we were awakened by serenaders—five horsemen circled around the carriage singing "Araby's Daughter." It was a beautiful starlight night. We were surrounded by bluffs in a little valley, and on being awakened by their song, seeing their panting steeds and looking around upon the wild country, it seemed as tho we were transported into Arabia. They were beautiful singers from Oregon; said they were exiles from home. They sang "Sweet Home" and several others. Invited us to stay and celebrate the 4th. Said they would make us a barbecue, but we were anxious to get

on and the affliction that we had just suffered unfitted us for such a scene.

31 July—Camped on the Snake. Indians came with salmon to sell. I let them have Helen's apron with a needle and thread and bought salmon enough for several meals. I wish you could [have eaten] with us. I certainly never tasted any fowl or fish half so delicious.

OREGON

3 September—Arrived at Milwaukie, and went into a house to live again, the first one that I had been in since we crossed the Missouri....

If a nearby family's dinner in Oregon was typical, the journey was worth it:

Well We had Rosted Ducks . . . And Fat Chickens And Rosted pig and Sausages And green Apl pie And Mince pies and Custard pies And Cakes of difrent kindes [and] Inglish goosburyes And Plums Blue And green gages And Siberian crab Apples And oregon Apples. . . . Like wise Buter And Sturson pikles and Beet pickles And Sauce And Bread and Mashed potatoes and Oister pie And Coffe And Tea to be shore. Now I Must tel you What other preserves that I have. I have peaches And citrons And Sweet Aples, Crab Aples Jelley And Tomatoes And Mince And pairs and Aple Butter. And now I will Tel you of the Rest of My Winter Suplies. I have A plentey of Butter And Milk And a Thousand poundes of Salman And plentey Cabage And Turnips And A Bout A Hundred and Fiftey Bushel of potatoes And plentey of dried fruits—Aples and Black Buryes the Best that I evr saw. . . . I never Saw Sutch Black Buryes And Ras Bryes As There Is in this Countrey in All My Life Time. . . . O yes I Have plentey Shougar Laid in For Winter This Year Two. And Salt   (new year's day, 1852)

A wayside grave on the route west. (*Courtesy, Library of Congress*)

political strength was in the North. In retaliation, southern Whigs rammed through a platform endorsing the Compromise, including the Fugitive Slave Law.

Saddled with a candidate unpopular in the South and a platform unpopular in the North, the Whigs lost disastrously in 1852. Franklin Pierce of New Hampshire, the Democratic candidate, carried twenty-seven of thirty-one states—the most lopsided election victory since 1820. Surveying the ruins, antislavery Whigs began to seek a new alliance.

Not long afterward, it was the Democrats whom the slavery issue divided. The Kansas-Nebraska Act bitterly antagonized northern antislavery Democrats, and their frustration found expression in the "Appeal of the Independent Democrats," composed in 1854 by Charles Sumner, Salmon P. Chase, and other antislavery Democratic congressmen. The appeal invited all opponents of slavery expansion to form a common front "to rescue the country from the domination of slavery."

This rebellion among antislavery Democrats made for a dramatic restructuring of northern politics. Antislavery politicians—former Whigs, breakaway Democrats, some of the more moderate abolitionists—struggled to create the coalition called for in the appeal. The new organization came formally into existence at a convention held in Ripon, Wisconsin, in February 1854; the delegates adopted a statement of principles proclaiming their opposition to the extension of slavery in the territories. The new party officially adopted the name "Republican" a few months later.

The "Know-Nothing" Party

For a time another party, the "Know-Nothings," was also in the field. The flood of Irish and German immigrants after 1840 had alarmed lower-class, old-stock Protestants, who feared that this predominantly Catholic immigration would undermine republican institutions. Those "governed by a head in a foreign land," exclaimed one nativist editor in reference to the Pope, where *"no genuine liberty, either civil or religious"* exists, must not "control the American Ballot Box." One nativist blamed "the vast influx of immigrants" for lowering wages, raising the price of food and rent, and bringing "a thousand evils . . . [on] the working class." The newcomers were also charged with corrupting the nation's morals. According to another nativist, they brought "grog shops like the frogs of Egypt upon us." The visit of a special papal envoy to the United States in 1853 triggered a series of riots in Cincinnati, Pittsburgh, and elsewhere. A mob in Charlestown, Massachusetts, burned a Catholic convent to the ground. In 1849 Charles B. Allen of New York had formed a secret "patriotic" society, the Order of the Star-Spangled Banner, anti-Catholic and anti-foreign. Party members, when questioned by outsiders, customarily answered, "I know nothing." For a few years the society remained an obscure local organization, but in 1854, hoping to capitalize on the breakup of the old party alignments, nativists went political and formed the American or "Know-Nothing" Party.

For a time the Know-Nothings demonstrated much political strength, capturing several state governorships and seventy-five seats in Congress. They were strongest in the Northeast and the border states. The Know-Nothings soon discovered, however, that as a bisectional party, they enjoyed no more immunity from the disruptive influence of the slavery question than the other parties. After a quarrel at the 1855 national convention, the party disintegrated. Most northern Know-Nothings went into the new Republican Party, which had been actively soliciting the nativists with pledges of "No Popery and Slavery."

The Republican Party

The 1856 Republican Convention resembled a revival meeting. "There is but a slight quantity of liquor consumed," a journalist reported, "very little profane swearing is heard, and everything is managed with excessive and intense propriety." The platform condemned slavery as a "relic of barbarism" and reaffirmed the "right and duty" of Congress to prohibit it in the territories. For President the Republicans nominated forty-three-year-old John C. Frémont, the dashing "Pathfinder" of western exploration. The Democrats bypassed President Pierce and Stephen A. Douglas, who were too closely identified with the Kansas-Nebraska Act, in favor of sixty-five-year-old James Buchanan of Pennsylvania. Buchanan was a veteran politician and diplomat who, happily, had been out of the country during the Kansas-Nebraska struggle. A third candidate, ex-President Millard Fillmore, was nominated by the still-existing southern wing of the Know-Nothing Party.

The election itself was not a three-cornered affair, but rather two separate contests—one between Buchanan and Frémont in the North, the other between Buchanan and Fillmore in the South. As the only

A Frémont campaign song demonstrated the feelings of the Republican Party toward the slave South:

The Freemont Train has got along,
Just jump aboard ye foes of wrong,
Our train is bound for Washington
It carries Freedom's bravest son.

CHORUS:

Clear the track, filibusters,
Now's no time for threats and blusters
Clear the track (or) ere you dream on't,
You'll be 'neath the car of Frémont.

Now don't you see we've just the man
To meet the foe?—for he who can
Brave torrents wild and mountain snows
Will fear no Brooks nor Southern blows.

So jump aboard the Frémont train
And soon the Capital we'll gain;
Then we'll rejoice there's one in power
Who never will to slavery cower.

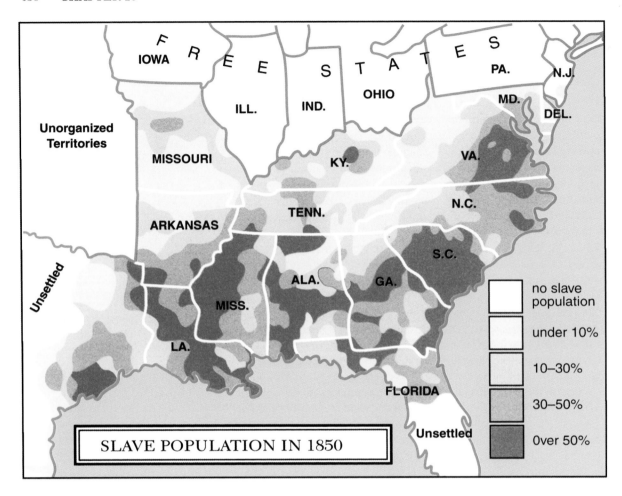

Unorganized
Territories

Unsettled

FREE STATES

IOWA

ILL.   IND.   OHIO   PA.   N.J.

MD.   DEL.

MISSOURI   KY.   VA.

TENN.   N.C.

ARKANSAS

ALA.   GA.   S.C.

MISS.

LA.

FLORIDA

Unsettled

☐	no slave population
☐	under 10%
☐	10–30%
☐	30–50%
☐	Over 50%

SLAVE POPULATION IN 1850

really national candidate, Buchanan benefited from the fear that a clear-cut sectional victory would split the Union. In November he won, carrying all the slave states but one, and gaining Pennsylvania, New Jersey, Indiana, Illinois, and California. In the other eleven free states, Frémont made a clean sweep—an impressive showing for a new party.

The real winner in 1856 was sectionalism: with the exception of Ohio, all eleven Frémont states were farther north than any of the twenty Buchanan states. No longer was the national political system a bond of union. Another of the cords holding the country together had snapped.

Sectionalism Ascendant

The year 1857 was auspicious, and ominous, for the United States. The *Dred Scott* decision by the United States Supreme Court undermined any hopes for future compromise on the issue of the expansion of slavery, the debate over the Lecompton Constitution in Kansas destroyed the northern branch of the Democratic Party, the Panic of 1857 convinced southerners of the superiority of the plantation economy, and the writings of Hinton Rowan Helper predicted the demise of slavery. The events of 1857 made political compromise between the North and the South all but impossible.

Dred Scott   After 1848 the slavery question, like some curse, transformed everything it touched. It divided churches, shattered political parties, turned Congress into a battleground, and ruined presidential careers. Only one institution—the Supreme Court—had remained unchanged. Pressure had been building on the Court for a definitive judgment regarding slavery in the territories. In 1857, in the case of *Dred Scott v. Sandford,* the Court's majority, sympathetic to the South, abandoned judicial impartiality in the hope of settling this nagging question once and for all. The justices assumed that respect for the Court would insure acceptance of its decision by all sides. Rarely had American public figures so misgauged the popular temper: rather than settling the slavery question, the *Dred Scott* decision pushed the country forward on the road to civil war.

The case involved a Missouri slave, Dred Scott, who had sojourned with his master for several years in Illinois and in Minnesota Territory. Upon returning to Missouri, Scott and his wife sued for their freedom, contending that they had been emancipated by virtue of their residence on free soil. Chief Justice Roger B. Taney, speaking for a majority of the Supreme Court, rejected the Scotts's claim on three grounds: as black people they could not be citizens and therefore had no right to bring suit in the federal courts; as residents of Missouri they did not fall within the law of Illinois prohibiting slavery; and their sojourn in the Minnesota Territory had not emancipated them, for the provision of the Missouri Compromise prohibiting slavery north of 36° 30' was unconstitutional. Congress, Taney declared, had no right to deprive citizens of their property in the territories without "due process of law," and he was defining slaves as property.

On nearly every point the Chief Justice's opinion was either plainly wrong or open to serious dispute. To declare that black people in general, and hence even free blacks, were non-citizens who, as Taney said, had "no rights [that whites] were bound to respect" defied American history. Free blacks had always been recognized as citizens in at least some northern states, and therefore did have the right to sue in the federal courts. In rejecting the principle that the status one state granted to an individual held for that person in another state, Taney ignored several earlier decisions in which Missouri courts had recognized the claim to freedom of slaves who had sojourned in free territory. The supreme authority of Congress over the territories had previously been upheld no less than three times by the Taney Court itself.

Taney's pronouncement that it was unconstitutional for Congress to exclude slavery in the territories provoked a storm of criticism in the North. Republicans dismissed the decision as part of the "slavepower conspiracy." According to Horace Greeley's *New York Tribune,* it was entitled "to just so much moral weight as would be the judgment of a majority of those congregated in any Washington bar-room." The decision also embarrassed northern Democrats such as Stephen A. Douglas. They had fixed their hopes on the doctrine of popular sover-

Dred Scott. The Supreme Court's decision in the Scott case—denying both the right of a slave to sue for freedom and the right of a territory to exclude slavery within its boundaries—further inflamed the antislavery factions. *(Courtesy, The Missouri Historical Society)*

eignty. But if Congress could not exclude slavery in the territories, then neither could it bestow on the people of a territory the authority to do so. Southerners, of course, hailed the *Dred Scott* decision as a vindication of their claim that slavery could not be excluded from the territories prior to statehood. By striking down popular sovereignty, the Supreme Court had destroyed just about the last device for sectional compromise. Meanwhile, events in Kansas deepened sectional division still further.

The Lecompton Constitution   In 1857 the proslavery faction in Kansas held a convention at Lecompton, drafted a constitution recognizing slavery, and applied for statehood. Although a clear majority of the territory's residents opposed the Lecompton Constitution, President Buchanan accepted it and asked Congress to admit Kansas to statehood. The President took this fateful step out of fear that a rejection of Lecompton would antagonize southern Democrats.

Buchanan's action outraged Stephen Douglas, who had proposed popular sovereignty as a democratic solution to the question of slavery in Kansas. Bucking the administration, he denounced the "Lecompton fraud" as a travesty on popular sovereignty and joined with Republican congressmen in opposing it. Douglas's opposition to Lecompton offended southerners and probably ruined his presidential prospects. After a struggle, Congress in 1858 sent the Lecompton Constitution back to the people of Kansas to be voted on again. This time a fair election was held, and Kansas rejected the "Lecompton fraud" by a margin of 11,300 to 1,788. Kansas remained a territory until after the Civil War had begun.

Buchanan's attempt to ram the Lecompton Constitution through Congress, coming so soon after the Kansas-Nebraska Act, broke the northern wing of the Democratic Party. Few northern Democrats who supported him on Kansas survived the 1858 mid-term elections. From this point on and for about a century thereafter, the white South was to identify with the Democratic Party.

In the North and West, meanwhile, within the Republican party antislavery sentiment was coalescing with economic nationalism.

Numbers of American statesmen, among them Hamilton, John Quincy Adams, and Henry Clay, had wished to make the national government an active partner in the shaping and strengthening of a unified American economy. But economic nationalist programs differed in detail. Adams would have kept a high price on public lands in the West and applied the revenues to his ambitious governmental programs for the enriching of the economy and culture. For a time, northeastern business interests also had wanted the price of public lands to remain high, for they feared that cheap land would drain away eastern labor to the West. But now industrialists could think differently: immigration was supplying labor for northern industry and a prosperous West could be a customer for northeastern manufactured goods. So northerners of varying economic condition, landhungry farmers along with ambitious businessmen, could unite behind a nationalist program that would have the government nurture northern industry, turn government land over to western settlers, and finance transportation connecting the Northeast to the West.

This economic nationalism had much common ground with the antislavery movement. Northerners wishing to settle in the West did not want the new lands dominated by the slave powers. Northern industrialists were at war politically with southern slaveholders who opposed protective tariffs. The Republican conviction that Congress had the authority to prohibit slavery in the territories blended with a larger belief in strong federal government, the kind that could legislate an active and continental economic program. Perhaps northerners who championed a vigorous program of economic development could even detect a cultural identity between their economic and their antislavery convictions, believing that industriousness and progress were the way of the free-labor North while indolence was the way of the southern slaveholding class.

In any event, Republicans sponsored legislation in Congress favoring free homesteads for settlers, agricultural colleges financed by grants of land, internal improvements aided by the federal government, and a protective tariff. Southern Democrats blocked each of these measures. By obstructing the dynamic economic forces then at work in the North and Midwest, the South pressed these two sections to work together.

Northern politics, like the northern economy, was now moving along an east-west axis. And the Republican program for the economy, like the Republican opposition to slavery, had the more generous view of how the republic could conduct its life, for the party was really looking beyond the localism of states' rights and proposing a cooperative commonwealth in which the resources of the entire nation would be put to the common welfare.

The Panic of 1857   In the midst of the civil war in Kansas and the debates over the Dred Scott case, the Ohio Life Insurance and Trust Company of New York City declared bankruptcy and triggered a financial panic throughout the major cities of the North and upper Midwest. A wide range of smaller financial institutions went under, as did dozens of brokerage firms and larger industrial concerns that could no longer secure credit. Unemployment spread. But the southern economy remained prosperous. Between 1836 and 1840 cotton producers had exported a total of $321 million of cotton, and that volume jumped to nearly $750 million between 1856 and 1860. The plantation South not only survived the panic of 1857; it experienced unprecedented prosperity.

The Panic of 1857 convinced southerners that their way of life was superior to that of the North. While northern businesses went broke or at best barely survived, southern plantations thrived. While northern workers lost their jobs and their homes, southern slaves were housed, fed, and clothed better than before. Southerners elevated their rhetoric once again, praising slavery as a moral good and an essential feature of the American economy. The Southern Commercial Convention, meeting in Vicksburg, Mississippi, in May 1859, went beyond even that and called for restoration of the Atlantic slave trade as a means of strengthening the southern economy.

Lydia M. Child had called attention to the mistreatment of blacks in the North:

"While we bestow our earnest disapprobation on the system of slavery, let us not flatter ourselves that we are in reality any better than our brethren of the South. Thanks to our soil and climate and the early exertions of Quakers, the *form* of slavery does not exist among us; but the very *spirit* of the hateful and mischievous thing is here in all its strength. . . .

Of the attempt to establish a school for African girls at Canterbury, Connecticut, Child wrote:

"Had the pope himself attempted to establish his supremacy over that commonwealth, he could hardly have been repelled with more determined and angry resistence. A colored girl who availed herself of this opportunity to gain instruction was warned out of town, and fined for not complying; and the instructress was imprisoned for persevering in her benevolent plan."

Hinton Rowan Helper

Hinton Rowan Helper, a native of the upper South, was not so sure about the virtues of the southern economy. Using statistics gleaned from the Census of 1850, Helper concluded that plantation slavery had actually impoverished the vast majority of southern whites. In New York in 1857 he published *The Impending Crisis of the South*. By implying that most southern whites would be better off in a free economy, Helper became *persona non grata* in the South. Southern state legislatures declared the book to be treasonous and provocative, and they prohibited its sale in bookstores and its distribution through federal post offices. A host of northern congressmen endorsed the book and even had more than 100,000 copies printed for distribution to their constituents. The stage was set for another confrontation between North and South.

Abe Lincoln of Illinois

Young Abraham Lincoln lost the 1858 election for senator of Illinois to Stephen A. Douglas, but beat Douglas and two other candidates to become President of the increasingly divided nation in 1860.

The Lincoln-Douglas Debates

The earliest principal contender for the Republican nomination in 1860 was William Seward. As governor of New York for four years and senator for twelve, he enjoyed a national reputation. But suddenly, in 1858, a new potential candidate appeared. Throughout that summer, newspapers carried reports of a series of debates between Stephen A. Douglas and a little-known Illinois lawyer and former congressman named Abraham Lincoln. The occasion was the contest for Douglas's seat in the Senate. Political feelings in the 1850s ran so strong that one debate, at Galesburg, drew many horse drawn floats; one carried thirty-two young women, one for each state, dressed in white, and a thirty-third in black labeled "Kansas" carrying a banner, "THEY WON'T LET ME IN." One woman who lived into the 1930s would remember the "electricity crackling in the air" and Douglas' remark that if Lincoln thought so much of the Negro he imagined Abe would like one for a wife. Replied Lincoln in his slow drawl: "No, I do not want a negro for a wife, neither do I want one for my slave." When the debates were over, Lincoln had lost the election but had become a figure to be reckoned with in the Republican Party. "You are like Byron," a friend wrote, "who woke up one morning and found himself famous."

The Supreme Court's *Dred Scott* decision, which in effect denied to the people of a territory the right to exclude slavery within its boundaries, had placed Douglas in a difficult situation. The "Little Giant" was the foremost advocate of popular sovereignty. If he accepted the Court's decision, he would probably lose the election in Illinois, where free-soil sentiment was strong. But if he reaffirmed the right of settlers to decide the slavery question for themselves, he would lose the support of southerners, which he desperately needed if he hoped to win the Democratic presidential nomination in 1860.

According to legend, Lincoln took advantage of Douglas's predicament to further his own political ends. At Freeport he asked Douglas whether, in light of Taney's opinion, the people could still exclude slavery from a territory. Douglas replied that they could, merely by withholding the police regulations and local laws that slavery needed in order to exist. The Freeport formula, summed up in the phrase "unfriendly legislation," supposedly assured Douglas's reelection to the Senate, but would cost him the support of southerners in 1860. Lincoln, so the legend goes, had thus with superhuman foresight sacrificed the short-run of a Senate seat in the interests of winning the big prize in 1860.

This story, like so many pieces of Lincoln lore, is more fiction than fact. In reality Douglas had announced his doctrine of "unfriendly legislation" months before the Freeport debate. And by the time of his confrontation with Lincoln, popular sovereignty was no longer a major issue. The real issue between the two men—and the one Lincoln strove to develop—was the ultimate one of the morality of slavery. Here Lincoln and Douglas differed fundamentally.

Douglas did not regard the question of slavery in the territories as a moral issue. He believed that blacks, whatever their status, would never achieve equality with whites. Whether they were subordinated as slaves, therefore, or merely as second-class citizens was not a matter of great concern for him, certainly not an issue worth breaking up the country over. Douglas disliked slavery; but what to do about it, he thought, should remain a local decision. Southerners had chosen to keep it. Northerners had decided to get rid of it. In the territories Douglas would let the local residents decide by popular sovereignty. He would never try to impose a single national policy on the slavery question. This position accorded with his friendly way with the voters: "I live with constituents," he once proudly asserted, "drink with them, lodge with them, pray with them, laugh, hunt, dance, and work with them. I eat their corn dodgers and fried bacon." He wanted them all to like him and, like Henry Clay before, wanted desperately to be President, thinking a middle ground the safest route to victory in national politics. But by temporizing in an era of polarization, he would lose both poles of the electorate.

For Lincoln slavery was a moral wrong. Although political considerations and respect for constitutional guarantees to slaveholders often impelled Lincoln to compromise his moral views in public, he never deserted them. Lincoln could never say, as Douglas said, that he did not care whether slavery was "voted up or voted down."

Lincoln differed from Douglas on another point: he insisted that slavery, as a national problem, required a national policy. Lincoln would not interfere with slavery where it existed; but he would not allow it to expand. Lincoln believed that the Founding Fathers, recognizing slavery as a wrong, had placed restrictions on it designed to produce its eventual extinction. Douglas and the Democrats, by refusing to recognize the moral wrong, had provided constitutional sanctions for slavery and made possible its expansion.

In 1858, Douglas narrowly won reelection to the Senate. But it was Lincoln who had sensed and shared the growing moral and emotional concern over the slavery issue in the North. This would be critical in the election of 1860.

As the election year approached, North and South ceased even to pretend to any interest in compromise. In 1859 Senator Jefferson Davis

A popular song of the time, referring both to the Compromise of 1850 and to popular sovereignty, pointed to the difficulty of Douglas' position:

Once we had a Compromise,
A check to Slavery's wrong,
Douglas crushed the golden prize,
To help himself along,
Then the North and then the West,
Arose with giant power,
Pierce succumbed to the South's behest,
But Douglas had to cower.
  Hi! Douglas! Sly Douglas!
  A Senator would be.

of Mississippi introduced resolutions in Congress designed to get the Democratic Party to support the extreme southern position on slavery in the territories. These upheld the constitutional right of slaveholders to go into territories and called for the creation of a federal slave code for those areas. Senate Democrats finally adopted the Davis resolutions, over the vigorous objections of Stephen Douglas. At about the same time some southerners launched a movement to revive the African slave trade. This proposal had no chance of success, even among southerners; its main purpose, successfully achieved, was to irritate northern sensibilities. During the 1850s several northern state legislatures had defied the Fugitive Slave Act by passing "personal liberty" laws. Most of these prohibited state officers from aiding federal officials in their efforts to reclaim fugitives. In 1854 the Wisconsin supreme court had carried defiance of the federal government a step farther by declaring the Fugitive Slave Act of 1850 unconstitutional. Eventually the United States Supreme Court overturned this judgment, whereupon the Wisconsin legislature, taking a line from the Kentucky Resolution of 1798, declared the Court's action to be "an act of undelegated power, void, and of no force." But going beyond these acts of North and South in prefiguring sectional war was John Brown's raid at Harpers Ferry, Virginia (see page 438).

The Election of 1860

The Democrats Meet in Charleston

In April 1960, the Democrats began their national convention at Charleston, South Carolina. For the Democrats, 1860 was the climax of the intra-party struggle between the dominant southern faction and the northerners, whose spokesman was Stephen Douglas. Ever since the split over Lecompton, both sides had been spoiling for a confrontation over the question of slavery in the territories. Most southern delegates came to Charleston pledged to the adoption of the Davis Resolutions opposing any limitation on slavery in the territories. When the convention rejected their inclusion on the platform, delegates from eight southern states left. The convention then reassembled at Baltimore on June 18, where the fight immediately resumed. This time delegates from eleven southern states (all the future states of the Confederacy) walked out. The remaining delegates nominated Douglas for President on a platform endorsing popular sovereignty. The bolters met in another hall and for President nominated John Breckinridge of Kentucky. Their platform upheld the Davis Resolutions. The split between the Democrats was complete.

A number of factors brought this fatal action by the southern Democrats. A few hotheads sought deliberately to split the party, precisely in order to produce the Republican victory that would, they anticipated, precipitate secession. Some delegates hoped merely to force the election into the House of Representatives. The Democrats had met amidst extreme excitement, and many delegates were simply swept away by the violent speeches of "fire-eaters," a term applied to agitators like William Yancey of Alabama. They bolted without fully considering the consequences. Right up to November, many of the bolters assumed that somehow the party would come back together.

The
Republicans
Convene in
Chicago

The Republican convention opened at Chicago on May 16. The Republican strategy in 1860 was simple: to win the presidency the party had only to win the same states Frémont had carried in 1856, and just 34 additional electoral votes. This meant carrying Pennsylvania (27 votes) and either Illinois (11), Indiana (13), or New Jersey (7). Each of these four states had reason to desire such Republican measures as the tariff and internal improvements. The delegates reaffirmed Republican opposition to the expansion of slavery, but promised to leave slavery alone where it existed.

This same concern for the swing states governed the choice of a candidate. The party pros settled on Abraham Lincoln as the safest: he resided in the state of Illinois and was a moderate on slavery.

In 1860 there were two campaigns. In the North the contest was between Lincoln and Douglas: Breckinridge and the unionist John Bell of Tennessee were also in the race, but barely. In the South Breckinridge divided votes with Bell, though the moderate Stephen Douglas was also

This cartoon employs a setting from the new game of baseball to argue that Lincoln won the 1860 election because he stood for equal rights and free territory. *(Courtesy, The New-York Historical Society, New York City)*

John Bell. *(Courtesy, Library of Congress)*

John Breckinridge. *(Courtesy, Library of Congress)*

John Brown. *(Courtesy, Library of Congress)*

on the ballot. On the real issue of the campaign, the possible dissolution of the Union, Lincoln and Breckinridge remained silent.

On election day each of the hard-line candidates won in his own section. Lincoln carried all the northern states except New Jersey; Breckinridge captured eleven slave states. Douglas ran well in the North, but carried only Missouri and three electoral votes in New Jersey. Bell, whose popular vote was the smallest, took Virginia, Kentucky, and Tennessee. In the country as a whole Lincoln won only thirty-nine percent of the popular vote, but his votes were concentrated in the populous North. As a result, he had a clear victory in the electoral college—180 votes against a total of 112 for his three opponents. He would have won even if the opposition to him had been united. Conservatives within the Republican Party hoped to appease the upper South with a policy of popular sovereignty instead of outright opposition to admission of any of the territories as slave states. But then came a further setback to the South: John Brown's nightmare attack at Harpers Ferry.

John Brown's Raid

In the fall of 1859, the nation seemed still capable of veering off the collision course on which its sections were hurtling. Then John Brown, who had avenged the murders of freestate settlers in Kansas with bloody retribution at Pottawatomie Creek, shocked the country with a bold and desperate stroke in the slave South.

Funded by the "Secret Six" prominent white northern abolitionists, and encouraged by additional contributions from meetings held by Ralph Waldo Emerson and Henry David Thoreau in Boston, the movement also collected money from African Americans who had moved to San Francisco during the Gold Rush. Leaders in the militant Black Convention Movement, begun in the 1830s, believed that the time for petitions was over because the *Dred Scott* decision by the U.S. Supreme Court in 1857 had declared that no black person, slave or free, was a citizen of the United States. This gave some credibility to Brown's utopian proposals and desperate plans for liberating slaves.

John Brown prepared a "Provisional Constitution and Ordinances for the Oppressed People of the United States" at Frederick Douglass's home in Rochester, New York, in 1858. These were approved in a convention held in a communal settlement of fugitives and free blacks in Canada, a group similar to that in which Brown's large family lived in the Adirondack Mountains, near Lake Placid, in New York, on land that was donated by the abolitionist Gerrit Smith, one of the "Secret Six."

Brown was riding a wave of wide public approval, especially in the Middle West, for his recent rescue of eleven slaves in Missouri who had asked his assistance—a number increased to twelve when a baby was born in Kansas in their wintry sojourn on the Underground Railroad in January 1859. He renewed his acquaintance with black and white militant abolitionists in New England and Ohio who had been discouraged by delay. Frederick Douglass, however, remained disaffected over infighting, and when told by Brown of his new plan to attack the federal weapons factory and arsenal at Harpers Ferry, Virginia, the most prominent African American leader in the country tried to dissuade him, calling the town situated at the confluence of the Potomac and Shenandoah rivers a "steel trap."

The small army of sixteen whites and five blacks stealthily entered the town on the rainy night of October 16, 1859, their Sharps' rifles hidden by long woolen shawls. Taking hostages among slaveholders, the group was aided by a number of local slaves and free blacks who soon saw themselves surrounded by local white railroad workers and militia. The white population within the area outnumbered blacks ten to one. After thirty-six hours, the United States marines led by Robert E. Lee besieged them. Ten of the party was killed, including two of Brown's own sons. John Brown resisted the efforts of his own second officer in command to leave the town, causing endless debates on the real motive for the attack: Did he intend to become a deliberate martyr?

"He is the gamest man I ever saw," admitted the governor of Virginia, upon questioning the wounded captive. Brown replied to every questioner at his interrogation and at his trial with crisp assurance born of clarity of purpose. His many letters after his conviction breathed saintly dedication to the biblical injunction to remember them that are in bonds as bound with them. Brown never wavered, showed no fear, no vindictiveness toward his captors, no selfish purposes at all. He awed his enemies and captured the respect of much of the North for a deed that few could actually condone. His surviving young army, several from his freestate Kansas battles, showed the same conviction. John Brown was executed on December 2, 1859, convicted of murder, inciting slaves to insurrection, and treason against the laws of slavery in the state of Virginia. Ralph Waldo Emerson predicted that Brown "will make the gallows as glorious as the cross."

At the time of John Brown's raid in October, 1859, the new Republican Party leader Abraham Lincoln disavowed the abolition attack and praised the local slaves for not beginning a bloody insurrection. But John Brown's willingness to die for his beliefs played upon the deepest chords of the Puritan conscience. That Protestantism, committed to the perfection of the individual, went with an energetic American belief in the moral conquest of social evil. John Brown's sacrifice on the gallows brought northerners an awareness of the futility of combating the entrenched institution of slavery with persuasive means. By the time Lincoln was re-elected President of the United States near the close of the Civil War in 1865, he was able to speculate in his Second Inaugural Address whether "every drop of blood drawn with the lash shall be paid by another drawn with the sword."

Suggested Readings

Books on the 1850s include William E. Gienapp, *The Origins of the Republican Party, 1852–1856* (1987), Deborah White, *Ar'n't I a Woman? Female Slaves in the Plantation South* (1985), Eugene D. Genovese, *Freedom and Progress in Southern Conservative Thought, 1820–1860* (1991), Michael F. Holt, *The Political Crisis of the 1850s* (1976), David M. Potter, *The Impending Crisis: 1848–1861* (1976), Gerald W. Wolf, *The Kansas-Nebraska Bill: Party, Section, and the Coming of the Civil War* (1977), Don E. Fehrenbacher, *The Dred Scott Case* (1978), and Eric Foner, *Free Soil, Free Labor, Free Men: The Ideology of the Republican Party Before the Civil War* (1970).

Other important studies are Mitchell Snay, *Gospel of Disunion: Religion and Separatism in the Antebellum South* (1993), Richard J. Carwardine, *Evangelicals and Politics in Antebellum America* (1993), George B. Forgie, *Patricide in the House Divided: A Psychological Interpretation of Lincoln and His Age* (1979), and Drew Gilpin Faust, *A Sacred Circle: The Dilemma of the Intellectual in the Old South, 1840–1860* (1978). Stephen B. Oates's biography of John Brown is entitled *To Purge This Land With Blood* (1970). A good discussion of *Uncle Tom's Cabin* appears in the opening pages of Edmund Wilson's *Patriotic Gore* (1961). Milton Rugoff's family history is entitled *The Beechers* (1981). See also Joan Hedrick, *Harriet Beecher Stowe: A Life* (1993).

Don E. Fehrenbacher, *The Dred Scott Case: Its Significance in American Law and Politics* (1978) is a definitive work. See also Philip Paludan, *A People's Contest: The Union and the Civil War* (1988), Kenneth M. Stampp, *America in 1857: A Nation on the Brink*, Leon F. Litwack, *North of Slavery: The Negro and the Free States, 1798–1860* (1961), and James Oakes, *Slavery and Freedom: An Interpretation of the Old South* (1990).

What Caused the Civil War?

Kenneth M. Stampp

During the 1850s the proslavery South had won a series of striking political victories. In the Compromise of 1850, it had obtained a new and more stringent Fugitive Slave Act, which gave slaveholders the assistance of federal commissioners in their efforts to recover runaways. In 1854 southern Senators forced [Illinois Senator Stephen A.] Douglas to agree to the repeal of the Missouri Compromise before giving their support to the Kansas-Nebraska Act. In 1857 the Supreme Court's Dred Scott decision affirmed the right of slaveholders to carry their property into all the territories of the United States. The year 1857, in fact, marked the high tide of the proslavery South's national political power. It had the sympathy of the Buchanan administration. It controlled the Supreme Court. It dominated the Democratic majority in both houses of Congress. Pressing on, aggressive proslavery leaders ignored the advice of more cautious proslavery spokesmen, such as the *Richmond Enquirer,* not to force their northern allies to support policies that would destroy them—in short, not to endanger the survival of the Democratic party as a national organization. Instead, they disregarded election frauds and the clear will of the Kansas majority and, with the wholehearted support of the administration, demanded congressional approval of the [pro-slavery] Lecompton constitution.

[The president] had concluded that it would be folly to oppose the Lecompton constitution simply because it protected the owners of a few hundred slaves! Looking back, knowing the ultimate consequences of Buchanan's policy decision, it stands as one of the most tragic miscalculations any President has ever made. . . . The Buchanan administration was discredited; southern control of the House of Representatives was lost in the elections [of 1858]; and the Democratic party was split. The Republican victory in the presidential election of 1860 was the logical result. . . .

Would all this have been avoided—would the course of the sectional conflict have been significantly altered—if Buchanan had remained true to his pledge and demanded the submission of the whole Lecompton constitution of the voters of Kansas? This is a question no historian can answer. It is doubtful that a firm stand by Buchanan would have resulted in southern secession, because the provocation would not have been sufficient to unite even the Deep South behind so drastic a response. Nor would it have been sufficient to produce a major split in the national Democratic party. Accordingly, without a divided and demoralized national Democracy, Republican successes in the elections of 1858 and the presidential election of 1860 would have been a good deal more problematic. . . .

How Buchanan, a shrewd and experienced politician, one of the best trained Presidents the country has ever had, could have been responsible for a political disaster of such magnitude has been variously explained by hostile contemporaries and by historians. According to his modern biographer, Buchanan was a legalist and accepted the constitution because the Lecompton convention was a legal body, and no law required it to provide for full ratification. . . . [Another] explanation for Buchanan's Lecompton policy is that there was no significant difference between his outlook and that of the Southerners in his Cabinet. They shared an extreme dislike of abolitionists and Republicans, and they saw no great wrong in the existence of black slavery.

Kenneth M. Stampp, *America in 1857: A Nation on the Brink* (New York: Oxford University Press, 1990), pp. 329–30.

[This account] of what Abraham Lincoln called the American Union's "fiery trial" seeks to refocus attention on slavery as the taproot of sectional discord and civil war. It represents, that is, a modest challenge to those historians who see slavery as a largely artificial or symbolic issue. Of course, slavery was not the only item on the political agenda in the troubled 1850s, but it was, I think, the most important. The North and South may not have *been* distinct cultures, but by mid-century each section *thought* of itself as possessing a distinct and superior way of life, one shaped most profoundly by the absence or presence of human bondage. The debate over slavery's right to expand not only aroused feelings of jealousy, honor, and regional pride, but raised fundamental questions about the future direction of American society. Unable to find common ground with such vital issues at stake, the Union broke asunder. . . .

The slaveholding South had good reason to take alarm at Lincoln's victory. Its perception of the Republican party as first and foremost an antislavery instrument was fundamentally correct. Even conservative Republicans, who stressed the danger of Slave Power aggression and showed scant concern for those in chains, damned slavery as a "blighting institution" and sought a congressional barrier against its spread. The events of the 1850s—Kansas-Nebraska, Dred Scott, Lecompton and "Bleeding Kansas," proslavery designs on Cuba, and talk of reopening the African slave trade—had progressively radicalized party moderates, producing a heightened sensitivity to the immorality of slavery and a determination, in Lincoln's words, to pursue its "ultimate extinction" throughout the land.

There were limits, of course, to the antislavery steps Republicans might take. . . . Still, Lincoln's triumph was a palpable menace to the South. Quite aside from the long-range damage to be expected once Congress and the Supreme Court also came under Republican control (namely, exclusion of slavery from all territories, abolition in the District of Columbia, an end to the interstate slave trade, repeal or drastic modification of the Fugitive Slave Law), the new president, acting solely on his executive authority, might make no end of mischief. By appointing Republicans to judgeships, collectorships, postmasterships, and other positions in the South he could foster an antislavery influence dangerous not only to the peculiar institution but, once it reached the slave quarters, to the very lives of Southern whites. Such patronage, moreover, might spawn Republican organizations in the South destructive to the unity on which the region's special culture depended.

In fact, Lincoln's election itself, independent of the policies he and his party might be expected to pursue, represented an assault on the honor and well-being of the South. By electing a candidate pledged to slavery's destruction, the Northern majority had grossly insulted the South and proclaimed its determination to make vassals—slaves—of Southern whites. To prideful Southerners, the voters' verdict amounted to "a declaration of war against our property and the supremacy of the white race," a slap in the face that demanded retribution. More practical considerations also fueled Southern indignation at Lincoln's victory. Many fretted that slave property, its value dependent upon an expectation of future returns, "must be greatly depreciated" under a "black Republican" administration. The *Charleston Mercury* estimated that "the submission of the South to the administration of the Federal Government under Messrs. Lincoln and Hamlin, must reduce the value of slaves in the South, one hundred dollars each," a loss to the region of more than $400 million. Worse yet, as slave prices skidded, planters in the upper South (where slavery was deemed a marginal investment) would feel pressure to sell off their chattels. Then, worried the *Mercury,* "the Frontier States [will] *enter on the policy of making themselves Free States.*" Meanwhile, word of the election of an antislavery president seemed in itself sufficient to promote bloody insurrections against the "master race." Finally, magnifying all such fears was the fear of the unknown. Abraham Lincoln would be the *first* Republican president and history offered no reassurances concerning his probable behavior in office.

Richard H. Sewell, *A House Divided: Sectionalism and Civil War, 1848–1865* (Baltimore: The Johns Hopkins University Press, 1988), pp. 11, 76–78.

A reconstruction by the lithography firm of Currier and Ives of the bombardment of Fort Sumter in Charleston Harbor, the attack that launched the Civil War. *(Courtesy, Hugh Cleland Collection)*

A Great Civil War 1861–1865

WAS THE CIVIL WAR NECESSARY?

Some wars are simple and unchanging in purpose. Upon their conclusion, observers can decide to what extent each side has obtained its objectives. Such, for example, was the Mexican War of the 1840s. The United States intended to take territory from its southern neighbor; Mexico intended to resist the land grab; the thieves got what they wanted and the victims lost.

Quite different was the course of the Civil War. Southern secession, which brought on the war, aimed to protect slavery. But the result of the war was the end of slavery as a legal institution. Had the rebel states not seceded and fought, slavery would have survived—at least until the coming of some later crisis. An appraisal of the intentions of the Union is more difficult.

The North fought, at least for the most part, to put down secession. At the war's beginning, the Union did not contemplate the ultimate loss of life: Doing so might have deterred it from fighting. The Lincoln Administration, less willing to attack slavery than the South was to keep it, was at first prepared to make unbreakable guarantees to the seceded states that if they returned to the Union their peculiar institution would be safe. Lincoln was not going to allow the extension of slavery into the newer western states. But the South, in the very fact of secession, had surrendered every right to the western territories anyway—their disposition was no longer at issue. Lincoln's decision to fight had as its immediate effect the spread of secession, sending Virginia, North

HISTORICAL EVENTS

1860
South Carolina secedes
from the Union

1861
Confederate States of America
formed • Jefferson Davis becomes
provisional President of the Confederacy • Morrill Tariff • Fort Sumter
attacked by Confederate forces
(April 12) and the Civil War begins
• Battle of Bull Run

1862
Homestead Act of 1862 • Morrill
Land Grant Act of 1862 • Lincoln
suspends some civil liberties • Union
begins recruiting blacks for military
service • Battle at Shiloh • Union
Army captures New Orleans • the
Merrimac vs. the *Monitor* • Battles of
Antietam • Emancipation
Proclamation

1863
National Banking Act of 1863
• General Hooker defeated at
Chancellorsville • Union victories at
Gettysburg and Vicksburg
• antidraft riot in New York City

continued

HISTORICAL EVENTS

1864
National Banking Act of 1864 • *ex parte Vallandigham* • Grant begins siege of Richmond • Lincoln reelected

1865
Sherman takes South and North Carolina • the Confederacy authorizes taking blacks into the army • Lee and Grant battle in Virginia • Lee surrenders (April 9) • the Thirteenth Amendment outlaws slavery

1866
Ex parte Milligan

Carolina, Tennessee, and Arkansas out of the Union. It would take four bloody years to beat them and their sister states back in.

Today, the war is judged more for its destruction of slavery than for its preservation of the Union. But before the 1860s no considerable portion of the northern population would ever have undertaken such a venture. And as for instigating a slave rebellion: only a few abolitionists, most notably the followers of John Brown, seriously considered such a thing. It was only because, on the northern side, a war began not over slavery but over the existence of the Union that by 1863 a war against slavery became possible.

Was the Civil War necessary? From the northern viewpoint, it was necessary only because the South had seceded. If, however, a bloodless end of slavery had to await the South's decision to end it, the war was certainly necessary to bring about emancipation any time soon. For a century after its defeat the South was able to keep much of the substance of slavery if not the form. That gives a hint of how long slavery might have lasted in the absence of a war.

That the outcome of the Civil War was so far from the initial purpose of either of the two belligerents is a comment on the quickness with which war can set its own terms. The Civil War in this sense was more like the American Revolution than the combat with Mexico. The war that began in 1775 had also started with fairly limited intentions. The British wanted to reassert parliamentary authority over a major part of their empire; the Americans wanted a larger degree of self-determination within that empire. The British, of course, did not get what they wanted; the American rebels who at the beginning of the conflict still looked to George III as their sovereign ended by rejecting the crown they had once revered. The results of both the Revolution and the Civil War would today be judged as reasonably satisfactory. But the twentieth century was to be a tale of wars that produced in new forms the horrors they were fought to overcome.

The Declaration of Independence, and the victory of the American rebels against imperialism, are taken as models even by peoples who define the United States as a new imperialist power. And the ending of slavery, the unplanned product of the Civil War, is now rightly celebrated as a triumph of morality and humanity.

The South Secedes

As soon as Lincoln's election was certain, the South Carolina legislature called for a state convention. On December 20, 1860, the convention met at Charleston and unanimously declared "that the Union now subsisting between South Carolina and other States of America is hereby dissolved." Similar declarations followed in rapid succession in Alabama, Georgia, Florida, Mississippi, and Louisiana. The smooth course of secession was upset only in Texas, where crusty old Governor Sam Houston, a staunch Unionist, refused to summon a special session of the legislature. The lawmakers met anyway, and called a convention without Houston's authorization.

Up to this point, the secession process had moved forward with electrifying speed. Moderates tried to avert the catastrophe. But too much blood had been shed in Kansas, too much noble madness displayed at Harpers Ferry. In the space of forty-two days, seven states, stretching from South Carolina to Texas, seceded from the Union. On February 4, 1861, however, the secessionist tide broke momentarily when the voters of Virginia elected a majority of convention delegates opposed to immediate secession. Subsequently the electorate in four other upper South states—Tennessee, North Carolina, Arkansas, and Missouri—voted in effect against secession. The three remaining slave states—Kentucky, Maryland, and Delaware—did not even call conventions. Having stronger ties to the North and smaller ratios of blacks in its population, the upper South was hesitant to secede. For the moment, the lower South was isolated.

Nonetheless, at Montgomery, Alabama, on February 7, 1861, delegates from the seven states proceeded to adopt a provisional constitution for the Confederate States of America. It was modeled closely on the United States Constitution, but several modifications safeguarded state sovereignty and slavery. The Confederate Constitution reserved to the states the power of amendment and even permitted them to impeach Confederate officials under certain circumstances. It guaranteed the property rights of slaveholders both in the existing states and in any future territory the Confederacy might acquire. To lead the new government the delegates chose Jefferson Davis of Mississippi as provisional President and Alexander H. Stephens of Georgia as Vice President.

President and Mrs. Jefferson Davis. In February 1861, the first seven Confederate States of America—there were to be eleven in all—elected Davis as President. (*Courtesy, Confederate Museum, Richmond, Virginia*)

A Compact of States   Declarations issued by the various state conventions spelled out the reasons for secession. South Carolina's was typical. The United States Constitution, the declaration begins, was a compact among sovereign states for the purpose of establishing "a government with defined objects and powers." Like all compacts, this one bound the contracting parties to certain mutual obligations. The failure of one of the parties to perform these obligations, in whole or in part, released the other from its bond. The northern states, continues the South Carolina declaration, had refused to fulfill their constitutional obligation to return fugitive slaves. They had tolerated abolition societies "designed to disturb the peace and steal the property of the citizens of other states." They had encouraged "servile insurrection"—a reference to John Brown. At last, a sectional party "hostile to slavery" had captured control of the federal government. This party, the declaration concludes, was dedicated not merely to excluding slavery from the "common territory," but to slavery's ultimate extinction.

Southerners might associate the case for slavery with the case for secession, claiming that both slaveholding and states' rights were old institutions strongly founded in law. But the two issues were in fact quite separate. In previous years northern opponents of slavery had proposed that free states refuse cooperation with a national government that protected slavery; and in 1860 some sympathizers with slavery were also supporters of the Union.

Earlier in the century political and constitutional quarrels had taken place over whether it was the Union or the states that possessed sovereignty. The argument looked back to the process of ratification, in which each state had held a convention to decide whether that state should adhere to the Constitution.

Nineteenth-century champions of state sovereignty concluded from this that ratification had been by individual states, each state retaining sovereignty and the right of independence. They believed that sovereignty belonged also to the states formed after ratification.   The opposite argument started with the proposition that at the time of the American Revolution it had been the whole people who asserted sovereignty, rebelling against the false claim of the British throne to be sovereign over British America. Thereafter that same whole and undivided sovereign people, following the Confederation period, voted for the Constitution, the states providing no more than convenient administrative units for the conduct of the vote. If the states at the time of ratification had been that—administrative units within the nation—they could not later present themselves as being sovereign and having been so in the eighteenth century. Americans who thought this way could believe that in opposing southern seccession they were opposing an illegal rebellion by a part of the people against the whole people.

The Union Responds   By early winter 1861 Lincoln was on his way to Washington. The seven states of the deep South had seceded and formed the Confederate States of America, with Montgomery, Alabama, as their first capital. The crisis was the greatest since the Revolution. Washington was astir with worry and excitement.

The nation's capital, tucked between the slave states of Virginia and Maryland, was a largely southern city. For decades southern politicians, or "northern men with southern principles," had dominated the political, business, and social life of the capital. The city still had slaves in its population, although since the 1850 Compromise the slave pens and auction blocks had gone. Now, in the country's greatest crisis, the southern sympathies of many Washingtonians were visible everywhere. At the city's many bars the imbibers of toddies and flips announced that Lincoln would never be inaugurated: proud "southrons" would not allow it. At the government executive departments young clerks wore secession cockades to show their support of the South.

Unionists who found themselves in the capital during the secession winter were apprehensive. The young Henry Adams, who had come to Washington as private secretary to his father, Congressman Charles Francis Adams of Massachusetts, thought the southerners "demented," so confident of independence that they were already cultivating the good will of their future Yankee customers. Senator Stephen Douglas,

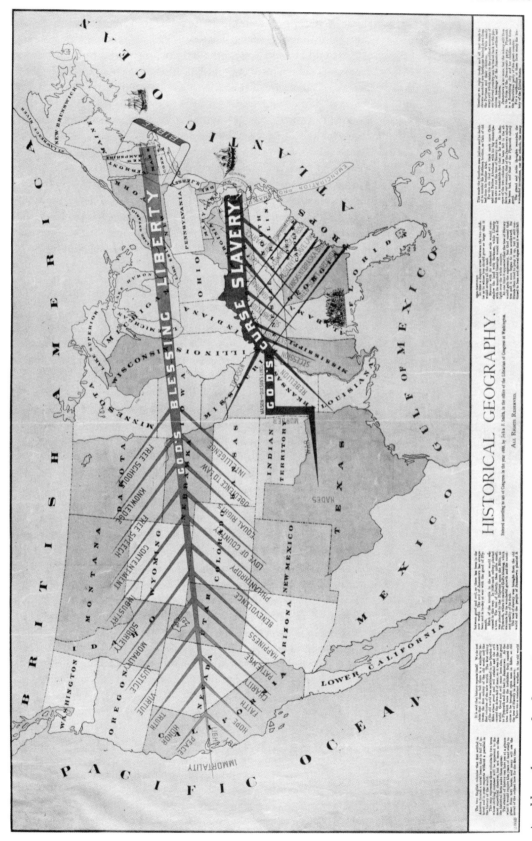

An old northern textbook map depicting the tree of Slavery (God's curse) branching out across the South and into Missouri, and the tree of Liberty (God's blessing) branching out across the rest of the nation. The traditional dividing line between North and South was the Mason-Dixon line, a 1769 survey of the Pennsylvania-Maryland border by Charles Mason and Jeremiah Dixon.

waiting for Congress to begin its session, talked darkly of the "slave power" conspiracy that had connived at defeating him for President and was now intent on breaking up the Union. Unionists charged that the conspirators could be found in President Buchanan's cabinet itself. Cabinet members Howell Cobb of Georgia, Jacob Thompson of Mississippi, and John B. Floyd of Virginia, they said, were providing the Confederacy with guns and ammunition from federal arsenals and threatening the weak-willed Buchanan that if he tried to move against the secessionists he would be either assassinated or impeached.

Indeed, from the Unionist view it looked at first as if the seventy-year-old James Buchanan had been terrified into inaction. The Democratic President had proclaimed secession illegal and declared the Union "perpetual." But he apparently doubted that the federal government had any constitutional authority to force the return of seceded states, and he feared that any attempt at coercion would make the situation worse. Buchanan attributed the whole trouble to fanatical abolitionists and to the menace the free-soil movement posed for the South. The President hoped for some new compromise that would still the issue of slavery as had the arrangements of 1820 and 1850.

Efforts at compromise were not wanting. The issue needing resolution was that of slavery in the territories. Early in 1861 the Washington Peace Convention, a gathering of statesmen under the chairmanship of former President John Tyler, looked for a solution. Congress also debated. A plan pressed by Senator John J. Crittenden of Kentucky would extend the Missouri Compromise line to the Pacific and add a constitutional amendment protecting slavery wherever it existed. But the extremists dominating politics in the cotton states would probably have turned down the plan, and it is doubtful that the Republican Party would have abandoned its principle of opposing an unrestricted right to slavery in the territories.

While attempts at compromise were unsuccessful, neither secession nor war appeared certain. Republican and Democratic upholders of the sovereignty of the United States perceived secession as an impulsive and irrational act that the South could decide to reverse. War, or at any rate a prolonged one, must have been almost unthinkable. While Unionists argued with assurance that secession was unconstitutional, it was not clear that the federal government had the constitutional right to prevent it by force. Nor could supporters of the Union have any confidence that the northern people would summon the will to march against the seceded states. For President-elect Lincoln and prospective members of his cabinet, the problem was to find a political solution to the crisis.

The Problem of the Forts

Lincoln in his inaugural address told the South that he would enforce the Fugitive Slave Law and support a constitutional amendment protecting slavery where it already existed. But he did not modify his position on free soil in the territories; and he condemned secession, pledging to "hold, occupy and possess" all Union property within the regions that had announced their secession.

By February 1861 federal forts, customs houses, and post offices throughout the lower South had fallen into the hands of the Confederate or state authorities. But two key posts held out, Fort Pickens at Pensacola, Florida, and Fort Sumter in Charleston harbor. For the secessionists to concede these to the United States meant accepting the intolerable presence of a foreign power in the new southern nation's domain. For the Union to surrender them would be acquiescence in southern independence. The situation of Fort Pickens was not acute, since Florida authorities had not challenged the presence there of federal troops. Fiery Charleston was a different story.

As the citizens of the southern port went about their business, they were aware of the drama at their doorsteps. Across the harbor they could see the Stars and Stripes flying defiantly over Sumter, while on Morris Island and at the city's main fortifications uniformed men loyal to the new Confederacy rushed here and there moving big guns, ammunition, and powder.

For weeks South Carolina officials had been negotiating with both the Washington authorities and Major Robert Anderson, the garrison commander, for evacuation of the fort. Anderson had holed up at Sumter when he concluded that his small force was inadequate to occupy all three federal strong points in the harbor, but from that grim, gray bastion he refused to depart. Soon after the new year Buchanan, his resolve stiffened by four new Unionist cabinet members, dispatched the *Star of the West,* an unarmed steamer, to reinforce Anderson with men and supplies. The Charleston authorities ordered their guns to fire at the vessel. Anderson came within an eyelash of returning the fire to protect the ship, but before he did, it turned back.

Upon his inauguration in March 1861, Lincoln had to confront the problem of Sumter. He sought advice from his cabinet members and other statesmen. William Seward of New York, his secretary of state, startled him with the suggestion that the administration bring the country together by getting into a war with Europe. On April 4, 1861, the President announced that he was sending a squadron for the relief of Fort Sumter. The ships would carry only food. If the secessionists allowed them through, the federal government would make no attempt to send men or ammunitions to Anderson.

News of Lincoln's intentions infuriated the Confederate authorities in Montgomery, who believed that the Republican President had assured them he would evacuate Sumter. Convinced that they could not avoid a clash without seeming to be weak, they reluctantly ordered an attack on Sumter before the promised reinforcement could arrive.

Charleston rejoiced. Happiest of all, perhaps, was the venerable Edmund Ruffin, a leading writer on southern agronomy. Now a silver-haired man of sixty-seven, Ruffin had been among the staunchest defenders of southern rights, long advocating secession. When his own state of Virginia proved slow to take up the northern challenge he came to fire-eating Charleston and, despite his age, joined the South Carolina infantry. When the order to attack Sumter was given early on the morning of April 12, the elderly gentleman was positioned at the great

A reconstruction by the lithography firm of Currier and Ives of the bombardment of Fort Sumter in Charleston Harbor, the attack that launched the Civil War. *(Courtesy, Hugh Cleland Collection)*

Columbiad cannon pointing at the federal fort. In reality his shot was preceded by a mortar barrage, but history has accorded him the symbolic honor of opening the war.

The bombardment lasted for a respectable several hours for the outnumbered Union force. Anderson, his food and gunpowder low, finally sent word that he was ready to surrender. The next day the flag of the Union was lowered and the Palmetto banner of South Carolina raised. No soldier was killed or seriously injured. But by seceding and then firing the first shot, the Confederacy brought together in defense of the Union a North that surely would not have chosen to fight the South on the question of slavery alone.

War Strategies

Immigrants or citizens in the Union army celebrated their experiences in their native languages:

Viva Grant! Viva Grant! ciudadanos,
que cinco años la guerra sostuvo,
y un ejército enorme mantuvo
en defensa de la libertad.

Y después de sangrientos combates,
do murieron valientes soldados;
fueron libres aquellos estados
que jamás pretendían la igualdad.
Dios te salve, caudillo del Norte!
Yo saludo tu sacra bandera,
que en el mundo flamea por doquiera,
ofreciendo la paz y la unión.

También México ensalza tu nombre
porque fuiste con el indulgente,
fuiste siempre y serás el valiente
que defiende la Constitución.

Ich in Gettysburg mit schlug,
Half erringen jenen Sieg,
Und die Kosten auch mit trug,
Wenn ich auch keinen Nickel krieg.
Hancock führte an, du sagst,
Im Gefecht ein grosser Mann,
Ob ich für ihn stimm', du fragst?
Nein, o nein, das geht nicht an.
Damals trug er Union Blau,
Jetzt liebt er Rebellen Grau.

Northern Strategy The attack on the fort began the Civil War. In the absence of Congress, which was not yet in session, President Lincoln issued a proclamation requesting 75,000 volunteers for putting down "combinations too powerful to be suppressed by the ordinary course of judicial proceedings." When Congress assembled, it gave its support to this proclamation along with other actions that Lincoln had taken in the military emergency.

Lincoln's call for troops confronted the upper South states with an unwelcome choice: either fight against the South or fight against the Union. Virginia, North Carolina. Tennessee, and Arkansas joined the Confederacy. Four slave states remained in the Union: Delaware, Maryland, Kentucky, and Missouri. Of these, only Delaware did so peaceably. In the other three states opinion was divided. President Lincoln used force to aid the Union cause in strategic Maryland. When a mob favoring the South attacked federal soldiers in Baltimore and cut the rail line between that city and Washington, he sent troops to subdue the disorder and arrest potential secessionists. Kentucky, birthplace of both Lincoln and Jefferson Davis, declared its neutrality, but within months both Union and Confederate troops had entered the state. Kentucky and Missouri were torn by guerrilla warfare, as supporters of both sides fought for control of the state governments. Although the Confederacy claimed these two states, both remained in the Union. In 1863, the federal government arranged to make into a separate state West Virginia, the northwestern region of Virginia where slaves were few and Unionist sentiment was strong.

For the North, the basic strategy was clear: use its advantage of vast material and human resources to subdue the South. Its population in 1860 numbered over twenty million, while the South had barely nine million, forty percent of whom were slaves. Nine-tenths of the country's manufacturing capacity was situated in the North, which also had two-thirds of the railroad mileage. Most of the nation's merchant shipping and financial resources were in northern hands.

General Winfield Scott, one of several southerners who was a high-ranking Union officer during the Civil War, was the first commander of the federal forces under Lincoln, who as President was Commander-in-Chief. At the war's beginning the ailing Scott in his short remaining tenure in office mapped out the basic northern strategy. He proposed blockading southern ports, dividing the Confederacy by an occupation of the Mississippi River, and sending in armies of invasion that would break the southern nation into bits. Northerners expected a short war, but once the reality of a long war sank in, they closely followed Scott's strategy, soon named after the anaconda, the snake that squeezes its prey. The anaconda policy was ultimately to conquer the Confederacy.

Southern Strategy   The Confederacy's crucial disadvantage was economic, though it also suffered from a deep moral isolation in a world that increasingly repudiated slavery as a loathsome and retrograde remnant of a benighted past. Having few mills, factories, and foundries, the South began the war with little more than a stockpile of captured or imported equipment. In spite of heroic efforts toward industrial self-sufficiency, the South could never replace equipment as rapidly as it wore out. Since the naval coils of the northern anaconda were meanwhile stifling southern commerce with the outside world, the Confederacy had no way of supplying itself with the means of waging a multi-sided, fully aggressive conflict.

Yet the South at the beginning of the war was not in a weak position. For while the Confederacy could not win a head-on conflict with the North, it did not have to do so. Against the North's enormous task of conquering a vast territory, the rebels needed to do no more than demonstrate to the northern people and to Europe, by one military strategy or another, that the old Union was no longer a single, workable nation.

On at least one count, the South made a major mistake. It invested a naive faith in the power of "King Cotton." Convinced that British industry could not long do without southern cotton, the new Confederate government in 1861 forbade all exports of this, the South's only major source of foreign credit. Starving British textile makers, Richmond thought, would force Britain to intervene in the Confederacy's behalf. But British manufacturers, expecting war in America, had stockpiled cotton. By the time the South realized its error, the northern blockade had closed tight. For the rest of the war the South's "white gold" rotted

Resources of the Union and the Confederacy, 1861		
	Union	*Confederacy*
Population	23,000,000	8,700,000*
Real and personal property	$11,000,000,000	$5,370,000,000
Banking capital	$330,000,000	$27,000,000
Capital investment	$850,000,000	$95,000,000
Manufacturing establishments	110,000	18,000
Value of production (annual)	$1,500,000,000	$155,000,000
Industrial workers	1,300,000	110,000
Railroad mileage	22,000	9,000
		*40 percent were slaves (3,500,000)

on the wharves while southerners lacked military supplies and civilian goods.

Harper's Weekly published this drawing of a "long" Lincoln, by which it meant length in character and ability. *(Courtesy, Library of Congress)*

Wartime Legislation   In 1861, just before Lincoln's inauguration, Congress passed the Morrill Tariff, a protectionist measure putting duties to the levels they had been at in 1846; and later the national legislature raised duties even higher. The war put a strain on the system of banking and currency. In response, Congress reformed the system in a way that agreed with the Republican concept of strong government in the service of a national economy. The National Banking Acts of 1863 and 1864 provided that, in return for investing one-third of their capital in federal banks, private banks could issue national bank notes that would serve as paper money: these could be in amounts up to ninety percent of the market value of the securities the banks had purchased from the government. The notes of state banks, which had circulated as a form of money, were unstable and injured the economy. In order to suppress them, Congress later placed a ten percent tax on the notes of all institutions that did not take part in the national bank system.

The Republican idea of supplying federal lands for settlers triumphed in the Homestead Act of 1862. A settler who filed a claim to a quarter-section of one hundred and sixty acres of federal land and lived on it for five years would get ownership of it after payment of a small fee. The act permitted single women as well as men to file a claim. In practice, women alone, or even women with children, had great difficulty in sustaining their claims. Men needed the assistance of a woman as much as women needed the assistance of a man, but when men and women settled together in a family unit, the man invariably held title to the claim and officially directed its operation. Nor did the law permit married couples to file claims. Later in the century considerable amounts of the land went to timber and mining companies that had employees put in claims for homesteads. But at the time of the adoption of the act, there was some expectation that it would pull labor from the East to the free lands. And because of the labor shortage that the war was bringing about, Congress authorized immigration of contract workers from Europe and the Orient, permitting employers who paid the laborers' passage to deduct that cost from the pay.

In another use of federal lands, the Morrill Land Grant Act of 1862 offered lands to states that in return would finance colleges offering schooling in agriculture, engineering, and military science. It was a less dramatic measure than others of these wartime years, but significant in making the national government a partner to modern technical education.

The absence of legislators from the deep South made it easier for Congress during the war to adopt a scheme for a transcontinental railway running through the middle of the country, from Omaha to California. Southerners would have fought for a more southerly road. During the 1860s the national legislature granted to railroad developers thirty million acres of federal land and made them millions in loans to see the project through. It was one of the first of many extensive projects in which the government has joined with business.

Civil Liberties   In the extraordinary danger that the nation faced at the time of the war, free civil institutions continued in the North and for the most part in the border states. Lincoln's government did not attempt in any major and consistent way to put those institutions aside. But it was conscious that disruption or demoralization among the people in the regions loyal to the Union could upset the entire conduct of the war.

Lincoln suspended the writ of *habeas corpus*—the power of a court to have a prisoner brought before it—in cases in which individuals were suspected of disrupting the war effort. The suspension meant that the federal government could hold people for long periods without trial. Despite protests, Lincoln in the autumn of 1862 issued a proclamation subjecting to martial law and to trial in military tribunals anyone who discouraged others from enlisting or committed any disloyal act. The War Department in the course of the conflict arrested at least thirteen thousand people, most of whom never came to trial.

The chief northern political opponents of the conduct of the war were the Peace Democrats, or Copperheads, as supporters of the war called them. The most prominent among those was Clement Vallandigham of Ohio, who insisted that the war was strengthening the central government at the expense of civil liberties. Vallandigham called for "the Constitution as it is, the Union as it was." In 1862 he was defeated for reelection to Congress. He continued his attacks on the war and a military tribunal finally sentenced him to prison for its duration. The affair was an assault on the constitutional right of free speech. Protest was so widespread as to become a political danger to the administration. To deflect the issue, Lincoln by use of his executive power banished Vallandigham to the Confederacy. But the Ohioan returned to the North and kept up his criticisms. The administration now left him alone. Vallandigham tried to get the Supreme Court to consider his claim that the government had been acting unconstitutionally. The Court in 1864 ruled in *ex parte Vallandigham* that it had no jurisdiction over the proceedings of military tribunals. In 1866, however, the Supreme Court did find the methods of the war administration to have been unconstitutional. In *ex parte Milligan* the Court held that martial law and the subjection of civilians to military trials were illegal when the civil courts were open and in full operation.

Stalemate: The Early Campaigns, 1861–1862

The American Civil War, like other wars, was shaped as much by geography as by generals. The removal of the Confederate capital from Montgomery to Richmond, only one hundred miles from Washington, focused the fighting in the East in a narrow theater between and around the capitals. Here rival armies marched and countermarched for four years, as each side sought to protect its capital and threaten that of its rival. The dramatic battles fought here—such as at Chancellorsville and, just north of Maryland, at Gettysburg—constitute the classic war so celebrated in Civil War legend.

Robert E. Lee, native son of Virginia, brilliant military strategist, and leader of the Confederate forces. *(Courtesy, Library of Congress)*

Robert E. Lee wrote of the Confederate Congress:

"been up to see the Congress and they do not seem to be able to do anything except to eat peanuts and chew tobacco, while my army is starving."

Robert E. Lee, who led the Confederacy's northern Virginia troops and would become the South's most prominent general, had been no enthusiast for secession. Family tradition opposed it: his father, "Lighthorse Harry" Lee, had been a Revolutionary War hero, and his mother's family had also played an honorable role in the founding of the United States. His wife was the great granddaughter of Martha Washington, and Lee had grown up in Alexandria, Virginia, surrounded by mementos of George Washington, upon whom he modeled himself. Educated at West Point, Lee before the Civil War spent all his adult life in the United States Army, distinguishing himself in the Mexican War, serving as the superintendent of West Point, and achieving some eminence as an army engineer. When secession came, the Lincoln Administration sounded him out about taking command of the Union army. Lee saw no choice but to resign his commission rather than to face the prospect of leading troops against his native state. In the end he was a Virginian first. When after 1865 the Confederacy was no more, he could find it relatively easy to resume his loyalty to the Union and to urge other southerners to follow his lead.

While the two warring governments were preoccupied with the territory between their capitals, the decisive theater of the Civil War was in the West. Here nature had formed a series of southerly-flowing rivers—the Cumberland, the Tennessee, the Mississippi—that thrust into the heart of the Confederacy. Union strategists recognized early the value of these rivers for rapid movement of men and supplies, and acted to control them. It was here, and in Sherman's later invasion of the deep South from the West, that the North won and the South lost the Civil War.

In April 1861 both governments were unprepared for war. Guns and ammunition were in short supply. Few officers on either side had commanded large bodies of men. The hastily-formed volunteer regiments lacked even the rudiments of military training. Some such units wore gaudy, impractical uniforms and adopted flamboyant names.

These amateur armies had their first taste of war in July 1861. Pressured by a public demand to take Richmond at once, Union General Irvin McDowell led his ill-trained army into northern Virginia, followed by carriages full of Washingtonians out to see the show. At Bull Run (or Manassas Junction), the Union troops met an equally ill-prepared army under General P.G.T. Beauregard. For some time the two armies fought with a courage beyond their experience. After early reverses, Confederate troops rallied behind General Thomas Jackson—"Stonewall," as he would soon be known for a moment at Bull Run when he and his troops stood against an enemy attack "like a stone wall." Retreat became chaos as green troops struggled with panic-stricken civilians along the roads to Washington. McDowell's army simply fell apart; soldiers threw down their guns, canteens, and coats, and ran. "One Southerner is equal to five Yankees," pronounced a southern newspaper. But the Confederate soldiers, nearly as disorganized, did not pursue; Jackson boasted that with 5,000 men he could have finished the job.

Bull Run awakened the North to reality. Lincoln gave the command to General George B. McClellan, a cautious soldier but brilliant

PENNSYLVANIA

MD

MARYLAND

Antietam
Sept. 1862

LEE

McCLELLAN

SHENANDOAH VALLEY

LEE

2nd
Bull Run
Aug. 1862

1st.
Bull Run
July 1861

Washington
D.C.

Chesapeake Bay

Fredericksburg
Dec. 1862

Potomac River

VIRGINIA

LEE

McCLELLAN

Richmond

James River

Monitor
vs.
Merrimac
Mar. 1862

THE CIVIL WAR
IN VIRGINIA, 1861–1862
☆ Battles
→ Union movements
→ Confederate movements

organizer. As McClellan trained his troops in the East, critical events were taking place in the West. Union attention here focused on the rivers, where Confederate strong points barred an advance southward.

Western Campaigns   In February 1862 an army under General Ulysses S. Grant, supported by a fleet of iron-clad gunboats, pushed up the Tennessee River and captured Fort Henry. Union forces also besieged Fort Donelson on the Cumberland. Grant took this fort, too, firing the North's imagination with his demand for "immediate and unconditional surrender."

Confederate troops struck back hard at Grant's army in April at Shiloh, on the Tennessee River near the northern border of Mississippi. Catching Grant off guard, they nearly pushed his troops back into the river. All day long the battle raged. "From right to left, everywhere," an Illinois soldier wrote, "it was one never ending, terrible roar, with no prospect of stopping." Grant's second in command, General William Tecumseh Sherman, was wounded twice, once in his hand and once in his shoulder, and a ball of shot passed through his hat; he also had several horses shot from under him during the day. At nightfall Union reinforcements turned the battle. Shiloh cost nearly 23,000 casualties.

At Shiloh the Confederacy lost its supreme bid to regain western

A New York soldier stationed in Louisiana wrote of the insensitivity the carnage had wrought:

"What hardened wretches we have become. The word came, 'Eph. Hammond is dead, hurry up and make a box for him.' He was one of the best-liked men in the regiment. Yet not a tear was shed, and before his body was cold he was buried in the ground. We will talk about him more or less for a day or two and then forget all about him. That is what less than a year has done to us."

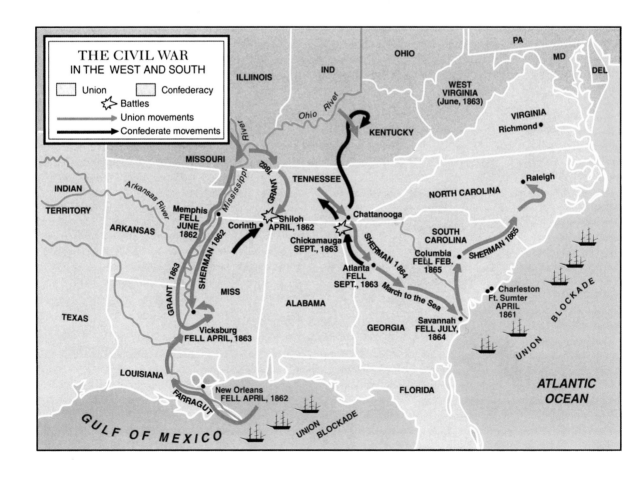

Tennessee. Other Union forces opened the upper Mississippi as far south as Memphis. That same April of 1862 the Confederacy suffered one of its greatest losses when Admiral David Farragut of Tennessee, one of the distinguished southerners who had remained with the Union, captured New Orleans, the South's biggest seaport. By midsummer the South's hold on the Mississippi was limited to a narrow stretch of river between Vicksburg, Mississippi, and Port Hudson, Louisiana.

Diplomacy and the Blockade   Late in 1861, the Union got for a moment into a dangerously confrontational situation with Britain. A federal ship stopped the British steamer *Trent* outside United States waters and seized two southern diplomats, James Mason, who was seeking to represent the Confederacy in Britain, and John Slidell, aiming to do the same in France. Anger flared in the British government and public. Lincoln quickly made amends of a sort by releasing the two. But the incident indicated the delicacy and the riskiness of relations between the United States and European countries as it patrolled the waters in pursuit of victory.

A particular point of risk was the blockade. While the North was pressing in on the Confederacy in the West, it was also pushing in from the sea. The blockade aimed at stopping foreign merchant ships and confiscating even nonmilitary goods that they were carrying to the Confederacy. Such seizures were questionable under international law, and France and Britain complained.

For a time the Union had to face the possibility that Great Britain or France, not displeased at a weakening of the United States and eager to resume full trade with the cotton South, might recognize the Confederacy as a separate nation. British recognition would give a tremendous lift to southern morale and injure that of the North, France might recognize the Confederacy in return for southern support of Napoleon III's plan to install a French puppet, Austrian Archduke Maximilian, on a specially created Mexican throne. But when federal troops in September 1862 stopped the rebel invasion at the Battle of Antietam (or Sharpsburg, as southerners called it), Great Britain decided to put off recognition of the Confederacy. The blockade remained safe from direct foreign interference.

The small Confederate navy was no match for the formidable Union fleet. For one day in 1862 in a battle off Hampton Roads, Virginia, however, the Confederate vessel *Merrimac* did much damage to Union naval forces. In a great technological innovation, the ship had been covered with iron plates, and against them northern naval guns had little effect. The next day the North set its own ironclad *Monitor* against the *Merrimac,* rendering it harmless. Later in the war northern commerce suffered from the raids of the Confederate ship *Alabama,* built in Britain by a private company. Charles Francis Adams, the United States minister to Britain, protested to the British government for its failure to stop the construction of the ship, and after the war the United States would win compensation from Britain for losses the ship had inflicted. The Union navy finally sank the *Alabama.*

Merrimac and ***Monitor.*** *(Courtesy, R. Burnes)*

The port of Norfolk, Virginia, a southerner confided to his diary on May 20,

"has been evacuated by the Confederate troops and the Merrimack has been destroyed. There ends for the present all hope of a southern navy. The loss of Norfolk involves that of the Navy yard at Portsmouth with its dry dock and ship building facilities. Yet, I believe, the destruction of the Merrimack produced a deeper mortification in the South than all the other losses that attended it. There had been among the people the most exaggerated expectations."

Confederate privateers could attack merchant ships, but were no threat to the northern navy. While the blockade could not keep the Confederacy from the sea trade, it was effective enough to deprive Confederate society of much that it needed to function smoothly.

Eastern Campaigns   In the East, General McClellan in 1862 drilled his Army of the Potomac for months, all the while ignoring the public clamor for action. (An exasperated Lincoln once said he would like to borrow McClellan's army if the general did not intend to use it.) Prodded by the President, McClellan finally proposed in the spring of 1862 a bold plan to take Richmond from the rear. Instead of fighting his way overland, he would make an amphibious landing on the James River Peninsula; from there he could march up the Peninsula and seize the Confederate capital. Lincoln approved, provided McClellan left enough men behind to protect Washington.

When McClellan embarked in March 1862, he did not leave behind the force intended for the defense of the capital. Lincoln thereupon recalled part of the Army of the Potomac. This nearly immobilized the cautious McClellan, who consistently overestimated Confederate strength: he in fact still had 90,000 men to the enemy's 70,000. The slowness of his progress up the Peninsula gave the Confederate troops, commanded by Lee, time to organize. In a series of battles known as the Seven Days, Lee hammered at McClellan's army and threw it back. In August McClellan began a slow withdrawal from the Peninsula. Command of the Army of the Potomac passed to General John Pope.

Sensing an opportunity to strike before the federal army could regroup, Lee took the offensive. On August 30 he smashed Pope's army at the second battle of Bull Run, then swung north into Maryland. But a copy of his battle plans fell into the hands of McClellan, whom Lincoln had hurriedly recalled to command. On September 17, McClellan engaged the invading Confederate troops at Antietam Creek. After the bloodiest single day's battle of the entire war—24,000 dead and wounded—Lee withdrew unpursued. Tactically the battle had been a draw, but measured against Confederate expectations it was a crushing defeat.

Although Lee had failed at Antietam, he was still unbeatable on his home ground. Twice during the winter of 1862–63, federal generals renewed the offensive against Richmond, each time with disastrous results. In December General Ambrose Burnside, a handsome West Pointer remembered for his legendary growth of side whiskers, and now in command in place of McClellan, was soundly defeated at Fredericksburg. At Chancellorsville in the spring of 1863, Lee and Jackson caught the army of Burnside's successor, General Joseph Hooker, straddling the Rappahannock River, and cut it to pieces. Lee paid a fearful price—"Stonewall" Jackson was mortally wounded, shot down by his own men in the confusion of battle as they waged hopeless frontal assaults against entrenched Union forces. After two years the northern drive on Richmond was back where it had started—on the Potomac.

The northern nurse Clara Barton evoked the sorrow and scope of battle:

"Antietam! With its eight miles of camping armies, face to face; 160,000 men to spring up at dawn like the old Scot from the heather! Its miles of artillery shaking the earth like a chain of Etnas! Its ten hours of uninterrupted battle! Its thunder and its fire! The sharp unflinching order—'Hold the Bridge, boys—always the Bridge.' At length, the quiet! The pale moonlight on its cooling guns! The weary men—the dying and the dead!"

War Fortunes Turn, 1863–1864

The victory at Antietam provided Lincoln with the political momentum he needed to move ahead with legally liberating the slaves in the rebellious states of the Confederacy. The President was looking to the election of 1864, and he was worried about his prospects. One group of Republicans, coming to be known as Radical Republicans, from whom Lincoln needed at least some support if he was to be renominated, was pushing hard for emancipation. He was also sincerely if cautiously committed to the principle of freeing the slaves. But if he liberated them in too bold a manner, he might lose valuable support in the slaveholding states still loyal to the Union. Lincoln would have to strike a fine balance.

Emancipation   At the beginning of the war the federal government was careful to insist that it was fighting only to preserve the Union and not to free the slaves. The war, said a resolution adopted by Congress, was not for "overthrowing or interfering with the rights or established institutions" of the seceded states. The government wanted to convince those proslavery southerners who were prepared to be sympathetic to the Unionist cause that the institution of slavery was not in danger. But it is reasonable to suppose that something beyond mere political strategy lay behind the caution of the President and Congress about interfering with slavery. Neither Lincoln nor most of the national legislators had been abolitionists. However distasteful slavery was to much of the government, the slave system was so firmly established, and so hedged with legal protections, that even opponents might have had doubts about the sudden military abolition of slavery. Politicians and statesmen, like the rest of humankind, are hesitant to imagine any workable society that is far different from whatever one they are accustomed to. It took time and the events of the war to make the government see the tangible possibility of wiping out slavery at a stroke.

General John C. Frémont jumped ahead of the government when he issued a military order freeing the slaves in Missouri. Lincoln modified Frémont's order, but he did ask Congress in 1862 to grant federal funds to any state adopting a scheme of emancipation. Congress did not respond, but in the Second Confiscation Act of 1862, authorizing the seizure of all rebel property, it declared that slaves who come into Union lines were to be free. It also empowered the President to recruit blacks into the army. The Act was both a substantial measure and a somewhat limited one. It did not apply to slaves held by southern Unionists. But the Second Confiscation Act signified that Union politicians were losing their timidity about abolishing slavery, and the very existence of the Act provided a certain momentum toward abolition. Abolitionists meanwhile were urging a wider policy of emancipation. Such a policy, moreover, could have desirable diplomatic effects. The apparent success of the South in maintaining its independence, and the advantage that European countries could gain from a division of the United States, raised the danger that they might recognize the Confederacy as a sovereign nation. That would greatly weaken the Union effort. Lincoln believed that if European nations could see the war as a struggle not merely between Union and secession but between freedom and slavery,

Northern soldiers. *(Courtesy, Library of Congrss)*

Confederates soldiers. *(Courtesy, Library of Congrss)*

they would be less likely to recognize the slave republic. And while Lincoln had not been an abolitionist, he had been a free soiler and a moral opponent of slavery. Surely his conscience welcomed the decision toward which political considerations were pushing him.

The Emancipation Proclamation The Confederate failure at Antietam gave Lincoln the opportunity to issue in September 1862 a preliminary Emancipation Proclamation, announcing that as of January 1, 1863, all slaves in those regions still in rebellion on that date would be free. Lincoln was offering to secessionists an alternative to loss of their slaves: if they voluntarily brought their communities back into the Union quickly enough, they might maintain the institution. The Emancipation Proclamation itself, issued on January 1, carried out the terms of the preliminary proclamation: it declared that all slaves in areas still in rebellion were "then, thenceforward, and forever free." Lincoln was drawing on the power he possessed as Commander-in-Chief; the Proclamation was essentially a military order, on somewhat the same principle as the instructions an officer might give his troops for the treatment of citizens and property. The Emancipation Proclamation, like the Second Confiscation Act, was of sharply limited scope; it freed no slaves immediately because it did not apply to the border states or to regions already under Union control. But it was understood at the time, as it has been understood ever since, as the great symbolic moral action of the war, a public statement that the war was now being fought for freedom. After the preliminary Proclamation the military had begun seriously taking in black volunteers.

Congress contained a variety of opinions on racial matters. At one extreme were several Democrats reluctant to make changes in existing institutions. At the other extreme, as the war progressed, was a small but important group of Republicans who wanted the strongest possible policy of abolition and protection of the rights of the freed slaves. Within this faction ideas emerged for going beyond emancipation and bringing about changes in the social and economic condition of black Americans. Congress in the course of the war repealed a law prohibiting blacks from carrying the mail and a ban on testimony of black witnesses in federal court. It outlawed slavery in the territories, and established a scheme for emancipation in the District of Columbia that would provide compensation to the slaveholders. Blacks were allowed in places from which they had once been excluded: the congressional visitor's gallery, lectures at the Smithsonian Institution. Some states got rid of a number of discriminating laws. The country was taking some halting steps beyond emancipation and toward equality or at least a concept of justice. When Congress passed and in 1865 the necessary number of states approved the Thirteenth Amendment outlawing slavery, the nation was confirming the policy to which events had been leading it.

Vicksburg and Gettysburg In the summer of 1863, Ulysses S. Grant won one of two battles that put the North on the way to final victory. For months his troops had besieged Vicksburg, the last Confederate stronghold on the Mississippi River. Situated high on a bluff above the river, with bayous

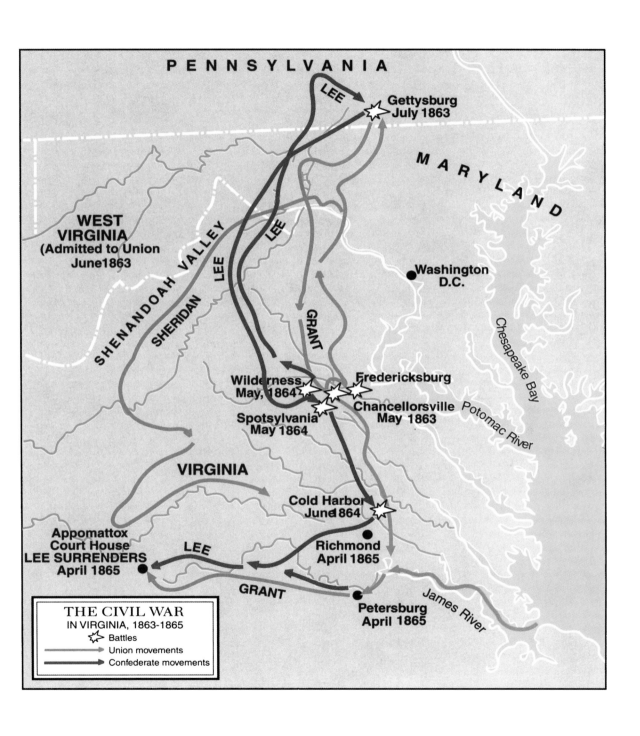

PENNSYLVANIA

LEE

Gettysburg
July 1863

MARYLAND

WEST
VIRGINIA
(Admitted to Union
June1863

SHENANDOAH VALLEY

SHERIDAN

LEE

LEE

GRANT

Washington
D.C.

Chesapeake Bay

Wilderness
May, 1864

Fredericksburg

Chancellorsville
May 1863

Spotsylvania
May 1864

Potomac River

VIRGINIA

Cold Harbor
June 1864

Appomattox
Court House
LEE SURRENDERS
April 1865

LEE

Richmond
April 1865

GRANT

Petersburg
April 1865

James River

THE CIVIL WAR
IN VIRGINIA, 1863-1865
☆ Battles
→ Union movements
→ Confederate movements

A Civil War Gallery

Confederate prisoner James Washington and union officer George A. Custer. They had been West Point classmates. *(Courtesy, Library of Congress)*

Union soldiers at Manasses, Virginia, July 1862. *(Courtesy, Library of Congress)*

Union nurses in the Civil War. *(Courtesy, Library of Congress)*

A Civil War volunteer soldier. *(Courtesy, Library of Congress)*

Black cooks during the Civil War. *(Courtesy, Library of Congress)*

A cockfight in a southern camp, 1864. *(Courtesy, Library of Congress)*

Overturned Confederate train. Similar problems plagued Confederate transportation. *(Courtesy, Library of Congress)*

Dead soldiers after a battle. *(Courtesy, Library of Congress)*

Armory Square Hospital (Union). *(Courtesy, Library of Congress)*

Union quartermasters camp. 1st Division, 9th Army Corps. *(Courtesy, Library of Congress)*

A public hanging for treason in Washington, D.C. *(Courtesy, Library of Congress)*

Libby Prison, Richmond, Virginia. *(Courtesy, Museum of Fine Arts, Boston)*

Trenches at Fredericksburg, Virginia. *(Courtesy, Library of Congress)*

Confederate camp, Warrington Navy Yard, Pensacola, Florida, 1861. *(Courtesy, Library of Congress)*

Lee surrenders to Grant at Appomattox Court House in Virginia. *(Courtesy, Library of Congress)*

Drawing by J. A. Arthur of Washington welcoming Lincoln to Heaven with a crown of laurels, 1865.
(Courtesy, Library of Congress)

General Grant's victories come at a great expense in lives.

"He is a butcher and is not fit to be at the head of army, 'declared Mary Lincoln.' He loses two men to the enemy's one. . . . He would depopulate the North." "But he has been very successful in the Field," quietly observed the President.

"Where the line stood the ground was covered in blue," a Georgia soldier recalled, speaking of the corpses of Union soldiers at Gettysburg. "I could have walked on them without putting my feet on the ground."

General Ulysses S. Grant.
(Courtesy, Library of Congrss)

on both flanks, the city seemed impregnable. After repeated failures to dislodge the Confederate defenders, Grant hit on a bold plan. Abandoning his supply base, he slipped around the city on the Louisiana side, marched downstream, and crossed below Vicksburg. With dazzling speed, he moved inland to Jackson, cutting Vicksburg's rail link with the Confederacy, then turned west to lock up the city from the land side. Cut off, Vicksburg surrendered on July 4, 1863. Grant had reopened the Mississippi and split the Confederacy in two, leaving the trans-Mississippi region isolated.

In the East, just a day before Grant's victory at Vicksburg, the Union army at Gettysburg had won what was to become the most famous battle of the war. Gettysburg was the devastating outcome of a daring Confederate attempt begun in June, when Lee marched his army north again in search of a decisive victory.

The South needed one. It was in trouble in the West, and the Union blockade was withering the southern economy.

In the first stage of the campaign that was to end at Gettysburg, Lee's army moved quickly out of the Blue Ridge Mountains into Maryland. Hooker followed, keeping to the east in order to protect Washington. As Lee drove into Pennsylvania, Lincoln replaced the timid Hooker with George G. Meade. Respectful of General Meade's abilities, Lee concentrated his forces at Gettysburg. Rushing forward, Meade collided with him at that Pennsylvania town, and on July 1, 2, and 3 they fought the greatest single battle of the war.

Lee struck first, before Meade could concentrate his army, and on July 1 nearly drove the federal army from the field. During the night Union troops arrived in strength and dug in. On the next two days Lee attacked at both flanks and the center of the Union line in a total effort to crush the Army of the Potomac. But nothing quite worked. The climax came on July 3 when 15,000 Confederate troops under General George Pickett made a gallant frontal assault on the Union center on—appropriately—Cemetery Ridge. On Pickett's men came, "an ocean of armed men . . . magnificent, grim, irresistible," as Union gunners fired triple loads of iron shot into their ranks. A few Confederate soldiers reached

The blood-soaked battlefield at Gettysburg after the fighting of July 1, 1863. *(Courtesy, Scribner's Archives)*

the Ridge; then suddenly Union reinforcements poured into the breach. The surviving Confederate troops retreated, leaving many of their number dead. The battle was over. On July 4, while a rainstorm washed the blood from the grass, the Confederate army withdrew. Meade, as paralyzed as his predecessors, did not pursue. Lee had lost 20,000 men—a third of his army. The Confederacy's offensive power was broken forever.

Life in the Confederacy

During the rush of enthusiasm following Sumter many southerners rejoiced at the prospect of glory and independence. "I feel as tho' I could live poetry," exclaimed Mrs. Catherine Edmonston, mistress of a North Carolina plantation. But within the South's white population some wondered whether their section had not made a colossal mistake.

Even slaveholders had their doubts. One Mississippi planter anticipated the defeat of the Confederacy and feared a time "when the northern soldier would tread her cotton fields, when the slave should be made *free* and the proud southerner stricken to the dust in his presence." And in the mountain backbone that split the older from the newer South, Unionist sentiment smoldered. There slaveholding was not extensive. Virginia's western counties would carry their dissent so far as to secede from Secessia and form the state of West Virginia. In eastern Tennessee, western North Carolina, and Kentucky—that state never seceded anyway—thousands of young men joined the Union army. In region upon region where small farmers tilled their acres with the sole help of their families or a few hired hands, the Union found some degree of favor. In places like northern Louisiana, Alabama, and Mississippi, however, Unionist sentiment was more difficult to act on than in the mountains.

Economic Problems After the early months of enthusiam passed, life in the Confederacy was difficult for everybody. The southern economy was not suited for swift adaptation to war production. The rail network could not efficiently transport troops and supplies. Most southern railroads were short lines. The rail system consisted of eleven different gauges, which meant that a railroad car fitted for one gauge would have to confine itself to some portion of the tracks. Nor was there enough railway equipment. The South in 1861 did only a fifth of the whole nation's manufacturing, and it lacked the knowledge and technology necessary for quick growth. By the award of generous contracts, the Confederate and state governments gave their encouragement to industries such as textiles and iron, and by the end of the war Atlanta had become a considerable industrial center. But some manufacturers had to be satisfied with makeshifts, such as lard in place of grease and cloths soaked in linseed oil as a substitute for machine belts. The Confederacy had to import much of its arms and civilian goods, slipping a large portion of them through the Union blockade. To support itself the Confederate government turned to "tithing in kind," collecting from farmers one-tenth of their produce in certain crops, and

A southerner's diary entries, for 1861 and 1865, tell the course of war:

Saturday, July 13, 1861. Events transcending in importance anything that has ever happened within the recollection of any living person in *our* country, have occurred since I have written last in my Journal. Since then *War* has been declared. Our ministers sent North to negotiate terms of peace have been treated with cool indifference. Our forts are still retained with the exception of Sumter. *There* the ever memorable victory was achieved which added fresh laurels to the glory of the gallant little state of South Carolina. Never shall I forget the state of intense excitement which pervaded the city of Augusta when it was announced that the fight was going on down at Sumter. Pa went down to Charleston just in time to witness from the top of the Charleston Hotel, the whole proceeding of the bombardment. It is needless to account the gallant achievement of Wigfall and others or to note the additional honour acquired by Gen Beauregard. . . .

Wednesday, March 29, 1865. I know I will regret hereafter that I have made no record of time and events which are fraught with so much interest, record of events which are hourly making history—but I cannot. I shrink from the task. At times I feel as if I was drifting on, on, ever onward to be at last dashed against some rock and I shut my eyes and almost wish it was over, the shock encountered and I prepared to know what destiny awaits me. I am tired, oh so tired of this war. I want to breathe free. I feel the restraint of the blockade and as port after port becomes blockaded, I feel shut up, pent up and am irresistibly reminded of the old story of the iron shroud contracting more and more each hour, each moment. I live too fast. A strange contradiction, yet true. A life of emotion, quick rapid succession of startling events will wear upon the constitution and weaken the physical nature. I may perhaps be glad hereafter that I have lived through this war but now the height of my ambition is to be *quiet.* . . .

One southern woman, Margaret Preston, wrote in her diary:

April 3d, 1862: . . .

"Darkness seems gathering over the southern land; disaster follows disaster; where is it all to end? My very soul is sick of carnage. I loathe the word —*War*. It is destroying and paralyzing all before it. Our schools are closed—all the able-bodied men gone—stores shut up, or only here and there one open; goods not to be bought, or so exorbitant that we are obliged to do without.

Sept. 4th: The worst has happened—our fearful suspense is over: Willy, the gentle, tender-hearted, brave boy, lies in a soldier's grave on the Plains of Manassas! This has been a day of weeping and of woe to this household. I did not know how I loved the dear boy. My heart is wrung with grief to think that his sweet face, his genial smile, his sympathetic heart are gone. My eyes ache with weeping. . . . Oh! his precious stricken Father! God support him to bear the blow! . . . Alas! the beloved son has been five days in his grave. My poor husband! Oh! if he were only here, to groan out his anguish on my bosom. I can't write more."

printed great amounts of paper money that worsened inflation. Shortages, invasion, and a sense of defeat were the lot of the rebel population as the war dragged on.

The price of flour in Richmond more than doubled in the first year of the war. Soap, made from scarce animal fat, went up a thousand percent in price. Imported coffee, selling for twelve cents a pound before the war, went to five dollars by 1863. In late December of that year, apples went in Richmond for $65 or $75 a barrel in Confederate money, while onions were $30 a barrel, Irish potatoes, $6 to $9 a bushel, sugar, $3.50 a pound, and eggs, $3 a dozen. Worst of all to one young soldier stationed at the Confederate capital was the price of whiskey. "It would cost about fifty Dollars to get tight here," he wrote his family in 1863.

At times essential commodities were unavailable at any price. Shortages were more common in the cities, swollen with war refugees and soldiers, than in the countryside. In the spring of 1863, three hundred Richmond women, some brandishing revolvers and others bowie knives, attacked the city's business district demanding affordable food. The riot soon got out of hand and the women looted the jewelry and clothing stores before they were stopped. And even in the country districts food and clothing shortages provoked direct action. In 1863 fourteen women armed with "guns, pistols, knives, and tongues" attacked a mill near Thomasville, Georgia, and seized a large supply of flour.

Changes in the South

War transformed the lives of southern white women. Many were fiery Confederate patriots. It has been said that southern belles, by favoring army volunteers and shunning young men who avoided the war, were the most effective recruiters for the Confederate army. Southern women of the middle and upper classes had always managed large households. As the war progressed, their administrative skills were put to running the plantations and businesses their husbands had left behind. Wives of ordinary farmers, too, took over managerial duties. The Confederate Treasury hired hundreds of women clerks. Some women found jobs in the South's factories or worked in Confederate hospitals. The visible presence of these women in the public sphere faded after the war.

States' rights, the doctrine upon which the Confederacy had been founded, was no help in wartime. Several governors, notably Joseph E. Brown of Georgia and Zebulon Vance of North Carolina, showed a narrow jealousy of every exercise of Confederate power. They developed revenue programs of their own and obstructed Confederate tax collections in their states. They retained control of state troops and even prevented them from leaving the state. In Georgia, men who wished to escape Confederate service could do so by enlisting in the state militia. Governor Vance hoarded food and supplies for North Carolina troops that Lee's starving army at Richmond desperately needed.

Ultimately the Confederate government resorted to measures of centralization that amounted to a revolution within a revolution. Davis declared martial law in "disloyal" areas. The Confederate Congress authorized the first thorough military draft on the North American

Slaves planting sweet potatoes on James Hopkinson's plantation, Edisto Island, South Carolina, 1862. Though there were no major uprisings, the old slave system began to disintegrate by late 1863 as blacks refused to work for their old masters or simply left the plantations. *(Courtesy, The New-York Historical Society)*

continent. Richmond took an increasingly active role in the southern economy, impressing food supplies from farmers, building factories to produce critical war materials, commandeering space on blockade runners for essential imports. In 1865 the Confederate government reached the ultimate measure of centralization when it authorized the military to take black men into the army.

For many years after the Civil War southerners with a nostalgic affection for the Confederacy would speak of how loyal slaves had been to their southern masters. When southern white men were off fighting Yankees and blacks had a chance to revolt, they remained at their jobs, providing the Confederacy with its food and manufactured goods. This romantic image of contented and loyal slaves is only partly accurate. The experience of the Pryor family of Georgia furnishes an example. In 1861 Shepard G. Pryor went off to fight, leaving his wife in charge of his farm and his thirteen slaves. Mrs. Pryor chose as her overseer a white man who had no control over the slaves. Eventually she made a crucial decision to appoint one of her slaves, Will, as overseer. The choice was fateful for the Pryors' corner of the slave system. For a while Will performed as his mistress wished, and he successfully managed the 1862 crop harvest. But soon Will was hiding slave runaways and in general refusing to cooperate with the slave system. The authorities finally arrested him for sheltering slave fugitives. By late 1863 the slave system was disintegrating in many parts of the South. Nowhere was there a major slave uprising, but black people were helping to pull the system apart in other ways. Whenever rumors spread of Yankee troops nearby the slaves of the neighborhood would desert the plantations in droves. Many of those who remained became disobedient and refused to work. One elderly slave was overjoyed when freedom came. She "dropped her hoe" and shouted at her mistress: "I'm free! Ain't got to work for you no more! You can't [sell me] now!"

Life in the Union

Initially the northern economy faltered as businessmen, fearful of disruption and disorder, sought to call in debts. In many northern cities, especially New York, Chicago, and Cincinnati, the loss of southern customers disrupted the economy. Some economic historians claim that on the whole the Civil War slowed economic growth. Yet the newspapers of the day suggest that, after the middle of 1862, the Union experienced an economic boom. The draining of men into the military left shortages of labor. On some farms women filled in. The North, however, had more machines than the South that could replace manpower; from 1860 to 1865 the McCormick Reaper Company received more orders for its harvesting machines than it could fill. The continuing influx of immigrants, almost half a million during the war years, relieved labor shortages in the cities. The demand for war supplies invigorated the northern economy, already fitted for manufacturing. Factories hummed and wages rose. Farmers benefited from the increase in demand for food. The effect of the war on the economy of the North was quite the opposite from the effect in the South, where invasion unsettled the normal pattern of production and trade and the blockade broke commerce with Europe.

Still, the Union had an inflation rate only slightly less staggering than that of the Confederacy. One reason for that was the policy of financing the war by a combination of heavy borrowing and paper money. Another was the scarcity of labor that machines and immigrants only partially offset. And the wartime prosperity bestowed itself unevenly. While consumer prices had risen by 1865 between seventy-five and a hundred percent, the wages of skilled workers went up during the same period about sixty percent, and those of common laborers rose just under fifty percent. Meanwhile the business and professional classes crowded Broadway in New York, Michigan Avenue in Chicago and Pennsylvania Avenue in Cincinnati, buying at the fashionable shops, attending the theaters, and dining at the fancy restaurants. Some of these people were profiteers who had made a good thing out of the swelling orders from the War and Navy Departments and the flow of greenback currency. Charging the government high prices for desperately needed supplies, some profiteers also provided uniforms and shoes that disintegrated at the first heavy rain, powder that would not explode, and beef, pork, and flour that were inedible.

Army Life

The Civil War sorely tested the American traditions of individualism and provincialism. In the beginning men on both sides enlisted in local regiments raised by the state governors. Each regiment wore its own uniform and many elected their own officers, a practice that discouraged strict discipline. Gradually all this changed. The Union and Confederate governments took over many duties of recruitment and the appointment of officers. Standardized uniforms were introduced. Drill and discipline tightened. The sons of a rawboned democracy slowly adjusted to become cogs in a larger machine. At the same time they accustomed themselves to a world beyond their own communities. Their care and feeding became increasingly the responsibility of central governments or national organizations like the United States Sanitary Commission.

Along with the Union victory, the experience of army life must have contributed to the nationalist element in American civilization that has struggled to maintain itself against the pull of loyalty to region, state, or locality.

At the same time that the armies were taking American farmboys and town dwellers away from their familiar surroundings, they were pulling in thousands of immigrants. The Union army especially spoke with many tongues, and in that sense represented what American cities were and would increasingly become in the years after the victory of the Union.

In the Field   Of about two million federal troops, 360,000 died. Among the more than one million who at some time served in the Confederate military, some 250,000 never came back. Only one in three of these died of battle wounds; the others succumbed to disease or accident. There were also about a half million wounded, many of them severely maimed.

During the Civil War, infantry weapons became highly destructive while infantry tactics continued to follow older concepts. Many soldiers carried rifles rather than smooth-bore muskets. These hurled a bullet for hundreds of yards with deadly accuracy. Yet until the very end of the war commanders on both sides frequently ordered their men to charge the enemy across open fields as if only the older, less accurate musket opposed them. Toward the end of the war attackers had to face the fast-firing breech-loaders with which more and more soldiers were being equipped.

If a man was wounded his chance for survival was precarious. Little was known about infections, and military surgeons performed operations without sanitary precautions. Soldiers contracted gangrene and other deadly infections. Though anesthetics were known, doctors did not always have them on hand, and shock, followed by death, was often the consequence of major surgery. Long delays occurred in getting the casualties to medical aid stations or hospitals.

Pests such as mosquitoes, lice, and biting flies infested the battlefront, spreading diseases that included malaria and yellow fever. Heat in the deep South and cold, particularly in the mountain areas and the upper South, afflicted the soldiers. Wool uniforms were standard year-round issue and soldiers of both armies simply shed as much as they could during the summer. Northern troops were often overdressed; rebels were often half naked. As the Union blockade took hold and internal transport broke down, Confederate soldiers found it difficult to get replacements for worn or torn uniforms. Many ended up wearing homemade garments sent by relatives and friends. Others relied on captured Yankee shoes and other clothes. Especially serious was the shortage of boots and shoes. In the last winter of the war many of the troops accompanying General J. B. Hood on his campaign through Tennessee marched barefoot through snow and sleet. The path of Hood's army, it was said, was marked by a trail of blood.

Few Union soldiers went hungry, but the diet of salt pork, bread, and coffee undermined health. The Confederate soldier's standard diet consisted of bacon, cornmeal, and coffee—when he could get them.

One experience of northern troops was firsthand observation of slaves whom they had known only through newspaper accounts and antislavery literature. One northerner wrote in his diary:

"Some of them were scarred from head to foot where they had been whipped. One man's back was nearly all one scar, as if the skin had been chopped up and left to heal in ridges. Another had scars on the back of his neck, and from that all the way to his heels every little ways; but that was not such a sight as the one with the great solid mass of ridges, from his shoulders to his hips. That beat all the antislavery sermons ever yet preached."

Following the battle of Seven Pines in mid-1862, wounded federal soldiers were carried to the rear for shipment to the hospitals around Washington. The trains were slow to arrive, a sensitive observer noted, and the men sometimes

"lay by the hundreds on either side of the railway track . . . exposed to the drenching rain . . . shivering from the cold, calling for water, food, and dressings . . . the most heart-rending spectacle. Many died from exposure, others prayed for death to release them from their anguish."

Soldiers soon lost their sense of the romance of war. A North Carolina volunteer wrote home in 1862:

"The dirt of a camp life knocks all its poetry into a cocked hat. . . . We had no tents after the 6th of August, but slept on the ground, in the woods or open fields, without regard to the weather. . . . I learned to eat fat bacon raw, and to like it. . . . Without time to wash our clothes or our persons, and sleeping on the ground all huddled together, the whole army became lousy more or less with body lice."

Coffee, an imported item that had to get through the Union blockade, went quickly; the bacon lasted longer, but it, too, was often in short supply and southern troops occasionally supplemented their meat rations with cuts of mule, horse, raccoon, and bear. Sometimes Confederate troops were reduced to consuming little more than parched corn. Chewing the grains, reported one southern soldier, was "hard work"; it made "the jaws ache and the gums so sore as to cause unendurable pain."

War Mobilization

During the Civil War, as during the Revolution, both sides required the mobilization of society as a whole in the service of the war effort. But the Civil War reflected social and economic changes that would also influence the nature of the civilian contribution. The nursing of soldiers acquired a far more organized and professional character. Under the auspices of the United States Sanitary Commission, Dorothea Dix organized nursing services for the Union side. In the early months of the war, Ladies Aid Societies sprang up throughout the North to provide volunteer services for soldiers, including sewing, assembling food, clothing, and supplies, and providing communication between soldiers and their families. These societies eventually joined in a unified national institution. In the South, comparable societies remained local, volunteer efforts. Southern women nursed the wounded soldiers of the Confederacy in what were frequently makeshift hospitals.

At the beginning of the war, both the North and the South had relied on volunteers and militia. In time, both sides resorted to a draft, the Union conscription law permitted a draftee to find a substitute. He could also make a payment in place of service; that feature drew charges that the law favored the wealthy. In neither North nor South was conscription popular. In 1863 an antidraft riot broke out among the Irish in New York City. Before federal troops could restore order, the rioters lynched several blacks and burned a black orphanage. But the Union military continued to attract volunteers. The large bounty the Union offered was an inducement, as was the lurking presence of the draft. Patriotism and in some cases hostiltiy to slavery also drew volunteers.

While it was not until the South was badly in need of additional troops at almost the end of the war that the Confederacy contemplated the recruitment of blacks, the Union was accepting them as early as 1862. Earlier Lincoln's government had held back, fearing that the presence of black soldiers would seem to indicate that the war was not only for restoration of the Union but for the abolition of slavery. The acceptance of black volunteers, from both the North and the South, came at the urging of black leaders and white abolitionists, and by the end of the war, blacks composed about a tenth of the federal army and a fourth of the navy. For most of the war, black privates got three dollars a month less than whites. Some were relegated to labor units. Some Confederate commanders declared a policy of putting black prisoners into slavery. Confederate General Bedford Forrest promised to kill any blacks in uniform. But in combat the black soldiers won the respect of their officers and helped to discredit further the remnants of the slave system.

In time, as blacks themselves went to war, attitudes in New York City changed, or so one account indicates:

"Eight months ago the African race in this City were literally hunted down like wild beasts. They were shot down in cold blood, or stoned to death, or hung to the trees or to the lamp-posts. . . . How astonishingly has all this been changed! The same men now march in solid platoons, with shouldered muskets, slung knapsacks, and buckled cartridge boxes down through the gayest avenues and busiest thoroughfares to the pealing strains of martial music, and everywhere are saluted with waving handkerchiefs, with descending flowers, and with the acclamations and plaudits of countless beholders."

One officer wrote of his black comrades:

"No officer in this regiment now doubts that the key to the successful prosecution of this war lies in the unlimited employment of black troops. Their superiority lies in that they have peculiarities of temperament, position, and motive which belong to them alone. Instead of leaving their homes and families to fight they are fighting for their homes and families. . . ."

The End Stage, 1864–1865

Generals Grant and Sheridan

In 1864 the Union organized for final victory. Lincoln called Grant to Washington and put him in overall command of federal armies. Grant outlined a coordinated Union campaign. In the East he would lead an army against Lee. From the West, which the victory at Vicksburg had placed firmly under northern control, Grant's trusted subordinate Sherman would press into Georgia.

In May Grant pushed south. In a region of Virginia known as the Wilderness, his army, larger than Lee's, drove relentlessly forward. Repeatedly Lee checked Grant's advance, but the northern troops did not retreat. After each battle Grant went around the Confederate right flank and continued south, never giving Lee the initiative. The brilliant Virginian had no chance to organize a counterstroke of the kind that had disrupted previous federal offensives. By the end of June the Confederate troops were bottled up around Richmond. There followed months of siege warfare suggestive of World War I, as Grant gradually squeezed Lee's troops.

In September and October of the same year, the Union won an important victory when forces under General Philip Sheridan of the cavalry drove the rebels out of Virginia's Shenandoah Valley. That combat produced one of the best remembered incidents of the war. On October 19, Confederate soldiers commanded by Jubal Early sent the federal troops into a confused retreat from Cedar Creek. Sheridan, away at the time, rode on horseback to rejoin his men and by skill and force of personality turned them to a counter attack. The rebels, victorious earlier in the day, were crushed, and the Shenandoah Valley belonged to the Union.

To the south of both Sheridan and Grant, further disaster was befalling the Confederacy. Sherman was hacking his way through the lower South, slashing to bits much of what remained of the rebel heartland.

Making possible Sherman's march had been hard fighting nearly a year earlier in eastern Tennessee, a region containing much Unionist sentiment. On September 19, 1863, at Chickamauga Creek, the intervention of the Virginia Unionist General George H. Thomas—henceforth known as the Rock of Chickamauga—kept a federal defeat from turning into a rout. But afterward, Union troops in east Tennessee, now under the command of Grant, had better fortunes, and in late November they won a major victory at Chattanooga, crowned by a heroic and successful assault up the steep slope of nearby Missionary Ridge. Thenceforth, eastern Tennessee was available to federal forces as a launching point for an invasion of the deeper South. It was after this triumph that Grant received command of all federal armies and initiated his campaign in Virginia. Simultaneously with that Virginia offensive, Sherman began an advance from Tennessee into Georgia. Joseph E. Johnston conducted a skillful retreat, and the invaders did not reach Atlanta until September. At this point Sherman changed the rules. Leaving sufficient troops behind to deal with Johnston, he marched off across Georgia, allowing his men to burn and loot as they went. Sher-

General William Tecumseh Sherman, second to Ulysses S. Grant among northern generals, marched through Georgia in 1864. His army, burning and looting, left a wide path of destruction in its wake. (*Courtesy, Library of Congress*)

A Union soldier describes Sherman's march through Georgia:

"You can form no idea of the amount of property destroyed by us on this raid. All the Roads in the state are torn up and the whole tract or country over which we passed is little better than a wilderness. I can't for the life of me think what the people that are left there are to live on. We have all their Cattle, Horses, Mules, Sheep, Hogs, Sweet Potatoes, and Molasses and nearly everything else. We burnt all the Cotton we met which was millions of pounds. Our teams with all their hard driving are better today by about 200 percent than they were when we started because we have more than 2/3 new mules, besides all the old ones we could bring with us. Those that couldn't travel we killed and the road is lined with those that died. A tornado 60 miles in width from Chattanooga to this place 290 miles could not have done half the damage we did."

—W.F. Saylor

man's army reached Savannah in December, leaving a fifty-mile-wide path of destruction in its wake. From there, Sherman slashed northward through the Carolinas, while Johnston tailed him, powerless to intervene.

The Election of 1864   To wage the war successfully, Lincoln needed as much popular support as he could get. In his 1864 reelection campaign he ran not as a Republican but as the candidate of a coalition of Republicans and Democratic supporters of the war, which called itself the Union Party. The vice-presidential candidate of the party was Andrew Johnson, a Tennessee Democrat who had remained loyal to the Union. The presidential candidate of the regular Democratic Party was General McClellan, who had been commander of the Union armies. McClellan was loyal to the war effort, and in effect he rejected the claim by some northern Democrats that the war was a failure. By the time of the campaign and election the war had been going so successfully for the North that Lincoln's victory was assured.

While winning the war was the most important objective for the Republicans, they were committed also to an entire political, social, and economic policy within which the emancipation of the slaves and the preservation of the Union were elements. Before the Civil War much of the antislavery movement had also wanted a more vigorous national government working for the achievement of an advanced industrial and agricultural economy. Some Americans had possessed a vision of what a powerful American economy and society might be: an industrialized Northeast trading its manufactured goods for the produce of a great agricultural West. The federal government, these people believed, should stimulate eastern manufactures through a protective tariff, populate the agrarian West by giving government lands to settlers, and tie together the two regions by a railroad system built with federal aid. Northern politicians who thought this way could wish to exclude slavery from the territories not only because they genuinely disliked slavery on moral grounds, but also because they desired that the western lands be reserved for free American farmers. And in the years before the Civil War they had clashed with the South on other political issues: the southern cotton interest opposed a protective tariff, wanting instead to bring manufactured goods more cheaply from Europe, and resisted the construction of a northern railroad from East to West, holding out for a southern route. It is fitting that political circumstances put the Republicans in command of the war to save the the Union; for the Union came to mean strong central government presiding over a vast and economically progressive nation, while secession would have broken the country into weaker republics. It is fitting also that the Republicans became the champions of federally enforced emancipation.

For decades after the Civil War, the Republicans would continue to be the party favoring a cooperative society and economy, centrally planned and nourished by the federal government. Not until the twentieth century, and especially the coming of the New Deal, did the Democratic Party assume that role, while the Republicans became the party favoring a shrinkage in government.

Appomattox   The Confederacy's end came swiftly in the spring of
Court House   1865. The Union blockade had a stranglehold on the
southern economy, while the Union occupation of
large sections of the South badly disrupted agricultural production.
Confederate troops were suffering for lack of food and clothing, and
desertion rates skyrocketed. Between January and March 1865, General
William Sherman's army moved through South and North Carolina,
laying waste to farms, plantations, towns, and cities along the way.
Farther to the north, in Virginia, the army of Ulysses S. Grant met the
army of Robert E. Lee for a final confrontation. Late in March, Lee
made a desperate attempt to break through the siege Grant had imposed, but the southern forces had neither the manpower nor the
resources to succeed. On April 2, Lee abandoned Petersburg and
Richmond and scrambled toward the south, hoping to get his troops into
North Carolina.

It was not to be. Within a week Lee's army, now down to only
30,000 men, was surrounded by the armies of Grant and William T.
Sherman. Grant caught up with Lee near Appomattox Court House. On
April 9, 1865, Lee surrendered his proud but exhausted Army of
Northern Virginia. General Joseph Johnston surrendered to General
Sherman a few days later. Some rebel troops in the West held out a little
longer. But the Civil War was over.

Civil War drum, Ninth Regiment,
Vermont Volunteers, U.S. infantry,
made about 1860. *(Index of
American Design)*

Suggested Readings

On the Civil War era see Philip Paludan, *"A People's Con-
test": The Union and the Civil War* (1988), Frederick Blue,
Salmon P. Chase (1987), Gerard Linderman, *Embattled
Courage: The Experience of Combat in the American Civil
War* (1987), John M. Priest, *Antietam* (1989), and Drew
Gilpin Faust, *The Creation of Confederate Nationalism*
(1988). See also Eugene Genovese's perceptive study, *The
Slaveholders' Dilemma: Freedom and Progress in Southern
Conservative Thought, 1820–1860* (1992).

A standard work is James G. Randall and David Donald,
The Civil War and Reconstruction (revised 1973). James
McPherson presents an excellent guide to the period in
Ordeal by Fire: The Civil War and Reconstruction (1982);
all of Bruce Catton's books make beautiful reading. See also
Frank Vandiver, *Blood Brothers: A Short History of the Civil
War* (1990). Emory L. Thomas analyzes *The Confederate
Nation* (1979), and studies its greatest military leader in
Robert E. Lee: A Biography (1995).

For biographies of Union and Confederate leaders see
David Donald's *Lincoln* (1995) and William C. Davis's *Jef-
ferson Davis: The Man and His Hour* (1991). See also
Stephen B. Oates, *With Malice Toward None* (1978) and
Clement Eaton's *Jefferson Davis* (1977). Two major books
on the response of intellectuals to the war are George
Fredrickson, *The Inner Civil War: Northern Intellectuals
and the Crisis of the Union* (1965) and Daniel Aaron, *The
Unwritten War: American Writers and the Civil War* (1973).

Other studies include Richard E. Beringer and others, *The
Elements of Confederate Defeat: Nationalism, War Aims,
and Religion* (1989), James M. McPherson, *What They
Fought For, 1861–1865* (1994) and two older works, *Abra-
ham Lincoln and the Second American Revolution* (1990)
and *Battle Cry of Freedom* (1988). See also Paul D. Scott,
*After Secession: Jefferson Davis and the Failure of Confed-
erate Nationalism* (1978), Herman Hathaway and Archer
Jones, *How the North Won: A Military History of the Civil
War* (1983), Burke Davis, *Sherman's March* (1980), James
L. Roark, *Masters Without Slaves: Southern Planters in the
Civil War and Reconstruction* (1977), Adrian Cook, *The
Armies of the Streets: The New York City Draft Riots of 1863*
(1974), and Harold M. Hyman, *A More Perfect Union: The
Impact of the Civil War and Reconstruction on the Consti-
tution* (1973).

Military tactics are treated in *Lincoln and His Generals* by
T. Harry Williams, Reid Mitchell, *Civil War Soldiers* (1988),
Joseph T. Glatthaar, *The March to the Sea and Beyond:
Sherman's Troops in the Savannah and Carolinas Campaign*
(1985), Grady McWhiney and Perry D. Jamieson, *Attack
and Die: Civil War Military Tactics and the Southern Heri-
tage* (1982), Charles Royster, *The Destructive War: William
Tecumseh Sherman, Stonewall Jackson, and the Americans*
(1991), and Stephen W. Sears, *Landscape Turned Red: The
Battle of Antietam* (1983).

Who Freed the Slaves?

James M. McPherson

After the battle of Antietam, Lincoln issued the preliminary Proclamation warning that on January 1, 1863, he would proclaim freedom for slaves in all states or portions of states then in rebellion against the United States. January 1 came, and with it the Proclamation applying to all or parts of ten southern states in which, by virtue of his war powers as commander in chief, Lincoln declared all slaves "forever free" as "a fit and necessary measure for suppressing said rebellion." . . .

Emancipation, then, became a crucial part of northern military strategy, an important means of winning the war. But if it remained merely a *means* it would not be a part of national strategy—that is, of the *purpose* for which the war was being fought. Nor would it meet the criterion that military strategy should be consistent with national strategy, for it would be inconsistent to fight a war using the weapon of emancipation to restore a Union that still contained slaves. Lincoln recognized this. Although restoration of the Union remained his first priority, the abolition of slavery became an end as well as a means, a war aim virtually inseparable from Union itself. The first step in making it so came in the Emancipation Proclamation, which Lincoln pronounced "an act of justice" as well as a military necessity. Of course the border states, along with Tennessee and small enclaves elsewhere in the Confederate states, were not covered by the Proclamation because they were under Union control and not at war with the United States and thus exempt from an executive action that could legally be based only on the president's war powers. But Lincoln kept up his pressure on the border states to adopt emancipation themselves. With his support, leaders committed to the abolition of slavery gained political power in Maryland and Missouri. They pushed through constitutional reforms that abolished slavery in those states before the end of the war.

Lincoln's presidential reconstruction policy, announced in December 1863, offered pardon and amnesty to southerners who took an oath of allegiance to the Union *and* to all wartime policies concerning slavery and emancipation. Reconstructed governments sponsored by Lincoln in Louisiana, Arkansas, and Tennessee abolished slavery in those states—at least in the portions of them controlled by Union troops—before the war ended. West Virginia came in as a new state in 1863 with a constitution pledged to abolish slavery. And in 1864, Lincoln took the lead in getting the Republican national convention that renominated him to adopt a platform calling for a Thirteenth Amendment to the Constitution prohibiting slavery everywhere in the United States. Because slavery was "hostile to the principles of republican government, justice, and national safety," declared the platform, Republicans vowed to accomplish its "utter and complete extirpation from the soil of the republic." Emancipation had thus become an end as well as a means of Union victory. As Lincoln stated in the Gettysburg Address, the North fought from 1863 on for "a new birth of freedom." . . .

Emancipation and the enlistment of slaves as soldiers tremendously increased the stakes in this war, for the South as well as the North. Southerners vowed to fight "to the last ditch" before yielding to a Yankee nation that could commit such execrable deeds. Gone was any hope of an armistice or a negotiated peace so long as the Lincoln administration was in power. The alternatives were reduced starkly to southern independence on the one hand or unconditional surrender of the South on the other.

Reprinted from James M. McPherson, *Abraham Lincoln and the Second American Revolution* (New York: Oxford University Press, 1990).

On Jan. 1, 1863, Abraham Lincoln promulgated his Emancipation Proclamation. A document whose grand title promised so much but whose bland words delivered so little, the Emancipation Proclamation has been an enigma ever since. Like contemporaries, historians have been unsure whether to condemn it as a failure of idealism or applaud it as a triumph of *real-politik*.

Lincoln's proclamation, as has often been noted, freed not a single slave. It applied only to the slaves in territories then beyond the reach of federal authority. It specifically exempted Tennessee and Union-occupied portions of Louisiana and Virginia, and it left slavery in the loyal border states—Delaware, Maryland, Kentucky and Missouri—untouched. Indeed, the Proclamation went no further than the Second Confiscation Act of July 1862, which freed all slaves who entered Union lines professing that their owners were disloyal, as well as slaves who fell under federal control as Union troops occupied Confederate territory. . . .

What then was the point of the Proclamation? It spoke in muffled tones that heralded not the dawn of universal liberty but the compromised and piece-meal arrival of an undefined freedom. Indeed, the Proclamation's flat prose, ridiculed by abolitionists as having the moral grandeur of a bill of lading, suggests that the true authorship of Afro-American freedom lies elsewhere—not at the top of American society but at the bottom.

From the first guns at Sumter, the strongest advocates of emancipation were the slaves themselves. . . . Steadily, as opportunities arose, slaves risked all for freedom by abandoning their owners, coming uninvited into Union lines and offering their help as laborers, pioneers, guides and spies.

Slaves forced federal soldiers at the lowest level to recognize their importance to the Union's success. That understanding traveled quickly up the chain of command. In time, it became evident even to the most obtuse federal commanders that every slave who crossed into Union lines was a double gain: one subtracted from the Confederacy and one added to the Union. The slaves' resolute determination converted many white Americans to the view that the security of the Union depended upon the destruction of slavery. Eventually, it tipped the balance in favor of freedom, even among those who had little interest in the question of slavery and no love for black people. . . .

As black laborers became essential to the Union war effort and as demands to enlist black men in the federal army mounted, the pressure for emancipation became inexorable. On Jan. 1, Lincoln fulfilled his promise to free all slaves in the states still in rebellion. Had another Republican been in Lincoln's place, that person doubtless would have done the same. Without question, some would have acted more expeditiously and with greater bravado. Without question, some would have acted more cautiously with lesser resolve. In the end, Lincoln did what needed to be done. His claim to greatness rests upon his reading of the moment.

The Emancipation Proclamation's place in the drama of emancipation is thus secure. To deny it is to ignore the deep struggle by which freedom arrived. It is to ignore the soldiers who sheltered slaves, the abolitionists who stumped for emancipation and the thousands of men and women who—like Lincoln—changed their minds as slaves made the case for universal liberty. In this sense, slaves were right in celebrating Jan. 1 as the Day of Jubilee. The Emancipation Proclamation reminds us that real change derives only from the actions of the people and that political leadership finds its truest moment when it acts upon the authentic will of the people.

Ira Berlin, "How the Slaves Freed Themselves," *Washington Post,* December 27, 1992. Reprinted by permission.

Ku Klux Klansmen in the South, ca. 1870. *(Courtesy, Hugh Cleland)*

15

"Been in the Storm So Long": Emancipation and Reconstruction

THE KLAN'S LYNCHING OF JIM WILLIAMS

On the night of March 6, 1871, a group of men mounted on horses gathered near Yorkville, South Carolina. Most wore black gowns with black face masks, and some had decorated themselves with horns. Meeting up with another party, they rode to the cabin of a black man, Jim Williams. There they demanded guns that they claimed were hidden. Then they took Williams away. The next day he was found hanged from a tree.

For its time and place the story is not unusual. What makes it noteworthy is that Williams had been captain of a militia unit organized by the Republican Reconstruction government of South Carolina. His murderers, of course, belonged to one of the innumerable local bands in the South that went under the general heading of the Ku Klux Klan. The killing was a moment in a paramilitary conflict that followed the formal end of the Civil War.

The war itself had not been merely a regional battle. In the mountains especially, many southern whites remained loyal to the Union. By the time of General Robert E. Lee's surrender, blacks had enlisted in large numbers in the Union army. After the war, its social character became clearer. White Unionists along with black southerners found themselves pitted against white former rebels of all social classes.

HISTORICAL EVENTS

1863
Lincoln presents "ten percent plan" of Reconstruction

1864
Lincoln vetoes Congress's Wade-Davis Reconstruction Bill

1865
Civil War ends (April) • Thirteenth Amendment • Freedmen's Bureau established • Lincoln assassinated • Andrew Johnson becomes President • all-white southern legislatures begin to pass Black Codes

1866
Civil Rights Act passed over Johnson's veto • first Ku Klux Klan is organized

1867
Tenure of Office Act • Johnson suspends Secretary of War Edwin Stanton • Freedmen's Bureau ends

1868
Fourteenth Amendment • Johnson impeached by House, acquitted by Senate • Ulysses S. Grant elected President

continued

HISTORICAL EVENTS

1869
Woman suffrage associations organized in response to Fourteenth Amendment

1870
Force Acts destroy Ku Klux Klan • Fifteenth Amendment

1873
Panic and depression

1875
Mississippi "Redeemers" oust black and white Republican officeholders

1877
Compromise of 1877 • Rutherford B. Hayes becomes President • federal troops withdrawn from the South

1880s
Tenancy and sharecropping predominate in South • disfranchisement and segregation of blacks under "Jim Crow" begins

"I have vowed," declared a Virginian toward the end of the war, "that if I should have children—the first ingredient of the first principle of their education shall be uncompromising hatred & contempt of the Yankee."

A North Carolinian—his sons killed and his home burned by Yankees—"hate[d] 'em. I git up a half-past four in the morning, and sit up till twelve at night, to hate 'em."

The origins of the Klan seem fairly clear—as clear as can be expected of a phenomenon that enforced secrecy. It began in 1866 as a fraternal society. A year later in Nashville, the Klan reorganized on more ideological lines. "Dens" of Klansmen appeared throughout the former Confederacy. All this suggests a central structure, but no general regional Klan existed. And even within the local dens, the ability of leaders to keep discipline was slight. Had it been greater, the brutality of the Ku Klux might have been somewhat lessened.

The Klan became quickly known for flamboyant costumes. For these there were two clear motives: secrecy—for the activities of Klans could bring trouble to their perpetrators—and the belief that freed blacks were gullible and could be made to think that ghosts, specifically of the Confederate dead, were abroad in the night. Robes of various colors Klansmen supplemented with simple cloth masks or hideous faces, horns, tall conical hats, and sometimes coverings for their horses. The announcement that a Klan had organized in a locality would go to a newspaper in declarations with references to "Serpent's Den," "Hollow Tomb," "dark and dismal hour," "Great High Giant," "Shrouded-Knight," or whatever else could convey a sense of dread mystery. Warnings could take the form of gallows or miniature coffins at the houses of victims.

As confrontation mounted between the Klan and its black and white Unionist Republican enemies and as the ranks of armed whites swelled, the Reconstruction governor of South Carolina disarmed the county militias, which left Republicans at the mercy of the Klan. Estimates have it that in about a year from September 1870 eleven murders occurred in York County alone, including that of Jim Williams. In 1871 more than three-fourths of the county's white adult males were Klansmen. In some districts almost all the black population slept in the woods for much of the year.

Soon the national government began implementing legislation imposing control over Klan activity. By the end of 1871 violence finally had subsided.

The South after the Civil War

Hatred crackled and seared among white southerners in the first post-war days, amidst other emotions: sadness, resignation, relief, doubtless in a few cases a renascent loyalty to the Union. The feelings of the freed slaves are easy to imagine: their joy at the dizzying prospect of freedom has been documented. "I'm free as a frog!" one exultant former slave exclaimed. The southern land, meanwhile, was in a physical disruption to match the broiling emotions of the more irreconciled of its inhabitants.

Wherever travelers went in the months following Appomattox they saw abandoned fields, twisted rails, and burned structures. People in creaking wagons drove their gaunt mules for miles to find fords across bridgeless streams. For decades to come, men hobbling on one leg or dangling an empty sleeve were to be common sights throughout Dixie. In 1866 the state of Mississippi would spend a fifth of its revenues on artificial arms and legs for Confederate veterans. The defeat of the Confederacy had also wiped out millions of dollars of bank capital and made all Confederate money worthless. But most unsettling of all the changes the war had brought was the end of slavery. For generations it had been the foundation on which the entire southern economy rested. Now that it was gone, what would take its place?

Some former slaves remained on farms and plantations, but many others had departed. Some had gone to the towns, where life seemed more interesting than in the sleepy countryside. Others took to the road to test their new freedom. Many went traveling to seek out lost relatives and friends separated years ago by the migration of white masters or by the domestic slave trade. Eventually most would return to the land somewhere in the South.

Lincoln and most other northerners had entered the Civil War determined only to preserve the Union. Southerners, believing they saw larger and more menacing aims on the part of the North, had been as determined to protect their independence. The Emancipation Proclamation gave the Union a moral purpose and confirmed the fears of many white southerners that victory for the Union would mean social revolution. It was the leveling of the southern social and racial hierarchy as much as it was the leveling of Atlanta that caused bitterness among southerners after General Robert E. Lee surrendered at Appomattox Court House.

Together, the ending of slavery and the social dislocations of defeat prepared the South for the very thing that white southerners had dreaded and most northern Unionists had not wanted. The South was ripe for social revolution. That revolution, in fact, had already come in the sheer numbers of black southerners free and in motion across the countryside. What form that revolution would take, how long it might endure: all this in 1865 was a matter of endless and unpredictable possibility.

Would liberty fulfill itself, as black southerners wanted, in the independence that comes of owning a plot of land? Would liberty amount to the freedom defined by northern capital: freedom on the part of workers, black and white, to sell their labor to the highest bidder? What form would black family life take on: the patriarchy of the white family or the community of affection that had developed in slave quarters? Would blacks achieve social equality and integration with whites? What were white southerners going to think about black freedom, now that they had to think about it?

Such questions would have been unimaginable two or three years earlier as immediate practical considerations. New conditions now made them inescapable. There could be no retreat.

"Right off colored folks started on the move," one ex-slave was to recall. "They seemed to want to get closer to freedom, so they'd know what it was—like it was a place or a city."

In northern Florida, a black preacher advocated testing freedom by moving. He told a large crowd of former slaves:

"You ain't, none o' you, gwinter feel rale free till you shakes de dus' ob de Ole Plantashun offen yore feet an' goes ter a new place whey you kin live out o' sight o' de gret house. So long ez de shadder ob de gret house falls acrost you, you ain't gwine ter feel lak no free man, an' you ain't gwine ter feel lak no free 'oman. You mus' all move—you mus' move clar away from de ole places what you knows, ter de new places what you don't know, whey you kin raise up yore head douten no fear o' Marse Dis ur Marse Tudder. Go whey you please—do what you please."

In the end, social revolution was not to endure. That failure has defined the character of American social and political life ever since.

Reconstruction

Blacks recalling slavery decades later had a wide spectrum of memories.

"Might as well tell the truth. Had just as good a time when I was a slave as when I was free. Had all the hog meat and milk and everything else to eat."
—HARDY MILLER

"De white folks wuz good ter us, an' we loved 'em. But we wanted ter be free 'cause de Lawd done make us all free."

—TOM WILCOX

"There was no such thing as being good to slaves. Many white people were better than others, but a slave belonged to his master, and there was no way to get out of it."

—THOMAS LEWIS

"I thought slavery wuz right. I felt that this wuz the way things had to go— the way they were fixed to go. I wuz satisfied. The white folks treated me all right. My young missus loved me, and I loved her. She whupped me sometimes—I think, just for fun, sometimes."

—JOE HIGH

"Some colored people say slavery was better, because they had no responsibility. It is true, they were fed, clothed, and sheltered, but I'm like the man that said, 'Give me freedom or give me death!' "

—BELLE CARUTHERS

Reorganizing the Union   The Confederate surrender opened a difficult constitutional question about the status of the defeated states. Did the former rebel states have the right, as members of the Union, to come straight back to Congress and resume their old political life under the Constitution? Would the government have no authority to set conditions that they would have to meet before they resumed their seats in the House and Senate? If so, Congress would lack the power to force on the South whatever reforms might be necessary for the protection of the freed slaves and the prevention of any future disloyalty. Republicans who favored a coercive policy toward the South argued that by the act of secession the Confederate states had forfeited their status of statehood and reverted to the condition of territories. If they were no longer states, they were not entitled to the rights of states and could therefore be directly subject to the will of the federal government.

Some fundamental reform of the South, at any rate, was necessary, especially since the southern states were imposing oppressive codes of conduct on the freed slave. In the absence of reform, the Union victory might actually give the South a stronger presence in the House of Representatives than the region had enjoyed before the war, and with no consequences to the white majority. For the Constitution had provided that in counting the population of a state to determine how many members it was to have in the House, three-fifths of the slaves in the state were to be counted in. But if slavery no longer existed and the blacks were legally free, the whole black population would be counted within the population of the state, and the South would gain about twenty House seats. And if former Confederate states should succeed in finding methods for denying full freedom for the black populace, the South would be getting extra seats without even having to give up its oppression of the black race.

Overshadowing all these issues was the question of the future status of the black people. By eradicating slavery, the country unwittingly confronted questions regarding the civil and political status of blacks. Would the ballot and citizenship be conferred on them?

Such questions had to be worked out amid a legacy of bitterness and frustration created by the war. White southerners found themselves in the unique position of being the only Americans to know defeat in wartime, their region burned and bare, their economy a shambles. The North had not suffered the physical and economic devastation experienced by the South. Even its human losses were proportionally less. But northerners had sacrificed to preserve the Union. They needed to know that their expenditures had gone for something, that their principles had been vindicated. They expected a measure of symbolic satisfaction from the South as well as physical surrender.

Lincoln's Reconstruction Plan

In the efforts during the war to settle on some scheme for restoration of the rebel states to the Union, President Lincoln generally favored policies that would make few demands on the South. He had originally hoped for a speedy end to the war and a rapid resumption of antebellum political ties. Although the prolonged struggle on the battlefield made that impossible, the President continued to advocate a moderate postwar Reconstruction. Lincoln had not been an advocate of black equality. He always approached racial issues cautiously. He had hoped that the process of emancipation would be gradual and under the direction of officials of the former slave states. Believing that the colonization of blacks outside the United States was the ideal solution, Lincoln's administration sponsored efforts to resettle blacks in the Caribbean and Central America. And Lincoln was a cagey politician. An ex-Whig himself, he may have had it in mind that moderate policies attractive to southern former Whigs might draw them to the Republican Party.

In December 1863 Lincoln outlined a formal plan for Confederate areas coming under Union control. It contemplated swift restoration, with no penalties for ex-rebels beyond loss of their slaves. It did not anticipate black participation in Reconstruction. Under Lincoln's "ten percent plan," whenever a total of whites equal to one-tenth the number who had voted in 1860 took an oath of future loyalty to the United States and its laws—which included the abolition of slavery—they could form a new state government. Before the war ended Lincoln had recognized "ten percent" governments in Arkansas, Tennessee,

WHAT WOULD LINCOLN HAVE DONE?

Historians have long speculated over how Lincoln would have approached the problem of postwar reconstruction had he not been assassinated. And in so doing they are merely following the lead of his contemporaries, most of whom claimed their own proposals reflected Lincoln's plans. The real question may be: did Lincoln have any plans?

It seems probable that he did, but Lincoln confided them to no one. In this matter, as in most others, he kept his own counsel. The result is that, following the assassination, people have tried to infer his postwar plans from his wartime programs. This is a very dubious enterprise. The reason is that Lincoln sought throughout the war to shorten it by enticing the seceding states back into the Union. The generous terms he offered were contingent on their willingness to lay down their arms. And so those terms should be seen as the carrot Lincoln used alongside the military stick. That they should not be seen as likely precedents for his postwar plans is suggested by this logic. Leniency was held out as a reward for voluntarily returning to the Union. None of the Confederate states earned that reward. That means that Lincoln, by his own terms, was free to deal with them as harshly as circumstances might demand. All this is technically true, and indicates Lincoln's essential conservatism. Yet there is a contrary truth to the Emancipation Proclamation. Lincoln knew what it implied, and so did the white South in its angry public reaction to the Proclamation. It was, by implication and beneath its limited surface, a declaration of war against slavery. We also have Lincoln's reaction to the Wade-Davis Bill to go by. He objected not so much to its rigor as that it would tie his hands in advance. Lincoln wanted to be free to deal with a defeated South as circumstances might suggest.

All in all it seems that we will never know what Lincoln would have proposed, much as we might like to think he would have striven for Negro equality. But the disastrous course of Johnson's attempts at reconstruction will always invite speculation on what Lincoln might have done had he lived.

Abraham Lincoln toward the beginning of the Civil War.
(Courtesy, Library of Congress)

Lincoln's second inaugural address described his postwar plans in humane but unspecific terms:

"With malice toward none; with charity for all, with firmness in the right, as God give us to see the right, let us strive on to finish the work we are in: to bind up the nation's wounds. . . ."

and Louisiana. But Congress refused to admit representatives from these states, and their votes were not counted in the 1864 presidential election. Lincoln agreed that Congress should take some role in the reconciliation process, but he always sought to keep restoration under presidential leadership.

The national legislators were looking for a plan more firmly ensuring that the new southern governments would remain loyal. The Wade-Davis Bill of 1864 required that before a formerly seceded state could form a government, fifty percent of the adult white males in that state would have to take an oath of loyalty to the Union. The state could then hold a constitutional convention to make a new government for itself. But voting for delegates to that convention would be limited to people who had taken an oath that they had never supported secession. The bill included legal equality for blacks, but did not provide them with the vote. Thinking the Wade-Davis Bill too severe and an invasion of presidential responsibility, Lincoln pocket vetoed it.

Neither Lincoln's plan nor the Wade-Davis Bill provided for blacks to be given the vote. But some Republicans in Congress wished to grant a wide range of rights to the freedmen. Legislators of this kind wanted the national government to have strong control over former rebel states, so that their legal and social systems could be thoroughly reshaped and white southerners would not get the chance to bring back the old slavery system in a new form.

During the final year of the war President Lincoln appeared to be moving somewhat toward a more active and progressive solution to the race question. In March 1864 he came out in favor of granting the vote to "very intelligent" black people and black Union soldiers. He pressed for the Thirteenth Amendment outlawing slavery. A month before his death Lincoln signed the bill creating a Freedmen's Bureau to aid the ex-slaves in their transition to freedom.

In the end, Reconstruction was to be in hands other than Lincoln's. But in the spring of 1865 the President and the Union public did have a brief period to savor victory.

Lincoln's Last Days   On April 4 Lincoln went to Richmond to view the Confederate capital now evacuated by the government of Jefferson Davis. Accompanied by his son and a military escort, he walked up Main Street to the Confederate executive mansion. Black men and women crowded around the presidential party and sang and shouted. When he entered the Confederate President's house and took a seat in Davis's chair, the Union troops, black and white, cheered. Later the President toured the captured city that for four bloody years had been the supreme goal of Union armies. Like many other large southern towns Richmond was in ruins: it was blackened by a fire set accidentally by the Confederate authorities before they withdrew.

Lincoln returned to Washington on April 9, the day Lee surrendered to Grant at Appomattox. The news reached Washington the next day and the government declared a holiday for its employees. On the tenth, throngs gathered on the streets of the capital. The crowds eventually converged on the White House, where Lincoln was working at his desk. They interrupted him several times by their shouts for a speech until he finally made an appearance. He would deliver some appropriate remarks the following evening, he said, but for the moment he would just order the bands to play "Dixie." The Confederate anthem, he noted, was now the lawful property of the Union.

The next evening the President came to the upper window of the White House as he had promised. He delivered a thoughtful address, his last, on the problems to come. If the crowd had wanted a rousing cock-crow of triumph, it was disappointed. At least one man in the audience, however, found himself deeply moved, but to rage and anger. John Wilkes Booth was a Marylander, an actor from a distinguished theatrical family. The defeat of the South had sent him into despair.

On the evening of April 14 the President, accompanied by his wife and several friends, went to see the comedy *Our American Cousin* at Ford's Theater. The President's party arrived late but quickly settled down to enjoy the story of a shrewd comic American visiting his English relatives. During the third act the sounds of a muffled shot and a scuffle came from the President's box. Suddenly a tall figure leaped from the box to the stage and shouted *Sic semper tyrannis!* (thus ever to tyrants), the motto of Virginia. Before he could be stopped Booth escaped into the night.

They carried the unconscious President to a house across the street. While high officials and family members gathered around, the doctors examined him. The bullet had entered the rear of his head and lodged near his eye. Nothing could be done. He died at 7:22 a.m.

Robert E. Lee at first would not believe the news of Lincoln's death. Then he told a visitor that he had "surrendered as much to [Lincoln's] goodness as to Grant's artillery."

Andrew Johnson

Like other Vice Presidents in American history, Andrew Johnson was selected without much consideration that he might become President. A self-educated tailor from east Tennessee and a strong Jacksonian Democrat, Johnson had been in 1861 the only senator from a secessionist state to support the Union. After Tennessee fell to Union troops, Lincoln made him war governor, a task he performed with vigor and fortitude. In 1864 the Republican Party, seeking to broaden itself into a Union party, turned naturally to Johnson, an ex-Democrat and a southern Unionist, to be Lincoln's running mate. Then suddenly, on April 14, 1865, he was the President.

Johnson, a President without a party, had to deal with a Republican Congress. And Johnson was a southern white supremacist, willing and perhaps happy to accept emancipation and some rights for black Americans but close in his thinking to southerners who wished to place strict controls over the black population. This brought him into conflict not only with the increasingly strong band of Radical Republicans in Congress but with moderates as well. Courageous and stubborn but belligerent and lacking in political tact, Johnson had one of the most troubled presidential administrations in American history.

Johnson wanted an easy restoration of the seceded states. There was not yet any clearly defined program that would instruct a rebel

Andrew Johnson's attempt to assume primary responsibility for Reconstruction after Lincoln's death alienated Congress, while his leniency toward the South increasingly angered northern voters. *(Courtesy, Library of Congress)*

state in how it must go about reorganizing itself so as to be accepted
back into the Union, and Johnson did not wait for Congress to recon-
vene (it was out of session until December) before dealing with the
problem. Like Lincoln, Johnson offered pardon to ex-rebels pledging
future loyalty. He asked only that the reorganized state governments
nullify their ordinances of secession, repudiate their Confederate
debts, and ratify the Thirteenth Amendment.

Assuming primary responsibility for Reconstruction, Johnson chis-
eled a policy bound to alienate Republicans in Congress. His leniency
toward the South angered Radicals. Southerners, moreover, took a
course that aroused northern resentment. They elected to state office
and to Congress prominent ex-rebels, including Confederate Vice
President Alexander Stephens and numerous generals. Some of the
reorganized state governments refused to repudiate their Confederate
debts or nullify their secession ordinances. A number of them passed
"Black Codes" defining the rights of emancipated slaves in ways that
severely restricted their freedom.

A typical code might bar blacks from jury duty and from testifying
in court against whites; it might forbid them to take up any occupation
except agriculture or to rent land on their own; some subjected unemployed blacks to arrest and forced labor. The character of the "restored" governments and the "Black Codes" seemed to indicate that
southerners remained rebels at heart. Mississippi's version of the Black
Codes contained a section levying fines and possible imprisonment for
former slaves "committing riots, routs, affrays, trespasses, malicious
mischief, cruel treatment to animals, seditious speeches, insulting ges-
tures, language, or acts, or assaults on any person, disturbance of the
peace, exercising the function of a minister of the Gospel without a
license . . . vending spiritous or intoxicating liquors, or committing any
other misdemeanor, the punishment of which is not specifically provided for by law."

Early Reconstruction

When Congress met in December 1865, it refused to seat newly
elected southern representatives, but disagreed on what to do next.
Radical Republicans demanded a thoroughgoing political and economic shake-up of the South. Congressman Thaddeus Stevens of
Pennsylvania and Senator Charles Sumner of Massachusetts led the
Radicals. Many southerners thought the Republican Congress wanted
to punish the South by providing numerous political and economic
rights for the freedman. Stevens in fact wanted Confederate lands
appropriated by Washington and given to blacks. At this point, however, moderates still dominated Republican policy. But they too
wanted to ensure the civil rights of black southerners. In 1865 Congress
passed a bill giving to a Freedmen's Bureau the power to try by military
commission anyone charged with depriving freedmen of their civil
rights. It also put through a bill that gave the freedmen citizenship and
civil rights. Johnson vetoed both bills as unconstitutional extensions of
federal power. Congress thereupon enacted the civil rights measure

A Freedmen's school, one of the more successful endeavors supported by the Freedmen's Bureau. Working with teachers from northern abolitionist and missionary societies, the Bureau founded thousands of schools for freed slaves and poor whites. *(Courtesy, Valentine Press, Richmond, VA)*

over his veto, passed a revised bill for a Freedmen's Bureau, and overrode Johnson's veto of it.

Congress's establishment of the Freedmen's Bureau departed from normal government policy by addressing various aspects of people's lives that had normally been left to private initiative. The Bureau, empowered also to care for white refugees, was essentially responsible for protecting blacks against reenslavement in the unsettled conditions of the southern states. Under its commissioner, Union veteran and general Oliver O. Howard, it provided direct aid to blacks, found them employment, supervised labor contracts, set up schools and courts, gave public recognition to marriages among black southerners, attempted to provide them with abandoned land and in general worked to ensure that freedom would be a reality.

The Fourteenth Amendment
Congress soon offered Johnson and the South another chance. It framed an elaborate Fourteenth Amendment covering a range of issues and gave each of the state governments favored by Johnson the opportunity to return to Congress if it should ratify.

The Fourteenth Amendment declared that "All persons"—the lawmakers were thinking particularly of black Americans—"born or naturalized in the United States, and subject to the jurisdiction thereof, are citizens of the United States and of the State wherein they reside." The Amendment prohibited the states from violating the "privileges or immunities of citizens of the United States," depriving "any person of life, liberty, or property, without due process of law," or denying "to any person within its jurisdiction the equal protection of the laws." The Amendment did not directly extend the right to vote. It attempted instead to entice the states to give the vote to blacks. The admentment disfranchised former confederate leaders. But provided that a state would lose seats in the House of Representatives in proportion to the number of its adult males denied the right to vote.

Miss M. A. Parker, a white schoolteacher, observed the hunger for education on the part of some black parents for their children:

Raleigh, N.C., Feb. 22, 1869
It is surprising to me to see the amount of suffering which many of the people endure for the sake of sending their children to school. There is one woman who supports three children and keeps them at school; she says, "I don't care how hard I has to work, if I can only sen[d] Sallie and the boys to school." . . . One may go into their cabins on cold, windy days, and see daylight between every two boards, or feel the rain dropping through the roof; but a word of complaint is rarely heard. They are anxious to have the children "get on" in their books, and do not seem to feel impatient if they lack comforts themselves. A pile of books is seen in almost every cabin, though there be no furniture except a poor bed, a table and two or three broken chairs.

—Miss M. A. Parker

The Freedmen's Bureau Commissioner in Mississippi and Louisiana wrote:

"I hear the people talk in such a way as to indicate that they are yet unable to conceive of the negro as possessing any rights at all. . . . To kill a negro they do not deem murder; to debauch a negro woman they do not think fornication; to take the property away from a negro they do not consider robbery. The people boast that when they get freedmen affairs in their own hands, to use the classic expression, 'the niggers will catch hell.'"

A state ratifying the Amendment could expect to be granted readmission without further reform. Implicit in the offer was a penalty for rejection: the process of restoring the state to the Union would begin anew, with Congress dictating terms. Had it not been for Johnson, the South might have ratified. But Johnson refused to bend. On his advice all the southern states except his Tennessee rejected the Amendment. Tennessee ratified and was readmitted to the Union. The other ten, said James A. Garfield, had "flung back into our teeth the magnanimous offer of a generous nation."

The break between the President and Congress was now complete. In the fall of 1866 Johnson stumped the North encouraging the defeat at the polls of leading Republican congressmen. The tour was a disaster for the President personally and politically. Forgetting that he was no longer a Tennessee stump-speaker, Johnson engaged in undignified arguments with hecklers and even suggested hanging leading Radicals. In November the Republicans swept the elections, winning over a two-thirds majority in both houses of Congress. That gave the Republicans in each house the ability, if they stood together, to muster the votes necessary to override a presidential veto of a bill. Reconstruction would begin anew, under the leadership of such Radicals as the Massachusetts Senator Charles Sumner and Representative Thaddeus Stevens of Pennsylvania.

Radical Reconstruction

The situation when Congress met in December 1866 was very different from that a year earlier. Events during 1866 had conspired to bring together moderate and Radical Republicans, at least temporarily. A majority in Congress now agreed on the necessity of creating new southern state governments on the basis of black suffrage and exclusion of the former rebel leadership from participating in the drawing up of state constitutions. Arming blacks with the ballot, Republicans hoped, would give them a weapon against white Democratic oppression and build a strong Republican Party in the South.

The Military Reconstruction Act of 1867 set the terms of the congressional program. It divided the South into five military districts. Military governors in each were to register voters, including blacks but not whites who had held public office before the Civil War and then supported the Confederacy. The governors would thereupon call elections for new constitutional conventions. These conventions had to write black suffrage into the new state constitutions. Once the voters had approved these constitutions and the Fourteenth Amendment, the states might apply to Congress for readmission. If the constitution met approval, the state would be readmitted to the Union and its representatives seated. Three other Reconstruction Acts followed the first. In 1868 the necessary number of states ratified the Fourteenth Amendment, and it became part of the federal Constitution.

Reconstruction had something in common with the economic policy of the Republican Party and with the party's defense of the

Union during the Civil War. It represented that commitment to strong and active central government toward which Republicans then tended. In the enforcement of civil rights, the effort to establish universal male suffrage, and the work of the Freedmen's Bureau, the federal government for the first time in its history was lending its resources to a political and social revolution.

To southern whites haunted by the old antebellum fear of slave insurrection, Radical Reconstruction seemed a nightmare come true. With their traditional leaders barred from office and illiterate ex-slaves enfranchised, they predicted a grim era of black rule.

The artist of this 1867 glorification of Reconstruction focuses on raising the missing pillars (the returning southern states) to form a rotunda of the reunited Republic. Clasped hands above the American eagle carry the words "Union and Liberty Forever." From heaven, the country's great leaders look down approvingly— Washington, Lincoln, Jefferson, Webster, Calhoun, and many more. Black and white babies (bottom, center), sleeping innocently in baskets, remind the viewer that "All men are born free and equal." Black and white children play together—a nation's noblest dream. *(Courtesy, Library of Congress)*

Massachusetts Senator Charles
Sumner (top) and Pennsylvania
Representative Thaddeus Stevens,
leaders of Radical Reconstruction.
(Courtesy, Library of Congress)

Who Were the Radicals? The earliest historians of Radical Reconstruction condemned it as a rape of southern society. Political opportunism and hatred of the South, so such critics argued, had motivated the Radical Republican policies: military rule and black suffrage violated the spirit, if not the letter, of the Constitution. Accounts sympathetic to the white South stressed the corruption of Reconstruction state regimes and the unruliness—by which some of them may have meant the claims to equality—of former slaves. Scholars denounced northern "carpetbaggers," who according to folklore had gone southward carrying carpetbag luggage and intending to profit from the helplessness of the ex-Confederacy. Their partners in evil, so the same version of history claimed, were southern "scalawags" who in greed turned against their own region and people and entered the Reconstruction state governments. Reconstruction was a "blackout of honest government." In this view, the political triumph on the state level of the "redeemers," some of whom were of the old planter class, rescued the South from the work of Radical Reconstruction and brought back constitutional government and proper race relations.

By the 1930s historians were becoming increasingly interested in explaining events by economic causes. That brought a new way of interpreting Reconstruction. Now writers looked back to the days before the Civil War when southerners had opposed such measures favorable to northern business as the protective tariff, which would force the South to buy its manufactured goods from the North rather than at cheaper European prices. Those scholars perceived the Radical Republicans as representatives of northeastern business interests. These interests had feared that a speedily reconstructed South might regain its political power and overturn the control of the national government acquired by northern business during the war years. It was for that reason, this interpretation would hold, that Republicans in Congress gave the vote to southern blacks, who were sure to vote for the Republican Party.

More recently, a generation influenced by the civil rights struggles of the 1950s and 1960s has begun describing Reconstruction as another phase in the black American search for justice. Radical Republicans, this analysis insists, represented the last moment of abolitionist idealism. The Radicals tried to provide national protection for the rights of the freed people and to extend some measure of social and economic assistance. Not particularly vindictive and not the tools of a capitalist conspiracy, congressional Republicans, moderates as well as Radicals, undertook their actions only after they realized the extent of white southern stubbornness and presidential obstructionism. And their measures were not especially severe, particularly when compared to the postwar policies of other victorious nations. The national government committed only a small number of troops to military Reconstruction, and the whole process lasted only a few years. This recent idea of Reconstruction would hold that if any fault is to be found with the policy, it is not for being too severe toward the defeated South but for not being thorough enough to win the black race full and permanent equality and justice. The very word "Radical" has been questioned, since most measures passed were compromises unsatisfactory to true radicals.

Impeachment of Johnson

Although his policies had clearly been rejected and Republicans now held two out of three seats in both houses, enough to pass legislation over his veto, President Johnson continued to resist Radical Reconstruction by every possible means. Using the authority he possessed as commander-in-chief, he issued orders curtailing the powers of the military commanders in the South. He also removed from office people friendly to Radical policies. Congress responded in 1867 and 1868 by trying to trim the President's powers so as to reduce his capacity for harm. In particular it passed the Tenure of Office Act, which forbade him to dismiss federal officials without the consent of the Senate. Another law required him to issue all orders to the army through its commanding general, U. S. Grant.

There had been talk among Radicals for some time of removing Johnson from office. Under the Constitution a President could be removed for "Treason, Bribery, or other high Crimes and Misdemeanors." Johnson had committed none of these. His only real offense was to refuse to cooperate in legislative policies that Congress and the public had approved. This might indicate bad political judgment. But bad judgment is not a high crime or misdemeanor.

Then Johnson, always his own worst enemy, made a major political blunder. In August 1867 he suspended Secretary of War Edwin M. Stanton, a close ally of the Radicals. There followed a comic opera in which Stanton barricaded himself in his office for two months while his successor periodically stood outside begging him to vacate. Outraged at Johnson's defiance, and convinced that he intended to destroy Radical Reconstruction, the House of Representatives in February 1868 impeached the President—that is, charged him with misconduct. Johnson stood accused of a number of doubtful offenses such as delivering "inflammatory and scandalous" speeches, but especially the offense of

Facsimile of a ticket to Andrew Johnson's impeachment trial. Though Johnson was guilty of no crime other than continued resistance to Radical Reconstruction, a switch of a single Senate vote would have removed him from office.
(*Courtesy, Library of Congress*)

dismissing Stanton in violation of the Tenure of Office Act. Impeachment meant that Johnson now had to go on trial before the Senate, which would decide whether to remove him from the presidency. For three months the Senate sat as a court, listening to arguments from attorneys for both sides. Johnson's lawyers argued that a President could be removed only for violation of criminal law; counsel for the House contended that Johnson had exceeded his presidential authority and therefore provided adequate grounds for removal. Suspense mounted as it became clear that Republican senators were divided over the question of Johnson's guilt. In the end, seven Republicans broke with their colleagues and voted with Democrats against conviction. As a result the Senate fell one vote short of the required two-thirds needed to remove the President from office.

Johnson's impeachment and trial were the product of nerves stretched to the limit after three years of feuding. So convinced were many northerners that Johnson had joined with unrepentant rebels to undo the results of the war that they sanctioned any means to drive him from office. Johnson's conviction—especially on such flimsy grounds—might have damaged permanently the role of the President in the American political system.

Blacks and the Land

Advertisements, angry or despairing, were placed in newspapers by blacks following the war:

"Information Wanted, of Caroline Dodson, who was sold from Nashville, Nov. 1st, 1862, by James Lumsden to Warwick, (a trader then in human beings), who carried her to Atlanta, Georgia, and she was last heard of in the sale pen of Robert Clarke, (human trader in that place), from which she was sold. Any information of her whereabouts will be thankfully received and rewarded by her mother. Lucinda Lowery, Nashville."

The Black Family

The country roads in the early days after Appomattox, crowded with newly freed slaves seeking lost loved ones, speak of the violence the slave system had done to the black family. Protecting their absolute right to their property, slaveholders had refused to give formal and legal recognition to slave marriages. Masters had often found it in their interest, however, to encourage slave unions: children were future laborers, and family responsibility would restrain rebelliousness. Yet when the economics of plantation life demanded it, husbands would be separated from wives, wives sold away from husbands, and children torn from mothers and fathers.

It is logical to suppose that in the absence of socially protected marriage, the mother would assume the primary parental role. Historians have described the slave family as matriarchal. That view is under question. Evidence indicates the presence within the slave community of males who performed the tasks of husband and father: providing their families with game or fish as dietary supplements, fashioning articles of furniture, passing along to a child some memory from an earlier time and a different land, and, when possible, protecting a wife or child against an abusive overseer or master.

But beyond these elements of similarity between black and white fatherhood, little division of responsibilities along gender lines existed within slave quarters. The necessities of plantation agriculture assured, for example, that the great majority of slave men and women worked alongside one another in the fields. Slave parents, faced with the problem of bringing children to maturity, rarely observed Victorian distinctions in sex roles. Both parents taught their children survival, the subtle art of accommodation to the plantation system. Yet whites might accept from a slave woman a degree of aggressiveness in defense of her children that they would not tolerate from black fathers.

Unable under the conditions of slavery to enjoy a secure and stable nuclear family life, blacks established an enlarged community of relations, stretching from one plantation to the next, of "brothers" and "sisters," "aunts" and "uncles" who took up family responsibilities. When the opportunity presented itself after the war, the freed slaves rejoined their immediate biological families and sought legitimacy and protection in legally recognized marriages. The Freedmen's Bureau presided over many of these unions and made them a matter of public record.

For blacks, gaining control of their own families was perhaps the most important immediate consequence of freedom. But emancipation also worked to alter relations within the black family. Slavery had flattened, though not entirely, the differences between men's and women's roles; emancipation made possible a differentiation between roles that the larger society endorsed. Black males most often went to work for whites in various jobs as they had done before the war, but now for hire. They generally preferred, however, that their wives not work for the white man, and many black females wished to create a conventional household and give their energies to raising children. In the years immediately following the war, white southern landowners complained of the scarcity of black women and children available for field work or domestic employment. For black men and women emancipation was supposed to mean at least the freedom whites enjoyed to organize a household.

Freed women when they stepped out from their homes encountered barriers already set up for the rest of their sex. Black women who had to seek employment complained to Freedmen's Bureau officials that they received wages lower than men were getting for the same work. Bureau policy required husbands to sign contracts for the labor of their wives. Though black men—for the most part temporarily—acquired more and more political liberty throughout the Reconstruction era, especially the right to vote and hold office, black women like their white sisters remained outside the political system. The experience of sexual equality that had belonged to slavery was being swallowed in theories of male primacy that came with freedom.

The black family, meanwhile, thrived in freedom. By 1870 a large majority of black children were growing up in households of two parents. Relations between the sexes, while not so nearly equal as under slavery, were not so sharply defined and as hierarchical as conventional morality might have demanded. Blacks, in any event, now had a stable home foundation on which to build wider forms of community and political organization.

Building the Black Community   From the earliest days of Reconstruction, there emerged into full public view an institution that had maintained a powerful place in slave society and among antebellum free blacks. Evangelical Protestantism spoke to the condition of American blacks. Most slave states had made it illegal to educate slaves. But the incomparable vocabulary of the King James Bible was available. Illiterate blacks could learn the cadences by ear; free blacks with schooling could read it, like slaves who had learned to read despite the prohibitions. A story of ancient Jews whose lot seemed close to that of the slaves; a language of bondage, flight, and deliverance, of suffering endured, rendered into prayer and devotion and in time ended: all was magnificent material for preaching and for hymns. With religion came a ministry of slaves and free blacks. During Reconstruction, blacks pressed for separate churches, nurturing their own congregations already established. The black ministry gained political leadership to supplement its spiritual role, taking a place within the black community that it would still occupy during the civil rights struggles of the 1950s and 1960s.

Side by side with the ministers in a position of leadership stood the teachers, now at liberty openly to instruct other blacks and to enlarge their own education. Ex-slaves and black southerners who had been free even in slavery times now joined with black and white teachers who had come from the North to serve in the new time of emancipation. Schools flourished: vast numbers of tiny schools ran on a shoestring; most received the countenance and aid, however meager, of the Freedmen's Bureau. The teachers might be passing on the fragments of learning they had snatched and hoarded in the days of slavery; pupils, eager for a schooling that Americans in general have traditionally prized as a means of success and a good in itself, might have the ambition to become teachers. The halting eloquence to be found among the papers of newly schooled Reconstruction blacks has its counterpart in the letters of immigrants, trying in their freshly acquired English to explain their place and hopes in their adopted country.

One freedman observed:

"Perhaps some will get an education in a little while. I *knows de next generation will*. But . . . we has been kep down *a hundred years* and I think it will take *a hundred years to get us back again*."

Another ex-slave would recall sending his children to school:

"We had no idea that we should see them return home alive in the evening. Big white boys and half-grown men used to pelt them with stones and run them down with open knives, both to and from school. Sometimes they come home bruised, stabbed, beaten half to death, and sometimes quite dead. My own son himself was often thus beaten. He has on his forehead today a scar over his right eye which sadly tells the story of his trying experience in those days in his efforts to get an education. I was wounded in the war, trying to get my freedom, and he over his eye, trying to get an education."

Community Voices

Even before the end of the war, black southerners in regions under control of federal troops were meeting to provide a voice for their community. The main insistence in the gatherings was on political and legal rights. More generally, they appear to have had as their objective the establishment of an organized and articulate presence in American society. Underlying this purpose was a fear that even the more enlightened of white Americans were likely to treat the freed slaves as no more than recipients of white benevolence. That was not going to be to the liking especially of blacks who had won for themselves an education, whether pieced together in defiance of laws forbidding literacy schooling for slaves or acquired in the precarious margins of southern society allowed to free blacks before the war. Blacks made more particular demands during the early days of Reconstruction for the right to vote, to serve on juries, to exercise the other freedoms of Americans. These demands too can perhaps best be understood as reflecting the determination to be an active rather than a passive component of the nation. The plan of Reconstruction imposed by Congress later in the decade would succeed, if only briefly, because there existed among southern blacks a roughly hewn political structure, a stratum of educated leaders, and a political will. These could respond to the congressional program for bringing the freed slaves into the nation's public life.

Humanitarian Efforts

During the Reconstruction years, the national government provided some assistance to the freed people in the South. The Freedmen's Bureau coordinated relief activities and tried to ease the difficult transition from slavery to freedom. Critics at the time generally indicted the Bureau for doing too much to assist blacks. Later historians have found quite the opposite. Many of the well-meaning officials were overly paternalistic; others displayed outright prejudice toward black people; some encouraged freedmen to enter into exploitive labor contracts; the agency did too little to enlarge opportunities for the former slaves. Yet the Bureau represented a notable though mild and temporary expansion of the social role of the federal government. In 1869, with its work still only a beginning, Congress cut its appropriation. This was a sign of northern retreat from Reconstruction. By 1872 the Freedmen's Bureau was defunct.

Private philanthropic and religious groups tried to aid freed people. Various churches, especially the Congregationalists and the Quakers, sent both money and volunteers to the South. Educational institutions related to the churches gave many black children and adults their first opportunity to learn to read and write. Blacks rushed to make use of the new schools, where northern female schoolteachers took an especially important role. Their devotion to the people they were teaching mingled with their commitment to inculcating them with northern, middle-class values. Church groups also helped establish black colleges and industrial schools, and the Freedmen's Bureau extended some financial assistance to missionary schools, including Howard University in Washington, D.C.

Many northern black churchmen and educators journeyed south to spread the Gospel and the schoolbook among the ex-slaves. Former slaves themselves put up schoolhouses and paid for teachers, established churches, organized conventions to lobby for equal rights and the ballot, and opened savings banks.

The Fifteenth Amendment

By the Fifteenth Amendment, ratified in 1870 by the necessary number of states, Congress brought the right to vote under federal control. The Amendment declared that a citizen's right to vote "shall not be denied or abridged . . . on account of race, color, or previous condition of servitude." The Amendment applied to black males in the North—much of the North had not allowed black Americans to vote—as well as to former slaves in the South. Most of the black vote went to Republicans, and some northern supporters of the Amendment may have been mainly concerned with strengthening the Republican Party. But others risked a white backlash to guarantee suffrage to the black man.

The vote that was granted to black males was denied to both black and white females. White leaders of the movement for women's rights were incensed. Before the war, they had worked within the abolitionist movement and then supported the Republican cause. In 1866, Susan B. Anthony, Elizabeth Cady Stanton, Lucy Stone, and Lucretia Mott organized the American Equal Rights Association to support suffrage for both white women and blacks. Some even asserted that white

Sarah Jane Foster, a Quaker volunteer teacher from Maine, wrote to her home town newspaper about her experiences during Reconstruction:

Letter from Martinsburg, West Va., Feb. 11th 1866

"My day school is growing larger. Its list is now seventy, while the night list approaches fifty. . . . I spoke of good spelling in my last letter. Week before last a boy of sixteen, named Willoughby Fairfax, who chanced to recite alone, spelled seventy-five long words and only missed *two*. At the beginning of the year he was in words of four letters. He is one of my best pupils. . . . I daily become more and more interested in the school, and in all that concerns the welfare of the colored people here."

Febr- 28

"The cognomen of 'nigger teacher' seems to have died out, and I occasionally hear my own name as I pass in the street, or, more frequently some person is notified that 'there goes the Freedmen's Bureau.' I have not met with any annoyance on the street but once, and then a white man addressed an insolent remark to me as I was going into the schoolroom door. I don't mind such things at all. Report has married or engaged me several times to men connected with the school, and, Mrs. Vosburgh was actually asked by a neighbor the day I was there 'if I was not part nigger.' I hope they will believe it, for then surely they could not complain of my teaching the people of my own race."

Harper's Ferry, April 20th, 1866 [May 9]

"The colored people here are scattered, and many of them in very destitute circumstances. They do not now come into school so well as they did last term. The older ones are gone out at service, and smaller ones, who have long distances to come, fear to do so without protection; for the white boys will molest them when they find an opportunity. . . ."

Susan B. Anthony (1820–1906)
and Elizabeth Cady Stanton
(1815–1902), the two most
influential leaders of the woman
suffrage movement, ca. 1870.
Both broke with their longtime
abolitionist allies after the Civil
War when they opposed the
Fifteenth Amendment. They
argued that the doctrine of
universal manhood suffrage
it embodied would give
constitutional authority to the
claim that men were the social
and political superiors of women.
(*Courtesy, Schlesinger Library,
Radcliffe College*)

women were better fitted to vote than black men. In the ensuing dispute about priorities, the Equal Rights Association split into two groups. Lucy Stone and Henry Blackwell formed the American Woman Suffrage Association, which in order not to jeopardize the vote for black men accepted the refusal to grant women the vote. Susan B. Anthony and Elizabeth Cady Stanton organized the more militant National Woman Suffrage Association. Bitter about what they took to be betrayal by male Republican leaders, they warned that women could not trust men, refused to support the freedmen's right to the vote, and even used racist arguments to explain that it was of greater importance to give the vote to white women. Although their racism declined after the passage of the Fifteenth Amendment, it left a disturbing legacy to the women's movement.

Reconstruction   In most southern states, Reconstruction lasted for
Governments   only a few years. In states with large white majori-
ties, conservatives regained political control rather quickly. Virginia was "redeemed" in 1869, Tennessee and North Carolina in 1870. Georgia fell under conservative rule in 1872, Alabama, Texas, and Arkansas in 1874, and Mississippi in 1875. In only three states—Louisiana, Florida, and South Carolina—did Radical Republican government last a full decade, and they were all "redeemed" in 1877.

Even in those states where blacks made up a majority of the voters, they did not dominate the reconstructed state governments. They formed a majority in one state constitutional convention, that of South Carolina, exactly one half the membership in the Louisiana convention, and a minority in eight others. After the new governments were formed, blacks never held a majority in both houses of a state legislature. No state had an elected black governor; only two black senators and fourteen black representatives were elected to the national Congress. At the local level, blacks never enjoyed a proportionate share of offices. In the constitutional conventions and in legislatures, blacks rarely pressed for equal access to public facilities. Still, during the Reconstruction era blacks were a significant force in southern politics.

The Reconstruction governments were far from being the corrupt and mischief-making institutions that an early generation of historians of the Reconstruction period were to describe. Much of the leadership of Republican regimes fell to native whites or to northerners who had resettled in the South after the war. Most of the local whites who supported or entered Reconstruction governments and became known derisively as "scalawags" were ex-Whigs seeking to reenter politics. These were not mere opportunists; as Whigs they had supported a vigorous federal government, and their beliefs accorded with the policies of congressional Reconstruction. The northerners whom their opponents labeled "carpetbaggers" defy easy characterization. On the average, they were well-educated middle-class professionals: physicians, lawyers, teachers. Many were former Union soldiers attracted by the South's climate and cheap land. Some undoubtedly were profiteers;

others, like Governor Adelbert Ames of Mississippi and Governor Daniel Chamberlain of South Carolina, were idealists. Any discussion of corruption must be measured against the records of previous white southern administrations and against the sorry performance of several northern governments during this era. On the whole, Reconstruction governments made substantial progress toward postwar recovery and social reform. They drafted progressive new constitutions, reapportioned legislatures to give backcountry districts equitable representation, expanded social services, improved roads, encouraged railroad construction, and established the South's first substantial public school system. Much of the so-called extravagance of Reconstruction legislatures merely represented expenditures for public services that previous regimes had neglected.

The Land Question	The blacks were legally free and had the vote. But they lacked the one essential basis of independence and equality: land or an equivalent property. Both

races in the postwar South recognized the importance of the land question. "The way we can best take care of ourselves is to have land and turn it and till it by our labor," contended a delegation of freed people in 1865. This is exactly what former slaveholders feared, and they determined early on to prevent blacks from owning land. Without access to employment except on land owned by whites, all the ballots and education in the world would be worthless. "They who own the real estate of a country control its vote," warned one observer. It is this as much as anything else that explains the successful overthrow of Reconstruction in the South.

A few antislavery activists had wanted to provide land for emancipated slaves. As early as 1862 Congress passed legislation confiscating plantations of Confederate sympathizers, and it was proposed to resettle blacks on them. But the Lincoln Administration showed little interest. In 1865 General William T. Sherman temporarily allotted to thousands of homeless ex-slaves small tracts of confiscated land along the South Atlantic coast. "Forty acres and a mule" became a byword among landless ex-slaves. The Freedman's Bureau attempted a scheme of renting abandoned land to blacks, who were to own it after three years.

This was as close as anyone came to providing a new life for blacks to move into when they moved out of slavery. Andrew Johnson restored confiscated lands to their previous owners and evicted the black tenants. Few northerners supported Stevens' plan to seize private property, even from slaveholders. Congress soundly defeated his watered-down confiscation plan in 1866. It did set aside certain public lands in the South for purchase by freed people. This scheme failed badly, however, because the land available was inferior, and because few ex-slaves had the capital to buy land and farm equipment.

In many areas, the first system to develop in the absence of slavery was that of wage labor. Guided and prodded by agents of the Freedmen's Bureau, blacks signed contracts to work for so much a month and were provided with cabins, often in the former plantation slave quar-

They were free, but the economic condition of most black tenant farmers and sharecroppers was not dramatically better than that of slaves. Redistribution of some confiscated plantation lands might have improved their lot, but the government undertook no such sizable programs. *(Courtesy, Library of Congress)*

ters, and sometimes with food. Yet work in the fields at the white man's bidding, on the white man's land, under the immediate supervision of a white overseer seemed far too much like old slavery in a new guise. Many blacks would have none of it and sabotaged the arrangement. One way was to collect wages during the planting and cultivating months and then decamp just before the crucial harvest, which left the owner with the problem of gathering in the cotton or tobacco without a workforce.

Sharecropping   The specific reason for the rejection of the gang labor system was that it suggested the organization of field work under slavery. But in looking for some alternative, the freed slaves were acting in keeping with an American tradition that identified personal independence with the possession of property. One estimate has a fifth of black farm workers owning land by the 1880s. For most, conventional ownership was not an immediate option. Sporadic attempts, soon after the defeat of the rebels, to seize the land of planters met with resistance by the federal government. An alternative, however inadequate, gave the black family an opportunity to work independently on a plot of ground. This land and labor system finally devised in the postwar South was sharecropping. In this form of tenancy the black worker contributed labor and perhaps the use of some tools and a mule, and received from the landlord some land to farm. At harvest time the cropper got to keep from one-half to two-thirds of the crop, the remaining portion going to the landowner.

The system had some advantages. Blacks now had some personal freedom; there was no overseer to supervise their work. Instead of living in the old slave quarters, moreover, each black family could reside apart on its own rented piece of land. Some blacks simply took their slave cabin from the old quarters to their own farm. Blacks could now decide how to spend their money. And they could arrange their own family division of labor.

The sharecropper system was nevertheless a poor substitute for landowning. Sharecroppers, like other tenants, had little incentive to improve the land they farmed since they did not own it. The credit system that grew up alongside sharecropping was its worst element. Tenants often could not wait until harvest to buy the things they needed during the year. Storekeepers sold them cloth, tools, knick-knacks, and even food on credit, taking out a lien, a kind of mortgage, on the crop as security until harvest time in the fall. Then, when the crop was sold, the storekeeper subtracted the debt from the cropper's share. Those caught in this crop-lien process might not ever see any cash once the storekeeper and the landlord had taken their shares. Goods bought on credit were far more expensive than those bought with cash. The system also allowed many opportunities for fraud. Storekeepers, themselves under considerable economic pressure, kept the accounts and sometimes juggled the books to make sure that the sharecropper remained permanently in debt. Such a tenant remained tied to the storekeeper as a perpetual customer, unable legally to deal with any other merchant until the debt was discharged. Some scholars have seen this debt peonage as the virtual reenslavement of the South's black population. It certainly weakened the possibility that sharecropping might become for any sizable number of former slaves a way station to land ownership.

As pursuers of the nineteenth-century American ideal of small property ownership, the ex-slaves had been from the beginning cousins to the middling and poor whites of the South. In Reconstruction days as before, landowning was common among whites who had possessed no slaves or few. In this respect much better off than the newly freed black population, the white plain folk in this time of uncertainty and open possibility had reason for antagonism to the planters who had led them on a fruitless war for the maintenance of a slaveholding system in which they had largely not shared. But no politics of cooperation materialized between blacks and whites. Racist psychology dominated, and instead of seeing blacks as fellow victims of planter hegemony, poor whites would soon come to view them as upstart competitors for the scraps and tatters of poverty. This gave added cause for the violence that blacks even a century later have suffered from their white neighbors.

As regional impoverishment continued throughout the remainder of the nineteenth century, increasing numbers of rural whites and blacks were ground down into sharecropping. All in all, racial animosity never gave way to a politics of class, but by the late 1880s there were to be some feeble beginnings of just such a politics. Tentative alliances between a few poor blacks and poor whites form a remarkable though faltering episode of late nineteenth-century southern history.

A SHARECROPPING CONTRACT

This contract made and entered into between A. T. Mial of one part and Fenner Powell of the other part both of the County of Wake and State of North Carolina—

Witnesseth—That the Said Fenner Powell hath bargained and agreed with the Said Mial to work as a cropper for the year 1886 on Said Mial's land on the land now occupied by Said Powell on the west Side of Poplar Creek and a point on the east Side of Said Creek and both South and North of the Mial road, leading to Raleigh, That the Said Fenner Powell agrees to work faithfully and dilligently without any unnecessary loss of time, to do all manner of work on Said farm as may be directed by Said Mial, And to be respectful in manners and deportment to Said Mial. And the Said Mial agrees on his part to furnish mule and feed for the same and all plantation tools and Seed to plant the crop free of charge, and to give the Said Powell One half of all crops raised and housed by Said Powell on Said land except the cotton seed. The Said Mial agrees to advance as provision to Said Powell fifty pound of bacon and two sacks of meal pr month and occasionally Some flour to be paid out of his the Said Powell's part of the crop or from any other advance that may be made to Said Powell by Said Mial. As witness our hands and seals this the 16th day of January A.D. 1886

Witness

> A. T. Mial [signed]   [Seal]
>
> his
>
> Fenner X Powell   [Seal]
>
> mark

W. S. Mial [signed]

A black newspaper in New Orleans predicted about sharecropping:

"A kind of general serfdom and humiliation is about to take the place of slavery."

The End of Racial Progress and the Compromise of 1877

Reconstruction remained, at least in fragments, into the 1870s. After white organizations, among them the Ku Klux Klan, began threatening and committing violence on black citizens for exercising their newly acquired rights, the national legislature in the early 1870s put through several Force Acts that aimed at restraining the terrorist groups. A law in 1870 made it a felony to interfere with the exercise of the right to vote. The administration of Ulysses S. Grant, elected President in 1868 as the candidate of the Republican Party, broke the Klan by the end of 1871. Grant had easily won reelection in 1872 against Horace Greeley, publisher of the *New York Tribune*, but his administration suffered from a number of political scandals that suggested widespread corruption. Crédit Mobilier, a dummy corporation formed by a circle of Union Pacific Railroad shareholders, extorted wealth from the company and distributed bribes to prominent congressmen. For a while into the 1870s, some southern states had Reconstruction governments that represented black as well as white voters. And in 1876 there were still a few federal soldiers in the South whose object was to defend the rights of the black community. But the era of Reconstruction was coming to an end.

Finally, in the events that followed the presidential contest of 1876 between the Republican candidate Rutherford B. Hayes of Ohio and

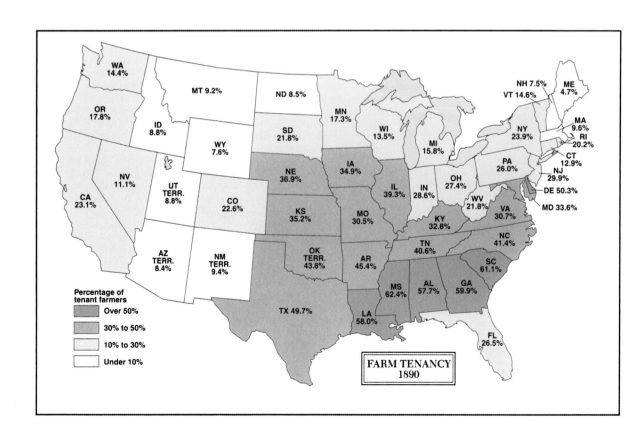

Percentage of tenant farmers

- Over 50%
- 30% to 50%
- 10% to 30%
- Under 10%

FARM TENANCY 1890

Democrat Samuel J. Tilden of New York, the Republican Party abandoned black southerners and their rights. After the general election, which chose the presidential electors who were to cast the actual vote for President, charges of irregularities had arisen concerning procedures in three southern states, South Carolina, Florida, and Louisiana. There the election boards that had counted the popular presidential vote, giving it in each case to the Republicans, were under the control of Republican Reconstruction forces; Democrats suggested that the vote in each state had actually gone for the Democrats. Both parties also claimed one disputed electoral vote in Oregon. Unless the Republican claims could stand in each of the four states, the majority in the whole electoral college would be Democratic and Tilden would be the next President. Democrats and Republicans worked out a scheme for a commission that was to decide among the disputed electors. It was supposed to be balanced between Democratic and Republican members, with one other member, Justice David Davis of the Supreme Court, who was a Republican but was expected to be independent of either party in his decisions. But in a twist of political events Davis resigned, Republican Justice Joseph P. Bradley was appointed in his stead, and the commission by a divided vote chose all the disputed Hayes electors. Democrats believed that they were about to have the election taken away from them. After the dispute had lasted for months, during which there was talk of renewed civil war, the parties came to a solution. In return for a Democratic agreement not to oppose the selection of Hayes electors, Republicans agreed that a Republican presidential administration would not only remove the remaining federal troops from the South but also give political patronage to white southerners and be friendly to economic legislation beneficial to southern states. Hayes, who had expressed concern for the rights of black southerners, presided over the end of a policy that by 1877 no longer had political support. The Republican effort to protect civil rights in the South had ceased.

Suggested Readings

Readings on Reconstruction could start with Eric Foner's volume of that title (1988). Kenneth Stampp's *The Era of Reconstruction, 1865–1877* (1965) is also thorough on the Reconstruction years. An important study of the consequences of freedom for blacks is Leon F. Litwack's *"Been in the Storm So Long": The Aftermath of Slavery* (1979). Harold M. Hyman analyzes the constitutional issues of the era in *A More Perfect Union* (1973). Michael Les Benedict, *The Impeachment and Trial of Andrew Johnson* (1973) is a superior analysis of the divisions and alignments within the Radical Reconstruction Congress and its relationships with the President, whom the author depicts unfavorably. See also Benedict's *A Compromise of Principle: Congressional Republicans and Reconstruction* (1974), which argues that the Radical Republicans found the Reconstruction measures mere compromises. C. Vann Woodward's *Reunion and Reaction* (1951) is about the Compromise of 1877; Keith Polakoff, *The Politics of Inertia* (1977), gives a differing interpretation.

See also John Hope Franklin, *Reconstruction After the Civil War* (1961), Willie Lee Rose, *Rehearsal for Reconstruction: The Port Royal Experiment* (1964), William Gillette, *Retreat from Reconstruction, 1869–1879* (1980), Eric McKitrick, *Andrew Johnson and Reconstruction* (1965), and Allen W. Trelease, *White Terror: The Ku Klux Klan Conspiracy and Southern Reconstruction* (1971). And see William E. Nelson, *The Fourteenth Amendment* (1988), and Richard Current, *Those Terrible Carpetbaggers* (1988).

On the Freedmen's Bureau there are George R. Bentley, *A History of the Freedmen's Bureau* (1965) and William S. McFeely, *Yankee Step-Father: General O. O. Howard and the Freedmen's Bureau* (1965). A good state study is Joe Gray Taylor's *Louisiana Reconstructed, 1863–1877* (1974).

Herbert Gutman in *The Black Family in Slavery and Freedom* (1976) argues that even under slavery there was often a strong nuclear family with the father in charge. See also Hans Trefousse's *Andrew Johnson: A Biography* (1989) and William S. McFeely's *Grant: A Biography* (1981).

Should Andrew Johnson Have Been Impeached?

Michael Les Benedict

As Americans for the first time seriously discussed the possibility of impeaching a president, they arrived at two opposing concepts of the law of impeachment. . . .

Democrats, Republicans who opposed impeachment, and most lawyers argued that a government officer could be impeached only for an act actually criminal, a violation of a criminal statute. Many historians have accepted this view as embodying the proper law of impeachment, accusing those who insisted on a broader interpretation of using impeachment wrongly in a purely political vendetta. But those who espoused the narrow view had an extremely difficult task in sustaining it, because in fact it was a novel argument, running counter to precedent, the overwhelming weight of American legal authority, and logic. . . .

Since legal authorities had almost unanimously adopted the broad view of impeachment, conservatives proceeded to the lawyerlike task of citing their testimony on questions not quite in point. They argued that the power of impeachment should be determined primarily by the words of the Constitution. The framers had authorized the House of Representatives to impeach government officers for "treason, bribery, or other high crimes and misdemeanors." Arguing that the language raised the presumption that impeachment lay only for actual crimes, despite the number of impeachments that seemed to imply the opposite, conservatives cited the great English constitutional commentators Blackstone, Wooddeson, and Hale to the effect that a crime was a violation of law and that laws must be known to the people. . . .

Radicals argued that the "misdemeanors" the Constitution referred to as grounds for impeachment included misfeasance and malfeasance in office as well as crimes indictable before criminal courts. . . .

The radicals' greatest strength resided in the unanimity with which the great American constitutional commentators had upheld the broad view of the impeachment power. . . .

As a practical matter, American constitutional commentators—[Supreme Court Justice Joseph] Story, [William A.] Duer, [James] Kent, [William] Rawle, and the authors of *The Federalist*—recognized that the maintenance of proper checks and balances in government, which they believed guaranteed liberty, depended upon the good faith and restraint of those entrusted with power. They recognized that the danger to liberty and the efficient workings of government lay not in the possibility that the president or lesser executive officers might act illegally, but rather that they might abuse the powers the Constitution *had* delegated to them. . . . The abuses commentators feared were precisely those "too artful to be anticipated by positive law, and sometimes too subtle and mysterious to be fully detected in the limited period of an ordinary investigation. . . ."

Had Republicans acted upon these doctrines, there can be no doubt that Andrew Johnson could have been impeached, tried, convicted, and removed at any time after December 1865, for his activities fitted precisely into the pattern Pomeroy, Rawle, and others had outlined. . . .

Historians have often interpreted the impeachment movement as part of a drive for congressional supremacy. Had it succeeded, some suggest, the government of the United States might have evolved into a parliamentary system. But in fact it had not been Congress but the President who had been claiming broad new powers. It was Andrew Johnson who had appointed provisional governors of vast territories without the advice and consent of the Senate, who had nullified congressional legislation, who claimed inherent quasi-legislative powers over Reconstruction. In many ways, Johnson was a very modern president, holding a view of presidential authority that has only recently been established. Impeachment was Congress's defensive weapon; it proved a dull blade, and the end result is that the only effective recourse against a president who ignores the will of Congress or exceeds his powers is democratic removal at the polls.

Michael Les Benedict, *The Impeachment and Trial of Andrew Johnson* (New York: W. W. Norton and Co., 1973). Reprinted by permission.

So Johnson had won. . . . To find the reasons for his victory, the political situation and the circumstances of the trial must be kept in mind. True, the Republicans enjoyed an overwhelming majority in both houses, the president had forfeited much of his popularity, and the country was anxious to proceed with Reconstruction, but it proved impossible to convict the executive on the charges presented. In the first place, they were dubious. From the very beginning, Thaddeus Stevens himself realized their weakness. "As the Committee are likely to present no articles having any real vigor in them," he wrote [Representative Benjamin F.] Butler on February 28, "I submit to you if it is not worth our while to attempt to add at least two other articles." The result was the addition of the last two charges [one accusing Johnson of having brought Congress into disrepute and the other summarizing the previous charges], which even radical newspapers and editors criticized as a mere afterthought. . . .

The House should have waited a few days before acting, Representative Thomas A. Jenckes heard from his home in Rhode Island. "Johnson would then have been mad enough to commit some further misdemeanor upon which you could have prosecuted him with the certainty of convicting him." The charges added up to a "penny whistle affair," thought Benjamin B. French, and Senator John B. Henderson characterized them as counts of "narrow bounds in offense both in act and intent."

If the case was weak, the managers' conduct did not help. "The managers of the House of Representatives have been poor judges of human nature and poor readers of human motives," wrote the Chicago *Tribune* on May 9. One could hardly call Johnson a "great" criminal as they had done. Butler, who had vowed to try the case as he would a horse case, appeared aggressive and offensive. Because the managers had a poor case, they took refuge in various legal devices, a tactic seen as a confession of weakness.

Constitutional considerations also played a role in Johnson's acquittal. The genius of the American system was widely believed to be founded on the tripartite division of government. The legislative, executive, and judicial branches operated each in its proper sphere, and as the impeachment trial coincided with attacks on the Supreme Court, there was widespread fear of the danger of legislative supremacy. Assessing the case many years later, Edmund Ross came to the conclusion that "the impeachment of the President was an assault upon the principle of coordination that underlies our political system and thus a menace to our established political forms, as, if successful, it would, logically, have been the practical destruction of the Executive Department." And [Senator Lyman] Trumbull, in justifying his vote for acquittal, stated: "Once set the example of impeaching the President for what, when the excitement of the hour shall have subsided, will be regarded as insufficient causes . . . no future President will be safe who happens to differ with a majority of the House and two-thirds of the Senate on any measure deemed by them important, particularly if of political character. . . . What then becomes of the checks and balances of the Constitution, so carefully devised and so vital to its perpetuity? They are all gone."

The short time left of Johnson's term was also a factor. "To convict and depose a Chief Magistrate of a great country while his guilt was not made palpable by the record, and for insufficient cause, would be fraught with greater danger to the future of the country than can arise from leaving Mr. Johnson in office for the remaining months of his term," Trumbull wrote in his opinion. Conviction would not have benefited Grant, and the Republicans were now determined to elect him president. Thus Republicans failed to find Johnson guilty, as he had gambled they would.

And what had the President accomplished by his victory? Above all, he had succeeded in preserving the Constitution that he admired so much. No other President would ever again be impeached for political differences with Congress; the separation of powers was preserved, and the United States retained its presidential form of government, which set it apart from the cabinet systems of European countries.

Hans L. Trefousse, *Andrew Johnson: A Biography* (New York: W. W. Norton and Co., 1989). Reprinted by permission.

Appendixes

The Declaration of Independence

When in the Course of human events, it becomes necessary for one people to dissolve the political bands which have connected them with another, and to assume among the Powers of the earth, the separate and equal station to which the Laws of Nature and of Nature's God entitle them, a decent respect to the opinions of mankind requires that they should declare the causes which impel them to the separation.

We hold these truths to be self-evident, that all men are created equal, that they are endowed by their Creator with certain unalienable Rights, that among these are Life, Liberty and the pursuit of Happiness. That to secure these rights, Governments are instituted among Men, deriving their just powers from the consent of the governed, That whenever any Form of Government becomes destructive of these ends, it is the Right of the People to alter or to abolish it, and to institute new Government, laying its foundation on such principles and organizing its powers in such form, as to them shall seem most likely to effect their Safety and Happiness. Prudence, indeed, will dictate that Governments long established should not be changed for light and transient causes; and accordingly all experience hath shown, that mankind are more disposed to suffer, while evils are sufferable, than to right themselves by abolishing the forms to which they are accustomed. When a long train of abuses and usurpations, pursuing invariably the same Object evinces a design to reduce them under absolute Despotism, it is their right, it is their duty, to throw off such Government, and to provide new Guards for their future security.—Such has been the patient sufferance of these Colonies; and such is now the necessity which constrains them to alter their former Systems of Government. The history of the present King of Great Britain is a history of repeated injuries and usurpations, all having in direct object the establishment of an absolute Tyranny over these States. To prove this, let Facts be submitted to a candid world.

He has refused his Assent to Laws, the most wholesome and necessary for the public good.

He has forbidden his Governors to pass Laws of immediate and pressing importance, unless suspended in their operation till his Assent should be obtained; and when so suspended, he has utterly neglected to attend to them.

He has refused to pass other Laws for the accommodation of large districts of people, unless those people would relinquish the right of Representation in the Legislature, a right inestimable to them and formidable to tyrants only.

He has dissolved Representative Houses repeatedly, for opposing with manly firmness his invasions on the rights of the people.

He has refused for a long time, after such dissolutions, to cause others to be elected; whereby the Legislative Powers, incapable of Annihilation, have returned to the People at large for their exercise; the State remaining in the mean time exposed to all the dangers of invasion from without, and convulsions within.

He has endeavoured to prevent the population of these States; for that purpose obstructing the Laws of Naturalization of Foreigners; refusing to pass others to encourage their migration hither, and raising the conditions of new Appropriations of Lands.

He has obstructed the Administration of Justice, by refusing his Assent to Laws for establishing Judiciary Powers.

He has made Judges dependent on his Will alone, for the tenure of their offices, and the amount and payment of their salaries.

He has erected a multitude of New Offices, and sent hither swarms of Officers to harass our People, and eat out their substance.

He has kept among us, in times of peace, Standing Armies without the Consent of our legislature.

He has affected to render the Military independent of and superior to the Civil Power.

He has combined with others to subject us to a jurisdiction foreign to our constitution, and unacknowledged by our laws; giving his Assent to their acts of pretended legislation:

For quartering large bodies of armed troops among us:

For protecting them, by a mock Trial, from Punishment for any Murders which they should commit on the Inhabitants of these States:

For cutting off our Trade with all parts of the world:

For imposing taxes on us without our Consent:

For depriving us in many cases, of the benefits of Trial by Jury:

For transporting us beyond Seas to be tried for pretended offences:

For abolishing the free System of English Laws in a neighbouring Province, establishing therein an Arbitrary government, and enlarging its Boundaries so as to render it at once an example and fit instrument for introducing the same absolute rule into these Colonies:

For taking away our Charters, abolishing our most valuable Laws, and altering fundamentally the Forms of our Governments:

For suspending our own Legislature, and declaring themselves invested with Power to legislate for us in all cases whatsoever.

He has abdicated Government here, by declaring us out of his Protection and waging War against us.

He has plundered our seas, ravaged our Coasts, burnt our towns, and destroyed the lives of our people.

He is at this time transporting large armies of foreign mercenaries to compleat the works of death, desolation and tyranny, already begun with circumstances of Cruelty & perfidy scarcely paralleled in the most barbarous ages, and totally unworthy the Head of a civilized nation.

He has constrained our fellow Citizens taken Captive on the high Seas to bear Arms against their Country, to become the executioners of their friends and Brethren, or to fall themselves by their Hands.

He has excited domestic insurrections amongst us, and has endeavoured to bring on the inhabitants of our frontiers, the merciless Indian Savages, whose known rule of warfare, is an undistinguished destruction of all ages, sexes and conditions.

In every stage of these Oppressions We have Petitioned for Redress in the most humble terms: Our repeated Petitions have been answered only by repeated injury. A Prince, whose character is thus marked by every act which may define a Tyrant, is unfit to be the ruler of a free People.

Nor have We been wanting in attention to our British brethren. We have warned them from time to time of attempts by their legislature to extend an unwarrantable jurisdiction over us. We have reminded them of the circumstances of our emigration and settlement here. We have appealed to their native justice and magnanimity, and we have conjured them by the ties of our common kindred to disavow these usurpations, which, would inevitably interrupt our connections and correspondence. They too have been deaf to the voice of justice and of consanguinity. We must, therefore, acquiesce in the necessity, which denounces our Separation, and hold them, as we hold the rest of mankind, Enemies in War, in Peace Friends.

We, therefore, the Representatives of the United States of America, in General Congress, Assembled, appealing to the Supreme Judge of the world for the rectitude of our intentions, do, in the Name, and by Authority of the good People of these Colonies, solemnly publish and declare, That these United Colonies are, and of Right ought to be Free and Independent States; that they are Absolved from all Allegiance to the British Crown, and that all political connection between them and the State of Great Britain, is and ought to be totally dissolved; and that as Free and Independent States, they have full Power to levy War, conclude Peace, contract Alliances, establish Commerce, and to do all other Acts and Things which Independent States may of right do. And for the support of this Declaration, with a firm reliance on the Protection of Divine Providence, we mutually pledge to each other our Lives, our Fortunes and our sacred Honor.

The Constitution of the United States

We the people of the United States, in Order to form a more perfect Union, establish Justice, insure domestic Tranquility, provide for the common defense, promote the general Welfare, and secure the Blessings of Liberty to ourselves and our Posterity, do ordain and establish this CONSTITUTION for the United States of America.

ARTICLE 1

Section 1.   All legislative Powers herein granted shall be vested in a Congress of the United States which shall consist of a Senate and House of Representatives.

Section 2.   The House of Representatives shall be composed of Members chosen every second Year by the People of the several States, and the Electors in each State shall have the Qualifications requisite for Electors of the most numerous Branch of the State Legislature.

No Person shall be a Representative who shall not have attained to the Age of twenty-five Years, and been seven Years a Citizen of the United States, and who shall not, when elected, be an inhabitant of that State in which he shall be chosen.

Representatives and direct Taxes shall be apportioned among the several States which may be included within this Union, according to their respective Numbers, which shall be determined by adding to the whole Number of free Persons, including those bound to Service for a Term of Years and excluding Indians not taxed, three fifths of all other Persons. The actual Enumeration shall be made within three Years after the first Meeting of the Congress of the United States, and within every subsequent Term of ten Years, in such Manner as they shall by Law direct. The Number of Representatives shall not exceed one for every thirty Thousand, but each State shall have at Least one Representative; and until such enumeration shall be made, the State of New Hampshire shall be entitled to chuse three, Massachusetts eight, Rhode-Island and Providence Plantations one, Connecticut five, New-York six, New Jersey four, Pennsylvania eight, Delaware one, Maryland six, Virginia ten, North Carolina five, South Carolina five, and Georgia three.

When vacancies happen in the Representation from any State, the Executive Authority thereof shall issue Writs of Election to fill such Vacancies.

The House of Representatives shall chuse their Speaker and other Officers; and shall have the sole Power of Impeachment.

Section 3.   The Senate of the United States shall be composed of two Senators from each State, chosen by the Legislature thereof, for six Years; and each Senator shall have one Vote.

Immediately after they shall be assembled in Consequence of the first Election, they shall be divided as equally as may be into three Classes. The Seats of the Senators of the first Class shall be vacated at the Expiration of the second Year, of the second Class at the Expiration of the fourth Year, and of the third Class at the Expiration of the sixth Year, so that one-third may be chosen every second Year; and if Vacancies happen by Resignation, or otherwise, during the Recess of the Legislature of any State, the Executive thereof may make temporary Appointments until the next Meeting of the Legislature, which shall then fill such Vacancies.

No Person shall be a Senator who shall not have attained to the Age of thirty Years, and been nine Years a Citizen of the United States, and who shall not, when elected, be an Inhabitant of that State in which he shall be chosen.

The Vice President of the United States shall be President of the Senate, but shall have no vote, unless they be equally divided.

The Senate shall chuse their other Officers, and also a President pro tempore, in the absence of the Vice President, or when he shall exercise the Office of the President of the United States.

The Senate shall have the sole Power to try all Impeachments. When sitting for that purpose, they shall be on Oath or Affirmation. When the President of the United States is tried, the Chief Justice shall preside: And no person shall be convicted without the Concurrence of two thirds of the Members present.

Judgment in Cases of Impeachment shall not ex-

tend further than to removal from Office, and disqualification to hold and enjoy an Office of honor, Trust, or Profit under the United States: but the Party convicted shall nevertheless be liable and subject to Indictment, Trial, Judgment, and Punishment, according to Law.

Section 4.   The Times, Places and Manner of holding Elections for Senators and Representatives, shall be prescribed in each state by the Legislature thereof; but the Congress may at any time by Law make or alter such Regulations, except as to the Places of Chusing Senators.

The Congress shall assemble at least once in every Year, and such Meeting shall be on the first Monday in December, unless they shall by Law appoint a different Day.

Section 5.   Each House shall be the Judge of the Elections, Returns and Qualifications of its own Members, and a Majority of each shall constitute a Quorum to do Business from day to day, and may be authorized to compel the Attendance of absent Members, in such Manner, and under such Penalties, as each House may provide.

Each House may determine the Rules of its Proceedings, punish its Members for disorderly Behavior, and, with the Concurrence of two thirds, expel a Member.

Each House shall keep a Journal of its Proceedings, and from time to time publish the same, excepting such Parts as may in their Judgment require Secrecy; and the Yeas and Nays of the Members of either House on any question shall, at the Desire of one fifth of those Present, be entered on the Journal.

Neither House, during the Session of Congress, shall, without the Consent of the other, adjourn for more than three days, nor to any other Place than that in which the two Houses shall be sitting.

Section 6.   The Senators and Representatives shall receive a Compensation for their Services, to be ascertained by Law, and paid out of the Treasury of the United States. They shall in all Cases, except Treason, Felony, and Breach of the Peace, be privileged from Arrest during their Attendance at the Session of their respective Houses, and in going to and returning from the same; and for any Speech or Debate in either House, they shall not be questioned in any other Place.

No Senator or Representative shall, during the Time for which he was elected, be appointed to any civil Office under the Authority of the United States, which shall have been created, or the Emoluments whereof shall have been encreased during such time; and no Person holding any Office under the United States shall be a Member of either House during his continuance in Office.

Section 7. All Bills for raising Revenue shall originate in the House of Representatives; but the Senate may propose or concur with Amendments as on other bills.

Every Bill which shall have passed the House of Representatives and the Senate, shall, before it become a Law, be presented to the President of the United States. If he approve he shall sign it, but if not he shall return it, with his Objections, to that House in which it shall have originated, who shall enter the Objections at large on their Journal, and proceed to reconsider it. If after such Reconsideration two thirds of that House shall agree to pass the bill, it shall be sent, together with the objections, to the other House, by which it shall likewise be reconsidered, and if approved by two thirds of that House, it shall become a Law. But in all such Cases the Votes of both Houses shall be determined by Yeas and Nays, and the Names of the Persons voting for and against the Bill shall be entered on the Journal of each House respectively. If any Bill shall not be returned by the President within ten Days (Sundays excepted) after it shall have been presented to him, the Same shall be a Law, in like Manner as if he had signed it, unless the Congress by their Adjournment prevent its Return, in which Case it shall not be a Law.

Every Order, Resolution, or Vote to which the Concurrence of the Senate and House of Representatives may be necessary (except on a question of Adjournment) shall be presented to the President of the United States; and before the Same shall take Effect, shall be approved by him, or being disapproved by him, shall be repassed by two thirds of the Senate and House of Representatives, according to the Rules and Limitations prescribed in the Case of a Bill.

Section 8. The Congress shall have Power To lay and collect Taxes, Duties, Imposts and Excises, to pay the Debts and provide for the common Defence and general Welfare of the United States; but all Duties, Imposts and Excises shall be uniform throughout the United States;

To borrow money on the credit of the United States;

To regulate Commerce with foreign Nations, and among the several States, and with the Indian Tribes;

To establish an uniform Rule of Naturalization, and uniform Laws on the subject of Bankruptcies throughout the United States;

To coin Money, regulate the Value thereof, and of foreign Coin, and fix the Standard of Weights and Measures;

To provide for the Punishment of counterfeiting the Securities and current Coin of the United States;

To establish Post Offices and Post Roads;

To promote the Progress of Science and useful Arts, by securing for limited Times to Authors and Inventors the exclusive Right to their respective Writings and Discoveries;

To constitute Tribunals inferior to the Supreme Court;

To define and punish Piracies and Felonies committed on the high Seas, and Offences against the Law of Nations;

To declare War, grant Letters of Marque and Reprisal, and make Rules concerning Captures on Land and Water;

To raise and support Armies, but no Appropriation of Money to that Use shall be for a longer Term than two Years;

To provide and maintain a Navy;

To make Rules for the Government and Regulation of the land and naval forces;

To provide for calling forth the Militia to execute the Laws of the Union, suppress Insurrections and repel Invasions;

To provide for organizing, arming, and disciplining the Militia, and for governing such Part of them as may be employed in the Service of the United States, reserving to the States respectively, the Appointment of the Officers, and the Authority of training the Militia according to the discipline prescribed by Congress;

To exercise exclusive Legislation in all Cases whatsoever, over such District (not exceeding ten Miles square) as may, by Cession of particular States, and the acceptance of Congress, become the Seat of Government of the United States, and to exercise like Authority over all Places purchased by the Consent of the Legislature of the States in which the Same shall be, for the Erection of Forts, Magazines, Arsenals, dock-Yards, and other needful Buildings—And

To make all Laws which shall be necessary and proper for carrying into Execution the foregoing Powers, and all other Powers vested by this Constitution in the Government of the United States, or in any Department or Officer thereof.

Section 9. The Migration or Importation of such Persons as any of the States now existing shall think proper to admit, shall not be prohibited by the Congress prior to the Year one thousand eight hundred and eight, but a tax or duty may be imposed on such Importation, not exceeding ten dollars for each Person.

The privilege of the Writ of Habeas Corpus shall not be suspended, unless when in Cases of Rebellion or Invasion the public Safety may require it.

No Bill of Attainder or ex post facto Law shall be passed.

No Capitation, or other direct, Tax shall be laid unless in Proportion to the Census or Enumeration herein before directed to be taken.

No Tax or Duty shall be laid on Articles exported from any State.

No Preference shall be given by any Regulation of Revenue to the Ports of one State over those of another: nor shall Vessels bound to, or from, one State, be obliged to enter, clear, or pay Duties in another.

No Money shall be drawn from the Treasury, but in Consequence of Appropriations made by Law; and a regular Statement and Account of the Receipts and Expenditures of all public Money shall be published from time to time.

No Title of Nobility shall be granted by the United States: And no Person holding any Office of Profit or Trust under them, shall, without the Consent of the Congress, accept of any present, Emolument, Office, or Title, of any kind whatever, from any King, Prince, or foreign State.

Section 10. No State shall enter any Treaty, Alliance, or Confederation; grant Letters of Marque and Reprisal; coin Money; emit Bills of Credit; make any Thing but gold and silver Coin a Tender in Payment of Debts; pass any Bill of Attainder, ex post facto Law, or Law impairing the Obligation of Contracts, or grant any Title of Nobility.

No State shall, without the Consent of the Congress, lay any Imposts or Duties on Imports or Exports, except what may be absolutely necessary for executing its inspection Laws: and the net Produce of all Duties and Imposts, laid by any State on Imports or Exports, shall be for the Use of the Treasury of the United States; and all such Laws shall be subject to the Revision and Control of the Congress.

No State shall, without the Consent of Congress, lay any duty of Tonnage, keep Troops, or Ships of War in time of Peace, enter into any Agreement or Compact with another State, or with a foreign Power, or engage in War, unless actually invaded, or in such imminent Danger as will not admit of delay.

ARTICLE II

Section 1. The executive Power shall be vested in a President of the United States of America. He shall hold his Office during the Term of four years,

and, together with the Vice-President, chosen for the same Term, be elected, as follows:

Each State shall appoint, in such Manner as the Legislature thereof may direct, a Number of Electors, equal to the whole Number of Senators and Representatives to which the State may be entitled in the Congress; but no Senator or Representative, or Person holding an Office of Trust or Profit under the United States, shall be appointed an Elector.

The Electors shall meet in their respective States, and vote by Ballot for two persons, of whom one at least shall not be an Inhabitant of the same State with themselves. And they shall make a List of all the Persons voted for, and of the Number of Votes for each; which List they shall sign and certify, and transmit sealed to the Seat of the Government of the United States, directed to the President of the Senate. The President of the Senate shall, in the Presence of the Senate and House of Representatives, open all the Certificates, and the Votes shall then be counted. The Person having the greatest Number of Votes shall be the President, if such Number be a Majority of the whole Number of Electors appointed; and if there be more than one who have such Majority, and have an equal Number of Votes, then the House of Representatives shall immediately chuse by Ballot one of them for President; and if no Person have a Majority, then from the five highest on the List the said House shall in like Manner chuse the President. But in chusing the President, the Votes shall be taken by States, the Representation from each State having one Vote; a quorum for this Purpose shall consist of a Member or Members from two-thirds of the States, and a Majority of all the States shall be necessary to a Choice. In every Case, after the Choice of the President, the Person having the greatest Number of Votes of the Electors shall be the Vice President. But if there should remain two or more who have equal votes, the Senate shall chuse from them by Ballot the Vice-President.

The Congress may determine the Time of chusing the Electors, and the Day on which they shall give their Votes; which Day shall be the same throughout the United States.

No person except a natural-born Citizen, or a Citizen of the United States, at the time of the Adoption of this Constitution, shall be eligible to the Office of President; neither shall any Person be eligible to that Office who shall not have attained to the Age of thirty-five years, and been fourteen Years a Resident within the United States.

In Case of the Removal of the President from Office, or of his Death, Resignation, or Inability to discharge the Powers and Duties of the said Office, the same shall devolve on the Vice-President, and the Congress may by Law provide for the Case of Removal, Death, Resignation, or Inability, both of the President and Vice-President, declaring what Officer shall then act as President, and such Officer shall act accordingly, until the disability be removed, or a President shall be elected.

The President shall, at stated Times, receive for his Services a Compensation, which shall neither be increased nor diminished during the Period for which he shall have been elected, and he shall not receive within that Period any other Emolument from the United States, or any of them.

Before he enters on the execution of his Office, he shall take the following Oath or Affirmation:— "I do solemnly swear (or affirm) that I will faithfully execute the Office of President of the United States, and will, to the best of my Ability, preserve, protect, and defend the Constitution of the United States."

Section 2.   The President shall be Commander in Chief of the Army and Navy of the United States, and of the Militia of the several States, when called into the actual Service of the United States; he may require the Opinion, in writing, of the principal Officer in each of the executive Departments, upon any subject relating to the Duties of their respective Offices, and he shall have Power to Grant Reprieves and Pardons for Offences against the United States, except in Cases of Impeachment.

He shall have Power, by and with the Advice and Consent of the Senate, to make Treaties, provided two thirds of the Senators present concur; and he shall nominate, and by and with the Advice and Consent of the Senate, shall appoint Ambassadors, other public Ministers and Counsuls, Judges of the Supreme Court, and all other Officers of the United States, whose Appointments are herein otherwise provided for, and which shall be established by Law: but the Congress may by Law vest the Appointments of such inferior Officers, as they think proper, in the President alone, in the Courts of Law, or in the Heads of Departments.

The President shall have Power to fill up all Vacancies that may happen during the Recess of the Senate, by granting Commissions which shall expire at the End of their next Session.

Section 3.   He shall from time to time give to the Congress Information of the State of the Union, and recommend to their Consideration such Measures as he shall judge necessary and expedient; he may, on extraordinary occasions, convene both Houses, or either of them, and in Case of Disagreement between them, with respect to the Time of Adjournment, he may adjourn them to such Time as he shall think proper; he shall receive Ambassadors and other public Ministers; he shall take Care that the Laws be faithfully executed, and shall Commission all the Officers of the United States

Section 4.   The President, Vice President and all civil Officers of the United States, shall be removed from Office on Impeachment for, and Conviction of, Treason, Bribery, or other high Crimes and Misdemeanors.

ARTICLE III

Section 1.   The judicial Power of the United States, shall be vested in one supreme Court, and in such inferior Courts as the Congress may from time to time ordain and establish. The Judges, both of the supreme and inferior Courts, shall hold their Offices during good Behavior, and shall, at stated Times, receive for their Services, a compensation, which shall not be diminished during their Continuance in Office.

Section 2.   The judicial Power shall extend to all Cases, in Law and Equity, arising under this constitution, the Laws of the United States, and treaties made, or which shall be made, under their Authority;—to all Cases affecting ambassadors, other public ministers and consuls;—to all cases of admiralty and maritime Jurisdiction;—to Controversies to which the United States shall be a Party;—to Controversies between two or more States;—between a State and Citizens of another State;—between Citizens of different States,—between Citizens of the same State claiming Lands under Grants of different States, and between a State, or the Citizens thereof, and foreign States, Citizens or Subjects.

In all Cases affecting Ambassadors, other public Ministers and Consuls, and those in which a State shall be Party, the supreme Court shall have original Jurisdiction. In all the other Cases before mentioned, the supreme Court shall have appellate Jurisdiction, both as to Law and Fact, with such Exception, and under such Regulations as the Congress shall make.

The trial of all Crimes, except in Cases of Impeachment, shall be by Jury; and such Trial shall be held in the State where the said Crimes shall have been committed; but when not committed within any State, the Trial shall be at such Place or Places as the Congress may by Law have directed.

Section 3.   Treason against the United States, shall consist only in levying War against them, or in adhering to their Enemies, giving them Aid and Comfort. No Person shall be convicted of Treason unless on the Testimony of two Witnesses to the same overt Act, or on Confession in open Court.

The Congress shall have power to declare the Punishment of Treason, but no Attainder of Treason shall work Corruption of Blood, or Forfeiture except during the Life of the Person attainted.

ARTICLE IV

Section 1.   Full Faith and Credit shall be given in each State to the public Acts, Records, and judicial Proceedings of every other State. And the Congress may by general laws prescribe the Manner in which such Acts, Records and Proceedings shall be proved, and the Effect thereof.

Section 2.   The Citizens of each State shall be entitled to all Privileges and Immunities of Citizens in the several States.

A Person charged in any State with Treason, Felony, or other Crime, who shall flee from Justice, and be found in another State, shall on demand of the executive Authority of the State from which he fled, be delivered up, to be removed to the State having Jurisdiction of the crime.

No Person held to Service or Labour in one State, under the Laws thereof, escaping into another, shall, in Consequence of any Law or Regulation therein, be discharged from such Service or Labour, but shall be delivered up on Claim of the Party to whom such Service or Labour may be due.

Section 3.   New States may be admitted by the Congress into this Union; but no new State shall be formed or erected within the Jurisdiction of any other State; nor any State be formed by the Junction of two or more States, or parts of States, without the Consent of the Legislatures of the States concerned as well as of the Congress.

The Congress shall have Power to dispose of and make all needful Rules and Regulations respecting the Territory or other Property belonging to the United States; and nothing in this constitution shall be so construed as to Prejudice any Claims of the United States, or of any particular State.

Section 4.   The United States shall guarantee to every State in this Union a Republican Form of Government, and shall protect each of them against Invasion; and on Application of the Legislature, or the Executive (when the Legislature cannot be convened) against domestic Violence.

ARTICLE V

The Congress, whenever two-thirds of both Houses shall deem it necessary, shall propose Amendments to this Constitution, or, on the Application of the Legislatures of two-thirds of the several States, shall call a Convention for proposing Amendments, which, in either Case, shall be valid to all Intents and Purposes, as part of this Constitution, when ratified by the Legislatures of three-fourths of the several States, or by Conventions in three-fourths thereof, as the one or the other Mode of Ratification may be proposed by the Congress; Provided that no Amendment which may be made prior to the Year One thousand eight hundred and eight shall in any Manner affect the first and fourth Clauses in the Ninth Section of the first Article; and that no State, without its Consent, shall be deprived of its equal Suffrage in the Senate.

ARTICLE VI

Debts contracted and Engagements entered into, before the Adoption of this Constitution, shall be as valid against the United States under this Constitution, as under the Confederation.

This Constitution, and the Laws of the United States which shall be made in Pursuance thereof; and the Treaties made, or which shall be made, under the Authority of the United States, shall be the supreme Law of the Land; and the Judges in every State shall be bound thereby, any Thing in the Constitution of Laws of any State to the Contrary notwithstanding.

The Senators and Representatives before mentioned, and the Members of the several State Legislatures, and all executive and judicial Officers, both of the United States and of the several States, shall be bound by Oath or Affirmation to support this Constitution; but no religious Test shall ever be required as a qualification to any Office or public Trust under the United States.

ARTICLE VII

The Ratification of the Conventions of nine States shall be sufficient for the Establishment of this Constitution between the States so ratifying the same.

Done in Convention by the Unanimous Consent of the States present the Seventeenth Day of September in the Year of our Lord one thousand seven hundred and Eighty seven, and of the Independence of the United States of America the Twelfth. In Witness whereof We have hereunto subscribed our names.

Signed by
George Washington
Presidt and Deputy from Virginia
(and thirty-eight others)

Articles in Addition to, and Amendment of, the Constitution of the United States of America. Proposed by Congress, and Ratified by the Legislatures of the Several States, Pursuant to the Fifth Article of the Original Constitution.

AMENDMENT I [1791]

Congress shall make no law respecting an establishment of religion, or prohibiting the free exercise thereof; or abridging the freedom of speech, or of the press; or the right of the people peaceably to assemble, and to petition the Government for a redress of grievances.

AMENDMENT II [1791]

A well regulated Militia, being necessary to the security of a free State, the right of the people to keep and bear Arms, shall not be infringed.

AMENDMENT III [1791]

No Soldier shall, in time of peace be quartered in any house, without the consent of the Owner, nor in time of war, but in a manner to be prescribed by law.

AMENDMENT IV [1791]

The right of the people to be secure in their persons, houses, papers, and effects, against unreasonable searches and seizures, shall not be violated, and no Warrants shall issue, but upon probable cause, supported by Oath or affirmation, and particularly describing the place to be searched, and the persons or things to be seized.

AMENDMENT V [1791]

No person shall be held to answer for a capital or otherwise infamous crime, unless on a presentment or indictment of a Grand Jury, except in cases arising in the land or naval forces, or in the Militia, when in actual service in time of war or public danger; nor shall any person be subject for the same offence to be twice put in jeopardy of life or limb; nor shall be compelled in any criminal case to be a witness against himself, nor be deprived of life, liberty, or property, without due process of law; nor shall private property be taken for public use, without just compensation.

AMENDMENT VI [1791]

In all criminal prosecutions, the accused shall enjoy the right to a speedy and public trial, by an impartial jury of the State and district wherein the crime shall have been committed, which district shall have been previously ascertained by law, and to be informed of the nature and cause of the accusation; to be confronted with the witnesses against him; to have compulsory process for obtaining witnesses in his favor, and to have the Assistance of Counsel for his defence.

AMENDMENT VII [1791]

In suits at common law, where the value in controversy shall exceed twenty dollars, the right of trial by jury shall be preserved, and no fact tried by a jury, shall be otherwise reexamined in any Court of the United States, than according to the rules of the common law.

AMENDMENT VIII [1791]

Excessive bail shall not be required, nor excessive fines imposed, nor cruel and unusual punishments inflicted.

AMENDMENT IX [1791]

The enumeration in the Constitution, of certain rights, shall not be construed to deny or disparage others retained by the people.

AMENDMENT X [1791]

The powers not delegated to the United States by the Constitution, nor prohibited by it to the States, are reserved to the States respectively, or to the people.

AMENDMENT XI [1798]

The Judicial power of the United States shall not be construed to extend to any suit in law or equity, commenced or prosecuted against one of the United States by Citizens of another State, or by Citizens or Subjects of any Foreign State.

AMENDMENT XII [1804]

The Electors shall meet in their respective States and vote by ballot for President and Vice-President, one of whom, at least, shall not be an inhabitant of the same State with themselves; they shall name in their ballots the person voted for as President, and in distinct ballots the person voted for as Vice-President, and they shall make distinct lists of all persons voted for as President, and of all persons voted for as Vice-President, and of the number of votes for each, which lists they shall sign and certify, and transmit sealed to the seat of the government of the United States, directed to the President of the Senate;—The President of the Senate shall, in the presence of the Senate and House of Representatives, open all the certificates and the votes shall then be counted;—The person having the greatest number of votes for President, shall be the President, if such number by a majority of the whole number of Electors appointed; and if no person have such majority, then from the persons having the highest numbers not exceeding three on the list of those voted for as President, the House of Representatives shall choose immediately, by ballot, the President. But in choosing the President, the votes shall be taken by states, the representation from each state having one vote; a quorum for this purpose shall consist of a member or members from two-thirds of the states, and a majority of all the states shall be necessary to a choice. And if the House of Representatives shall not choose a President whenever the right of choice shall devolve upon them, before the fourth day of March next following, then the Vice-President shall act as President, as in the case of the death or other constitutional disability of the President.—The person having the greatest number of votes as Vice-President, shall be the Vice-President, if such number be a majority of the whole number of Electors appointed, and if no person have a majority, then from the two highest numbers on the list, the Senate shall choose the Vice-President; a quorum for the purpose shall consist of two-thirds of the whole number of Senators, and a majority of the whole number shall be necessary to a choice. But no person constitutionally ineligible to the office of President shall be eligible to that of Vice-President of the United States.

AMENDMENT XIII [1865]

Section 1.   Neither slavery nor involuntary servitude, except as a punishment for crime whereof the party shall have been duly convicted, shall exist within the United States, or any place subject to their jurisdiction.

Section 2.   Congress shall have power to enforce this article by appropriate legislation.

AMENDMENT XIV [1868]

Section 1.   All persons born or naturalized in the United States, and subject to the jurisdiction thereof, are citizens of the United States and of the State wherein they reside. No State shall make or enforce any law which shall abridge the privileges or immunities of citizens of the United States; nor shall any State deprive any person of life, liberty, or property, without due process of law; nor deny to any person within its jurisdiction the equal protection of the laws.

Section 2.   Representatives shall be apportioned among the several States according to their respective numbers, counting the whole number of persons in each State, excluding Indians not taxed. But when the right to vote at any election for the choice of electors for President and Vice-President of the United States, Representatives in Congress, the Executive and Judicial officers of a State, or the members of the Legislature thereof, is denied to any of the male inhabitants of such State, being twenty-one years of age, and citizens of the United States, or in any way abridged, except for participation in rebellion, or other crime, the basis of representation therein shall be reduced in the proportion which the number of such male citizens shall bear to the whole number of male citizens twenty-one years of age in such State.

Section 3.   No person shall be a Senator or Representative in Congress, or elector of President and Vice-President, or hold any office, civil or military, under the United States, or under any State, who, having previously taken an oath, as a member of Congress, or as an officer of the United States, or as a member of any State legislature, or as an executive or judicial officer of any State, to support the Constitution of the United States, shall have engaged in insurrection or rebellion against the same, or given aid or comfort to the enemies thereof. But Congress may by a vote of two-thirds of each House, remove such disability.

Section 4.   The validity of the public debt of the United States, authorized by law, including debts incurred for payment of pensions and bounties for services in suppressing insurrection or rebellion, shall not be questioned. But neither the United States nor any State shall assume or pay any debt or obligation incurred in aid of insurrection or rebellion against the United States or any claim for the loss or emancipation of any slave; but all such debts, obligations, and claims shall be held illegal and void.

Section 5.   The Congress shall have the power to enforce, by appropriate legislation, the provisions of this article.

AMENDMENT XV [1870]

Section 1.   The right of citizens of the United States to vote shall not be denied or abridged by the United States or by any State on account of race, color, or previous condition of servitude—

Section 2.   The Congress shall have power to enforce this article by appropriate legislation.

AMENDMENT XVI [1913]

The Congress shall have power to lay and collect taxes on incomes, from whatever source derived, without apportionment among the several States, and without regard to any census or enumeration.

AMENDMENT XVII [1913]

The Senate of the United States shall be composed of two Senators from each State, elected by the people thereof, for six years; and each Senator shall have one vote. The electors in each State shall have the qualifications requisite for electors of the most numerous branch of the State legislature.

When vacancies happen in the representation of any State in the Senate, the executive authority of such State shall issue writs of election to fill such vacancies: *Provided,* That the legislature of any State may empower the executive thereof to make temporary appointments until the people fill the vacancies by election as the legislature may direct.

This amendment shall not be so construed as to affect the election or term of any Senator chosen before it becomes valid as part of the Constitution.

AMENDMENT XVIII [1919]

Section 1.   After one year from the ratification of this article the manufacture, sale, or transportation of intoxicating liquors within, the importation thereof into, or the exportation thereof from the United States and all territory subject to the jurisdiction thereof for beverage purposes is hereby prohibited.

Section 2.   The Congress and the several States shall have concurrent power to enforce this article by appropriate legislation.

Section 3.   This article shall be inoperative unless it shall have been ratified as an amendment to the Constitution by the legislatures of the several States, as provided in the Constitution, within seven years from the date of the submission hereof to the States by the Congress.

AMENDMENT XIX [1920]

The right of citizens of the United States to vote shall not be denied or abridged by the United States or by any State on account of sex.

Congress shall have power to enforce this article by appropriate legislation.

AMENDMENT XX [1933]

Section 1.   The terms of the President and Vice-President shall end at noon on the 20th day of January, and the terms of Senators and Representatives at noon on the 3d day of January, of the years in which such terms would have ended if this article had not been ratified; and the terms of their successors shall then begin.

Section 2.   The Congress shall assemble at least once in every year, and such meeting shall begin at noon on the 3d day of January, unless they shall by law appoint a different day.

Section 3.   If, at the time fixed for the beginning of the term of the President, the President elect shall have died, the Vice-President elect shall become President. If a President shall not have been chosen before the time fixed for the beginning of his term, or if the President elect shall have failed to qualify, then the Vice-President until a President shall have qualified; and the Congress may by law provide for the case wherein neither a President elect nor a Vice-President elect shall have qualified, declaring who shall then act as President, or the manner in which one who is to act shall be selected, and such person shall act accordingly until a President or Vice-President shall have qualified.

Section 4.   The Congress may by law provide for the case of the death of any of the persons from whom the House of Representatives may choose a President whenever the right of choice shall have devolved upon them, and for the case of the death of any of the persons from whom the Senate may choose a Vice-President whenever the right of choice shall have devolved upon them.

Section 5. Sections 1 and 2 shall take effect on the 15th day of October following the ratification of this article.

Section 6. This article shall be inoperative unless it shall have been ratified as an amendment to the Constitution by the legislatures of three-fourths of the several States within seven years from the date of its submission.

AMENDMENT XXI [1933]

Section 1. The eighteenth article of amendment to the Constitution of the United States is hereby repealed.

Section 2. The transportation or importation into any State, Territory, or possession of the United States for delivery or use therein of intoxicating liquors, in violation of the laws thereof, is hereby prohibited.

Section 3. This article shall be inoperative unless it shall have been ratified as an amendment to the Constitution by conventions in the several States, as provided in the Constitution, within seven years from the date of the submission hereof to the States by the Congress.

AMENDMENT XXII [1951]

No person shall be elected to the office of the President more than twice, and no person who has held the office of President, or acted as President, for more than two years of a term to which some other person was elected President shall be elected to the office of the President more than once.

But this Article shall not apply to any person holding the office of President when this Article was proposed by the Congress, and shall not prevent any person who may be holding the office of President, or acting as President, during the term within which this Article becomes operative from holding the office of President or acting as President during the remainder of such term.

AMENDMENT XXIII [1961]

Section 1. The District constituting the seat of Government of the United States shall appoint in such manner as the Congress may direct:

A number of electors of President and Vice President equal to the whole number of Senators and Representatives in Congress to which the District would be entitled if it were a State, but in no event more than the least populous State; they shall be in addition to those appointed by the States, but they shall be considered, for the purposes of the election of President and Vice President, to be electors appointed by a State; and they shall meet in the District and perform such duties as provided by the twelfth article of amendment.

Section 2. The Congress shall have power to enforce this article by appropriate legislation.

AMENDMENT XXIV [1964]

Section 1. The right of citizens of the United States to vote in any primary or other election for President or Vice President, for electors for President or Vice President, or for Senator or Representative in Congress, shall not be denied or abridged by the United States or any State by reason of failure to pay any poll tax or other tax.

Section 2. The Congress shall have the power to enforce this article by appropriate legislation.

AMENDMENT XXV [1967]

Section 1. In case of the removal of the President from office or his death or resignation, the Vice President shall become President.

Section 2. Whenever there is a vacancy in the office of the Vice President, the President shall nominate a Vice President who shall take the office upon confirmation by a majority vote of both houses of Congress.

Section 3. Whenever the President transmits to the President pro tempore of the Senate and the Speaker of the House of Representatives his written declaration that he is unable to discharge the powers and duties of his office, and until he transmits to them a written declaration to the contrary, such powers and duties shall be discharged by the Vice President as Acting President.

Section 4. Whenever the Vice President and a majority of either the principal officers of the executive departments, or of such other body as Congress may by law provide, transmit to the President pro tempore of the Senate and the Speaker of the House of Representatives their written declaration that the President is unable to discharge the powers and duties of his office, the Vice President shall immediately assume the powers and duties of the office as Acting President.

Thereafter, when the President transmits to the President pro tempore of the Senate and the Speaker of the House of Representatives his written declaration that no inability exists, he shall resume the powers and duties of his office unless the Vice President and a majority of either the principal officers of the executive departments, or of such other body as Congress may by law provide, transmit within four days to the President pro tempore of the Senate and the Speaker of the House of Representatives their written declaration that the President is unable to discharge the powers and duties of his office. Thereupon Congress shall decide the issue, assembling within 48 hours for that purpose if not in session. If the Congress, within 21 days after receipt of the latter written declaration, or, if Congress is not in session, within 21 days after

Congress is required to assemble, determines by two-thirds vote of both houses that the President is unable to discharge the powers and duties of his office, the Vice President shall continue to discharge the same as Acting President; otherwise, the President shall resume the powers and duties of his office.

AMENDMENT XXVI [1971]

Section 1. The right of citizens of the United States, who are eighteen years of age or older, to vote shall not be denied or abridged by the United States or by any State on account of age.

Section 2. The Congress shall have power to enforce this article by appropriate legislation.

AMENDMENT XXVII [1992]

No law, varying the compensation for the services of the Senators and Representatives, shall take effect, until an election of Representatives shall have intervened.

Admission of States to the Union

1	Delaware	Dec. 7, 1787	26	Michigan	Jan. 26, 1837
2	Pennsylvania	Dec. 12, 1787	27	Florida	Mar. 3, 1845
3	New Jersey	Dec. 18, 1787	28	Texas	Dec. 29, 1845
4	Georgia	Jan. 2, 1788	29	Iowa	Dec. 28, 1846
5	Connecticut	Jan. 9, 1788	30	Wisconsin	May 29, 1848
6	Massachusetts	Feb. 6, 1788	31	California	Sept. 9, 1850
7	Maryland	Apr. 28, 1788	32	Minnesota	May 11, 1858
8	South Carolina	May 23, 1788	33	Oregon	Feb. 14, 1859
9	New Hampshire	June 21, 1788	34	Kansas	Jan. 29, 1861
10	Virginia	June 25, 1788	35	West Virginia	June 19, 1863
11	New York	July 26, 1788	36	Nevada	Oct. 31, 1864
12	North Carolina	Nov. 21, 1789	37	Nebraska	Mar. 1, 1867
13	Rhode Island	May 29, 1790	38	Colorado	Aug. 1, 1876
14	Vermont	Mar. 4, 1791	39	North Dakota	Nov. 2, 1889
15	Kentucky	June 1, 1792	40	South Dakota	Nov. 2, 1889
16	Tennessee	June 1, 1796	41	Montana	Nov. 8, 1889
17	Ohio	Mar. 1, 1803	42	Washington	Nov. 11, 1889
18	Louisiana	Apr. 30, 1812	43	Idaho	July 3, 1890
19	Indiana	Dec. 11, 1816	44	Wyoming	July 10, 1890
20	Mississippi	Dec. 10, 1817	45	Utah	Jan. 4, 1896
21	Illinois	Dec. 3, 1818	46	Oklahoma	Nov. 16, 1907
22	Alabama	Dec. 14, 1819	47	New Mexico	Jan. 6, 1912
23	Maine	Mar. 15, 1820	48	Arizona	Feb. 14, 1912
24	Missouri	Aug. 10, 1821	49	Alaska	Jan. 3, 1959
25	Arkansas	June 15, 1836	50	Hawaii	Aug. 21, 1959

Population of the United States, 1790–1990

YEAR	NUMBER OF STATES	POPULATION	PERCENT INCREASE
1790	13	3,929,214	
1800	16	5,308,483	35.1
1810	17	7,239,881	36.4
1820	23	9,638,453	33.1
1830	24	12,866,020	33.5
1840	26	17,069,453	32.7
1850	31	23,191,876	35.9
1860	33	31,443,321	35.6
1870	37	39,818,449	26.6
1880	38	50,155,783	26.0
1890	44	62,947,714	25.5
1900	45	75,994,575	20.7
1910	46	91,972,266	21.0
1920	48	105,710,620	14.9
1930	48	122,775,046	16.1
1940	48	131,669,275	7.2
1950	48	150,697,361	14.5
1960	50	179,323,175	19.0
1970	50	203,235,298	13.3
1980	50	226,504,825	11.4
1990	50	249,632,692	10.2

The Vice Presidents and the Cabinet

SECRETARY OF STATE
(1789–   )

Thomas Jefferson	1789	Daniel Webster	1850	Elihu Root	1905
Edmund Randolph	1794	Edward Everett	1852	Robert Bacon	1909
Timothy Pickering	1795	William L. Marcy	1853	Philander C. Knox	1909
John Marshall	1800	Lewis Cass	1857	William J. Bryan	1913
James Madison	1801	Jeremiah S. Black	1860	Robert Lansing	1915
Robert Smith	1809	William H. Seward	1861	Bainbridge Colby	1920
James Monroe	1811	E. B. Washburne	1869	Charles E. Hughes	1921
John Q. Adams	1817	Hamilton Fish	1869	Frank B. Kellogg	1925
Henry Clay	1825	William M. Evarts	1877	Henry L. Stimson	1929
Martin Van Buren	1829	James G. Blaine	1881	Cordell Hull	1933
Edward Livingston	1831	F. T. Frelinghuysen	1881	E. R. Stettinius, Jr.	1944
Louis McLane	1833	Thomas F. Bayard	1885	James F. Byrnes	1945
John Forsyth	1834	James G. Blaine	1889	George C. Marshall	1947
Daniel Webster	1841	John W. Foster	1892	Dean Acheson	1949
Hugh S. Legaré	1843	Walter Q. Gresham	1893	John Foster Dulles	1953
Abel P. Upshur	1843	Richard Olney	1895	Christian A. Herter	1959
John C. Calhoun	1844	John Sherman	1897	Dean Rusk	1961
James Buchanan	1845	William R. Day	1897	William P. Rogers	1969
John M. Clayton	1849	John Hay	1898	Henry A. Kissinger	1973

Cyrus Vance	1977
Edmund Muskie	1979
Alexander M. Haig, Jr.	1981
George Shultz	1982
James A. Baker, III	1989
Warren Christopher	1993
Madeleine K. Albright	1997

SECRETARY OF THE TREASURY (1789–   )

Alexander Hamilton	1789
Oliver Wolcott	1795
Samuel Dexter	1801
Albert Gallatin	1801
G. W. Campbell	1814
A. J. Dallas	1814
William H. Crawford	1816
Richard Rush	1825
Samuel D. Ingham	1829
Louis McLane	1831
William J. Duane	1833
Roger B. Taney	1833
Levi Woodbury	1834
Thomas Ewing	1841
Walter Forward	1841
John C. Spencer	1843
George M. Bibb	1844
Robert J. Walker	1845
William M. Meredith	1849
Thomas Corwin	1850
James Guthrie	1853
Howell Cobb	1857
Philip F. Thomas	1860
John A. Dix	1861
Salmon P. Chase	1861
Wm. P. Fessenden	1864
Hugh McCulloch	1865
George S. Boutwell	1869
William A. Richardson	1873
Benjamin H. Bristow	1874
Lot M. Morrill	1876
John Sherman	1877
William Windom	1881
Charles J. Folger	1881
Walter Q. Gresham	1884
Hugh McCulloch	1884
Daniel Manning	1885
Charles S. Fairchild	1887
William Windom	1889
Charles Foster	1891
John G. Carlisle	1893
Lyman J. Gage	1897
Leslie M. Shaw	1902
George B. Cortelyou	1907

Franklin MacVeagh	1909
William G. McAdoo	1913
Carter Glass	1918
David F. Houston	1920
Andrew W. Mellon	1921
Ogden L. Mills	1932
William H. Woodin	1933
Henry Morgenthau, Jr.	1934
Fred M. Vinson	1945
John W. Snyder	1946
George M. Humphrey	1953
Robert B. Anderson	1957
C. Douglas Dillon	1961
Henry H. Fowler	1965
David M. Kennedy	1969
John B. Connally	1970
George P. Shultz	1972
William E. Simon	1974
W. Michael Blumenthal	1977
G. William Miller	1979
Donald T. Regan	1981
James A. Baker, III	1985
Nicholas Brady	1988
Lloyd Bentsen	1993
Robert Rubin	1995
Lawrence H. Summers	1999

SECRETARY OF WAR (1789–1947)

Henry Knox	1789
Timothy Pickering	1795
James McHenry	1796
John Marshall	1800
Samuel Dexter	1800
Roger Griswold	1801
Henry Dearborn	1801
William Eustis	1809
John Armstrong	1813
James Monroe	1814
William H. Crawford	1815
Isaac Shelby	1817
George Graham	1817
John C. Calhoun	1817
James Barbour	1825
Peter B. Porter	1828
John H. Eaton	1829
Lewis Cass	1831
Benjamin F. Butler	1837
Joel R. Poinsett	1837
John Bell	1841
John McLean	1841
John C. Spencer	1841
James M. Porter	1843
William Wilkins	1844
William L. Marcy	1845

George W. Crawford	1849
Charles M. Conrad	1850
Jefferson Davis	1853
John B. Floyd	1857
Joseph Holt	1861
Simon Cameron	1861
Edwin M. Stanton	1862
Ulysses S. Grant	1867
Lorenzo Thomas	1868
John M. Schofield	1868
John A. Rawlins	1869
William T. Sherman	1869
William W. Belknap	1869
Alphonso Taft	1876
James D. Cameron	1876
George W. McCrary	1877
Alexander Ramsey	1879
Robert T. Lincoln	1881
William C. Endicott	1885
Redfield Proctor	1889
Stephen B. Elkins	1891
Daniel S. Lamont	1893
Russell A. Alger	1897
Elihu Root	1899
William H. Taft	1904
Luke E. Wright	1908
J. M. Dickinson	1909
Henry L. Stimson	1911
L. M. Garrison	1913
Newton D. Baker	1916
John W. Weeks	1921
Dwight F. Davis	1925
James W. Good	1929
Patrick J. Hurley	1929
George H. Dern	1933
H. A. Woodring	1936
Henry L. Stimson	1940
Robert P. Patterson	1945
Kenneth C. Royall	1947

SECRETARY OF THE NAVY (1798–1947)

Benjamin Stoddert	1798
Robert Smith	1801
Paul Hamilton	1809
William Jones	1813
B. W. Crowninshield	1814
Smith Thompson	1818
S. L. Southard	1823
John Branch	1829
Levi Woodbury	1831
Mahlon Dickerson	1834
James K. Paulding	1838
George E. Badger	1841

Abel P. Upshur	1841
David Henshaw	1843
Thomas W. Gilmer	1844
John Y. Mason	1844
George Bancroft	1845
John Y. Mason	1846
William B. Preston	1849
William A. Graham	1850
John P. Kennedy	1852
James C. Dobbin	1853
Isaac Toucey	1857
Gideon Welles	1861
Adolph E. Borie	1869
George M. Robeson	1869
R. W. Thompson	1877
Nathan Goff, Jr.	1881
William H. Hunt	1881
William E. Chandler	1881
William C. Whitney	1885
Benjamin F. Tracy	1889
Hilary A. Herbert	1893
John D. Long	1897
William H. Moody	1902
Paul Morton	1904
Charles J. Bonaparte	1905
Victor H. Metcalf	1907
T. H. Newberry	1908
George von L. Meyer	1909
Josephus Daniels	1913
Edwin Denby	1921
Curtis D. Wilbur	1924
Charles F. Adams	1929
Claude A. Swanson	1933
Charles Edison	1940
Frank Knox	1940
James V. Forrestal	1945

SECRETARY OF DEFENSE
(1947–   )

James V. Forrestal	1947
Louis A. Johnson	1949
George C. Marshall	1950
Robert A. Lovett	1951
Charles E. Wilson	1953
Neil H. McElroy	1957
Thomas S. Gates, Jr.	1959
Robert S. McNamara	1961
Clark M. Clifford	1968
Melvin R. Laird	1969
Elliot L. Richardson	1973
James R. Schlesinger	1973
Donald Rumsfeld	1974
Harold Brown	1977
Caspar Weinberger	1981

Frank Carlucci	1988
Richard Cheney	1989
Leslie Aspin, Jr.	1993
William Perry	1994
William Cohen	1997

POSTMASTER GENERAL
(1789–1970)

Samuel Osgood	1789
Timothy Pickering	1791
Joseph Habersham	1795
Gideon Granger	1801
Return J. Meigs, Jr.	1814
John McLean	1823
William T. Barry	1829
Amos Kendall	1835
John M. Niles	1840
Francis Granger	1841
Charles A. Wickliffe	1841
Cave Johnson	1845
Jacob Collamer	1849
Nathan K. Hall	1850
Samuel D. Hubbard	1852
James Campbell	1853
Aaron V. Brown	1857
Joseph Holt	1859
Horatio King	1861
Montgomery Blair	1861
William Dennison	1864
Alexander W. Randall	1866
John A. J. Creswell	1869
James W. Marshall	1874
Marshall Jewell	1874
James N. Tyner	1876
David M. Key	1877
Horace Maynard	1880
Thomas L. James	1881
Timothy O. Howe	1881
Walter Q. Gresham	1883
Frank Hatton	1884
William F. Vilas	1885
Don M. Dickinson	1888
John Wanamaker	1889
Wilson S. Bissell	1893
William L. Wilson	1895
James A. Gary	1897
Charles E. Smith	1898
Henry C. Payne	1902
Robert J. Wynne	1904
George B. Cortelyou	1905
George von L. Meyer	1907
F. H. Hitchcock	1909
Albert S. Burleson	1913
Will H. Hays	1921

Hubert Work	1922
Harry S. New	1923
Walter F. Brown	1929
James A. Farley	1933
Frank C. Walker	1940
Robert E. Hannegan	1945
J. M. Donaldson	1947
A. E. Summerfield	1953
J. Edward Day	1961
John A. Gronouski	1963
Lawrence F. O'Brien	1965
W. Marvin Watson	1968
Winton M. Blount	1969

ATTORNEY GENERAL
(1789–   )

Edmund Randolph	1789
William Bradford	1794
Charles Lee	1795
Theophilus Parsons	1801
Levi Lincoln	1801
Robert Smith	1805
John Breckinridge	1805
Caesar A. Rodney	1807
William Pinkney	1811
Richard Rush	1814
William Wirt	1817
John M. Berrien	1829
Roger B. Taney	1831
Benjamin F. Butler	1833
Felix Grundy	1838
Henry D. Gilpin	1840
John J. Crittenden	1841
Hugh S. Legaré	1841
John Nelson	1843
John Y. Mason	1845
Nathan Clifford	1846
Isaac Toucey	1848
Reverdy Johnson	1849
John J. Crittenden	1850
Caleb Cushing	1853
Jeremiah S. Black	1857
Edwin M. Stanton	1860
Edward Bates	1861
Titian J. Coffey	1863
James Speed	1864
Henry Stanbery	1866
William M. Evarts	1868
Ebenezer R. Hoar	1869
Amos T. Ackerman	1870
George H. Williams	1871
Edwards Pierrepont	1875
Alphonso Taft	1876
Charles Devens	1877

Wayne MacVeagh	1881
Benjamin H. Brewster	1881
A. H. Garland	1885
William H. H. Miller	1889
Richard Olney	1893
Judson Harmon	1895
Joseph McKenna	1897
John W. Griggs	1897
Philander C. Knox	1901
William H. Moody	1904
Charles J. Bonaparte	1907
G. W. Wickersham	1909
J. C. McReynolds	1913
Thomas W. Gregory	1914
A. Mitchell Palmer	1919
H. M. Daugherty	1921
Harlan F. Stone	1924
John G. Sargent	1925
William D. Mitchell	1929
H. S. Cummings	1933
Frank Murphy	1939
Robert H. Jackson	1940
Francis Biddle	1941
Tom C. Clark	1945
J. H. McGrath	1949
J. P. McGranery	1952
H. Brownell, Jr.	1953
William P. Rogers	1957
Robert F. Kennedy	1961
Nicholas Katzenbach	1964
Ramsey Clark	1967
John N. Mitchell	1969
Richard G. Kleindienst	1972
Elliot L. Richardson	1973
William Saxbe	1974
Edward H. Levi	1974
Griffin B. Bell	1977
Benjamin R. Civiletti	1979
William French Smith	1981
Edwin A. Meese, III	1985
Richard Thornburgh	1988
William P. Barr	1992
Janet Reno	1993

SECRETARY OF THE INTERIOR (1849–   )

Thomas Ewing	1849
T. M. T. McKennan	1850
Alexander H. H. Stuart	1850
Robert McClelland	1853
Jacob Thompson	1857
Caleb B. Smith	1861
John P. Usher	1863
James Harlan	1865
O. H. Browning	1866

Jacob D. Cox	1869
Columbus Delano	1870
Zachariah Chandler	1875
Carl Schurz	1877
Samuel J. Kirkwood	1881
Henry M. Teller	1881
L. Q. C. Lamar	1885
William F. Vilas	1888
John W. Noble	1889
Hoke Smith	1893
David R. Francis	1896
Cornelius N. Bliss	1897
E. A. Hitchcock	1899
James R. Garfield	1907
R. A. Ballinger	1909
Walter L. Fisher	1911
Franklin K. Lane	1913
John B. Payne	1920
Albert B. Fall	1921
Hubert Work	1923
Roy O. West	1928
Ray L. Wilbur	1929
Harold L. Ickes	1933
Julius A. Krug	1946
Oscar L. Chapman	1949
Douglas McKay	1953
Fred A. Seaton	1956
Steward L. Udall	1961
Walter J. Hickel	1969
Rogers C. B. Morton	1971
Thomas S. Kleppe	1975
Cecil D. Andrus	1977
James G. Watt	1981
William P. Clark, Jr.	1983
Donald P. Hodel	1985
Manuel Lujan	1989
Bruce Babbit	1993

SECRETARY OF AGRICULTURE (1889–   )

Norman J. Colman	1889
Jeremiah M. Rusk	1889
J. Sterling Morton	1893
James Wilson	1897
David F. Houston	1913
Edwin T. Meredith	1920
Henry C. Wallace	1921
Howard M. Gore	1924
William M. Jardine	1925
Arthur M. Hyde	1929
Henry A. Wallace	1933
Claude R. Wickard	1940
Clinton P. Anderson	1945
Charles F. Brannan	1948
Ezra Taft Benson	1953

Orville L. Freeman	1961
Clifford M. Hardin	1969
Earl L. Butz	1971
John A. Knebel	1976
Bob Bergland	1977
John R. Block	1981
Richard E. Lyng	1986
Clayton Yeutter	1989
Edward Madigan	1991
Mike Espy	1993
Dan Glickman	1995

SECRETARY OF COMMERCE AND LABOR (1903–1913)

George B. Cortelyou	1903
Victor H. Metcalf	1904
Oscar S. Straus	1906
Charles Nagel	1909

SECRETARY OF COMMERCE (1913–   )

William C. Redfield	1913
Joshua W. Alexander	1919
Herbert Hoover	1921
William F. Whiting	1928
Robert P. Lamont	1929
Roy D. Chapin	1932
Daniel C. Roper	1933
Henry L. Hopkins	1939
Jesse Jones	1940
Henry A. Wallace	1945
W. A. Harriman	1946
Charles Sawyer	1948
Sinclair Weeks	1953
Lewis L. Strauss	1958
F. H. Mueller	1959
Luther Hodges	1961
John T. Connor	1965
A. B. Trowbridge	1967
C. R. Smith	1968
Maurice H. Stans	1969
Peter G. Peterson	1972
Frederick B. Dent	1973
Elliot L. Richardson	1974
Juanita M. Kreps	1977
Philip M. Klutznick	1979
Malcolm Baldrige	1981
C. William Verity, Jr.	1987
Robert Mosbacher	1989
Ronald H. Brown	1993
Mickey Kantor	1996
William Daley	1997

SECRETARY OF LABOR
(1913–   )

William B. Wilson	1913
James J. Davis	1921
William N. Doak	1930
Frances Perkins	1933
L. B. Schwellenbach	1945
Maurice J. Tobin	1948
Martin P. Durkin	1953
James P. Mitchell	1953
Arthur J. Goldberg	1961
W. Willard Wirtz	1962
George P. Schultz	1969
James D. Hodgson	1970
Peter J. Brennan	1974
John T. Dunlop	1975
W. J. Usery, Jr.	1976
Ray Marshall	1977
Raymond J. Donovan	1981
Elizabeth Dole	1990
Lynn Martin	1991
Robert B. Reich	1993
Alexis Herman	1997

SECRETARY OF HEALTH, EDUCATION, AND WELFARE
(1953–1979)

Oveta Culp Hobby	1953
Marion B. Folsom	1955
Arthur S. Flemming	1958
Abraham A. Ribicoff	1961
Anthony J. Celebrezze	1962
John W. Gardner	1965
Wilbur J. Cohen	1968
Robert H. Finch	1969
Elliot L. Richardson	1970
Caspar W. Weinberger	1973
Forrest D. Matthews	1974
Joseph A. Califano, Jr.	1977

SECRETARY OF HEALTH AND HUMAN SERVICES
(1979–   )

Patricia R. Harris	1979
Richard S. Schweiker	1981
Margaret Heckler	1983
Otis R. Bowen	1985
Louis W. Sullivan	1989
Donna E. Shalala	1993

SECRETARY OF HOUSING AND URBAN DEVELOPMENT
(1966–   )

Robert C. Weaver	1966
George W. Romney	1969
James T. Lynn	1973
Carla Anderson Hills	1974
Patricia Harris	1977
Moon Landrieu	1979
Samuel R. Pierce, Jr.	1981
Jack Kemp	1989
Henry G. Cisneros	1993
Andrew Cuomo	1997

SECRETARY OF ENERGY
(1977–   )

James R. Schlesinger	1977
Charles W. Duncan, Jr.	1979
James B. Edwards	1981
Donald Hodel	1982
John S. Herrington	1985
James Watkins	1989
Hazel R. O'Leary	1993
Frederico Peña	1997
Bill Richardson	1998

SECRETARY OF TRANSPORTATION
(1967–   )

Alan S. Boyd	1967
John A. Volpe	1969
Claude S. Brinegar	1973
William T. Coleman	1975
Brock Adams	1977
Neil E. Goldschmidt	1979
Andrew L. Lewis, Jr.	1981
Elizabeth Dole	1983
James L. Burnley, IV	1987
Samuel Skinner	1989
Frederico Peña	1993
Rodney Slater	1997

SECRETARY OF EDUCATION (1979–   )

Shirley M. Hufstedler	1979
Terrel Bell	1981
William J. Bennett	1985
Lauro F. Cavozos	1988
Lamar Alexander	1991
Richard W. Riley	1993

SECRETARY OF VETERANS AFFAIRS
(1989–   )

Edward Derwinski	1989
Jesse Brown	1993
Togo D. West, Jr.	1998

VICE PRESIDENT

John Adams	1789–97
Thomas Jefferson	1797–1801
Aaron Burr	1801–05
George Clinton	1805–13
Elbridge Gerry	1813–17
Daniel D. Tompkins	1817–25
John C. Calhoun	1825–33
Martin Van Buren	1833–37
Richard M. Johnson	1837–41
John Tyler	1841
George M. Dallas	1845–49
Millard Fillmore	1849–50
William R. King	1853–57
John C. Breckinridge	1857–61
Hannibal Hamlin	1861–65
Andrew Johnson	1865
Schuyler Colfax	1869–73
Henry Wilson	1873–77
William A. Wheeler	1877–81
Chester A. Arthur	1881
Thomas A. Hendricks	1885–89
Levi P. Morton	1889–93
Adlai E. Stevenson	1893–97
Garret A. Hobart	1897–1901
Theodore Roosevelt	1901
Charles W. Fairbanks	1905–09
James S. Sherman	1909–13
Thomas R. Marshall	1913–21
Calvin Coolidge	1921–23
Charles G. Dawes	1925–29
Charles Curtis	1929–33
John Nance Garner	1933–41
Henry A. Wallace	1941–45
Harry S Truman	1945
Alben W. Barkley	1949–53
Richard M. Nixon	1953–61
Lyndon B. Johnson	1961–63
Hubert H. Humphrey	1965–69
Spiro T. Agnew	1969–73
Gerald R. Ford	1973–74
Nelson A. Rockefeller	1974–77
Walter F. Mondale	1977–81
George Bush	1981–89
J. Danforth Quayle	1989–93
Al Gore	1993–

Presidential Elections, 1789–1996

Year	Candidates	Party	Popular Vote		Electoral Vote
1789	**George Washington**				69
	John Adams				34
	Others				35
1792	**George Washington**				132
	John Adams				77
	George Clinton				50
	Others				5
1796	**John Adams**	Federalist			71
	Thomas Jefferson	Democratic-Republican			68
	Thomas Pinckney	Federalist			59
	Aaron Burr	Democratic-Republican			30
	Others				48
1800	**Thomas Jefferson**	Democratic-Republican			73
	Aaron Burr	Democratic-Republican			73
	John Adams	Federalist			65
	Charles C. Pinckney	Federalist			64
1804	**Thomas Jefferson**	Democratic-Republican			162
	Charles C. Pinckney	Federalist			14
1808	**James Madison**	Democratic-Republican			122
	Charles C. Pinckney	Federalist			47
	George Clinton	Independent-Republican			6
1812	**James Madison**	Democratic-Republican			128
	DeWitt Clinton	Federalist			89
1816	**James Monroe**	Democratic-Republican			183
	Rufus King	Federalist			34
1820	**James Monroe**	Democratic-Republican			231
	John Quincy Adams	Independent-Republican			1
1824	**John Quincy Adams**	Democratic-Republican	113,122	(30.9%)	84
	Andrew Jackson	Democratic-Republican	151,271	(41.3%)	99
	Henry Clay	Democratic-Republican	47,531	(12.9%)	37
	William H. Crawford	Democratic-Republican	40,856	(11.1%)	41
1828	**Andrew Jackson**	Democratic	642,553	(55.9%)	178
	John Quincy Adams	National Republican	500,897	(43.6%)	83
1832	**Andrew Jackson**	Democratic	701,780	(54.2%)	219
	Henry Clay	National Republican	484,205	(37.4%)	49
	William Wirt	Anti-Masonic	100,715	(7.7%)	7
1836	**Martin Van Buren**	Democratic	763,176	(50.8%)	170
	William H. Harrison	Whig	550,816	(36.6%)	73
	Hugh L. White	Whig	146,107	(9.7%)	26
	Daniel Webster	Whig	41,201	(2.7%)	14
1840	**William H. Harrison** **(John Tyler, 1841)**	Whig	1,275,390	(52.8%)	234
	Martin Van Buren	Democratic	1,128,854	(46.8%)	60

Year	Candidates	Party	Popular Vote		Electoral Vote
1844	**James K. Polk**	Democratic	1,339,494	(49.5%)	170
	Henry Clay	Whig	1,300,004	(48.0%)	105
	James G. Birney	Liberty	62,103	(2.3%)	
1848	**Zachary Taylor**	Whig	1,361,393	(47.2%)	163
	(Millard Fillmore, 1850)				
	Lewis Cass	Democratic	1,223,460	(42.4%)	127
	Martin Van Buren	Free Soil	291,501	(10.1%)	
1852	**Franklin Pierce**	Democratic	1,607,510	(50.8%)	254
	Winfield Scott	Whig	1,386,942	(43.8%)	42
1856	**James Buchanan**	Democratic	1,836,072	(45.2%)	174
	John C. Frémont	Republican	1,342,345	(33.1%)	114
	Millard Fillmore	American	873,053	(21.5%)	8
1860	**Abraham Lincoln**	Republican	1,865,908	(39.8%)	180
	Stephen A. Douglas	Democratic	1,382,202	(29.4%)	12
	John C. Breckinridge	Democratic	848,019	(18.0%)	72
	John Bell	Constitutional Union	591,901	(12.6%)	39
1864	**Abraham Lincoln**	Republican	2,218,388	(55.0%)	212
	(Andrew Johnson, 1865)				
	George B. McClellan	Democratic	1,812,807	(44.9%)	21
1868	**Ulysses S. Grant**	Republican	3,013,650	(52.6%)	214
	Horatio Seymour	Democratic	2,708,744	(47.3%)	80
1872	**Ulysses S. Grant**	Republican	3,598,235	(55.6%)	286
	Horace Greeley	Democratic	2,834,761	(43.8%)	66
1876	**Rutherford B. Hayes**	Republican	4,034,311	(47.9%)	185
	Samuel J. Tilden	Democratic	4,288,546	(50.0%)	184
1880	**James A. Garfield**	Republican	4,446,158	(48.2%)	214
	(Chester A. Arthur, 1881)				
	Winfield S. Hancock	Democratic	4,444,260	(48.2%)	155
	James B. Weaver	Greenback-Labor	305,997	(3.3%)	
1884	**Grover Cleveland**	Democratic	4,874,621	(48.5%)	219
	James G. Blaine	Republican	4,848,936	(48.2%)	182
	Benjamin F. Butler	Greenback-Labor	175,096	(1.7%)	
1888	**Benjamin Harrison**	Republican	5,443,892	(47.8%)	233
	Grover Cleveland	Democratic	5,534,488	(48.6%)	168
1892	**Grover Cleveland**	Democratic	5,551,883	(46.0%)	277
	Benjamin Harrison	Republican	5,179,244	(42.9%)	145
	James B. Weaver	People's	1,024,280	(8.5%)	22
1896	**William McKinley**	Republican	7,108,480	(51.0%)	271
	William J. Bryan	Democratic; Populist	6,511,495	(46.7%)	176
1900	**William McKinley**	Republican	7,218,039	(51.6%)	292
	(Theodore Roosevelt, 1901)				
	William J. Bryan	Democratic; Populist	6,358,345	(45.5%)	155

Year	Candidates	Party	Popular Vote		Electoral Vote
1904	**Theodore Roosevelt**	Republican	7,626,593	(56.4%)	336
	Alton B. Parker	Democratic	5,082,898	(37.6%)	140
	Eugene V. Debs	Socialist	402,489	(2.9%)	
1908	**William H. Taft**	Republican	7,676,258	(51.5%)	321
	William J. Bryan	Democratic	6,406,801	(43.0%)	162
	Eugene V. Debs	Socialist	420,380	(2.8%)	
1912	**Woodrow Wilson**	Democratic	6,293,152	(41.8%)	435
	Theodore Roosevelt	Progressive	4,119,207	(27.3%)	88
	William H. Taft	Republican	3,486,383	(23.1%)	8
	Eugene V. Debs	Socialist	900,369	(5.9%)	
1916	**Woodrow Wilson**	Democratic	9,126,300	(49.2%)	277
	Charles E. Hughes	Republican	8,546,789	(46.1%)	254
1920	**Warren G. Harding** **(Calvin Coolidge,** 1923)	Republican	16,133,314	(60.3%)	404
	James M. Cox	Democratic	9,140,884	(34.1%)	127
	Eugene V. Debs	Socialist	913,664	(3.4%)	
1924	**Calvin Coolidge**	Republican	15,717,553	(54.0%)	382
	John W. Davis	Democratic	8,386,169	(28.8%)	136
	Robert M. La Follette	Progressive	4,814,050	(16.5%)	13
1928	**Herbert C. Hoover**	Republican	21,411,991	(58.2%)	444
	Alfred E. Smith	Democratic	15,000,185	(40.7%)	87
1932	**Franklin D. Roosevelt**	Democratic	22,825,016	(57.4%)	472
	Herbert C. Hoover	Republican	15,758,397	(39.6%)	59
	Norman Thomas	Socialist	883,990	(2.2%)	
1936	**Franklin D. Roosevelt**	Democratic	27,747,636	(60.7%)	523
	Alfred M. Landon	Republican	16,679,543	(36.5%)	8
	William Lemke	Union	892,492	(1.9%)	
1940	**Franklin D. Roosevelt**	Democratic	27,263,448	(54.7%)	449
	Wendell L. Willkie	Republican	22,336,260	(44.8%)	82
1944	**Franklin D. Roosevelt** **(Harry S Truman,** 1945)	Democratic	25,611,936	(53.3%)	432
	Thomas E. Dewey	Republican	22,013,372	(45.8%)	99
1948	**Harry S Truman**	Democratic	24,105,587	(49.5%)	303
	Thomas E. Dewey	Republican	21,970,017	(45.1%)	189
	J. Strom Thurmond	States' Rights	1,169,134	(2.4%)	39
	Henry A. Wallace	Progressive	1,157,057	(2.3%)	
1952	**Dwight D. Eisenhower**	Republican	33,936,137	(55.1%)	442
	Adlai E. Stevenson	Democratic	27,314,649	(44.3%)	89
1956	**Dwight D. Eisenhower**	Republican	35,585,245	(57.3%)	457
	Adlai F. Stevenson	Democratic	26,030,172	(41.9%)	73
1960	**John F. Kennedy** **(Lyndon B. Johnson,** 1963)	Democratic	34,221,344	(49.7%)	303
	Richard M. Nixon	Republican	34,106,671	(49.5%)	219

Year	Candidates	Party	Popular Vote		Electoral Vote
1964	**Lyndon B. Johnson**	Democratic	43,126,584	(61.0%)	486
	Barry M. Goldwater	Republican	27,177,838	(38.4%)	52
1968	**Richard M. Nixon**	Republican	31,783,148	(43.4%)	301
	Hubert H. Humphrey	Democratic	31,274,503	(42.7%)	191
	George C. Wallace	Amer. Independent	9,901,151	(13.5%)	46
1972	**Richard M. Nixon**	Republican	47,170,179	(60.6%)	520
	George S. McGovern	Democratic	29,171,791	(37.5%)	17
1974	**Gerald R. Ford**	Republican	Appointed on August 9, 1974, as President after the resignation of Richard M. Nixon.		
1976	**Jimmy Carter**	Democratic	40,828,587	(50.1%)	297
	Gerald R. Ford	Republican	39,147,613	(48.0%)	240
1980	**Ronald Reagan**	Republican	43,899,248	(50.7%)	489
	Jimmy Carter	Democratic	35,481,435	(41.0%)	49
	John Anderson	Independent	5,719,437	(6.6%)	
	Ed Clark	Libertarian	920,859	(1.0%)	
1984	**Ronald Reagan**	Republican	54,451,521	(58.8%)	525
	Walter F. Mondale	Democratic	37,565,334	(40.5%)	13
1988	**George H. Bush**	Republican	47,946,422	(54.0%)	426
	Michael S. Dukakis	Democratic	41,016,429	(46.0%)	112
1992	**Bill Clinton**	Democratic	43,682,624	(43.2%)	378
	George H. Bush	Republican	38,117,331	(37.7%)	168
	H. Ross Perot	Independent	19,217,212	(19.0%)	0
1996	**Bill Clinton**	Democratic	45,628,667	(49.9%)	379
	Robert Dole	Republican	37,869,435	(41.5%)	159
	H. Ross Perot	Independent	7,874,283	(8.6%)	0

Glossary

abolitionism: The campaign, strengthened by religious passion, for the immediate end of slavery. Among the most famous abolitionists were William Lloyd Garrison and Theodore Dwight Weld. Themselves always in the minority, abolitionists combined with more compromising opponents of slavery to form a wide antislavery movement in the North by the eve of the Civil War.

agrarian: Relating to agriculture

amnesty: General pardon granted usually for political offenses.

Anglo: A term in the Southwest for English-speaking whites.

antebellum South: The South in the decades before the Civil War.

antinomianism: The belief among Christians that salvation depends on the indwelling presence of the Holy Spirit, not obedience to earthly laws and codes.

apocalypse: A revelation or discovery. Christianity teaches that the final victory will be realized through the redemptive powers of Christ's Second Coming. Revelations, the Bible's final chapter, provides an apocalyptic vision of that fateful, final day.

appeasement: Giving concessions to enemies to maintain peace.

apprentice: A person bound to work for a time in exchange for instruction in a trade.

aqueduct: A device to transport water from a remote source.

arbitration: Parties to a dispute submit their case to the judgment of an impartial person or group.

armistice: A truce agreement between military opponents. The armistice that ended World War I, for example, was signed on November 11, 1918.

Articles of Confederation: The form of national government in the early days of the United States. The Articles, adopted in 1777, gave each state so much independence that the central government had difficulties in collecting revenue and establishing a national policy.

artisan: A skilled craftsman such as a blacksmith or carpenter.

assembly line production: A method of assembling standardized, interchangeable parts into an automobile or other item of mass consumption. Workers are assigned small, specialized tasks along the route of assembly, which increases efficiency, reduces production costs, and consequently lowers prices for the consumer. Of the nation's industrialists, Henry Ford was most closely identified with this form of production, using a conveyor belt system and making automobiles affordable to the middle class buyer.

assimilate: To absorb a culturally distinct group into the prevailing culture.

astrolabe: An instrument that navigators used to calculate their ship's location by measuring proportional distance to stars.

baby boom: Sudden increase in the birthrate after World War II from about 1947 through the 1950s.

balance of payments: The margin between the value of a nation's exports and the value of its imports.

balance of power: A system of international relations in which opposing alliances of countries seek to balance each other's military and diplomatic power. The confrontation between NATO (the North Atlantic Treaty Organization) and the Soviet-dominated Warsaw Pact is an example. See also **collective security**.

Bank of the United States: A centralized financial institution designed to regulate the nation's economy through selective distribution of capital (loans and related transactions). As envisioned by Alexander Hamilton, the first Bank of the United States was to stimulate general economic growth through commercial investment, which in turn would make individual states more dependent on a strengthened national government. Andrew Jackson, in his assault upon the Second Bank of the United States, argued that such centralized control threatened the authority of the states and favored wealthy interests to the detriment of others.

banknotes: Paper money issued by private banks and backed by the assets of those banks but not by any governmental agency.

barrio: A Spanish-speaking community, often economically impoverished.

bear market: A period of declining prices in the stock market or in any market. Speculators who agree to sell at some point in the future at lower than current prices are called bears since they can make a profit only if prices fall. See also **bull market**.

beat culture: A movement of the 1950s that rejected the nation's dominant values and mass culture. Beats, or beatniks, found little of worth in the decade's aggressive and confident capitalism and the generally rapid pace of American life. Instead they espoused individualism and nonconformity, which included Eastern religions, improvisational jazz, marijuana, and life on the road.

belligerent: A nation formally at war.

benign neglect: The British policy of non-enforcement of regulations on the American colonies in return for loyalty and mutual economic benefit.

black nationalism: The belief that African Americans should seek an independent national or cultural existence. Marcus Garvey was the major proponent of this viewpoint in the 1920s. Black Muslims continue to promote this view. See also **pan-Africanism**.

Bleeding Kansas: A phrase to describe the violent struggle between proslavery and antislavery forces in the Kansas territory after passage of the Kansas-Nebraska Act. Outside activists from both camps urged migration to Kansas to gain majority control of the territorial government and its decisions concerning slavery. Two separate governments were established, vigilante violence spread, and Congress, which had attempted to avoid the slavery issue, was forced to deal with the much intensified struggle. See also **popular sovereignty**.

blockade: The use of naval force to shut off passage to and from a hostile port or country. Used by England in its wars against Europe and the United States, by the North against the South during the Civil War, and by the United States in the twentieth century against such nations as Cuba and Iraq, blockades are designed to cripple a nation's economy and war machine by cutting off needed supplies.

bloody shirt (waving the): Taken from the waving in political campaigning of a shirt, actually or apparently bloody, said to belong to a supporter of the federal government killed by white southerners. The term "waving the bloody shirt" came to refer to the practice on the part of some Republican politicians late in the nineteenth century of arousing feelings among northern voters against the South, widely associated with the Democratic Party.

blue laws: Local laws, typically promoted by Protestant reformers, designed to keep Sundays reserved exclusively for worship and religious contemplation. Various immigrant and Catholic communities viewed the laws as discriminatory because they closed places used by these groups for social gatherings and cultural activities.

bond: A certificate of debt guaranteeing payment of an investment plus interest by a specified future date.

border states: Those states located between the North and the deep South, such as Delaware, Maryland, Kentucky, and Missouri, where slavery was legal but the plantation system was not widespread. A major task of Lincoln during the Civil War was to keep the border states in the Union.

brains trust: A popular nickname for the advisers Franklin D. Roosevelt gathered during his New Deal administration in the 1930s. Trust was another term for monopoly.

broadside: An advertisement or public notice printed on one side of a sheet of paper.

bull market: A stock market in which values are rising, to the benefit of investors who have bet on an increase in prices.

bullion: Gold used as backing for currency. See also **specie**.

cajun: People of southwestern Louisiana descended from those expelled by the British in the eighteenth century from Nova Scotia (Acadia, of which cajun is a variant).

capitalism: An economic system in which the means of production and exchange are privately owned (although one or more governmental agencies may regulate both) and market exchanges establish prices. Also referred to as the "free enterprise system." See also **socialism**.

carpetbagger: Negative southern term for the northerners who came South after the Civil War to take part in Reconstruction.

cartel: Business organizations that cooperate to control the production, pricing, and marketing of goods.

cash crops: Agricultural produce grown for sale rather than for the farmer's own use. In the nineteenth century, cotton was the nation's most valuable cash crop.

Chautauqua: Educational, religious, and recreational activities for adults that began in Chautauqua, New York.

checks and balances: The principle embedded in the Constitution that each branch of government be able to prevent any other from unilaterally deciding policy or imposing its will. The President, for example, can veto legislation and Congress can, with a two-thirds majority, override that veto.

civil liberties: Those rights of the individual citizen, as enumerated in the Bill of Rights in the Constitution, that limit the powers of the government. The First Amendment to the Constitution, for example, prohibits Congress from making any law that would restrict the free exercise of religious liberty.

civil rights: Rights to legal and social equality that everyone is supposed to possess regardless of race, creed, color, country of origin, age, gender, sexual orientation, or disability.

closed shop: The practice, made illegal by the Taft-Hartley Law, of requiring employers to hire only trade union members. See also **open shop** and **union shop**.

collective bargaining: Negotiations between organized workers and employers to determine wages and working conditions.

collective security: A system of diplomatic arrangements in which countries agree to act in unison to defend any one party to the agreement that is under armed attack or the threat of it. The United Nations seeks to embody this system on a global scale. See also **balance of power**.

commodity market: Financial market where brokers buy and sell agricultural products determining the prices paid to farmers.

conscription: Also known as the draft; a system in which young men (but, so far, not young women) are chosen and required to serve in the military for a specified period of time.

contraband: Goods legally prohibited from being imported or exported.

cooperative: A business enterprise in which workers or consumers share in ownership.

cost analysis: Study of the cost of operations intending to make them more efficient.

covenant: An agreement, like the Mayflower Compact, uniting a group of people for an expressed purpose. These agreements formed the basis for town settlement and government organization in regions where Puritan or Separatist groups took root. When establishing a new town, settlers signed a document (covenant) stating the spiritual purpose of their community and agreed to abide by Christian beliefs in their daily lives.

craft or trade union: Labor union that organizes skilled workers engaged in a specific craft or trade.

crop lien: A claim against a growing crop, usually held by a store in exchange for extending credit.

cult of domesticity: The belief that women's proper role lay in domestic pursuits.

currency: Money, whether specie (that is, gold or silver) or paper. The total amount of money in circulation at any one time is the total of all currency not held in bank reserves, plus all outstanding credit orders.

dark horse (candidate): An office seeker regarded as a long shot in a race. A person who achieves unexpected support as a political candidate.

de facto: Existing in practice, not established by law.

deflation: A period of declining prices and, therefore, of increasing purchasing power. During the last quarter of the nineteenth century, the longest sustained deflationary period in the nation's history, prices fell by a quarter, or a third. See also **inflation**.

deism: The belief that God created the universe so that no divine intervention was necessary for its operation.

de jure: According to law.

depression: A severe economic slump in which the total amount of goods and services produced declines sharply. The decline in production decreases employment, the result is that the public has less money with which to purchase goods, and that further discourages production. A less severe decline is called a **recession**.

deterrence: Measures taken by one country to discourage another from attacking it.

direct primary: A primary where party voters choose their candidates directly.

disarmament: A policy of reducing the size of a nation's military. Countries may undertake such a policy as part of an agreement with one or more other states. In that case the policy is called multilateral disarmament. Or it may disarm alone. That is called unilateral disarmament. Disarmament may involve particular weapons or types of weapons, such as intermediate range nuclear missiles, or may entail a general reduction in a country's military.

Dixiecrats: The name given to southern Democrats who bolted the 1948 nominating convention in protest over a civil rights plank in the party's platform. Forming the States Rights Party and nominating James Strom Thurmond as a third party presidential candidate, the Dixiecrats put forward a conservative program that pledged to preserve "social custom."

Dollar Diplomacy: A policy adopted by the United States during the administration of William Howard Taft (1909–1913) that relied upon economic incentives to persuade Latin American countries to cooperate with the policy initiatives of the United States.

domino theory: If one nation comes under Communist control, then neighboring nations will also become Communist.

dry farming: Farming that uses available moisture efficiently.

dry goods: Textiles, clothing, and materials.

effigy: A likeness, usually three-dimensional.

the elect: According to Calvinism, the people preordained by God for salvation.

Electoral College: Under the Constitution voters cannot directly elect the President or Vice President. Instead the Constitution provides that states are to elect the members of the Electoral College, who in turn elect the President and Vice President. Electors are not obligated to vote for the candidate with the highest popular vote in their state although, with rare exceptions, they have done so.

emancipation: Release from slavery.

embargo: A government decree banning trade with other nations.

Enlightenment: Also known as the Age of Reason, this term refers to the scientific and philosophical achievements from the late seventeenth century to the outbreak of the French Revolution at the end of the eighteenth. "Enlightened" thinkers emphasized the power of human reason to discover scientific "laws" of human behavior.

entail: Legal limitation preventing property from being divided or alienated.

established church: The official church of a government or state.

fascism: A political doctrine, adopted in Italy in the 1920s and then in Germany under the Nazis in the 1930s, that exalted the state and military power.

federalists: Supporters of ratification of the Constitution; believers in a strong central government.

fellow-traveler: Person who sympathizes with the Communist party, but not a member.

feminism: The belief that women should have equal rights to those of men.

flapper: In the 1920s, a young woman with short hair and short skirt.

foreclosure: Confiscation of property by a bank when mortgage payments are delinquent.

franchise: Government grant allowing a private company or person to provide a public service.

franchise (or suffrage): The right to vote.

free soil: The political doctrine, embodied in the Wilmot Proviso of 1846 and the Free Soil Party in the presidential election of 1848, that western territories should be closed to slavery.

free trade: The policy of permitting other countries to sell their goods in a nation's domestic markets without paying fees or taxes, called tariffs. In the nineteenth century Great Britain adopted this policy with the expectation that the resulting free competition would reward its advanced manufacturing capabilities. See also **protectionism**.

freedmen: Generic term used in reference to all black men, women, and children freed from slavery during the Civil War. The Freedmen's Bureau, passed by Congress over Andrew Johnson's veto, was established to minister to the needs of these former slaves.

frontier: Technically, the line marking the extent of settlement in the western territories; more broadly the term refers to the early period of settlement before such instruments of civilization as schools and churches had been established.

frontier thesis: Frederick Jackson Turner's argument that the American frontier shaped the American character, more especially implanting habits of democracy, individualism, and enterprise.

fundamentalism: The belief in the literal truth of the Bible. For centuries it had been habitual for Christians to take the Bible as being literally accurate, but among some conservative Christians in the United States that way of reading Scripture became particularly insistent early in the twentieth century in reaction to scientific theory and to historical interpretation of the Bible. It is to this recent reaction that the term "fundamentalism" is applied.

gauge: Distance between the iron rails in a railroad track.

general store: A small store, common in rural areas, that sells a lot of different goods.

general strike: A strike by all union members in a particular area.

gold standard: A monetary policy in which the amount of currency in circulation is based upon the amount of a country's gold reserves. The gold standard is often associated with the term "hard money."

Gospel of Wealth: The view, most strongly associated with Andrew Carnegie, that the wealthy were "stewards" of their riches and were to use them to benefit society. Carnegie's own philanthropy emphasized education and world peace.

grandfather clause: Some southern states restricted suffrage to those whose ancestors could vote in 1867, depriving blacks of the vote.

Great Plains: The arid, treeless area of the United States between the Dakotas in the north to parts of Texas in the south.

Great Society: The label given to Lyndon B. Johnson's domestic program. Johnson, having grown up politically during Franklin D. Roosevelt's years in office, sought during his own presidency a program to fulfill the promise of the New Deal and complete the work left undone by John F. Kennedy's New Frontier.

greenbacks: Paper money first issued by the Lincoln Administration and not redeemable in gold.

habeas corpus: The right of anyone to be brought before a court to determine whether the person is being held legally.

hard money: Currency backed by specie or redeemable in it. See also **soft money**.

harrow: A farm machine of heavy frame and sharp teeth, used to smooth plowed ground.

holding company: A corporation that holds stock in other corporations and is therefore able to establish a monopoly.

impeachment: The first part of a process whereby a President, Vice President, or federal judge can be removed from office. The word refers to a finding by the House of Representatives, by a two-thirds majority, that there is reasonable evidence that the officeholder in question committed "high crimes or misdemeanors." After impeachment by the House, the official goes on trial before the Senate. If a majority of two thirds of that body present finds the charges to be true, the defendant is removed from office.

imperialism: The policy of one nation's conquering other portions of the world and exercising political dominion over them. The term can also be applied to economic or cultural domination of one society by another.

implied power: Power not specifically granted by the Constitution but allegedly needed to carry out the governing duties listed in the Constitution.

impressment: Seizing men and forcing them into military service; the British thereby obtained crews for its ships in the War of 1812.

indentured servant: An individual bound by a contract, called an indenture, to work for a specified period of time. During the length of the contract the servant is not free to leave his master's employ. Indentured service was common during the colonial era. Many entered into such contracts to finance their migration to North America. See also **redemptioners**.

industrial union: Labor union that organizes all workers in an industry, skilled or unskilled.

industrialization: The process of substituting machine for human power in the manufacture of goods. In the United States this first happened on a large scale in the cotton textile industry, water power providing the primary source of energy.

inflation: A period of rising prices and therefore of decreasing purchasing power. Debtors favor inflation since it permits them to repay loans in dollars that are worth less than the ones they borrowed. Creditors have a corresponding preference for **deflation**.

infrastructure: Basic units that a society needs to function, such as transportation systems, water and power lines, and public institutions.

initiative: A proposed law is voted on by the electorate after a required number of signatures are obtained.

injunction: A court order sometimes to force strikers to return to work.

integration: The policy of ending the legal or customary segregation (separation) of the races. It may also entail the adoption of active measures such as school busing to achieve racial balance.

internal improvements: The policy, first associated with the Federalists under Hamilton and later with the Whigs under Henry Clay, of getting the federal government to finance the construction of roads, railroad lines, canals, bridges, and other public works.

interposition: A states rights theory whereby the state interposes itself or comes between the people and the federal government to protect the rights of the people.

isolationism: The conviction that the United States could, and should, stay clear of "foreign entanglements." It was especially popular following the First World War. In its extreme form it called for the United States to abandon all unnecessary contact with the rest of the world; a more moderate version called upon the United States to act alone in protecting its interests.

Jim Crow: A colloquial name for the system of legal segregation of African Americans formally adopted in the South in the late 1890s and 1900s. See also **integration**.

junta: Military officers who rule a country after seizing power.

kitchen cabinet: Unofficial but important advisers of President Andrew Jackson.

laissez-faire: The economic doctrine, especially popular during the nineteenth century, that holds that the government should not interfere with the free working of economic markets.

lame duck: An officeholder who has not been reelected but has the remainder of a term to serve, or a President serving a second and therefore by law a final term.

land grant college: A college instituted and funded by

resources made available under the Morrill Land-Grant College Act of 1862. Each state was allotted federally owned land in proportion to the size of its congressional delegation, to be sold by the state for the establishment of an agricultural college.

lobby: To attempt to influence public officials for or against a specific cause.

loyalists: Those colonists who retained their allegiance to Great Britain during the American Revolution. They were also called Tories.

manifest destiny: The belief, especially popular in the 1840s, that the United States was destined to rule all or most of the Western Hemisphere. Supporters of the War with Mexico used it to justify the invasion of that country and the seizure of a third of its territory.

manumit: To free from slavery or bondage; emancipate.

Medicare: A program of health care for the elderly championed by Lyndon B. Johnson and passed into law in 1965. During the next two years legislation was passed extending benefits to the needy under the Medicaid program.

melting pot: America as a place where immigrants lose their distinctive cultural identities and are absorbed into a uniform culture.

mercantilism: An economic policy under which a nation seeks to maximize exports and minimize imports on the theory that there is a finite amount of wealth and that one nation's gain is therefore another's loss. As applied by Great Britain during the eighteenth century, the policy held that colonial trade should be regulated in the interests of the empire as a whole as London perceived that whole.

merchant marine: A country's commercial ships.

mestizo: One of mixed Spanish and Indian ancestry.

middle passage: In the triangular trade among New England, Africa, and the West Indies, the voyage between Africa and the West Indies, when ships carried slaves held in nightmarish conditions.

migrant workers: Laborers who travel from one area to another to obtain work.

militiamen: Ordinary citizens ready to serve in military in event of emergency.

millennialism: The religious doctrine that the Second Coming of Jesus Christ will begin a thousand-year-long reign of the just, or alternatively, that the Coming will follow the reign of the just. Millenarians have often tried to predict the exact date of the Second Coming.

Model T: Automobile produced by Henry Ford from 1908 to 1927 and sold at the lowest possible price.

monopoly: Effective control over the supply of a product or service such that the holder can dictate its price. Some economists distinguish between "natural" monopolies, such as over a city's water supply, which should be permitted and regulated, and "artificial" ones, such as John D. Rockefeller's Standard Oil Company.

Monroe Doctrine: The policy adopted by the United States in 1823, proclaiming that in the future no European nation may establish a colony in the Western Hemisphere. See also **Roosevelt Corollary.**

moratorium: Suspension of an activity.

muckrakers: Progressive era writers who wrote articles exposing corruption in industry and government.

muckraking: A derogatory term coined by Theodore Roosevelt for the investigative journalism of the Progressive Era.

Mugwumps: Republican reformers in the 1880s and 1890s, who might cross party lines.

mulatto: One of mixed black and white ancestry.

nationalize: To convert an industry from private to governmental ownership.

nativism: Hostility to immigrants that has typically fed upon anti-Catholic or anti-Semitic notions or upon the belief that foreigners are the source of political radicalism. It is sometimes linked to racism when the immigrant group in question is non-white.

naturalized: Granted full citizenship after having been born in a foreign country.

naval stores: Timber, tar, resin, pitch, and turpentine used in building wooden ships.

navigation acts: A series of measures enacted by the British Parliament to regulate colonial commerce. See **mercantilism.**

Nazism: The German variant of Fascism. Nazis under Hitler sought German supremacy in Europe, the extermination of "lesser" races such as Jews and Gypsies, as well as homosexuals, and a totalitarian social order.

neutrality: A position of non-alignment adopted by a nation with respect to a real or potential international conflict. At the start of World War I, for example, President Woodrow Wilson pledged the United States to be neutral.

nullification: The constitutional theory, most notably associated with John C. Calhoun, that individual states could nullify and declare void within their own borders those acts of Congress the state believed to violate the Constitution. Used early by James Madison and Thomas Jefferson in their arguments against the Alien and Sedition Acts, and culminating in the nullification of the United States Constitution itself during southern secession, this theory was put aside as legitimate constitutional interpretation with the defeat of the Confederacy and its radical assertion of states' rights. See also **secession.**

nullify: To declare invalid.

old-stock: Families in the United States for a lengthy period.

Open Door (policy): The policy, adopted by Theodore Roosevelt's administration, that called for all states to have equal access to markets in China. By the end of the nineteenth century, several European powers had established spheres of influence in China that included monopolies of portions of that country's international trade.

open shop: The practicing of hiring nonunion as well as union employees. See also **closed shop** and **union shop.**

pacifist: A person opposed to war or violence to resolve disputes.

pan-Africanism: The vision of the uniting of all "colored races" in a single, free African state. Promoted in one form by Marcus Garvey, the idea gained additional popular support among urban African Americans after World War I. It quickly lost momentum when Garvey fell prey to legal and financial troubles, culminating in his deportion to Jamaica in the late 1920s.

panic: A sharp economic downturn, believed to be caused by a sudden loss of confidence in one or more markets. Panics normally follow bursts of speculative investing in which values rise very rapidly and many speculators overextend their holdings by buying on credit.

peculiar institution: A southern euphemism for slavery.

piecework: Work, usually textiles, paid for according to the number of items turned out.

piedmont: Land at the foot of a mountain range.

platform: A formal statement of principles on which a political party bases its appeal to the public.

political machine: A single-party political organization that dominates government and controls policy and practice. Most closely associated with the Democratic party in large northern cities during the late nineteenth and early twentieth centuries, the machine used patronage and corruption to consolidate a political power base that in turn provided opportunity for profit. George Washington Plunkitt, a boss in New York City's Tammany Hall machine, justified these practices, claiming they were merely the product of "honest graft."

poll tax: A fee some southern states required as a prerequisite to voting to discourage black participation.

popular sovereignty: A concept of self-rule built into the Kansas-Nebraska Act and other pre–Civil War legislation. People in the newer organized territories were empowered to decide whether to establish or prohibit slavery. Stephen Douglas and other architects of the policy hoped in vain to avoid contentious congressional and national debate over the extension of slavery, but in practice tensions between North and South intensified as evidenced by episodes such as "Bleeding Kansas."

populism: A radical political movement centered in the agricultural regions of the South and West of the late 1880s and the 1890s. Populists called for the federal regulation of railroads, the direct popular election of senators, federally guaranteed credit for farmers, the free coinage of silver, and numerous other reforms.

portage: Carrying boats or supplies overland between waterways.

pragmatism: An American philosophy most closely associated with William James, Charles Peirce, and John Dewey arguing that the truth value of an idea is its utility in enabling the thinker to accomplish some purpose. This use of utility to assess truth is referred to as the "pragmatic test."

primogeniture: Legal right of the eldest son to inherit the entire estate of his father.

privateer: A ship of war owned and equipped by a private individual, yet sanctioned by a government to seize and plunder enemy vessels during war. Englishmen John Hawkins and Sir Francis Drake, for example, profited greatly in ventures against the Spanish during the sixteenth century, as did many Americans against the English during the War for Independence.

progressivism: A moderate political reform movement of the early twentieth century. Progressives sought to eliminate governmental corruption at all levels, to make cities safer and more liveable, and to use the federal government to correct abuses in business.

prohibition: The policy of enforcing temperance by outlawing the sale and nonmedicinal use of alcohol. The Eighteenth Amendment to the Constitution, adopted in 1919, established prohibition throughout the nation. The Amendment was repealed in 1933.

protectionism: The economic policy of placing special fees or taxes (tariffs) on foreign imported goods. The idea, in addition to raising revenue, is to aid domestic manufacturers whose goods would enjoy a protected position in their home markets.

protective tariff: Tax on imported goods to make them more expensive than similar domestic goods.

protectorate: A country partially controlled by a stronger power that protects it from foreign threats.

public domain: Federally-owned land.

racism: The belief that humanity is divided into distinct racial stocks and that one race is superior to others.

recall: Voters' petition to remove an elected official from office.

recession: See **depression**.

redeemers: Southern Democrats who hoped to bring the Democratic Party back into power during Reconstruction.

redemptioners: Laborers who contracted their services to pay for passage to the New World. Unlike indentured servants, who contracted through agents while still in Europe, redemptioners agreed to terms only after the Atlantic crossing. Most of them upon arrival were given two weeks to secure alternative means of payment through friends or family. If this failed, the newcomer's services would then be auctioned off. While indentured servants came singly, redemptioners generally came as whole families or even as small communities.

referendum: The submitting to the public for approval of proposed law.

reparations: Payments exacted from Germany, principally by Great Britain and France, after World War I in payment for damage that, so the victors claimed, Germany had done during the war. The Treaty of Versailles of 1919 authorized the payments under a "war guilt" clause that assigned blame to Germany for causing the war.

revenue sharing: The policy of sharing federal tax dollars with state and local governments.

revivalism: A season of spiritual renewal among evangelical Christians. Revivalists, beginning with Jonathan Edwards in the eighteenth century, have called upon sinners to acknowledge their own sinful natures and throw themselves upon Jesus' infinite love and forgiveness. The revived believer is said to be converted and seeks to reorganize his life.

right-of-way: The right to build facilities that cut across land belonging to others.

romanticism: Movement characterized by interest in nature, emphasis on emotion and imagination, and rebellion against social conventions.

Roosevelt Corollary (to the Monroe Doctrine): In 1904 Theodore Roosevelt added to the Monroe Doctrine that the United States pledged to police the hemisphere to make sure, for example, that Latin American countries did not default upon debts to other nations.

scalawag: Negative southern term for white southerners who aligned with the Republican Party.

secession: As a specific term in American history, the act of the eleven states of the Confederacy in removing themselves from the Union; also the doctrine justifying that decision. The theory of secession held that the Union was made up of sovereign states each of which retained the right to go its separate way.

sectionalism: A term used to describe the growing division between the North, South, and West in the decades prior to the Civil War. Each section increasingly identified more with its own regional interests than with national concerns.

secular: Related to or oriented toward worldly, nonreligious issues.

sedition: Conduct or language against the authority of a government.

segregation: The policy of maintaining a racially separate society. In 1896 the Supreme Court, rendering its decision in *Plessy v. Ferguson,* ruled that segregated "separate but equal" public facilities did not violate the Fourteenth Amendment. In 1954 the Court reversed itself through its decision in *Brown v. Board of Education,* holding that separate facilities were "inherently unequal."

separatists: Dissenting Christians who believed that virtual separation from the Anglican Church and the establishment of independent congregations were necessary for the practice of a purified spiritual life.

settlement house: Community center run by social workers in slums to aid the poor.

shaman: Acting between the visible and invisible spirit world, a shaman healed the sick, conducted religious ceremonies, and foretold the future.

sit-down strike: Strike where workers refuse to leave their factories until demands are met.

slave codes: Laws regulating slaves in the Old South. Codes typically required slaves to possess a pass from their master in order to travel, prohibited slaves from learning to read, and banned slaves from testifying in court against whites. During Reconstruction these codes were revised, becoming known as black codes, as a means of controlling the freed slave population and subsequently enforced by newly formed vigilante groups, including the Ku Klux Klan.

Social Darwinism: The nineteenth-century social philosophy teaching that human progress mimics animal evolution, in which the strong and most "fit" win out, and that therefore government programs or private charities that seek to help the less "fit" such as the poor actually retard progress.

Social Gospel: Reform movement of the twentieth century led by Protestant clergymen, who advanced social justice for the poor.

socialism: An economic system in which the workers collectively own the means of production. In the former Soviet Union, collective ownership had translated into ownership by the state. Socialist thought in the West has envisioned control by smaller collective units with participation on the part of the individual worker.

soft money: Paper money not backed by specie (coin or hard money).

sharecropping: An agricultural system of tenancy in which landlord and tenant share the crop. The landlord provides the land and often credit for supplies; the tenant provides the labor. After the Civil War, this became a dominant system in the South.

specie: Gold or silver used as currency.

sphere of influence: Area where a foreign nation has considerable authority.

spoils system: The winning party in an election distributes government jobs to its supporters.

states' rights: Maximum self-government by the individual states.

subculture: A group of people united by ethnicity, social class, behavioral tendencies, or other defining characteristics that are identifiably distinct from the dominant culture. In the United States since the middle of the twentieth century, the term has often been used in reference to countercultural groups such as the beat generation of the 1950s or the cultural radicals of the 1960s.

subsidy: Financial aid from a government in support of an enterprise in the public interest.

suburbanization: The movement of urban dwellers to surrounding areas or "bedroom communities." Advances in transportation, especially the automobile, made it possible for individuals to live at considerable distances from the workplace. After World War II, suburban developments such as Levittown, Long Island, provided thousands of nearly identical, inexpensive homes for first-time buyers. Here, the "baby boom" flourished, and the power also of television, along with that of mass market consumerism, made American life appear increasingly standardized.

suffrage: The right to vote. During Reconstruction the Fifteenth Amendment was ratified, granting the vote to African-American males. Women remained without a federal guarantee of the vote until 1920 when, after a century of organized political pressure, the Nineteenth Amendment was ratified.

summit meeting: Conference of highest-rank officials of two or more governments.

sweatshop: A shop where employees work long hours at low wages under bad conditions.

tariff: A tax imposed upon goods or services imported into a country. When such taxes are used simply to help finance governmental operations, they are called revenue tariffs. When they are used to give domestic manufacturers a favored position by raising the prices of their foreign competitors, they are called protective tariffs.

tarring and feathering: Covering a person with hot tar and rolling the victim in feathers.

temperance: The campaign against the nonmedical use of alcohol. It was one of the largest reform movements of the nineteenth and early twentieth centuries.

Texians: Non-Hispanic settlers in Texas in the nineteenth century.

Third World: A term used to designate non-Western countries that have yet to industrialize. The United States and its industrialized trading partners, and the former Soviet Union and its former satellites, make up the first two worlds respectively.

tidewater: Low coastal land drained by tidal streams.

tribute: A payment of valuables made as a price of security.

trust: A combination of companies or other economic units that have joined to act in restraint of trade by setting prices or eliminating competition.

union shop: The practice of requiring new employees to join a trade union, usually within thirty to ninety days. Unlike the closed shop system, the union shop allows the employment of workers who are not members of a union at the time of their hiring; unlike the open shop, the union shop system forces them thereupon to join a union. See also **closed shop** and **open shop**.

vigilantes: Individuals who band together extralegally to enforce particular codes of behavior. In the South after the Civil War, white gangs lynched African Americans and whites who challenged the system of white supremacy; on the western frontier, vigilantes sometimes hanged cattle rustlers.

welfare state: The set of governmental programs that provides minimal care for the poor, the elderly, the disabled, and the unemployed. All industrialized societies have adopted welfare measures. In the United States the origins of the welfare state lie in Franklin Roosevelt's New Deal.

writs of assistance: General search warrants giving customs officers authority to search ships and storage houses for smuggled goods.

yellow journalism: Newspapers that exaggerate events or give prominence to scandals to attract readers.

SUCCEEDING IN
HISTORY COURSES

By John McClymer

STUDYING HISTORY AND
STUDYING FOR EXAMS

The instructor who designed this course hopes you will take advantage of the opportunity to learn about the American past. Your own objectives in taking the course may be somewhat different. You may be taking it because it fulfills some requirement for graduation or because it fits into your schedule or because it seems less objectionable than the alternative you could be taking.

In a better world, these differences between your objectives and those of the course would not matter. The studying you do to perform well on exams and papers would involve your learning a fair amount of history. And so your grade would certify that you had indeed left the course with a more informed and thoughtful understanding of the American past than you had when you entered it. In the world we must actually live in, the connection between studying history and studying for exams in history is not necessarily so clear or straightforward.

Many students manage to prepare themselves for mid-terms and finals without permanently adding to their understanding. There they sit, yellow hi-liting pens in hand, plodding through the assigned chapters. Grim-faced, they underline every declarative sentence. Then they trace and retrace their tracks trying to commit every yel-

lowed fact to memory. As the time of the test draws near, they choke back that first faint feeling of panic by trying to guess the likeliest question. The instructor is never, they say to themselves, going to ask us to identify George Washington. But what about Silas Deane? And Pinckney? No, wait. There were TWO Pinckneys! That means there is almost certainly going to be a question about ONE of them. So it is that some students devote more energy to Thomas and Charles Cotesworth Pinckney than they do to George Washington. By such tactics they may get ready for the exam, but sabotage their chance of gaining any insight into American history.

Life does afford worse tragedies. This one, however, is remediable. And this introduction can help. It is designed to help you do well in the course, and to help you learn some history. It is, in fact, dedicated to the proposition that the easiest and most satisfying way to succeed in a history course is to learn some history. It makes very little sense, after all is said and done, to spend your time trying to keep the Pinckneys straight or running down a fact or two about Silas Deane. What will it profit you? You may pick up a few points on the short answer section of the exam, but those few points are a small reward for hours of studying. And, in the meantime, your essay on Washington as a political leader was distinctly mediocre. Clearly something is wrong.

Studying for exams is a poor way of learning history. Studying history, to the contrary, is an excellent way of preparing for exams. If you had, for example, thought about American relations with France during John Adams' presidency, you would very probably remember who Charles C. Pinckney was. And you would scarcely have had to memorize anything.

Conserve your yellow pens. All that hi-liting simply lowers the resale value of the book. If you underline everything you read, you will wind up with a book of underlinings. There may be some psychological comfort in that. All of that yellow does provide visible evidence that you read the material. But it will not leave you with a useful guide to what to review. You have hi-lited too much.

You have created a democracy of facts. All names, dates, and events are equally yellow. The Pinckneys and Silas Deane, in other words, have just become as noteworthy as George Washington or John Adams. You need, more than anything else, some way of determining what is important.

The next step may prove harder. You will have to give up trying to learn history by rote. A certain amount of memorizing may be unavoidable in a course, but ultimately it is the enemy of understanding. That is because many people use it as an alternative to thinking. Have you ever wished there were a better way? Well, there is. If you understand what Lincoln had hoped to accomplish with the Emancipation Proclamation, for example, you will not need to memorize its provisions. You will know why it did not promise freedom to any of the slaves in states (like Maryland or Missouri) that remained loyal to the Union. You will know why the Proclamation did not go into effect until one hundred days after it was issued. You will not, in short, stumble over a question like: "Whom did the Emancipation Proclamation emancipate?"

Facts are by no means unimportant. It is essential to have something to think about. But it is generally more fun to pay attention to ideas. Lincoln, to pursue this example, was interested above all else in restoring the Union. He was perfectly willing, he said, to keep slavery if that would accomplish his purpose; he was equally willing to abolish slavery if that would do the trick. So there is no mystery that in the Emancipation Proclamation he gave the states of the Confederacy one hundred days to return to the Union on pain of losing their slaves if they did not. The same reason explains why the Proclamation did not apply to slave states still in the Union.

If you take care of the ideas, the facts will assemble themselves. That has to do with the way in which textbooks are written and courses taught. It also relates to how people learn.

No historian, including the authors of the text and your instructor, pretends that history is the story of everything that ever happened. Many things happened for which there are no surviving records. More importantly, scholars use the records that have survived in a highly selective way. Even though they are always interested in finding new information, and in finding new ways of using information already known, each individual work of history—be it an article, a doctoral dissertation, a monograph, a textbook, a course of lectures—represents hundreds and thousands of choices about what to include and what to omit. Much more is known, for example, about the signers of the Declaration of Independence than you will read in any textbook. The information you actually encounter in this course, as a result, is there because the text authors or your teacher decided for some reason to include it. Usually the reason is that this particular bit of information helps explain or illustrate some pattern of behavior or thought. Focus on these patterns. They are what you should be thinking about.

In doing so you will have the approval of learning theorists. They have found that while it is difficult for people to recall disconnected bits of data (for example, which Pinckney was an emissary to France during the XYZ affair), it is comparatively easy to remember details of coherent stories. This is not a very startling finding. Details make sense once you see how they fit together. Let us return to the example of the Emancipation Proclamation. Lincoln's actions followed from his political priorities in which the integrity of the Union outranked achieving peace or ending slavery; his analysis of the course of the war, and his perception of the choices open to him. Had Lincoln valued peace or ending slavery more highly than preserving the Union, had easy victory or actual defeat seemed near at hand, had other inducements to the states of the Confederacy to return to the Union seemed more promising, he would have acted differently. Once Lincoln's perception of the situation becomes clear to you, you will have little, if any, difficulty remembering what he did.

Neither compulsive underlining nor prodigious memorization will help you to understand these patterns. What will? Rephrase the question: What does it mean to read and listen intelligently? For most students, reading and listening are passive forms of behavior. They sit and wait to be told. Someone else, they expect, will provide the answers. Even worse is that they expect someone else will provide the questions. And, of course, they do. At best, this situation leaves them with a more or less adequate record of what someone else thinks they should know.

Most of what passes for studying involves not a conscientious effort to wrestle with the subject, but a determined effort to be prepared to answer likely questions. That is why we pay more heed to Silas Deane than to George Washington. It is why studying for exams is such a poor way to learn history.

Letting your teacher or the authors of the text do your thinking for you leads to tedium. Passivity is boring. Yet people rarely blame themselves for being bored. It cannot be your own fault. You are only "taking" the course. Someone else is "giving" it, and so you look to the instructor to liven things up a touch. Maybe some audio-visuals or a bit of humor, you think, would make the course less dreary. These hopes are misplaced, for while humor is a blessed thing and audio-visuals have their place, it is the substance of the course that should interest you.

Boredom is almost always a self-inflicted wound. Students are bored because they expect the instructor always to be interesting when it is they who must themselves take an interest.

Taking an interest involves learning to read and listen actively. Intellectual activity begins with questions—your own questions directed, in the first instance, to yourself and then to your teacher. Why is it, you might wonder, that the United States is the only industrialized country without a comprehensive national system of health care? Why were New England authors drawn to the innocence or the mysterious evil of the wilderness in nature and the soul? Why did slavery last so long in the American South? And why did a party system develop even though the founders were bitterly opposed to political parties?

You will not always find satisfactory answers. But you will have started to think about the American past. And when you do, something quite desirable happens to all of those facts. They will take on life and become evidence, clues to the answers you are seeking. The questions will give you a rational basis for deciding which facts are important. And George Washington will finally receive his well-deserved place over the Pinckneys.

All of this leads directly to the question of how you should study for a course. It is too easy to assume that the sole reason why students are sometimes ill-prepared is that they did not spend enough time getting ready. This is a half-truth, and a dangerous one. It ignores the inefficiency of much reviewing itself.

How do you get ready for an exam? Do you get out your textbook and notes and pour over them again and again until the time runs out or the sheer boredom of it all crushes your good intentions? If so, then you have lots of company—a consolation of sorts. Available, on the other hand, is a better way.

Find a quiet and comfortable spot. Bring along a blank pad and something to write with. Then jot down, just as they occur to you, whatever items you can remember about the course. Do not rush yourself. And do not try, at this stage, to put things in order. Just sit there and scribble down whatever pops into your mind. After a while you will have quite a large and varied mix of facts. Then see how much of this you can put together. You do not need to write out whole sentences or paragraphs. An arrow or a word or two will frequently be enough. You are not, after all, going to hand in these scribbles. You are just collecting your thoughts. Do not be concerned if this process seems to be taking up some of the limited time you have to study. It will prove to be time well spent.

Now look over what you have written. Where are the gaps? You will find that you know a fair bit about the material just from your previous reading of the text and from listening in class. But some topics will still be obscure. Now you know what you should be studying. Why study what you already know? And here is the nub of the matter, for an intelligent review focuses on what you need to refresh your mind about.

You will doubtless have noticed that this

strategy presupposes that you have read the text-book and taken good notes in class. Just what, you might wonder, are good notes? Many students think that the closer they come to transcribing the instructor's every word the better their notes are. They are mistaken, and for several reasons.

One is that unless you are an expert at short-hand, you will not succeed. Instead you will be frantically scrambling to catch up. At the end of class you will have a sore hand, a great deal of barely legible notes, and little if any idea of what the class was about.

Another reason not to attempt to transcribe lectures—taping them usually wastes time—is that you will spend much of your hour taking down information you either already know or can easily find in the textbook. How often do you need to see that Jefferson Davis was the president of the Confederacy?

The most important reason not to take down everything is that it prevents you from doing what you ought to be doing during class, listening intelligently. Your instructor is not simply transmitting information but also seeking to explain the principles of the discipline. It is these explanations you should be listening for, and your notes should concentrate on them. It is much easier to do this if you have read the relevant textbook chapters first. That way you will already know much of the information. And you will have some questions already in your mind, something to listen for. You can take notes sensibly. You can fill in explanations of points that had puzzled you, jot down unfamiliar facts, and devote most of your time to listening instead of writing. Your hand will not be sore; you will know what the class was about; and your notes will complement rather than duplicate what you already knew.

So far we have dealt mainly with the mechanics of studying—taking notes, reviewing for exams, and the like. Valuable as knowing the mechanics can be, the real secret to studying is learning how to think within the ultimate intentions and boundaries of the field. History is a way of thinking about the human condition. Scholars of literature quarrel about the essence of their topic, but together they study the imagination of writers and the means by which words sharpen and express that imagination. And so, as you learn the details of the subject and the ways those details relate to one another, think even more broadly what the

field of study is all about. Consider both the specific causes of the Civil War and the universal motives of pride and greed and loyalty that found expression in those times.

HOW TO TAKE EXAMS

In the best of worlds examinations would hold no terrors. You would be so well prepared that no question, no matter how tricky or obscure, could shake your serene confidence. In the real world, it seems, preparation is always less than complete. "Of course," you say to yourself, "I should have studied more. But I did not. Now what?" This section will not tell you how to get A's without study, but it will suggest some practical steps that will help you earn the highest grade compatible with what you do know.

Before you begin answering any of the essay portion of the exam, look over the entire essay section. It is impossible to budget your time sensibly until you know what the whole exam looks like. And if you fail to allow enough time for each question, two things—both bad—are likely to happen. You may have to leave some questions out, including perhaps some you might have answered very effectively. How often have you muttered: "I really knew that one"? The other unhappy consequence is that you may have to rush through the last part of the exam, including questions you could have answered very well if you had left more time.

How do you budget your time effectively? The idea, after all, is to make sure that you have enough time to answer fully all the questions you do know. So the best plan is also the simplest. Answer those questions first.

Answering question #7 before #4 may seem odd at first, but you will soon enough get used to it. And you will find that, if you still run out of time, you at least have the satisfaction of knowing you are rushing through questions you could not have answered very well anyway. You will have guaranteed that you will receive the maximum credit for what you do know. Answering questions in the order of your knowledge has an immediate psychological advantage too. Most students are at least a little tense before an exam. If you answer the first several questions well, that tension will likely go away. As you relax, you will find it easier to remember names, dates, and other bits of information. If you get off to a shaky start, a simple case of pre-exam jitters can become full-scale panic. Should that happen, you may have trouble remembering your own phone number.

Let us suppose you have gotten through everything you think you know on the exam and still have some time left. What should you do? You can now try to pick up a few extra points with some judicious guessing. Trying to guess with essay questions is of little use. In all probability you will write something so vague that you will not get any credit for it anyway. You should try instead to score on the short-answer section.

Some types of questions were made for shrewd guesswork. Matching columns are ideal. A process of elimination will often tell you what the answer has to be. Multiple choice questions are almost as good. Here too you can eliminate some of the possibilities. Most teachers feel obliged to give you a choice of four or five possible answers, but find it hard to come up with more than three that are plausible. So you can normally count on being able to recognize the one or two that are there just as padding. Once you have narrowed the choices to two or three, you are ready to make your educated guess. Always play your hunches, however vague. Your hunch is based on something you heard or read even if you cannot remember what it is. So go with it. Do not take your time. If you cannot think of the answer, just pick one and have done with it. Try to avoid changing answers. A number of studies show that you are more likely to change a right answer than to correct a wrong one.

Identifications are the type of short-answer question most resistant to guesswork. Don't spend much time on questions for which you have little idea of an answer, but try to come up with something better than a slapdash hunch. (This does not contradict the advice about playing hunches on multiple-choice questions. Such questions offer alternatives, one of which may tickle your memory.) You want the exam as a whole to convey what you do know. Supplying a mass of misinformation usually creates a presumption that you do not know what you are talking about even on those sections of the exam for which you really do. So be careful about wild guesses. Be prepared to present your instructor with a solid assemblage of good factual answers that will indicate that while you have achieved a critical understanding of the themes of the course, you have also respected the facts to which those themes speak.

These suggestions are not substitutes for studying. They may, however, help you get the most out of what you know. They may, that is, make the difference between a mediocre and a good grade.

HOW TO WRITE BOOK REVIEWS

One goal of book reviews is to set forth clearly and succinctly who would benefit from reading the work in question. It follows that a good review indicates the scope of the book, identifies its point of view, summarizes its main conclusions, evaluates its use of evidence, and—where possible—compares the book with others on the subject.

You have probably written book reviews in high school or in other college courses. You may then be in danger of approaching this kind of assignment with a false sense of security. It sounds easy, after all, to write an essay of five hundred words or so. And you have written lots of other reviews. But did those other reviews concentrate clearly on the questions a good review must address? If they did not, your previous experience is not going to prove especially helpful. You may even have developed some bad habits.

Easily the worst habit is that of summarizing not the book's argument but its contents. Let us suppose you are reviewing a biography of George Washington. The temptation is to write about Washington rather than about the book. This is a path to disaster. Washington had an eventful but widely known career. You are not, in all probability, going to find much that is fresh or interesting to say about him. Meanwhile, you have ignored your primary responsibility, which is to tell the reader what this study has to say that is fresh or interesting.

So you need to remind yourself as forcefully as possible that your job is to review the book and not the subject of the book. Does the book fix narrowly on Washington or does it also go into the circle to which he belonged? Is the author sympathetic to him? Does the writer attempt to psychoanalyze him or stick to questions of his political leadership? Is the book in firm command of the available evidence (this requires you to read the footnotes)? Does the author have something new to say about Washington and his times? If so, how well documented is this new interpretation?

You should generally not comment on

whether you enjoyed the book. That is undoubtedly an important consideration for you, but it is of little interest to anyone else. There are occasions when you need to suffer in silence. This is one of them.

HOW TO SELECT A
TERM PAPER TOPIC

Doing research, as you may already have had occasion to learn, is hard work. It is sometimes boring. Typically it involves long periods of going through material that is not what you were looking for and is not particularly interesting. It also involves taking detailed and careful notes, many of which you will never use. These are the dues you must pay if you are ever to earn the excitement that comes when you finally find the missing piece of evidence and make sense of things.

Not everything about doing research is boring. Aside from the indescribable sensation of actually finding out what you wanted to know are occasional happy accidents when you stumble across something that while not relevant to your research nonetheless pricks your imagination. Many a scholar studying an old political campaign has read up on the pennant races or fashions or radio listings for that year. These are, as one scholar puts it, oases in the desert of evidence. But, as he quickly adds, no one crosses the desert just to get to the oasis. The truth is that you have to have a good reason for getting to the other side. This dictates a topic you are genuinely interested in.

The point cannot be overemphasized. If you have a question you really want to answer, you will find it much easier to endure the tedium of turning all those pages. You will have a motive for taking good notes and for keeping your facts straight. If you are not interested in your topic, you are going to be constantly tempted to take shortcuts. And even if you resist temptation, you will find it hard to think seriously about what you do find.

So the topic has to interest you. That, you may be thinking, is easy to say. But what if your interest in the subject is less than compelling? Are you then going to be stuck with some topic you could care little about? The answer is No. No, that is, unless it turns out that you have no curiosity about anything at all; and if that is the case, you are probably dead already. Anything that can be examined chronologically is fair game for the historian.

Histories exist of sports and of sciences, of sexual practices and jokes about them, of work and of recreation. Surely your imagination can find a topic on which you and your instructor will agree. This being true, if you wind up writing on some question you are not passionately concerned with answering, you alone are at fault.

Once you have such a topic you need to find ways of defining it so that you can write an intelligent essay. "The Automobile in American Life" could serve as the subject for a very long book. It is not going to work as a subject for a term paper. You could not possibly search out so vast a topic in the time you have to work with. And your paper, however long, is not going to be of book length, so you would be stuck with trying to compress an immense amount of information into a brief essay. You need to fix on some element of the general topic that you can intelligently treat in the space and time you have to work with.

Students usually look at this problem backwards. They complain about how long their papers have to be. They should complain about how short they have to be. Space is a luxury you normally cannot afford. If you have done a fair amount of research on an interesting topic, your problem is going to be one of finding a way of getting into your paper all you have to say. Writing consists of choices about what you want to say. And if you have done your work properly, the hard choices involve deciding what to leave out.

"Fair enough," you may be thinking, "but I do not want to get stuck investigating some minute bit of trivia, the 'gear shift level from 1940 to 1953,' for example. I want to study the automobile in American life." Here we come to the core of the matter. Your topic must be narrowly defined so that you can do it justice, but it must also speak to the broad question that interested you in the first place. The trick is to decide just what it is about your topic—cars in this instance—that really interests you. Cars are means of transportation, of course, but they are also status symbols, examples of technology, and much else. Because of the automobile, cities and suburbs are designed in ways very different from how they were when people traveled by trolley or train. The automobile has dictated even teenage dating patterns. Having a driver's license, and regular access to a car, has become for some teenagers an obsession.

The point is that you have to think about your

topic and then decide what within it to examine. If you end up doing a treatise on differing methods of changing tires, you are your own enemy. You could have been studying sex and sexism in automobile advertising.

HOW TO LOCATE MATERIAL

Once you have worked up an interesting and practical topic for your term paper, you are ready to begin your research. For many students this means ambling over to the library and poking around in the computer catalog. This may not be the best way to begin. The librarians who catalog the library's holdings, while skilled professionals, cannot possibly anticipate the needs of every individual student. So they catalog books by their main subject headings and then include obvious cross-references. But much of what you need may not be obvious. So, for example, if you are interested in the causes of the Civil War, you will have no trouble finding under "U.S. History, Civil War" a title such as Kenneth Stampp's *And the War Came*. But will you find Roy Nichol's *Disruption of the American Democracy*? Your subject, however, may have a general guide, such as the *Harvard Guide to American History*. In that case, draw titles from it.

Now you have the beginnings of a decent bibliography. Your next act should be to introduce yourself to the research librarian. This person's specialty is helping people look for information. Yet many students never consult with a librarian. Do not pass up an opportunity to make your work easier. Often a librarian can point you to more specialized bibliographical guides, show you where to learn of the most recent books and articles, and help you refine your topic by indicating what questions are easiest to get information on.

You now have a reasonably extensive set of cards. And you can now safely consult the computer catalog to see which of these titles your library has. Prepare yourself for some disappointments. Even good undergraduate libraries will not have everything you need. They will have some (unless your library is very weak or your topic esoteric). Almost all college libraries participate in the interlibrary loan system. This system, which the library staff will gladly explain to you, permits you to get virtually any title you could wish for. The only catch is that you must give the library enough lead time. For books and articles that are not especially rare this normally means from a day or two to two weeks.

HOW TO TAKE NOTES

Sifting through the material you have found, you will need to take careful notes. As you do, you should write down on a notecard each piece of information you believe might prove relevant. For each piece of information you also will have to specify the full source.

Following these two bits of advice will save you much time and trouble. Finding information in your sources is trouble enough. You do not want to have to find it all over again when you sit down to write your paper. But this is often just what students have to do because they failed to write down some bit of data (which, perhaps, seemed only marginally important at the time) or took all of their notes on loose leaf paper and now must search through every page to find this one fact. It is far easier, over the long run, to have a separate card for each piece or group of closely related pieces of information. Tell yourself that you are the last of the big time spenders and can afford to use up index cards as though they were blank pieces of paper, which is what they are.

The general rule is that in compiling your research notes you should take extra care so that the actual writing will be as trouble-free as possible. It follows that you should take lots of notes. Do not try to determine in advance whether you are going to use a particular bit of data. Always give yourself the margin of safety. Similarly, do not try to decide in advance whether you will quote the source exactly or simply paraphrase it. If you take down the exact words, you can always decide to make the idea your own by qualifying it in various ways and putting it in your own words.

WRITING TERM PAPERS AND OTHER ESSAYS

You have no doubt already learned that next to mastery of the subject matter nothing is more important for earning good grades than effective writing. You surely know people who despite weak study habits get high grades. The reason may be their ability to write well.

Students who are not among that relatively small group who write well sometimes think it unfair that writing skills should count so heavily. The course, some complain, is American history and not expository writing, and so their prose should not influence their grade. But teachers continue to believe that the ability clearly and forcefully to express what you know is an indispensable measure of how well you have learned the subject. Writing well is an invaluable skill, and not only in college. Many of the most desirable jobs involve writing correspondence, reports, memoranda. The writing will never stop.

No matter how poorly you write, if you can speak English effectively you can learn to write it effectively. It is simply a matter of expressing your ideas clearly. This you can learn to do. It requires not genius but merely patience and practice.

Charity, St. Paul said, is the chief of all the virtues. In expository prose, however, the chief virtue is clarity. And like charity, it covers a multitude of sins. If your sentences, however homely, are clear, they will receive a sympathetic reading.

It has perhaps crossed your mind that on some occasions you are not very eager to get to the point. Sometimes you may not be sure just what the point is. Sometimes you do know, but are not convinced that your point is a very good one. At such times, a little obfuscation may seem a better idea than clarity. It is not. Nothing is more troubling than reading a paper in which the author tried to hedge bets or fudge ideas. The very worst thing you can do is leave it up to your reader to decide what you are trying to say. So no matter how weak your ideas seem to you, set them forth clearly. Something is always better than nothing. Most teachers are interested in helping students. It is much easier to help you if your instructor can figure out what you were trying to say.

And teachers delight in watching students improve. The reason is obvious: They see it as proof that they are doing a good job. They take special pleasure in the progress of students who start off poorly but steadily get better over the course of the semester. You can do a lot worse than be one of those students.

If you have the energy, learn to write gracefully. But in any event, write clearly.

WHEN AND HOW TO USE FOOTNOTES

Many students apparently believe that the only thing worse than having to read footnotes is having to write them. It is easy to understand why they feel that way, but they are making much ado about very little. Footnotes inform the reader where the information in the body of the paper can be found. That is the substance of the matter.

So when should you use a footnote? One occasion is when you are referring to someone's exact words whether by direct quotation or by paraphrase. (If your paper does not require footnotes, you need only mention the author's name at the time you quote.) The other is when you are referring to some bit of information that is not already well known or is someone's interpretation of the facts. How, you might wonder, can you tell whether or not something is already well known? A simple rule is that nothing you can find in a standard textbook needs to be footnoted. Hence, for example, you do not have to footnote that George Washington was the first President of the United States. You may need to footnote an exact quotation from his "Farewell Address." You do not need to footnote that Abraham Lincoln wrote the Gettysburg Address. If you are in doubt about a particular case, you still have two steps open to you. One is to ask your instructor, the reader you are seeking to inform in the first place. The other, if you find it impracticable to reach your teacher, is to use the footnote. Having an unnecessary footnote is a minor flaw. Not having a necessary one is a serious omission. So you can simply err on the safe side.

Now that you know when to use footnotes, you can consider the matter of how to use them. Several formats are in common use. Simply ask your instructor which one is preferred. If your teacher has no preference, invest in the inexpensive Modern Language Association (MLA) style sheet. It is brief, clearly written, reliable, and cheap. It is very unlikely you will encounter a question it will not answer. If you think your writing needs improvement, try Brandywine Press's *Thinking and Writing*. It costs less than ten dollars.

WHAT TO INCLUDE IN YOUR BIBLIOGRAPHY

Early in your research you compiled a list of possible sources. The temptation is to type out a bibliography from those cards. This is fine provided that you actually used all of those sources. Your bibliography should include all the sources you consulted and only those sources. So even though you have all sorts of cards, and even though your bibliography would look far more authoritative if you included sources you looked up but did not use, do not do so. It is most unlikely that padding your bibliography will impress.

A WORD
ABOUT PLAGIARISM AND
ORIGINALITY

Plagiarism is the act of claiming another's work as your own. It is about as serious an academic offense as you can commit. Many colleges require teachers to report all instances of plagiarism, and while the punishment can vary, it is always stiff. And of all the various ways of cheating, teachers find plagiarism the easiest to detect.

Some students plagiarize without realizing that this is what they are doing. They quote from a book or article without so indicating by quotation marks or citing the author and the work, or they paraphrase a passage without proper acknowledgment. They have unintentionally passed off someone else's work as their own. Sometimes this results in nothing worse than a private lecture

from the instructor on the necessity of correctly attributing all information. Even so it is embarrassing, and it creates the impression that you do not know what you are doing. So be sure you indicate the sources not only of your information but also of the interpretations or ideas you include in your papers.

Teachers will often tell their students that their papers should be original. Scholars use this word in a somewhat different sense from what you might expect. In ordinary speech something is original if it is the first of its kind or the only one of its kind. Scholars mean something less dramatic. We refer to research as "original" if the researcher did the work. We do not mean that the conclusions have never been reached before or that no one else has ever used the same source materials. The way you put together familiar information and ideas may be original.

Do not hesitate to make use of ideas from other scholars. No one with any sense expects beginning students to make startling discoveries or to develop radically new perspectives. It is, accordingly, perfectly legitimate for you to use other people's insights. The only hitch is that you must always acknowledge where they came from.

Index

A

Abolitionism, 364–366, 389–395;
  Free Soil Party, 332, 404; Liberty
  Party, 392–393, 404; *also see*
  Antislavery
Abraham and Straus, 523
Abraham Lincoln Brigade, 845
Acadians, 112
Acheson, Dean, 895, 898, 919
Acquired Immune Deficiency
  Syndrome (AIDS), 983, 1004, 1005
Adams, Abigail, 141
Adams, Brooks, 661
Adams, Charles Francis, 446, 457
Adams, Henry, 446
Adams, John, 126, 132, 137, 140,
  141, 190, 267, 287; defends
  British soldiers in court, 128,
  165; title of President, 192;
  elected to presidency, 204–205;
  compromises with France, 209;
  defeated in 1800, 210–211;
  appoints midnight judges, 211
Adams, John Quincy, early career,
  287; Treaty of Ghent, 244;
  Monroe's secretary of state,
  287–292; Monroe Doctrine,
  290–292; in election of 1824,
  292–294; policies, 294–296;
  defends Creek Indians, 296;
  Panama conference, 296–297;

in election of 1828, 299–301;
  antislavery congressman, 297;
  cooperates in lowering tariffs, 317;
  defends *Amistad* slave mutineers,
  332; defeats gag rule, 389–390
Adams, Samuel, 124, 126, 128, 132,
  138, 184
Adams, Samuel Hopkins, 707
Adams, Sherman, 917
Adams-Onis Treaty, 290
Adamson Act, 749
Addams, Jane, 646, 647, 650, 712;
  opposition to war, 755, 764; *also
  see* Hull House; Settlement
  houses
Adet, Citizen, 205
Administration of Justice Act, 131
Affirmative action, 1017
Afghanistan, 995, 996, 998, 1009
Africa, history of, 15–20; Tuskegee
  graduates teach in, 581; British
  clash with Boers in South Africa,
  669; Marcus Garvey and Pan-
  Africanism, 785–786; Italian
  fascist invasion of Ethiopia, 844;
  North African campaigns in
  World War II, 855, 857, 862; civil
  war in Rwanda, 1021; *also see*
  Egypt
African Americans, *see* Blacks;
  Slavery
Agnew, Spiro, 973, 974

Agrarians, southern (school of social
  criticism), 517
Agricultural Adjustment Acts and
  Agricultural Adjustment
  Administrations (AAA), 816, 818,
  819, 825, 828
Agricultural Marketing Act, 791, 798
Agriculture, tobacco in colonial
  South, 58–60, 83, 88–89; rice in
  colonial South, 83–85; farming in
  the republic's first days, 174,
  227–228; mid-nineteenth-century,
  379–380; farming in the
  antebellum West, 380; antebellum
  urban exchange with western
  agriculture, 381; southern plain
  folk, 382–383; South, mid-
  nineteenth-century, 382–386;
  growth in the late nineteenth
  century, 501; mechanization and
  industrialization, 550–551, 576,
  611–612; cattle industry, 571–576;
  farming in the farther West,
  576; farming in the Cherokee
  Strip, 576–577; education and
  research in agriculture, 452;
  George Washington Carver's
  experimentation in agricultural
  products, 581; colleges provided
  for under Morrill Land Grant
  College Act offer agricultural
  and other technical schooling,

Agriculture—(continued)
610–611; Hatch Act establishes agricultural experimental stations, 611; agrarian discontent in the later nineteenth century, the Grange and Granger laws, 613–615; the Alliances, 614–615; Populism, 615–617; President Wilson's farm policy, 748; Smith-Lever Act establishes cooperation between land-grant colleges and state extension stations teaching methods to farmers, 748; farm troubles and politics during the 1920s, 790–791; McNary-Haugen proposal for agricultural surplus, 791; President Hoover's support of agricultural cooperatives, 791; New Deal programs, 816, 828; during 1960s and afterwards, United Farm Workers organize migrants, 987; *also see* Cotton; Cooperatives; Currency

Aguinaldo, Emilio, 678, 679
Air pollution, 971
Airline Deregulation Act, 994
Aix-la-Chapelle, Treaty of, 112
Alabama, 457
Alamo, battle of, 371–374
Albany Plan of Union, 113
Albany Regency, 312
Aldrich-Vreeland Act, 694
Aldrin, Edwin, 970
Alexander I, Czar, 291
Algeciras Conference, 683, 684
Alger, Horatio, 526, 810
Alianza, 986
Alien and Sedition Acts, 207–208
Allen, Charles B., 429
Allen, Ethan, 138, 363
Allende, Salvador, 964, 966
Alliance for Progress, 931
Alliances (farmers' organizations), 614–615
Altgeld, John Peter, 533, 642, 647
Alvarez de Piñeda, Alonso, 25
Amalgamated Association of Iron and Steel Workers, 533
Amalgamated Clothing Workers Union, 708
American Anti-Boycott Association, 710
American Antislavery Society, 390
American Asylum, 350
American Colonization Society, 364

American Equal Rights Association, 497–498
American Federation of Labor (AFL), formed and organizes skilled labor, 530; shifting positions on black workers, 583–584; Gompers does not support free silver, 644; early policy, 708–709; in World War I, 710; bad fortunes in 1920s, 790; clash within, over industrial unionism, 817–818
American Indian Movement (AIM), 989
American Indians, *see* Indians; North American Indians
American League, 626
American Legion, 778, 838
American Magazine, 707
American Party, *see* Know-Nothings
American Protective Association, 601, 638
American Republican Party, 360
American Revolution, 149–158; social classes, 133–138; Declaration of Independence, 140–143; armies, 149–150; rebel methods of fighting, 150–151; British methods of fighting, 152
American Slavery as It Is, 366
American Social Science Association, 538
American Sugar Refining Company, 544, 750
American System, 293
American Tobacco Company, 580
American Tract Society, 349–350
American Woman Suffrage Association, 498
Americanization, 624, 715, 716
Americans for Democratic Action, 891
Ames, Adelbert, 499
Ames, Fisher, 183, 200
Amherst, Sir Jeffrey, 114
Amistad, 331–332
Amsterdam News, 784
Anarchism, 634
Anderson, Marian, 814
Anderson, Major Robert, 449–450
Anderson, Sherwood, 786
Andros, Edmund, 63
Anglicans, during Revolution, 135; *also see* Church of England
Annapolis meeting, 178

Anthony, Susan B., 357, 497–498
Anthracite, 524, 531, 698, 733–735
Anthracite coal strike, 524, 733–735
Antietam, battle of, 457, effect, 459, 460
Anti-Federalists, 189, 190
Anti-imperialism, 676, 679, 681
Anti-Imperialist League, 676
Anti-Masons, 327
Antinomianism, 46
Anti-Semitism, 602, 712, 823, 898
Antislavery, Quaker opposition to slavery, 89; Federalist and Whig opposition to slavery, 225, 266, 285, 328; World Anti-Slavery Convention, 337, 392; abolitionism, 364–366; antislavery movement connects to economic nationalism, 432–433; *also see* Liberty Party; Free Soil Party; Republican Party; *individual activists*
Antiwar movement during conflict in Vietnam, 956–959, 960–962
Anzio, 865
Apache, 561
Apollo space program and the moon landing, 970–971
Appeal of the Independent Democrats, 428
Appeal to Reason, The, 725
Appleton, Frank, 323
Appomattox Court House, 477, 483, 486
Arapaho, 563
Architecture, 608–610, 719–720
Arena, 707
Argonne Forest, battle of, 760
Aristide, Jean-Bertrand, 1020
Arizona, 852
Arkwright, Richard, 284
Armenians as American ethnicity, 603
Armory show, 719
Armour Company, 725
Armstrong, Neil, 970
Arnold, Benedict, 138, 152, 157
Aroostook War, 396
Artemus Ward (character by Charles F. Browne), 363
Arthur, Chester A., 609, 635
Arthur, Timothy Shay, 351
Articles of Confederation, 166–168; economic troubles in period of

Confederation, 168–169; daily life, 174–177

Arts, Monticello, 218–219; literary and other artistic expression at mid-nineteenth century, 252–253, 361–363; architecture in the late nineteenth and the early twentieth centuries, 608–610, 719–720; photography, 718–719, 832–833; Ashcan and abstract schools of painting, 718–719; literature at turn of twentieth century, 720; Greenwich Village, 720–721; literature in recoil from First World War, 765; Harlem Renaissance, 769–771, 783; silent movies and first talkies, 630–631, 787–788; literature in nineteen twenties, 783, 786; during Great Depression, 832–833; rhythm and blues, rock and roll, 923; beats, 923, 924, 981; folk revival and hard rock, 923–924; *also see individual artists*

Asbury, Francis, 347

Asch, Joseph, 689

Ashcan School, 718, 719

Ashley, Lord, 54

Assembly line, 696

Astor, John Jacob, 288

Asylums, reform of, 354

Atahualpa, 27

Atchison, Topeka and Santa Fe railroad, 552, 554

Atlantic and Pacific Tea Company (A&P), 523, 697

Atlantic Charter, 851, 854

Atom bomb, *see* Nuclear power

Attica prison, 969, 970

Attlee, Clement, 880

Attucks, Crispus, 128

Auburn prison, 354

Auld, Sophia, 366

Auschwitz, 839

Austin, Stephen F., independence of Texas, 372

Austria, in World War I, 753; Nazis absorb, 845–846; Nazi rule collapses, 871–872; enters North Atlantic Treaty Organization, 887

Austrian Succession, War of, 112

Automobiles, early, 696 (assembly line), 699–700

Ayatollah Khomeini, 996, 1008

Aztecs, 3, 5, 26–28, 670

B

Baby boom, 909, 921

Bacon, Nathaniel, 62

Bacon's Rebellion, 61–62, 85–86

Bad Axe Massacre, 310

Baez, Joan, 981

Bagot, Charles, 288

Baker, James, 1013, 1016

Baker, Newton D., 647

Baker, Ray Stannard, 706

Baker v. Carr, 940

Balboa, Vasco Núñez de, 25

Ballinger, Richard A., 742, 743

Ballinger-Pinchot controversy, 742, 743

Baltimore, 227, 242

Baltimore, Lord, *see* Calvert, Cecil; Calvert, George

Baltimore and Ohio Railroad (B and O), 530–531, 631, 805

Bank holiday, 815

Bank of Augusta v. United States, 326

Bank of the United States, 193–194, 195–196; state banknotes after expiration, 269; *also see* Second Bank of the United States

Banking Act of 1933, *see* Glass-Steagall Act

Bankruptcy Act of 1841, 324

Banks, Dennis, 989

Baptists, 198; Second Great Awakening, 343

Barb (Berkeley), 981

Barbary Pirates, 171, 229

Barbour, Edmund, 511

Barnett, Ida Wells, 704

Barré, Major Isaac, 118

Barrow, Clyde, 832

Barton, Bruce, 789

Baruch, Bernard, plan for international control of nuclear power, 884

Baseball, 626, 628, 639, 779, 830, 831, 841, 909, 924

Bataan, battle of, 855; death march, 855, 878

Batista, Fulgencio, 912, 930

Battle of, Alamo, 371–374; Antietam, 457, effect, 458, 459, 460; Argonne Forest, 760; Bataan, 855, death march, 855, 878; Belleau Wood, 760; Brandywine Creek, 154; Breed's Hill, 136; Brooklyn Heights, 154; Buena Vista, 399; the Bulge, 866; Bull Run, 454, second, 458; Cerra Gordo, 399; Chancellorsville, 453, 458; Chattanooga, 475; Chickamanga, 475; Concord, 133–135; Coral Sea, 861; Corregidor, 855; Fallen Timbers, 162; Fort Sumter, 447; Fredricksburg, 458; Germantown, 155; Gettysburg, 468–469; Guadalcanal, 861–862, 867; Guam, 867; Horseshoe Bend, 245; Iwo Jima, 869; Lake Champlain, 237; Lake Erie, 236–237, 240; Lexington, 133–135; Leyte, 869; Little Big Horn River, 564; Lundy's Lane, 241; Marne River, 760; Midway, 861; Monterrey, 399; New Orleans, 245–246; Okinawa, 872; Saratoga, 155; Savo Island, 861; Shiloh, 456–457; Stalingrad, 862; Thames, 235; Tippecanoe Creek, 234, 237; Trenton, 154; Vicksburg, 457, 460, 462, 475

Bay of Pigs, 932

Beard, Charles A., 650, 843

Beats, 923, 924, 981

Beauregard, General P.G.T., 454

Beauvoir, Simone de, 984

Becknell, William, 398

Bedford, Duke of, 114

Beecher, Catharine, 353

Beecher, Harriet, *see* Stowe, Harriet Beecher

Beecher, Henry Ward, 423

Beecher, Lyman, 353, 360, 409

Beecher's Bibles, 423

Belgium, German invasion in World War I, 753, 762; Herbert Hoover supplies relief, 796; after *Kristallnacht*, admits refugees, 838; Nazis invade, 847; Allies enter, 866

Bell, Alexander Graham, 509, 511, 698

Bell, John, 437–438

Bellamy, Edward, 634

Belleau Wood, battle of, 760

Bellecourt, Clyde, 989

Belmont, August, 641

Bentley, Arthur F., 649

Benton, Thomas Hart, 314, 404

Berbers, 18

Berger, Victor, 709

Bergman, Ingrid, 860

Berkeley, William, 53, 62, 86

Berle, Adolf A., 814

Berlin Decree, 230

Berlin, Allied occupation after World War II, Berlin airlift, 886, 887; Berlin wall, 931; the Berlin wall torn down, 1011

Bermuda, 849

Bernard, Francis, 124, 126

Bessemer steel process, 512, 514, 609, 696

Beveridge, Albert, 662, 677

Bible Society, 349–350

Bicycling, 626

Biddle, Nicholas, 272–273, 319–320, 322

Big Three, 863, 869, 880

Bill of Rights (U.S.), 191

Bingham, George Caleb, 361

Birmingham, Alabama, demonstrations, 927; also see New South

Birney, James G., 392–393

Black Codes, 488

Black Hawk, 310

Black Panthers, 970

Black power, 938, 939

Blackmun, Harry, 969

Blacks, in colonies, 87–89, 100; in American Revolution, 139; at turn of nineteenth century, 226; in War of 1812, 240, 245; free northern blacks on colonization, 364; antislavery activity, 390; in South during Civil War, 460, 471; in military during Civil War, 459, 474, 486; and Ku Klux Klan after Civil War, 481–482; postbellum blacks and the land, 483, 499–501; labor contracts for freed slaves, 489, 495, 497, 499–500; quest for education, during Reconstruction, 489, 495–496, 497; family before and after Civil War, 494–495; evangelical religion among slave and freed blacks, 495–496; political leadership during Reconstruction, 496, 498; black labor, southern and northern, in the late nineteenth century, 551, 582–584; George Washington Carver experiments with agricultural products, 581; Booker T. Washington, Tuskegee, 581; Atlanta Compromise, 581,

585–587; *Plessy v. Ferguson* allows states to segregate, 584, 913; Jim Crow, 584–585; W. E. B. Du Bois, 585, 710–711, opposes Atlanta Compromise, 586, part in the Niagara Movement and the formation of the National Association for the Advancement of Colored People, 711–712; Brownsville, and Theodore Roosevelt's attitudes towards race, 737; Chicago race riot of 1919, 776; Harlem Renaissance, 769–771, 783; the great migration, 783–785; Marcus Garvey and pan-Africanism, 785–786; discrimination against blacks in New Deal projects, 829; discrimination in the military during World War II, 858; NAACP wins *Brown v. Board of Education of Topeka*, 913; Montgomery bus boycott, 914–915; Little Rock, 913–914; Greensboro sit-ins, 907–908; freedom riders, 926; Albany, Georgia, 926–927; James Meredith integrates University of Mississippi, 927; struggle in Birmingham moves President Kennedy to action, 927; March on Washington, 928; civil rights acts of 1964 and 1965, 937–938; efforts to desegregate housing, 938; racism confronts Martin Luther King, Jr. in Chicago, 938; Malcolm X, 938; black power, 938, 939; killings at Jackson State University, 966; Black Panthers, 969–970; Attica, 970; affirmative action, 1017; also see Black Panthers; King, Martin Luther; Malcolm X; Reconstruction; Slavery

Blackwell, Elizabeth, 356–357

Blackwell, Henry, 498

Blaine, James G., 635, 636, 664–667

Blair, Ezell, 907

Bland-Allison Silver Purchase Act, 519

Bleeding Kansas, 423–425

Blitzkrieg, 847, 849, 866

Bloomer costume, 336, 357

Blough, Roger, 929

Blue laws, 638

Blum, Léon, 845

Board of Trade (English), 101–102

Bogart, Humphrey, 860

Boleyn, Anne, 29, 30

Bolívar, Simón, 291, 296, 297

Bolshevism, 753, 759, 763, 771, 772, 775, 778, 792–793, 844, 918; *also see* Communism; Soviet Union

Bond, James, 930

Bonhomme Richard, 149, 157

Bonus Army, 805

Booth, John Wilkes, 487

Boquet, Colonel Henry, 115

Borden, Gail, 262

Boston, early prerevolutionary resistance to Britain, 119, 123, 125–126; Boston Massacre, 127–128; Boston Tea Party, 129–131; closing of port, 131; rebels besiege British troops, 133–138; at turn of nineteenth century, 226

Bourne, Randolph, 715, 764

Bowdoin, Governor James, 184–185

Bowie, Jim, 372

Boxer Rebellion, 681

Boxing, 606, 627, 730, 779

Braddock, General Edward, 113–114

Braddock, James, 831

Bradford, William, 41, 46

Bradley, Justice Joseph P., 503

Bradstreet, Anne, 75

Bradwell, Myra Colby, 536

Brains Trust, 814

Brandeis, Louis D., 649, 705, 745

Brandt, Willy, 964

Brandywine Creek, battle of, 154

Brattle, Thomas, 92

Brazil, 508

Breckinridge, John, 436–438

Breed's Hill, battle of, 136–137

Brewster, William, 41

Breyer, Steven G., 1020

Brezhnev, Leonid, 966, 995, 996, 1009

Briand, Aristide, 793

Bridgman, Laura, 350

Britain, early English explorations, 29–31; colonization, 31, 37–56 *passim*; imperialism, 57–60; imperial system preceding American Revolution, 115–133; restricts entrance of the U.S. to the British West Indies, 170; military posts in the Northwest, 170–171; war with revolutionary France, 200; Jay Treaty, 201–202;

impressment, 205–206; interference with American commerce, 229–234 *passim*; War of 1812, 236–246; Treaty of 1818, 288; and Monroe Doctrine, 292; during U.S. Civil War, 457; Clayton-Bulwer Treaty of 1850 and Hay-Pauncefote Treaty of 1901, 655–656; Venezuelan crisis, 668–669; Algeciras Conference, 683–684; in World War I, 753–755, 760; intervenes in Russia against Bolsheviks, 771, 772; at Washington Naval Conference, 791; abandons gold standard, 799; after *Kristallnacht*, accepts refugees, 838; in World War II, 846–848, 853–854, 855, 862–872; enters North Atlantic Treaty Organization, 887; joins France and Israel in attack on Egypt, 920; enters Southeast Asia Treaty Organization, 950; in Gulf War, 1015

British East India Company, 129–130

British Protestants as American ethnicity, 375–376

British West Indies, 170

Brook Farm, 348

Brooklyn Bridge, 609, 713, 718

Brooklyn Heights, battle of, 154

Brooks, Preston S., 425

Brown, John, 424, 436, 438–439

Brown, Joseph E., 470

Brown Berets, 986

Brown v. Board of Education of Topeka, 913

Browne, Charles F., 363

Bruce, Louis, 989

Bryan, William Jennings, in campaign of 1896, 642–644 (Cross of Gold, 643); volunteer in war with Spain, 674; supports annexationist treaty with Spain, 677; resigns as secretary of state, 754; at Scopes trial, 780

Brzezinski, Zbigniew, 995

Buchanan, James (inventor of threshing machine), 611

Buchanan, James, proposes extending Missouri Compromise line to Pacific, 404; victorious Democratic presidential candidate in 1856, 429–430; supports Lecompton Constitution, 432; succession, 448, 449

Buchanan, Patrick, 1018, 1022

Buddhists in Vietnam, 951, 955

Buena Vista, battle of, 399

Bulganin, Nikolai A., 918

Bulgaria, 753, 867, 881

Bulge, the, battle of, 866

Bull Run, battle of, 454, second, 458

Bullitt, William, 841

Bunau-Varilla, Philippe, 656, 657

Bunker Hill, *see* Breed's Hill

Bureau of Agriculture, 610

Bureau of Corporations, 740, 748

Bureau of Indian Affairs, 567

Burford, Ann Gorsuch, 1005

Burger, Warren E., 969

Burgoyne, John, 136, 155

Burke, Edmund, argues for leniency toward colonies, 130

Burns, Lucy, 705

Burnside, General Ambrose, 458

Burr, Aaron, 210–211, 225–226

Bush, George, rival to Ronald Reagan in presidential primaries in 1980, 998; campaign of 1988, 1010; presidency, 1010–1018; Gulf crisis and war, 1012–1015

Bush, George W., 1024–1025

Business, *see* Commerce

Butler, Andrew P., 425

Byrd, William, 85

Byrnes, James, 884

C

C. Turner Joy, 952

Cabot, John, 23, 29

Cabot, Sebastian, 23

Cabrillo, Juan Rodriguez, 28

Cadore, Duc de, 233

Cahan, Abraham, 715

Calhoun, John C., War Hawk, 234; nationalist, 234, 247, 268; Monroe's secretary of war, 266–267; advocate of slavery, 287; and John Quincy Adams, 292–293, 299; opposes Panama conference, 296; and Van Buren, 312–314; and states' rights, 314–319; cooperates against Jacksonians, 327; and Texas treaty, 397; and slavery in territories, 404; and Compromise of 1850, 411–414

Californios, 403

Calley, Lieutenant William, 959, 960

Calvert, Cecil (second Lord Baltimore), 49, 65

Calvert, George (Lord Baltimore), 49

Calvin, John, 15, 43

Calvinists, 44; *also see* Calvin, John

Cambodia, once part of French empire, 947; Geneva accords acknowledge independence, 949; Southeast Asia Treaty Organization extends shield to Cambodia, 950; campus reaction to South Vietnamese and American invasion, 956–958, 966; Communists victorious, 968, 991

Cambridge Agreement, 41

Camp David, 921, 995

Canada, taken by British, 109–111, 114; designs of War Hawks, 235; in War of 1812, 236–238, 239–242; in 1817 and 1818, Britain and U.S. resolve claims, 288; in World War II, 866; enters North Atlantic Treaty Organization, 887; *also see* Webster-Ashburton Treaty

Canals, 251–254, 257

Canning, George, 291

Cannon, Joseph G., 735, 736

Cantor, Eddie, 630

Cape of Good Hope, 22

Capehart, Homer, 897

Capone, Al, 779

Capra, Frank, 811

Carey Act, 559

Carmichael, Stokeley, 939

Carnegie, Andrew, 513–516, 533–535, 586, 679, 710, 897

Caroline affair, 396

Carpetbaggers, 492, 498

Carranza, Venustiano, 752

Carson, Rachel, 916

Carswell, Harrold G., 969

Carter, James, campaign of 1976, 992; presidency, 992–996; policy on human rights, 993–994, 1001–1002; Iran and hostage crisis, 996; campaign of 1980, 995

Carteret, George, 53, 54

Cartier, Jacques, 29

Cartwright, Peter, 347

Carver, George Washington, 581

Casals, Pablo, 732

Casey, William, 1008

Cass, Lewis, 404

Castlereagh, Robert Stewart, Viscount, 288

Castro, Fidel, 912, 930, 931, 972, 1001

Catherine of Aragon, 29

Catholicism, *see* Roman Catholicism

Catlin, George, 738

Catt, Carrie Chapman, 706, 764

Cavelier, Robert (Sieur de La Salle), 57

Cellini, Benvenuto, 14

Central Intelligence Agency (CIA), formed, 888; switches from its early policy of seeking to strengthen non-Communist left, 896; orchestrates Bay of Pigs, 930–931; engineers military coup in Chile, 966; involvement in Iran-Contra, 1008

Central Pacific railroad, 551–552, 554, 861, 867

Central Powers, 753, 755, 759

Cerra Gordo, battle of, 399

Cervera, Admiral Pascual y Topete, 676

Chain stores, 522–524

Chamberlain, Daniel, 499

Chambers, Whittaker, 897

Chancellorsville, battle of, 453, 458

Chaney, James, 939

Chaplin, Charlie, 787

Charles I of England, 41, 50

Charles I of Spain (Charles V of the Holy Roman Empire), 29

Charles II of England, 50, 51, 53, 54–55, 57, 59, 61, 62

Charles River Bridge, 326

Charleston, in 1800, 227

Chase, Salmon P., "Appeal of the Independent Democrats," 428

Chattanooga, battle of, 475

Chautauqua, 631–632

Chavez, Cesar, 986, 987

Chemistry, in late nineteenth and early twentieth centuries, 696–697

Cherokee, 86, 172, 307–310, 562, 576, 577

Chesapeake, colonies, 58

Chesapeake, 230–231, 235

Chesnut, Mary, 355

Cheyenne, 561, 563

Chiang Kai-shek, as Nationalist leader of China, 800; joins with Communists in resistance to Japan, 848; war against Japan,

869; China in UN, 880; Communist defeat, 893, 894, 896, 948

Chicago, site of Republican convention of 1860, 437; Haymarket Square bombing, 532–533, 633; Slavic immigration to, 600; site of Democratic convention of 1896 that nominates William Jennings Bryan, 642–643; race riot of 1919, 776; disturbances at Chicago convention of 1968, 961–962

Chicano movement, 986

Chickamauga, battle of, 475

Chickasaw, 172, 516

Chief Joseph, 565

Child labor, 540–542, 639, 704, 735, 749, 819, 828

Children, in colonial times, 99

China, trade with U.S., 171–172; Boxer Rebellion, 680–681; Japan attacks, 800; becomes Communist, 893–895; enters Korean War, 900; rupture with Soviet Union, 932–933; President Nixon begins détente, 965–966; Tiananmen Square, 1020–1021

Chinese as American ethnicity, temporary workers before the Civil War, 377–378; workers on the construction of the Central Pacific, 551; subject to prejudice in California, 602

Chinese Exclusion Act, 602

Chivington, Colonel John, 563

Choctaw, 172, 310

Chou En-lai, 900, 965, 966

Church of England, 30, 50; colonial Anglican ministers and laity as Tories during American Revolution, 135; southern Anglican patricians support Revolution, 135

Church of Jesus Christ of Latter-Day Saints, *see* Mormons

Churchill, Winston, 847, 849, 851, 862, 863, 870, 871, 880, 884

Cíbola, 28

Cinqué, leader of rebel slaves on *Amistad*, 331–332

Cities, eastern, in mid-nineteenth century, 379; midwestern, in mid-nineteenth century, 381; growth of cities in the late nineteenth century, 592–594; squalor and

filth in late nineteenth century cities, 595; poor in the late nineteenth century, 595–596, 605; electrical transportation changes composition of, 596–597, 599; life among new-immigrant ethnicities, 599–601, 603–605, 712–714; prostitution, 605–606; political machines, 606–608; architecture in late nineteenth and early twentieth centuries as expression of new technology, 608–610, 719–720; urban public schools in the nineteenth century, 623–624; emergence of participatory and spectator sports, 625–628; Triangle Shirtwaist fire and its reformist outcome, 689–692; political reform before and during the progressive era, 702–703; prohibitionist and nativist suspicion of, 779

Civil Aeronautics Board (CAB), 994

Civil liberties, 453, 762, 764, 841, 937

Civil rights legislation in the nineteenth century, 489–490

Civil rights movement, *Brown v. Board of Education of Topeka*, 913; Montgomery bus boycott, 914–915; Little Rock, 913–914; Greensboro sit-ins, 907–908; freedom riders, 926; Albany, Georgia, 926–927; James Meredith integrates University of Mississippi, 927; struggle in Birmingham moves President Kennedy to action, 927; March on Washington, 928; civil rights acts of 1964 and 1965, 937–938; efforts to desegregate housing, 938; racism in Chicago, 938; Student Nonviolent Coordinating Committee works for black voter registration in Mississippi, 938–939; Freedom Summer and Mississippi Freedom Democratic Party, 938–939; *also see* King, Martin Luther

Civil War, impending crisis of the South, 430–432; secession, 444–446, 450; Fort Sumter, 448–450; northern strategy, 450–451; southern strategy, 451–452; Union blockade, 451, 457–458, 473; campaigns and battles, 454, 456–457, 458, 460, 468–469, 475–477; fate of civil liberties, 453; diplomacy and the war, 451, 459–460; Unionist sentiment in South, 469, 487; economic problems in South, 469–470; northern economy, 471–472; conscription, 470–471, 474; Confederate Congress authorizes enlistment of blacks, 471; immigrants in both militaries, 473; army life, 472–474; war mobilization, 474; blacks in the Union military, 459, 474; election of 1864, 476; surrender of Lee and Johnston, 477; *also see entries for specific battles and leaders*

Civil wars, in England, 50–51

Clark, J. Reuben, 793

Clark, William, 222–223

Clark Memorandum, 793

Clay, Henry, War Hawk, 233–234; Treaty of Ghent, 244; and Madison, 247; American System, 293; in election of 1824, 293–294; becomes secretary of state, 294; Panama conference, 296–297; bank troubles, 320; loses to Jackson in 1832, 321, 327; American Colonization Society, 364; and Tyler, 396; Compromise of 1850, 412, 414

Clay, General Lucius D., 887

Clayton Antitrust Act, 748

Clayton-Bulwer Treaty, 421, 655

Clean Air Act, 1010

Clemens, Samuel L., 421, 520

Cleveland, Grover, Pullman strike, 533; preserves watershed land, 559; meets with Frederick Douglass, 586; campaign of 1884, 635–636; campaign of 1888, 636; second term, 640–642; foreign policy, 667–669; prepared to resist war with Spain, 671

Clifford, Clark, 959, 960

Clinton, De Witt, 251, 285, Erie Canal, 252–253

Clinton, George, 190

Clinton, Henry, 136, 157

Clinton, Hillary Rodham, 1021

Clinton, William, campaign of 1992, 1019; troubles in early administration, 1019–1020; pushes through an energy tax, 1020; wins approval for North American Free

Trade Agreement, 1020; policy toward Haiti, China, and Bosnia, 1021; failure of health care plan, 1021, 1022; election of 1996, 1021–1022; second term, 1022–1024;

Cobb, Howell, 448

Cockburn, Sir George, 242

Coercive or Intolerable Acts, 131, 132, 133

Cohan, George M., 760

Cohens v. Virginia, 274

Cold War, Moscow's wish for hegemony in East Europe, 884–885, 886–887; containment policy, 884–885; Marshall Plan, 885–886; Berlin airlift, 886–887; North American Treaty Organization formed, 887–888; Republican platform of 1948 in effect endorses, 890; National Security Council Paper No. 68 further defines containment policy, 895; conservatives attack containment, 895–896; in administration of President Eisenhower, West Germany joins NATO, 918; Moscow forms Warsaw Pact, 918–919; Eisenhower relies on massive nuclear retaliation, 919; first summit meeting, 919; Eisenhower Doctrine for Middle East, 920–921; Southeast Asia Treaty Organization formed, 949–950; President Kennedy and, 930; Peace Corps, 930; Bay of Pigs, 930–931; Alliance for Progress, 931; Berlin Crisis of 1961, and Berlin Wall, 931; Cuban missile crisis, 932; peaceful coexistence and Test Ban Treaty, 932–933; under President Nixon, SALT I, 963–964; détente with Communist China, 965–966; détente with Moscow, 966; Soviet Union invades Afghanistan, 995; President Reagan's policy for Central America, 1002; Grenada, 1002; Reagan's plan for Strategic Defense Initiative, 1002–1003; Reagan supports Contras in Nicaragua, 1007–1008; Gorbachev, Reagan, and full détente, 1009–1010; East European Communist regimes

collapse and Berlin Wall torn down, 1011; *also see* Communism; Korean War; Vietnam

Cole, Thomas, 361

Collier, John, 988

Collier's, 707

Collins, Mike, 970

Colombia, and 1846 treaty, 421; Panamanian revolution sponsored by U.S., 656–658; indemnity to Colombia, 793

Columbian Exchange, 3–4, 32–33

Columbus, Christopher, 1–4, 22–23, 215

Comanche, 381, 561

Commerce, Europe–Asia trade routes, precolonial, 11–12; tobacco, colonial, 58–60; colonial and transatlantic, 75–77; rum manufacture in eighteenth-century New England, 116; Spain closes New Orleans port, 169–170; trade with China, 171–172; urban crafts in early republic, 175; Hamilton's Reports, 192–194; during war between Britain and France, 205; industry in Pittsburgh in 1899, 227; panic of 1819, 270–271; *Dartmouth College v. Woodward* strengthens corporations, 273; boom in 1820s and after, 323; land speculation and panic of 1837, 323–324; depression of 1837–1841, 324; *Charles River Bridge* case weakens corporations, 326; panic of 1857, 430, 433; in South during Civil War, 469–470; in North during Civil War, 471–472; investment bankers in the late nineteenth century, 519–520; mergers, 520–521; retailing in the late nineteenth century, 521–524; Interstate Commerce Commission established, 543; Sherman Antitrust Act, 543–544; railroads and the West in the late nineteenth century, 551–554; depression of the 1890s, 639–641; corporations in the early twentieth century, 694; welfare capitalism, 710, 789; Theodore Roosevelt and the trusts, 732–733, 740, 743; New Nationalism against New Freedom on question of consolidation, 744–745; Federal

Commerce—(continued)
Reserve Board established, 747;
Federal Trade Commission
established, 748–749; Clayton
Antitrust Act, 748–749;
Republican ascendancy during the
1920s, 788–790; Herbert Hoover
as spokesman for enlightened
capitalism and technology, 796;
causes of Great Depression,
796–797; President Hoover's
Reconstruction Finance
Corporation and Federal Home
Loan Banks, 798–799; Hoover's
policy toward war reparations and
international debts, 799–800; the
Depression, the New Deal, and
the economy, Chapter 24 *passim*;
World Economic Conference and
early New Deal positions on
international economics, 839–840;
during World War II, government
organizes the economy for
wartime production, 855–856;
Marshall Plan, 885–886; the
economy during the 1950s, 915;
President Kennedy's economic
policies, and conflict with United
States Steel, 928–929; President
Johnson's Economic Opportunity
Act, 936; inflation during Richard
Nixon's ninety-day freeze on
wages and prices, 971; stagflation
during the 1970s, 991; oil
embargo and prices during the
1970s, 992; energy problems
during presidency of Carter, 993;
also see Agriculture; Bank of the
United States; Currency; Labor
and work; Technology and science
Committee of Secret
Correspondence, 139
Committee on Industrial
Organization, 817–818; *also see*
Congress of Industrial
Organizations
Committee on Public Information,
761
Committee to Re-Elect the President
(CREEP), 972–973
Committees of correspondence, 128,
132
Common Sense, 140, 142
Commons, John R., 649, 715
Commonwealers, 623

Commonwealth v. Hunt, 378
Communism, *see* China; Cold War;
Communist Party (U.S.A.); Cuba;
Korean War; Soviet Union;
Vietnam
Communist Party (U.S.A.), Eugene
Debs at odds with, 775; supports
Moscow's Popular Front, 822;
endorses Henry Wallace, 891;
and second Red Scare, 896–898
Compromise of 1850, 403, 411–416;
ruptures Whig Party, 426,
427–428
Compromise of 1877, 502–503
Concord, battle of, 133–135
Confederate States of America,
formed, 445–446; *also see Chapter
14 passim*
Congregationalists, 199; education of
freed blacks, 497
Congress of Industrial Organizations
(CIO), organizes steel during
Great Depression, 535; Industrial
Workers of the World (IWW)
anticipate industrial unionism,
710; CIO leaves AFL, 818; sit-
down strikes, 827
Conkling, Roscoe, 635
Conquistadores, 25–28
Conscience Whigs, 427
Conscription, 757, 762–764
Conservation, federal government
protects watershed lands in West
and develops policy on water,
558–559; origins of conservation,
movement, 737–738; Theodore
Roosevelt's policy, 738–739;
nature for human use against
nature for its own value, 739–740;
Ballinger-Pinchot controversy,
742–743; Civilian Conservation
Corps, 815; questions of energy
and environment, President Nixon
on clear water and air, 971; Arab
oil boycott, and price of oil in
1970s, 992; Three-Mile Island,
993; conservation of energy in the
late twentieth century, 993, 1005;
President Carter's energy policy,
993; Reagan Administration favors
lessening controls, 1005
Constantinople, 12
Constitution, division of powers and
checks and balances, 187–188;
ratification, 189–190; Bill of

Rights, 191; concept of implied
powers, 196, 274; counterclaims
over nature of ratification,
445–446; text in appendix; *also
see* Supreme Court
Constitution, 238
Constitutional Convention, 185–188
Consumer goods, 521, 638, 697, 757,
796, 797, 829, 856, 909, 921, 992
Consumerism and mass culture,
922–923, 924
Continental Association, 133
Continental Congress, *see* First;
Second
Continentals (currency), 159–160
Contras, *see* Nicaragua
Cooley, Thomas M., 543
Coolidge, Calvin, as governor of
Massachusetts attacks Boston
police strikers, 776; Vice
President under Warren G.
Harding, 774; becomes President
on death of Harding, 788;
character of administration,
788–790; elected to full term, 795;
foreign policy, 792–793; refuses to
run for second term, 795
Cooper, James Fenimore, 361–362
Cooperatives, 529, 530, 613, 615,
790, 791, 822
Copley, John Singleton, 176
Copper ore, 516, 521, 571
Copperheads, *see* Peace Democrats
Coral Sea, battle of, 861
Corliss steam engine, 508
Cornwallis, Charles, 158
Coronado, Francisco Vásquez de, 28
Corporations, as organized bodies,
258–259, 265; as modern form of
business organization, 258–259;
from public interest to self-
interest, 259, 265; *also see*
Commerce
Corregidor, battle of, 855
Cortés, Hernán, 26
Cortina, Juan, 403
Corwin, Thomas, 402
Cosmopolitan, 707
Costello, Frank, 902
Cotton, in 1800, 227; cotton gin and
other inventions, 227, 262, 263,
284; revival of slavery, 284;
cultivation moves westward, 382;
King Cotton, 451; cotton belt, 807
Cotton, John, 43

Cotton gin, 227, 262, 263, 284
Coughlin, Rev. Charles, 823, 824
Country music, 921
Courier (Pittsburgh), 784
Court of the Star Chamber, 29
Cowrie shells (as currency), 20
Cox, Archibald, 973
Cox, James, 773
Coxey, Jacob, and Coxey's Army, 621–623
Craft unionism, 530, 817
Crane, Hart, 783
Crawford, William H., 266, 292–294, 313
Cream tester, 611
Crédit Mobilier, 502
Creek (Indians), 296, 563, 576
Creel, George, 761, 762
Crisis, The, 586
Crittenden, John J., proposes plan for ending secession crisis, 448
Croats, 1021
Crockett, David, 260, 281, 329, 372; at the Alamo, 372
Croly, Herbert, 745
Crompton, Samuel, 284
Cromwell, Oliver, 50
Cromwell, Thomas Nelson, 656, 657
Cronkite, Walter, 946, 959
Crook, George, 563
Crop-lien system, 501
Cross of Gold speech, 643
Crusade for Justice, 986
Crusades, 11
Cuba, proposed annexation of, 419–420; rebellions, 669–671; prelude to war, 671–673; Spanish-American War, 673–676; early U.S. relations with Cuban republic, 679–680, 912; Bay of Pigs, 930–931; missile crisis, 932; President Reagan's view of, 1001
Cullen, Countee, 770, 783
Cult of true womanhood, 356, 358, 578
Cumberland Road, *see* National Road
cummings, e e, 765, 783
Currency, Currency Act of 1764 forbids colonial issue of paper, 117; states issue paper money during Confederation, 168–169; Shays's Rebellion, 184; state banknotes after expiration of first Bank of the United States, 269;

second Bank of the United States, 269–270; Jacksonian opponents of paper, 324; paper flood after decline of second Bank, 322–323; National Banking Acts of 1863 and 1864, 452; greenbacks, in Union during Civil War, 472, and as a political question later, 517–518, urban workers and some varieties of farmers unattracted to silver, 638; meeting of farm Alliance and Knights of Labor supports, 615; Coxey's Army calls for public works financed by greenbacks, 639–640; the question of silver, 518–519, 614; Populists advocate free coinage, 615–616; Grover Cleveland supports gold, 640–641; William Jennings Bryan fights for silver, 642–645; gold Democrats split with Bryan wing of party, 643; New Deal challenges the gold standard and devalues the dollar, 839, 840
Currency Act of 1764, 117
Cushing, Caleb, 420
Custer, George Armstrong, 509, 549–550, 564
Cuzco, 3
Czechoslovakia, Nazis occupy, 845, 846; Communists stage coup d'état, 886; freedom of expression and spring of 1968, 963; Communist power collapses throughout East Europe, 1011
Czechs as American ethnicity, 593, 599, 600, 713, 717
Czolgosz, Leon, 729

D

Dachau, 839
Daley, Richard, 961
Dall, Caroline, 538
Danbury Hatters, 544
Dare, Ananias, 39; Elenora, 39; Virginia, 39
Darrow, Clarence, 780
Dartmouth College v. Woodward, 273
Darwin, Charles, 525
Darwinism, 525, 609, 720; Social Darwinism, 525, 648, 650, 660–661; clash with

fundamentalism in Scopes trial, 780
Daugherty, Harry, 788, 790
Davis, David, 503
Davis, Jeff (governor of Arkansas), 728
Davis, Jefferson, and Mexican War, 402; in 1859 introduces senatorial resolutions supporting extreme southern position, 435–436; becomes President of Confederacy, 445; declares martial law in portions of Confederacy, 470; flees from Richmond, 486
Davis, John, 31
Davis resolutions, 435–436
Dawes, William, 134
Dawes plan, 793
Dawes Severalty Act, 567, 988
Day, Doris, 924
Dayton (Ohio), site of Bosnian peace talks, 1021
Dayton (Tennessee), site of Scopes trial, 780
D-Day, 865
Dean, James, 924
Deane, Silas, 155
Dearborn, Henry, 239
Debs, Eugene, leader of American Railway Union, 633; a founder of Socialist Party, 633; Socialist candidate for President in 1912, 709, 744; during World War I, goes to prison for opposing the draft, 763, 775; opposes Communism, 775; supports Robert La Follette in 1924, 795
Decatur, Stephen, 238
"Declaration of the Causes and Necessities of Taking Up Arms," 139
Declaration of Independence, 140–143; text in appendix
Declaration of Indian Purpose, 989
Declaration of Panama, 848
Declaration of Sentiments (of the Seneca Falls Woman's Rights Convention), 338–339
Declaratory Act, 121
Deere, John, 262, 263
Defender (Chicago), 784
De Gaulle, Charles, 847, 948
Delaware (Indians), 173

Delaware Prophet, 115

De La Warr, Lord Baron, 38

Delcasse, Theophile, 683

De Leon, Alonso, 57

De Leon, Daniel, 633

De Lessups, Ferdinand, 655

Demobilization, after World War I, 774; after World War II, 881–882

Democracy, in New England, 43

Democratic Party, in nineteenth century, 296, 299; acquires coherent ideas, 325, 326–327; in campaign of 1840, 329–331; Kansas-Nebraska Act disrupts, 423, 428; in election of 1856, 429–430; Lecompton Constitution devastates northern branch, 430, 432; in 1860, breaks into two factions, 436; Peace Democrats in Civil War, 453; war Democrats, 476; nineteenth-century party of limited government, 476

Democratic Republicans, 299; *also see* Democratic Party

Denmark, Seward wants to buy Virgin Islands, 659; transfers Virgin Islands to the United States, 681; Nazis invade, 847; Nazi rule collapses, 871–872; enters North Atlantic Treaty Organization, 887

Department stores, 522–524, 697

Depository Institutions Deregulation and Monetary Control Act, 994

Deregulation, 994, 1003

Desert Fox (General Irwin Rommel), 855

Desert Land Act, 558

Desert Shield, 1012

Desert Storm, 1012–1015

Desha, Joseph, 234

De Soto, Hernando, 28

Detroit, Slavic immigration to, 600

Dewey, Alice Chapman, 648

Dewey, Admiral George, 674

Dewey, John, 648, 649, 692, 715

Dewey, Thomas E., 870, 890, 892

Dias, Bartholomeu, 22

Dickens, Charles, on Erie Canal, 253–254

Dickinson, John, 124, 166–167

Dien Bien Phu, 948–949

Digger (Indians), 560

Diggers (San Francisco

communitarian anarchists), 982

Dillinger, John, 832

Dillingham report, 715

Dillon, Douglas, 929

Dinwiddie, Robert, 112

Dirksen, Everett, 933

Disney, Walt, and Disneyland, 924

Dix, Dorothea, 354, 355, 474

Dix, Morgan, 592

Dixiecrats (States' Rights Party), 891, 892

Doenitz, Admiral Karl, 855

Doheny, Edward L., 788

Dole, Robert, 1022

Dollar diplomacy, 666, 750

Dominican Republic, Seward wants naval base in, 659; U.S. occupations, 684–685, 793

Dominion of New England, 63–64

Domino, Fats, 923

Dom Pedro, Emperor of Brazil, at Centennial Exposition, 507–508, 509

Doniphan, A. W., 401

Donnelly, Ignatius, 616

Doolittle, Jimmy, 861

Dorr, Thomas W., and Dorr's Rebellion, 341

Dos Passos, John, 765, 783

Douglas, Helen Gahagan, 898

Douglas, Stephen A., war with Mexico, 402; Compromise of 1850, 414–415; popular sovereignty and Kansas-Nebraska Act, 422–423, 429; and *Dred Scott* decision, 431–432; on Lecompton Constitution, 432; in senatorial contest with Lincoln, 434–435; objects to Jefferson Davis's senatorial resolutions, 436; in 1860, nominee of northern Democrats, 436–438; convinced of slave-power conspiracy, 446, 448

Douglass, Frederick, 350, 366, 390, 409

Dow, Neal, 350, 351

Dow Chemical, 958

Downie, Captain George, 241

Draft riots during Civil War, 474

Drake, Sir Francis, 28, 30–31

Dred Scott v. Sandford, 430, 431–432, 434

Dreiser, Theodore, 783

Drew, Thomas R., 389

Drugs (illegal), among cultural rebels, 981, 982; beliefs among conservatives, 997, 998; social effects of crack, 1004

Duarte, Napoleon, 1002

Dubcek, Alexander, 963

Du Bois, W. E. B., opposed to Booker T. Washington's Atlanta Compromise, 586; convictions and activities, 710–712, 785

Duchamp, Marcel, 719

Dukakis, Michael, 1010

Dulles, John Foster, 918–919, 920, 931, 949

Dumbarton Oaks, 880

Dunmore, Earl of, 138–139

Duryea, Charles E., 699

Dutch Reformed, 101

Dutch West India Company, 53

Dylan, Bob, 958, 981

E

Early, General Jubal, 475

East Berlin, *see* German Democratic Republic

East India Company, 129

Eastman, George, and Kodak camera, 698

Eaton, Peggy, 313–314

Economic nationalism, 267; Hamiltonian, 192–194, 432; Madison adopts, 247; John Marshall facilitates, 273–275; Henry Clay's American System, 293, 432; John Quincy Adams's program, 295, 432; Whig mentality, 328; in Republican Party, finds common ground with antislavery movement, 432–433, 476

Economic Opportunity Act, 936

Economy, the, *see* Commerce

Economy Act, 815

Ecuador, 964

Eddy, Mary Baker, on Monroe Doctrine, 290

Eden, Anthony, 920

Edison, Thomas, 511, 597, 630

Edmonston, Mrs. Catherine, 469

Education, higher, in colonial times, 93–94; industrialism and literacy, 265; public education and middle-class behavior, 352; public schooling, 352–353, 353–354; growth of higher education in nineteenth century, 353; education and research in agriculture, 452; quest among blacks during Reconstruction, 489, 495–496, 497; women's colleges, 537, 625; time for schooling as reason for abolishing child labor, 541; George Washington Carver's experimentation in agricultural products, 581; colleges provided for under Morrill Land Grant College Act offer agricultural and other technical schooling, 610–611; Hatch Act establishes agricultural experimental stations, 611; agrarian discontent in the late nineteenth century, 613–617; the Grange and Granger laws, 613–615; the Alliances, 614–615; public schools as agents of assimilation among new ethnicities, 623–624; development of research institutions, 624–625; Chautauqua, 631–632; Sputnik awakens concern over American schooling, 916; remedial and vocational schooling in Job Corps, 936; aid to elementary and secondary education in Johnson Administration, 936–937; Students for a Democratic Society and Berkeley's Free Speech movement, 956–957; campus radicalism, 956–958

Edwards, Jonathan, 90, 92

Egypt, ancient, 17–18; Six-Day War with Israel, 964–965, 991; war of 1973 with Israel, 991; Anwar Sadat rejects demands of militants for destruction of Israel, and Israel cedes part of occupied territory, 992; in 1978, President Carter arranges peace treaty between Sadat and Israel's Menachem Begin, 995–996; President Carter helps arrange a peace treaty with Israel, 995; invasion of Lebanon, 1002

Eighteenth Amendment, 757, 779–780, 810, 818

Eisenhower, Dwight D., oversees European theater of World War II, 865–866, 871; in election of 1952, 901–903; domestic policy, 916–917; employs federal troops to integrate Little Rock high school, 914; foreign policy, 918–921

Eisenhower Doctrine, 920

El Salvador, 1001, 1002

Elections, presidential, 1789, 190; 1796, 204–205; 1800, 209–211; 1808, 232; 1816, 246–247, 266; 1820, 267; 1824, 292–294; 1828, 299–301; 1832, 321, 327; 1836, 323; 1840, 328–331; 1844, 397; 1848, 404–405; 1852, 427–428; 1856, 429–430, 437; 1860, 436–438; 1864, 476; 1868, 502; 1872, 502; 1876, 502–503, 635; 1880, 635; 1884, 636; 1888, 636; 1892, 636, 639; 1896, 642–644; 1900, 729; 1904, 735; 1908, 741; 1912, 744–745; 1916, 756; 1920, 773–774; 1924, 795; 1928, 795–796; 1932, 807, 811–812; 1936, 824–825; 1940, 849–850; 1944, 870; 1948, 890–892; 1952, 902–903; 1956, 917; 1960, 925–926; 1964, 935; 1968, 960–963; 1972, 971–972; 1976, 992; 1980, 998; 1984, 1006–1007; 1988, 1010; 1992, 1018–1020; 1996, 1021–1022; 2000, 1024–1025

Electric motors, 696

Electric streetcar, 597

Electricity, 511, 695, 703, 789, 981

Elevated railway, 597

Elizabeth I of England, 30–31, 39

Elk Hills, 788

Elkins Act, 733, 735, 741

Ellington, Duke, 770

Ellis Island, 715

Ellsberg, Daniel, 973

Ely, Richard T., 649

Emancipation Proclamation, 460, 483

Embargo Act of 1807, 231–232

Emergency Price Control Act, 856

Emergency Relief Appropriation Act, 819

Emerson, Ralph Waldo, 348, 361, 362, 438

Empiricism, 92–93

End Poverty in California (EPIC), 822

Energy crisis, 991

England, see Britain

Enlightenment, 91–92

Enola Gay, 877

Environmental Protection Agency (EPA), 1005

Equal Employment Opportunity Commission, 937–938, 1017

Equal Rights Amendment (ERA), 985

Equiano, Olaudah, 20–21

Era of Good Feelings, 266–267

Erie Canal, 251–254

Erskine, David, 233

Ervin, Sam, 972, 973

Esch-Cummins Act, 774

Eskimo, 6, 659

Essay Concerning Human Understanding, An, 65

Essay on Civil Disobedience (1846), 400

Estonia, 1015

Ethiopia, 844

Europe, at time of colonization, 10–15

Evangelical religion, see Religion

Evans, George Henry, 340

Evans, Oliver, 262

Evans, Walker, 807, 832

Everett, Edward, 365

Everly brothers, 924

Ex parte Milligan, 453

Ex parte Vallandigham, 453

Expansion, British attempt to regulate settlement beyond Appalachians, 115–116, 117; Virginia cedes western land to federal government, 167; Northwest Ordinance, 173–174, 364; Louisiana Purchase, 222–225; Tecumseh resists white settlement, 234; War Hawks, 235; western territories widen controversy over slavery, 285–286, 287; westward settlement in early nineteenth century, 279–280; Secretary of State William Seward achieves purchase of Alaska and acquisition of Midway, 659; end of internal frontier spurs thought of overseas expansion, 580, 661; Alfred Thayer Mahan on sea power, 661; American commerce perceived as a benevolent expansion of the national ethos, 662; the moral argument, 662–663; Spanish-American War,

Expansion—(continued)
673–676; debate over acquisition of Philippines, 676–677; U.S. subdues and governs Philippines, 677–679; U.S. acquires Guam and Puerto Rico, 679–680; American interests in China, 680–681; U.S. acquires Panama Canal Zone, 655–657, 681; U.S. purchases Virgin Islands, 681; also see Land
Export-Import Bank, 840

F

Fair Deal, 733, 892–893, 902
Fair Labor Standards Act, 828
Fall, Albert, 788
Fallen Timbers, 162
Fallwell, Jerry, 997
Farm Credit Act, 816
Farm Holiday, 823
Farragut, Admiral David, takes New Orleans, 457
Fascism, in Europe, Italy, Germany, Spain, 844; Spain, 845; Nazis absorb Austria, 845–846; Nazis occupy Czechoslovakia, 846; Kristallnacht and subsequent atrocities, 837–839; Japanese imperialism, 848, 851–852; in United States, 821
Federal Bank Deposit Insurance Corporation (FDIC), 815
Federal Communications Commission, 818, 922
Federal Farm Board, 791
Federal Farm Loan Act, 748
Federal Home Loan Bank Act, 798
Federal Housing Administration (FHA), 816, 909
Federal Judiciary Act, 192
Federal land banks, 748
Federal Power Commission, 774
Federal Republic of Germany, enters North Atlantic Treaty Organization, 918; Germany reunified, 1011
Federal Reserve Board, 747, 915, 993, 1000
Federal Securities Act, 815
Federal Trade Commission (FTC), 748, 929
Federalist, The, 190
Federalists, beliefs, 203–204, 220, also see Hamilton, Alexander;

Alien and Sedition Acts, 207–208; oppose slavery, 225, 285; oppose War of 1812, 236, 246–247; party declines, 266
Ferdinand of Aragon, 1, 22
Ferdinand, Franz, 753
Ferraro, Geraldine, 1006–1007
Fessenden, William Pitt, 426
Fetterman, William, 564
Fifteenth Amendment, 497, 498
Filibusterers, 420
Fillmore, Millard, Anti-Mason, 327; becomes President, 414; supports Compromise of 1850, 414, 415, 427; becomes presidential candidate of remnant of Know-Nothing Party, 429
Finland, war of resistance against USSR, 847
Finney, Charles Grandison, 342, 343, 350, 366
First Amendment, 191, 763, 780, 818, 826
First Continental Congress, 132–133
Fisk, James, 514
Fitzgerald, F. Scott, 783
Fitzgibbon, James, 239
Fitzhugh, George, 378, 389
Five-Power Pact, 791–792
Fletcher v. Peck, 273
Florida, Spain cedes to U.S., 290
Floyd, John B., 448
Foch, General Ferdinand, 760
Folk music revival, 981, 983
Folsom points, 6
Food Administration, 757
Football, 627, 831, 857, 908, 924
Foote, Samuel A., 314
Foraker Act, 680
Forbes, Charles R., 788
Force Acts, 502
Ford, Gerald, becomes President, 989; tone of presidency, 989–990; economy, 991; foreign policy, and Arab oil embargo, 991–992
Ford, Henry, 696, 699, 700
Ford, Patrick, 651
Forestry Service, 739
Formosa, see Taiwan
Forrest, General Nathan Bedford, 474
Forrestal, James V., 884, 888
Fort Caroline, 29
Fort Duquesne (Fort Pitt), British seize, 114
Fort Henry, Union captures, 456

Fort Laramie, Treaty of, 563
Fort McHenry, in War of 1812, 242
Fort Niagara, British seize, 113–114
Fort Stanwix, Treaty of, 173
Fort Sumter, 449–450
Fort Sumter, battle of, 447
Fort Ticonderoga, 114, 138, 155
Four Freedoms, 851
Fourteen Points, 771, 773
Fourteenth Amendment, 489–490; business rights under, 542, 544; in Plessy v. Ferguson, Supreme Court accepts "separate but equal," 584, 913; in Brown v. Board of Education of Topeka, Court overturns Plessy v. Ferguson, 913
Fox sisters, 346
Frame of Government (1682), 55
France, early explorations, 28–29; settlements, 57; loses Quebec, 109–111; in Canada, 111–114; and American Revolution, 139; French Revolution, 199–200; at war with Britain, 200–201; XYZ affair, 206; naval war with U.S., 206; sells Louisiana, 222–225; interference with American commerce, 229–234 passim; ambitions in Mexico, and Civil War, 457; Free French and underground, 847; enters North Atlantic Treaty Organization, 887; in Gulf War, 1015
Francis I of France, 28
Franco, Francisco, 844, 845
Franco-American alliance, 155–156, 159
Frank, Leo, 602
Frankfurter, Felix, 814
Franklin, Benjamin, kite experiment, 91; Poor Richard, 99, 363; Albany Plan of Union, 113; and American Revolution, 133; Declaration of Independence, 140; envoy to France, 155–156; and Treaty of Paris, 159; at Constitutional Convention, 186
Franklin, William, 133
Fredericksburg, battle of, 458
Free Soil Party, 332, 404
Free Speech Movement (FSM), 956, 957
Freedmen's Bureau, established, 486, 488–489; on labor contracts, 489, 495, 497, 499–500; education of

freed slaves, 489, 496, 497; addresses land question, 499

Freedom Summer, 938–939

Frémont, John C., and Mexican War, 399; Republican nominee in 1856, 429–430; orders freedom for slaves in Missouri, 459

French and Indian War, 109–114

French Canadians as ethnicity in the U.S., 604, 716

French Revolution, initial American reactions, 199–200

Freud, Sigmund, 783

Frick, Henry Clay, 516, 533–535, 634

Friedan, Betty, 984

Frobisher, Martin, 31

Frontier thesis, 579

Frontier women in the trans-Mississippi West, 577–579

Frost, Robert, 783

Fuchs, Klaus, 897

Fuel Administration, 757

Fugitive Slave Act (1793), 395

Fugitive Slave Law of 1850, 412–416; Northern state legislatures resist, 436; to win back the secessionists, President Lincoln agrees to enforce, 448

Fugitive slaves, 394–395

Fulbright, William, 958

Fuller, Margaret, 348

Fulton, Robert, 256–257, 261, 263, 274

"Fundamental Constitutions of Carolina," 54

Fundamental Orders of Connecticut, 47

Fundamentalism, 780

G

Gable, Clark, 811

Gadsden, Christopher, 132

Gadsden, James, 418

Gadsden Purchase, 418–419

Gag rule, 389–390; John Quincy Adams attacks, 390–391

Gage, Thomas, 122, 133, 134, 135–136

Galbraith, John Kenneth, 796

Gallatin, Albert, 219, 244, 254, 298

Gallaudet, Thomas, 350

Galloway, Joseph, 132–133

Gama, Vasco da, 22

Garbo, Greta, 788

Gardoqui, Dom Diego de, 170

Garfield, James A., on southern refusal to ratify Fourteenth Amendment, 490; President, 635, 664

Garland, Hamlin, 593

Garrison, William Lloyd, abolitionism, 350, 365–366, 389, 390, 392–393; on Mexican War, 402

Garvey, Marcus, 585, 785–786

Gaspée, 128–129

Gates, Horatio, 155

Gates, Thomas, 38

General Motors, 810, 827, 883

General stores, 522

Genet, Citizen Edmond, 201

Geneva accords, after defeat of French in Vietnam, 949, 950

George, Henry, 610, 634

George III of England, 115; upon repeal of Stamp Act, New Yorkers do honor to, 121; Continental Congress in 1775 acknowledges allegiance to, 139; portrayed in Common Sense, 140, 142, and in the Declaration of Independence, 141, 142–143; position after defeat at Yorktown, 158

Georgia (in East Europe), 1015

German Catholics as antebellum American ethnicity, 376–377

German Democratic Republic (GDR–East Germany), Moscow does not want to allow to join with West Germany, 919; Berlin Wall, 931; West German Chancellor Willy Brandt holds talks with, 964; Germany reunified, 1011

German Lutherans as antebellum American ethnicity, 376–377

Germans as American ethnicity, 55–56, 77–79, 101, 376–377, 593, 603, 627, 633, 717; hostility to German Catholics, 328, 359–360, 429 ; also see German Catholics; German Lutherans

Germantown, battle of, 155

Germany, interest in Samoa, 666; confrontation with Britain and France over North Africa settled by Algeciras Conference, 683–684; American relations with, 1914–1917, 753–756; U.S. as belligerent in World War I,

756–757, 759–766; question of reparations, 773, 797–798, 799–800; under Nazism, 837–839, 844–846; U.S. as Ally against Germany in World War II, 853–861, 862–867, 870–872; postwar occupation, 881; Soviet isolation of Berlin, and Allied airlift, 886–887; West Germany enters North Atlantic Treaty Organization, 918; Communists seal off East Berlin and build Wall, 931; collapse of East German Communist regime, and reunification of Germany, 1011

Gerry, Elbridge, XYZ affair, 206

Gettysburg, battle of, 453, 468–469

Ghent, Treaty of, 244–245, 246, 287

Ghormley, Vice Admiral Robert C., 861

GI Bill of Rights, 882

Gibbons, Thomas, 274

Gibbons v. Ogden, 256, 274–275

Gibson, Charles Dana, 689

Gibson girl, 689

Giddings, Franklin, 661

Gideon, Clarence Earl, and Gideon v. Wainright, 940

Gilbert, Humphrey, 31

Gillespie, Elizabeth Duane, 508

Gingrich, Newt, 1021

Ginsberg, Allen, 923, 924

Ginsburg, Ruth Bader, 1020

Girard, Stephen, 271

Gladden, Washington, 650

Gladstone, William, 745–746

Glass-Steagall Act (Banking Act of 1933), 815

Glorious Revolution, 64, 65

Goebbels, Joseph, 838

Gold bloc, 839

Gold Rush, 405; Indians survival of 566; Hispanics, 568

Gold standard, 519, 636, 638, 640–645, 799, 839

Gold Standard Act, 645

Goldbergs, The, 830

Golden Hind, 31

Golden spike, 551–552

Goldman, Emma, 634, 762

Goldwater, Barry, 935, 937, 962, 969

Gompers, Samuel, 530, 644, 708–710, 749

Gomulka, Wladyslaw, 919

Gonzalez, Rodolfo, 986

Good Neighbor Policy, 841–843

Goodman, Andrew, 939
Goodman, Benny, 829
Gorbachev, Mikhail, 884, 1009, 1015
Gore, Al, 1018, 1022, 1025
Gothic Line, 865
Gould, Jay, 514, 528
Gowen, Frank B., 531
Grady, Henry, 580
Graham, Billy, 924
Grand Army of the Republic (GAR), 637
Grange (Patrons of Husbandry), and Granger laws, 612, 613
Grant, General Ulysses S., in early western campaign of Civil War, 456–457; at Vicksburg, 460, 462; appointed commander of federal forces, 475; at Wilderness, 475; at Appomattox Court House, 477; elected President in 1868 and reelected in 1872, 502, 635; at Centennial Exposition, 508
Grateful Dead, 982
Gray, Captain Robert, 171, 288
Great Awakening, 89–91; Second, 342–343
Great Basin, 555–560, 569, 577; Indians, 560
Great Depression, 807–811, 829–832
Great Northern railroad, 551, 732
Great Plains, see Plains
Great Society, 733, 936, 941, 999
Great Train Robbery, 631
Greece, 599, 881, 885
Greek Revival, 361; also see Monticello
Greeks as American ethnicity, 593, 599, 603
Greeley, Horace, 327, 431; runs against Grant in 1872, 502
Green, William, 127, 635
Greenbacks, 517–519, 615, 639, 640
Greene, Nathanael, 150, 155, 284, 363
Greenglass, David, 897
Greensboro sit-ins, 907–908
Greenwich Village, 720, 782, 923
Greer, Germaine, 984
Greer, 851
Grenada, U.S. invasion, 1002
Grenville, George, 115–118
Gresham, Walter, 668
Grimké, Angelina and Sarah, 350, 366, 390
Groton school, 812

Grundy, Felix, 234
Guadalcanal, battle of, 861–862, 867
Guadalupe Hidalgo, Treaty of, 568, 986
Guam, 679; battle of, 867
Guatemala, twentieth-century military regimes, 1002
Guerrière, 238
Gulf of Tonkin, 952, 958
Gulf War, 1013–1015
Guthrie, Woody, 851
Gutierrez, José Angel, 986

H

Haig, Alexander, 975
Haight-Ashbury, 982
Haiti, independence, 223–224, 297; U.S. intervention, 750, 751; U.S. withdraws, 842; President Clinton opposes military government, 1020
Hakluyt, Richard, 29
Haldeman, John, 973, 975
Hale, Nathan, 363
Half-Way Covenant, 51, 90
Halsey, Vice Admiral William F., 861
Hamburg-Amerika Line, 713
Hamer, Fannie Lou, 939
Hamilton, Alexander, at Constitutional Convention, 178, 186; on Constitution, 188; and The Federalist, 190; Reports on economy, 192–194; opposition, 195–196; concept of implied powers, 196, 265–266; Whiskey Rebellion, 197–198; Hamiltonian persuasion, 198–199; response to French Revolution, 200
Hamilton, Andrew, 95
Hammond, James H., 390
Hampton, Fred, 970
Hancock, John, 123, 126, 185
Hancock, Winfield Scott, 635
Hanna, Mark, 642, 644, 731–732, 733, 734
Hanson, Ole, 775
Harding, Warren G., wins presidential election of 1920, 773–774; presidency, 788; orders troops to subdue labor unrest in West Virginia coal fields, 817
Hargreave, James, 284
Harlem Renaissance, 769–771, 783
Harper, William, 389

Harpers Ferry, 438–439, 445
Harrington, Michael, 915
Harrison, Benjamin, wins presidential election of 1888, loses in 1892, 636; presidency brings back James G. Blaine as secretary of state, 664; diplomatic conflict with Chili, 665; sets aside forests as watersheds, 559
Harrison, William Henry, at war with Tecumseh, 234–235, 240; election of 1840, 329–331; death in office, 395
Hartford Convention, 243–244, 266
Harvester, 532, 611
Hat Act of 1732, 102
Hatch Act, 611
Hawaii, Albert Beveridge looks to acquisition, 662; American missionaries transform Hawaiian culture, 663; Hawaii late in the nineteenth century, 666–668; attack on Pearl Harbor, 852–853
Hawkins, John, 30
Hawthorne, Nathaniel, 254, 348, 362–363
Hay, John, 656, 657, 680–681
Hay-Herran Treaty, 656
Hayes, Rutherford B., in disputed election of 1876, 502–503; end of Reconstruction, 503, 635
Haymarket Square bombing, 532–533
Hayne, Robert Y., 314–315
Haynes, Elwood, 699
Haynsworth, Clement, 969
Haywood, William "Big Bill," 709, 721
"Headright," 39
Hearst, William Randolph, 670–672, 821
Heller, Walter, 929
Helper, Hinton Rowan, 430–431, 434
Hemingway, Ernest, 765, 783
Hennessey, David, 602
Henri, Robert, 718
Henry, Patrick, 118, 132, 189
Henry the Navigator, Prince, 22
Henry VII of England, 23, 29
Henry VIII of England, 29–30
Hepburn, Katherine, 811
Hepburn Act, 736, 741
Hermitage, 247
Herne, James, 628
Hessian mercenaries, 149, 154
Hickel, Walter, 971

Higginson, Thomas Wentworth, 416
Hill, Anita, 1017
Hill, David, 642
Hillquit, Morris, 709
Hiroshima, 760, 853, 872, 877–879
Hispanics, treatment by Anglos in the nineteenth century, 568–569; Mexican, Puerto Rican, and Cuban ethnicities in the twentieth century, 910–912; poverty, 915; Chicano movement, 986–987; question of bilingualism, 987–988; in Gulf War, 1014
Hiss, Alger, 897, 902
Hitler, Adolf, on race, 831, 844; expands into Eastern Europe, 845–847; pact with Stalin, 846–847; invasion of Poland, war with Britain and France, and war with Soviet Union, 847; early battlefield successes, and war plans, 855, 862; desperate to save eastern front, 866; death, 871
Ho Chi Minh, leads war against the French, 899, 947–949; in war against Americans, 952, 954–956, 959–960
Ho Chi Minh City, 991
Ho Chi Minh Trail, 955
Hodges, Luther, 908
Hoffman, Julius, 970
Holding companies, 520
Holding Company Act, 820
Holly, Buddy, 924
Holmes, Mary Jane, 363
Holmes, Oliver Wendell, Jr., 544, 649, 763, 775
Home Missionary Society, 349–350
Home Owners Loan Corporation (HOLC), 816
Homestead Act, 340, 452, 558, 577
Homestead steel strike, 533–535, 634
Homosexuals, Nazi persecution, 839; labeled security risks, 896; fight against discrimination, 982–983
Hood, General J. B., 473
Hooker, General Joseph, 458, 468
Hooker, Thomas, 47, 49
Hooper, Johnson, 363
Hoover, Herbert, administrator during World War I, 757; supplies relief to Europe, 796; secretary of commerce, 788, 790; election of 1928, 795–796; troubled presidency, 796–799, 805–807; diplomacy, 799–801; offers to

sponsor Jewish refugee children, 838
Hoover-Stimson doctrine, 800
Hope, Lugenia, 704
Hopi, 567
Horizontal integration, 516
Horseshoe Bend, battle of, 245
Hortelez et Companie, 139
Horton, Willie, 1010
Hosea Bigelow (character by James Russell Lowell), 363
House, Edward M. (Colonel House), 755
House of Burgesses, 40
House Un-American Activities (HUAC), 896
Houston, Sam, in battle of San Jacinto, 373–374; seeks annexation of Texas, 397; opposes secession of Texas, 445
Howard, Bronson, 628
Howard, Oliver O., 489
Howe, Frederic C., 702
Howe, Richard, 152, 154
Howe, Samuel Gridley, 350
Howe, William, 136, 152, 154–155
Hoyt, Charles, 628
Huckleberry Finn, 421
Hudson, Rock, 924
Hudson River School, 361
Huerta, Victoriano, 751–752
Hughes, Charles Evans, governor of New York, adopts progressive Wisconsin Idea, 728; Republican presidential candidate in 1916, 756; praises Charles Lindbergh, 794; under President Harding, becomes secretary of state, 788; at Washington Naval Conference, 791–792; chief justice, 824
Hughes, Langston, 769, 770–771, 783
Huguenots, 29
Hulbert, William A., 626
Hull, Cordell, 839–841
Hull, Isaac, 238
Hull, William, 236–237
Hull House, 646, 647
Human rights, President Carter applies to both right-wing and leftist regimes, 993–994; Moscow resents, 995; Reagan's policy, 1002; left attacks North American Free Trade Agreement for ignoring, 1021
Hummingbird, 26
Humphrey, Hubert, 890, 961–963

Hundred days, 623, 814–816, 818–822
Hungary, U.S. objects to Austrian suppression of Hungarian revolt, 662; Austria-Hungary as a Central Power, 753; brief Communist revolt in Hungary after World War I, 840; Hungarian rebellion, 919–920
Hunt, E. Howard, 972
Hunter, Robert, 713
Huron, 957, 983
Hurston, Zora, 771, 783
Hurt, Mississippi John, 981
Hussein, see Saddam Hussein
Hutchinson, Anne, 46–47, 165
Hutchinson, Thomas, 119, 128, 129–130, 135, 165
Hydroelectric power, 696, 739, 774, 816

I

Ickes, Harold, 814, 817
Il Proletario, 714
Illiteracy, 491, 496, 599, 842, 933, 936, 988
Immigration and ethnicities, immigration up to 1860 and reasons for, 374–378; Irish, 376; German, 376–377; Scandinavian, 376–377; Chinese, 377–378; immigrants in the two Civil War militaries, 473; the new immigrants, 599–601; life among the new-immigrant ethnicities, 599–601, 603–605, 712–714; at the turn of the century, domestic responses to immigration, 602–603; public schools as agents of assimilation among new ethnicities, 623–624; drawn to Democratic Party, 638–639; Americanization movement, 715–716; assimilation of immigrant ethnicities to mass culture, 716–718; hostility to the Treaty of Versailles and the League of Nations, 772–773; hostility to prohibition, 779, 780; Immigration and Nationality Act of 1965, 939; Chicano movements, 986–988; also see Nativism; specific ethnicities
Immigration and Nationality Act, 939

Immigration Restriction League, 638

Impressment, 205–206, 230, 233

Inca, 5, 27–28, 670

Income tax, Knights of Labor call for, 530; Supreme Court finds unconstitutional first income tax, 542; Populist Party in 1892 endorses, 616; Wisconsin first state to levy income tax, 728; Sixteenth Amendment makes possible on federal level, 542; tax early in President Wilson's administration, 747; in 1920, Congress reduces, 790; reduction, proposed by President Kennedy, enacted in 1964, 929, 936; reduction under President Reagan, 999

Indentured servants, 97–98

Independent Treasury Bill, 325, 330

Indian Defense Association, 988

Indian Removal Act of 1830, 309–310, 381

Indians, discovered by Columbus, 1–4; Columbian exchange, 32–33; and colonies, 60–62, 85–86; *also see* North American Indians; *Chapter 17 passim*

Indochina, *see* Cambodia; Laos; Vietnam

Industrial unionism, *see* Committee on Industrial Organization (Congress of Industrial Organizations); Industrial Workers of the World

Industrial Workers of the World (IWW), Western Federation of Miners contributes to formation, 571; character, 709–710, 721; hostility to, 761, 775, 776, 778

Industry, *see* Commerce

Initiative as device of direct democracy, 616, 727

Insular Cases, 680

Interchangeable parts, 262, 263, 264

Internal improvements, Madison's change of mind, 247, 267–268; Gallatin proposes, 254; turnpikes, 255–256; steamboats, 256–257; canals, 251–254 (Erie Canal), 257; railroads, 258; Monroe vetoes funds for completion of National Road, 281–282; Jackson and federal funding, 315

International Ladies' Garment Workers Union (ILGWU), 691

Interstate and Defense Highway System Act, 916

Interstate Commerce Act, 543

Interstate Commerce Commission (ICC), formed, 543; nineteenth-century Supreme Court decisions weaken, 728–729; Elkins Act strengthens, 732–733; Hepburn Act gives additional authority, 736, 741; as does the Transportation Act, 774; Attorney General Robert Kennedy orders ICC to ban segregation in interstate bus terminals, 926; effect of Motor Carrier Act of 1980, 994

Intolerable Acts, 131–132

Inuit, *see* Eskimo

Inventions, *see* Technology and science

Iran, under the Ayatollah Khomeini seizes Americans, 996; effect of hostage crisis on American politics, 998; war with Iraq, 1006, 1008, 1012, 1013; Iran-Contra, 1007–1008, 1010

Iraq, war with Iran, 1006, 1008, 1012, 1013; Gulf War, 1012–1015

Irish Catholics as American ethnicity, 376; support early Democratic Party, 327; nativist hostility to, at mid-nineteenth century, 328, 359–360, 429, 601; Molly Maguires rumored to have origins in Irish secret society, 531; Irish women in domestic service, 540; Irish workers on Union Pacific, 551; Irish before 1880s distinctive for settling in cities, 593; dominant in late nineteenth-century Catholic clergy, 600; city bosses, 607–608; boxers, 627; animosity towards, 639; political oratory against British, 668; in boundary dispute between U.S. and Venezuela, offer to serve as military, 669; great concentrations in Boston and New York City, 716; dislike of League of Nations, 772–773; prohibitionists associate Irish with drinking, 779; John F. Kennedy's connections with, 925

Iron Act of 1750, 102

Iron ore, 516

Iroquois confederation, 9; fate after formation of U.S., 172, 173, 310

Irving, Washington, 361

Isabella of Castile, 1, 22

Islam, *see* Muslims

Isolationism, among progressives before U.S. enters World War I, 755; between world wars, 843, 848–849; among conservatives in early days of Cold War, 886, 895; in 1992, 1018

Israel, joins Britain and France in attack on Egypt in 1956, 920; takes land in Six-Day War, 964–965, 991; Yom Kippur War of 1973, 991–992; President Carter helps arrange a peace treaty with Egypt, 995; invasion of Lebanon, 1002; missile attacks on Israel during Gulf War, 1013; meeting in 1991 with Arab leaders, 1016

Isthmus of Panama, Clayton-Bulwer Treaty, 655; U.S. obtains Canal Zone, 655–658

Italians as American ethnicity, patterns of settlement, 599–600; hostility to, 602; occupations of early immigrants, 604, 713; family patterns, 714; survival of city neighborhoods, 717

Italy, in World War I, 753, 759; at Washington Naval Conference, 792; fascism, 844; intervention in Spanish civil war, 845; Allies invade, 863, 865; joins Allies, 866; enters North Atlantic Treaty Organization, 887

Iwo Jima, battle of, 869

J

Jack Downing Papers, 363

Jackson, Andrew, early life, 297–298; battle of Horseshoe Bend, 245; battle of New Orleans, 245–246; as hero, 247, 266, 363; invades Florida, 289–290; in election of 1824, 293–294; in election of 1828, 299–301; and Chrokees, 308–310; inaugural, 311–312; and nullification controversy, 318–319; and Van Buren, 312–320; and Calhoun, 312–320; and Second Bank of the United States, 320–321; hostility to Bank, 321–323; veto of Bank recharter, 321; wins second term, 321;

opponents of, 327–328; and annexation of Texas, 396
Jackson, Helen Hunt, 567
Jackson, Jesse, 1006
Jackson, Rachel, 300–301
Jackson, General Thomas "Stonewall," at Bull Run, 454; dies at Chancellorsville, battle of, 458
Jackson State, 966
Jamaica, and Marcus Garvey, 785, 786
James, William, 648, 676, 692, 711
James I of England, 37, 41
James II of England (Duke of York), 53, 63–64, 65
James River, 37
Jamestown, 37–40
Japan, at war with Russia, 682–683; Gentlemen's Agreement limits Japanese immigration to U.S., 683; Root-Takahira Agreement, 683, 750; intervenes in Russia against Bolsheviks, 772; Japanese immigration to U.S. banned, 782; invades Manchuria and attacks China, 800; tension between Japan and U.S., 851–852; Pearl Harbor, 852–853; war between Japan and U.S., 861–862, 867–869, 872; Hiroshima and Nagasaki, 872, 877–879; American occupation, 893
Japanese as American ethnicity, 603; Gentlemen's Agreement limits Japanese immigration to U.S., 683; Japanese immigration to U.S. banned, 782; discrimination against during World War II, 858–859
Java, 238
Jaworski, Leon, 974
Jay, John, 170; negotiations with Spain over the port of New Orleans, 170; *The Federalist*, 190; first Chief Justice, 192; Jay Treaty, 201–202; opposes slavery, 285
Jeffers, Robinson, 783
Jefferson, Thomas, 161, 165, 171; Declaration of Independence, 140–143; on western lands, 167; opposes Hamilton's economic plans, 195–196; Jeffersonian persuasion, 198; early response to French Revolution, 200; becomes Vice President, 204; Kentucky Resolution, 208; elected to

presidency, 210–211; and Sally Hemings, 215–217; inauguration, 217; Monticello, 218–219; limited government, 219–221; Lewis and Clark expedition, 222–223; Louisiana Purchase, 222–225; policy toward Britain, 231–232
Jefferson Airplane, 982
Jews, persecution under Nazism, 837–839, 844; New Immigrants, 593, 599, 600, 603, 712, 713; occupation of early immigrants, 604; family life, 714; survival of city neighborhoods, 717; dislike of East European territorial settlements at Versailles, 773; President Truman courts, 891
Jim Crow, 584, 826
Job Corps, 936
Johnson, Andrew, Union Party nominee in 1864, 476; plans for Reconstruction, 487–488; restores land that had gone from owners to blacks, 499; appoints commission that makes peace with Plains Indians, 563; opposes Republican plans, 488–489, 490; impeachment and trial, 493–494
Johnson, Edward, 42
Johnson, Hiram, 728
Johnson, Hugh (of National Recovery Administration), 817, 819
Johnson, Hugh S. (agricultural marketing), 791
Johnson, Jack, 627
Johnson, James Weldon, 711, 783
Johnson, Lyndon, New Dealer, 934; Kennedy's vice-presidential candidate, 925, 934; interim presidential term, 933, 935; election of 1964, 935; domestic policy and war on poverty, 936–941; Vietnam, 945, 946, 952–956; Democratic opposition, 958–959; announces will not seek another presidential term, 960
Johnson, Samuel, 120
Johnson, Tom, 702
Johnson, William, 114
Johnson Act, 781
Johnston, General Joseph E., 475–476, 477
Jolson, Al, 788
Jones, John Paul, 149, 157
Jones Act, 679, 774
Joplin, Scott, 630

Jordan, 964, 1016
Jordan Marsh, 523
Judiciary Act of 1801, 211, 221

K

Kansas, Kansas-Nebraska Act and Bleeding Kansas, 422–428; Lecompton Constitution, 430, 432
Kansas-Pacific Railroad, 557, 573
Katzenbach, Nicholas, 960
Kazakhstan, 1015
Kearny, Dennis, 602
Keating-Owen Act, 749
Kefauver, Estes, 902, 925
Kelley, Abby, 357
Kelley, Florence, 647, 705
Kelley, Oliver, 612–613
Kellogg, Frank, 792
Kellogg-Briand pact, 792
Kemp, Jack, 1022
Kendall, Amos, 389
Kennan, George F., 884–885
Kennedy, Edward, 961
Kennedy, John F., in Senate, 925; issue of Catholicism, 796, 925–926 (campaign of 1960); civil rights movement, 926–927; domestic policy and New Frontier, 928–929; Special Forces and Peace Corps, 930; Bay of Pigs, 930–931; Berlin, 931; Cuban missile crisis, 932; negotiates treaty with Khrushchev banning nuclear testing above ground, 933; assassination, 933; Kennedy and Vietnam, 950–952
Kennedy, Joseph, 929
Kennedy, Robert, attorney general protects freedom riders and orders desegregation of interstate bus terminals, 926; advises against immediate air strike on Cuban missiles, 932; in cabinet, advises course of disengagement from Vietnam, 952; in 1968 Democratic primaries, 960–961; supports Cesar Chavez's United Farm Workers, 987; assassination, 961
Kent State, 966
Kentucky Resolution, 208, 436
Kerensky, Alexander, 759
Kerouac, Jack, 923, 924
Kerr, Clark, 957
Kettle Hill, 675

Key, Francis Scott, 242, 244, 363

Keynes, John Maynard, 828, 882

Khmer Rouge, 991

Khrushchev, Nikita, on Berlin, 931; Cuban missiles, 932; easing tensions between Moscow and the West, 932–933

Kidder Peabody, 520

Kimmel, Admiral Husband E., 852

King, Martin Luther, Jr., at Montgomery bus boycott, 915; commitment to nonviolence, 987; in civil rights movement, 926–928

King, Rufus, 246–247, 266, 285

King George's War, *see* Austrian Succession, War of

King Philip's War (1675–76), 60–61

King William's War, *see* League of Augsburg, War of

Kissinger, Henry, 963, 965, 966, 967

"Kitchen Cabinet," 312–313

Knights of Labor, formation and character, 530; invites blacks into membership, 583; common cause with farmers' Alliance, 615; Populist Omaha convention of 1890 supports Knights, 616, 646; temperance advocate Frances Willard joins, 646

Know-Nothings, 361, 429–430

Knox, Philander C., 732, 734, 750

Knox College, 353

Koch, Robert, 594

Kohl, Helmut, 1011

Konoye, Fumimaro, 852

Korean War, United Nations intervenes against North Korean invasion of South, 899; MacArthur's Inchon landing breaks North Korean army, 899; Chinese troops drive back UN forces, 900

Kósciuszko, Tadeusz, 155

Ku Klux Klan, 481–482, 502, 778, 780, 781, 926

Kuhn, Loeb, 520, 694

Kurds, 1012, 1015

Kush, 18

Kuwait, 1012–1013, 1015

L

Labor and work, crafts in eighteenth-century Philadelphia, 81; colonial slave labor, 83–85, 86–88; craft in 1800, 175; farming in 1800, 227–228, 339–340; pace of work in early nineteenth century, 254; domestic or putting-out system, 259; Waltham system, 259–261; continuance of craft in twentieth century, 265; political organization in 1830s, 340; professionalization, 341; factories before Civil War, 378; task and gang systems for antebellum slave labor, 383–385; slave craftsmen, 385; northern labor during Civil War, 472; labor contracts for freed slaves, 489, 495, 497, 499–500; sharecropping, 500–501, 527, 551, 577, 582–583; labor and the workplace in the late nineteenth century, 527–529; National Labor Union and particular unions after the Civil War, 529; Knights of Labor, 530; railroad strike of 1877, 531; McCormick International Harvester strike and Haymarket Square, 532–533; formation of the American Federation of Labor, 530; Pullman strike, 533; Homestead strike, 533–535; women wage earners in the late nineteenth century, 535–536, 539–540; professionalization of teaching, nursing, and social work, 537–539, and of middle-class work in general 700–701; child labor at the turn of the twentieth century, 540–541; black labor, southern and northern, in the late nineteenth century, 582–584; craft unions, 584, 710; perfecting the detail of work, 695–696 (Frederick Winslow Taylor); condition of wage workers in the early twentieth century, 708–709; Industrial Workers of the World, 709–710, 776; welfare capitalism addresses working conditions, 710; anthracite strike of 1902, 733–735; Clayton Antitrust Act recognizes rights of organized labor, 748–749; Ludlow massacre of 1914, 776–777; labor strife in San Francisco in 1916, 776–777; President Wilson's wartime policy, 759; labor unrest after World War I, 775, 776, 777; women in the workforce during the Great Depression, 808–809; effect of the Depression on the workforce, 809–810; dispute within AFL during Great Depression over industrial unionism, 817; New Deal work projects, 815–816, 817, 819–820, 823; unionism during the Depression, 817–818, 820, 827; in art of the Depression, celebration of work, 832–833; government during World War II, 856; women during the war, 856, 983; women in the work force after World War II, 983–984; postwar labor unrest, 883; the service economy that follows World War II, 921–922; Employment Act of 1946, 882–883; Taft-Hartley Act, 889; Job Corps and vocational schooling, 936; Neighborhood Youth Corps, 936; United Farm Workers organize migrants, 987; *also see* American Federation of Labor; Congress of Industrial Organizations; *other specific unions*

Lafayette, Marquis de, 154, 155, 199

Laffer, Arthur, 997

Laffite, Jean, 245, 246

La Follette, Robert M., progressive governor of Wisconsin, 727–728; enters Senate, 729; comments on means of regulating railroad rates, 736; opponent of President Taft, 743; shepherds Seaman's Act through Congress, 749; candidate for presidency on Progressive ticket, 692

Lake Champlain, 237

Lake Erie, battle of, 240

Land, Land Ordinance of 1785, 172; early nineteenth-century sectional disagreement on land sales, 282–283; northeastern manufacturers endorse cheap land, 432; Republicans call for free homesteads, 433, 476; Homestead Act, 340, 452; postbellum blacks, 483, 499–501; sharecropping, 500–501, 527, 551, 577, 582–583; crop-lien system, 501; federal land grants, to individuals for settlement, Homestead Act and subsequent grants for individual development of western lands, to colleges, 452, 558; Morrill Land Grant College Act, 452, 610; land-grant colleges coeducational, 537; for railroad connecting Great Lakes to Gulf of Mexico, 553; for first transcontinental road, 554; to Texas and Pacific, 558; reclamation of lands, 559, 817, 833; Smith-Lever Act establishes cooperation between agricultural extension stations and land-grant colleges, to railroads, 553; *also see* Expansion

Land banks, 748, 816

Land Ordinance of 1785, 172, 553

Landon, Alfred, 824

Lange, Dorothea, 807

Laos, once part of French empire, 947; Geneva accords acknowledge independence, 949; Southeast Asia Treaty Organization extends shield to Laos, 950; President Kennedy avoids direct confrontation with Communists, 931–932; Ho Chi Minh Trail runs from North Vietnam through Laos to Communists in South, 955; in 1971, South Vietnam with American assistance launches offensive against Communists, 967; Communists victorious, 968, 991

La Raza Unida, 986

La Salle, Sieur de, 57

Las Casas, Bartolomé de, 26

Lathrop, Julia, 742

Latrobe, Benjamin, 361

Latvia, 1015

Laurens, Henry, 119, 135, 148

Laval, Pierre, 799

Lawrence, D. H., 782

Lawrence, William and Amos, 323

Lazarus department store, 523

League of Augsburg, War of, 112

League of Nations, President Wilson's Fourteen Points, 771; political fight and defeat for American participation, 772–774; ineffectually condemns Japanese aggression against China, 800;

fails to act against Italian invasion of Ethiopia, 844; United Nations displaces, 880

Lease, Mary Elizabeth, 616

"Leatherstocking Tales," 252, 361

Lebanon, during civil strife, President Eisenhower sends troops, 920–921; in 1982, Israel invades, seeking to injure Palestinian Liberation Organization, 1002; Iran-Contra aims to rescue American hostages held in Lebanon, 1007, 1008; represented at the Madrid conference on peace in Mideast, 1016

Lecompton Constitution, 430, 432

Lee, Ann, 343

Lee, Arthur, 155

Lee, "Light Horse Harry," 189, 454

Lee, Richard Henry, 132, 140, 166, 185, 189

Lee, Robert E., 189; in Mexican War, 402; in assault on John Brown at Harpers Ferry, 439; commands Confederate forces, 454; confronts Peninsula Campaign, 458; at Antietam, 458; at Chancellorsville, 458; at Gettysburg, 468–469; at Wilderness, 475; at Appomattox Court House, 477, 483, 486

Legal realism, 649

Legree, Simon, 410

Leisler, Jacob, 64

Lend-lease, 850–851, 862

L'Enfant, Pierre, 209

Lenin, V. I., 759, 772, 840

Leopard, 230–231

Lever Act, 748, 757

Levittown, 909

Lewis, John L., during strife in 1920s, represents coal miners, 790; leader of industrial unionism promoted by CIO, 817–818; in 1946, orders strike by members of United Mine Workers, 883; known for militancy, 889

Lewis, Meriwether, 222–223

Lewis, Sinclair, 783, 786

Lexington, battle of, 133–134

Lexington, 861

Leyte, battle of, 869

Liberator, The, 365–366

Liberty League, 822

Liberty Party, 392–393, 404

Liddy, G. Gordon, 972

Liliuokalani, Queen of Hawaii, 667–668

Lincoln, Abraham, 446; in senatorial contest with Douglas, 434–435; Republican nominee in 1860, 437–438; at beginning of presidency, makes offer to secessionists, 448–449; decision to provision Fort Sumter, 449; calls for volunteers, 450; suspends writ of *habeas corpus*, 453; politics and morality of emancipation, 459–460; Emancipation Proclamation, 460; in election of 1864, 476; Second Inaugural Address, 444; on reconstruction, 485–486; last days, 486–487

Lincoln, Benjamin, 183

Lincoln-Douglas debates, 434–435

Lindbergh, Charles A., 793–794, 970

Lister, Joseph, 594

Literature, *see* Arts

Lithuania, 1015

Little Belt, 235

Little Big Horn, 509, battle of, 549–550, 564

Little Richard, 923

Little Rock, 913–914

Little Steel, 856

Litvinov, Maxim, 841

Livingston, Robert, drafting of Constitution, 140; participation in Louisiana Purchase, 223–225, 287; partner of Robert Fulton in steamboat enterprise, 256, 274

Lloyd George, David, 759

Lochner v. New York, 544

Locke, John, 54, 65

Locofocos, 325

Lodge, Henry Cabot, in 1890, tries to get legislation protecting rights of southern blacks to vote, 638; Lodge Corollary to Monroe Doctrine, 685; fights against entering League of Nation without reservations, 772, 773

Lodge Corollary to Monroe Doctrine, 685

Log Cabin campaign, 329–331

London Company (or Virginia Company), 37, 39–40, 41

London Naval Conference, 810

López, Narciso, 419

López de Santa Ana, Antonio, in Texas war, 372–373, 401
López Tijerina, Reyes, 986
Lord Baltimore (George Calvert), 49; (Cecil Calvert), 49, 65
Louis, Joe, 831
Louis XVI of France, 155–156, 159; and French Revolution, 199, 200
Louisiana, 246
Louisiana Purchase, 222–225
L'Ouverture, *see* Toussaint L'Ouverture
Lowell, Francis Cabot, Waltham system, 259–261
Lowell, James Russell, 363
Loyalists during American Revolution, *see* Tories
Ludendorff, Erich, 759–760
Ludlow, Colorado, strike and massacre, 776
Luks, George, 718
Lundy, Benjamin, 365
Lundy's Lane, battle of, 241
Lusitania, 754
Luther, Martin, 14–15
Lutherans, 101, 377
Lynd, Robert and Helen, 786
Lyon, Mary, 353
Lyon, Matthew, 208

M

MacArthur, General Douglas, suppresses Bonus Army, 806; commands losing defense of Philippines from Japanese, 855; drives toward Japan from south, 867; forces land in Philippines, 869; predicts costs of invading Japan, 870; governs Japan, 893; Inchon landing in Korea, 899; President Truman dismisses, 900
MacDonald, Ramsay, 799, 801
Macdonough, Thomas, 241
Macedonian, 238
Machado, Geraldo, 842
Machu Picchu, 27
Macon's Bill No. 2, 233
Macy's department store, 522
Maddox, 952
Madero, Francisco, 751–752
Madison, Dolley, 232, 242
Madison, James, at Constitutional Convention, 186; favors Constitution, 189–190; *The*

Federalist, 190; opposes Hamilton's economic plans, 195–196; Virginia Resolution, 208, 395; Jefferson's secretary of state, 221; becomes President, 232; policy toward Britain and France, 233, 235–236; flees from Washington, 242; adopts economic nationalist policies, 247, 267–268
Magellan, Ferdinand, 25
Maginot line, 847
Magruder, Jeb Stuart, 972–973
Mahan, Alfred Thayer, 661, 674
Maine, enters as free state in balance to Missouri, 286
Maine, 671–673
Malcolm, Daniel, 123
Malcolm X, 938
Malenkov, Georgi, 918
Malone, Vivian, 927
Manchuria, in Russo-Japanese War, Japanese troops push out Russians, 682; peace treaty grants Japan paramount interest in southern Manchuria, 683; Japanese envision as part of empire, 792; Japan undertakes conquest, 800; Allies in World War II agree on return of Manchuria to China, 893; at Potsdam, Stalin agrees to send troops against Japanese, 880–881; in Korean War, China fears threat to, 900
Manifest Destiny, 418–422, 558
Manila Bay, 674
Mann, Horace, 352–353
Mann-Elkins Act, 741
Manufactures, *see* Commerce
Mao Zedong, 800, 848, 893, 896, 948
Marbury, William, 221
Marbury v. Madison, 221–222
March on Washington, 783, 928
Marco Polo, *see* Polo, Marco
Marie Antoinette, 200
Marin, John, 718
Marne River, battle of, 760
Marsh, George Perkins, 738
Marsh brothers, 611
Marshall, George C., tries to arrange cease-fire between Nationalists and Communists in China, 895; Marshall Plan, 885–886, 888; secretary of defense, perceives General MacArthur

as insubordinate, 900; Joseph McCarthy attacks, 898, 902
Marshall, John, XYZ affair, 206; appointed Chief Justice, 211; judicial review, 221; economic nationalism, 273–275; Indian removal, 309; a founder of the American Colonization Society, 364
Marshall, Thurgood, 913, 1017
Marshall Plan, 885–886, 888
Martin, Luther, 186
Marx, Karl, 632
Marx brothers, 810
Maryland Toleration Act, 49, 51
Mason, George, 186, 188, 189
Mason, James, 457
Massachusetts Bay colony, 41; resistance to British imperial measures, 119, 125–128, 129–131, 132, 133–137
Massachusetts Bay Company, 41–43, 61
Massachusetts Gazette, 189
Massachusetts Government Act, 131
Mather, Cotton, 72, 73
Mather, Increase, 72
Maximilian, Archduke, 457, 658
Maximum Freight Rate Case, 543
Maya, 3, 5, 27
Mayaguez, 991
Mayflower Compact, 41
Mayo, Admiral Henry T., 752
Maysville turnpike, 315
McCain, Franklin, 907
McCain, John, 1024–1025
McCarthy, Eugene, 946, 960–962
McCarthy, Joseph, and McCarthyism, 896–898, 902, 903, 925
McClellan, General George B., assumes command of Union army, 454, 456; Peninsula Campaign, 458; at Antietam, 458; Democratic nominee in 1864, 476
McClure, Samuel S., and *McClure's* magazine, 706, 707
McCord, James, 972
McCormick, Cyrus, 262, 263
McCormick Reaper Company, 472
McCoy, Joseph, 573
McCulloch, James, 274, and *McCulloch v. Maryland*, 274
McDougall, William, 781
McDowell, General Irvin, 454
McGovern, George, 971
McGuire, Peter, 530

McKay, Claude, 770, 783

McKinley, William, on tariff, 636; presidential campaign of 1896, 642–645; resists U.S. entrance into war with Spain, 671–673; endorses annexation of Philippines, 677–678; reelected and assassinated, 729

McLeod, Alexander, 396

McNamara, Robert, 952

McNary-Haugen proposal for agricultural surplus, 791

McNeil, Joseph, 907

McParlan, James, 531

McVeigh, Timothy, 979

Meade, General George G., at Gettysburg, 468–469

Means, Russell, 989

Meany, George, 971

Meat Inspection Act, 725, 726, 737

Meatpacking, 516, 725–726, 737

Medicaid, 937, 1017

Medicare, 937, 1017

Mellon, Andrew, 788, 790

Melville, Herman, 254, 363

Mencken, H. L., 782, 789

Mental institutions, reform of, 354

Mercantilism, 102, *also see* Commerce

Merchant Marine Act, 774

Meredith, James, 927

Meroë, 18

Merrimac, 457

Messenger, 783

Methodists, 175, 198, 343; character and influence, 264, 346–347

Metropolitan Opera House, 629

Mexican War, 399–403

Mexicans as ethnicity in U.S., 403, 568, 910–911, 986–987

Mexico, Texas war of secession, 371–374; Mexican War, 399–403; Gadsden Purchase, 418–419; French install Archduke Maximilian, 457; Lodge Corollary to Monroe Doctrine aimed at Japanese attempt to gain Mexican port, 685; Mexican revolution and U.S. intervention, 751–753; Zimmermann letter, 756; question of U.S. oil interests, 792–793

Michelangelo, 14

"Middle Passage," 87

Midway, acquisition, 659; battle of, 861

Miles, Manly, 611

Military Reconstruction Act, 490

Millay, Edna St. Vincent, 783

Millennialism, 345–346

Miller, Phineas, 284

Miller, William, millennialism, 345–346

Miller, William (Barry Goldwater's running mate), 935

Millet, Kate, 984

Millis, Walter, 843

Mills, Robert, 361

Minute Men, 133–135

Missile crisis, 932

Missionary Ridge, 475

Mississippi Freedom Democratic Party (MFDP), 939

Missouri Compromise, 285–286, 403

Missouri Pacific railroad, 572

Mitchell, John (attorney general under President Nixon), 973

Mitchell, John (of United Mine Workers), 524, 710, 733–734

Mitchell, Maria, 536

Mittelberger, Gottlieb, 77

Moby Dick, 363

Mohawk, 989

Molasses Act of 1733, 102, 116

Moldavia, 1015

Moley, Raymond, 814

Molly Maguires, 531

Molotov, Vyacheslav, 918

Mondale, Walter, 1006–1007

Mongols, 10–11

Monitor, 457

Monroe, James, opposes Constitution, 189; Louisiana Purchase, 224–225; elected to presidency, 246–247, 266; on panic of 1819, 271; vetoes funds for completion of National Road, 281–282; foreign policy, 287–292

Monroe Doctrine, formation, 290–292; at end of Civil War, Secretary of State William Seward confronts Spanish ambitions in Latin America and France over occupation of Mexico, 658; Secretary of State James G. Blaine looks for influence in hemisphere, 665; U.S. conflict with Britain over Venezuela, 668–669; Roosevelt Corollary, 684–685; Lodge Corollary, 685; reservations to Covenant of League of Nations would include protection of, 773; Clark Memorandum defines limits of, 793; President Franklin D. Roosevelt's policy of consultation with Latin America, 842

Montcalm, General Louis de, 110–111, 114

Monterrey, battle of, 399

Montgomery, Alabama, first capital of Confederacy, 445; bus boycott, 914–915

Montgomery, General Bernard, 862

Montgomery, Richard, 138

Montgomery, Ward, 524, 697

Monticello, 218–219

Montreal, taken by British, 114

Moral Majority, 998

Moravians, 101

Morehead v. New York ex rel. Tipaldo, 825

Morgan, J. P., Morgan investment house, 520, 694; early user of electric lighting, 511; enables President Cleveland to rescue gold standard, 641; organizes steel merger, 515; President Theodore Roosevelt confronts Morgan over Northern Securities merger, 732–733; backs arbitration in coal strike of 1902, 734; Roosevelt approves Morgan's proposed purchase by United States Steel of Tennessee Coal and Iron, 740; President Taft moves against steel monopoly characterized by purchase, 743

Morgenthau, Henry, 814

Mormons, 343–345; hostility to, 344, 360; women converts on frontier, 577; Utah Mormons give women the vote, 579

Moroccan crisis, 683

Morrill Land Grant Act, 452, 610

Morrill tariff, 452

Morris, Gouverneur, 188, 199

Morris, Robert, 158, 164, 171

Morrow, Dwight, 793

Morse, Samuel F. B., 360, 510

Morse, Wayne, 952

Morton, Thomas, 44

Moses, Robert (New York commissioner of public works), 830

Moses, Robert Parris (civil rights worker), 938

Motion pictures, silent and first talkies, 620–621, 787–788; during the Great Depression, 810–811;

Motion pictures—(continued)
during World War II, 860; red-hunting in Hollywood, 896; during the 1950s, 924

Motor Carrier Act, 994

Mott, Lucretia, 337–338, 497

Mound Builders, 3, 8

Mount, William Sidney, 361

Mount Holyoke, 353, 625

Muckrakers, 703, 706–707

Mugwumps, 636, 639, 676

Muir, John, 739

Muller v. Oregon, 544, 649

Munn v. Illinois, 542, 613

Murchison letter, 636

Murray, John, Earl of Dunmore, 147–148

Murrow, Edward R., 860

Muscle Shoals, 816

Muslims, 10–12; in Africa, 18–19, 21–22; conflict with Christians in Lebanon, 920–921; Islamic militants, 996 (Ayatollah Khomeini in Iran), 1002, 1007, 1008; Bosnian Muslims, 1021; Kosovo, 1024

Mussolini, Benito, 844, 845, 853, 863

My Lai, 959

N

Nagasaki, 760, 853, 872, 877–878

Nagy, Imre, 919

Napoleon Bonaparte, agrees to end naval war with U.S., 209; sells Louisiana, 222–225; issues Berlin Decree against ships carrying British goods, 230; further actions against American commerce, 233

Napoleon III, 457, 658

Nashoba, 347–348

Nasser, Gamal Abdul, 920–921, 964–965

National American Woman Suffrage Association, 764

National Association for the Advancement of Colored People (NAACP), Niagara movement and formation, 711–712; at odds with Booker T. Washington, 586; response to Marcus Garvey, 785; victory in Brown v. Board of Education, 913

National Banking Acts of 1863 and 1864, 452

National Congress of American Indians, 988

National Defense Education Act, 916

National Housing Act, 816, 828, 893

National Industrial Recovery Act (NIRA), 817, 818; Supreme Court decision in Schechter v. United States finds unconstitutional, 819, 825

National Labor Relations Act, 820

National Labor Relations Board (NLRB), 999

National Labor Union, 529

National Monetary Commission, 694

National Organization for Women (NOW), 984

National Recovery Administration (NRA), 817; Supreme Court decision in Schechter v. United States finds unconstitutional, 819, 825

National Republicans, 299, 321

National Road, 255–256; Monroe vetoes funds for completion, 281–282

National Security Act, 888

National Security Council, 895, 948, 990

National Security Council Paper Number 68, 895

National Silver Republicans, 642

National Trades Union, 340

National War Labor Board, 759

National Woman Suffrage Association, 498

National Youth Administration (NYA), 820

Native Americans, see Indians; North American Indians

Nativism, hostility to Roman Catholicism, 328, 359–360, 429, 601–602, 638, 779, 780, 781; connections with reform in mid-nineteenth century, 359–360; hostility to Italians, 602; late nineteenth-century prejudice against Chinese, 602; Immigration Restriction League, 602–603; labor and social-reformist nativism, 714–715; hostility after World I to immigrants as radicals, 778; hostility to big-city culture, 779; prohibitionist and fundamentalist hostility to

immigrant ethnicities, 779, 780; Ku Klux Klan, 780, 781; laws of 1921 and 1924 restricting immigration, 780–782; treatment of Japanese Americans during World War II, 858–859

Nauvoo, 344

Navaho, 33, 567, 988

Navarre, General Henri, 948–949

Navigation Acts, 57, 58–59, 61, 66, 67, 81

Nazism, concept of superior Aryan race, 831, 844; Kristallnacht and subsequent atrocities, 837–839

Neoconservatism, 998

Neoorthodoxy, 924

Netherlands, after Kristallnacht, admits refugees, 838; Nazis invade, 847, 852; Allies enter, 866; enters North Atlantic Treaty Organization, 887

Neutrality Acts, 843–844

Neutrality, during World War I before 1917, 753–756; during World War II before December 1941, 843–844, 848–851

New Deal, Chapter 24 passim; Great Depression, 807–811; opposition from the right, 821–822, and from the left, 822; Huey Long, 823; Fr. Charles Coughlin, 823; Francis E. Townsend, 823–824; the artistic temper of the 1930s, 832–833

New England, settlement of, 40–43; Hartford Convention, 243–244, 266; Yankees as social reformers, 261, 427

New England Confederation, 60

New England Emigrant Aid Society, 423

New Freedom, 745; antitrust legislation during Wilson's presidency in spirit of New Freedom, 748; much of legislation during Wilson's presidency departs from New Freedom, 747, 774

New Guinea, 861, 867

New Harmony, 347

New Jersey Plan, 187

"New Lights," 90–91

New Nationalism, 743, 745, 774

New Netherland, 52–53, also see New York City

New Orleans, during Spain's possession, 169–170, 202–203,

223; Spain's cession to France, 222–223; U.S. acquires, 224–225; Union seizes, 457

New Orleans, battle of, 245–246

New Panama Canal Company, 655

New Right, 997

New South, 580, 582

New York City, as New Amsterdam, 53; first seat of government under the Constitution, 190; in 1800, 226–227; draft riot during Civil War, 474

New Zealand, 594, 950

Newlands Act, 559, 738

Newspapers, colonial, 75; and media coverage, early twentieth century, 622; Yellow press, 670

Nez Percé, 381, 564–565

Nguyen Cao Ky, 954

Nguyen Giap, 948, 990

Nguyen Khanh, 952

Nguyen Van Thieu, 954

Niagara movement, 586, 711–712

Nicaragua, possibility of isthmian canal, 656; British seize custom house, 668; U.S. troops in, 750, 751; Nicaraguans under Augusto Sandino resist U.S. occupation, 792; Sandinistas win control, 1001; Reagan Administration supports Contras, 1001; Congress resists military aid to Contras, 1001, 1012; Iran-Contra, 1007–1008; Sandinistas agree to hold free elections, 1009–1010; Sandinistas defeated in elections, 1012

Nightingale, Florence, 537

Nimitz, Admiral Chester, 861, 867, 869, 872

Nine-Power Pact, 792, 800

Nineteenth Amendment, 706, 983

Nixon, John, 142

Nixon, Richard M., investigation of Alger Hiss, 902; Eisenhower's vice-presidential candidate in 1952, 902; presidential campaign of 1960, 925–926; presidential campaign of 1968, 962–963; foreign policy, 963–965, 965–966; Nixon Doctrine, 963; approach to Communist China, 965–966; Vietnam, 946, 966–968; domestic policy, 968–971; campaign of 1972, 971–972; Watergate and resignation, 972–975

Nixon Doctrine, 963

"Noble savage," 32

Nonimportation agreements, as colonial resistance, 120, 124

Non-Intercourse Act, 232–233

Nonviolence, in civil rights movement under Martin Luther King, 915 (Martin Luther King at Montgomery), 926–927, 938–939 (Student Nonviolent Coordinating Committee in Mississippi)

Normandy, Allies land, 865–866

Norris, Frank, 720

Norris, George W., 816–817

North, Lord Frederick, in 1768, orders British troops to Boston, 124; Tea Act of 1773, 129; makes peace overtures to rebellious Americans, 139

North, Colonel Oliver, 1008

North American Free Trade Agreement (NAFTA), 1020

North American Indians, 4–10; in New England, 47–49; problems with colonists, 60–62; in Middle Colonies, 80–81; in Southern colonies, 85–86; in French and Indian War, 113, 114; Indian frontier after 1763, 115–116; and American Revolution, 162–163; Tecumseh resists advance of white settlement, 234–235; antebellum settlement presses upon Indians, 381–382; in West during late nineteenth century, 560–566; shifting governmental policies toward assimilation, 566–568 (Dawes Severalty Act), 988 (Wheeler-Howard Indian Reorganization Act and later changes); political and cultural activism in the later twentieth century, 988, 989 (American Indian Movement); also see entries for specific ethnicities and tribes

North Atlantic Treaty Organization (NATO), formation, 887–888; Eisenhower becomes commander, 901; West Germany joins, 918; Southeast Asia Treaty Organization (SEATO), a version for Asia and Pacific, 949–950; question during Reagan's presidency of arming with new intermediate range missiles, 1002–1003; reductions in American contribution after decline of Soviet Union, 1016; intervenes in Bosnian conflict, 1021; in Kosovo, 1024

Northern Pacific railroad, 554, 732

Northern Securities Company, and Northern Securities Company v. United States, 732–733

Northwest Ordinance, 161, 162, 173–174, 364

Northwestern Alliance (farmers' organization), 615

Norway, Germany invades, 847; enters North Atlantic Treaty Organization, 887

Noyes, John Humphrey, 348–349

Nuclear power, Hiroshima and Nagasaki, 872, 877–879; standoff between Moscow and the West, 883–884, 896; Bernard Baruch proposes international control, 884; espionage cases, 897; Eisenhower Administration relies on nuclear deterrent, 919; Cuban missile crisis, and treaty banning atmospheric testing, 932–933; first Strategic Arms Limitation Treaty (SALT I), 963–964, 995; in Carter's presidency, SALT II stalls in Senate, 995; during Reagan's presidency, USSR and U.S. disagree over control of nuclear armaments and over Strategic Defense Initiative, 1002–1003; Reagan and Mikhail Gorbachev effect treaty eliminating intermediate nuclear forces, 1009

Nullification, 315–317

Nye, Gerald P., 843

O

Oberlin College, 353, 366

Ochs, Phil, 981

Office of Economic Opportunity (OEO), 936

Office of Price Administration, 856

Ogden, Aaron, 274

Oglethorpe, James, 85

Ohio Company, 172

Ohio idea, 518

Okinawa, battle of, 872

Oklahoma (present state of), destination of removed Indians, 307; farming in the Cherokee Strip, 576–577
Oklahoma City bombing, 979–981
Old Joseph, 565
"Old Lights," 90–91
Olds, R. E., 699
Olive Branch Petition, 139
Oliver, Andrew, 119
Oliver, James, 611
Olmsted, Frederick Law, 737
Olney, Richard, 533, 668–669
Omnibus Crime Bill, 941
Oñate, Juan de, 56
O'Neale, Peggy, see Eaton, Peggy
Oneida community, 348–349
Onis, Luis de, 290
Open Door policy toward China, formation and purposes, 680–681, 750; signatories to Nine-Power Pact agree to respect, 792; expansionist Japan threatens, 851–852
Open hearth furnace for steel, 696
Open shop, 535, 777
Operation TORCH, 862
Order of the Star-Spangled Banner, 429
Orders in Council, 233, 235
Oregon, Treaty of 1818, 288; annexation of, 397–398
Organization of Petroleum Exporting Countries (OPEC), 992
Ortega, Daniel, 1001, 1009–1010
Osage, 381
Osceola, Chief, 310
Ostend Manifesto, 419–420
O'Sullivan, John L., 397, 419
Oswald, Lee Harvey, 933
Otis, Harrison Gray, 267
Otis, James, 117
Ottawa (Indians), 115, 173
Ottoman Empire, 12
OVERLORD, 865
Overman Act, 757
Owen, Robert, 347
Owen, Robert Dale, 347, 348

P

Pacific Railroad bill, 423, 554
Packenham, Sir Edward, 246
Page, Thomas Nelson, 584
Paine, Thomas, Common Sense, 140

Paiute, 560
Pakenham, Sir Edward, 246
Palestine, Palestinian guerrillas, 965; agreement between Israel and Egypt leaves unresolved the fate of Palestinian refugees, 995–996; in 1982, Israel invades Lebanon seeking bases of Palestine Liberation Organization (PLO), 1002; attends Madrid peace conference, 1016
Palestine Liberation Organization (PLO), 1002, 1016
Palmer, A. Mitchell, 775, 777
Palmer raids, 777
Pan-Africanism, 785
Panama, U.S., seeking canal route, supports independence, 655–658; U.S. pays Colombia indemnity for Panama, 658, 793; U.S. returns Canal Zone to Panama, 993; also see Panama Canal
Panama Canal, 655–658, 681, 740, 750, 993
Panama Congress, 296–297
Panay incident, 848
Panic of 1819, 270–271
Panic of 1837, 323–324
Panic of 1857, 430, 433
Panic of 1893, 519, 728
Paper money, see Currency
Paris, Treaty of (1763), 114; Treaty of, at end of Spanish-American War, 676
Paris accords, 918
Parker, Alton B., 735
Parker, Bonnie, 832
Parks, Rosa, 914–915
Parton, James, 591
Pasteur, Louis, 594
Paterson, William, 187
Patriot classes in American Revolution, 135
Patrons of Husbandry, see Grange
Patton, General George, 857, 863
Paul, Alice, 705, 764
Paulus, General, 862
Pawnee, 381
Paxton Boys, 115
Payne-Aldrich tariff, 742, 743
Peabody, Endicott, 812
Peace Corps, 930, 933, 936
Peace Democrats, 453, 637
Peale, Charles, 176
Peale, Norman Vincent, 925
Peek, George N., 791

Peirce, Charles Sanders, 648
Pelly, William Dudley, 821
Pendleton, George, 518
Pendleton civil service reform, 635
Peninsula Campaign in Civil War, 458
Penn, William, 54–56, 80, 81–82
Pensions for Union veterans, as political issue, 636, 637
Pentagon Papers, 972
Pequot War, 47–49
Peralta, Don Pedro de, 56
Percy, George, 40
Perkins, Frances, 814
Perkins, George, 710
Perot, Ross, 1018, 1019, 1022
Perry, Commodore Matthew, 420, 658
Perry, Oliver Hazard, 239, 240
Pershing, General John J., 752, 760
Pershing missiles, 1003, 1009
Personal liberty laws, 395, 436
Peru, Johnson's administration, 964
Pet banks, 322, 325
Petersburg, in Civil War, 477
Phagan, Mary, 602
Philadelphia, site of Constitutional Convention, 185–188; in 1800, 226
Philadelphia and Reading railroad, 524, 531
Philip II of Spain, 30, 31
Philippine Government Act, 679
Philippines, Admiral Dewey seizes Manila Bay, 673–674; U.S. acquires, 676–677; Americans impose rule on islands, 677–679; William Howard Taft as governor general, 740; Tydings-McDuffie Act provides for independence, 679; Japanese seize, 855; Americans land, in WWII, 869
Photography, photography as instrument of analysis and art, 718–719, 832–833
Pickering, Timothy, 208, 225
Pickett, General George, 468–469
Pickford, Mary, 631
Pierce, Franklin, 418, 420, 428
Pilgrims, 41
Pinchot, Gifford, 739, 742–743
Pinckney, Charles Cotesworth, 206, 232
Pinckney, Thomas, 202–203, 205
Pinckney Treaty, 202–203
Piñeda, see Alvarez de Piñeda

Pingree, Hazen, 702, 703

Pinkerton detective agency, agent James McParlan engaged to infiltrate Molly Maguires, 531; Pinkertons hired to break Homestead strike, 533, 534–535

Pitcairn, Major John, 134

Pitcher, Molly, 151

Pitt, William, 115; calls for repeal of Stamp Act, 121; argues against imposing punitive measures on colonists, 130

Pittsburgh, at turn of nineteenth century, 227

Pizarro, Francisco, 27–28

Plague, in Europe, 13

Plains, 555–560; Plains Indians, 8, 33, 371, 560–561, and relations with whites, 549–550, 562–564, 565–566

Plains of Abraham, 109–111

Platt, Orville H., 731

Platt Amendment, 680

Plessy v. Ferguson, 584, 913

Plunkitt, George Washington, 702

Pocahontas, 37–38

Poe, Edgar Allan, 254, 362

Poindexter, John, 1008

Poland, Hitler exploits presence of German minority, 845, 846; Nazi Germany and the USSR invade, 847; Warsaw uprising, 866–867; Moscow and President Truman dispute future of, 880, 881; Poznan, 919; Communist regime falls, 1011

Poles as American ethnicity, 593, 599, 600, 604–605, 712, 713, 716, 717

Political action committees (PACs), 998

Political theory in colonial period, 121

Polk, James K., 397–403, 419

Pollock v. Farmers' Loan and Trust Company, 542

Polo, Marco, 12

Ponce de León, Juan, 23

Pontiac, Ottawa chief, 115

Pools, form of industrial concentration, 521, 543

Pope, General John, 458, 463

Pope Leo XIII, *Rerum Novarum*, 651

Popular Front, 822, 847

Popular sovereignty, 422–423, 431–432

Populism (People's Party), formation, 615–616; in election of 1892,

616–617, 639; in election of 1896, 643

Port Huron Statement, 957, 983

Porter, Peter, 233–234

Portugal, early explorations, 21–23; enters North Atlantic Treaty Organization, 887

Post, Louis F., 777

Potawatomi, 310

Potsdam conference, 880

Pottawatomie Creek, John Brown at, 424, 438

Pound, Ezra, 783

Powderly, Terence, 530

Powell, General Colin, 1014

Powell, John Wesley, 738

Powell, Lewis, 969

Powhatan Confederacy, 61

Poznan, Polish revolt, 919

Pragmatism, 648

Preparedness measures, before American entrance into World War I, 756

Presbyterians, 101

Prescott, Colonel William, 136

President, 235

Presley, Elvis, 924

Preston, Captain Thomas, 127–128

Prevost, Sir George, 241–242

Prigg v. Pennsylvania, 395

Printing, beginnings of, 13

Prisoner of war issue, at Vietnam peace talks, 967

Prisons, reform of, 354

Pritchett, Laurie, 927

Proclamation of 1763, 115–116, 117

Proctor, Redfield, 672

Professionalization of work, 341, 537–539

Progressive education, 648

Progressivism, social and cultural sources, 689–721 *passim*; progressive politics, 725–749 *passim*

Prohibition, *see* Temperance and prohibition

Prophet, The, 234

Prussia, 867

Ptolemy, 10

Public Works Administration (PWA), 817

Puerto Rico, 679–681, 750, 842, 911

Pujo, Arsene, heads House investigation of banking, 694, 747

Pullman cars, 514, 533, 633, 699, 783, 830

Pullman strike, 533, 633

Pure Food and Drug Act, 737

Puritans, 41–49

Putman, Israel, 136

Q

Qaddafi, Muammar, 1007

Quakers, 54–56, 59, 80, 81–82, 101; opposition to slavery, 89; education of freed blacks, 497

Quartering Acts and quartering, 122, 124, 125–126

Quayle, Daniel, 1010, 1018

Quebec (city), taken by British, 109–111, 114

Quebec Act, 131–132

Queen Anne's War, *see* Spanish Succession, War of

Quetzalcoatl, 26

Quincy, Josiah, 128, 165

Quitman, John A., 419

R

Race riots, 481, 585, 711, 776

Radical Republicans, during Civil War call for emancipation, 459; at end of war, seek thorough reconstruction of South, 488; Radical Reconstruction, 490–493; Reconstruction governments, 498; in Louisiana, 482

Radio, opens the hinterland, 787

Radio Act, 787

Ragtime, 629–630

Rail Act, 994

Rail Administration, 757

Railroad brotherhoods, 710, 883

Railroads, early, 258; transcontinental, 421–422; Union Pacific and Crédit Mobilier, 502; railroads in the West in late nineteenth century, 552–555; early twentieth century passenger service, 698

Raleigh, Walter, 30–31, 38–39

Randolph, A. Phillip, 783

Randolph, Edmund, 186, 189–190, 196, 198

Randolph, John, 232

Raskob, John J., 796

Rath, Ernst vom, 837

Rationing, 757, 856

Rauschenbusch, Walter, 650

Reagan, Ronald, in 1976 primaries, 992; in campaign of 1980, 995, 998; support on the right, 997–998; domestic policy, 998–1001; Central America, 1001–1002; bombing of marine barracks in Lebanon, and invasion of Grenada, 1002; relations with Soviet Union, 1002–1003; election of 1984, 1006–1007; Iran-Contra, 1007–1008; friendship with Gorbachev, 1009; the affluent in the 1980s, 1003–1004, 1008–1009

Reaganomics, 998, 1000

Reaper, 262

Recall of officials, 727

Reclamation of lands, 559, 817, 833

Reclamation Service, and Newlands Act, 559

Reconcentration camps, in Cuba, 670, 672

Reconstruction, question of congressional authority, 484; Lincoln's ten-percent plan, 485–486; Wade-Davis Bill, 486; Freedmen's Bureau, 486, 488–489, 495, 496, 497, 499–500; black codes, 488; Johnson's plans, 487–488, 489; Fourteenth Amendment, 489–490; Military Reconstruction Act, 490; quest among freed slaves for education, 489, 495–496, 497; black family and community, 494–496; political leadership, 496; Fifteenth Amendment, 497–498; Reconstruction governments in South, 498–499; end of Reconstruction, 502–503

Reconstruction Finance Corporation (RFC), 798

Red Scare, after World War I, 634, 774–776, 777–778 (Palmer raids), 780, 822; after World War II, second Red Scare begins, 896; also see McCarthy, Joseph

Reformation, 14–15

Reformed (faith), 103

Refugee bill, 838

Rehnquist, William, 969

Reich, Charles, 892

Religion, revivalism, 175; antebellum religion and reform, 264–265, 328, 339, 349–350; perfectionism,

342; evangelical religion among slave and freed blacks, 495–496; in civil-rights movement, 915 (Martin Luther King, Jr., at Montgomery), 926–927, 928 (March on Washington), also see Nonviolence; religious right, 997; for other entries involving religion, see Roman Catholicism; Puritanism; Antislavery; Great Awakening; Social reform; entries under specific denominations

Remington company, 511

Renaissance, 13–14

Reno, Milo, 822

Reparations, required of Germany after World War I, 773, 797–798, 799–800

Republican Party (first), beliefs, 203–204, also see Jefferson; adopts Federalist policies, 247

Republican Party (second), formed, 428; in 1856, nominates Frémont, 429–430; fuses antislavery position with an activist federal economics, 432–433; in 1860, nominates Lincoln, 437–438; in 1864, merges into Union Party, 476; nineteenth-century party of active federal government, 476, 490–491; also see Radical Republicans

Republicanism as mentality, 165–166, 264–265

Reservations, Indian, 563–565, 567, 576, 915, 988

Resettlement Administration, 820

Retail outlets, 522

Reuben James, 851

Reuther, Walter, 883

Revenue Act of 1764, 116–117

Revere, Paul, 128, 132, 134

Revivalism, 175, 264

Rhode Island, founded, 46; charter colony, 52; Dorr's rebellion of, 341

Rhythm and blues, 921, 923–924

Ribicoff, Abraham, 962

Rice, plantations in South, 83–85

Richmond, in Civil War, 453, 470, 477, 486

Riesman, David, 922–923

Rillieux, Robert, 262, 263

Ripley, George, and Brook Farm, 348

Ritchie, Jean, 981

Rittenhouse, David, 92

Roanoke colony, 39

Robertson, Roy W., 806

Robin Moor, 851

Robinson, Jo Ann, 914

Robinson, Robert T., 826

Rock music, 921, 922, 923–924, 956, 981, 982

Rockefeller, John D., 521, 732

Rockefeller, Nelson, 962, 970

Rockingham, Marquis of, 121

Roe v. Wade, 969, 1005

Roebling, John, 609

Rogers, Edith Nourse, 838

Rogers, William P., 963

Rolfe, John, 40

Rolling Stones, 985

Rolling Thunder, 945, 954

Roman Catholicism, confronted by Reformation, 12, 28; nativist hostility to, 328, 351, 359–360, 601, 638, 779, 780, 781; Catholic opposition to prohibitionism as cultural force, 779, 780, 796; John F. Kennedy's Catholicism in election of 1960, 925–926

Romanians as American ethnicity, 717

Rommel, General Edwin, 855, 862, 866

Roosevelt, Eleanor, 813–814, 879

Roosevelt, Franklin D., background and character, 811–812; assistant secretary of the navy, 812; governor of New York, 805, 812–813; New Deal, 814–821 passim; election in 1936 to a second term, 824–825; foreign policy in interwar period, 840–843; opposition to isolationism, 848–851; decision to seek third term, 849–850; as wartime President, 852–871 passim

Roosevelt, Theodore, rancher, 575; governor of New York, 731; leads Rough Riders in war with Spain, 675–676; becomes President, 729; foreign policy, 656–658 (acquires Panama Canal Zone), 681–685; domestic policy, 726, 731–740; trusts, 732–733; conservation, 737–740; reelected in 1904, 735; New Nationalism, 743, 745; candidate of Progressive Party in 1912, 744–745

Roosevelt Corollary to Monroe Doctrine, 684–685

Root, Elihu, 751
Root-Takahira agreement, 683, 750
Rosenberg, Julius and Ethel, 897
Rosie the Riveter, 856
Ross, Edward A., 715
Ross, Harriet, 416–418
Rostow, Walt, 963
Roszak, Theodore, 982
Roth, Henry, 601
Rough Riders, 675, 731, 737
Rovere, Richard, 898
Ruby Ridge, 980
Ruckelshaus, William, 1005
Ruffin, Edmund, 449–450
Ruffin, Josephine St. Pierre, 704
Ruhr, 793
Rundstedt, Karl Rudolf Gerd von, 866
Rural Electrification Administration (REA), 820
Rush, Dr. Benjamin, 222
Rush, Richard, and Rush-Bagot agreement, 288
Russia, probes southward from Alaska, 291; U.S. purchases Alaska, 659; Russo-Japanese War, 682–683; the eastern front in World War I, and Russian defeat, 759; democratic revolutionary government overthrown by Bolsheviks, 759; *also see* Soviet Union
Russian-American Company, 291, 659
Russians as American ethnicity, 593, 712
Ryan, Fr. John, 627, 651

S

Sacajawea, on Lewis and Clark expedition, 223
Sacco, Nicola, 778
Sadat, Anwar, 991–992, 995
Saddam Hussein, 1012, 1013, 1015
Sage Brush Rebellion, 1005
Sahara, 15, 17
St. Augustine, Florida, 29
St. Cecilia Society, 175
Salem witchcraft, 71–74
Salutary neglect and its ending, 115
Sam, Vilbrum, 751
San Juan Hill, 675; *also see* Kettle Hill
San Martín, José de, 291
Sand Creek massacre, 563

Sanders, George N., 399
Sandinistas, *see* Nicaragua
Sanger, Margaret, 705
Santa Anna, *see* López de Santa Ana
Santa Clara Co. v. Southern Pacific Railroad, 542
Santo Domingo, 660; *also see* Dominican Republic
Saratoga, battle of, 155
Saratoga, 241
Saudi Arabia, 1012, 1013, 1015
Savings and loan troubles, 1003–1004, 1006, 1010
Savo Island, battle of, 861
Sawyer, Dianne, 1005
Scalawags, 492, 498
Scandinavians as American ethnicities, 376–377
Scarlet Letter, 362
Schechter v. United States, 819, 825
Schmeling, Max, 831
Schuyler, General Philip, 138
Schwarzkopf, General Norman, 1014
Schwerner, Michael, 939
Scientific management, 695–696, 708
Scopes, John, 780
Scotch-Irish as American ethnicity, 79; frontiersmen, 115 (Paxton boys)
Scott, Dred, 431; *also see Dred Scott v. Sandford*
Scott, Winfield, in War of 1812, 239, 241; removal of Indians, 307; ordered to put down nullification, 318; Whig nominee in 1852, 427–428; devises Union anaconda strategy, 450–451
Seale, Bobby, 970
Sears, Roebuck and Company, 524, 593, 631, 697
Secession of southern states, 444–445; South defines Constitution as compact among states, 445–446; second wave of secession, 450
Second Bank of the United States, established, 247, 267; intended to control flow of paper, 269–270; issues own paper, 270; panic of 1819, 271–272; Nicholas Biddle takes over, 272–273; hostility over, 319–321; Jackson destroys, 321–323
Second Confiscation Act of 1862, 459, 460
Second Continental Congress, 137–138, 139, 166; Declaration

of Independence, 140–143; seeks French aid, 139, 166; issues paper money, 166
Second Great Awakening, 342–343
Second hundred days, 819–821
Second party system, 298–299, 303, 328, 332–333
Second Treatise of Civil Government, 65
Securities and Exchange Commission (SEC), 818
Sedition Act (during U.S. participation in World War I), 762, 775
Seminole, 88; Andrew Jackson presses in Florida, 290
Seminole War, 310
Seneca Falls Woman's Rights Convention, 337–339, 355
Separatism, 41
Sequoyah, 308, 309
Serapis, 149, 157
Serbs as American ethnicity, 593, 600; in Bosnian War, 1021; Kosovo, 1024
Settlement houses, 607, 646, 703, 714, 715
Sewall, Samuel, 63, 75, 89
Seward, William, Anti-Mason, 327; a leader of young Republican Party, 434; Lincoln's secretary of state, 449
Seymour, Horatio, 635
Shakers, 343
Shantung, 772
Share Our Wealth, 823
Sharecropping, 500–501, 527, 551, 577, 582–583
Shawnee, 173
Shays, Daniel, and Shays's Rebellion, 183–185
Shenandoah Valley, in Civil War, 475
Sheridan, General Philip, 475, 477, 658
Sherman, Roger, 140
Sherman, General William Tecumseh, at Shiloh, 456; march through the South, 475–476, 477; allots confiscated lands to freed slaves, 499
Sherman Antitrust Act, 543–544, 729, 732, 741, 748
Sherman Silver Purchase Act, 519, 640
Shiloh, battle of, 456–457
Shipping Board, 774

Shirley, Governor William, 114

Shoshone, 560

Sibley, Colonel Henry, 563

Sierra Club, 738

Silver currency, as late nineteenth-century political issue, 518–519, 614; Populists advocate free coinage, 615–616; Grover Cleveland supports gold, 640–641; William Jennings Bryan fights for silver, 642–645; gold Democrats split with Bryan wing of party, 643; urban workers and some farmers unattracted to silver, 638

Silver Shirts, 821

Simon Slugs (character by Johnson Hooper), 363

Sinai, 920, 992, 995

Sinclair, Upton, 725–726, 737, 822

Sioux, 561, 563, 564, 566, 567, 989

Sirhan Bishara Sirhan, 961

Sirica, 972, 973

Sit-down strikes, 827

Sitting Bull, 509, 564

Sixteenth Amendment, 542, 742, 747

Slavery, early slavery trade, 4, 19–20, 40; in colonial times, 83, 85, 86–89; colonial slave women, 97–98; and American Revolution, 147–149; freedom offered to slaves who desert patriot masters and join loyalists, 139; after American Revolution, 161–162; and Northwest Ordinance, 161, 364; foreign slave trade forbidden as of 1808, 283; cotton and cotton gin revive slavery, 284–285; Missouri Compromise, 285–286; South tightens institution, 286–287; *Amistad* incident, 331–332; life in the South, 383–385; profitability of, 385–386; and race control, 387–388; and black family, 387–388; and "gag" rule, 389–390; in the West, 393–394; personal liberty laws, 436; in 1833, Kansas-Nebraska and Bleeding Kansas, 423–425; emancipation, 459–460; *also see* Abolitionism; Antislavery

Slavs as American ethnicities, 593, 600, 602, 604, 713, 716, 717

Slidell, John, 399–400, 457

Slovaks as American ethnicity, 600, 717

Smallpox, 3, 26, 32

Smith, Adam, 325, 524

Smith, Alfred E., on New York State Factory Investigation Commission, 692; object of anti-Catholicism, 781, 795–796; in campaign of 1928, 795–796; in 1932, Franklin D. Roosevelt defeats for Democratic nomination, 811; foe of New Deal, 822; contrast between Smith's and John F. Kennedy's handling of issue of Catholicism, 926

Smith, Bessie, 770

Smith, Erminnie, 536

Smith, Gerald L. K., 823, 824

Smith, John, 37–38, 40

Smith, Joseph, and Mormons, 343–344, 360

Smith, Seba, 363

Smith-Lever Act, 748

Snake (Indians), 560

Snyder, Gary, 923

Social Darwinism, 525, 648, 650, 660, 661

Social Democratic Party, 633

Social Gospel, 592, 650–651, 692

Social reform, 261, 266, 328, 350; evangelical religion and reform, 264–265, 328; perceptions of society among antebellum reformers, 349–350, 352; varieties of reform, 350–358; science of reform in antebellum days, 354–355; antebellum women as reformers, 355–356; professionalization of social work, 537–539; late nineteenth-century responses to prostitution, 605–606; Women's Christian Temperance Union, 645–646; settlement houses, 646–647; *also see* Antislavery; Temperance and prohibition

Social Security, 820, 826, 827–828, 890, 892, 935, 937

Socialism, 632–634; antagonism between democratic socialism and state Communism, 822; *also see* Eugene Debs, Red Scare, Norman Thomas

Society and social practice, in colonial settlements, 44–46, 49–50, 74–77, 83, 93–94, 95–98, 102–104; during the Revolution and its aftermath, 164, 174–177; backcountry in 1800, 227–229; social stratification in era of Jackson, 302; democratization of dress and manners, 341–342; public education and spread of middle-class behavior, 352; antebellum southern whites, 382–383; social life among antebellum slaves, 384, 387; black family and society before and after Civil War, 494–496; among Indians of the West during the nineteenth century, 560–561; on the mining frontier, 569–571; on the cattlemen's frontier, 572–574; among the wealthy in the late nineteenth and early twentieth centuries, 591–592, 695; squalor of late nineteenth-century cities, 595; condition of the urban poor in the late nineteenth century, 594–596, 605; urban electrical transportation changes the composition of cities, 596–597, 599; suburbs at the turn of the twentieth century, 597, 599; life among the new-immigrant ethnicities, 599–601, 603–605, 712–714; city prostitution, 605–606; emergence of participatory and spectator sports by the end of the nineteenth century, 625–628; entertainments and lectures in the late nineteenth and early twentieth centuries, 628–632, 698; middle-class consumer society by the early twentieth century, 697–698; assimilation of immigrant ethnicities to mass culture, 716–718; radio makes for a common culture, 787, 829–830; Great Depression affects character of family life, 808–809; the wealthy during the Depression, 810; leisure and entertainment during the Depression, 829–831; entertainment and fads during World War II, 860–861; suburbs after World War II, 909–910; consumerism and mass culture, 922–923, 924; the beats, 923;

counterculture, 981–982; wealth and the affluent in the 1980s, 1003–1004; underclass in the 1980s, 1004–1005; *also see* Women

Society of Friends, *see* Quakers

Solidarity, Polish resistance to Communist state, 1001

Somalia, 1019–1020

Somoza, Anastasio, 1001

Sons of Liberty, 118, 119–120, 121, 124, 128, 134

Soulé, Pierre, 419

South Carolina, and nullification, 315–317; secedes, 444–445

Southeast Asia Treaty Organization (SEATO), 949–950

Southern agrarians, 517

Southern Commercial Convention, 433

Southern Pacific railroad, 542, 552, 554

Southworth, Mrs. E.D.E.N., 363

Soviet Union, Communists establish, 778; Popular Front strategy, 822; pact with Nazi Germany, 846–847; invasion of Finland, 847; in Allied camp, 862–863, 866–867; Tehran, 863, 865; Yalta, 870–871; Potsdam, 880–881; dominates eastern Europe, 883–884; attempt to seal off Berlin foiled by airlift, 886–887; Soviet Union gains nuclear explosive, 895; aftermath of Stalin, 918; suppresses Hungarian rebellion, 919–920; supports East German sealing off of East Berlin and building of wall, 931; Cuban missile crisis, 932; invasion of Afghanistan, 996; under Gorbachev, eases repression and achieves détente with West, 1009–1010; end of Soviet Union, 1015–1016

Space exploration, Sputnik, 920; moon landing, 970–971

Spain, 1; and slavery, 4; early explorations, 23–28; settlements, 56–57; closes New Orleans port, 169–170; Pinckney Treaty temporarily opens New Orleans, 202–203; cedes Louisiana to France, 222–223; in Adams-Onis Treaty, cedes Florida to U.S., 290; slave ship *Amistad* seized,

331–332; Spain in Cuba, 669–670; war spirit in U.S., and *Maine*, 670–673; war with U.S., 673–677; Spain loses Cuba, Puerto Rico, Guam, and Philippines, 676–677, 679; fascism, 844; civil war, 845, and Communist treatment of anti-fascist allies, 847

Spanish-American War, 673–677

Spanish Armada, 31

Spanish Succession, War of, 112

Specie Circular, 323, 324

Spoils system, 302

Spokane (Indians), 381

Sports, 606, 625, 627–628, 730, 787, 831

Spot resolution, 402

Sprague, Frank L., 597

Spruance, Admiral Raymond A., 861, 867

Sputniks, 916, 917, 920, 922

Stalin, Joseph, President Franklin D. Roosevelt approaches Soviet Union, 840–841; ruthlessness, 844; pact with Hitler, 846–847; at Tehran, 863, 865; halts advance into Poland and Nazis crush Warsaw revolt, 867; desires German industrial plants, 870; at Yalta, 870–871; at Potsdam, 880–881; wants compliant regimes in eastern Europe, 883–884; pressures Turkey for control of Bosporus Straits, 885; fears resurgent Germany, 886; effort to cut off Berlin foiled by airlift, 886–887; boycotting United Nations security council at time UN votes to resist North Korea, 899; death, 918, 949

Stalingrad, battle of, 862, 866

Stamp Act, 117–121, 122

Stamp Act Congress, 118, 120–121

Stanton, Edwin M., 493–494

Stanton, Elizabeth Cady, 337, 338, 357, 497–498

Staple Act (1663), 58

"Star-Spangled Banner," 242, 363

Star Wars, *see* Strategic Defense Initiative

Starr, Ellen Gates, 646

Starr, Kenneth, 1023

Statue of Liberty, 508

Steam engine, 263, 508, 509

Steamboats, 256–257

Steel, Bessemer process, 512, 514, 609, 696–697; open hearth furnace, 696–697

Steel plow, 262

Steffens, Lincoln, 702, 706, 707

Stein, Gertrude, 783

Stephens, Alexander, becomes Vice President of Confederacy, 445; elected to Congress, 488

Steuben, Baron von, 150

Stevens, John L., 667

Stevens, Thaddeus, 327; Radical, 488, 490

Stevenson, Adlai, 902, 917

Stieglitz, Alfred, 718

Stimson, Henry L., 800

Stone, Lucy, 357, 497–498

Stono Rebellion, 85

Stowe, Harriet Beecher, 353, 409–411

Strait of Magellan, 25

Strasser, Adolph, 530

Strategic Arms Limitation (SALT I and SALT II) talks, 963–964, 966, 995, 998

Strategic Defense Initiative (SDI), 1003

Strong, Josiah, 664

Stuart, Gilbert, 176

Student Nonviolent Coordinating Committee (SNCC), 938–939

Students for a Democratic Society (SDS), 956–958, 983

Sturm, John, 377

Stuyvesant, Peter, 53

Submarine warfare, in World War I, 759, 762, 843

Suburbs, 597, 599, 909–910

Sudetenland, 845, 846

Suez, 655, 855, 920

Suffolk Resolves, 132

Sugar Act of 1733, 77; of 1764, 116–117, 121

Sullivan, John L., 627

Sullivan, Louis, 609, 696, 719

Sumner, Charles, 425; "Appeal of the Independent Democrats," 428; Radical Republican, 488, 490

Sun Dance, 561

Sung dynasty, 10

Supreme Court, judicial review, 125; *Marbury v. Madison*, 221–222; *Gibbons v. Ogden*, 256, 274–275; *Dartmouth College v. Woodward*, 273; Marshall and economic

Supreme Court—*(continued)* nationalism, 273–275; *McCulloch v. Maryland*, 274; Taney and economic authority of states, 326; *Dred Scott v. Sandford*, 430, 431–432; *Plessy v. Ferguson*, 584, 913; judgments of state and federal economic and social legislation in late nineteenth and early twentieth centuries, 542 and 613 (*Munn v. Illinois*), 542 (*Santa Clara Co. v. Southern Pacific Railroad; Wabash, St. Louis and Pacific Railroad Company v. Illinois;* and *Pollock v. Farmers' Loan and Trust Company*), 543 (*Maximum Freight Rate* case), 544 and 732 (*United States v. E. C. Knight*), 544 (*Lochner v. New York*), 544 and 649 (*Muller v. Oregon*), 790 (*Bailey v. Drexel Furniture Company* and *Adkins v. Children's Hospital*); on restriction on dissent during World War I, 763; conflict with New Deal legislation, 819, 825–826; *Brown v. Board of Education of Topeka*, 913; Warren Court, 912–913, 940–941; *also see individual decisions*

Sussex, 755

Sutter, John, 399

Syngman Rhee, 899

Syria, 1016

Syrians as American ethnicity, 603, 713, 717

T

Taft, Robert A., favors public housing, 883; Taft-Hartley Act, 889, 891, 892; defeated for Republican nomination in 1948, 890; as isolationist, opposes alliance against Moscow, 887; charges that Communist victory in China was connected to sympathizers in State Department, 894–895; endorses Joseph McCarthy, 898; speaks of sufferers under Communism, 900; competes with Dwight D. Eisenhower for Republican nomination in 1952, 901–902

Taft, William Howard, first governor general of Philippines, 740;

service to Theodore Roosevelt, 740–741; in 1908, elected President, 741; a reformist President, 741–742; policy toward rest of Hemisphere, 750; Ballinger-Pinchot controversy, 742–743; Roosevelt turns against, 743; election of 1912, 744–745

Taft-Hartley Act, 889, 890, 891, 892

Taiwan, 863, 894, 899, 900, 965–966

Talleyrand, Charles Maurice de, Louisiana Purchase, 223, 287

Tallmadge, James, and Tallmadge Amendment, 285–286

Tammany Hall, 607, 780, 795

Taney, Roger B., 326; supports President Jackson on Second Bank, 322; *Dred Scott* decision, 431–432

Tappan, Arthur, 366, 389, 390

Tappan, Lewis, 366, 390

Tarbell, Ida, 706

Tariff of 1816, 247, 267, 268, 281; of 1818, 269; of 1824, 316–317; of 1828, 316–317; of 1832, 316–319; of 1833, 319; Morrill tariff of 1861, 452; Wilson-Gorman tariff of 1894 (attempts to levy income tax), 542; McKinley tariff of 1890, 636; Payne-Aldrich tariff of 1909, 742; Underwood tariff (includes income tax made possible by Sixteenth Amendment), 747; Fordney-McCumber tariff of 1922, 788

Tarleton, Banastre, 157

Tax Reform Act, 1007

Taylor, Frederick Winslow, and Taylorism, 695–696

Taylor, General Maxwell, 930, 952

Taylor, Zachary, 399–400, 402, 404–405, 411

Tea Act, 129–130

Teapot Dome, 788

Technology and science, cotton gin, 227, 262, 263, 284; Monticello as embodiment of applied technology, 218–219; Erie Canal advances engineering knowledge, 253; steamboats, 256–257; reasons for invention in early republic, 261–262; technology perceived as expression of virtue, 264–265; inventors and important inventions 1793–1859, 262, 263; interchangeable parts, 262, 263,

264; steam engine, 508, 509; steel, Bessemer process, 512, 514, 609, 696–697, and open hearth furnace, 696–697; education and research in agriculture, 452 and 610–611; George Washington Carver's experimentation in agricultural products, 581; Hatch Act establishes agricultural experimental stations, 611; assembly line, 695, 696; perfecting the detail of work, 695–696 (Frederick Winslow Taylor); hydroelectric power and electric motors, 696; automobiles, 696, 699–700; chemistry in the late nineteenth and early twentieth centuries, 696–697; consumer technology in the late nineteenth and early twentieth centuries, 697–698; photography, as enhancement of leisure, 698, and as an instrument of analysis and art, 718–719, 832–833; early aircraft, 793–794 (Charles Lindbergh); radio, 787; silent movies and first talkies, 630–631, 787–788; consumer technology after World War II, 922; *also see* Railroads; Nuclear power; Space exploration

Tecumseh, 234–235, 240

Telephone, as invention, 509, 511

Temperance and prohibition, antebellum temperance movement, 350–352; connections with nativism and anti-Catholicism, 351, 779, 780; Women's Christian Temperance League, 645–646; prohibition during the nation's engagement in World War I, 757, 759, 779; Eighteenth Amendment, 757, 759, 778–779, 779–780 (effects); hostility to big-city culture, 779; opposition to Amendment, 779, 780, 795; repeal, 780, 818

Ten percent plan, 485

Tenements, 595–596, 605, 608, 713–714, 717, 909

Tennessee Coal and Iron dispute, 740, 743

Tennessee Valley Authority (TVA), 816–817, 935

Tenochtitlán, 3, 26

Tenure of Office Act, 493–494

Teresa, Empress of Brazil, 508
Tertium Quids, 232
Test Ban Treaty, 933
Tet offensive in Vietnam, 945–947, 959
Texas, war for independence, 371–374; annexation of, 396–397; *also see* Battle of the Alamo
Thames, battle of, 235
Thirteenth Amendment, 460, 486, 488
Thomas, Clarence, 1017
Thomas, Gabriel, 54
Thomas, General George H., 475
Thomas, Jesse B., 286
Thomas, Norman, 764, 822
Thompson, Jacob, 448
Thoreau, Henry David, 400, 402
Three Mile Island, 993
Threshing machine, 611
Thurmond, Strom, 891, 892
Tiananmen Square, 1020–1021
Tierra del Fuego, 25
Tilden, Samuel J., 502–503, 635
Tillman, Benjamin, 642
Time Inc. v. Hill, 962
Tin Pan Alley, 629
Tippecanoe Creek, battle of, 234, 237
Tituba, 72, 73
To Secure These Rights, 891
Tobacco, 58–60, 83, 88–89
Tobacco Control Act, 818
Tocqueville, Alexis de, 254, 302, 354
Todd, Dolley, *see* Madison, Dolley
Tories (in North America), 119, 126, 133, 135, 139
Toussaint L'Ouverture, 224, 297
Tower, John, 1008
Townsend, Francis F., 823–824
Townshend, Charles, 117–118, 122–124
Townshend duties, 122–124
Trade, *see* Commerce
Trail of Tears, 307–310
Transcendentalism, 348
Transcontinental railroad, antebellum North and South quarrel over route, 553–554; Congress during Civil War adopts plan, 452; construction, 551–552; Mormon leaders, fearing the road will bring settlers outside the faith, grant women the vote, 579; Secretary of State Seward sees road as a route into the Pacific and Asia, 659

Transportation revolution, 251–258, 267–268
Travis, William Barret, 372–373
Treaty of 1818 with Britain, 288
Treaty of Fort Laramie, 563
Treaty of Fort Stanwix, 162
Treaty of Greenville, 162
Treaty of Guadalupe Hidalgo, 402–403
Treaty of New Echota, 307
Treaty of Paris 1763, 114; (1783), 159
Treaty of Tordesillas 1494, 28
Trent Affair, 457
Trenton, 154
Triangle Shirtwaist fire, 689–692
Trinity Church, 591–592
Tripartite Pact, 853
Trist, Nicholas P., 402
Trotter, William Monroe, 586
Troup, George, 296
Troy Seminary, 353
Truman, Harry S, senator and Vice President, 879–880; becomes President on death of FDR, 879; Potsdam, 880–881; demobilization and early domestic policy, 882–883; establishes policy of containing Communism, 884–888; veto of Taft-Hartley overridden, 889; liberal domestic policy in first term, 889–890, 891–892; whistle-stop campaign of 1948, 891; Fair Deal in second term, 892–893; policy for Far East, 893–895; begins system of loyalty boards to search for subversives in government, 896; Korean War, 898–900; dismisses General MacArthur, 900
Truman Doctrine, 885
Trumbull, John, 176
Trusts, as form of industrial concentration, 521, 543
Truth, Sojourner, 358
Tubman, Harriet, 416–418
Tugwell, Rexford, 814, 842
Turkey, 715, 753, 885
Turner, Frederick Jackson, and frontier thesis, 579, 661
Turner, Nat, 213, 317, 366, 387, 388
Turnpikes, 255–256
Twain, Mark, *see* Clemens, Samuel L.
Tweed, William Marcy, 607, 608
Twenty-first Amendment, 780, 818
Twenty-fourth Amendment, 938
Tydings, Millard, 898

Tydings-McDuffie Act, 679
Tyler, John, Harrison's running mate in 1840, 329; becomes President after Harrison's death, 395–396; and annexation of Texas, 396–397; chairman of Washington Peace Convention, 448

U

Ukraine, 1015
Ulstermen, 79
Uncle Tom's Cabin, 409–411
Underground railroad, 393, 417
Union Pacific Railroad, 502, 551–552, 554, 557, 805, 807
Union Party in 1864, 476
United Farm Workers, 987
United Fruit Company, 750, 931
United Mine Workers (UMW), 708, 710, 733, 817, 883, 889
United Nations, structure, 880; decides to defend South Korea, 899; wages Gulf War, 1013–1015
United States Sanitary Commission, 472, 474
United States Steel, 515, 521, 533, 535, 740, 743
United States v. Butler, 819
United States v. E. C. Knight, 544, 732
Upshur, Abel P., 397
Utopian communities, 347–349

V

Valentino, Rudolph, 788
Vallandigham, Clement, 453
Van Buren, Martin, Jackson's political ally, 299, 303, 312–320; wins vice-presidential term, 321; presidential victory in 1836, 323; handling of depression, 324–325; Democratic candidate in 1840, 328–331; wishes to return *Amistad* mutineers, 332; later opponent of slavery, 332; and annexation of Texas, 396–397
Vance, Zebulon, 470
Vandenberg, Arthur, 886
Van Devanter, Willis, 826
Vanzetti, Bartolomeo, 778
Vaudeville, 630, 714

Veblen, Thorstein, 526
Venezuela, 668–669, 684
Venice, 631
Vergennes, Comte de, 139
Verrazano, Giovanni da, 28
Vertical integration, 516
Vesey, Denmark, 286–287, 317
Vespucci, Amerigo, 23
Vicksburg, battle of, 457, 460, 462, 475
Vicksburg, lynching, 602
Vienna, 594, 846, 931
Vietnam, once part of French empire, 947; Dien Bien Phu, 948–949; Geneva accords acknowledge independence, 949; U.S. assists South Vietnamese regime of Ngo Dinh Diem, 949; Southeast Asia Treaty Organization extends shield to Vietnam, 950; National Liberation Front appears, 950; Diem overthrown, 952; Gulf of Tonkin resolution, 952; U.S. fully enters war, 954–956; antiwar movement, 956–958; Tet and My Lai, 945–947, 959–960; peace talks, 960, 967; antiwar sentiment splits Democratic Party, 958–959, 960–962; President Nixon invades Cambodia, 966; peace talks bring agreement, 968; Communists overrun South Vietnam, 991
Vikings, 1
Villa, Pancho, 751, 752
Villard, Oswald Garrison, 712
Virginia Company, see London Company
Virginia Plan, 186–187
Virginia Resolution, 208
Virginia Resolves, 118
Vizcaíno, Sebastián, 28
Vo Nguyen Giap, 948
Volunteers in Service to America (VISTA), 936
Voting rights, 521, 892, 938
Voting Rights Act, 938

W

Waco, Texas, and Branch Dividian Compound, 980
Wade-Davis Bill, 486
Wagner, Robert F., 692
Wagner, Robert F., Jr., 817, 820, 838

Wagner Act, 820, 826
Wagner-Steagall National Housing Act, 828
Waite, Morrison, 542
Wald, Lillian, 712
Walker, David, 364
Walker, Patrick, 127
Walker, William, 420
Walla Walla, 381
Wallace, George, 962–963
Wallace, Henry A., 814, 849, 870, 880
Wallace, Henry C., 788
Walters, Barbara, 1005
Waltham system, 259–261
Wanamaker, John, 522
Wanamaker's department store, 522, 523
War Finance Corporation, 759, 798
War Hawks, 233–235
War Industries Board, 759
War Labor Board, 759, 856
War Manpower Commission, 856
War of 1812, 235–247; impressment of American sailors, 230; preliminaries, 229–235; War Hawks, 233–235; major engagements, 240 (Lake Erie), 242 (burning of Washington), 245–247 (New Orleans); Treaty of Ghent, 244–245
War on Poverty, 936, 941
Warehouse Act, 748
Warren, Earl, 912, 933, 962
Warsaw Pact, 918, 1011
Washington, Treaty of, 660
Washington, Booker T., Tuskegee, 581; Atlanta Compromise, 585–586; President Theodore Roosevelt's courtesy, 586, 732; black opposition, 586, 710–711; political organization, 596–597; speaks essentially for southern blacks, 785
Washington, D.C., choosing of capital, 195; in first days, 209–210; British burn, 242–243; Compromise of 1850 prohibits slave trade in, 446; southern city on eve of Civil War, 446
Washington, George, 170; in war with France, 112–113; land speculation, 117; calls for support of Boston, 131; commander of Continental army, 137–139, 154–158; on weakness of the

Confederation, 185; presides at Constitutional Convention, 185–186; favors Constitution, 189–190; assumes presidency, 190–191; title of President, 192; accepts concept of implied powers, 196; early response to French Revolution, 199; Whiskey Rebellion, 198; Farewell Address, 204, 290, 291; national hero, 363–364
Washington Naval Conference, 791–792
Washington Peace Convention, 448
Water Power Act, 774
Water Quality Act, 937
Water rights, 558
Watergate, 966, 972–975, 989
Waters, Ethel, 770
Watson, Doc, 981
Watt, James, 1005
Wayne, Anthony, 162
Wealth Tax Act, 820
Weathermen, 983
Weaver, James, 616–617, 644
Weaver, Randy, 980
Weaver, Robert C., 926
Webster, Daniel, *Dartmouth College* case, 273; Webster-Hayne debate, 314–315; and Bank troubles, 320; a leader of the Whig Party, 328; as secretary of state, concludes Webster-Ashburton Treaty, 396; Seventh of March speech, 412–413; dismisses value of far West, 549;
Webster, Noah, 185, 353
Webster-Ashburton Treaty, 396
Weed, Thurlow, 329
Weems, Mason Locke, 364
Weld, Theodore Dwight, 350, 365–366, 390, 409
Welk, Lawrence, 924
Wesley, John, 90, 91, 346
West, Benjamin, 176
West Germany, see Federal Republic of Germany; under Social Democrats, 964; approves deployment of American Pershing missiles, 1003; unifies with East Germany, 1011
West Point, (Benedict Arnold), 901
West Virginia, becomes separate state, 450
Western settlement, 381–382
Westmoreland, William, 945, 946

Weyler, General Valeriano, 670, 671

Wheeler-Howard Indian Reorganization Act, 988

Whig Party (American), forms, 327–328; character, 328; in campaign of 1840, 329–331; conscience Whigs, 397; Compromise of 1850 rips party, 426, 427–428; former Whigs in postbellum South, 485, 498

Whig philosophy in eighteenth century, 121–122

Whiskey Rebellion, 196–198

White, Hugh Lawson, 327–328

White, John, 39

White House tapes, 973

Whitefield, George, 90, 91, 92

Whitman, Walt, 363

Whitney, Asa, 421

Whitney, Eli, cotton gin, 227, 262, 263; interchangeable parts, 262, 263, 264, 284–285; Henry Ford's assembly line extends principle of interchangeable parts, 696

Wickersham, George W., 741

Wigglesworth, Michael, 75

Wildcat banks, 324

Wilderness campaign, in Civil War, 475

Wiley, Dr. Harvey W., 737

Wilkinson, James, 225

Willard, Emma, 353

Willard, Frances, 646

William III of England (William of Orange), 64, 65

Williams, Jim, 481–482

Williams, Roger, 46, 47, 52

Wilmot, David, and Wilmot Proviso, 404; on free labor, 423

Wilmot Proviso, 404, 411

Wilson, Charles, 919

Wilson, Thomas Woodrow, president of Princeton University and reform governor of New Jersey, 745–747; New Freedom and election of 1912, 744–745; domestic policy, 747–749; policy toward the rest of the Hemisphere, 750–753; during European war, attempts to maintain neutrality, 753–756; war President, 756–764 passim; Fourteen Points and fight for the League of Nations, 771–773

Winthrop, John, 42, 44, 74, 96

Wirt, William, candidate of Anti-Masons, 327

Wisconsin idea, 728, 731

Witches, in Salem, 71–74

Wobblies, see Industrial Workers of the World

Wolfe, General James, 109–111, 114

Women, in colonial times, 96–99; Abigail Adams on Revolution, 141; in American Revolution, 151–152; after American Revolution, 163; isolation in backcountry, 228–229; Waltham system, 259–261; response to exclusion from World Anti-Slavery Convention, 337; Seneca Falls Woman's Rights Convention, 337–339, 355; higher education for women in nineteenth century, 353; cult of true womanhood, 356, 358, 578; women as reformers, in antebellum period, 355–356; press for women's rights at mid-nineteenth century, 356–358; during Civil War, 470, 474; black women, slave and freed, 494–495; quest for suffrage after the Civil War, 497–498; women wage earners in the late nineteenth century, 535–536, 539–540; in the late nineteenth century, women's colleges and questions about higher education for women, 537, 625; women as teachers, nurses, and social workers, 537–539; frontier women in the trans-Mississippi West, 577–579; Women's Christian Temperance Union, 645–646; settlement houses, 646–647; women as reformers in the progressive period, 703–706; Margaret Sanger and birth control, 705; responses to World War I among women reformers, 764; Nineteenth Amendment, 764; women in the workforce during the Great Depression, 808–809; during World War II, women take the place of male workers in uniform, 856, 983; women in workforce after the war, 983–984; President Kennedy's Commission on the Status of Women, 984; Civil Rights Act of 1964 includes prohibition of sexual

discrimination, 984; political action in women's movement, 984–985; radical feminism, 985; affirmative action, 1017

Women's Christian Temperance Union (WCTU), 645–646

Wood, General Leonard, 756

Woodford, Stewart, 671, 673

Woodstock festival, 982

Wool, John, 241

Wool Act of 1699, 102

Woolman, John, 89

Worcester v. Georgia, 308–309

Works Progress Administration (WPA), 819–820, 830, 833

World Anti-Slavery Convention, 337, 392

World Court, 792

World Economic Conference, 839, 843

World War Foreign Debt Commission, 793

World War I (participation by U.S.), mobilization, 756–757, 759; war spirit, 760–762; repression of radicalism, 762–763; dissent, 763–764, 764–765; black Americans, 769; combat, 760

World War II (participation by U.S.), mobilization, 855–857; the national temper, 857, 860–861; discrimination against blacks and Japanese Americans, 858–859; combat, 861–863, 865–869, 871–872; diplomacy, 863, 865, 869–871

Wounded Knee, 550, 566, 989

Wovoka, 566

Wright, Chauncey, 648

Wright, Fanny, Nashoba, 347–348

Wright, Orville and Wilbur, 698

Writs of assistance, 116, 117

Wyandot, 173

X

XYZ affair, 206

Y

Yakima, 381

Yalta, 869–871, 880

Yamasee, 86

Yancey, William, 436

Yates, Robert, 186
Yellow press, 670
Yellowstone Park, 738
York, on Lewis and Clark expedition, 223
Yorktown, battle of, 158
Yorktown, 861

Young, Brigham, 345, 360
Young, Owen D., and Young Plan, 793
Young America, 399
Young Men's Christian Association (YMCA), 715, 762
Yuppies, 1004

Z

Zapata, Emiliano, 751
Zenger, John Peter, 94–95
Zhukov, Georgy, 918
Ziegfeld, Florenz, 630
Zimmermann, Arthur, 756

NOTES

NOTES

NOTES

NOTES

NOTES

NOTES

NOTES

NOTES

NOTES

NOTES

ARCTIC OCEAN

GREENLAND
(Den.)

NORTH

ALASKA
(U.S.)

Dawson

Anchorage

Baffin
Bay

Reykjavik

Juneau

60°

C A N A D A

Hudson
Bay

NEWFOUNDLAND

Edmonton

Winnipeg

Montréal

St. John's

45°

Vancouver

Seattle

AMERICA

Ottawa

Detroit

Chicago

New York

AZORES
(Port.)

San Francisco

UNITED STATES

Washington

Atlanta

30°

MIDWAY IS.
(U.S.)

Los Angeles

Houston

New Orleans

CANARY ISLANDS
(Sp.)

Tropic of Cancer

HAWAIIAN ISLANDS
(U.S.)

MEXICO

Gulf of Mexico

BAHAMAS

ATLANTIC

Havana

CUBA

CAPE VERDE

Mexico City

Veracruz

HAITI

DOM. REP.

PUERTO RICO (U.S.)

MA

BELIZE

JAMAICA

GUADELOUPE (Fr.)

SENEGAL

15°

PACIFIC

GUAT.

HOND.

Caribbean
Sea

MARTINIQUE (Fr.)

Dakar

THE GAMBIA

EL SAL.

NIC.

BARBADOS

GUINEA-BISSAU

COSTA
RICA

TRINIDAD AND TOBAGO

SIERRA LEONE

LE

PANAMA

Caracas

GUYANA

PALMYRA
(U.S.)

VENEZUELA

Georgetown

SURINAME

Bogotá

FRENCH GUIANA

COLOMBIA

0°

Equator

GALAPAGOS ISLANDS
(Ecua.)

Quito

Belém

KIRIBATI

ECUADOR

Manaus

Fortaleza

SOUTH

MARQUESAS IS.
(Fr.)

Lima

PERU

BRAZIL

Recife

15°

SAMOA

OCEAN

AMERICA

OCE

Salvador

AMERICAN
SAMOA

La Paz

BOLIVIA

Brasília

TONGA

COOK
ISLANDS
(N.Z.)

TAHITI

Sucre

PARAGUAY

Rio de Janeiro

Tropic of Capricorn

FRENCH POLYNESIA

Antofagasta

São Paulo

EASTER ISLAND
(Chile)

ARGENTINA

30°

Valparaíso

URUGUAY

CHATHAM IS.
(N.Z.)

ARCH. DE JUAN
FERNÁNDEZ
(Chile)

Santiago

Buenos
Aires

Montevideo

45°

FALKLAND IS.

SOUTH GEORGIA
(U.K.)

Punta Arenas

TIERRA DEL FUEGO

SOUTH SANDWICH

SOUTH ORKNEY IS.
(U.K.)

60°

SOUTH SHETLAND IS.
(U.K.)

Weddell
Sea

Antarctic Circle

75°

Scale 1:100,000,000; one inch to 1578 miles
Robinson Projection

0   400   800   1200   1600   2000 Miles

0   600   1200   1800   2400   3000 Kilometers

180° 1   165° 2   150° 3   135° 4   120° 5   105° 6   90° 7   75° 8   60° 9   45° 10   30°

ARCTIC OCEAN

A

75°

ZEMLYA FRANTSA-IOSIFA

NOVAYA ZEMLYA

FINLAND

St. Petersburg

B

60°

RUSSIA

DEN
EST
LAT
NTH
Warsaw
POLAND
BELARUS
Moscow
Kiev
UKRAINE

Okhotsk

BERING

SEA

C

Novosibirsk

Irkutsk

Sea of Okhotsk

SAKHALIN

45°

HUNG
ROM
MOLD.
KAZAKHSTAN
ASIA
Ulan Bator
MONGOLIA

ALB
GREECE
Istanbul
Ankara
TURKEY
UZBEKISTAN
KYRG.
TURKMENISTAN
TAJIK.
Beijing

Vladivostok
HOKKAIDŌ
NORTH
KOREA
Seoul
SOUTH
KOREA
HONSHŪ
JAPAN
Tōkyō

D

CRETE
CYPRUS
LEB
SYRIA
ISRAEL
Tehrān
Kābol
AFGHANISTAN
CHINA

Sea of Japan
KYŪSHŪ

Athens

Tripoli
IRAQ
Baghdad
JORDAN
IRAN
PAKISTAN
New Delhi

Shanghai

30°

Cairo
KUWAIT
QATAR

LIBYA
EGYPT
SAUDI
ARABIA
Riyadh
Mecca
U.A.E.
OMAN
Karachi

NEPAL

Guangzhou
TAIWAN
Macau
Hong Kong

PACIFIC

Tropic of Cancer

E

RICA
CHAD
SUDAN
YEMEN
Aden
DJIBOUTI

Mumbai
INDIA

BANG.
MYANMAR
(BURMA)
LAOS
Ho Noi

HAINAN

South China
Sea

NORTHERN MARIANA
ISLANDS (U.S.)

WAKE
(U.S.)

15°

CENTRAL AFRICAN
REPUBLIC
OON
ETHIOPIA
Abeba
Addis

SOCOTRA
(Yem.)

ARABIAN
SEA

LAKSHADWEEP
(INDIA)

Chennai

Colombo

SRI LANKA

Bay of
Bengal

THAILAND
Bangkok

CAMBODIA
VIETNAM
Thanh Pho
Ho Chi Minh

Yangon

Manila
PHILIPPINES

GUAM
(U.S.)

PALAU

OCEAN

F

CONGO
RWANDA
BURUNDI
KENYA
Nairobi
SOMALIA
Mogadishu

MALDIVES

MALAYSIA
BRUNEI

FED. STATES OF
MICRONESIA

MARSHALL
ISLANDS

Equator

DEM. REP.
OF THE
CONGO
TANZANIA
Dar es Salaam
SEYCHELLES

SINGAPORE
BORNEO

NEW GUINEA

G

Kinshasa

Luanda

SUMATRA

Jakarta
INDONESIA

PAPUA
NEW GUINEA

SOLOMON
ISLANDS

ANGOLA
ZAMBIA
COMOROS

INDIAN

JAVA

COCOS
ISLANDS
(Austl.)

EAST TIMOR
(UN Admin.)

15°

ZIMBABWE
MADAGASCAR

Darwin

CORAL SEA

VANUATU

FIJI

NAMIBIA
BOTSWANA
MOZAMBIQUE
Antananarivo
MAURITIUS

NEW
CALEDONIA
(Fr.)

Tropic of Capricorn

H

Pretoria
SWAZILAND
Maputo
REUNION
(Fr.)

OCEAN

AUSTRALIA

Brisbane

SOUTH
AFRICA
Durban
LESOTHO

Perth

Sydney

30°

Town

Canberra

Auckland
NORTH I.

Melbourne

NEW ZEALAND
Wellington

I

ÎLES KERGUÉLEN
(Fr.)

TASMANIA

Hobart

SOUTH I.

45°

J

60°

Antarctic Circle

K

75°

© RMC. R.L. 02-2-47
www.randmcnally.com
N-QRF10005-P1- -2

NTARCTICA

L